THE STUDY OF MINISTRY

THE STUDY OF MINISTRY

A comprehensive survey of theory and best practice

EDITED BY MARTYN PERCY
WITH IAN S. MARKHAM, EMMA PERCY
AND FRANCESCA PO

First published in Great Britain in 2019

Society for Promoting Christian Knowledge
36 Causton Street
London SW1P 4ST
www.spck.org.uk

British Library Cataloguing-in-Publication Data
A catalogue record for this book is available from the British Library

ISBN 978–0–281–08136–3
eBook ISBN 978–0–281–07301–6

Typeset by Manila Typesetting Company
First printed in Great Britain by TJ International
Subsequently digitally reprinted in Great Britain

eBook by Manila Typesetting Company

Produced on paper from sustainable forests

Contents

Part 3
MINISTRY IN CHRISTIAN TRADITION

Part 4
STYLES OF CHRISTIAN MINISTRY

Part 5
ISSUES IN CHRISTIAN MINISTRY

Contents

Contributors

The Revd Canon Dr Alan Billings is the Police and Crime Commissioner for South Yorkshire. He has been an Anglican parish priest in inner-city Sheffield, where he was also Deputy Leader of the City Council, and in Kendal, Cumbria. He has been Vice Principal of Ripon College Cuddesdon, Principal of the West Midlands Ministerial Training Course, and Director of the Centre for Ethics and Religion at Lancaster University. He was one of the authors of *Faith in the City* (Church House Publishing, 1985). He has written a number of books about contemporary ministry, including *Secular Lives, Sacred Hearts* (SPCK, 2004), *God and Community Cohesion* (SPCK, 2009), *Making God Possible* (SPCK, 2010) and *Lost Church* (SPCK, 2013).

The Revd Dr Amanda Bloor is Priest in Charge of the parish of Bembridge, Isle of Wight, and Assistant Director of Ordinands for the Diocese of Portsmouth. Her doctoral research investigated the expectations and experiences of those entering ordained ministry and she maintains an interest in the discernment, encouragement and sustaining of vocations. Amanda has been a bishop's chaplain, a diocesan advisor in women's ministry, and a diocesan director of ordinands (DDO). She has contributed to Tim Ling's book, *Moving On in Ministry* (Church House Publishing, 2013), and writes Bible studies for the Bible Reading Fellowship (BRF). She enjoys the challenges and controversies posed by feminist theologies.

The Revd and Worshipful Dr Rupert Bursell QC is currently Chairman of the Legal Advisory Commission to the General Synod. He is a retired Diocesan Chancellor of the Diocese of Durham and a one-time senior circuit judge, and writes and teaches on ecclesiastical law.

Dr Hywel Clifford is Tutor in Old Testament at Ripon College Cuddesdon, Oxford, and a member of the University of Oxford's Faculty of Theology and Religion. He is also a member of the Society of Biblical Literature (SBL), the Society for Old Testament Study (SOTS) and the European Association of Biblical Studies (EABS). Hywel has published on Amos, Isaiah 40—55 and Philo of Alexandria. He edited and contributed to the *Companion to the Old Testament: Introduction, Interpretation, Application*

(SCM Press, 2016). His areas of interest are monotheism, early Greek philosophy, the history of biblical interpretation, and the archaeology of biblical lands.

The Revd Prof. Mark Cobb is a senior chaplain and a clinical director at Sheffield Teaching Hospitals NHS Foundation Trust. He holds honorary academic appointments in health faculties at the University of Liverpool, the University of Sheffield and Sheffield Hallam University, where he lectures, supervises students, and contributes to research in the fields of health-related spirituality, palliative care and clinical ethics. He is widely published in academic journals and healthcare texts, and he most recently contributed to and co-edited the *Oxford Textbook of Spirituality in Healthcare* (Oxford University Press, 2012) and *A Handbook of Chaplaincy Studies* (Ashgate, 2015).

Prof. Douglas J. Davies is Professor in the Study of Religion and Director of the Centre for Death and Life Studies at Durham University, trained in social anthropology and theology. An Oxford Doctor of Letters (DLitt), Honorary Doctor of Theology of Uppsala, Fellow of the Learned Society of Wales, Fellow of the UK Academy of Social Sciences, and of the British Academy, his publications include *Mors Britannica: Lifestyle and Death-style in Britain Today* (Oxford University Press, 2015), *Emotion, Identity, and Religion: Hope, Reciprocity, and Otherness* (Oxford University Press, 2011), *Anthropology and Theology* (Berg, 2002), *The Theology of Death* (T&T Clark, 2008), *Death, Ritual, and Belief* (Bloomsbury, 2002) and *Private Passions* (Canterbury Press, 2000, Archbishop of Wales' Lent Book).

Prof. Abby Day is Professor in Race, Faith and Culture in the Department of Sociology, Goldsmiths, University of London, where her teaching, research, writing and supervisions cover sociology of religion, media, culture and critical criminology. Former Chair of the Sociology of Religion Study Group in the British Sociological Association, her work focuses on improving the academic and public understanding of complex religious and non-religious identities, from 'Christmas Christians' to the most loyal, and now dwindling, active generation of Anglican laywomen.

Prof. Norman Doe is a professor at Cardiff University Law School. His books include studies on medieval law, Anglican canon law, law and religion in Europe, and Christian law. A visiting professor at Paris University and KU Leuven, he was a visiting fellow at Trinity College Oxford (2011) and scholar at Corpus Christi College Oxford (2015), and acted as a consultant on canon law to the Anglican Communion, served on the Lambeth Commission (2003–4) and is Chancellor of the Diocese of Bangor. He is Director of the Master of Laws degree (LLM) in Canon Law at Cardiff.

The Revd Bonnie Evans-Hills is Interfaith Adviser in the Diocese of St Albans, and a parish priest. She serves on the Church of England's Presence and Engagement Task Group, resourcing multifaith parishes, and participates in United Nations initiatives for ending genocide and for response to the current humanitarian crisis. She has also worked on various interfaith initiatives with the Anglican Communion, as well as the World Council of Churches. Alongside Canon Michael Rusk, she is co-author of the book *Engaging Islam from a Christian Perspective* (Peter Lang, 2015).

The Revd Prof. James Farwell is Professor of Theology and Liturgy at Virginia Theological Seminary, USA. He teaches liturgical and sacramental theology and practice, ritual theory, comparative theology and theologies of religious plurality. His publications include *This Is the Night* (T&T Clark, 2005), on the Triduum liturgies, *The Liturgy Explained* (Morehouse, 2013), and essays and articles on inter-religious ritual, the Eucharistic Prayer and inter-religious dialogue. His current research explores the borderlands between liturgical and comparative theology, focusing on Christian–Buddhist inter-rituality and the bearing of Dōgen's non-dualism on eucharistic theology and practice.

The Revd Dr John Fitzmaurice is Director of Ordinands and Vocation in the Diocese of Worcester. Originally from Ireland, he trained as a musician at the Guildhall School of Music and Drama in London. He trained for ordination at the College of the Resurrection, Mirfield, and holds a master's degree in the Psychology of Religion from Heythrop College, as well as a doctorate from King's College London. He has served in parish ministry in the dioceses of Derby and Coventry, and has been involved in facilitating ministerial development and training in a variety of contexts. He is the author of *Virtue Ecclesiology* (Routledge, 2015).

The Revd Prof. Robin Gill held the Michael Ramsey Chair of Modern Theology in the University of Kent, Canterbury, for 20 years and is now Emeritus Professor of Applied Theology. He chaired the Archbishop of Canterbury's Medical Ethics Advisory Group and remains an Honorary Provincial Canon of Canterbury Cathedral. Previously he held the William

Leech Research Chair of Applied Theology at the University of Newcastle. Now editor of *Theology*, he has written some 40 books, among them *Moral Passion and Christian Ethics* (Cambridge University Press, 2017), *Theology in a Social Context: Sociological Theology* (3 volumes, Ashgate, 2012–13) and *A Textbook of Christian Ethics* (4th edition, Bloomsbury, 2014).

The Revd Dr David Gortner is Associate Dean for Church and Community Engagement at Virginia Theological Seminary, USA, where he has also served as Director of the Doctor of Ministry Program and Professor of Evangelism and Congregational Leadership. David is author of *Transforming Evangelism* (Church Publishing, 2007), *Varieties of Personal Theology* (Routledge, 2013), *Around One Table* (College of Bishops, 2009, online), as well as articles on clergy leadership and vocational development. He is the primary author of the Clergy Into Action website (<http://into-action.net>).

The Revd Canon Dr Robin Greenwood is Visiting Fellow at St John's College, Durham. For almost five decades as an Anglican priest, he has ministered in parishes, diocesan staff teams and cathedrals. He has written and contributed to conferences on ecclesiology, mission, ministry and spirituality. He has acted as consultant to the Lutheran Church in Sweden and the New York Synod of the Evangelical Lutheran Church of America, and with Anglicans in Australia and New Zealand. From 2005 to 2013 he was Vicar of St Mary's, Monkseaton, Newcastle Diocese, and from 2013 to 2015 held a William Leech Fellowship at Durham University. Among his other publications with SPCK are *Transforming Priesthood: A New Theology of Mission and Ministry* (fifth impression 2001), and *Sharing God's Blessing: How to Renew the Local Church* (2016).

The Revd Prof. James Barney Hawkins IV is Vice President for Institutional Advancement and the Arthur Carl Lichtenberger Professor in Pastoral Theology and Continuing Education at Virginia Theological Seminary. He has 21 years of parish experience and is currently Honorary Associate at Immanuel Church-on-the-Hill in Alexandria, Virginia. He has published a book on ministry: *Episcopal Etiquette and Ethics* (Morehouse, 2012), and *The Wiley-Blackwell Companion to the Anglican Communion* (Wiley-Blackwell, 2013). Hawkins has served on the boards of Episcopal Relief and Development, and Kanuga Conferences, Inc. Presently he serves as President on the North American Committee of St George's College, Jerusalem.

The Revd Prof. Robert S. Heaney is Associate Professor of Christian Mission and Director of the Center for Anglican Communion Studies, Virginia Theological Seminary, USA. He is an Anglican priest-scholar ordained in the Church of Ireland and has experience serving the Church and academy in Europe, Africa and the USA. He teaches and writes on mission theology, post-colonial theology and Anglicanism. He is the author of the book, *From Historical to Critical Post-Colonial Theology* (Wipf & Stock, 2015).

The Revd Canon Dr Sarah Hills has been Canon for Reconciliation at Coventry Cathedral since 2014. She was born in South Africa and brought up in Northern Ireland, qualifying in medicine from the University of Sheffield. She worked as a psychiatrist, specializing in psychotherapy until her ordination in 2007. She was awarded her PhD in the theology of reconciliation at the University of Durham in 2015. She is a Visiting Fellow of St John's College, Durham, and a Visiting Practice Fellow at the Centre for Trust, Peace and Social Relations at Coventry University. She works and teaches in the areas of conflict and reconciliation in the national Church and internationally, particularly in South Africa with reconciliation processes in the wake of the establishment of the Truth and Reconciliation Commission (TRC).

The Revd Prof. Ruthanna B. Hooke is Associate Dean of Chapel and Associate Professor of Homiletics at Virginia Theological Seminary, USA. She is also Executive Program Director of 'Deep Calls to Deep', a programme to strengthen Episcopal preaching. Hooke's publications include *Transforming Preaching* (Church Publishing, 2010), 'The Personal and Its Other in the Performance of Preaching' in *Preaching and the Personal* (Lutterworth, 2013) and 'Real Presence: Sacramental Embodiment in Preaching' in *Preaching and the Theological Imagination* (Peter Lang, 2015). A Designated Linklater Voice Teacher, Hooke teaches courses in preaching, voice, performance and biblical storytelling.

The Revd Prof. Thomas Hughson is a Catholic priest in the Society of Jesus. He served as Director of the Pontifical Biblical Institute, Jerusalem, from 1986 to 1989. Retired Emeritus from the Faculty of Theology at Marquette University, he had been Director of Graduate Studies for some years. Now on the editorial board of *Modern Believing*, his most recent books are *Connecting Jesus to Social Justice: Classical Christology and Public Theology* (Rowman & Littlefield, 2013) and an edited volume, *The Holy*

Spirit and the Church: Ecumenical Reflections with a Pastoral Perspective (Routledge, 2016). His pastoral activity mostly has been spiritual accompaniment in the light of St Ignatius' Spiritual Exercises.

The Revd Dr Tom Keighley is Dean of Self-Supporting Ministers (SSMs) in the Barking Diocesan Area. His PhD in Ecclesiology illuminated organizational issues facing SSMs. He is also a freelance nurse consultant, working with the various European agencies and governments facilitating the development of healthcare delivery and the education of healthcare professionals, and as assessor and evaluator of innovations in healthcare. He has held academic positions at universities in the UK and Canada. He is currently heavily engaged in projects in the countries of the former Yugoslavia.

Prof. Lisa Kimball is Associate Dean for Lifelong Learning, Director of the Center for Ministry of Teaching, and Professor of Christian Formation and Congregational Leadership at Virginia Theological Seminary, USA. Her current research, teaching and writing focus on faith transmission in a hyperconnected digital age and how religious pluralism and declining religious affiliation are opportunities for reimagining being church. Committed to deep listening in diverse cultural contexts, Kimball travels extensively across the United States and prioritizes collaboration, working closely with local congregations, ecumenical bodies and her chosen academic guilds.

The Revd Dr Tess Kuin Lawton is Chaplain and Fellow at Worcester College, University of Oxford. At the Diocese of Oxford, she was the Ecumenical Adviser during the implementation of the Anglican-Methodist Covenant. Her PhD asks 'Is There an Anglican Theology of Religious Pluralism?' and considers this wider form of ecumenism through an historical investigation into the Anglican *via media* of the sixteenth century.

Canon Keith Lamdin retired in 2015 from his post as Principal at Sarum Theological College. Before that he led the training and ministry department for the Diocese of Oxford. Both in Oxford and at Sarum he was at the forefront of developing leadership programmes for clergy and senior leaders in the churches. He writes and teaches on leadership and organizational development. His latest book was *Finding Your Leadership Style* (SPCK, 2012).

The Revd Dr Justin Lewis-Anthony is Deputy Director of the Anglican Centre in Rome. Before that, he was the Associate Fellow of the Oxford Centre for Ecclesiastical and Practical Theology at Ripon College Cuddesdon, and Dean of Students at Virginia Theological Seminary, USA. He is author of *If You Meet George Herbert on the Road, Kill Him* (Mowbray, 2009) and *You Are the Messiah and I Should Know* (Bloomsbury, 2013). He was educated at the London School of Economics (LSE) and Oxford University, and has been ordained for more than 25 years, working in parishes (and a cathedral) across the UK.

The Revd Dr Benjamin McNair Scott is an ordained Anglican priest based in the Diocese of Guildford. He is currently the school chaplain and a teacher of Religious Studies at St Catherine's School, Bramley, a leading independent school in Surrey. He was a doctoral student at King's College London under the supervision of Prof. Andrew Walker and is the author of *Apostles Today: Making Sense of Contemporary Charismatic Apostolates: A Historical and Theological Appraisal* (Pickwick, 2014), which was based upon his doctoral thesis and is a subject on which he has lectured at the University of Winchester.

The Revd Prof. Ian S. Markham is Dean and President of Virginia Theological Seminary, USA, and Professor of Theology and Ethics and Priest Associate at St Paul's Episcopal Church in Alexandria, Virginia. He is the author of several books and articles, including *Introduction to Ministry* (with Oran Warder, Wiley-Blackwell, 2016) and *A Theology of Engagement* (Blackwell, 2003). He has delivered several significant lectureships, including the Teape Lectures (India, 2000), the Frank Woods Lecture (Trinity College, Australia, 1996), the F. D. Maurice Lectures (King's College London, UK, 2015) and the Orr Lectures (Huron University College, Canada, 2016).

The Revd Prof. Jolyon Mitchell is Professor of Communications, Arts and Religion, and Director of the Centre for Theology and Public Issues (CTPI) at the University of Edinburgh. President of TRS-UK and a Fellow of the Royal Society of Arts (FRSA), Prof. Mitchell's research and teaching focuses on Religion, Violence and Peacebuilding, with particular reference to the arts and media. Ordained in the Scottish Episcopal Church, and a former BBC World Service producer and journalist, his books include *Promoting Peace, Inciting Violence: The Role of Religion and Media* (Routledge, 2012), *Martyrdom: A Very Short Introduction* (Oxford University Press, 2012) and *Media Violence and Christian Ethics* (Cambridge University Press, 2007).

The Revd Dr Mark Newitt is a specialist practitioner chaplain at Sheffield Teaching Hospitals NHS Foundation Trust. He is interested in what a virtue-based approach to chaplaincy has to offer and how appropriate liturgy and ritual might help people through times of liminality. He co-edited *Being a Chaplain* (SPCK, 2012) and has published articles exploring both theoretical and practical perspectives on chaplaincy in journals as diverse as the *British Medical Journal, Health and Social Care Chaplaincy* and *Infants, Midwives, and Practical Theology.*

The Revd Kyle Matthew Oliver is a doctoral student in the Communications, Media and Learning Technologies Design Program at Teachers College, Columbia University, and an assistant priest at St Michael's Church in New York City. Previously he was Digital Missioner in the Center for the Ministry of Teaching at Virginia Theological Seminary, USA. In that role, he was the principal organizer for the e-Formation Learning Community, a peer-training network for practising ministry in a digital world. He studies new media literacies with a focus on religious leadership and practice.

The Revd Dr Emma Percy is currently Chaplain, Fellow and Welfare Dean of Trinity College Oxford, and a member of the Faculty of Theology and Religion. She was one of the first generation of women priests in the Church of England and is chair of WATCH (Women and the Church). Her research interests include feminist theology, the theology of mothering and the theology of Anglican ministry. Her two recent books are *Mothering as a Metaphor for Ministry* (Ashgate, 2014) and *What Clergy Do: Especially When It Looks Like Nothing* (SPCK, 2014).

The Very Revd Prof. Martyn Percy writes and teaches on ministry and mission in the contemporary Church. He was Principal of Ripon College Cuddesdon, before being appointed Dean of Christ Church, Oxford in 2014. Since 2004, he has been a member of the Faculty of Theology and Religion at the University of Oxford, and Professor of Theological Education at King's College, London. His work is the subject of a recent study: *Reasonable Radical? Reading the Writings of Martyn Percy* (eds I. S. Markham and J. Daniels, Pickwick, 2018).

The Right Revd Prof. Stephen Pickard is Executive Director of the Australian Centre for Christianity and Culture, Director of the Strategic Research Centre in Public and Contextual Theology, and Professor of Theology, Charles Sturt University, Canberra, Australia. He is also an assistant bishop in the Anglican Diocese of Canberra and Gouburn. He has served in a range of ministerial and academic appointments over three decades in Australia and the UK. His teaching and writing includes *Theological Foundations for Collaborative Ministry* (Ashgate, 2009), *In-Between God: Theology, Community and Discipleship* (ATF, 2011) and *Seeking the Church: An Introduction to Ecclesiology* (SCM Press, 2012).

Francesca Po is a scholar of religion educated at the University of Oxford, the California Institute of Integral Studies, and the University of California at Berkeley. Her primary research interests are in religious change, non-religion and new religious movements. Previously, she served in the US Peace Corps in Kazakhstan, and was a religious studies educator and a high-school campus minister. She is a member of the Strategic Advisory Council and the Liaison to Wisdom Traditions at the Metta Center for Nonviolence, California.

The Revd Joshua Rey is an Anglican clergyman and was recently appointed as Chaplain to the Bishop of Southwark, before which he was a curate in inner south London. Before training for ordination at Ripon College Cuddesdon, he worked as an investment banker at J. P. Morgan in London and New York; as an aid worker with Medair in Afghanistan, Albania and other locations; and in a number of Whitehall roles in the field of employment and skills policy.

Prof. Robert C. Roberts is Distinguished Professor of Ethics, Emeritus, at Baylor University, Texas, and Chair of Ethics and Emotion Theory at the Jubilee Centre, University of Birmingham. He is the author of *Spiritual Emotions* (Eerdmans, 2007), *Taking the Word to Heart* (Eerdmans, 1993) and, most recently, *Emotions in the Moral Life* (Cambridge University Press, 2015). He is currently working on a book tentatively titled *Kierkegaard's Psychology of Character*, which will be published by Eerdmans.

Dr Cathy Ross is Tutor in Contextual Theology at Ripon College Cuddesdon, MA Coordinator for Pioneer Leadership Training at the Church Mission Society (CMS) and Lecturer in Mission at Regent's Park College, Oxford. She has previously worked in Rwanda, Congo and Uganda with the New Zealand Church Missionary Society (NZCMS). Her recent publications include *Life-widening Mission: Global Anglican Perspectives* (Regnum, 2012), *Mission in Context* (with John Corrie, Ashgate, 2012), *The Pioneer Gift* (with Jonny Baker, SCM Press, 2014), *Mission on the Road to*

Emmaus (with Steve Bevans, SCM Press, 2015) and *Pioneering Spirituality* (with Jonny Baker, SCM Press, 2015). Her research interests are in the areas of contextual theologies, world Christianity, feminist theologies, and hospitality.

The Revd Sally Ross is the team leader of the Chaplaincy and Spiritual Care department at Sheffield Health and Social Care, a hospital trust supporting people with mental health needs and learning difficulties. Previously, she has studied for an English degree, lived and worked in a L'Arche community with people with learning difficulties, and ministered as a priest in a variety of Anglican parishes.

The Revd Dr Allison St Louis joined the faculty of Virginia Theological Seminary (VTS) in 2010. She serves as Director of Field Education and the Second Three Years Program and teaches in the area of Practical Theology. A member of Phi Beta Kappa, she holds Doctor of Philosophy, Master of Science and Bachelor of Science (*summa cum laude*) degrees in Clinical Psychology from Howard University and a Master of Divinity (*cum laude*) degree from VTS.

The Revd Dr Susanna Snyder is Lecturer in Theology and Director of Non-Residential Training at Ripon College Cuddesdon. She is also an Associate of the Centre for Theology and Modern European Thought at the University of Oxford. She writes on theological, ethical and pastoral responses to migrants and refugees, and her books include *Asylum-Seeking, Migration, and Church* (Ashgate, 2012). A priest in the Church of England, she completed her curacy in the Diocese of London and has taught in seminaries in the United States.

The Revd Dr Chris Swift is Director of Chaplaincy and Spirituality for Methodist Homes (MHA). Previously he was a senior chaplain in the National Health Service for over 20 years. During his time in the NHS he completed a PhD in contemporary healthcare chaplaincy and continues to teach on MA courses, conduct research, advise on PhD projects and write for publication. Swift is a past president of the College of Health Care Chaplains (2004–7) and led the development of new national chaplaincy guidelines for NHS England in 2015.

The Revd Canon Dr Andrew Todd is Director of the Professional Doctorate in Practical Theology at Anglia Ruskin University and the Cambridge

Theological Federation. For over ten years he was Director of the Cardiff Centre for Chaplaincy Studies. He has published widely on chaplaincy and related issues, and was editor of the first ever *Handbook of Chaplaincy Studies* (Ashgate, 2015) with Chris Swift and Mark Cobb. He is a practical theologian and ethnographer, with particular interests in contemporary religion and spirituality and their interaction with longer-established faith traditions. He is a past president of the Cambridge Theological Federation.

The Revd Canon Dr Ian Tomlinson (1950–2016) was the rector of the Ragged Appleshaw benefice in the Diocese of Winchester from 1979 to 2016. He was also the founder and overseer of the Diocesan Pastoral Care and Counselling Service. Ian studied at London, the Open, Hull and Oxford universities, and at the Richmond Fellowship College and the Tavistock Clinic in London. He was a Professional Associate of the Grubb Institute of Behavioural Studies, and a pioneer in using psychotherapy to inform understandings of ministry.

The Revd Prof. Fraser Watts is currently Visiting Professor of Psychology of Religion at the University of Lincoln, and Executive Secretary of the International Society for Science and Religion. Formerly he was Reader in Theology and Science, Director of the Psychology and Religion Research Group, and a Fellow of Queens' College in the University of Cambridge. His books include *Psychology for Christian Ministry* (with Rebecca Nye and Sarah Savage, Routledge, 2002), *Forgiveness in Context* (with Liz Gulliford, T&T Clark, 2004), *Spiritual Healing: Scientific and Religious Perspectives* (Cambridge University Press, 2011) and *Psychology, Religion and Spirituality* (Cambridge University Press, 2017).

Prof. Ryan West is Assistant Professor of Philosophy at Grove City College (Grove City, Pennsylvania, USA). His research and teaching interests include ethics, philosophical psychology (moral and intellectual character, emotions), ancient philosophy and philosophy of religion. His work has appeared in such journals as *Canadian Journal of Philosophy, Faith and Philosophy* and the *Journal of Religious Ethics*. In addition to his academic work, he has over a decade of experience serving as a music minister.

Dr Catherine Wilcox lectures in Creative Writing in the Department of English at Manchester Metropolitan University. She was educated at Durham and London universities and has a degree in English and a doctorate in Theology. Writing as Catherine Fox, she is the author of six novels that explore themes of the spiritual and the physical with insight and humour. Her Lindchester Chronicles are published by Marylebone House/SPCK.

The Revd Canon Professor James Woodward PhD is Principal of Sarum College in Salisbury, an ecumenical Centre for Christian Study and Research. This work includes a wide range of courses alongside postgraduate teaching and research and the formation of women and men for ministry. He is also visiting Professor of Theology at the University of Winchester. He is a practical and pastoral theologian who has written widely in the area of old age, end-of-life care and reflective theological practice.

Introduction

The history and development of ministry

MARTYN PERCY

Why should one study ministry today? And what might the study of ministry tell us about church, society, culture and change? This survey sets out to study ministry empathetically and critically, from perspectives that are theological as well as rooted in a range of social sciences. The book consciously sets out to open up the study of ministry – it seeks to be a broad foundation for further reflection rather than a comprehensive guide. It is, in effect, a *conspectus* – a survey of a vast and complex field; and we seek to offer some signs, directions and destinations in such a space.

Denominations subscribe to a wide range of theologies and practices of ministry, each of which has its own distinctive ethos, and can trace its shape and roots not only back to scriptures and traditions, but beyond – to the ministry of the Father, Son and Holy Spirit throughout creation. Paradigms for such ministries are prevalent. Whether Jesus or Paul, Peter or John the Baptist, Elijah or Jeremiah, Mary or Phoebe, early Church Fathers or Reformers, the Church finds that the people it looks towards to shape its ministry necessarily lead us towards a considerable diversity of understandings and practices.

The Church, however, is also bound to make sense of ministry in every age. And while that can often be done with confidence within the Church, it is perhaps now less easy than in the past. A person set aside for a symbolic, pastoral and priestly role in any community or context is in an increasingly unusual (some would say unique) position today. The work is not paid, at least in the strict sense of remuneration; but there is often some sort of stipend. The role is not 'work', strictly speaking, in the way that the world might understand the concept. There are few prescribed hours, duties and tasks – and yet the role is highly demanding and, at times, intensive. The kind of leadership that one gives in a (largely) voluntary institution is not the same as that given in an organization with clarity between employers, employees and those whom the organization serves. Ministry is easy to describe on a day-to-day basis in terms of tasks; and supporting paradigms – rooted in people and practices drawn from the richness of

Christian tradition – are numerous. Yet curiously, ministry remains difficult to *define*, and the roles remain increasingly hard to articulate.

What, then, is ministry *like*? It is not like teaching, nursing or counselling; nor is it like being a doctor, social worker, solicitor or other profession.
It is, perhaps uniquely, a role in a community – whether a parish, prison or
other sector – that lies beyond the normal vocabulary for defining work.
As the poet Stewart Henderson puts it:

> So, what does a priest do?
> ... visits hospices, administers comfort,
> conducts weddings, christenings –
> not necessarily in that order,
> takes funerals
> consecrates the elderly to the grave
> buries children, and babies,
> feels completely helpless beside
> the swaying family of a suicide.[1]

The French Dominican theologian, Yves Congar, was deeply troubled
about how the Church's ongoing tension with the secular world was leading it to redefine ministry and 'to adopt very much the same attitudes as
temporal power, to conceive of itself as a society (or organization), as a
power, when in reality it was a communion of ministers and servants'.[2]
It is of course possible for any generation to reimagine Christian ministry. Part of the issue before the Church today may lie in the slow and
developing expansion of the term 'vocation' that has taken place since the
Reformation. Martin Luther broadened the term to include all Christians,
however they laboured and worked. John Calvin saw industry and commerce as evidence of God's blessing upon those who gave themselves to
the tasks God had assigned them. By the seventeenth century, the English
Puritans saw that faithfulness to God could be expressed through fidelity
to a job or a trade. So the idea of a vocation changed, in just a few hundred
years, from being a special calling to sacred orders or enclosed religious life
to being something that every Christian could practise in his or her sphere
of work. All occupations were now equal callings that came from God.

This, of course, has meant that the identity of ministry has undergone
degrees of specialization and intensification in direct proportion to its

---

[1] Stewart Henderson (1996), 'Priestly Duties', *Limited Edition* (London: Plover Books).
Reproduced by permission.
[2] Yves Congar (1967), *True and False Reform in the Church* (Collegeville, MN: Liturgical Press),
pp. 3–21.

gradual marginalization. This is something that Anthony Russell's work identifies, suggesting that clergy in the nineteenth and twentieth centuries reinvented themselves as assiduous visitors and preachers, or as 'technicians of the sanctuary'.[3] Yet many of the pivotal pastoral functions of the clergy continued to be reassigned to the local church, resulting in a deepening crisis of professional identity.[4]

So, if ministry today is now something 'for the whole people of God', pastoral work something that can be done by locally deployed teams, and many other aspects of ministry carried out by hired-in specialists provided by the diocese, district or region, then the role of the clergyperson shifts, almost imperceptibly, from being specialist and essential to being general and managerial. This is partly why professionalization has become a double-edged sword for clergy roles and clerical identity. On the one hand it increases the public sense of specialization – the uniqueness of priestcraft – at a time when the general fabric of civic life is being challenged. On the other hand its subsequent compression lays it open to further marginalization and rationalization.

Moreover, ministerial development reviews, diocesan strategies, aims, objectives, outcomes, organization and reorganization – all of which are rooted in secular forms of organizational theory and practice – never quite ring true in an institution that is primarily voluntary in character. With its clergy symbolic and vicarious, and training them as much about character and virtue as skills and techniques, the role and identity of clergy is not easy to articulate in contemporary culture. Towler and Coxon, writing over 30 years ago, also seem to have understood the ambiguity of the role of clergy in the late twentieth century. Their articulation of a crisis of identity and function is worth reflecting upon:

> Now the clergyman, more than anyone else on the contemporary scene, is a jack of all trades. He occupies a unique position, but the uniqueness of his position has nothing to do with unique skills, or even with unique competence. There is nothing which he does that could not be done equally well by a lawyer or bricklayer in the congregation whom the bishop had ordained to the Auxiliary Pastoral Ministry. He does not have a job at all in any sense which is readily understandable today, and today, more than ever before, a person must have a job in order to fit into society. The clergyman, however, is in a position which is marginal to society and at the same time highly visible. He is a public person who, alone in our society, wears a distinctive uniform

---

[3] Anthony Russell (1980), *The Clerical Profession* (London: SPCK), pp. 235ff.
[4] Martyn Percy (2006), *Clergy: The Origin of the Species* (London: Bloomsbury/Continuum).

at all times. When he discards the uniform, as many clergymen do today, he evades the problem posed by his marginality, but he does not solve it.[5]

Towler and Coxon described ministry not as work, or as a profession, or as labour – but as an 'occupation'. A rather quaint word, granted; but an 'occupation' is something, in other words, that consumes time, energy and lives, but was not paid or recognized as 'work' in the way that the secular world now comes to understand the term. This, they argued, made ministry an uncommon occupation – a sphere of activity where remuneration was no longer linked to the value of the endeavour (which in itself was hard to measure), either for the practitioner or for the public at large. This, they argued, made understandings of ministry more marginal, even though its symbolic and public functions remained public and at times highly visible.

So, what is ministry like today, and in particular, in relation to the training and formation of clergy? Clearly, it is important to engage first, not with ministry, but with theology itself, and to understand something of its nature, which in turn, might provide an important clue as to how the primary discipline of ministry (theology) shapes its contours. We begin by making a simple observation: 'the theologian is always beginning in the middle of things'.[6] For our purposes, this is a vital insight into theological training and formation. The 'map' of any curriculum cannot be laid out like a periodic table of the kind one might find in chemistry, or perhaps a genealogy from history. All doctrine is pastoral, biblical and applied. All theology is contextual. All of it is historical, ideological, philosophical and to some extent sociological. Theology refuses to be neatly organized. It cannot be coaxed into neat silos. Studying apologetics, and practising preaching, requires biblical and pastoral knowledge, cultural nuance and discernment, as well as historical and doctrinal comprehension.

For this reason alone, formation, as a concept, is highly significant in theological training. The person being shaped and formed for ministry is not merely banking knowledge, or simply acquiring new skills. He or she is being shaped and moulded into a person of character and virtue too, which is why this kind of theological training is a collective and shared exercise, and cannot be done alone. It also follows from this observation – namely that all theology begins in the middle of things – that the diversity of churches and denominations (a simple fact of ecclesiology) lies at the root of our diverse approaches to theological education. There

---

[5] A. Towler and A. P. M. Coxon (1979), *The Fate of the Anglican Clergy* (London: Routledge), pp. 54–5.
[6] Rowan Williams (2000), *On Christian Theology* (Oxford: Blackwell), p. xii.

is no agreement on where theology begins and ends, because the Church touches the whole of a person's life, and indeed, the whole of creation. Our theologies then – whether subjects or disciplines – are not in fact agreed 'core elements', but rather complex compounds and alloys that do not necessarily engender precise agreement on their nature and make-up, even though some consensus may be found.

Then again, the Church of this present age has found itself increasingly drawn into a more secular shaping of its pedagogy, and of the organization of the Church more generally. Contracts, for example, are clear to all parties. But contracts are also about interests, and being clear about these and the risk to all parties. In the Church, however, interests are not always clear; and they are, in any case, subject to repentance, transformation and transfiguration. This is why the Church tends to talk more about covenants, and not contracts. The former is about identity, not interests; and how our identities are shaped through relationships of reciprocity, and the renewal that God brings. Yet theological training is not so much about the acquisition of knowledge as it is about a growth in wisdom.

Clearly, it is important to engage with the Church in its concrete form, and to acknowledge the challenges we face. To reimagine, we must first be able to engage with the present, and, in view of this, it is appropriate to make a number of brief observations. First, formation is primarily about shaping individual vocations into public ones, and this requires social and community dynamics. Theological education and formation is done *together*; it cannot be done alone. 'Convert' and 'conversation' come from the same Latin words, meaning 'to turn'. Which is why formation is done together; crucially, we cannot all turn to the Lord on our own. We gather for training and formation because we gather for prayer and worship: eating, learning and worshipping together are crucial, shared activities that form the individual and body.

Second, theological training is about the ongoing renewal of a vocation. Renewal can be taken in three senses here: the recovery of what is lost; an improvement of what is in the present; or a complete exchange of the present for the future. So 'the renewal of our minds' (see Romans 12.2) for ministry takes 'renewal' to mean all three senses of that word. Renewal is a primary calling in a vocation, which itself requires an appreciation of the breadth of God, the depth of a call, and how God calls: through myself, through others and for others.[7]

---

[7] See Edward Hahnenberg (2010), *Awakening Vocation: A Theology of Christian Calling* (Collegeville MN: Liturgical Press).

Third, ministry is symbolic and vicarious. As clergy, we are representing more than our own identities and interests. This is why character and virtue are, rightly, so important in formation. And why learning how to disagree theologically with others, or having the humility to acknowledge what we do not yet understand or cannot comprehend, is as important as acquiring more information and skills. Knowing that theology is not neat and tidy, and cannot easily be organized, is a useful life-skill: for life itself. But in the midst of that, we believe and represent more than our selves. Ministers are, as the poet Stewart Henderson reminds us, as priests,

> transformed by The Priest
> that death prised open
> so that he could be our priest
> martyred, diaphanous and
> matchless priest.[8]

What, then, is ministry about? Thomas Tweed has recently suggested that there might be something quite common in what faiths (and their ministers) do for us. To paraphrase, leadership in faith communities can intensify joy and confront suffering, through drawing on the life and power of God to make homes and cross boundaries.[9]

We are rather drawn to this idea. At its best – and one presumes a passionate real faith in a real God as a basis – good ministry performs four important tasks that churches will know much about. First, it intensifies joy. It takes the ordinary and makes it extraordinary. It knows how to celebrate lives, love and transitions. It blesses what is good, and raises hope, thanks and expectation in prayer and praise. It lifts an institution and individuals to a new plane of existence – one of the blessing and thankfulness for what is and can be. And it not only moves, but also intensifies. So, just as a birth becomes even more in a baptism, so in mission and ministry does a ceremony become more with prayer and celebration. Second, suffering is confronted. Working with pain, bereavement, counselling and consolation will be familiar to all ministers and churches – providing the safe space and expertise that holds and slowly resolves the suffering that individuals and institutions carry inside them. Third, the making of homes is a profoundly analogical and literal reference to the function of faith. Making safe spaces of nourishment, well-being, maturity, diversity and individuation, our 'faith homes' (or households – *oikos*) are places both of open

---

8 Henderson, 'Priestly Duties'. Reproduced by permission.
9 Thomas Tweed (2006), *Crossing and Dwelling: A Theory of Religion* (Cambridge, MA: Harvard University Press), p. 12.

hospitality and security. Fourth, faith helps us to cross boundaries – to move forward and over the challenges of life to new places. It can be crossing deserts to find promised lands; or passing from darkness to light. Faith never keeps us in one place; even with our homes, it moves us on as our minds are renewed.

This might all sound like a lot of effort for those engaged in mission and ministry. And to some extent it is. However, I also want to suggest that the manner in which we engage with our institutions is just as important as the actual programmes and events that might be offered. Sometimes, it is the way of being and the character of individual ministry that carries more weight and resonance than those things that seem concrete and planned. This is not surprising, since faith communities often make contributions to social capital that are not easily calculated or calibrated.

Sometimes clergy foster and focus distinctive values which are derived from the process of training (often through hidden curricula rooted in shaping virtues and character) and which then go on to provide leaven in complex contexts. Here, ministers and faith communities often find themselves promoting forms of goodness that secular and utilitarian organizations might miss. In this respect, Bruce Reed explains how Christian ministry partly functions by drawing on an analogy from nature:

> If bees could talk, and we came across them busy in a flower garden and enquired what they were doing, their reply might be: 'Gathering nectar to make honey.' But if we asked the gardener, he would most certainly answer: 'They are cross pollinating my flowers.' In carrying out their manifest function to make food, the bees were performing a latent function of fertilizing flowers. The mutual dependence of bees and flowers is an analogue of churches and society.[10]

Here, Reed offers us a vivid picture of mission and ministry that we might recognize. Through a simple ministry of 'deep hanging out' with the people we serve, involving attentiveness, hospitality, care and celebration, ministers often do more good for the parishes, communities and institutions they serve than they can ever know. This may simply be through the offering of regular lunches, simple visiting, or open house for tea and coffee at any time. These are manifest intentions. But the potency of the gesture and practice lies more in their latency, and is significant for ministry, making it strangely effective. Much as Jesus' was, simply walking from place to place.

---

[10] Bruce Reed (1978), *The Dynamics of Religion: Process and Movement in Christian Churches* (London: Darton, Longman & Todd), p. 139.

The practice of being engaged in an occupation of this kind says something about the possibilities for different kinds of spaces in communities – social, pastoral, intellectual, spiritual, to name but a few. They open up a different side of the humanity of the institution to those individuals within it. In being there with programmes and events, as well as in being purposefully hospitable, churches actually enable the institution to begin transcending itself. Put simply, the ministry says 'there is more to life than what you are currently absorbed by'; 'look deeper'; 'think with your heart'; 'let your mind wander and wonder'; 'we are all beginners in prayer'.

What is ministry like? In some respects, it is rather like intentional parenting. That is to say, there are indeed plans and structures, and there is no getting away from the essential value of these for cultivating healthy individuals and relationships. A loving and cherishing home underlies this ecology. But mature parenting is also about accepting the fact that despite the intentionality of plans and structures, life, like ministry, is a constant stream of interruptions, disruptions and surprises – some of which are welcome, but not all. Ministry, like parenting, is a relatively boundless occupation. Theological education and formation – in both its highly formed and rather unformed states – prepares the minister for this world, and this type of occupation. Which is why it is important that the structuring of training oscillates between the systematic and unsystematic, and the planned and the fluid: our wisdom is found in the dialectic.

Somewhere, between the kinds of sentiments expressed in ACCM 22[11] and (highly) process-driven planning, the Spirit is at work. This is how we discover our emotional and ecclesial intelligence. The variegation of our theologies and our ecclesiologies cannot be managed by a process, because the sheer fact of their diversity expresses some crucial truths about the nature of God and of Christian faith. That Christians do not possess the truth, but are rather possessed by the truth; that the contestability of Christianity is a gift, not a curse; that God will not be organized, rationalized or homogenized by our curricula; that while humanity plans, God laughs, as the old proverb has it.

Now, this is not to say that theological education and formation can afford to be a kind of relaxed and aimless meander through subjects and issues that merely take the fancy of individuals or institutions. Theology is, crucially, a *discipline*. Just as religion is surrender and submission, and not acquisition. Theology is, however, not the normal kind of subject

---

[11] Advisory Council for the Church's Ministry (ACCM) (1987), 'Education for the Church's Ministry', Occasional Paper no. 22 (London: Church House Publishing).

discipline – insofar as it does not behave like a science, or even some of the humanities. Theological education is clearly not a process that is easily described or organized. It often leads its students into confusion and complexity before there is clarity. And with clarity comes humility, and perhaps some greater wisdom. Theology is not a discipline in which the shape and contents are easily agreed. The wisdom of theology is seeing that even an apparently applied and simple topic such as apologetics could be positioned in a number of categories: either mission, ministry, New Testament, doctrine, liturgy, pastoral theology or church history; to say nothing of potential interactions with the social sciences.

That said, theological education and formation for ministry has normative sources of authority that need appropriate attention, respect, and, in context, reverence and awe. The place of Scripture, for example, is fluid – not just to be scrutinized, but also to judge, sift, weigh and convict the reader on her or his vocational journey. The creeds are not optional, but integral. *The Ordinal* is essential for many – but unknown to some. Canon law is non-negotiable. *The Rule of Benedict* is highly desirable, but not known to all. The structuring of the Church – through synods, or in the threefold order of deacons, priests and bishops – is a given. In other words, the structuring of theological education and formation for ministry must include *some compulsory* elements, despite the fact that theology itself, as a more general discipline, is less prescriptive. This is where, once again, policy and praxis need to walk together; wisdom and knowledge need to be bound in communion; process and freedom affirmed as equally valuable, but neither of them optional.

Put another way, we might say that theological education and formation is an invitation into the perpetual vocation 'to be transformed, by the renewing of your mind' (see Romans 12.2). This is a continuous process, not merely an educational chore or a set of pedagogical hoops to jump through. The renewing of our minds is a fundamental part of our vocations that enables service, leadership, ministry and mission. This is precisely why we teach students in formation to negotiate issues through Scripture, tradition, reason and culture. It is why exemplars matter for formation. For we are formed not only by ideas, but also by the lives of those ambassadors of Christ who have gone before us:

> Certainly, ministers need to be schooled for what they do. Yet the nature of the ministry requires a schooling unknown in some other vocations because of the requisite character required to do the job faithfully. That is why pastors testify that the best schooling they receive tends to be apprenticeship – looking over the shoulders of a master, someone who has mastered the craft

of biblical interpretation, or homiletics, or pastoral care, or church history, and perhaps even more so, the art of self-mastery . . . We become persons of character by submitting to formation by persons of character, both the living and the dead . . . All ministerial education worthy of the name consists of various forms of apprenticeship because the goal is the formation of consistent clerical character.[12]

Charles Foster, in his exemplary *Educating Clergy* (2006), notes that pedagogies for practising religious leadership enact those dispositions and habits in specific responsibilities and roles associated with clergy practice.[13] They are directed to forming skills, but even more to forming patterns of leadership in which the theories clergy espouse are congruent with the theories embedded in the dispositions and habits that shape how they negotiate the interplay between institutional processes and the people who participate in them. As Spohn puts it:

Spiritual practices train the *affections*, the deeper emotions and dispositions. It is important to distinguish the affections from feelings. *Feelings* are transitory occurrences that may be genuine or not. The affections behind the Christian moral life are not simply spontaneous, like feelings. They can be tutored and evoked, for example, by the language of prayer or the rhythm of ritual. They can also be deliberately shaped by specific practices like hospitality, caring for the sick, sharing possessions, and forgiveness . . .

Since relationships are defined by the persons who are related, Christian prayer should lead individuals and communities into closer conformity with the character of Jesus, the Way that leads to God. Scripture provides the profile of Jesus that becomes normative for the practices of spirituality. These practices are regular, concrete activities that tutor Christians in the ways of Christ. Embodied spirituality, therefore, links the content of the story of Jesus to lives that express the gospel. The practices of Christian spirituality provide pedagogical avenues by which, under the power of God's spirit, the transformation called for by the Gospels is able to occur.[14]

What, then, is the minister to be or do today? Clearly, it is tempting to be seduced by recipes and formulae that deliver clarity and perhaps suggest achievement or potential success. But I would suggest that a fresh focus on the role and identity of the minister is a more fruitful path towards

---

[12] W. Willimon (2000), *Calling and Character: Virtues of the Ordained Life* (Nashville, TN: Abingdon Press), pp. 43–4.

[13] Charles R. Foster, Lisa E. Dahill, Lawrence A. Golemon and Barbara Wang Tolentino (2006), *Educating Clergy: Teaching Practice and Pastoral Imagination* (San Francisco, CA: Jossey-Bass).

[14] William Spohn (1999), *Go and Do Likewise: Jesus and Ethics* (New York: Continuum), pp. 13–14, 41, 48–9.

encouraging super, natural, organic church growth. This is where space for watchfulness becomes important. The training and formation of clergy is not about agreeing curricula. It is about forming and reforming communities of wisdom that can discern, foster and nourish vocations. This requires the renewing of our minds; and the daily renewal of vocations to serve God and the world. As Rowan Williams noted:

> Within and beyond all the debates about the detail of theological education and ministerial formation these days, the largest question still remains too often unanswered: what is the shape and unity of the Christian view of creation itself? What is the comprehensive story we tell? This is not a question about having more 'doctrine' in a course, but about how the whole process of ministerial education makes us natives in the landscape into which Jesus has invited us, and gives us some of the tools for celebrating how God has acted to introduce us into this place. We are not called on to give a bit more room to one module among others here, but to see this actual and present world joyfully and consistently in the light of God's being and doing, in the light of the Trinitarian life and the incarnation of the Word.[15]

In view of this, four final hallmarks for mission and ministry, and for priesthood and a priestly Church, are offered here, by way of a brief conclusion.

First, ministry is Sacramental-Transformative. To be a priest or a priestly Church is to have an understanding that ordinary material (such as bread, wine, water) can be transformed by prayer and worship into something through which God speaks to us and spiritually nourishes us. But one cannot confine this axis to the standard tokens of the sacramental life of the Church. Congregations and ministers find that casual conversations, pastoral encounters, acts of service and other activities are also sacramental and transformative; they become 'places' where the life of God meets the life of the world. The more alert a congregation is to how God feeds and sustains his people, the more likely it is that this food will be shared, and more people transformed.

Second, ministry is Reciprocal-Representative. That is to say, that while the minister or priest may undoubtedly represent Christ to the people, the congregation continually looks for the ways in which Christ is present both within itself and outside itself. This is an important dimension in mission, for it affirms the activity of the Holy Spirit beyond the borders of the Church, and reminds parishes and congregations that Christ can be encountered in new and alien ways, for which the Church needs to be

---

[15] Rowan Williams (2004), 'The Christian Priest Today', lecture at Ripon College Cuddesdon, Oxford, 28 May.

receptive. At a contextual level, churches that grow organically will tend to have deep partnerships with a variety of secular agencies that complement its work and mission, so that the 'common good' and the blessing of social capital becomes an enlarged and shared task.

Third, ministry has a Sacrificial-Receptive dynamic. Obviously, priesthood, as with other forms of ministry, is costly. But the cost is often found not in the output, but in the receptivity to the input. Individuals will confess and confide in priests and pastors all kinds of things that can go no further; or ask them to believe what they cannot (vicariously). Here, priests have a role as absorbers of pain; of receiving knowledge that cannot be shared; of taking upon themselves burdens that are being finally deposited, once and for all. There is some salvific and cathartic value here, to be sure. But it can also be noted that when an individual finally feels that he or she 'can tell you anything' (and not be judged, but simply loved), that person finally feels free to belong to the body of Christ. The costly ministry of sacrificially receiving people's lives and stories allows individuals to be grafted into the Church.

Fourth, ministry is also a delicate combination of the Pastoral-Prophetic. The old English adage expresses it well – clergy are there to 'comfort the afflicted and afflict the comfortable'. The imperative to offer love, nurture and tenderness has to be balanced with the responsibility to speak out, which can be costly. Sometimes, numerical growth and popularity must be sacrificed to truth and justice. The natural and organic growth that God gives to individuals or congregations sometimes requires heavy pruning and some interventionist cultivation. Yet, in all of this, it must be remembered that it is God alone who gives the growth. It can be engineered, and such engineering can sometimes be effective in terms of intellectual growth or the development of skills for ministry. But I remain convinced that the only true growth is the natural and deep kind that God invariably bestows upon a faithful, hopeful and joyful people.

This may be a deeply unfashionable note on which to conclude, but perhaps the most important thing about being a minister is, after all, to be vested in the notion of occupation. Our ministers are to be occupied with God. And then to be preoccupied with all the people, places and parishes that are given by God into our care: to dwell among, care for and love those people and places as Christ would himself. This is an uncommon occupation, to be sure. But one that comes only from the deepest sense of vocation, and that profound and humbling wisdom that calls us to be perpetually renewed before the face of Christ.

Part 1

UNDERSTANDING MINISTRY

1

The developing philosophy of ministry

JOHN FITZMAURICE

Context – from Reformation to postmodernism

Ministry is peculiar and particular. Those being licensed for ministry in the Church of England are reminded in the preface of the Declaration of Assent that they are to proclaim the faith afresh in each generation – that the ministry of the Church is uniquely expressed in its context, and reimagined for every new context. Thus ministry seeks to be responsive to the particularity of its situation. But what are the factors or criteria that shape that ministry, and how are those involved in the tasks of ministry to best exercise their ministries? What are the deep signposts that guide those who exercise ministry in the name of the Church? In this ever-changing and dynamic task, what is our philosophy of ministry to be?

It's important to recognize that the Church's understanding of ministry has always been contested. Indeed one of the great motivations for both the English and Continental Reformations was the reform of ministerial practice. The subsequent rewritings of the Anglican Ordinal witness to an attempt to articulate a fresh and reinvigorated ministerial vision. Clericalism and the cultic and sacerdotal practices that surrounded it is replaced with a much clearer vision of the relationship between priest and people. Webster suggests that the trajectory of the post-Reformation ordinals was away from a sacerdotal model of priesthood towards a more didactic one, and indeed that Cranmer's reworking of the eucharistic rite was not an exclusion of sacrificial understanding, but rather a radical reworking of it.[1] He suggests that the motivation for this was a move away from an understanding of the role of the priest as a mediator of sacrifice to that of a minister of word and sacrament, refocusing the salvific sacrificial action on that of Christ.[2] This shift of emphasis was not uncontroversial,

---

[1]   J. B. Webster (1988), 'Ministry and Priesthood', in S. Sykes and J. Booty (eds), *The Study of Anglicanism* (London: SPCK), pp. 285–96.
[2]   Webster, 'Ministry and Priesthood', p. 288.

causing some to question the validity of Anglican orders and suggesting a breech in apostolicity. For Evangelicals the fear was that that revised emphasis was not reformed enough. Such tensions lingered on until they were reignited in the revivals of the nineteenth centuries, Anglo-Catholics seeking to re-establish a clear link between Anglican orders and the historic Church, notably the early Church, while Evangelicals sought faithfulness to Scripture and an openness to the Spirit. In 1896 a further dynamic was added by Pope Leo XIII's declaration in *Apostolicae Curae* that Anglican orders were to be considered null and void.

The twentieth century, particularly its latter half, saw a renewed emphasis on the ministry of the whole Church and alongside it a search to articulate a theology of ordination within that wider context, something that Webster suggests tended towards functionalism.[3] The last few decades of the twentieth century within the Church of England were coloured by the extensive and passionate debates surrounding the ordination of women as priests.

So within the Church, the nature of ministry has always been contested, and that continues into the twenty-first century as we shall see. However, that societal context in which ministry is exercised has also changed dramatically. The contemporary context, which can variously be described as postmodern, secularist, post-Christian and even post-secular, has significant and lasting implications for how the Church understands and exercises its ministry, and it is essential that the Church deeply understands that context if it is to minister effectively to it.

Postmodernism is, of course, characterized by its rejection of metanarrative – there is no objective truth because all meaning is socially constructed – a key consequence of which is a relativistic approach to moral and ethical issues. How the Church, rooted as it is in a clear metanarrative, responds to such a challenge is a fundamental question as it tries to develop a philosophy of ministry.

Foundational to our understanding of both postmodernism and secularism is a recognition of their complexity. J. K. A. Smith, drawing on Taylor,[4] points to the paradox of this, noting that proponents of secularism view it as neutral, unbiased, objective, rational and a-religious, while the reality is that secularism is an alternative metanarrative that seeks to exclude religious voices from the public square. The problem as Smith

---

[3] Webster, 'Ministry and Priesthood', p. 293.
[4] J. K. A. Smith (2014), *How (Not) to Be Secular: Reading Charles Taylor* (Grand Rapids, MI: Eerdmans); C. Taylor (2007), *A Secular Age* (Cambridge, MA: Harvard University Press).

points out is that life is difficult and complex and secularist accounts don't help us understand it. Increased rationality does not lead to an abandonment of religion, as religion actually handles complexity better, and thus, Smith suggests, ultimately renders secularism untenable and unsustainable. David Lyall writes:

> In the midst of complexity and ethical ambiguity the pastoral task is not to provide easy answers or to lead people to believe that such answers exist (if indeed they ever did). Rather, the pastoral task is to 'hold' people in the midst of the complexity and ambiguity and to help them to catch a vision or be grasped by a grace which is more profound than the easy answer.[5]

The exclusion of religion, and with it transcendence, from the public square leaves a vacuum, which Smith and Taylor both suggest is filled with a creation of secularism, namely exclusive humanism. This is characterized not simply by what is left when religious discourse and the notion of transcendence is removed from the public square, but by the creation of a substitute. However, both Smith and Taylor suggest that the remaining immanent framework is subject to what they describe as 'cross-pressure' from the complexity of postmodernity. The postmodern marketplace of ideas contains many alternative narratives of meaning and significance, and thus both the exclusive humanism of secularity, and the faith of devout religious belief, are subject to an increased contestability. Thus, they claim, secularity changes belief rather than doing away with it – doubt becomes more common for the religious believer but also for the espoused atheist. The implications of this are significant as we grope our way towards a developing philosophy of ministry.

Postmodern ministry and secular discourse

The complexity of the contemporary context and the swirling morass of undifferentiated discourses of meaning and significance have challenged the Church in how it goes about its ministry. Whereas in pre-modern and modernist times any debates about the nature of ministry were largely internal to the Church and undertaken within the prevailing Christian metanarrative, with the onset of postmodernism the Church and its ministry has found itself, for better or for worse, engaging with non-theological discourses. How is the Church to handle non-theological data? How is the minister to discern its appropriateness in ministry offered in the name

---

[5] D. Lyall (2001), *The Integrity of Pastoral Care* (London: SPCK), p. 74.

of the Church? To understand this more clearly, we will examine two examples: the influence on the life of the Church and on the practice of ministry of psychodynamic theory and pastoral counselling, as well as theories and practices of leadership and management.

Pastoral counselling

David Lyall, in his excellent study of the Christian ministry of pastoral care, *The Integrity of Pastoral Care* (2001), notes the achievements of the modern counselling movement. No major tragedy can occur without those being caught up in it being offered counselling; specific forms of counselling such as marriage counselling, bereavement counselling and debt counselling are now endemic. It has become a well-organized, professionally accountable movement with high standards of training and practice. In the UK it can be accessed via the National Health Service (NHS) and, perhaps more commonly, privately. Yet Lyall notes a shadow side to all this as well – people cannot be 'given counselling' as if it were a commodity; for the process to be effective it requires the intentional commitment of the client to a real openness and engagement. He also notes that a mere paper qualification doesn't guarantee the personal or relational skills required. Perhaps the real risk identified by Lyall is the deskilling of those who have traditionally cared for others, and who feel disenfranchised in the new world of trained, qualified and certified counsellors.

This sense of deskilling has been prevalent in clergy and others in Christian pastoral roles. Alongside the deskilled and demotivated there have been those in pastoral ministry who have fully embraced the insights and tools of counselling, and have undertaken subsequent training in one of its disciplines. Trained or not, few of those involved in pastoral work today are unaware of the fundamentals of good listening and appropriate responding and their transformational impact on those they seek to help.[6] Such practices interrogate the Church's traditional practice of pastoral care at a profound level. How is the Church, and those who minister in its name, to respond to this new repertoire?

Leadership

A similar dilemma faces the Church in its interface with leadership and management theory.[7] Ever since the publication in 1994 of *Working as One Body*, the Church of England has increasingly embraced aspects of secular

---

[6] Lyall, *Integrity of Pastoral Care*, p. 5.
[7] For more on this see Chapter 29, 'Critical paradigms of ministry'.

business theory and practice.[8] This reached its zenith in September 2014 with the publication by a committee chaired by Lord Stephen Green, former group chairman of HSBC and a non-stipendiary priest in the Church of England, of a report entitled *Talent Management for Future Leaders and Leadership Development for Bishops and Deans: A New Approach* that quickly became known as the Green Report.[9] In brief the report suggests the provision of a special programme training bishops and deans in strategic organizational leadership skills, and the creation of a talent pool from where the next generation of bishops and deans may be called. The programme, which includes a mini-MBA, will be 'capable of delivering sustainable organisational change'.[10]

It is significant that the report is explicit is rejecting the Church's theological education institutions and internal trainers as potential deliverers of the new programme, preferring instead 'a major university or business school'.[11] The report goes on to say:

> External perspectives will be supplied from organisations like the National Trust, BBC, NHS Health Trusts and the Armed Services. The module will conclude with examining the importance of measurement and controls, including an overview of financial and other measurement tools and techniques.[12]

Here we see the Church clearly taking advantage of the complex marketplace of meaning and significance provided by postmodernism and embracing its insights in the hope of gaining a wisdom that will enable it to better fulfil its missionary task. But we also see a clear rejection of its own processes and structures as being not up to the job.

Another report published at almost the same time took a more circumspect view. *Senior Church Leadership: A Resource for Reflection* was published in early 2015 by the Faith and Order Commission under the chairmanship of Bishop Christopher Cocksworth.[13] This report recognizes the hold that the language around leadership already has on the Church,

---

[8] Archbishops' Council (1995), *Working as One Body: Report of the Archbishops' Commission on the Organisation of the Church of England* (London: Church House Publishing).

[9] Archbishops' Council (2014), *Talent Management for Future Leaders and Leadership Development for Bishops and Deans: A New Approach* (online): <http://www.thinkinganglicans.org.uk/uploads/TalentManagement.pdf> (accessed 12 October 2018).

[10] Archbishops' Council, *Talent Management*, p. 10.

[11] Archbishops' Council, *Talent Management*, p. 10.

[12] Archbishops' Council, *Talent Management*, p. 12.

[13] Archbishops' Council (2015), *Senior Church Leadership: A Resource for Reflection* (online): <https://www.churchofengland.org/sites/default/files/2017-10/senior_church_leadership_faoc.pdf> (accessed 12 October 2018).

and seeks to answer the question 'what are the underlying theological principles that inform the exercise of leadership within the church?'[14] The report identifies the emergence of talk about leadership after the Second World War, developing in the 1960s and coming into full bloom in the 1980s. Interestingly the report suggests two motivations for the increase in the use of such language: (1) the growing commitment to ecumenical relationships and in some cases shared working, and (2) the apparent avoidance of hierarchical implications of other attributions – leadership seemed to be a term that all those involved could gather around without the 'denominational and traditional baggage' of other terms.[15] Yet the report's authors are significantly more coy than those of the Green Report. They write:

> We will be discussing . . . the fact that the use of leadership language to talk about Christ's church is not particularly biblical – and the fact that this is not necessarily a problem (since the church is always unavoidably involved in borrowing and transforming language from elsewhere). Nevertheless, it is a telling fact that the New Testament authors seem consciously to have avoided the most obvious words for 'leader' in their culture, presumably because they wanted to avoid buying in to the kinds of behaviour and organization that were associated with that language.[16]

Here we have a sense that some sort of discretion is needed, some sort of dialogue between the received discourse of Scripture (and tradition) and the more recent culture of leadership. But it is to be a wise and respectful dialogue, with a clear focus. The authors write:

> We have been speaking as if there were a straightforward opposition between the desire for stronger leadership and criticisms of the increased focus on leadership in the church. That does not, however, do justice to the situation in which we find ourselves. On both sides the same question is being asked: What is needed for the ministry and mission of the church to flourish?

They realize that they and others can only begin to answer that question if they pay 'deeper attention to the nature of the church and its calling, and to the God who calls it'.[17]

These two examples portray clearly the tensions and dilemmas that those who minister in the name of the Church face in a postmodern age. How

---

[14] Archbishops' Council, *Senior Church Leadership*, p. 6.
[15] Archbishops' Council, *Senior Church Leadership*, p. 11.
[16] Archbishops' Council, *Senior Church Leadership*, p. 14.
[17] Archbishops' Council, *Senior Church Leadership*, p. 20.

are we to relate to secular discourse that at first sight seems to have much to offer, and yet is not part of the narrative that forms the community of the Church? Such questions cut at the root of our philosophy of ministry.

Before we can go on and begin to sketch an answer to such questions, and indeed a developing philosophy for ministerial practice, we need to reiterate explicitly the nature of secular discourse and its implications. As we saw above, part of the narrative of secularism is that it is neutral, unbiased, objective and rational, uncontaminated by religious speculation and irrationality; this belief, for that is what it is, is carried over into its disciplines, including pastoral counselling and leadership theory, and many in the Church, including those active in ministerial practice, have been convinced by it. Those in the Church who have embraced such insights have done so in the belief that these tools are agenda-free, morally neutral tools. The claim of secularism described above, however, bears further exploration. As the work of both Taylor and Smith has demonstrated, postmodernism and its concomitant secularism is far from philosophically neutral. At the root of all of this is the Enlightenment notion that as human beings we have all that we need to solve our own problems, to plan our own destinies – if something is amiss we just need a better strategic plan, be it corporate or personal, rendering the need for transcendence obsolete. Indeed some have gone so far as to suggest that secularism and its attendant disciplines have the hallmarks of a pseudo or even alternative religion,[18] with its own gurus and rituals.

Does this mean then that those involved in ministerial work should reject the tools of the secular world in favour of some allegedly 'purer' form of ministerial philosophy, uncontaminated by culture? I would suggest not, not least because as we saw at the outset, ministry activity is always contextual, always in dialogue with the surrounding culture, both personal and societal. I would, however, suggest that the ministerial dialogue with secular disciplines needs to be undertaken with real discernment and wisdom.

Applied theology

David Lyall is anxious. Writing about pastoral practice, he fears a capitulation of practitioners, consciously or unconsciously, to counselling models.[19] He is clear that pastoral care has its own integrity, and while

---

[18] See S. Pattison (1997), *The Faith of the Managers: When Management Becomes Religion* (London: Cassell).

[19] Lyall, *Integrity of Pastoral Care.*

there may be things the Church can learn from certain secular disciplines, it should guard against becoming dependent upon them, not least because it has no need to. What is needed, he suggests, is a retrieved confidence in the Christian community's own practice of ministry and care, and while this is very much open to engagement to the prevailing culture, it is not its prisoner.

Lyall, however, rejects the isolationist approach in ministry whereby the practitioner simply 'applies' pre-learned theological formulas to any and every situation. Such an approach is not relational, compassionate, or indeed just. It is based on a false assumption about the nature both of theology and of the ministerial task. He describes it thus:

> That assumption is that theology is essentially propositional and is learned from lectures or found in books in libraries. And if in any given situation one does not have the 'right' theological answer, then the only recourse is to return to the place where the answers are to be found, namely the books, where surely someone will have something relevant to offer.[20]

Because of the dynamics of power that surround this purist, isolationist approach, it prefers hierarchical models of ministry – the person with the theory (the minister) is not on an equal footing with the individual or group being helped; this is a very top-down model of care. It also misunderstands the relationship between theory and practice, as Ballard and Pritchard point out:

> We are finding out today, however, that there is no simple, deductive relationship between theory and practice. Rather there is a dialectical exchange between them. In theological terms: beliefs have been hammered out in the very practical struggles and controversies of Christian history; while at the same time the deeds of witness and service have been informed by a living faith.[21]

Engaged theology

So if we are to reject a ministerial model of 'applying' preformed theological truths to any given situation, what other options are open and available to us? A more dialogical mode of doing pastoral theology is that of critical correlation. Ballard and Pritchard trace the lineage of this methodology

---

[20] Lyall, *Integrity of Pastoral Care*, p. 28.
[21] P. Ballard and J. Pritchard (1996), *Practical Theology in Action: Christian Thinking in the Service of Church and Society* (London: SPCK), p. 60.

from Paul Tillich to the detailed work of Don Browning.[22] Tillich suggested that the context, the critical incident, posed the question and that the narrative and symbols of Christian faith provide an answer that addresses the questions asked; thus question and answer are in dialogue. Lyall quotes George Stroup as describing it thus: 'Revelation becomes an experienced reality at that juncture where the narrative identity of an individual collides with the narrative identity of the Christian community.'[23]

This correlation method then allows a full interplay between critical incident, context and the Christian narrative. Ballard and Pritchard offer three manifestations of this methodology.[24] First, a simple dialogue between an issue/experience and the tradition. This, they suggest, is not as straightforward as it might seem – neither the issue/experience, nor the perception of those involved with it, nor the tradition is ever that straightforward. Thus, the task of truly mapping the issue and its potential interface with the theological tradition becomes very complex very quickly. Their second manifestation of the critical correlation method centres on the interface between pastoral concerns and ethics. This involves resourcing those involved from within the Christian ethical and theological tradition to make better decisions in relation to the incidents/events in which they are caught up. The third method of critical correlation identified by Ballard and Pritchard finds its origins in the discipline of hermeneutics. How are we to interpret any given issue or critical incident and what tools does the tradition offer us for such an interpretation? But it doesn't end there; as with all hermeneutics the dynamic can be reversed – what does this issue or critical incident tell us about our understanding of the narrative of faith? Not only does faith interrogate experience, but experience interrogates faith. This can be expanded to include context and culture in the interpretative interchange. How do the secular disciplines interrogate experience and faith, and how does faith interrogate those disciplines and their interpretations of experience? Here, then, we begin to have a truly postmodern method of doing ministerial theology that is open and responsive to the insights of experience, of context and culture, and of the narrative and practices of faith. This has the potential to be a rigorous and vital dialogue which is captured in the methodology of theological reflection, or the pastoral cycle (experience > exploration > reflection >

---

[22] See, among others, D. S. Browning (1996), *A Fundamental Practical Theology: Descriptive and Strategic Proposals* (Minneapolis, MN: Augsburg).

[23] Lyall, *Integrity of Pastoral Care*, p. 34.

[24] Ballard and Pritchard, *Practical Theology in Action*, pp. 62ff.

action).[25] Ballard and Pritchard emphasize the importance of engaging with this process fully (and completing it) if it is to be theologically and ministerially fruitful.

This enables us to begin to recognize a methodology for ministerial practice and pastoral or practical theology that is appropriate to our ministerial context and recognizes the legitimacy of experience, of the secular context and its tools (notwithstanding our reservations about their provenance), and the tradition of faith. It enables us to engage and dialogue robustly with any relevant insights in any given situation and then to try out our responses and subsequently interrogate the new experience and context that emerges as a response to so doing.

But there remains another method for engaging experience, context and faith, and it is from this that we can begin to discern a developing philosophy for ministry.

Habitus and virtue

Ballard and Pritchard also describe the 'habitus' model of practical or ministerial theology. This is less about a specific methodology and more about the cultivation of Christian character. They write: 'So the task of theology, and practical theology in particular, is not in the end to provide methodology or skills, but a training of mind and heart . . . what is needed is a Christian instinct and a Christian nerve.'[26]

It's this Christian character formed in a Christian minister that allows faithful and effective ministry. It means that the minister's instincts are honed and will react appropriately in most situations. This requires in the minister the ability to access and to trust his or her intuitions. When operating in this mode ministers instinctively know when it is appropriate to use the tools of secular discourse to shed light on a problem and when the use of such tools would be inappropriate and only add confusion and dissonance. But the goal of this mode of ministerial theology is the development of Christian character not simply in the minister, but also in the individual and community being ministered to. There are no short cuts to this – the development of character takes place over time and is a result of a life committed to prayer, study and service of others in God's name.

So, in all of this, can we discern a developing philosophy of ministry? Well, I would suggest that we can. The issues we have been exploring have

---

[25] See Ballard and Pritchard, *Practical Theology in Action*, pp. 73ff.; and also L. Green (1990), *Let's Do Theology: A Pastoral Cycle Resource Book* (London: Mowbray).

[26] Ballard and Pritchard, *Practical Theology in Action*, p. 68.

been examined by philosophers, particularly moral philosophers, over time as well, and the approaches we have explored map neatly on to the three key approaches to moral philosophy and, I believe, offer the minister a helpful map for the ministerial task.

The issues around the uncritical importation of secular disciplines into theological discourse and ministerial practice are clearly a manifestation of utilitarianism. Utilitarianism had its origins in the work of Jeremy Bentham, and argued that the key determinator of the correctness of an action was whether it led to the best outcome for the greatest number of people; indeed Bentham believed that this could be statistically calculated. Utilitarianism is all about getting the job done by the most efficient means; in terms of ministerial theology, this means that any tool that helps the Church and its ministers achieve what they think they want to achieve is considered legitimate, regardless of the fact that there might be some concerns about its nature.

Conversely the 'applied' theology method can be seen to have its origins in the deontologicalism of Immanuel Kant. This approach is clear that there is a correct way to act, and this is the way a person should act regardless of the consequences – experience and context are of little or no importance.

What both these approaches have in common is a lack of dialogue. Utilitarianism seeks to get the job done, deontology to obey the rules. Ministerially, neither of these can be considered to be adequate.

The third approach of moral philosophy, which correlates entirely with that of the habitus model of ministerial theology and practice, is that of virtue ethics, an approach brought to wide attention by the publication of Alasdair MacIntyre's book *After Virtue*.[27] MacIntyre, drawing on Aristotle, suggested that it wasn't enough simply to do the right thing; it was necessary to do it for the right reason. Thus moral action, right action, involved not just the external training of a person, but an internal reorientation as well. In ministerial terms this means that ministry is less about learning the skills to be effective or the rules to obey, but rather allowing the mind of Christ to be formed in us. For MacIntyre there are a number of conditions that enable character to be developed. The first is that the person concerned (in our case, the minister) is situated within a *community* – virtuous living and indeed Christian ministry is a corporate activity.

---

[27] A. MacIntyre (1981), *After Virtue: A Study in Moral Theory* (London: Duckworth). For a more extended exploration of virtue ethics and ecclesiology see J. Fitzmaurice (2016), *Virtue Ecclesiology: An Exploration in the Good Church* (Farnham: Ashgate).

MacIntyre says that this community must be shaped by a *narrative* – in the case of Christian ministry, that of Scripture. How this narrative is understood and handed down from one generation to the next will create a *tradition*, which MacIntyre describes as 'a historically extended, socially embodied argument'.[28] Another key part of the formation of character is the undertaking of *practices*. MacIntyre's explanation of practices is complex, but boils down to the fact that we develop character by doing the things we wish to develop; for example, if someone wants to be compassionate he or she needs to do compassionate things. For Christians generally, and particularly for those in public ministry of some sort, these practices will be in the areas of prayer, study and service. And from all of this comes what MacIntyre calls *phronesis* or practical wisdom. Practical wisdom equates to that ministerial intuition we explored above.

'Faithful improvisation'

It is this deep ministerial character that ultimately allows those in ministry to navigate the complexities of the lives of the people they meet, and the wider paradoxical postmodern zeitgeist. It allows, in the words of the Faith and Order Commission's report we examined above, 'faithful improvisation', an improvisation that understands, and is obedient to, the deep underlying structures of the faith, while having the confidence to respond appropriately to any given context. The authors of this report write:

> faithful improvisation in leadership requires communities and individuals deeply grounded in the Christian faith, knowing it well enough and richly enough to be able to see new ways of living it out appropriate to new contexts in which they find themselves.

> Tradition and innovation are not opposed, because deep immersion in tradition is not an awkward constraint upon improvisation but its enabling condition. The more improvisation we want, the deeper the forms of education we will need – and the deeper those forms of education will need to take us into the knowledge of the tradition and knowledge of the scriptures.[29]

Such an approach will be essential as the Church develops over the forthcoming years into an unpredictable, if hopeful, future. However unpredictable the future shape of the Church and its ministry may be, the report notes that some things remain unchanging: the need to keep God at the

---

[28] MacIntyre, *After Virtue*, p. 222.
[29] Archbishops' Council, *Senior Church Leadership*, p. 82.

centre, the need to minister in the midst of people while attending to the context of that ministry, the need to remain disciples as well as ministers and to acknowledge failure when required.

So how are those involved in the tasks of ministry to best exercise their ministries? What are the deep signposts that guide those who exercise ministry in the name of the Church? Can we identify a developing philosophy of ministry? The signposts that guide ministry are, as they have always been, holiness and wisdom, lives committed to, and devoted to, the work of witnessing to the kingdom. Postmodern, secular society offers a new and complex context in which to live these virtues, undergirded by the realization that ministry is not a skill-set to be acquired, but rather a life to be lived in the fullness of our beings.

2

Hermeneutics of ministry

IAN TOMLINSON

ἑρμηνεύειν – make intelligible; interpret; explain; make clear; express; give utterance to.

Setting the scene

One clue to a hermeneutics of ministry lies in the word 'ministry' itself, and is to be found in a possible Latin derivation of the term: *minus*, less; *stare*, to stand – 'He must increase, but I must decrease.'[1] That saying can be understood as a basis and a motivation for a hermeneutics of ministry. John the Baptist interprets for his hearers what they can see for themselves: Jesus proclaiming and embodying the kingdom of God in his own ministry. The disciples, for example, in response to Jesus' parables, do not comprehend immediately that to minister, to serve others, is primarily an implication and an outcome of kingdom values and engagement. They become stuck in a dispute about power, authority and precedence, as to who is the greatest in the kingdom of heaven. Later, ministry becomes institutionalized as a matter of church order and hierarchy, but initially, the challenge and the calling belong to everyone to construe his or her life by exposure to the gospel, having heard the word and kept it. This can be true for people now. There can be a hermeneutical and a humane immediacy to minister, whenever need expresses itself, and the authority for acting morally and practically is self-evident in acts of kindness or justice or love.

The dynamic of ministry is therefore experienced as self-authenticating, and is, thereby, a universal activity in the human potential to care and be pastoral.

The Christian tradition of 'a cup of cold water',[2] given in Christ's name, is said in the gospel to be a focused expression of such a general principle

---

[1] John 3.30 NRSV.
[2] Matthew 10.42 NRSV.

of ministry. The twentieth-century missionary Bishop John V. Taylor, for instance, echoed this recommended radical behaviour by advising an ordinand always to 'stand small' whenever ministering in the parish to which he was licensed. It was enabling advice.

However, in any hermeneutical, or interpretative, process, there is both the question of 'What do you mean by that?' (in this case, an act of ministry) and its correlative, 'How am I to understand what has just happened to me?' (as the recipient of this particular act of ministry). There is an exchange of power and dependence, as well as the chance to check out whatever authority the minister is representing, having taken up the authority in that moment, or over time, to minister to the other. In different circumstances, that 'other' may indeed be the minister, so he or she, too, might be found on the receiving end of specific ministry, negotiating the question 'What is happening to me and why?'[3] In such cases, are ministers acting, for example, 'in persona Christi', or on their own say-so, or as a functionary of the organization of the Church to which they belong, or is their hermeneutic a subtle combination of these and other ways of thinking about ministry and its manifestations, now and heretofore?

A way forward

To explore this hermeneutical dynamic process further, I intend to concentrate on a particular methodology of systemic thinking, developed during the twentieth century and since, and to apply this way of interpretation to the practice of (Christian) ministry. However, this is but one of many hermeneutics available, and might be thought an unconventional way to proceed. The literature is vast when exploring the Western classical, traditional methodologies of ministerial hermeneutics: biblical categories and patterns; patristic developments and definitions; mediaeval hierarchies; Reformation disputes; Counter-Reformation certainties; Latitudinarian practices; Enlightenment challenges; Evangelical revivals; Catholic antiquarianism; nineteenth-century professionalization; twentieth-century secularization, and the present-day emphasis on collaborative baptismal lay ministry, alongside the questioning of predominant clerical paradigms and practices of ministry, personal and professional; and their successes and failures. All these conventional academic approaches can be referenced

---

[3] W. Carr, *The Pastor as Theologian: The Formation of Today's Ministry in the Light of Contemporary Human Sciences*, SPCK, London 1989, 2008.

throughout the rest of this book, in detail, and complement my analysis from a Human Relations stance. Hermeneutics, by definition, requires a multi-aspect approach to the subject under scrutiny, in this study ministry, in order for any insights to emerge.

For example, the necessary analyses of the disciplines of sociology and psychology, anthropology and philosophy, in relation to making ministry intelligible, need to be taken into account, not only internally to the Church but also externally to society and local communities. The advance of the discipline of congregational studies,[4] for instance, has discovered the similarities of expectations of different faith communities to ministry, in whatever form they take, particularly in the roles fashioned by religious leaders, as teachers, arbitrators, welfare workers, spokespersons, worship celebrants and so on, in relation to their congregants. Indeed, the recent UK government provision of secular celebrants at weddings and funerals, as well as naming ceremonies, illustrates the boundary management of 'liturgy', when people meet to welcome a new baby, marry or register a civil partnership, or bid farewell to their dead. How far is this imitative of Christian ministry, received over many centuries as the norm, so that parishioners, for example, might ask the parish priest to minimize the religious content of, say, a cremation service and, rather, emphasize what they have seen at events led by civil celebrants, such as eulogizing the departed rather than praying for the repose of his or her soul?

Here the grammar of hermeneutics comes to the fore for describing what happens when someone, or a community, ministers. A common language has to be achieved, taking into account all the narratives already alluded to in the development over the centuries, as social norms change, of what it means to minister.[5]

For some, from the Catholic and Orthodox traditions, the very nature of their ordination will determine that both the content and the relationship or relatedness of any ministerial action will have an ontology that is given, by virtue of the laying on of hands by a bishop and fellow presbyters. This sacramental stamp is conferred, and the ordained minister's character is thus formed and develops, as the Spirit grows in that minister, throughout the acted-out vocation of the individual throughout his or her life, recognized and authorized by the Church. This notion that a minister is identified by who a minister is, rather than what they do, is symbolized

---

[4] M. Harris, *Organising God's Work: Challenges for Churches and Synagogues*, Macmillan, London 1998.

[5] P. Bühler, 'Hermeneutics', in *The Oxford Companion to Christian Thought*, Oxford University Press, Oxford 2000.

as a norm for all other extended forms of lay ministry, and is not superior, but complementary, to the ministry of, say, teacher, pastor, parent, worker, carer, prophet, evangelist, or the responsibility of engaging in daily work, civic duty and so on.

The context for this understanding of the exercising of ministry is the whole creation, and, immediately, the world, society and local community. Although, in contrast to this bold assertion of its universal nature, this tradition of the meaning of ministry, and the constituency of who recognizes and determines ministry, the opposite may be perceived and experienced as, rather, a narrow ecclesiology, because of the way this expression of ministry has been exercised in a formal, legalistic framework over centuries in the Church as an organization, mirroring societal patterns of governance, nevertheless, its universalist aetiology can be found, in embryo, in the New Testament, especially worked through in the Pastoral Epistles.

In the Evangelical and Protestant traditions, ministry is a function. It emerges from baptismal living, and is a response to the experience of the New Testament Church, being differentiated as gifts of the Holy Spirit as listed, for instance, in 1 Corinthians 12: apostles; prophets; teachers; deeds of power; gifts of healing; forms of leadership; various kinds of tongues. The primary calling for a minister is to preach God's word; all flows from that. Therefore, other derived ministries are, in the first place, to the congregation. In this sense, ministry is pragmatic. Any external stimulus to respond ministerially to those outside the gathered faithful is essentially a missional opportunity. This plays out noticeably, for example, in the engagement with the occasional offices of the Church: baptism, marriage and funerals. In a parochial system, such as in the Church of England, there can be a tension in ministry, and in its delivery by both laity and clergy to those outside the immediate 'flock', and when the parson has the cure of souls of everyone in the parish, in how to prioritize time spent pastorally, on whom and when, and in what circumstances.

Hermeneutics recognizes this plurality in understanding and practice, especially when the Liberal tradition of the interpretation of ministry intervenes, in what is often represented as the middle ground of praxis. A contemporary practical situation can be presented: two gay members of the congregation, as well as being exemplary citizens, loyal to each other for decades, and over the same time-span devout in their discipleship and membership of the weekly worshipping community, want their civil marriage blessed. How am I, as the local minister, to respond to this request? Did the members of the local church understand what was being told them when the enquiry came? What is meant here about marriage, sexuality and the sacraments of the Church? Those who give the message and those who receive it are affected, and self-understanding is tested. The hermeneutics of ministry comes to the fore: theory and practice conflict and converse.

Each generation has had the same dynamic ethical process to face and tackle, but with different subjects over the centuries: capital punishment; slavery; divorce; artificial birth control; marriage after divorce; Just War theory; ecology and climate change; migration and refugees, and so on – the moral setting for ministry: deontological (principles) and teleological (outcomes) factors continuously informing and shaping what ministers think and do, with and for others, when decisions in ministering have to be made and lived with.

When formulating any theological rationale associated with issues such as those listed above, a foundational working model is crucial. The doctrine of the Trinity should always undergird any hermeneutic of ministry.[6] That is, any interpretation should have an integrated relational rationale and demonstrate the co-inhering love that is at the heart of the Godhead: *perichoresis* – a divinely inspired empathetic *kenosis*, in which ministers are emptied of self-interest and filled with a compassion that enables ministry to flow for the benefit of others. In such a way is ministry authenticated and becomes a matter of integrity in its performance. Hermeneutics of ministry is, therefore, Trinitarian – Persons co-inhering in mutual love – the lover and the beloved and the love between them, demonstrating ministry at its best, worth it for its own sake, and for the good of the recipient and the minister – service at its most practical and effective and pastoral.

Person, system and role

Although the use of the word 'person', when referring to the Godhead, is not technically the same as the common usage of the term 'person' in the human sphere, nevertheless, the implications of the origin of both, as categories, are that they mutually predicate relational position and activity. It is, therefore, not surprising that ministry is expressed typically as a personal matter, as reflecting a personal God – 'I AM'.

A sharp focus in any testing of a hermeneutic of ministry is vocation.[7] This is, first, conventionally spoken about as a personal interior calling, tested by the discernment of external examiners, and second, judged

[6] P. S. Fiddes, *Participating in God: A Pastoral Doctrine of the Trinity*, Darton, Longman & Todd, London 2000.
[7] J. Macquarrie, *The Church and the Ministry: Ministerial Character*, Additional Curates Society, undated.

against the criteria of the Church's needs and emphases in ministry, during any particular era, with elements remaining the same throughout history, in terms of the ongoing tradition, since biblical times, of God's call to peoples and individuals to fulfil their destiny.

However, this approach can be very limiting if the personal dimension is solely relied on to manifest ministry and its associated activities. Relationships abound in the sustaining of such a way of working, which can drain the emotional, theological and other internal resources available to the minister. Because God is available all the time, so the minister, lay or ordained, can be caught up in a fantasy of spiritual omnipotence, put on to them by the endless demands of the job and the unrealistic expectations of others. Especially when the modern manifestations of the place of the clergy, for instance, in the social fabric and network of national life are seen to be diminishing, in terms of status and assumed functions in the occasional offices of the Church, which are now met elsewhere, in secular surroundings and with a consumer choice of celebrant, the temptation is to work harder at self-promotion and justification. This can lead to breakdown and loss of faith at worse, or, at least, a disorientated malaise in ministerial living, when running the local church managerially can replace the prophetic, priestly and pastoral vision of the minister's original vocation.

An antidote to this personal emphasis in ministry is role.[8] Role can be said to be the patterning of ideas by which a person organizes his or her behaviour in relation to a specific situation, seen as a system. That ministry is concerned with role, or a series of roles, is a hermeneutic that can bring release, through an understanding of the person who finds, makes and takes up the many different roles required to be a minister, in a series of activities within a boundary that constitute the contexts and the relatedness to the task engaged with, at any particular time, such as presiding at the Eucharist, hearing confessions, preaching a sermon, visiting the sick, chairing meetings, studying the Bible, leading groups, teaching in school, helping at a food bank, praying for others – the list is endless, and determined by what is going on in the Church and society at any particular time. This is a flexible interpretation of ministry that brings with it a realistic immediate accountability in the public sphere through the acknowledgement of the place of representation and dependence, which oscillate between autonomy and reliable availability to others by the minister, within negotiated boundaries, by means of a clear distinction between the exercising of personal power and legitimate authority to act.[9]

---

8   B. D. Reed, *An Exploration of Role*, The Grubb Institute, London 2001.
9   The Grubb Institute, *Relationship and Relatedness*, London 1988.

This psycho-social dynamic interpretation of ministry can be tested in what might be called the 'critical incidents'[10] of working and personal life for a parish priest, incidents that have been characterized as sometimes finding oneself 'lost in familiar places'.[11] Hermeneutics are at the heart of such experiential encounters. A couple, for instance, applying to the vicar for the christening of their child may bring with them all sorts of cultural and social expectations about the sacrament, in terms of a rite of passage. The vicar, on the other hand, may have in his or her mind language about their becoming members of the Church and see them as future congregants. The parents hope for a quiet ceremony on the Sunday afternoon with their families and friends. The vicar favours the rite with the entire usual Sunday congregation present in the morning. The expected input is the request for baptism, the assumed output different to both parties.

This sort of misunderstanding can lead to national exposure in the press whenever there is an unresolved disagreement. Even when the vicar has given thorough instruction in the Christian faith, bringing out all the nuances of the sacrament and its meaning, there is still the question of what the pouring of water will signify. The vicar may never see the couple again, or perhaps not until the baptism of the next child. He or she is disappointed, as they seem not to have understood about commitment to the Church. However, the parents are completely happy. They came for a christening, and that is what they received. The outcome at the antenatal clinic may be that they speak of the event positively; for it is there that the parish's baptismal policy is to be articulated and discovered by parishioners, rather than, say, at the Deanery Synod, by the members attending and making official baptismal policy. It is as though the parents know instinctively that God loves their child and that the sacrament of baptism asserts that prevenient grace. How sensitively the vicar handles the occasion may facilitate the sense of responsive commitment that he or she so longs for as a caring pastor.

Thus a dynamic model of role is discovered in the many exchanges, liturgical and pastoral, in which clergy and laity are involved. To achieve this stance, the minister's self-perception is as a 'person-in-role'. This counteracts the allegation of hypocrisy so common in complaints about the way in which the clergy are often perceived as behaving. This 'insincerity' is not only to be found in the caricature of the 'stage parson', but also

---

[10] J. Newton, S. Long and B. Sievers (eds), *Coaching in Depth: The Organizational Role Analysis Approach*, Karnac, London 2006.

[11] E. Shapiro and W. Carr, *Lost in Familiar Places: Creating New Connections between the Individual and Society*, Yale University Press, New Haven, CT, and London 1991.

when in taking a service a clergyman or woman is thought to be distant or cold. However, what the individual cleric may be doing is keeping to task, such as not breaking down uncontrollably at a particularly tragic funeral, for example. This can be a cause of preventing any opportunity for the mourners to grieve during the service, as they seek to comfort the minister in distress. However, by maintaining the role, as celebrant of the liturgy, the person of the minister may emerge as empathetic through the words used, for example in the panegyric.

This is a flexible and immediately useful way of being a pastor to and with others, by means of a person-in-role relatedness, rather than by trying to sustain personal relationships with everyone for whom I have responsibility as the vicar, leading to potential exhaustion in the attempt to sustain such a network, or, from the opposite perspective, by relating to people rigidly in formal roles, resulting in a perceived 'professional' aloofness towards parishioners, which cannot enable sympathy or empathy when pastoring them.

An analogy is that of sailors who know the general direction they are heading but are continually adjusting the sails and tiller to take the best advantage they can of the prevailing conditions of wind and tide to achieve their goal.[12]

Practical theology

Hermeneutically, it is the Incarnation that provides the distinctively Christian template for ordained and other ministries, because of an earthed identification with the human condition and human behaviour by God the Holy Trinity in the person of Christ, and the representative nature of ministry, ordained and lay, in relation to that identification. It is, therefore, not without significance that anything said about the psychological components of that ministry would be equally demanding. So, in any theological reflection on ministry, the person of Christ will be a particular influence, and there will need to be a hermeneutical attempt at congruence between the two.

In trying to follow this paradigm of Jesus, I have found that power-broking in ministry remains a constant challenge to those who wear the clerical collar, whether literally as ordained ministers or, metaphorically, as those laity in positions that attract unconscious ministerial projections

---

[12] J. Hutton, *Working with the Concept of Organisation-in-the-Mind*, The Grubb Institute, London 2000.

and transferences, as well as processing the phenomenon of counter-transference. This comes about when there is a confusion between role authorization in public ministry and a personal sense of vocation or a leadership style that is motivated by an autocratic rather than a consultative style, such as in arranging a wedding, for example, as people approach the vicar with their requests for photographs or confetti (or both) and wonder what his or her reasons for and against either or both are, and then hear what the rationalizations of the vicar's decisions will be, when challenged by the couple making enquiries, as to why they can or cannot have photographs and confetti.

Such a questioning of motivation can be understood as a rational explanation undermined by an emotional attachment, literally in this case in the Solemnization of Holy Matrimony, to paraphernalia (traditions associated with pagan bridal dowry accoutrements) outside the scope of a Christian, or clerical, interpretation of the sacrament or ceremony, and yet, for the couple, difficult to disentangle from the liturgical rites themselves. Indeed, an informed awareness of those unconscious processes – transference and projection – in a wedding preparation interview, for instance, can be of great assistance in interpreting what is happening to me (my person) and why (my roles) in any individual ministerial encounter or engagement or any communal gathering for worship, pastoral care or administrative business in groups, such as organizing one of the occasional offices of the Church, or when chairing a Parochial Church Council meeting, for example, where people behave in an irrational way, for no apparent reason, and cannot complete their work, and would rather squabble than keep to task. It is precisely at that moment in chairing the group that I resist the move to set up the vicar to 'lead' in the sense outlined below, or 'pair' with a member to resolve the impasse, or waste time in 'fight/flight', a case of an institutional defence against anxiety. It would also undermine years of encouraging the laity to see their primary vocation to serve God in the world, and not in running the Church.

Hermeneutically, therefore, I have particularly found helpful recognizing the theoretical bases of a 'basic assumption' life of groups, small, medium and large.[13] They are 'dependence', when a leader is thrown up by the group to obviate the need to work. The next is 'pairing', when the group unconsciously chooses a couple to get on with the work so that a saviour figure will be produced to provide a hopeful solution. The third option is 'fight/flight', in which the group either gets on with the work or avoids it, often swinging violently between the two reactions. Although echoing

---

[13] W. R. Bion, *Experiences in Groups*, Tavistock Publications, London 1961.

the way in which, as individuals, we encounter these similar feelings and activities at different stages of our personal development, nevertheless, we are required by this schema to address the group manifestation of what has been called 'anti-task' behaviour.

In terms of analysing and interpreting what is going on in any particular pastoral or organizational situation, to be unaware of the possibility that there are unconscious processes taking place in groups and individuals, such as leaders, congregants, parishioners and colleagues, can lead to a much greater confusion than already exists in any human endeavour, which is always messy and unfinished, no matter how rationally the conscious behaviour is undertaken.

Moreover, such an informed understanding of so dense a mental model can be a helpful tool for the work of ministering and pastoring contemporary lay or clergy people; and yet, it is no substitute for the distinctively theological and liturgical, scriptural and pastoral traditions that accompany and inform their roles in the Church in relation to society. Thus can such insights be used alongside, and in conversation with, inherited models of ministry, rather than trumping them with new-fangled 'superior' methodologies, as though now we practitioners really know what is going on in our parishioners' minds, which they demonstrate and disclose through their behaviour in the presence of the clerical cognoscenti.

Hermeneutically, it is worth reiterating that the accessing of a psycho-social dynamic way of thinking for clergy and authorized lay ministers must be scrutinized by the integrity of the encounter itself with the system in which it is set, so as to avoid labelling of parishioners by pastors as psychological types and, therefore, suitable only to certain tasks in the congregational life and parish work and mission. It might be attractive to modern ministers to label other people and to look for repeated patterns in parishioners' and congregants' behaviour. But the deeper attraction to engage with others ministerially might lie far more productively in the area of figurative language, employed in both the biblical and psychological narratives of discerning what constitutes the human person, and the roles they inhabit to express their personalities and responsibilities in relation to themselves and others. This is hermeneutically both a primary stance and a task outcome.

Dependence

When dealing with pastoral situations, the pastor is managing what constitutes a dependent relationship between the pastor and parishioner or congregant. Dependence[14] can also be seen as a characteristic of an understanding of the life of God the Holy Trinity, with implications as well for human social, political and organizational behaviour. This reflection on the nature of dependence as an expression of what God is like can be earthed in the exercise of ministry on all sorts of levels. The liturgical elements express this dependence in a variety of opportunities for pastoral work of all sorts, especially at liminal moments in rites of passage and at the significant stages of a person's life, both individually and corporately. As has already been indicated in reflecting on the place of the unconscious above, it is one of the dangers of this psycho-social approach to interpreting the behaviour of others who appear to be in the grip of events that have negative outcomes for them, especially in relationships at work and for them in their public personas, to brand them as being lacking in self-awareness and of not having any conscious knowledge of how their behaviour affects others. What may be seen by others as their being at the mercy of their unconscious may be experienced by them as being nothing more than misunderstandings by others or as misinterpretations of noble motives and sentiments. Hypotheses, using psychological and group dynamic categories for understanding what is going on, can be tested by using evidence to prove them false or verifiable, but the key for authenticity and integrity for me is constantly to return to the basic challenge, 'What is happening to me and why?', in any particular situation or set of circumstances. This is not a necessarily idiosyncratic exercise, but rather the avoidance of second-guessing the behaviour of others without first checking out with them what they think is going on.

This explanation for the causes of disruptions in human behaviour and the motivations of individuals and groups, which lie outside rather than inside and between people, is representative of a standard Christian understanding of the process of temptation and occasions of sin, repentance, forgiveness, penance and redemptive restitution. In other words, it is a recognition that human beings are caught up in a mythic struggle between good and evil, in which the salvific drama of the incarnation and redemption of Christ is a significant means of solution to these problems for the individual, rather than needing hours of psychoanalysis, psychotherapy, counselling or the ministry of a psychologically aware minster.

---

[14] E. Miller, *From Dependency to Autonomy: Studies in Organization and Change*, Free Association Books, London 1993.

Representation

In terms of dependence, as already described, theological distinctions between differentiated roles in the ministry of the Church, in serving the world, are not the only issue to consider. There is the matter of ministry as representation.[15] Whatever model of ministry is used in the Church, ministers themselves, ordained or lay, commissioned or authorized, priests, bishops, superintendents, moderators, or whatever their official or unofficial designation, will display, consciously or unconsciously, representative attributes and receive a whole range of appropriate and inappropriate psychological projections from those whom they seek to serve.

Christian ordained ministers find that their representative function and being are equally vital parts of their work. When they preside at worship, do they think that they are there on behalf of the assembly or instead of them, in the sense that the congregation are getting on with their own personal spiritual agendas and the presidents with theirs, with little correlation? Here is a challenge as to what, or whom, a Christian minister thinks she or he is representing, and whether or not there is a correspondence between theological or ecclesiological expressions of representation, in rituals, ceremonial, dress and the exercising of power and authority in the Church in relation to society.

The role of representative can be a very helpful one, releasing the individual to take up his or her actual responsibilities, both in terms of those represented and the one representing, as well as for those who can share the role of representative by being present, observing and participating in an event, such as those who take up the position of worshipper. If I take up my role in a system, it gives others the opportunity to take up theirs.

Representation is also used in the Christian tradition as a means of discerning how God is disclosed to human beings, especially in Jesus Christ, as one who acts *on behalf of* the world. Christian ministry, as both the functional manifestation of the Church and its *raison d'être*, responds to this particular Christological slant by employing dynamics and practices that are derived, not only from the pattern of Jesus Christ, but also from psychological and social understandings of representation in human culture. Hermeneutically, ministry shares in that representative process when worshipping and serving others, the style and content of that worship and service being determined by cultural and psychological influences in any particular era. In carrying out Christian ministry, it is necessary to

---

[15] W. Carr (ed.), *The New Dictionary of Pastoral Studies*, SPCK, London 2002.

distinguish between theological and social understandings of representation, so that attempts can be made to speak of one in terms of the other.

Conclusion

A deep insight into this ontological–functional–dependent–representative calling to exercise contemporary ministry can be found in Ancient Eastern mystical, monastic and desert practices. Bishop Rowan Williams, the systematic theologian, characterizes the hermeneutic of these creative tensions in the different traits in vocation to minister by distinguishing between two complementary, but distinctive, types of monks, represented by Abba Arsenius and Abba Moses. He writes:

> two large boats . . . were shown . . . In one of them sat Abba Arsenius and the Holy Spirit of God in complete silence. And in the other boat was Abba Moses, with the angels of God: they were all eating honey cakes. What could put more clearly the sense of the distinctiveness of vocations? . . . Silence and honey cakes are not competing achievements to be marked out of ten . . . there is no hint that Moses or Arsenius lost any sleep over their diversity.[16]

Such a parable is at the heart of any modern hermeneutics of ministry. A priori, there is plenty of theory available to the student and practitioner about how to do ministry; a posteriori, we discover who a minister is by how he or she behaves with and for others. The universal and particular hermeneutical ministerial standard is the life, teaching, example and Spirit of Jesus Christ. The rest is reflective interpretation and the practice of grace.

---

[16] R. Williams, *Silence and Honey Cakes: The Wisdom of the Desert*, Lion, Oxford 2003, p. 43.

3

Anthropology of ministry

ABBY DAY

She finally stopped crying.

What a relief! I had tried to remain composed and impartial listening to her story, as any good academic researcher should be, but it was difficult. Being academic is not the antithesis to being human, but we are reminded constantly, at least in some circles, to be 'objective'. Hearing her story had nearly moved me to tears because it was so heartfelt, immediate; drenched in sadness and pierced by hope. In other words, human.

The attempt of the anthropologist-researcher to remain objective and distant is, I began to learn, the exact opposite of what anthropology is and what the anthropologist needs to be. Like the priest, we are privileged to be touching so often the hearts and, perhaps, even the souls of the people with whom we are paid professionally to interact.

It was a priest who was at the heart of the young woman's story. She was describing to me what her life had been before she had met him, that day when she had happened to be walking by the church. Desolate, worried, depressed, she was pushing one child in a pram while the other, grumpily, walked beside her. Her marriage had just broken up, she had money problems, and the future looked bleak. She had barely noticed the man sweeping the steps outside the church until he spoke to her. He said hello, and she had mumbled something in return. He spoke again, asking her if she was all right, adding that she looked very sad, and wondering if she might like to pop in and have a cup of tea and a chat. It was a chat that would change her life, she told me, crying with the memory of her pain and his kindness. He was gentle, and seemed to understand the terrible mess she was in. What was more, he seemed not to be judging her, or even offering advice, but had just made her feel welcome, as if she almost belonged. From then on, she and her children became part of the life of his church and she drew close to her God.

Her story seemed to fit well into the theories I had already developed, which is always gratifying to an academic. Believing in belonging was by then my niche, and her story would only help to enrich it. There was one part, however, that continued to niggle at me: what was the priest doing that day, *really*? Did the steps always need sweeping, or was the act an excuse to be outside the church, positioned in the hope that a potential new recruit might be passing by? A technique for church growth, perhaps, or maybe, on reflection, it was both an act and a metaphor: sweeping in the sad souls of the modern, atomized, urban landscape. He may have been practising what I have come to understand as an anthropology of ministry, a way of being a priest that put the 'human' with 'the spirit' at the heart of practice.

In this chapter I intend to develop further ideas about what that practice appears to be in the churches I have studied, and to offer some reflections on its future. First, I will review some of the anthropological methods and theories that have most, in my view, influenced an academic understanding of religion in general, and Christianity in particular.

Anthropological practice

Anthropology is an holistic discipline with several sub-disciplines, ranging from physical or biomedical anthropology, through to social anthropology, cultural anthropology, cognitive anthropology, evolutionary anthropology and more. The distinctive focus is on *anthropos* or humankind, which makes it a study not just of people but also of relationship: of the self to another. The anthropology of religion is concerned with the relationality of religious people with each other, with their objects of worship, be they human or other-than-human, and with those outside their immediate religious group – politicians, educators, and others who interact with religious people or organizations. Anthropologists of religion are usually interested in symbols, languages, group processes and rituals.[1] What is generally left out of the study is the 'object of worship' itself.

The method of study adopted by anthropologists, and held as sacred as their singular mark of practice, is 'ethnography'. The American Anthropology Association (AAA) describes ethnography as

> the researcher's study of human behavior in the natural settings in which people live. Specifically, ethnography refers to the description of cultural systems or an aspect of culture based on fieldwork in which the investigator

---

[1] For a review of introductory textbooks on the anthropology of religion, see Abby Day and Simon Coleman (2016), 'Textbooks for Teaching the Anthropology of Religion: A Review', *Religion* 46.2: 209–20.

is immersed in the ongoing everyday activities of the designated community for the purpose of describing the social context, relationships and processes relevant to the topic under consideration. Ethnographic inquiry focuses attention on beliefs, values, rituals, customs, and behaviors of individuals interacting within socioeconomic, religious, political and geographic environments. Ethnographic analysis is inductive and builds upon the perspectives of the people studied. Ethnography emphasizes the study of persons and communities, in both international and domestic arenas, and involves short or long-term relationships between the researcher and research participants.[2]

The AAA further describes ethnography as including a variety of techniques, such as unobtrusive direct observation, participant observation, structured and unstructured interviewing, focused discussions with individuals and community members, analysis of texts, and audio-visual records. The distinctive qualities of ethnography compared to other methods, such as interviewing without participant observation, surveys or historical techniques, is the proximity of researcher to researched. This is not an arm's-length discipline, but more a hands-dirty (or 'up to the elbows in dishwater', as I describe my research with elderly church laywomen)[3] exercise. Rather than feared, subjectivity is an aspect to be cultivated. The goal, as the founder of ethnography, Bronislaw Malinowski, described it, is to 'to grasp the native's point of view, his relation to life, to realize *his* vision of *his* world'.[4] Malinowski, like many people of his time, including missionaries, soldiers and teachers who worked in European colonies, carried an inherently colonial view of his 'subjects'. Just as missionaries assumed the 'natives' needed civilizing and bringing-to-Jesus, there ran through Malinowski's private, posthumously published diary aggressive comments about his informants, indicating his dislike of their attitudes and behaviours.[5] Raymond Firth's second Introduction to the diary's second edition reflects on the critical reception to the first edition, concluding:

> It is not merely a record of the thinking and feeling of a brilliant, turbulent personality who helped to form social anthropology; it is also a highly

---

2   See <http://bit.ly/20ld4OB>.
3   See Abby Day (2015), 'The Spirit of "Generation A": Older Laywomen in the Church', *Modern Believing* 56.3: 313–23; Abby Day (2017), *The Religious Lives of Older Laywomen: The Last Active Anglican Generation* (Oxford: Oxford University Press).
4   Bronislaw Malinowski (1961 (1922)), *Argonauts of the Western Pacific* (New York: E. P. Dutton), 25.
5   Bronislaw Malinowski (1967), *A Diary in the Strict Sense of the Term* (London: The Athlone Press).

significant contribution to the understanding of the position and role of a fieldworker as a conscious participator in a dynamic social situation.[6]

The process of reflection on one's role is what has become known in anthropology as 'reflexivity': active engagement with our own prejudices and coloured perceptions. It would be, perhaps, similar to the priestly practice of prayer and contemplation about one's own flaws and culpability. Just as priests occupy themselves with moral questions and problems, so too is anthropology concerned with ethics, values and what it means to be good, or bad.[7]

To adopt an anthropological approach to ministry would thus encompass three main ingredients:

1 centring on the 'human';
2 awareness of the context;
3 reflexivity.

Methodologically, anthropologists generally adopt a 'methodological atheism'. Their goal is to study how people enact their religion, or relationship to a god or higher power – not whether such an entity exists. Sensible on the surface, closer inspection may reveal a standard normative position. The stance is not neutral: if, for example, we were to study how people feel about their current political leaders, it would be startling to discover that their allegiance was wholly misplaced if Prime Minister Theresa May did not actually exist.

There is therefore often embedded in early anthropological studies an assumption that the people being studied might be well intentioned, but wrong. Such an assumption is not surprising as it was the core belief (if we can apply such an emotive term to social scientists – and why not? – as will be discussed below) behind the person who became the world's first Professor of Anthropology at Oxford University: Edward Burnett Tylor.[8] He made his mark initially through his work on religion, particularly his idea that animism, or faith in the soul, stems from an individual's mistaken belief in spiritual beings.

Tylor's Quaker background may have had two significant impacts on his understanding of belief. His religious upbringing may have predisposed

---

6   Malinowski, *A Diary*, xxxi.
7   See, for example, Joel Robbins (2004), *Becoming Sinners: Christianity and Moral Torment in a Papua New Guinea Society* (Berkeley: University of California Press); Joel Robbins (2013), 'Beyond the Suffering Subject: Toward an Anthropology of the Good', *Journal of the Royal Anthropological Institute*, 19: 447–62.
8   Edward Burnett Tylor (1958 (1871)), *Primitive Culture* (New York: Harper).

him to accepting a wider, non-theistic view of religion, while his religious status as a Quaker barred him initially from being accepted into Oxford or Cambridge, as Quakers and Catholics were not allowed until 1871 to study there. He first learned about other cultures while travelling in Central America, and returned to England determined to understand more about what became known as 'cultural anthropology'. Once he ceased being a Quaker he was admitted to Oxford and became a reader, then professor. There is something pleasingly ironic about a religious-scholar outcast becoming one of the most significant anthropologists of religion.

Tylor argued that religion started from the tendency of people to explain why they saw visions of deceased ancestors. They concluded that they had a dual nature, spirit and material. The visions of their ancestors were, they believed, their actual ancestors returning to their worldly position, and they would therefore need to be cared for and honoured by providing food or gifts at their graves or household shrines. As the ancestors were then accorded a controlling or at least overseeing role, they became what we would now describe as gods, and their worship was the origin of religion. Thus, the root of religion was ancestor worship. Tylor went further than this and developed theories of animism – the belief that everything, material and non-material, has a soul. While reasonable, according to some kind of primitive logic, those conclusions were, he argued, simply wrong. They were similar to beliefs held by children, out of which they would grow as they became older and wiser. Societies also develop, he thought, as they become more rational and correct-thinking through the benefit of science. A man of his Victorian time, embracing the ideas of evolution, Tylor universalized his theory to a grand narrative that explained the development of religion everywhere. Writing as he did more than a century ago, Tylor might now be surprised to find the continuing presence and, in many 'evolved' Euro-American countries, the growth of animist beliefs, sometimes described as New Age, Pagan and Neo-Pagan.

Such ideas can seem threatening, and many Protestant traditions will oppose practices such as lighting candles for deceased loved ones, while at the same time increasingly offering services for the departed on All Souls' Day. In one church I visited I noticed a printed card next to a box of tea lights explaining that it was perfectly acceptable to light a candle in memory of a departed loved one. This was not superstitious, the text explained, but an acceptable means of commemoration. Priests who also accept this may be keeping in step with popular conceptions. Large-scale surveys support the view that belief in life after death is a common phenomenon: Haraldsson's 2006 paper based on analysis of the European Values Survey, for example, showed that a majority of those surveyed from Nordic countries believe in life after death and 43 per cent in reincarnation.[9] I have argued elsewhere that belief in life after death arises from the experience of extraordinary relationality and can be understood as a late modern Euro-American form of ancestor veneration that serves to preserve social relations and, particularly, patriarchal gender norms.[10] Further, I have called for a re-conception of the term 'religious experience' to acknowledge that most of those so-called experiences are more humanly than divinely inspired.

Hay and Hardy conducted research similar to mine, involving in-depth interviews, and heard similar stories about people's experience of something outside their 'everyday selves'.[11] In reviewing what people said, and to what or whom they attributed that presence, Hay concluded that other than the named experience of God, experiences such as 'premonitions, encounters with the dead and encounters with an evil presence were often ruled out of the category religious'.[12] He concluded, however, by suggesting:

> On the basis of what people have said to us, then, I feel that 'religious experience' is not quite the right term for what we have been describing. I would be more correct to say that it is a type of experience which is commonly given a religious interpretation. For reasons of shorthand I intend to continue to use the word 'religious' while recognising that this is only one way of looking at it.[13]

And yet, from his research alone it was evident that most people's experiences were not given a religious interpretation, thus rendering his 'shorthand' as rather obscuring the significance of the beliefs of people who reported such experiences. Anthropologists resist creating overly generalized categories because they have a tendency to creep into an emerging canon and can be used to suit all manner of theories and agendas. Questionnaires, for example, that persist in asking if people believe in 'heaven' fail to separate a religious trope of 'heaven' as a place for the godly and good from heaven as a place for continuing adherent relationships.

---

9   Erlendur Haraldsson (2006), 'Popular Psychology, Belief in Life after Death and Reincarnation in the Nordic Countries, Western and Eastern Europe', *Nordic Psychology* 58.2: 171–80.

10 Abby Day (2012), 'Extraordinary Relationality: Ancestor Veneration in Late Euro-American Society', *Nordic Journal of Religion and Society* 25.2: 57–69.

11 David Hay (1982), *Exploring Inner Space: Scientists and Experience* (Harmondsworth: Penguin); A. C. Hardy (1979), *The Spiritual Nature of Man: A Study of Religious Experience* (Oxford: Oxford University Press).

12 Hay, *Exploring Inner Space*, 152.

13 Hay, *Exploring Inner Space*, 162–3.

Many priests have told me that their parishioners frequently experience what they describe as the presence of a deceased loved one and yet rarely admit it, so burdened are they with the guilt of affording the status of 'spirit' to anything less than God. Those experiences may reflect some otherworldly phenomena, but also a specific way of conceiving *this* world that anthropologists have long been interested in. Those extraordinary, supra-human experiences[14] may be similar to what Lévy-Bruhl described as a 'law of participation' where distinctions between the material world and the spiritual worlds are irrelevant and all interactions are experienced emotionally and perceived as relational.[15] This is, he says, different from the 'laws of contradiction' that are taught and reinforced in our society. Even today, he concluded, people in contemporary society are also at times 'pre-logical' as they seek the ecstasy experienced through a sense of total participation. Although such terms as *pre-logical* forced much criticism of his work, Luhrmann points out that Lévy-Bruhl's idea of interconnection is the core of many contemporary spiritualist and witchcraft beliefs.[16] For many of my informants there was no obvious distinction between the everyday and the ever-after. Transcendence is here shifted to an everyday, human, social scale, relocating a transcendent 'other' to an everyday experience of the ever-after. As Wood observed, the so-called spiritual experiences that sometimes may appear to be fluid and free-floating, such as certain forms of New Age spirituality, are in practice often deeply rooted in social and particularly kinship networks.[17] The manner in which accounts were related in my study contributed to my theories about beliefs arising from and being performed through relational social engagement. Beyond belief, there are ritual practices that indicate belief in life after death.

A legacy of Tylor's work is not only his view of the evolutionary, universalistic nature of religion, but also his definition of religion itself as a 'belief in spirits'. He argued that religious belief resulted from the need to explain uncanny events and would therefore eventually be replaced with the benefit of scientific knowledge and other civilizing influences as societies evolved through a linear series of predictable stages. Many theorists

---

[14] These ideas are further elaborated in Abby Day (2013 (2011)), *Believing in Belonging: Belief and Social Identity in the Modern World* (Oxford: Oxford University Press).

[15] L. Lévy-Bruhl (1926), *How Natives Think* (London: George Allen & Unwin), 76.

[16] Tanya M. Luhrmann (2007), 'How Do You Learn to Know That It Is God Who Speaks?', in D. Berliner and R. Sarró (eds), *Learning Religion: Anthropological Approaches* (New York and Oxford: Berghahn Books), 83–102.

[17] M. Wood (2004), 'Kinship Identity and Nonformative Spiritual Seekership', in S. Coleman and P. Collins (eds), *Religion, Identity and Change: Perspectives on Global Transformations* (Aldershot: Ashgate), 191–206.

today, such as those advocating 'rational choice' and evolutionary social science, can trace their intellectual lineage to Tylor. In common with other anthropologists of the nineteenth and early twentieth centuries, Tylor gained his knowledge from reading the accounts of other people, largely missionaries and colonials, and then tended to universalize their findings into general theories. As Lambek noted, Tylor's theories 'remain congenial to many contemporary thinkers and [are] indeed almost a part of western "common sense" on the subject'.[18]

Tylor formed his theories in isolation from the people he was actually studying, which must have influenced his theories to some extent. Those early anthropological theorists are sometimes dismissed as 'armchair anthropologists'. Their distance from the real, messy, confusing reality of human experience can possibly incline them towards their accounts of religion and belief being wholly propositional, rooted in an apparently coherent system of ideas, rather than in lived experience and collective beliefs and practices.

While Tylor's view of belief could be described as intellectualistic, psychological, universal, evolutionary, it is also profoundly individualistic. The idea that belief serves to explain uncanny events and gives meaning to life is a strong theme that arises frequently within the sociology of religion and religious studies, and has consequently influenced hundreds of researchers. Taking a more anthropological and ethnographic approach, other scholars have constructed anthropological theories that religion was not individualistic but was a product of collective, human behaviour that had real impact on people and wider society.

From theology to theodicy

The individualistic tendency in anthropology was partly corrected by Edward Evan Evans-Pritchard who concluded that the people he studied were wrong, but not irrational. Following Malinowski's example, Evans-Pritchard absorbed himself in the life of those he studied, becoming fluent in their languages and making detailed observations. His work moved anthropological thinking along in several ways, probably most notably in showing how social systems and people's cosmologies – or worldviews about meaning and causation – intersect and are mutually dependent.

---

[18] Michael Lambek (ed.) (2002), *A Reader in the Anthropology of Religion* (Malden, MA: Blackwell), 21.

In his study of Azande witchcraft belief,[19] Evans-Pritchard discussed with people about what they thought, and observed how they conducted their lives, the actions they took and the results that occurred. He demonstrated that while an 'intellectualist' outsider might perceive some of their witchcraft beliefs as contradictory, when understood in terms of their own logic and the function that belief performed, there was no contradiction. Standing back to both understand and respect why people believe what they do is the mark of both the sensitive anthropologist and the priest. There is something discomfiting at academic conferences about seeing people smile or even snigger when a presenter is discussing the beliefs and activities of a group of people being studied. What appears to be a contradiction may instead be a pattern we have not yet recognized.

The problem Evans-Pritchard investigated will be one familiar to the contemporary priest: he found in his everyday life that people were sometimes troubled by vexing questions about why misfortune happened. At those times of unforeseen tragedy they asked such questions as 'Why me?' For example, to find cover from the sun, people might occasionally sit in the shade of a granary, a large barn-like structure on stilts that held their grain. Over time, it would become rotten and sometimes it would collapse – sometimes killing the people who were sitting beside it. Evans-Pritchard found that the people understood that the instability would be caused by a natural force, such as termites. They did not need a supernatural answer for the question of why the granary collapsed, any more than people today need a supernatural answer to why a car careering off the road was able to strike and kill a passer-by. Their question was ontological, not scientific: why the collapse just then, on to that person? Why the car accident at that time and place, killing this person? The Zande people believed that such things would be explained best by the curse of a witch, and if their local priest, or shaman, agreed, then the question would be to find who might have a reason to curse them. Whom might they have wronged? With whom should they seek reconciliation?

Pritchard observed how those beliefs in witchcraft helped balance social relations, particularly because only some people could be accused of witchcraft – not, notably, close kin or the ruling princes. By not dismissing the Azande witchcraft beliefs as silly superstition, Evans-Pritchard could see how they not only made sense at that time and in that place, but also were vital for calibrating and maintaining a social system. The Zande

---

[19] E. E. Evans-Pritchard (1976 (1937)), *Witchcraft, Oracles, and Magic among the Azande* (Oxford: Clarendon Press).

sustained what we may theoretically see as a contradiction – why not close family members? Why not rulers? What matters to them is the preservation of social and kin relations. A contemporary priest may counsel similar actions in similar circumstances: repent, reconcile, forgive.

The beliefs of the Zande, like those of most people today, were not perfectly worked out. They were 'hardly precise enough to be called a doctrine', said Evans-Pritchard.[20] But they worked, and they worked because the task of explaining such tragedies is hard, intellectual and spiritual labour. There remains an unanswered question about just how close Evans-Pritchard came to accepting Zande beliefs. He famously described seeing one night a light when strolling in his garden that could have been a fire, and could have been the 'light of witchcraft'. That he leaves it open, and converted in later life to Catholicism, suggests that his own beliefs were complex. But does this matter? Everyone believes something. Most anthropologists would agree that the important matter is to be reflexive about our own researcher position, and scrupulous when making claims about others. Evans Pritchard made a lasting impact on anthropology, altering a view that so-called primitive people held unsophisticated beliefs to an understanding that people's beliefs are consistent with their social system and to that extent entirely rational.

The granary question, however, poses only part of the problem. Bad things might happen by accident to good people, indeed, but if people do not believe in witchcraft but, instead, believe that there is an all-powerful, all-loving god controlling the universe, the question becomes how such a god can allow bad things to happen. Monotheistic religions struggle with that common problem, sometimes described as the problem of evil, or of meaning. It inevitably arises in monotheistic religions as adherents face an apparent contradiction between their view of a loving, omnipotent, omniscient, omnipresent God and the presence of suffering in the world. The means by which people try to resolve this problem is known as a theodicy (divine being or god (*theos*) and justice (*dike*), a term originally coined by the eighteenth-century rationalist philosopher Gottfried Wilhelm Leibniz). Anthropologists turn often to Max Weber, who wrote extensively about rationalization, and most importantly the relationship between rationality and belief.[21] Discussing 'rational' in the sense of a means to achieve an end, Weber contributed to anthropology by challenging the idea that 'primitive man' was irrational. Religious rituals

---

[20] Evans-Pritchard, *Witchcraft, Oracles, and Magic*, 2.
[21] Max Weber (1978 (1922)), *Economy and Society* (Berkeley: University of California Press).

were a logical means to achieving an end, he argued. A rationally derived theodicy enables people to restore order to their worldview, making sense of the apparent discontinuity between perfect, all-powerful love and terrible events. Weber argued that believing in divine, benign intervention stems from a belief in magic, with petitioners having to please, influence, cajole or collaborate with a magician-like God and, in prayer, try to show God why they are deserving.

Ministry is often concerned with creating theodicies, unlike magicians, who do not seek so much to change worldviews as to alter materiality and the course of events. American anthropologist Tanya Luhrmann carried out fieldwork in London on contemporary witchcraft, trying to understand how 'modern', educated, intelligent people could sustain a belief in magic, defined by her as the ability to affect material objects by non-material means – 'casting a spell'.[22] She showed how the members of a coven supported their logic of witchcraft through extensive, collective discourses of rationalization. My own ethnographic study of a Baptist women's prayer group reached a similar conclusion.[23] I had observed that many of their prayers were not answered, and I therefore sought to understand how they collectively reconciled unanswered prayer. The 'sociology of prayer' I devised explicitly mapped their conversations and revealed patterns of conversation that helped them restore their worldview. In sharing my findings with them, I found them to be polite and interested, but unconvinced. They did not accept my idea of 'unanswered prayer', preferring to see it as 'differently answered prayer'. Further, any resolution and comfort they found was not, as I had suggested, an outcome of social discursive processes, but rather the grace of God.

Of most difficulty to anthropologists is the apparent separation of belief, knowledge and experience, such that an anthropological turn in the 1970s led many to dispense with the idea of 'belief' altogether. Rodney Needham began to historicize the way belief has been used by, primarily, anthropologists and philosophers.[24] Needham provided an exhaustive review of 'belief', mainly from the philosophical literature, and concluded that it was a mistake to universalize it. He argued that the broadly anthropological literature and, more specifically, ethnographic literature consistently fails to interrogate how scholars are using the term 'belief'. He concluded that

---

[22] Luhrmann (2007), 'How Do You Learn to Know that It Is God?'

[23] Abby Day (2005), 'Doing Theodicy: An Empirical Study of a Women's Prayer Group', *Journal of Contemporary Religion* 20.3: 343–56.

[24] Rodney Needham (1972), *Belief, Language and Experience* (Chicago, IL: Chicago University Press).

it should be abandoned as a useful concept in research because it could not be universalized. Needham forced a more careful interrogation about belief and its Christian-centric roots. Malcolm Ruel, following Needham, identified what he describes as four 'fallacies' common to the treatment of belief: that it is central to all religions, in the same way that it is central to Christianity; that belief guides and therefore explains behaviour; that belief is psychological; that it is the belief, not the object of belief, that is most important.[25]

Anthropologists sometimes mistakenly think we can separate what people believe about the world from the world itself. As Ruel puts it: 'A distinction made frequently today is between "belief in" (trust in) and "belief that" (propositional belief)'.[26] Ruel concludes it is best to use the term 'belief' as we might use 'faith' if what we mean is 'trust': Ruel says that the original Greek word for faith was *pistis*, expressing the idea of trust, or conduct that honoured an agreement or bond and thus had a social orientation.

This may be familiar ground to those in ministry, but for others it can be, perhaps, a fruitful reminder to pause and reconsider what is meant by belief, believer and unbeliever. If one's faith is based on just a piece of doctrine or a section of Scripture, one might lose the power of relationality that anthropology brings. A woman deacon I spoke to during my research described to me how her role was helping the congregation live practically as a coherent community while the (male) priest busied himself 'with the magic'. This was not said in altogether complimentary tones. Many people with whom I spoke as I carried out research in the churches talked more about the parties than the pieties. In his research about people leaving Anglicanism, Callum Brown interviewed people who often described their teenage years and the role of the Church. The social life was a primary draw. For example, he related his conversation with a woman who described how the local church was competing with her other activities as a teenager, until a young 'charismatic' priest arrived and started a youth group, which 'made her "happy enough" in her religious connection'.[27]

Happy enough may, indeed, be enough.

---

[25] M. Ruel (1982), 'Christians as Believers', in J. Davis (ed.), *Religious Organization and Religious Experience*, ASA Monograph 21 (London / New York: Academic Press), 9–32.

[26] Ruel, 'Christians as Believers'.

[27] Callum Brown (2015), 'An Oral History of Becoming Secular: How Anglicans Lose Religion', in Abby Day (ed.), *Contemporary Issues in the Worldwide Anglican Communion: Powers and Pieties* (Farnham: Ashgate), 252.

Being human

The above discussion has positioned anthropology as a discipline committed to exploring what it means to be human. In so doing, it privileges the human, or social, over the apparent divine. An anthropology of ministry may contrive to do both, to hold in comfortable tension this world/other world. By way of conclusion, I will offer a few reflections from others closer to the everyday field than I. This is what Martyn Percy described as the ministry of 'deep hanging out' through many activities, from visiting to offering open house: 'Much as Jesus' was, simply walking from place to place.'[28]

The idea of the priest simply walking from place to place evokes the original idea of the anthropological 'field', as a place within walking distance.[29] When the then Archbishop of Canterbury Rowan Williams addressed the Synod of Bishops in Rome in 2012, he recalled the importance of anthropology as a means of returning to the human:

> But one of the most important aspects of the theology of the second Vaticanum was a renewal of Christian anthropology. In place of an often strained and artificial neo-scholastic account of how grace and nature were related in the constitution of human beings, the Council built on the greatest insights of a theology that had returned to earlier and richer sources – the theology of spiritual geniuses like Henri de Lubac, who reminded us of what it meant for early and mediaeval Christianity to speak of humanity as made in God's image and of grace as perfecting and transfiguring that image so long overlaid by our habitual 'inhumanity'.[30]

Such a practice of humanity would not escape the notice of congregations, whose members are rarely as concerned about theology as they are about theodicy and the possibility of a congregation having a busy and vibrant life.

The experience on the ground is often transformative. For example, between 1983 and 1984, Alyson S. Peberdy conducted doctoral research

---

[28] Martyn Percy (2015), 'Theological Education and Formation for an Uncommon Occupation', in Day (ed.), *Contemporary Issues*, 235.

[29] The idea of field has been deconstructed and problematized to invite closer attention to its multiple permutations (see, for an excellent overview, Simon Coleman and Pauline von Hellerman (2011), *Multi-sited Ethnography: Problems and Possibilities in the Translocation of Research Methods* (London: Routledge)) and to its invention by the fieldworkers themselves (see also Simon Coleman and Peter Collins (2006), *Locating the Field? Changing Contexts of Fieldwork and Ethnography*, ASA Series (Oxford: Berg)).

[30] See <http://rowanwilliams.archbishopofcanterbury.org/articles.php/2645/#sthash.FAwOl354.dpuf>.

among six Church of England parishes to explore people's responses to women priests. As women were not yet admitted to the Church of England priesthood, the women ministering were deaconesses, occupying a role that was the nearest equivalent to that of a priest. Her discussions focused on how women ministers are received, what actions they perform, and how they feel about their roles and levels of acceptance. In the introduction to her pamphlet *A Part of Life*, John Tinsley, former Bishop of Bristol, chastised those who considered the issue of women's ordination to be a matter of theology: 'This is to do theology badly because an incarnational religion like Christianity impels us to do our theological and other thinking inductively working from actual facts, real data and considered experience.'[31] Speaking like a true anthropologist, Tinsley points to inductive learning and 'data' drawn from real experience, considered through what anthropologists today would describe as 'reflexivity'. Peberdy's research found that the 'data' often did not support initial expectations. There was no correlation between the theology of a parish and the extent to which women ministered there. As she spoke with people about women priests, she noticed that most people with good experiences of the deaconesses were in favour of the idea, thought it was 'normal' and found it difficult to remember their earlier opinions of opposition. 'Such forgetting of earlier views is a normal part of the adoption of new attitudes', she noted.[32]

Peberdy quoted one man at length to illustrate the effect of being raised in a parish that had been strongly opposed to women's ordination. John, an accountant in his late thirties, was speaking about Penny, their deaconess, when he admitted that his views had changed significantly because he had

> always thought that there was something wrong with a woman leading a service simply because I was brought up to see a man doing it . . . but I've changed my mind because of the way Penny conducts services and now my feelings against women preaching and so on have completely disappeared.[33]

He not only found it acceptable that Penny carried out the role, but he changed his mind to accept wholeheartedly the wider principle of women's ordination. Data, as anthropologists know, informs experience. One woman expressed her fears that a woman priest might not engage sufficiently with the women of the congregation. Given that laywomen did

---

[31] Alyson Peberdy (1985), *A Part of Life: A Study of Lay-people's Response to Women's Ministry in the Church of England* (London: The Movement for the Ordination of Women), Foreword.

[32] Peberdy, *A Part of Life*, 23.

[33] Peberdy, *A Part of Life*, 24.

most of the church labour, such a concern is understandable. Pat said that she liked her church's deaconess, Anne, because:

> She's let us have our say and then drawn us on starting from our level . . . The talents that have come forward are quite amazing. Anne is always there in the background, being supportive. Jobs you thought you couldn't do you find yourself doing.[34]

Letting the women have their say is another way of describing 'trust', or 'believing in' somebody. During my research with elderly laywomen I described as Generation A, I often heard stories about the priests they liked and those they did not.[35] The contrast was clear: an engaged priest who listened to them and trusted them was accommodated. Those priests who did not were simply ignored. Some priests felt that the women, being conservative and traditional, were holding their church back and failing to allow it to modernize. On the subject of women priests alone, they are probably right. Whether that explains the continuing decline of the Church of England is contestable; we may find future anthropological research is necessary to fully explain it. This may be conducted by academic researchers or by engaged priests, wanting to immerse themselves in others' lives and find what messages may be drawn inductively from their data. Standing on the church steps for a spot of sweeping may be a good place to start.

---

[34] Peberdy, *A Part of Life*, 18.
[35] Day, 'Spirit of "Generation A"'; Day, *Religious Lives of Older Laywomen*.

4

Sociology of ministry

DOUGLAS DAVIES

Ministry is work in the Christian care of people. Usually conducted by persons set apart by church authorities after special selection, theological and pastoral training, and ordination into paid occupation within an ecclesial hierarchy, this work underpins Christian churches. While some groups, however, regard ministry as the mutual work of Christian communities, all ministry is legitimized by theological traditions and influenced by wider social-political, economic and gender factors.

In terms of the Church of England, the focus of this chapter, we find a kaleidoscope of 'traditions' from Catholic-Sacramental to Protestant-Evangelical, with Liberal and Charismatic styles also being in evidence. These make for complex ecclesial decision-making as with the ordination of women priests in 1994, and bishops in 2015. Issues of legitimate authority for 'ministry' also involve those licensed to conduct some but not all religious services. Such intricacies of 'ministry' reflect the interplay of the historical bureaucracy of churches with the personal sense of faith, a complexity captured in the idea of vocation and priesthood, notions explored sociologically by Max Weber. This included the 'rational training and discipline of priests', with 'doctrine' being the 'rational system of religious concepts', and with priesthood being, 'the specialization of a particular group of persons in the continuous operation of a cultic enterprise, permanently associated with particular norms, places, and times, and related to specific social groups'.[1]

Weber also touched on the nature of the parish and the fact that 'the priesthood must frequently meet the needs of the laity in a very considerable measure' if status is to be maintained.[2] Accordingly, he identified preaching and pastoral care as core aspects of 'congregational religion', with preaching being a kind of 'imitation' of prophecy, but with

---

[1] Max Weber (1922), *The Sociology of Religion* (Boston, MA: Beacon Press), 29–30.
[2] Weber, *Sociology of Religion*, 65.

Protestantism having largely replaced the notion of 'priest' with that of 'preacher'.[3] While preaching often failed to influence much of daily life, he took 'pastoral care in all its forms' to be 'the priests' real instrument of power (*sic*)',[4] especially within the 'workaday world' framed by an ethical attitude.[5] Some of these early twentieth-century insights remain fruitful, as does much of his extensive interest in the very notion of vocation, not only in priests but also in 'the man of vocation'[6] and the dedicated organization of everyday life, especially as worked out in his Protestant Ethic thesis.

Vocation

As Weber well knew, vocation or 'calling' draws from ancient biblical roots, from ecclesial traditions of authority and, potentially, from more individualized ideas of self. Biblically, God called certain individuals to witness to the divine, to call people to responsible ethical living and to care for their ensuing lives. From the prophets of the Hebrew Bible to Jesus and his apostles in the Christian New Testament there emerges a key sense of people called by and to work for God in a scheme of division of labour within the Christian community. Its language of ministry, which is often expressed theologically as a variety of gifts of members of the 'body' of Christ, can be expressed sociologically as a division of labour. Theologically speaking, ministry has the Holy Spirit as its driver with the Spirit's presence sustaining 'life' as a phenomenon that transcends ordinary living. The Spirit demarcates the Christian community as the 'body of Christ', itself a remarkably odd expression but one that enhances the notion of ministry as care for that body. While body-care is, one might say, a most natural symbol, perhaps one of the more universal symbols of humanity, care for the body of Christ becomes its Christian manifestation. To speak in this way is not to set ministry above all 'ordinary' work but to show how it is valued by the churches themselves. 'Vocation' thus describes a spectrum of understanding from a person's private sense of God's call to devote his or her life to the service of others to the formal institutional evaluation of a person's qualities and subsequent establishment in post. This description of ministry acknowledges the influence of theological ideas, emotional experiences and intuitive processes within Christian narratives worked out in ritual and ethical practices.

---

3   Weber, *Sociology of Religion*, 74–5.
4   Weber, *Sociology of Religion*, 75.
5   Weber, *Sociology of Religion*, 77.
6   Weber, *Sociology of Religion*, 183.

Narrative worlds

People are remarkable for using narrative when describing and coping with life. Meaning-making, especially when intensified in one's sense of identity, takes shape through biographical narratives with Christians also setting autobiography as refractions of the enfolding story of God's engagement with the world. The once popular phrase 'salvation history' outlined divine interaction with humanity, and ritualized it in liturgy, to give a sense of identity and destiny. This grand, and grandly personal, narrative, framed by denominational emphases, still frames many approaches to Christian life and ministry. Despite the fact that some contemporary trends, notably linked to ideas of postmodernity, prefer to think in terms of fragmented meaning or even of meaning's absence, ministry remains as work possessed of a long tradition. Sociologically speaking, sacred narrative occupies both a central ritual space and a core theological focus for most Christian communities and their ministers as their appropriation of Christian tradition 'performs' it anew today.

Dividual ministry

Tradition is especially dominant in formal rituals of ordination that confer leadership status. In Catholic, Orthodox, Lutheran and some Anglican traditions priesthood is understood as a profound continuation of Christian practice from Christ's authoritative calling of his first disciples whose transformation into apostles heralded the work of ministry. Such hierarchically organized institutions pinpoint the office of bishop as holding an authoritative oversight that is shared with new priests. In some Protestant groups, however, the congregation itself is seen as the holder of authority, and as such it calls a person to be its new minister. Whether in ordination or setting apart, rites highlight the complementarity of minister and people.

This background of tradition, its scriptural and ecclesial narratives, and the double sense of vocation easily sets the scene for describing ministers and ministry not in terms of 'individual identity' and 'individual work' but of 'dividual identity' and 'dividual work'. The background to this anthropological concept stems from societies where a person's identity and life is much caught up in the lives and identities of others.[7] Dividuality

---

[7]   McKim Marriott (1976), 'Hindu Transactions: Diversity without Dualism', in B. Kapferer (ed.), *Transaction and Meaning: Directions in the Anthropology of Human Issues* (Philadelphia, PA: Institute for the Study of Human Issues), 109–42; Marylin Strathern (1988), *The Gender of the*

marks the essentially interactive nature of identity: persons are entailments of the lives of their parents, kin and networks. Dividuality stands apart from the word 'individual' with its connotations of discrete and even isolated individuality, and which often dominates some sociological and Western European notions of 'self' and of postmodern conditions, appropriate perhaps for contexts of grand narrative absence.

The strong relational characteristic of dividuality is already found in Christian notions of believers being 'members one of another', in ideas of fellowship and its Greek notion of *koinonia*. Similarly, widespread South African cultural notions of *ubuntu* popularized by Archbishop Desmond Tutu foster the community-focused notion of the mutual embeddedness of lives. This cluster of notions indicating the strong relationality of a complex 'self' is especially important for understanding ministry where the person's life not only stands within the long narrative, scriptural and ecclesial-ritual contexts of life, but where that person's work embraces the joys and sorrows of others. Additionally, no sociological description of ministry can ignore the reported place of God in community life, even if interpreted as a social or psychological effect. Dividuality, then, becomes important for collective and private aspects of ministry as we now show for pastoral ministry and then for ritual.

Pastoral ministry

Pastoral work has long depended on the historically significant system of geographical parishes within major denominations, even if industrialization and urbanization proved to be straining. Parish ministry also served civic functions of registration of birth, marriage and death until state institutions took over those functions and, in the process, removed that aspect of ministerial work. Developing earlier ideas of military, educational and prison chaplains, the later twentieth century witnessed innovatory support for a wide variety of 'ministry' performed by work-based chaplains for sports teams, shopping malls or even railways, each involving distinctive issues of identity with workplace and church authorities. Such interpersonal ministry embraces life's anxieties, crises, joys and celebrations, with this interaction arousing sociological interest if the minister is viewed as the trained, professional 'service provider' and others as 'service users',

Gift: Problems with Women and Problems with Society in Melanesia (Berkeley, CA: University of California Press); Chris Fowler (2004), *The Archaeology of Personhood: An Anthropological Approach* (London: Routledge).

terminology that may appear quite inadequate to ministers for whom the 'human' contacts and their need looms large, as does their own personal emotional investment. Here the role of ministry as 'weeping with those who weep and rejoicing with those who rejoice' assumes significant proportions, for this is where ministry as the management of emotion looms large.

Sociologically, this is not only where institutional status and personal identity interact but also where the theme of God again becomes relevant in a distinctive fashion. There are cases of bereavement where, for example, when two people speak about the deceased, the narrative seems to bring a sense of the deceased into the conversational present.[8] This engendering of 'otherness-present', as we might call it, may also apply to other faith-linked pastoral contexts where the biblical text promising that where 'two or three' are 'gathered together' in the name of Christ he is there with them is enormously telling (Matthew 18.20). Here the pastoral moment transforms from a simple twofold interaction into what may be experienced as threefold, with the divine or transcendent element comprising the 'third party'. Acts of prayer, private or public, may prompt this sense of an 'other' as being present, which then becomes its own legitimation of ministry. Though some may foster such relationship moments more than others, given that its psycho-social dynamics are doubtless complex, this kind of phenomenon should not be ignored in sociological accounts of ministry. The cumulative effect of 'sensed others' upon Christian ministers reflects Strathern's study with its emphasis on the fact that 'persons are frequently constructed as the plural and composite site of the relationships that produced them'.[9] Such an approach is as applicable to pastoral contexts as to ritual at large. From this awareness of the divine within more personal experience of ministry, we now move to more corporate ritual, something that is usually given primacy in the sociology of religion.

Ritual and liturgy

The sociology of religion's early expression in Emile Durkheim and, before him, in Scotland's William Robertson Smith recognized the self-transcendence engendered through ritual, with folk feeling stronger, communally integrated and sensing themselves at one with their deity. Much

---

[8]   Christine Valentine (2008), *Bereavement Narratives: Continuing Bonds in the Twentieth Century* (Abingdon: Routledge).

[9]   Strathern, *Gender of the Gift*, p. 13.

subsequent research shows similar benefit from privately more contemplative as well as publicly expressive modes of ritual behaviour.[10] As ritual communities, churches anticipate in their ministerial leader a presentation of self as a ritual actor. In Catholic-Sacramental-style churches this involves priests eschewing what many Western sociologists define as individual styles of behaviour. Adopting formal-traditional activity and priests' liturgical dress, as at the Eucharist, 'covers' individuality, and indicates dividual rather than individual identity. Centuries of tradition, albeit represented through contemporary expression, fully set out liturgical action, allowing minimal personal diversity at some points in the service, but never for core formulae. Personal ideas in sermons might even embrace suitable humour, but no 'joke' is acceptable when, for example, uttering the words 'This is my body which is given for you', or 'This is my blood that is shed for you'. For the eucharistic celebrant exists in a complex ritual-symbolic state; 'being' or 'representing' Jesus Christ, as depicted in the biblical texts of the Last Supper, he or she allows the faithful mind of the devotee to imagine the crucifixion itself, providing a fertile field for the foundational dynamics of 'gift' to be evoked in the context of a recipient's life.

Marriott's 'dividuality' is also valuable when considering the Eucharist, especially his assertion that, 'dividual persons . . . are always composites' of 'the substance-codes that they take in'.[11] While 'substance-codes' might initially seem a strange concept, it is a fruitful way of referring not only to the literary and ritual narratives whose familiarity can become 'first nature', but also to sacramental phenomena that pervade a person's piety, sense of identity, and even destiny. Eucharistic bread and wine are one of the more obviously powerful substance-codes whose material culture, spiritual import and rules of administration inform the work of ministry. These 'codes' are, contextually, aligned with the fact that the priest stands at an altar that is normally in a church's sanctuary, an echo of Weber's itemizing place, cult and priest. Spatial and doctrinal dynamics interplay with silence, music and the subdued movement of devotees to furnish an arena where substance-codes find expression. Here caution is needed, for although a minister might seek to foster fruitful emotive piety in a congregation, his or her own mode of embodiment may differ from that congregational mood. The same might be said for the 'ministry' of church organists, whose focused technical playing may differ from the congregational passive hearing and spiritual appreciation of the sound.

---

[10] Roy Rappaport (1999), *Ritual and Religion in the Making of Humanity* (Cambridge: Cambridge University Press).

[11] Marriott, 'Hindu Transactions', p. 111.

Flow

However, with experience of long-term ritual performance, leaders can assume self-transcendent awareness when the liturgical text becomes one with the minister's emotive piety. Much the same might be said of the customary informal formalities of churches that consider themselves free of 'tradition' but where spontaneity is not always spontaneous. So, too, in many contemporary forms of worship and praise, often in buildings that are not architectural 'churches', where the extensive use of popular music, music groups, lighting effects and 'worship leaders' would seem to encourage a unity of emotional tone between performers and congregational audience.

Here the concept of **flow** is invaluable for describing moments when people sense themselves to be at one with their action and its goals. Shifting from an instrumental state of careful, self-conscious performance, they simply act: 'doing' coheres with 'being'. 'Flow' is often used in terms of sport and athletic performance, with the phrase 'being in the zone' capturing the mode.

'Liturgical flow' is similar, and is possible against a base of deep familiarity with words and actions; it is aided by familiar music or silence. When priests are, for example, using a quite new liturgical text or are in a quite unfamiliar ritual setting, their conscious focus on what needs to be done is unlikely to be conducive to 'flow'. By contrast a minister utterly familiar with a form of worship, textual or otherwise, being 'at home' in a worship context and perhaps being in a life situation allowing freedom from anxiety, is in a situation conducive to flow. The same can be said for actors and concert musicians.

It is precisely at this liturgical core of ministry, not least where flow is possible, that the individual 'ends' and the corporate identity flowers. This is a relatively unusual human social experience and it takes time for due appropriation. It is worth stressing this absorption of and in a role, for it is intimately aligned with the ideas now to be considered as **habitus** and **embodiment**.

Habitus and embodiment

While it is relatively easy to discuss the social status and institutional nature of ministry, it is equally important, though more complex, not to forget the minister as a person, especially recalling what has already been said about dividual identity. Here we may capture the 'personal' element through the three concepts of ***Homo duplex***, **habitus** and **embodiment**. Durkheim spoke of human beings as *Homo duplex* to stress the interplay of social values and personal aspects of life, as though a social being is grafted on to the person. Max Weber, Marcel Mauss and, more familiar still, Pierre Bourdieu took the classical Latin notion of *habitus* to refer to characteristic attributes of a way of life that is appropriated by people as they are formed through a particular culture. This body-focus is further caught in the notion of embodiment, a topic Mauss pinpointed in his sketched 'techniques of the body'. These various idioms depict how religious leaders come to express emotionally toned core cultural ideas through their bodily practice.

This is as present in learning how to conduct religious ritual, including preaching, as in pastoral activity, including adopting facial expressions of concern, kindliness or welcome. While much occurs by imitation, such a habitus develops once a person is ordained or formally adopted as a minister. The psychological dynamics of the interplay of external behaviour expected by church congregations and the more internal 'state of mind' or felt embodiment experienced at different periods in a minister's life also raise distinctive issues that cannot be pursued here. Suffice it to say that the well-established notion of flow might also be given a negative turn by taking the notion of cognitive dissonance and rephrasing it as habitus-dissonance to portray the sensation of disruption between expectation and 'reality' in ministerial contexts.

Cultural purity and betrayal

Just how ministers appropriate the values of their Church and religion opens issues of their own, for prized leaders are frequently drawn from those who successfully embody the ideals of the religion in their personal life. Trust is especially important in religious leaders, both in terms of the leadership hierarchy of their Church as a social institution and of their relationships with church members. Christian religion is built on the ideals of revealed truth, of theological reflection on it, on its teaching, and on forging ways of life consonant with those ideals. Some ministers are extremely successful in achieving this consonance, many others strive with it and a few fail – some catastrophically. Despite the theological ideal describing the Christian Church as an institution comprised of and for sinners, the expectation that salvation and a life of grace should foster worthy lives sets high standards of behaviour and practice for ministers, as those set aside as the face and hands of the institution.

When major faults of behaviour occur, sins in theological terms, then it is feasible to speak of betrayal. Part of the embodiment motif is that core religious values are and should be nurtured in the ministerial life. The closing decades of the twentieth century, for example, witnessed many cases of child sex abuse, acts that can be best evaluated as a betrayal of ministerial expectations.

In social-scientific terms this kind of social criminality and ecclesial sin can be fruitfully approached through the anthropological idea of ritual purity and impurity, where 'purity' describes the status needed for dealing with core cultural values in doctrine, ritual and ethics. Christian religion sees itself as dealing with the expression or revelation of divine character, especially as scripturally depicted in the person of Jesus, developed through centuries of theological reflection refracted in corporate liturgy, ethics and private devotion. Because Christian ministers are especially charged to hold and to foster such truths, often with a distinctive community or congregation as their prime responsibility, while some may fail in this in relatively 'small' ways, it is when major acts of immorality occur that culpability assumes major import. This is why 'betrayal' seems an appropriate description of such an act, and renders a minister ritually 'impure'. In practical terms this has resulted not only in public criminality and imprisonment but also in debarring from ministry. Sociologically, at least, such a person could be reckoned as not embodying 'truth'.

Celibacy, marriage, partnerships

For the vast majority of ministers, however, life is lived neither as a perfect example of embodied truth nor as flagrant disregard but amidst the many tensions of a high calling and daily vicissitudes of life. While this includes changes in formal belief over the life-course of ministry, it also embraces the nature of married, single, complex relationships, and celibate forms of Christian leadership. Just how persons manage their thoughts, property, wealth or poverty, relationships, emotions, sexuality, and their mode of domestic and church life involves utterly complex issues.

Over time, local cultures arrive at a conventional patterning of these, while periods of social change influence them, sometimes quite dramatically. This was evident, for example, when the Protestant Reformation largely adopted married clergy as against the Roman Catholic Church's celibate male clergy and, indirectly, against Eastern Orthodoxy's largely married clergy and celibate bishops.

Arguments for celibacy often dwell on issues of ministry, seeing it as allowing a priest's full attention to be given to his ministry, without all the cares of domestic relationships. Churches with married clergy have argued for a greater understanding of those very domesticities among the people served. Sociologically speaking, it is important to say not only that Catholic celibacy ensures a significant control over a priest's life, time and property, but also that it enhances the very notion of priesthood as an ecclesial sacrament. Celibacy frames ministry in a most distinctive fashion, not simply because of this intensified focus of life upon institutional forms of organization and practice but also because of its prime sexual significance. Sexuality exists as one of the strongest human energies, and its entailments in intimate relationship, procreation, life-investment in children, and in its own form of self-understanding are inestimable. For married ministers these family outcomes also provide their own form of communication with married church members.

There is no knowing just *how* millions of church members think about their leaders, but it is likely that opinion lies on a spectrum from those who idealize the celibate priest as free from the 'lusts of the flesh' and devoted to his holy work, notably in his representative role as celebrant at the Eucharist, through those who are glad their married minister understands their own domestic joys and sorrows, to lesbian, gay and transgender persons whose sexuality is not simply aligned with heterosexual patterns, whether celibate or not. These are issues that have assumed significant proportions in the late twentieth and early twenty-first centuries, as some Protestant churches have ordained women, and debated and responded to other patterns of sexuality.

Symbolic complexities

Embedded within these debates are issues of considerable psychological-cultural complexity associated with embodiment, sexuality and ritual/symbolism. This is particularly important for the three areas of baptism, Eucharist and funerary rites. The major religions of the world, including Christianity, have, for millennia, used male priests for such initiation and intensification rites, and only in recent decades has this been significantly changed as a result of widespread cultural revaluation of persons and gender under the imperative of equality and social justice.

However, the gender division remains highly influential in Roman Catholicism and Orthodoxy, and in some Protestant Evangelical contexts. The reasons for past and continuing regimes are complex: some find legitimation in biblical texts that assert male headship and leadership over women, while some extrapolate from Jesus' apparent decision to choose only male disciples to a rule for male-only priesthood. The core theological doctrine of Jesus as a divine Incarnation has framed approaches to human bodies and materiality, and to ministry, in quite profound ways.

Moreover, while a significant element lies in social power exerted through male authority in many societies – something that feminist theorists have done much to document – it is likely that some distinctive embodiment factors of men and women have also played a part, albeit largely implicitly.

One theme involves the fact that women give birth, and inherent in that capacity lies the allied fact of menstruation which, in numerous traditional societies, involved periodic restrictions over aspects of domestic and social life, including religious functions. Menstrual blood has to do with core cultural values of fertility, reproduction, motherhood and the ongoing nature of 'human' existence. Though it is difficult to generalize over ideas that have often varied cross-culturally, it is worth speculating on the theme that Christianity has more than a minor concern with transcending the ordinariness of life. In the Christian streams of thought associated with both the Gospel of John and Paul's letters, the flesh is ordered against the spirit; the vitality of human parentage is raised to a higher order by the Holy Spirit as a vehicle for 'spirit-life'. There is, then, a sense in which male priests came to conduct formal rites of initiation into that supernatural domain.

Due to cultural, textual and theological developments, early Christians found themselves aligning Jewish ideas of Passover and cultural deliverance through a lamb's blood sacrifice with the death of Jesus and his shed blood. Blood discourse became one firm medium of communication of the idea of salvation. This was fostered over centuries, not least through medieval philosophical theology of the ritual of the Mass, and through later Protestant ideas of blood atonement and salvation. The ensuing 'blood language' of eucharistic liturgy raises difficult cultural issues in that traditional liturgical language deals explicitly with the sacrificial blood of salvation completely identified with Jesus as both a man and a divine agent. Because there is no immediate blood symbolism associated with priests as men compared with women as mothers, they can appear as simple agents of and for the sacramental blood. Even circumcision, whose blood is important in Christianity's Jewish roots, was formally abandoned by Christianity, thus eliminating blood language from Christian men. However, the association of blood with menstruation carries a potential breadth of symbolic significance that is seldom discussed in mainstream Christian theology.

Christianity's own early theological sense of male–female gender divisions being transcended through a common Christian identity (Galatians 3.28) has seldom led to pragmatic implementation as far as eucharistic leadership in major world churches is concerned.

Ideas, emotions and more

Here it is worth considering one scheme that integrates several of the above concerns and which bears application to Christian ministry and truth. It begins with ideas, or with ideas in the form of doctrine. As such there are thousands of 'ideas' in the world, and so too with many doctrines. Some of these, however, come to be pervaded by emotion as people are drawn to them and invest part of their life-energy in them. At this point we might argue that an 'idea' becomes a 'value'. When such a 'value' contributes to the sense of identity of a person, and much the same applies to a group, it can be regarded as a 'belief'; and when that 'belief' is seen as framing a person's destiny it becomes a 'religious belief'.

> Idea
> Idea + emotion = value
> Value for identity = belief
> Identity for destiny = religious belief

This simple scheme is helpful for interpreting many aspects of social and cultural life. Football is an obvious idea. For millions it is a simple idea, for keen fans it may assume 'value' status, while for some of those it functions as a 'belief' when some aspect of a person's identity is framed by fan behaviour and commitment. It probably stops at that point, though it is quite telling when a few folk have their funeral in a club-coloured coffin, or have their cremated remains placed at locations provided by that club.

'Ministry' is another such term. At one level it is a simple idea; many churches find emotion attached to it, and ministry becomes a value. It can, however, become an identity-conferring value, at which point we can accord it belief status. More than that, even, it may be regarded as affecting the destiny of persons served by it, and then it becomes a religious belief. This approach is helpful, for example, when considering Roman Catholic and Protestant views of leadership, especially given the former's doctrinal identification of priestly work in the sacraments as vehicles of salvation.

The key work of ministry, notably in traditions emphasizing priesthood and the primacy of sacraments, lies in baptism and the Eucharist, as well as in other 'sacraments' of particular churches: tasks existing to expand and sustain the church community. Interestingly, most contemporary Christian ministry also engages in the fundamental work of conducting funeral rites.

Rites of passage, intensification and gifts

In anthropological terms baptism and funerals, as also with marriage rites, confirmation and rites at the end of life, express the anthropological idea of **rites of passage**, a notion formulated by Arnold van Gennep in terms of shifts in the social status of a person. He illustrated it in the idea of passing over thresholds, taking the Latin *limen* – or threshold – to arrive at pre-liminal, liminal and post-liminal phases of a status-change ritual. Given that van Gennep spoke of 'society' as taking people by the hand and help-ing them through such periods of change, we can easily relate these rites to the work of ministry and to divine assistance. Further nurturing falls to ministry through what anthropology has described as rites of **intensifica-tion**, the formal and informal acts of worship or other congregational life that recharge Christian identity and reaffirm group cohesion.

Though lying beyond this study, the other influential sociological idea pervading ministry is that of reciprocity theory and the whole debate about what counts as **gift**.[12] Once Christian ministry is understood in terms of a narrative and ritual tradition engaging with contemporary dynamics of faith, it becomes transformed into an ecclesial 'cumulative tradition' received as its own form of gift that now needs passing on to others and to future generations. Ministry becomes a gift-reception and gift-donation way of life with the dynamic of the Holy Spirit fostering the entire process. Ministry becomes an embodiment and expression of gift.

Hope: emotions of ministry

Whether in rites of passage or of intensification, the work of ministry is indelibly aligned with human identity, emotions and the salvation-goal of churches. Theologians often speak of the 'theological virtues' of faith, hope and love (1 Corinthians 13.13), as distinct from classical antiqui-ty's 'cardinal' or 'natural' virtues of prudence, temperance, justice and fortitude. Sociologically speaking, hope deserves special attention for the work of ministry, especially if regarded as the cultural manifestation of what is, at the more biological level, the drive to survive. Hope's Christian threefold setting, alongside faith and love, fosters a communal venture set upon biblical narrative and community relationship, alongside a sense of the divine 'other'. Baptism and Eucharist, for example, initiate and sus-tain hope, while the ongoing pastoral work of ministry exists to foster the same positive outlook. This is vital in innumerable contexts where people

---

[12] Douglas J. Davies (2002), *Anthropology and Theology* (Oxford: Berg), 53–80, 195–210.

easily lose hope through negative life-circumstances. Anxiety, depression and despair beset most lives, and while they can be addressed both psychologically and in terms of pastoral work they should not be ignored in terms of the survival and long-term flourishing of a social institution such as a church. For it is through such long-term institutional survival that the more immediate and personal work of ministers is made possible over centuries. Sociologically speaking, it is also the ongoing existence of major churches that makes possible, and perhaps even incites, the protest of sectarian movements with their emphasis on an even more intense sense of community.

Blessing and authority

One way of encapsulating the work of ministry is through the notion of dual sovereignty, which links two complementary forms of authoritative 'power', **legal or jural authority** on the one hand and **mystical authority** on the other.[13] The former is necessary for the maintenance of institutions and societies, including churches whose ministers need to adhere to the laws of the land and of their Church. But such legality is only half the picture of ministry and calls out for a complement in 'mystical authority', a term describing how faith is fostered and human well-being nurtured. In this way, dual sovereignty embraces blessing and salvation.

---

[13] Davies, *Anthropology and Theology*, 75–6.

5

Congregational studies and ministry

DAVID GORTNER

The effectiveness of clergy's ministry and leadership depends on their capacity and willingness to read and understand their congregations and surrounding communities with sustained and generous curiosity, and nuance. A congregational study can be revelatory when conducted well, in partnership with lay leaders. Discoveries deepen understanding of the complexity of congregational life and its community impact. A shared process of discovery with lay leaders develops congregational leadership. The habits and practices of multifaceted contextual exegesis learned in this process help shape and regularize informal day-to-day practices of reading and understanding one's context of ministry. Clarity about congregational identity, purpose, spiritual life and mission emerges.

Congregational studies emerged as a field of enquiry and research to explore, test and establish sound, consistent methods to catalogue and understand the dynamic, complex world of a congregation. For decades, and especially since the first Congregational Studies Consultation in 1982,[1] scholars and practitioners have gathered insights from various fields of theory and research to construct a distinct field of study devoted to understanding congregations in community context. These tools offer better assessment of congregational vitality and suggest pathways for change and growth.

Contextual exegesis is fundamental for grasping and framing local theology,[2] and for engaging in sound theological reflection on local reali-

---

[1] Jackson W. Carroll, Carl S. Dudley and William McKinney (eds), *Handbook for Congregational Studies*, Nashville, TN: Abingdon Press (1986). The Preface contains a brief history of congregational studies' emergence as a field of applied research, bringing together American scholars 'from the Alban Institute, Auburn Theological Seminary, Candler School of Theology, Hartford Seminary, McCormick Theological Seminary, and the research offices of the Presbyterian Church (U.S.A.) and the United Church Board for Homeland Ministries'. This handbook was an early result of their work.

[2] Robert J. Schreiter, *Constructing Local Theologies*, Maryknoll, NY: Orbis Books (1985/1999).

ties in relation to theological traditions and broader cultural sources of insight.[3] It undergirds practices of mission,[4] pastoral care[5] and practical theology.[6] Richard Osmer describes practical theology in ministry as a continuous cyclical process of descriptive enquiry, interpretative investigation, prescriptive evaluation and pragmatic solution.[7] Descriptive enquiry seeks to answer the question 'What (really) is going on?' through purposeful, sustained listening and observing that is both expansive and incisive.[8] Osmer echoes Don Browning, a principle architect of contemporary practical theology, who summarized the process this way:

> For a practical theology to be genuinely practical, it must have some *description* of the present situation, some *critical theory* about the ideal situation, and some understanding of the *processes, spiritual forces, and technologies required* to get from where we are to the *future ideal*, no matter how fragmentarily and incompletely that ideal can be realized.[9]

Both Osmer's and Browning's starting place reveals a fundamental hermeneutical principle in contextual exegesis: that a context, like a text, must be read and understood *from within*. For this reason, Moschella, in *Ethnography as a Pastoral Practice*,[10] presents contextual exegesis ethnographic methods as essential for wise, faithful and insightful pastoral ministry and leadership – and argues for a process of balanced emic (insider) and etic (outsider) discovery. This embraces the hermeneutic circle involved in deep sympathetic reading and interpretation of, and conversation with, a text.[11]

---

3   James D. Whitehead and Evelyn Eaton Whitehead, *Method in Ministry: Theological Reflection and Christian Ministry*, Lanham, MD: Rowman & Littlefield (1981/1995).

4   D. Bosch, *Transforming Mission: Paradigm Shifts in Theology of Mission*, Maryknoll, NY: Orbis Books (1991/2011).

5   Margaret Kornfeld, *Cultivating Wholeness: A Guide to Care and Counseling in Faith Communities*, New York: Continuum (2000/2012); Charles W. Taylor, *The Skilled Pastor: Counseling as the Practice of Theology*, Minneapolis, MN: Fortress (1991).

6   D. S. Browning, *A Fundamental Practical Theology: Descriptive and Strategic Proposals*, Minneapolis, MN: Augsburg (1995); Bonnie J. Miller-McLemore (ed.), *The Wiley-Blackwell Companion to Practical Theology*, Malden, MA: Wiley-Blackwell (2014).

7   Richard Osmer, *Practical Theology: An Introduction*, Grand Rapids, MI: Eerdmans (2008), p. 4.

8   Osmer, *Practical Theology*, pp. 31–76.

9   Don Browning, 'Practical Theology and Political Theology', *Theology Today* 42(1), April 1985, p. 15, emphasis added.

10 Mary Clark Moschella, *Ethnography as a Pastoral Practice: An Introduction*, Cleveland, OH: Pilgrim Press (2008).

11 The process of 'getting inside' a text and its world of meaning ultimately leads to transformation of the reader. See Hans-Georg Gadamer, *Philosophical Hermeneutics*, Berkeley: University of California Press (1977).

Contextual exegesis always begins with *description*, preceding interpretation. Describe as richly and as accurately as possible the current life, patterns and situations of the setting – the congregation, community, group, culture or person. Then begin to consider how these descriptions reveal values and ideals embedded in the context. Following this, bring these contextual values and ideals into conversation with broader perspectives from Christian tradition and from interdisciplinary wisdom and social factors that shape contextual reality. This trialogical process (as outlined by Whitehead and Whitehead in *Method in Ministry*) resonates deeply with similar Anglican and Methodist theological methods traced back to Richard Hooker[12] and John Wesley.[13]

A robust congregational study includes both basic and more nuanced elements. It marks historical as well as current patterns and signs of life and vitality. Such a study should document the following: changes and developments in congregational size and budget, demographics, congregational structures and groups, culture, identity and mission, key lay and ordained leadership, the demographics of the surrounding community, that community's relative assets and challenges, and the congregation's theological identity, practices of discipleship, ministry and mission, and the congregation's impact. Such a study will also encourage the analysis of congregational dynamics from eight different perspectives. These perspectives are as follows:

1 personal faith stories;
2 interpersonal networks and connections;
3 'the numbers' (numerical data);
4 shared congregational history;
5 surrounding community (numerical and qualitative data);
6 espoused and operant theology;
7 congregational dynamics (interaction, power, communication or leader development);
8 oneself as leader.

Each perspective requires different perceptual lenses, methods of research, sources of data, and questions to drive analysis and interpretation. Each yields a different picture of congregational life, identity and vitality. Those

---

[12] Richard Hooker, *Of the Laws of Ecclesiastical Polity: The Fifth Book*, London: Macmillan (1597/1902), p. 36. Hooker noted the importance of Scripture, reason and tradition in Christian life and thought – in that order of primacy.

[13] John Wesley (ed. Albert C. Outler), *John Wesley*, New York: Oxford University Press (1964). Wesley added experience to Hooker's triad.

lenses relating to the congregation are described more fully below, with organizing questions and methods of study.

1 Personal faith stories

In their efforts to build and strengthen the institution, clergy can forget to take time to learn about people's lives, their experiences of faith and doubt, and their relationships with God. Increasingly, people construct meaning and encounter moments of spiritual importance beyond the Church and the collective life of the congregation. Consider conducting 8–12 planned one-to-one conversations with a sampling of different congregants, in which study team-members spend about 40 minutes asking each person about his or her life. Questions like 'What brought you here to live, and what kept you here?' can open the conversation. Questions about meaning and purpose should be part of such conversations: 'What matters most to you here and now, at this point in your life? What concerns you most? What do you celebrate most?' I have found that people are responsive to questions about their beliefs and the world ('What kind of a place is the world to you, in general?'), life purpose ('What is your sense of your place, or fit or purpose in the world?') and values ('Are there core principles and values that you try to live by – and are there values that you shun or ignore?').[14] People are willing to share their thoughts, and will often discuss key experiences that shape their beliefs and values. It is important to offer something of one's own story, so that it is an exchange of mutual discovery and enrichment. Concluding the conversation with questions about God and faith is important: 'Who is God to you? How have you met God in your life?' Following these questions, it is fine to ask people directly about their experiences of God and faith in the Church, and specifically in the congregation. But it is important to begin with a wider view – beginning with questions about the Church and the local congregation automatically restricts the conversation and one's implied definition of what is important and what defines the person.

This exercise helps clergy and dedicated church leaders step beyond an ecclesiology-in-practice narrowed by habit. Any sound theology of the Church dispersed, the *missio Dei*, and God's freedom of movement and action in people's lives requires a broader view of how God is at work.

---

[14] In *Varieties of Personal Theology*, Burlington, VT: Ashgate (2013), David Gortner showcases responses of young adults to these questions, revealing consistent themes and patterns in contemporary Americans' 'fundamental theology'.

Furthermore, hearing the stories of people's lives and experiences of God and faith that stretch beyond the bounds of the Church radically expands leaders' perspective of the breadth and depth of Christ's body that happens to gather and connect with that congregation and place.

When done with intention and open-ended curiosity, this process, inviting and listening to people's narratives, yields new insights about the theological beliefs and values, spiritual experiences and faith journeys that emerge from people's lives, and the ways in which they are similar to and different from the expected threads of theological identity of a local congregation, diocese, or broader ecclesial or academic claims about what is 'normative'. Ellen Clark-King's study of working-class English women's narratives of faith and belief in God revealed a very different real-life pattern from that anticipated and affirmed among many feminist theologians.[15] Joyce Mercer's conversations with teenage girls and my own interviews with young adults (ages 18–25) uncovered beliefs, values and relationships with God that went much deeper than the surface 'moralistic therapeutic deism' identified as normative among American youth and young adults by sociologist Christian Smith[16] – more akin to the varieties of 'redemptive narratives' brought to the surface by psychologist Dan McAdams.[17] This only happens when one suspends assumptions and judgements, becomes inquisitive, listens deeply, and asks questions that are not restricted to a single context or system of meaning.

2 Interpersonal networks and chains of informal influence

Many clergy are surprised – even taken aback – by the ways in which information moves through a congregation and community, and the ways ministry initiatives can be quickly supported, redirected or reversed. Web-based social networks transmit ideas, judgements and valuations even more rapidly – and with fewer self-editing filters. But networks preceded the Internet. People are connected in complex networks that function for different purposes. There are networks of kinship and affinity, role, action

---

[15] Ellen Clark-King, *Theology by Heart: Women, the Church and God*, Peterborough: Epworth Press (2004).

[16] Joyce Ann Mercer, *Girltalk, Godtalk: Why Faith Matters to Teenage Girls – and Their Parents*, San Francisco, CA: Jossey-Bass (2008); Christian Smith and Melina Lundquist Denton, *Soul Searching: The Religious and Spiritual Lives of American Teenagers*, New York: Oxford University Press (2005).

[17] Dan P. McAdams, *The Redemptive Self: Stories Americans Live By*, New York: Oxford University Press, rev. edn (2013).

and decision, information and impact, just to name a few. The study of human networks is rooted in social psychologist Kurt Lewin's field theory of social influence,[18] sociologist Charles Kadushin's work on informal sources of support and power,[19] and a variety of anthropologists' field studies of relationships and genealogies in different cultures.[20] The study of human networks has illuminated kinship bonds, interaction patterns and decision chains,[21] thickness of social capital in relation to social class and wellness,[22] scholarly and professional heritage chains through mentoring,[23] and the power of adolescent peer networks in academic and social life.[24] Studies of social networks inform and continue to emerge from web-based commerce and social media sites.

Human network study receives remarkably little attention in the training of religious leaders. But interpersonal networks and informal chains of influence are realities of all human communities. They are inherently neither good nor bad – they just are. *How* they are used and for what purposes are matters of moral assessment. Exploring how they function and who they involve reveals much about the nature of a human community.

Imagine asking congregants about specific people in the church to whom they turn for help, for three purposes: (a) to move a decision or action forward; (b) to gather people for a shared event or purpose; and (c) to bring deeper understanding to what is happening in the congregation. The next step in network analysis is to repeat these questions with the new people identified. A third and, if necessary, fourth round will allow mapping of the informal decision networks, socialization networks and insight networks in the congregation. These networks are never identical.

---

[18] Kurt Lewin, *Field Theory in Social Science: Selected Theoretical Papers*, New York: Harper & Row (1951).

[19] Charles Kadushin, *Understanding Social Networks: Theories, Concepts, and Findings*, Oxford and New York: Oxford University Press (1966/1968/2012).

[20] John A. Barnes, 'Class and Committees in a Norwegian Island Parish', *Human Relations* 7, 1954, pp. 39–58; Ileana Baird (ed.), *Social Networks in the Long Eighteenth Century: Clubs, Literary Salons, Textual Coteries*, Newcastle-upon-Tyne: Cambridge Scholars (2014); Jeremy Boissevain, *Factions, Friends, and Feasts: Anthropological Perspectives on the Mediterranean*, Oxford and New York: Berghahn Books (2013); John Scott, *Social Network Analysis*, 3rd edn, Los Angeles, CA: Sage (2012).

[21] See these classics: Margaret Mead, *Coming of Age in Samoa: A Psychological Study of Primitive Youth for Western Civilisation*, New York: W. Morrow & Co. (1928); Napoleon A. Chagnon, *Yanomamö: The Fierce People*, New York: Holt, Rinehart & Wilson (1968/1981).

[22] Nan Lin, *Social Capital: A Theory of Social Structure and Action*, New York: Cambridge University Press (2001).

[23] Howard Gardner, Mihaly Csikszentmihalyi and William Damon, *Good Work: When Excellence and Ethics Meet*, New York: Basic Books (2001).

[24] John Cotterell, *Social Networks in Youth and Adolescence*, Hove: Routledge (2007).

They may or may not match the formal organizational charts of membership on church councils and committees. With people named in the third or fourth rounds (and any other focal people emerging from earlier rounds), it is worthwhile asking about what matters most to them in their congregation's life and ministry, and what they hope to foster in the congregation.

It is important to keep the process confidential, and to keep names anonymous for any sharing of insights from network analysis with the congregation. But for those in leadership, a network analysis helps reveal the following:

- recognized leaders' values and interests;
- important threads of connection;
- depth or shallowness of influence among congregants;
- similarities and differences between informal networks and formal structures;
- foundational data for exploration using family systems theory, power and influence dynamics, and paths of volunteer and leader development.

Create visual network depictions using marks and arrows, mapping who seeks whom for help in each area. Present these without names to the whole congregation, as a visual point for discussion about network complexity, reach, and inclusion or exclusion. Such discussions bring to the surface and make conscious the patterns of influence that may be known but undiscussed.

3 The numbers

Numerical data provide a description that is transportable and generally consistent, and allows for comparisons. Congregational annual reports often include summaries of numerical data, such as total number of living members or communicants in good standing, average Sunday or weekly attendance, and budgetary information. These types of records have been kept for centuries by churches. Not all of these are equally useful or reliable, however. For instance, membership rosters are not always carefully maintained, leading to a deceptive appearance of increasing or decreasing membership over time. Likewise, overall budget revenues can mask the degree to which total revenue is dependent on an endowment rather than current congregational habits of stewardship.

More useful are data on Sunday or weekly attendance and giving over the course of a year. The following are standard annual measures:

- average Sunday attendance (ASA) or average weekly attendance (AWA – including worship services on other days);[25]
- marriages, baptisms, confirmations and funerals;
- Sunday School and youth group attendance;
- average weekly or total annual 'plate and pledge' offering (non-endowment).

Comparisons year by year provide clearer indicators of growth and decline in church involvement. These benchmarks, in addition to membership (or claimed affiliation) and overall budget revenue and expenditure, mirror typical measures in sociological studies of religious affiliation, attendance and commitment, and also sociological patterns in affiliation with institutions and voluntary organizations.[26]

Demographic figures for membership and attendance are also important. In our increasingly multicultural and multi-ethnic societies, the numbers – and percentages in relation to the whole – of people in the congregation who are from differing racial, tribal and ethnic backgrounds, cultures, and levels of education and income, reveal an explicit picture.

Other matters worth closer attention are member age distribution, number of programmes and events outside of worship, numbers of adults volunteering time for different programmes, and budget allocations for different ministries.

Current numbers become more meaningful in relation to numbers that span ten years, or five- or ten-year increments, revealing patterns of growth, stability, stagnation or decline. Specific congregation numbers come into sharper focus when compared to parallel indices from the neighbourhood or community surrounding the church (for example, population density). Again, these comparisons gain value when read across years and decades.

Particularly helpful are comparisons with overall trends in a diocese, a nation, a geographic region – and among congregations that share similarities (size, institutional age, urbanicity, ethnicity, wealth). The Episcopal Church website provides data on ASA/AWA, membership and 'plate and pledge' giving for a ten-year span, for every congregation

---

[25] There are increasing arguments that ASA or AWA does not accurately represent the impact of a church. Many are experimenting with indicators of 'average weekly touch' (AWT), to account for services and ministries provided throughout the week by the congregation and through partnerships.

[26] See 2015 websites for the Pew Foundations religious research; Robert Wuthnow, *After the Baby Boomers: How Twenty- and Thirty-Somethings Are Shaping the Future of American Religion*, Princeton, NJ: Princeton University Press (2007); and Robert D. Putnam, *Bowling Alone: The Collapse and Revival of American Community*, New York: Simon & Schuster (2001).

and diocese. Through partnership with Mission Insite, Inc.,[27] it also provides census-based data for a three-mile radius around each congregation in the Episcopal Church.

Researchers and practitioners observe distinctive congregational patterns and dynamics that coincide with numerical attendance and membership data. Arlin Rothauge first mapped types of congregations by size – specifically, by ASA.[28] These church size descriptions have become commonplace across Protestant denominations in America and throughout the Anglican world. Family-sized congregations (ASA 50 or fewer) have different cultures of leadership, fellowship and cooperation than pastoral-sized congregations (ASA 51–150), programme-sized congregations (ASA 151–350), and corporate- or resource-sized congregations (ASA over 350). My research has confirmed Rothauge's observations of differing size-related dynamics, including variance in congregations' openness to change, activity level and organizational stability (all typically stronger in larger congregations), and in sense of community (typically stronger in smaller congregations).[29] As church consultants like Alice Mann have documented, one of the great challenges church leaders face is helping congregations adjust their habits, expectations and dynamics as they move from one size to another.[30]

Numerical accounting does not automatically yield objectivity. What one tracks is itself a choice with meaning, one that gains importance because of focused attention. What is not accounted may also be important – but more telling is the fact that it is not being accounted (consider a church's careful accounting of age demographics but no account of ethnic demographics, or a church ledger that attends meticulously to every expenditure in music but makes broad unmarked allocations for social outreach ministries).

Loren Mead, in an article titled 'Lay Ministry Is at a Dead End', suggested that part of the challenge of supporting vigorous lay ministry is an implicit focal bias in data collection for parochial reports from congregations. Priests are not asked to report how many lawyers, teachers and medical personnel offer pro bono services in the wider community, but they

---

[27] See <http://missioninsite.com> for an introduction.
[28] Arlin J. Rothauge, *Sizing Up a Congregation for New Member Ministry*, New York: Episcopal Church Center (1986).
[29] David Gortner, 'How Congregational Size Changes Congregational Climate', presented at the American Psychological Association Annual Meeting, Toronto, Ontario, 2003.
[30] Alice Mann, *Raising the Roof: The Pastoral-to-Program Size Transition*, Lanham, MD: Rowman & Littlefield (2001).

are prompted to report how many people come to special programmes or liturgies on social justice.[31] There is a tendency in congregational data reporting to focus only on what is happening inside or under the direct jurisdiction of the church. This erodes a greater sense of the total ministry of laity and the church in daily life.

4 A congregation's history

People live among their history, experiencing the juxtapositions of old, very old and new side by side. Sigmund Freud adopted the metaphor of archaeology for his work in psychoanalysis, referring to the many layers that might lie beneath the surface of current life, the interplay and influence of old and new.[32] Organizations and institutions have histories too, as do communities. Learning this history requires a blend of methods, including attention to physical evidence, archival exploration, and enquiry through conversations with individuals and groups to understand how past structures, processes, relationships, and systems of meaning and symbol interact with current congregational life.

The historical work of a congregational study, especially when done as a team and in conversation with the congregation, becomes a rich process that raises discussion about the church's identity, culture and mission over time. Work undertaken in this phase of congregational study will take the team into contact with archives, old memories, and the stored accumulation of history tucked away in odd places and out in the open. It will also bring to the surface stories of the experiences and memories of church members.

Congregational history lives in the artefacts of physical structures and objects, in written records and collected documents, in the oral traditions of long-term members and their families, and in a shared process of discussing history together. Written records will hold information about the who, what, when, where, how and why of buildings, objects, gathering patterns, processes and decisions, and ministry aims and purposes. Written records will also provide insight into patterns in membership, attendance, involvement in ministries and programmes, and age-groups in the community of faith – and this information can help inform and frame more contemporary numerical data. James Wind recommends asking the

---

[31] Loren Mead, 'Lay Ministry Is at a Dead End', *LayNet* 15 (2004), p. 7.

[32] Sigmund Freud, 'Constructions in Analysis' (1937), *The Standard Edition of the Complete Psychological Works of Sigmund Freud: Volume XXIII (1937–1939)*, London: Hogarth Press (1964), pp. 257–69.

following basic questions in each exploration of a community of faith's history:[33]

- What happened when? What was done when? Who were the people involved?
- Where did people come from? Where has the congregation been? Where did it and people move?
- How did things happen? Why did they happen?

Congregations do not emerge, develop or continue in a bubble. They unfold in relation and response to other systems that surround and interact with them and their members. Attention in historical enquiry to changes and developments in the broader community, society and culture will reveal how context has influenced and interacted with the life of the congregation. What are the contextual realities that have had direct, symbiotic and indirect impact on the congregation? What were the major events, enduring patterns, direct and indirect influences, social movements and cultural meaning-systems that shaped the life of a community of faith? And what impact did the community of faith have on these surrounding systems? As a team considers various surrounding contextual realities, it is worth considering the *tone* of relationship between congregation and surrounding contexts over the course of the congregation's history.[34]

Oral histories are an essential component of congregational history. There are individuals in most congregations who carry stories undocumented in written materials that can reveal much about the spirit and tone of a congregation at different points in its life. These individuals can often thread connections between different events, and will note people who played important roles at various points. For those working with dispersed or travelling communities of faith, conversations and interviews will be the primary means of learning history. Furthermore, to expand the frame of history and to ensure that less dominant narratives have a voice, it is important to interview a few individuals with outlier perspectives or who have left the congregation. Email or direct mail can be another means of inviting people to share history; but there are distinct advantages to the oral tradition.[35]

---

[33] James P. Wind, *Places of Worship: Exploring Their History*, Nashville, TN: American Association for State and Local History (1990).

[34] See H. Richard Niebuhr's *Christ and Culture* (New York: Harper & Brothers (1951)) or Keith Ward's *Religion and Community* (Oxford: Clarendon Press (2000)) for an interpretative framework for cultural interaction.

[35] Excellent web-based resources, guides and examples for oral history (created by different universities and historical organizations) are available. See Linda Shopes, 'Making Sense of

The 'congregational timeline' method, described in the congregational studies manuals, is worth making the heart of collective oral history work. This approach allows a team to engage the congregation as a whole, inter-generationally, to chart historical moments and patterns, and benefits congregational life through the collective sharing of stories. Begin with a long sheet of butcher paper or newsprint rolled out sideways across a long wall, marked horizontally across the middle with the central timeline for the congregation (from founding date to present). This becomes the basis for a series of adult and intergenerational gatherings where congregants are asked to mark the timeline with the following:

- first personal memories of contact with members of the congregation (with names or initials);
- starting and ending dates of significant leaders – clergy and lay;
- starting and ending dates of families and/or groups that are remembered;
- high and low points in membership, attendance, money, children;
- important events, programmes and projects in the congregation's life – successes and failures;
- important conflicts and crises;
- important deaths, relationship changes;
- important broader societal events and shifts (e.g. war, factory closure, building campaigns).

Structuring the time should allow people freedom to converse and write, and make space to discuss themes and insights concluding each session. An extended period of display allows other groups in a church to interact with and mark the timeline.[36]

There are organizing features for a well-threaded congregational history: source stories, essential clues, formal and informal structures, and dominant and subordinate plot lines. Here are patterns and experiences to address in a congregational history:

Oral History', in *History Matters: The U.S. Survey Course on the Web*: <http://historymatters.gmu.edu/mse/oral> (February 2002), for an introduction and set of guidelines. Sample oral history interview questions can be found at sites like <http://home.earthlink.net/~ahickling/interviewsuggestions.html>, or at Texas A&M University's AgriLife Extension Services: <http://fcs.tamu.edu/families/aging/reminiscence/oral-history-techniques-and-questions/> (26 June 2015).

[36] As suggested in Carl S. Dudley, *Effective Small Churches in the Twenty-first Century*, Nashville, TN, Abingdon Press (2003), and in the congregational studies manuals: Carroll, Dudley and McKinney (eds), *Handbook for Congregational Studies*; N. T. Ammerman, J. W. Carroll, C. S. Dudley and W. McKinney (eds), *Studying Congregations: A New Handbook*, Nashville, TN: Abingdon Press (1998).

- What has been the life cycle of significant movements, ministries and organizations in the congregation and overlapping with the congregation?
- What are peak experiences (the 'highs') of the congregation? What are dark or empty times experienced (the 'lows')? What events were most important in people's memories? Are there events now mostly forgotten that were once important?
- How has the congregation been shaped by – and how has it contributed to – its surrounding contexts? What local, regional and denominational realities have left their mark?

5 The surrounding community

Communities have their own stories and identities, their own dynamics related to changes in economics, migration and demographics, their unique needs, passions and concerns, and gifts and assets. Hence, many methods used for internal study in congregations apply to the study of surrounding context: demographic data, observation of physical environment and of people, interviews and conversations, and mapping of connections and sources of influence. There is a recent resurgence of concern that churches connect more with their surrounding communities. While a steady stream of scholar-practitioners over decades have called the Church to greater public engagement,[37] voices are now providing theological leadership in this effort to refocus our pastoral, prophetic and partnering presence in our communities.[38]

Demographic data in many countries are available from civic, regional or state offices, and are increasingly online. These data, along with published historical and contemporary descriptions of communities, provide a view of a community that may often escape those working or living day to day in it. If in a large city, restrict the range of data to a neighbourhood,

---

[37] John M. Perkins (ed.), *Restoring At-Risk Communities: Doing It Together and Doing It Right*, Grand Rapids, MI: Baker (1995); Dennis A. Jacobsen, *Doing Justice: Congregations and Community Organizing*, Minneapolis, MN: Fortress (2001); Sara Miles, *Take This Bread: A Radical Conversion*, New York: Ballantine (2008); Harvey Cox, *The Secular City: Secularization and Urbanization in Theological Perspective*, New York: Macmillan (1965); Ray Bakke, *A Theology as Big as the City*, Downers Grove, IL: IVP (1997); Martin Luther King Jr, 'Letter from Birmingham Jail', in *Why We Can't Wait*, New York: Harper & Row (1964), pp. 77–100.

[38] For example, Miroslav Volf, *A Public Faith: How Followers of Christ Should Serve the Common Good*, Grand Rapids, MI: Baker (2013); and Willis Jenkins, *The Future of Ethics: Sustainability, Social Justice, and Religious Creativity*, Washington, DC: Georgetown University Press (2013).

postal area, parish boundary or census region immediately around the church. Key data available online and from published regional data sources include total population and population density, ethnicity, age groups, income, types of households, health and mortality, crime, education levels, occupations and businesses, and major organizations or institutions – and their changes over time. With access to satellite images through Google Maps and others, it is possible for a team – and a whole congregation – to get a truly visual bird's-eye picture of the church's surrounding context.

However, one does not know a context until one walks its streets and paths, sits with others in public places, and spends time in places of work, education, family and leisure. Just as with mission work, urban and rural field research relies upon direct interaction with people who live in the context being explored. It is important for a congregational study team to intentionally explore the surrounding public world, through observation, tours with informed residents, and one-on-one relational conversations with people who live and work there.

A 'prayer walk' of a neighbourhood is a first-level evangelistic practice that involves openness to God's leading of one's attention and awareness, to become more attuned to and aware of the needs, joys, concerns and strengths embedded in a community's buildings, streets and paths, parks and fields, and patterns of life. It is valuable to listen to and join in conversations at public gathering places, and on the streets, to hear people's concerns and joys. Asking shop owners, police officers, teachers or long-term residents to help you get to know the neighbourhood will open doors to deeper conversations about community concerns and lead to more introductions.

The one-on-one relational conversation is the backbone of any community-based work by a Christian body of faith, be it evangelism, church planting, community organizing, or partnership development for ministry and mission. Through conversation, one learns directly about gifts and capacities, interests and passions, and needs of individuals, groups and organizations in a community. It is also through these conversations that one can discern the spiritual yearnings and joys of a community through the art of evangelistic listening. To conclude (but not to begin) such conversations, congregational study team members can ask people in the community about their perceptions of the local church: is it known, how is it known, and for what is it known?

There are critical practices for effective one-on-one relational meetings. First, let curiosity take the lead – be interested in and inquisitive about the person. Second, remember that the conversation needs to be mutual– sharing some of one's own story, passions and talents makes the conversation more of an exchange and shared discovery than an interview. Third, follow the hints of someone's passions, concerns and talents – the purpose is to begin to understand deeper issues in a community and to discover hidden resources of strength.[39] Fourth, be attuned to someone's spiritual yearnings and expressions of 'personal theology'.[40]

Once a group completes a series of relational conversations, review themes and patterns, looking for common and diverse concerns, perceptions of needs that could be addressed, talents and strengths revealed that could be tapped, and common spiritual yearnings and theological ideas. Following this exploration and rediscovery of the surrounding community, a congregation can then review its activities, ministries and community connections to evaluate more honestly how its members engage with the needs, passions and gifts of their context. This review helps clarify the degree of impact of the church in its surrounding context.

In an increasingly fluid social world, in which people who do attend church choose where to do so based on qualities of congregational life more than on location, churches often find themselves becoming 'destination churches' rather than neighbourhood churches.[41] A more honest community assessment in such congregations should include mapping the communities represented among congregants, and intentional deeper study of communities where a higher percentage of congregants live, in addition to the community in which the church is physically located.

6 A congregation's explicit and implicit theology

All information gathered up to this point contributes to deeper analysis and discernment of the congregation's explicit and implicit theology.

---

[39] Michael Gecan discusses the power and practice of relational meetings in his short books, *Effective Organizing for Congregational Renewal*, Skokie, IL: Acta Publications (2008) and *Going Public*, Boston, MA: Beacon Press (2012). John McKnight and Peter Block discuss the art (to be recovered in consumptive cultures) of drawing forth the assets, gifts and natural associations in communities in *The Abundant Community*, San Francisco, CA: Berrett-Koehler (2010).

[40] Gortner, *Varieties of Personal Theology*: asking questions about people's beliefs about the world and their place in the world, and about their most strongly held values, reveals much about how individuals and segments of communities think implicitly – and differently – about the cosmos, being and God.

[41] For example, see Aubrey Malphurs' discussion of Arn's study of driving time to church – the majority of attenders in this American study lived over five minutes' drive away. Malphurs discusses this in his chapter, 'Who Will Be Reached?', as a contrast with his discussion in the same chapter about the importance of a church reaching and embedding itself in its surrounding community (*The Nuts and Bolts of Church Planting: A Guide for Starting Any Kind of Church*, Grand Rapids, MI: Baker (2011)).

Explicit theology is that which is stated in print, engraved or painted on the building itself, and claimed consistently in congregants' and clergy's descriptions of the church's identity, beliefs, values and intended mission. Implicit theology is revealed in other ways, and can be discerned partly through the information gathered through observation and research. How people talk about God, faith and life in their personal narratives reveals the range of beliefs, values and experiences of the divine held by the people of a congregation – as well as how people experience the church in relation to their lives. Numbers such as demographics, particularly in comparison to the demographics of the surrounding community, reveal how the church engages in evangelism, welcome and cultural adjustment. Budget allocations and patterns of giving reveal how a church invests in what it claims to believe and value. Patterns of growth and decline in relation to internal patterns of leadership and the values pursued, neglected or rejected by those leaders reveal an ordering of priorities in the congregation over time. Social networks for decision-making, gathering and discernment reveal informally recognized leadership and its relationship to formal leadership structures and roles, as well as its influence on enacted values and purposes. Connections and gaps between a church's ministries and the surrounding community's needs, concerns and strengths reveal consistencies and inconsistencies between the explicit and implicit theology of a congregation's relationship to the world. These sources of information bring to light the implicit beliefs and values of the congregation in its day-to-day life – beliefs and values about the church's identity, purpose, ministry and mission, and also about God's presence, purposes and calling to the church in its context. How these align with more explicit beliefs and values embodied in church mission statements, 'slogans' and emblematic symbols, common quotations, sermon themes and core affirmations is an important point of analysis and discussion that helps guide, redirect and redefine a congregation's trajectory.

There are other ways of reading both explicit and implicit theology. The shared spiritual practices of a congregation, as well as individual and familial spiritual practices, paint a descriptive landscape of how congregants understand their relationship with God, one another, themselves and the world around them. For instance, how and for what does a congregation pray? What are treasured practices and traditions, inside and outside formal worship? How do congregants speak about and invite conversation about faith in their daily lives – with those inside and outside the church? How does the congregation celebrate and mourn? Authors like Richard Foster, Dorothy Bass, Don Richter, Diana Butler Bass, Stephanie Paulsell and Ragan Sutterfield are just a few who have written recently about spiritual practices in relation to a wide range of topics of daily life such as care of our bodies, care of our 'stuff' (our possessions) and care of our time.[42] Together, the range of shared and individual spiritual practices reveals much about a congregation's implicit (as well as explicit) theology.

People's preferences about church also reveal much about implicit theology. Surveys with Likert-scale questions, checklists and open-ended questions can produce a telling picture of a congregation's – or denomination's – spiritual passions and desires, and central theological ideals.[43] But the relationship between expressed passions (in surveys and forums) and actual behaviour may also be telling. Such revealed discrepancy can lead congregants and clergy into a pointed discussion about their commitments to discipleship.

Stories also carry with them a theological narrative. Congregations differ in their response to times of distress, conflict, betrayed trust, tragedy or trauma. Like individuals, faith communities vary widely in their dealing with anger, guilt, shame, grief or shock. Some more easily find narratives of new hope and new life through experiences of seeking and finding the grace of resilience, redemption, responsibility, recovery or restoration. Others struggle for a long time to find a 'redemptive narrative'[44] and find themselves moving towards narratives of inevitability, cynicism or suspicion, woundedness or resolute resistance. Still others may not find a new narrative, adrift in continuing sadness unnamed or anger un-faced. In his classic book, *Congregation,* James Hopewell recommended listening deeply for the theological narrative of a congregation about itself and its ways of understanding God's action in the members' own history.[45] Drawing on

---

[42] See Richard Foster, *Celebration of Discipline: The Path to Spiritual Growth,* San Francisco, CA: HarperSanFrancisco (1978/1998); Dorothy C. Bass, *Practicing Our Faith: A Way of Life for a Searching People,* San Francisco, CA: Jossey-Bass (1997/2010); Diana Butler Bass, *The Practicing Congregation: Imagining a New Old Church,* Herndon, VA: Alban Institute (2004); Stephanie Paulsell, *Honoring the Body: Meditations on a Christian Practice,* San Francisco, CA: Jossey-Bass (2002); and Ragan Sutterfield, *This Is My Body: From Obesity to Ironman,* New York: Convergent Books (2015).

[43] David Gortner, *Around One Table: Exploring Episcopal Identity,* Stanford, CA: College for Bishops / CREDO Institute Inc. (2009), reveals results of a nationwide survey in the USA of Episcopal bishops, key leaders, priests and congregation members regarding most central theological values of the Episcopal Church: <https://www.episcopalchurch.org/files/aot_report.pdf>).

[44] McAdams, *The Redemptive Self.*

[45] James F. Hopewell, *Congregation: Stories and Structures,* Philadelphia, PA: Fortress (1987).

Northrop Frye's classic narrative typology,[46] he suggested that congregations will develop a dominant narrative that is either comic (exuberant, moving from strength to strength), romantic (moving from difficulties to triumphs and breakthroughs), tragic (moving from joyful beginnings into events that lead to continuing losses) or ironic (both starting and concluding with difficulties). In each congregational narrative type, God is experienced and understood differently. To complicate matters, each narrative type can be deeply honest or a habitual cover-story. To discern implicit theology at this level requires deep listening over time.

7 Congregational dynamics

Much can be discerned about congregational dynamics from the information gathered in these prior sections without need for much additional research. Identifying congregational dynamics becomes an exercise of thoughtful interpretation, ideally in conversation with a few others, as one considers patterns in social networks, communication and leadership, both in the current life of the congregation and in its history, to divulge the following at play in congregational life:

- patterns of power and influence exercised, and key players in times of conflict;
- dynamics of closeness and distance, direct and indirect communication, and attempts to change or preserve known patterns;
- arising, support and development of leaders and key contributors;
- patterns of communication, including what is said and what is intentionally or unintentionally left unsaid.

To help guide such interpretation, I suggest clergy and teams read classic works on power, family systems, volunteer and leadership development, and organizational communication.

8 Leadership

The entire process of conducting a congregational study, especially with a team from the congregation, brings one face to face with one's own habits and choices in leadership – and forces one to engage directly in leading the various efforts of discovery. What one learns along the way will cast light

---

[46] Northrop Frye, *Anatomy of Criticism: Four Essays*, Princeton, NJ: Princeton University Press (1957).

on oneself as well, as a leader of a congregation: retrospectively, shedding light on how one has led so far; and prospectively, assessing what is needed and what needs to be learned as a leader. Some of these important matters of perspective for more effective leadership are discussed in the final chapter of this volume.

A congregational study is an act of ministry and will produce change – especially when conducted as a team. As Nancy Ammerman affirms:

> leading a congregation toward change is best accomplished when everyone takes seriously and appreciatively the need for a disciplined understanding of the present reality of the congregation. It is important to begin with a clear picture of where you are. But that understanding is best achieved when the congregation and its leaders are working in concert to discover what they need to know in order to move ahead.[47]

A truly rich, productive and insightful congregational study will make use of these varied lenses to yield a thicker, more multifaceted description and understanding of a congregation and the community in which it is embedded. Such a multi-focal approach breaks open the assumptions and attachments of clergy and lay leaders alike. It helps develop what Ronald Heifetz calls 'adaptive leadership': by requiring teams to practise greater complexity and integration when perceiving and interpreting their congregations and surrounding communities, they will begin to shape and direct new conversations, decisions and actions in their contexts of ministry and leadership.[48]

---

[47] Ammerman, Carroll, Dudley and McKinney (eds), *Studying Congregations*, p. 10.
[48] Ronald A. Heifetz, Marty Linsky and Alexander Grashow, *The Practice of Adaptive Leadership: Tools and Tactics for Changing Your Organization and the World*, Cambridge, MA: Harvard University Press (2009).

6

Psychology of ministry

FRASER WATTS

It will be helpful to begin this overview of the psychology of ministry with some general points about the nature and scope of psychology. Psychology is both a basic science, studying psychological processes and phenomena, and a profession that applies psychology in a variety of contexts, such as health, education, organizations and prisons.

The area of psychological investigation that is most obviously relevant to ministry is the psychology of religion, a body of knowledge that is by now quite well developed, though it focuses largely on Anglo-American Christianity. I will draw largely on recent surveys of my own.[1] The area of professional psychology that is most relevant is clinical and counselling psychology, which is applicable to pastoral care in ministry and draws on a broader understanding of personal development.[2] Other areas of psychology are also potentially relevant, as I and others have argued.[3] For example, educational psychology is relevant to education in churches; organizational psychology is relevant to how churches function as organizations;[4] and clergy can be studied from the perspective of occupational psychology.[5]

Psychology is particularly interested in differences between people, and in changes in people over time. In this, it differs from sociology, which tends to generalize about what people in any given society have in common. Differences between people are highly relevant to ministry, as

---

[1]   F. Watts (2016), *Psychology, Religion and Spirituality: Concepts and Applications* (Cambridge: Cambridge University Press); F. Watts (2018), *Living Deeply: A Psychological and Spiritual Journey* (Cambridge: Lutterworth Press).

[2]   J. Rose (2013), *Psychology for Pastoral Contexts: A Handbook* (Norwich: Canterbury Press).

[3]   F. Watts, R. Nye and S. B. Savage (2002), *Psychology for Christian Ministry* (London: Routledge).

[4]   S. B. Savage and E. Boyd-MacMillan (2007), *The Human Face of Church: A Social Psychology and Pastoral Theology Resource for Pioneer and Traditional Ministry* (London: SCM Press).

[5]   L. J. Francis and S. H. Jones (1996), *Psychological Perspectives on Christian Ministry: A Reader* (Leominster: Gracewing / Fowler Wright).

different kinds of people benefit from different approaches to ministry. Processes of development and change are also relevant, as the Christian gospel is about transformation, and psychology is the academic discipline that tries to understand how human transformation takes place.

I will take a broad, inclusivist view of what is meant by psychology. Psychology sometimes works with narrow self-imposed limitations, such as B. F. Skinner's attempt to restrict psychology to the study of observable behaviour. These limitations have often been linked to the prioritization of one particular methodology over others. Psychology should be concerned with a broad range of relevant phenomena, such as cognition, emotion, behaviour and experience, and attempts to exclude any part of its natural subject matter should be resisted. I also suggest that it should draw on a broad range of methodologies and types of data, again with no arbitrary exclusions.

Psychology is also both a biological and social science, and tries to hold the two together. Biological psychology functions as a natural science. Social psychology can be a human, interpretative science (though some approaches to social psychology try to make it as much like a natural science as possible). I suggest that this broad bio-social approach to human nature is an advantage. Applications of psychology, such as to Christian ministry, should be open to both the biological processes in which all human functioning is rooted and grounded, and the social context in which individuals operate. There has sometimes been a tendency to reduce everything in psychology to biology, but biological factors can be considered without following that reductionist path. Psychology is sometimes criticized for being too individualistic but, in fact, social psychology takes full account of the social context in which individuals are embedded.

The diversity of Christians

Religious people are so diverse that it is almost impossible to generalize about them. Many problems in ministry arise from one kind of Christian failing to understand that other Christians see things in a completely different way. It is hard to achieve a balanced position on this. The tendency is often to assume that other Christians are essentially similar to oneself, and to be puzzled and surprised when that turns out not to be the case. Alternatively, once you have realized how different some Christians are, it is tempting to denigrate them as standing for something entirely inferior to what you believe in yourself. Looked at with psychological eyes, the focus of such attacks sometimes looks misplaced. One or two specific issues, such as the interpretation of Scripture or attitudes to homosexuality, can stand in for a much broader difference in mindset.

Though there is strong evidence for diversity among Christians, there is as yet no widely accepted classification, but there are several useful approaches.[6] One was developed by Gordon Allport in post-war America, and arose from research on social attitudes among Christians. Initial research suggested that religious people had more social and racial prejudice than non-religious people. However, Allport doubted whether that was true of all Christians, and he developed a distinction between 'intrinsic' religious types (people for whom religion was their dominant motivation) and 'extrinsic' religious people (whose involvement in religion was motivated by extraneous factors, such as social benefits). Though extrinsic religious people were more prejudiced than non-religious people, intrinsic religious people were *less* prejudiced than non-religious people. These two groups of religious people thus differed from non-religious people in opposite directions.

Similar differences emerged for mental health. Intrinsic religious people had better mental health than non-religious people, while extrinsic types had worse mental health. Though many religious people believe in being altruistic towards others, they don't always actually display helping behaviour. Subsequent research has identified a third type of religious people, the 'quest' type, who seem the most likely to be helpful towards other people in practice. It is worth noting that attitudes to race and homosexuality are expressed very differently among Christians, and it is quite common for Christians to be liberal on race but conservative on homosexuality.

There is also an interesting body of work on 'faith development' carried out by James Fowler.[7] However, the assumption that it deals with a set of stages of development that follow one another in an orderly sequence is not well supported by the evidence, and Fowler's work may be better seen as pointing to different types of faith, rather than as setting out a developmental sequence. (For simplicity I will ignore here Fowler's stages 0 and 6, and focus just on the central five stages/types.) For some people faith is 'intuitive-projective', focusing on felt experience and a sense of mystery. For others, faith is 'mythic-literal', focusing on the literal interpretation of simple ideas. For yet others, faith is 'synthetic-conventional' and

---

[6] Watts, *Psychology, Religion and Spirituality*, ch. 10.

[7] J. Fowler (1981), *Stages of Faith: The Psychology of Human Development and the Quest for Meaning* (San Francisco, CA: Harper & Row).

is primarily a form of loyalty. Faith can also be 'individuative-reflective', focusing on the personal religious journey. There is also a 'conjunctive' form of faith, which integrates some of these different elements; it is a form of faith that is particularly helpful for those in Christian ministry who need to relate sympathetically to a variety of other faith types.

There are also interesting leads from work on how religion relates to openness to experience, one of the 'big five' dimensions of current psychology of personality. It seems that some religious people have high levels of openness to experience, while others have unusually low levels. That is likely to have important implications for what form their religious life takes, and may be one of the key factors that differentiates conservative Christians from Charismatic and liberal ones.

There are at least two personality dimensions with significant heritability that are relevant to religion, even though they affect other things too.[8] One is conservatism, which dominates much contemporary religion, though there is nothing in Christianity that necessarily links it to conservatism. Religion is often linked to low levels of cognitive complexity, namely to a preference for black-and-white thinking, and a failure to integrate different frameworks and perspectives. Another dimension that is relevant to religion but again of broader significance is openness to unusual and anomalous experience. That leads to a more experiential Christianity, very different from conservatism.

Differences between Christians are often reflected in how they came to faith, or what kind of conversion they had, which is always an interesting thing to know about a fellow Christian. People who had a sudden conversion tend to be more conservative in both religious and social matters than those who had gradual conversions. Some Christians regard sudden conversions as superior to gradual ones, though it is not clear that there is any good theological rationale for that.

It seems that relatively few people are converted by intellectual arguments, though the widespread assumption that there are intellectual objections to religious belief may be a significant obstacle to conversion. Another possible route into faith is through religious experience. In most surveys, about a third of the population report having had an important religious experience of some kind. However, many keep such experiences to themselves, and they often do not lead to joining a church or other faith community. The social conversion route is probably one of the most

---

[8] Watts, *Psychology, Religion and Spirituality.*

important routes into faith, that is, people join a church because they identify with the values and lifestyle of church members.

Religious understanding

Much ministry is concerned with cognitive aspects of religion. There are two sides to this. On the one hand there is the role of the minister in teaching and interpreting the faith; on the other there is the question of how Christians receive the faith, what they believe and how they think about it. These come together, of course, in how ministers facilitate exploration of the faith. Religious education is now often seen more as facilitating people's growth in religious understanding than as communicating correct teaching.

Some of the ways in which Christians differ from one another affect how they understand their faith. It is important to keep a clear distinction between *what* people believe and *how* they believe it (i.e. the cognitive style with which they hold their beliefs). Some people think mainly in pictures, others mainly in words. Some think quite concretely, others in a more abstract way. Some focus on one thing at a time; others take a lot of background, contextual features into account. Some think in binary black-and-white categories; others deal more in shades of grey. It is very challenging to undertake teaching or preaching with people who have very different cognitive styles.

Many tensions between Christians seem to arise from assuming that, because other Christians have a different cognitive style and hold beliefs in a different way, they actually believe different things. However, many differences are more about the *how* than the *what* of belief. It is often possible to make progress towards reconciliation between Christians who assume they have fundamental disagreements by helping them to understand each other's different cognitive styles.[9] It can be quite a breakthrough to realize that the same basic beliefs can be held in very different ways. However, recognizing that is in itself a movement towards a more complex cognitive style.

Sometimes differences in mood or emotion affect where people put the emphasis in their religious beliefs. Understandably, people often tend to gravitate towards a version of Christianity that fits their personality and outlook. So, those with a strong sense of guilt may emphasize God's judgement, while those who feel more positively about themselves may

---

9   S. B. Savage (2013), 'Head and Heart in Preventing Religious Radicalization', in F. Watts and G. Dumbreck (eds), *Head and Heart: Perspectives from Religion and Psychology* (Philadelphia, PA: Templeton Press), pp. 157–94.

emphasize God's love and forgiveness. While this is entirely understandable, the sad thing about it is that people's religious beliefs often keep them entrenched in being the kind of people they already are, rather than broadening and rebalancing their outlook in a way that might be liberating.

Differences between Christians often surface in connection with what Christians believe about Jesus' work on the cross. Different theories of atonement may speak most powerfully to people with different personalities. So, emphasizing Jesus' victory over sin and evil may speak powerfully to anxious types, whereas emphasizing how Jesus bore our guilt may speak powerfully to those with a strong sense of guilt. It is very helpful in Christian ministry to be aware of this cross-talk between personality and belief, and to be aware of why people emphasize the things they do, and what personal significance their religious beliefs have for them. There has been growing interest in how people's image of God intersects with their patterns of belief, and how that can be explored in spiritual counselling.[10]

Particular issues arise about the religious education of children. Children initially understand things in a pre-linguistic way. At first their linguistic understanding is quite concrete, and often in narrative form. Abstract thinking develops later, roughly around age 11. So, children are not initially able to really understand more abstract theological formulations. However, it is important to recognize that children can and do understand religion in their own way, just not in the same way as adults. In fact they often seem to have quite a rich world of spiritual experience, broadly defined, which may fade somewhat as their capacity for intellectual understanding develops.[11] They seem well able to connect with what is happening in the Eucharist in an intuitive, imaginative way, even if they couldn't explain eucharistic theology. The best approaches to the religious education of children, such as Godly Play, facilitate the development of children's own understanding, playing to the strengths of children, rather than trying to impart adult understandings.

Prayer and spirituality

There is a psychological angle to most aspects of religious life and practice, and an awareness of this is very helpful in giving people spiritual help and guidance. It is important to emphasize that this is not to 'reduce' religion

---

[10] G. Moriarty and L. Hoffman (2007), *God Image Handbook for Spiritual Counseling and Psychotherapy: Research, Theory and Practice* (Binghamton, NY: Routledge/Haworth).

[11] R. Nye (2009), *Children's Spirituality: What It Is and Why It Matters* (London: Church House Publishing).

to just a matter of psychology. For example, to take an interest in how prayer works psychologically and how it can transform people is not to say that there is nothing more to prayer than psychological processes. The psychology of prayer is perfectly compatible with assuming that it involves relationship with a transcendent being, though it is equally compatible with the assumption that there is no such being.

In giving practical guidance about how to pray, the psychology of prayer may in some ways be of more help than an abstract, intellectual theology of prayer. However, putting it like this may be to overstate the distinction between the theology and psychology of prayer, as there is much practical psychological wisdom intertwined with theology in such religious practitioners as Ignatius or Teresa of Avila. Indeed the psychology of the religious life may sometimes just be saying things in the modern, accessible language of psychology that previous ages would have said in a more explicitly religious language. In Christian ministry, theology and psychology provide complementary perspectives; religious life is understood better with the binocular vision that occurs when they are both used together.

A useful route into the psychology of prayer is through traditional categories such as adoration, confession, thanksgiving and supplication (the latter including both petition for oneself and supplication for others). Different psychological processes arise in different facets of prayer. Some aspects of prayer such as adoration and intercession encourage perspective-taking, and help to alleviate egocentricity. There is an interesting convergence between prayers of thanksgiving and current psychological work on gratitude. Regular exercises in gratitude seem to have psychological benefits, and thanksgiving to God has probably long had comparable psychological benefits. Confession involves helpful processes of self-exploration, enhancing self-awareness about the adverse effects one's actions may have had on other people (though it is important psychologically that such awareness is balanced by encouragement to receive and accept forgiveness). Praying for oneself promotes a different aspect of self-awareness, and provides an opportunity to probe beneath what might give immediate gratification to what might bring more enduring fulfilment. It seems important that all this is done in the context of the felt presence of God; the sense that God is present seems to make an important psychological difference.

Similar issues arise about meditation and contemplative prayer. Though meditation methods such as mindfulness have come out of a religious stable, they have largely become secularized and decoupled from their religious origins. Mindfulness comes from Indian religious traditions, but similar methods can be found within the Christian tradition. As with prayer, the psychology of meditation can be interpreted in a purely secular way, but it is equally compatible with seeing meditation as part of the practice of the presence of God. Most methods of meditation involve a combination of mental alertness and physical relaxation. They also involve a focusing of attention and a way of avoiding mind-wandering; that can be achieved in various ways, such as focusing on breathing, or on a simple mantra.

The Jesus Prayer of the Eastern Christian tradition combines both. Contemplative prayer often sees the journey inwards as also being a journey into God. In the imagery of St Teresa of Avila it is a journey to the inner room of the interior castle where God is to be found, deep within. This maps easily on to psychological frameworks such as those of C. G. Jung that postulate a true or higher Self that stands behind the ego, the everyday centre of consciousness. In giving pastoral guidance in silent prayer it is again helpful to be able to draw on psychological approaches as well as more traditional religious formulations.

Funerals and public liturgy

There is also a helpful psychological perspective on liturgy and public worship. This is perhaps most clearly evident in pastoral liturgy such as a funeral service which, at best, can make a significant contribution to the grieving process and help people to come to terms with their loss. Grieving often passes through different stages, and Kübler-Ross has suggested that these are denial, bargaining, anger, guilt, depression and acceptance. It is doubtful whether things are often quite as neat as this scheme suggests, but at least this approach draws attention to the multifaceted nature of grieving in which different aspects are in the ascendancy at different times.

Funeral services can play different roles for different people depending on their personality and where they have got to in the grieving process. There is often a subtle path to be steered. It is also usually helpful for the congregation to be emotionally engaged during the funeral service, but for the service to provide a strong enough framework that it can contribute to transformation and working through grief. It is important on the one hand to recognize the reality of the loss and not to collude with denial, but on the other hand to assert the reality of a new form of life for the deceased person with God.

It is possible for somewhat similar processes of transformation to take place in regular liturgy, such as a Eucharist. That is probably less often achieved, though again psychology can contribute a useful perspective, so that those who lead worship are more aware of the impact their approach will have on those present. There is no single psychology of the Eucharist, as there is a huge difference between a handful of people holding an informal open-air Eucharist and a formal High Mass in a large church building. One emphasizes community and presence; the other emphasizes awe and mystery. Some people have a strong preference for one approach or the other, but many people find that different ways of doing a Eucharist can be helpful on different occasions. In most cases the Eucharist takes people on a spiritual journey towards the moment when bread and wine are blessed and received. At best, the preparation for that moment can take individuals, or indeed a community, on a journey of preparation that is not unlike the contemplative journey into the inner room of the castle.

Confession and forgiveness

Confession and forgiveness have long been central aspects of the religious life, and there is a helpful psychological perspective on them that can assist Christian ministry. The sense of guilt is troublesome for many people; it is something that they need help with and for which Christians have relevant resources. However, it is worth noting that feelings of guilt are quite varied. Some guilt is realistic and appropriate; other guilt is excessive and disproportionate. In the first case the primary problem is with the person's behaviour whereas in the latter case the main problem is with his or her emotions, and that calls for different responses. Making confession, and the preparation for doing so, can be useful in clarifying this and in pinpointing what actually calls for confession. Appropriate confession and absolution can bring huge relief and can be transformative. However, there is also a danger that over-frequent confession can foster an excessive sense of guilt.

Psychology has recently taken a good deal of interest in the practice of forgiveness and has developed forgiveness as a kind of therapy.[12] There are indeed many negative consequences of harbouring resentment, and people often feel better if they can bring themselves to forgive, or be helped to do so. Most psychological approaches emphasize the importance of preparatory work before forgiveness itself, such as finding positive things about the offending person to reflect on, and recognizing that one has caused offence to others oneself. However, forgiveness is not always

---

[12] E. L. Worthington (2003), *Forgiveness and Reconciliation* (New York: Routledge).

possible, however beneficial it might be. It is important not to add to people's burdens by making them feel bad about their inability to forgive.

A religious approach to forgiveness differs in subtle ways from the psychological one. Religious people are more likely to see forgiveness as something bigger than themselves in which they can join, rather than something that they decide to initiate; that makes it feel very different. They also tend to see forgiveness as something that arises from a long-standing path of personal and spiritual development rather than as something one can do 'out of the blue'. There has also, so far, been a curious neglect in psychology of how difficult it can be to receive forgiveness, and religion may be able to contribute something to that.

Healing

Prayers for healing have become an important part of Christian ministry, often with laying on of hands and anointing. Again, there is a helpful psychological perspective.[13] That is not to imply that healing is just a psychological matter, though psychology can contribute a useful perspective on how the benefits of healing ministry might be mediated. There is a tendency for people to go to extremes about spiritual healing and to assume that it is either a miracle or worthless. However, there are many sensible in-between positions; there is now strong evidence that a personal spiritual life can have beneficial effects on both mental and physical health, so it is not surprising if praying for healing with others can often produce similar benefits.

There is sometimes a curious reticence about whether or not healing is supposed to actually help. My own experience is that it often can, though not in ways that are completely predictable. It is, of course, more likely to help if those involved expect it to do so. There are many pathways through which spiritual and psychological processes can contribute to physical health and experience. For example, how much pain people experience depends on a range of mental and emotional processes, not just on physical tissue damage.

It is often helpful for a minister to pray with someone who comes for pastoral care. It puts things in the larger context of the presence of God, and is one of the distinctive things about Christian pastoral care. Praying with someone can play a special role in building a pastoral relationship and

---

[13] F. Watts (2011), *Spiritual Healing: Scientific and Religious Perspectives* (Cambridge: Cambridge University Press).

contributes to social bonding. Frequently it seems to provide the resources to enable a pastoral conversation to become transformative; it adds a kind of energy and focus that secular counselling often lacks. It brings into the conversation a God's-eye perspective which helps people to look at things in a way that is more balanced, benign, honest and perceptive.

Personal problems and pastoral care

In any Christian congregation there are people with personal issues and problems, some of whom will turn for help to an ordained minister, or to others in the community who undertake pastoral work. There is now a much broader range of services to whom such people can turn than in previous ages, which raises issues about what should be attempted by those who minister in church and what should be directed elsewhere. There is no simple answer to that. It depends partly on the pastoral competence of the person exercising ministry. For example, some will have received training in counselling, while others won't. In general, it is good for those in ministry to use their skills to help others, as far as time allows, and within the limits of their pastoral competence. There is also a growing trend for counselling to include consideration of spirituality.[14]

There is no space here for a complete survey of the range of personal problems a minister may encounter. However, it is worth saying something about depression, as an example, as it occurs frequently and raises interesting issues. Christian people can get depressed like anyone else, and it should not be seen as indicating a lack of faith, or as being a judgement from God. Depression affects people in many ways. When depressed, people feel sad, and sometimes guilty and angry too. They think very negatively about themselves, the world and the future. They become lethargic and withdrawn, and lacking in energy. Relationships become difficult, and are often negative and demanding. Eating and sleeping may become difficult too.

Christian virtues are relevant to depression. Though people often feel unloved when they get depressed, they need love and support more than ever, that is, they need people who understand them, spend time with them and want the best for them. Depressed people often feel pessimistic but, even if they no longer expect a bright future, it is sometimes still possible for them to sustain hope in the sense of maintaining a positive,

---

14 K. I. Pargament (2011), *Spiritually-Integrated Psychotherapy: Understanding and Addressing the Sacred* (New York: Guilford Press).

determined attitude that is built upon their faith in God. Depressed people strip away the rosy glow with which many of us see things, and there can be something helpful about that stark realism, if they can avoid being overwhelmed by it.

Pastoral care often involves listening and giving advice. Pastoral care should always start with good listening. It is important to create a relaxed, unhurried non-judgemental atmosphere in which individuals can talk honestly about what they are feeling and what is troubling them. It is sometimes helpful to prompt people by asking questions, provided that is not done in an inquisitorial way. However, it is sometimes possible just to be non-directive in the manner of Carl Rogers, just reflecting back what people say, as a prompt for them to say more. If people are to engage in constructive self-exploration it is important that they should experience in their listener a positive regard for them, as well as genuineness and accurate empathy.[15] Good listening is helpful to the other person in itself, but a minister who listens well will be more sure-footed, because he or she understands the situation better.

Sometimes it is appropriate to give advice, though people differ in how much they benefit from that. Some people can work out for themselves what they should do, provided they come away feeling understood, and able to understand themselves better. Others look for good advice more than anything else and will only feel they have been helped if they receive it. Much pastoral advice is really common sense, and doesn't require much professional expertise. However, there are some basic principles underlying cognitive-behaviour therapy, which in many ways is a systematization of practical common sense.

- In many problems a vicious circle is set up, in which there are things the person does or thinks repetitively that make the problem worse; it is helpful to identify those things and to try to avoid them. For example, depression is largely maintained by thinking negative thoughts.
- Equally, there are often things that the person could do, and perhaps has done in the past, which would be helpful; it is useful to identify those things and for the person to make an effort to do them. For example, a person who has become very withdrawn will probably feel better if he or she makes the effort to get back into contact with people.

---

[15] B. Thorne (2012), *Counselling and Spiritual Accompaniment: Bridging Faith and Person-Centred Therapy* (Oxford: Wiley-Blackwell).

- There are sometimes situations that lead on to things that drag the person down; it is helpful to identify what situations put the person at risk, and to avoid them.
- There are also often things the person wants to be able to do but which are proving difficult; they generally get easier with practice, especially if the person approaches them in a graded way, starting with easier situations and moving on to more difficult ones.

Conclusion

There can be mutual enrichment between psychology and Christian ministry. Psychological approaches to care can be enhanced by including spiritual aspects. Equally, psychology can bring wider horizons to Christian ministry, raising awareness and furnishing additional practical resources. This is not to reduce Christian ministry to psychology but to augment it. Psychology can make a helpful contribution to almost every aspect of Christian ministry.

7

Ministry in fiction

CATHERINE WILCOX

Introduction

A few years ago, a young clergyman was invited to a twenty-first birth-day party in a working men's club in the north-east of England. He had recently taken a funeral for the same family, and this had established a pastoral link. The evening came. He was running late, and did not have time to go home and change out of his clerical shirt. To his bewilderment, his arrival in the club was greeted by whistles, and cries of 'Get your kit off!' Since *real* vicars do not get invited to twenty-first birthday parties in clubs, obviously the male stripper had just arrived. In vain the hosts flapped their hands and mouthed, 'No! No! *He really is one!*' The cheering continued.

There may well be a similar dynamic when vicars appear in contem-porary literature. What is going on here? Is this for real? In a bygone age, when clergy were a normal part of the social landscape, fictional priests came as no surprise to the reader. But in a modern novel, some kind of explanation is probably necessary.

This chapter will explore the phenomenon of clergy in novels. The first section takes a nostalgic look at The Good Old Days, when clergy were a familiar sight; an era when clerics were central to their local community and required no explanation. They were simply there, like elm trees. In the second section we will look at some of the ways in which clergy have been deployed in more recent works of fiction.

It goes without saying that everyone reading this will be scandalized by the glaring omissions. How can she not have mentioned X? No two lists of Top 20 fictional priests will be the same. A quick search on the Internet throws up a wide spectrum, from the scholarly – 'Representations of Clergy in Victorian Literature' – to the racy – 'Hot and Sexy Historical Romances with Vicars, Priests, and Men of God' (aka cassock-rippers). What follows is a small idiosyncratic collection from which I will seek to make general observations. It is an overwhelmingly Church of England list, for which (as I once overheard an ordinand say in a quintessentially passive-aggressive Anglican manner) I am sorry, but I make no apology.

Part 1: The Golden Era

Before we begin our trawl of novels, we must pause to genuflect in the direction of Geoffrey Chaucer. *The Canterbury Tales* gives us the first pen portraits of English churchmen and women, from saintly to scurrilous, *in English.* Chaucer's decision to eschew the language of the powerful elite – French – helped shape our literary canon, and we all stand in his debt.

The first notable cleric to stride through the pages of the English novel is Henry Fielding's Parson Abraham Adams (*Joseph Andrews*). We are told Adams was 'an excellent scholar' and 'besides, a man of good sense, good parts, and good nature'. But – the reader knows there is a *but* coming – *but* he was 'at the same time as entirely ignorant of the ways of this world as an infant just entered into it could possibly be'. Abraham Adams is the ancestor of every fictional parson who has ever blinked behind his round spectacles, said 'Well, bless my soul!' and forgotten to remove his bicycle clips. This stereotype is a hardy perennial of the fictional herbaceous border – the good but unworldly man of God. Septimus Harding in Trollope's *The Warden* is another. These men are lovable, harmless and often comic.

There are, however, plenty of fictional clerics who manage to be comic without being harmless and lovable. It is a truth universally acknowledged that Jane Austen's Mr Collins is one of the least attractive fictional vicars ever to crawl off the page. 'Can he be a sensible man, sir?' asks Elizabeth Bennet, after hearing Mr Collins's introductory letter read out. 'No, my dear,' replies her father. 'I think not. I have great hopes of finding him quite the reverse.' Mr Bennet's hopes are speedily gratified in *Pride and Prejudice*. Unlike her father, Elizabeth cannot always laugh off her cousin's absurdities. His obsequious behaviour in public impinges on her, and makes her ridiculous by association. As an Anglican, I fleetingly share Elizabeth's embarrassment. He makes the Church ridiculous by association, too. How I long for vicars – both real and imaginary – who do not let the side down.

Mr Elton (in *Emma*) runs Mr Collins a close second. In comparison, he *is* a sensible man. Emma herself, we are told, 'thought very highly of him as a good-humoured, well-meaning, respectable young man ... *whom any woman not fastidious might like*' (my emphasis). Let us pause to relish that backhander. Emma, of course, is fastidious. Misunderstandings and wounded vanity follow, and Mr Elton shows his true colours. He emerges from behind his charming façade as socially ambitious and vain. Worse, he is capable of spite; a vice – when coupled with intelligence – that is less easily laughed off than Mr Collins's 'mixture of servility and self-importance'. Certainly, the narrative punishes 'Mr E' with a suitably ghastly name-dropping wife; while Mr Collins is more fortunate in meeting 'one of the very few sensible women who would have accepted him, or have made him happy if they had'.

So far, so disheartening. Who on earth recommended these men for training?

The ministerial selection processes glimpsed in Jane Austen's novels are – on the face of it – not rigorous. We have a rare sight of someone being turned down, when Mr Darcy heads off the caddish Wickham's request to be presented to a living. ('I knew that Mr Wickham ought not to be a clergyman.') Elsewhere, though, gentlemen (and it was always gentlemen in those days, of course) appear to 'take orders' in much the same way that one might buy an army commission – without any nonsense about testing your vocation or ministerial formation. One had an Oxbridge degree. What more did one require? – other than a patron to provide a living of enough hundreds of pounds a year to live on respectably. We are told in passing in *Mansfield Park* that Edmund was going 'to a friend near Peterborough in the same situation as himself, and they were to receive ordination in the course of the Christmas week'. Sorted.

Edmund is rare in articulating his sense of vocation (needled into it by Mary Crawford telling him, 'A clergyman is nothing'). He replies that he

> cannot call that situation nothing, which has the charge of all that is of the first importance to mankind, individually or collectively considered, temporally and eternally – which has the guardianship of religion and morals, and consequently of the manners which result from their influence.

I wish I could love Edmund Bertram as much as the novel implies he deserves. He is very kind and thoughtful, but he is very *earnest*. Ah, those naughty witty Crawfords, with their dangerous worldly glamour! Would it have been so very terrible to pair off Edmund with Mary, and Fanny with Henry?

But we are not here to rewrite *Mansfield Park*.

This leaves the question, are there *no* good clergymen at all in Jane Austen? Mr Morland, father of the heroine of *Northanger Abbey*, attracts no censure (apart from the misfortune of being called Richard). Yet, once again, he and his wife are a little earnest. Let us refine the question: are there no good clergy, who do not make us want to stick a whoopee cushion under their kneeler at evensong? Fortunately, yes: there is Henry Tilney in *Northanger Abbey*. He is 'a clergyman, and of a very respectable family in Gloucestershire', and 'if not quite handsome, was very near it'. He makes up for this slight deficiency by possessing, in spades, what other Jane Austen clerics lack: a good sense of humour (GSOH).

At their first meeting, Henry makes the heroine laugh with his Regency fop impression: 'Then forming his features into a set smile, and affectedly softening his voice, he added, with a simpering air, "Have you been long in Bath, madam?"' If Elizabeth is the wittiest of Austen's heroines, Henry Tilney is a contender for wittiest hero. I bless him for that. Those who move in church circles know there are plenty of witty clerics around to defy the earnest or pompous stereotype. However, Tilney does not operate within the text primarily as a clergyman. Hence, the novel's preoccupation with those characteristics (good looks, sense of humour, fortune) that belong more properly to the romantic hero than the parson. What difference would it have made to the plot if the closing line of Chapter 3 had read, 'He was an army officer, and of a very respectable family in Gloucestershire'?

Very little, I suspect. Tilney's professional duties seem light. At one point he mentions that he has to be in his parish 'on Monday to attend the parish meeting, and [will] probably be obliged to stay two or three days'. Considerably more time in the novel is devoted to dancing, country walks and flirting. Nevertheless, we are not invited to judge Henry as a slacker in danger of being clapped into Clergy Disciplinary Measures. We are to assume he is a respectable and dutiful clergyman. Novels cannot show us everything, or the protagonist would never finish getting out of bed in the morning. They selectively show us what is important. The business of Austen's novels is not the ordained ministry. It is matrimony.

By contrast, there are novels whose business is very much the ordained ministry. What difference would it make to *Barchester Towers* if Archdeacon Grantly or Mr Slope were not ordained? The book simply could not function. I reread all the Barchester novels a few years ago when I moved to live in a medieval cathedral close. My overwhelming impression was 'Good grief – nothing's changed!' Well, of course it hasn't. Trollope was writing about the venerable historic institution of the Church of England, and about human nature. The institution has changed superficially, of course. These days new bishops are not appointed quite as swiftly as Dr Proudie was; nor may cathedral canons discharge their duties *in absentia*, and spend their lives butterfly-hunting in Italy.

What has not changed is the human heart. Trollope's genius is to present the reader with a cast of memorable characters, to put them in predicaments that are all too agonizingly plausible – and make us care what happens next. The cathedral close in Barchester is riven with factions, high church pitted against low church. There is scheming, manoeuvring and back-stabbing. None of the characters is exemplary. All are flawed. I will focus on one representative of each faction: Dr Theophilus Grantly, archdeacon (high), and Obadiah Slope, bishop's chaplain (low).

The irascible Grantly ('Good heavens!') is a firm favourite among churchy readers. He is as beloved as the bishop's chaplain is loathed. Slope has no redeeming qualities – except possibly his nose. Yes, Trollope concedes that Slope's nose is his redeeming feature: 'It is pronounced, straight and well-formed.' Even so, Trollope cannot bear to let this go unqualified: 'I myself would have liked it better did it not possess a some-what spongy, porous appearance, as though it had been cleverly formed out of a red-coloured cork.' So much, then, for Mr Slope's redeeming nose. He is a 'priestly charmer' of the ladies, and has 'a pawing greasy way with him'. 'How on earth such a creature got ordained! – they'll ordain anybody now,' concludes the archdeacon.

Trollope himself does the job of comparing the archdeacon and the chaplain: 'and despite the manifold faults of the former, one can hardly fail to make it much to his advantage.' Both men love to wield power. Both are ambitious. Indeed, the novel opens with Grantly's ambition to be the next bishop of Barchester:

> He certainly did desire to play first fiddle; he did desire to sit in full lawn sleeves among the peers of the realm; and he did desire, if the truth must out, to be called 'My lord' by his reverend brethren.

For all that, the author is on his side. 'Our archdeacon was worldly – who among us is not so?' The reader is given a firm steer: we are to indulge and forgive.

No such mercy is extended to Slope. Trollope frankly owns up to this bias: 'My readers will guess from what I have written that I myself do not like Mr Slope.' Here we stumble upon another trope. It is the fate of Evangelicals in ecclesiastical fiction to be loathed. They fare particu-larly badly in the hands of Dickens. Witness the (alcoholic) temperance preacher Mr Stiggins of *The Pickwick Papers* ('He was a prim-faced, red-nosed man, with a long, thin countenance, and a semi-rattlesnake sort of eye – rather sharp, but decidedly bad'); and the oleaginous Mr Chadband ('attached to no particular denomination') in *Bleak House*. Dickens hits off Chadband's Nonconformist preaching style mercilessly, the cadences of which will still be familiar today to those who move in the right circles:

'Peace, my friends,' says Chadband, rising and wiping the oily exudations from his reverend visage. 'Peace be with us! My friends, why with us? Because,' with his fat smile, 'it cannot be against us, because it must be for us; because it is not hardening, because it is softening; because it does not make war like the hawk, but comes home unto us like the dove.'

Ladies and gentlemen, the Dickensian Evangelical: thin and snake-like, or fat and oily. It is scant comfort for the Anglican reader that these two cant-ing hypocrites are Nonconformists. Why this persistent trope, I wonder? Is it simply because the novelists themselves are allergic to Evangelicalism? Where are the *good* Evangelical fictional clergy?

Maybe we should be asking: where are the Evangelical *novelists*? Have their works sunk without trace? Perhaps in the nineteenth century they were far too busy writing improving works for the Religious Tract Society to produce mainstream fiction. A novel that is 'just' a novel is potentially troubling to the Evangelical mind. (I am not taking cheap shots here – I self-identify as Evangelical.) Surely, *surely* (as Mrs Proudie might say), fiction by Christians ought to commend the gospel, enshrine Christian values, avoid bad language and explicit sex (or at least make it clear that these are to be repented of)? This ambivalence about the purpose of novels continues to this day – witness the buoyant market for Christian genre fiction, particularly in the USA. This is the place to hunt for romances written for readers of purer eyes than to look upon the F-word, or for fantasies with the right kind of magic (i.e. Narnia, not Harry Potter) – lest child readers slither down the slippery slope into the Occult.

But let us return to my question: where are the *good* Evangelical fic-tional clergy? Unless we stray once more into the wilds of fictional Nonconformity (where we encounter Dinah Morris, the Methodist preacher of George Eliot's *Adam Bede*) we will struggle to find a sympa-thetic portrayal of an Evangelical minister. Evangelicals seldom escape from stereotype sufficiently to engage the reader's affections. (I will enter a caveat here – Evangelicals and Nonconformists fare better in American fiction, from Reverend Alden in the Laura Ingalls Wilder books, through to John Ames in Marilynne Robinson's *Gilead*.)

We need to pause here, however. Stereotypes – with their broad brush-strokes – tell a certain bald kind of truth. The thing about the Evangelical stereotype is that its flaws are at the cool end of the sin spectrum. The sins are not passionate and vibrant – drunken leg-overs, sweariness and wrath. They are more your cold dingy grey sins, your dull-as-ditchwater sins: hypocrisy, narrow-mindedness and judgementalism – not forgetting our old friend, earnestness. Of course, if they set their mind to it, novelists can persuade the reader to root for almost any character, no matter how unpleasant. We have our cunning tricks. But writers, like readers, are only human. We write about what we find interesting, and few of us are intrigued by the inner workings of the Evangelical conscience. No, I fear Evangelicalism is destined to remain a convenient shorthand for everything *not on the side of life* (rather as the killjoy Roman Catholic priest operates in Joanne Harris's *Chocolat*).

It is worth bearing in mind the social dimension of churchmanship in an earlier age. Evangelicalism, with its chapel associations, carried with it a whiff of vulgarity. It was the religion of the lower classes, not the gentry. Consider the following, in George Eliot's *Middlemarch*. Mrs Farebrother is the mother of a vicar, and is here lamenting the passing of the old days: 'It was not so in my youth: a Churchman was a Churchman, and a clergyman, you might be pretty sure, was a gentleman if nothing else. But now he may be *no better than a Dissenter*' (my emphasis).

We cannot leave the Golden Era without a look at the clergy in the novels of George Eliot. While we encounter the familiar dour Evangelicals (for example, Mr Tynan in *Scenes of Clerical Life*), churchmen of other stripes also figure unsympathetically. Who (other than the idealistic Dorothea Brooke) could find it possible to love the pedantic scholarly Mr Casaubon in *Middlemarch*? 'This was the first time that Mr Casaubon had spoken at any length. He delivered himself with precision, as if he had been called upon to make a public statement.' We have all met clergymen like that. Casaubon's faults, too, lie at the chilly end of the spectrum. It is rather easier to warm to Mr Farebrother, whose chief foible is gambling at cards. But once again, these two men are not operating primarily as clergymen in this text. We are much more interested in Casaubon the unlikely suitor, the chilly husband, the failed scholar, Casaubon wracked with jealousy and suspicion – Casaubon *the man*. In short, the beating heart of the book is relationships, not theology. Some of the doctrinal disputes of the day are canvassed, but they are not the central concern of the novel. Despite its title, Eliot's *Scenes of Clerical Life* is not primarily focused on matters clerical, either.

Where are the novels that deal primarily with clergy *as clergy*? Even in Trollope's Barchester novels, there is a certain reticence about what we might term hardcore vicaring. He offers this disclaimer in *Barchester Towers*:

It would not be becoming were I to travesty a sermon, or even to repeat the language of it in the pages of a novel. In endeavouring to depict the characters of the persons of whom I write, I am to a certain extent *forced to speak of sacred things* [my emphasis].

'Sacred things' – prayer, preaching, the inward life of the spirit, personal devotion – these are things from which Trollope's narrative fastidiously averts its gaze. Despite their church setting, Trollope's Barchester novels are not theologically driven. There are Victorian novels that grapple with issues of faith and doubt (notably Mrs Humphry Ward's runaway best-seller, *Robert Elsmere*), but these works have not retained a lasting place in readers' affections in quite the same way. Trollope's strategy of eliding 'sacred things' has risks: his clerical characters tend to appear worldly. That said, to devote pages to inner spiritual wrestling has risks too – the characters will tend to appear tediously sanctimonious. Worse, the novel may start to sound didactic. Keats once wrote, 'We hate poems that have a palpable design on us.' The same is true for novels.

To summarize, in the novels I have mentioned, clergy characters are here (as the song goes) *because they're here*. That was in the good old days, before secularization fretted away the church garments like a moth, and declining numbers took their toll.

Part 2: The glory has departed

How are clergy portrayed in novels now they are no longer simply part of the social furniture? In a range of sometimes surprising ways. Those of us who know vicarage life intimately may wonder why there are so many clerical sleuths in the pages of novels. It is less surprising to encounter vicars being deployed for comic relief, or as Aunt Sallies for satirists to take pot shots at. As we have seen, there is a tiresomely long tradition for this. It is not hard to see why a novel seeking to explore acute moral dilemmas might fasten on a priestly protagonist to heighten the tension. Yet we might still wonder why there are so few novels that seem to tell 'our' story – the life of faith – sympathetically. We will look at these different strands in turn.

Clerical detectives

There are so many of these I sometimes wonder whether some kind of Sleuthing Module ought to be part of clergy theological formation. Religious murder mysteries have a long and venerable lineage. A fictional chronology presents us first with pre-Reformation sleuths (Ellis Peters' much-loved Brother Cadfael novels; Umberto Eco's *The Name of the Rose*). In the so-called Golden Age of the whodunnit, we encounter the granddaddy of them all, G. K. Chesterton's Father Brown; and Margery Allingham's Canon Hubert Avril (who operates as an unofficial sleuth alongside his more famous nephew, Albert Campion). Then in the fictional 1950s we meet James Runcie's Canon Sidney Chambers. Encouragingly, clerical sleuthing is by no means a male bastion. Witness Kate Charles' Revd Callie Anderson and Phil Rickman's Revd Merrily Watkins.

Clergy will always be amateur sleuths. They star in whodunits, not in police procedural novels. We look in vain for similar numbers of accountants- or teachers-turned-detective, though. What accounts for this riot of clerical colour in whodunit genre? Two things, I think. There is the Father Brown factor: 'A man who does next to nothing but hear men's real sins is not likely to be wholly unaware of human evil.' Here we encounter the trope of the priest as shrewd observer of human nature, and recipient of secrets. Logically, we might argue that GPs are similarly placed, but they lack the mysterious glamour of church paraphernalia. The other factor is the 'small world' of the whodunit, where the crime takes place in a closed community (country house, English village, island, train, ship, Oxbridge college). The parish is another such small world, and the priest, of course, is at the centre. But there is a bit of slippage here. Are *real* clergy *really* still at the centre? Or is the clerical whodunit by definition going to be old-fashioned, and shot through with nostalgia? Notice that Sidney Chambers inhabits a 1950s, not a present-day, Grantchester.

Comic clerics

There is something potentially hilarious about vicars, I fear. The funny clothes, the otherworldliness, the arcane institution that cannot really be taken seriously any more – all these are fair game to the novelist. The works of Barbara Pym are gentle comedies of post-Second World War English manners, and they contain many fine skewerings of clergy (in the Jane Austen tradition). Here is an example from *Jane and Prudence*:

> Nicholas [the vicar] accepted his two eggs and bacon and the implication that his own needs were more important than his wife's with a certain amount of complacency, Jane thought. But then, as a clergyman he had had to get used to accepting flattery and gifts gracefully.

This is a world of spinsters, distressed gentlewomen and jumble sales. Pym chronicles an era when the Church had been displaced from centre stage in national and local affairs. If the Church has increasingly become an irrelevance, then her clergy seem to embody this in their comic ineffectuality. Pym admitted, 'I suppose I criticise and mock at the clergy and the Church of England because I'm fond of them.' The novels breathe an affection for something much loved, but faded and shabby – an old sofa, perhaps – that one is not ready to part with.

By contrast, the Church in A. N. Wilson's novels – to press my analogy to extremes – is a purple plush sofa with empty gin bottles and porn stashed down the back, occupied by camp young men calling one another by women's names. When it was published in 1978 *Unguarded Hours* was regarded by many as a wildly over-the-top comic creation. Insiders, however, acknowledged it was a wickedly accurate portrait of *a certain institution*. This divide in opinion is understandable. The reading public comes with certain expectations of The Cloth. The unchurched will read through the filter of limited experience and stereotypes. These may be wildly outdated (the 'trendy' vicar strumming his guitar to 'Kum Ba Ya' – we stopped singing *that* in the 1970s). The churched are prone to read via the weapon slit of their own particular bunker. Fiction risks being dismissed as unrealistic when it offers a view of clergy behaving in unexpected ways. 'I have moved in church circles all my life and have never encountered this kind of thing.' Yet it is a risk worth taking. The act of reading a novel opens up new worlds and may extend our capacity to empathize with those different from ourselves.

Priests with awful dilemmas

The Church of England may still be the established Church, but it has receded to the edges of public life. This is a serious loss to novelists interested in exploring moral dilemmas. Adultery these days is a matter of cheating on your spouse. This is subject matter enough for many a novel, of course, but it lacks that spiritual depth-charge of novels from an earlier age. It is as if modern novelists are organists who can no longer play on the bad boys – those massive 32-foot pipes, whose sound is off the bottom of the range of human hearing but which shakes the very air with doom and awe. Before the Sea of Faith withdrew, actions had eternal as well as temporal implications. So it is understandable that novelists will still seek out this lost territory by focalizing their narrative through men and women of the cloth. When Patrick Gale explores an array of vexed questions in *A Perfectly Good Man*, the issues are brought into sharper focus by making the good man of the title, Barnaby Johnson, an Anglican priest.

It's true: a dog collar always ups the ante, even now. Asking 'Why are there so few nice ordinary fictional clergy?' is like asking why the news is full of disasters and scandals. Drunk drivers are ten a penny, but a bishop caught over the limit is a story. Gale is rare in setting out to write about a perfectly good man. Bad men offer far more for novelists to get their teeth into.

On the subject of bad men in fiction, we should note that the Roman Catholic (RC) Church commonly acts as a lightning conductor for society's anxieties about child abuse, and the white-hot anger over hypocrisy and cover-ups. Thus the recurring appearance of the RC priest as paedophile monster (while middle-of-the-road Anglicans are more likely to be busy committing adultery, and Evangelicals embezzling the funds). Virtue, like happiness, tends to write white. Sin always shows up nicely on the page.

Who is telling our story?

Who, then, is writing the tales of ordinary clergy going about their normal lives in the twenty-first century? Why is nobody telling our story? To put it brutally (and the world of publishing is a bit brutal): *because nobody cares.* The Church is unfashionable to the extent that mainstream publishers view it as a marketing liability. When my third novel came out – the protagonist was a woman curate – Penguin suppressed all mention of the Church on the jacket, on the grounds that it would put people off buying the book.

Novelists who already have a proven record will fare better. (I daresay J. K. Rowling's agent could get a bidding war going for a 'Chaplain of Hogwarts' book proposal.) During the 1980s and early 1990s bestselling novelists Joanna Trollope (*The Rector's Wife, The Choir*) and Susan Howatch (the Starbridge Series) turned their attention to church matters, bringing tried-and-tested narrative strategies to bear. This was a hugely exciting era for Anglican novel-readers. Finally, we got to read about our world! A handful of other authors have found a way past the publishing gatekeepers to tell church tales (Jonathan Tulloch's vicar in *Give Us This Day*, the clergy in Michael Arditti's novels). But alas, these novels have remained an exception; rocky church outcrops in a wide secular plain.

Dare we hope for a soaring mountain of a church novel? Perhaps we can. Perhaps we should remember Marilynne Robinson's *Gilead* (and *Home* and *Lila*) and strengthen our feeble knees. It *is* possible to publish and sell stories about ministers preparing sermons, praying, discussing Karl Barth and pondering Bible commentaries. Let us pray the Lord of the Harvest to send out more great novelists to labour in the heat of the twenty-first century.

Conclusion

It seems to me, then, that portrayals of Anglican clergy in fiction follow the same trajectory as the role of clergy in real life. When Jane Austen set to work on her 'three or four families in a country village' (which she considered to be 'the very thing' to make a novel out of), a vicar was an inevitable member of the cast. Everyone knew the vicar. These days, clergy have largely receded to the margins – apart from at those moments of crisis and change (births, deaths and marriages). Clergy are only there when there is a good reason for it, both in the pages of novels and in the lives of most ordinary people. I tend to lose sight of this, living and writing as I do, in the thick of church life.

Is it all bleak, then? No. Here is where I draw courage in the face of church decline and implacable publishers: it is personal encounters that make the difference. The genuine pastoral moment that changes a life. The stripper who turns out to be a real vicar after all. Or else the made-up characters who are so 'real' that readers end up caring what happens to them, and understanding the world of faith, or the human condition, a little better. Even if those fictional characters are Anglican priests. Even (shudder!) if they are Evangelicals.

8

Ministry in television and film

JOSHUA REY AND JOLYON MITCHELL

Introduction: intimacy, prophecy and power

Think of a clergyman in a movie. If you chose Rowan Atkinson's stumbling Father Gerald in *Four Weddings and a Funeral* you are in good company.[1] For ministry is very often experienced at weddings and funerals, and at other times of vulnerability and heightened emotion. This shapes its screen portrayal. Moreover, whereas other visitors at times of crisis (medics, police officers and lawyers) intrude whether we want them or not, the minister (cleric, priest and pastor) is invited in. So the minister's role is distinctively intimate.

At the same time, ministry offers not just service but also challenge; and ministers challenge by bringing to bear something beyond their own personality. Viewers will have different ideas about what this is: divine power, psychological insight, or the effect of oppression and superstition down the ages. Whatever the source of this power, the minister is distinctive in being both invited in to the intimate spaces of lives, and also, when there, empowered both to comfort and to disturb. This enigmatic mixture of closeness and prophetic challenge is a significant factor informing diverse dramatic screen portrayals and interpretations of ministry.

It is important to acknowledge that any paradigm has limits. Several exceptions to the main thesis of this chapter will be discussed below. Nevertheless, striking structural similarities often emerge between superficially divergent portrayals. To examine these structural elements, we consider portrayals of ministry on two axes: benignity and efficacy. Is the minister portrayed as good or evil, as seeking the well-being of others or as motivated by power and self-interest? And is the minister portrayed as having power to get things done and change lives, or as being impotent, whimsical and ineffectual?

---

[1] *Four Weddings and a Funeral*, dir. Mike Newell, 1994.

Benign but ineffectual: the established vicar

A great DVD to chillax with on a Sunday afternoon . . . you'll be lulled into a cosy, fuzzy sense of security with, among other things . . . vicars, strolling through gardens . . .[2]

I'm so weak – why did I give in?[3]

(Revd Major Mary Greenstock)

Few portrayals of ministers in British media question their benignity. Bernice Woodall, vicar of Royston Vasey in the dark, surreal comedy *League of Gentlemen*,[4] is an exception, though by the end of the big-screen spin-off, *The League of Gentlemen's Apocalypse*,[5] she has regained her faith. Major Mary Greenstock, the army padre in the British comedy drama about a bomb disposal team in Afghanistan, *Bluestone 42*,[6] has her flaws. She is portrayed as defying her conscience and professional obligations to have sex with Captain Nick Medhurst (series 2, episode 5). But this is a comic and innocent passion: Nick's opening gambit when they meet in series 1, episode 1, is 'Cup of tea?' In her final scene, Mary regains integrity, provoking a moment of concern for the other in the self-centred Medhurst: as she rejects his kiss he says 'Just thought it'd be fun' and she answers 'Who for?'[7]

The normative British TV clergy of the last 50 years are all high in benignity. The Revd Geraldine Granger in the sitcom *The Vicar of Dibley*[8] is a challenging comic character precisely because she is so persistently good. Portrayed as a good-humoured, compassionate, motherly figure, comic lines tumble from her lips: 'Everyone is welcome here in the bosom of my bosoms',[9] as she puts up with her idiosyncratic parishioners. Indeed some even claim her portrayal made a far greater impact than the dozens of speeches, sermons and reports supporting the value of the ordination of

---

[2]   Paraphrase of *That Mitchell and Webb Look*, series 3, episode 6, BBC2, 16 July 2009.

[3]   Kelly Adams, *Bluestone 42*, series 2, episode 6, BBC3, 27 March 2014.

[4]   *The League of Gentlemen*, BBC2, 1999–2002.

[5]   *The League of Gentlemen's Apocalypse*, dir. Steve Bendelack, 2005.

[6]   *Bluestone 42*, BBC3, 2013–15.

[7]   *Bluestone 42*, series 2, episode 6, 27 March 2014.

[8]   BBC1, 1994–2007. Alongside 20 episodes, there have also been six briefer comic relief specials, including three between 2007 and 2015.

[9]   Dawn French in 'The Handsome Stranger', *Vicar of Dibley*, Christmas special, BBC1, 25 December 2006. For more on 'motherhood as a metaphor for ministry' see a book with that title by Emma Percy (Farnham: Ashgate, 2014).

women.[10] Not without weakness, in her choices she always favours the other and the truth. Adam Smallbone's typical story arc in an episode of the inner-city London drama *Rev.*[11] is to meet a challenge, to take the course of weakness, self-interest or fear, and then to repent and, often sacrificially, to do the right thing. His weaknesses are real and sometimes damaging, but they are weaknesses of execution, not evils of intent. Even Derek Nimmo's Mervyn Noote, in the sitcom *All Gas and Gaiters,*[12] though not as other-focused as Granger and Smallbone, and not above self-interested carelessness, is at worst harmless. The setting of *All Gas and Gaiters* is, in any event, the isolated world of the cathedral close: there is no ministry, because there is nobody to minister to.

Few iterations of Rowan Atkinson's comic vicar are anything but well-intentioned. Like a slapstick Adam Smallbone, Father Gerald's failings are of competence, not kindness. It's particularly instructive to consider a film where this comic turn takes centre stage. At the start of *Keeping Mum,*[13] the vicar of Middle Wallop is immersed in work, and neglectful of his wife who resorts to an affair with the golf pro. By the end he has found a sense of humour and a literal reading of the Song of Songs, and reintegrated ministry with marriage. He starts off good but repressed, and ends good and less repressed. In case the viewer should fail to discern his moral condition, his name is Walter Goodfellow.

In two British detective dramas set in the 1950s, the eponymous *Father Brown*[14] and Sidney Chambers in *Grantchester*[15] are, as detectives, *ipso facto* on the side of right: but they are also benign as ministers, validating ordinary experience and debunking hypocritical piety. They are frank about their own weaknesses, forgiving of others. Chambers drinks and is sometimes moderately violent, but the audience is not encouraged to doubt his goodwill.

The other common factor in these depictions is low efficacy. Padre Mary is terrified by a mortar attack that leaves everyone else underwhelmed.[16] Geraldine Granger's triumphs in Dibley are mitigated: for example, she

---

[10] Joy Carroll Wallis, upon whom Dawn French's character was based, argued for 'The Importance of *The Vicar of Dibley*', suggesting that it 'helped everyone to receive women priests into the community and into the fabric of society': <https://www.youtube.com/watch?v=d9NIoX-2zJ8c> (accessed 17 December 2015).

[11] BBC2, 2010–14.

[12] BBC1, 1966–71.

[13] *Keeping Mum*, dir. Niall Johnson, 2005.

[14] 2013 – present.

[15] 2014 – present.

[16] *Bluestone 42*, series 1, episode 7, BBC3, 16 April 2013.

raises £11,000 to repair a window, but the final scene reveals that she has instead donated the money to an earthquake relief appeal.[17] Granger's efficacy is so other-oriented that it is largely off screen: she does not achieve her stated goal, and, as we see her, is rendered ineffectual. One might think this inefficacy is inherent to the sitcom genre, in which the situation must be preserved, denying the protagonist a large field of efficacy. By the end of series 3 of *Rev.*,[18] however, Adam Smallbone is no longer a vicar and his church has closed. The situation has changed dramatically, and through Smallbone's agency: his abortive non-affair brings down the wrath of the local newspaper and the bishop. Smallbone is not denied efficacy by the conventions of his genre; he just is ineffectual. The Atkinson comic vicar derives his comedic effect from ineffectuality: perhaps the least funny Atkinson vicar, Walter Goodfellow, is also the one who, towards the end of the film, is stumbling towards efficacy.

This portrayal of ministers of the Established Church in England is mirrored in portrayals of ministers in other church settings. In locally produced Ghanaian video dramas ministers from the historic mission churches (such as Methodists, Presbyterians and Anglicans) are well intentioned but marginal to the outcome of the story. A contrast is drawn with pastors from independent Pentecostal or Charismatic churches, typically dynamic and spiritually powerful.[19] In the Americas, Stewart Hoover offers a close reading of Pastor Harding, a character in the Alaskan-based *Northern Exposure* (1990–5).[20] Though well intentioned, Harding, wearing 'the classic black suit and clerical collar', is a paradigm of 'ineffectualness'.[21] The Established Church of Scotland is portrayed much the same way: the always depressed Revd I. M. Jolly's parodies of late-night television reflections illustrate how an inept cleric can become a figure of fun.

The clergy detectives, Brown and Chambers, are exceptions, part of a distinctive and interesting category.[22] Apart from them, though, all these screen ministers are benign but largely ineffectual. We would trust Mary Greenstock or Adam Smallbone to want the best for us. We would invite

---

[17] *The Vicar of Dibley*, series 1, episode 4, BBC1, 1 December 1994.

[18] BBC2, 2010–14.

[19] Jolyon Mitchell, 'Towards an Understanding of the Popularity of West African Video Film', in Jolyon Mitchell and S. Brent Plate, eds, *The Religion and Film Reader* (London and New York: Routledge, 2007), pp. 103–12.

[20] See Stewart M. Hoover, 'Visual Religion in Media Culture', in David Morgan and Sally Promey, eds, *The Visual Culture of American Religions* (Berkeley: University of California Press, 2001), pp. 146–59.

[21] Hoover, 'Visual Religion in Media Culture', p. 149.

[22] See below in the section on sleuths.

Geraldine Granger or Walter Goodfellow to share the significant moments of our lives. But they do not threaten or challenge us.

Efficacy, but questionable benignity: warrior priests and false icons

There's nothing like a good, strong pickaxe handle.[23]

(The Preacher)

You're going to heaven. I'm going to jail and you're going to heaven.[24]

(Sonny Dewey)

The good, gentle and laughable ministers of the established churches in British screen drama could scarcely be more different from the free church ministers often portrayed in the USA. The first thing one notices is their sheer physicality. The Preacher in *Pale Rider*[25] is certainly more Samson than St Paul, injuring and killing dozens of men with a hammer, a gun and a hickory pickaxe handle. By these means he improves the position of the characters with whom we are invited to have sympathy, the impoverished mining community outside town. Burt Lancaster, as the title character in *Elmer Gantry*,[26] the salesman-turned-revivalist preacher, gives another highly physical portrayal of a minister. In one scene he ascends to his preaching dais by performing a baseball slide. He has a compelling and resonant voice; his charisma and quick wit fills revival tents; he raises money. Though he too ends up chastened and transformed, Elmer Gantry is (for ill as for good) the antithesis of Adam Smallbone.

Both Gantry and the Preacher are, not to put too fine a point on it, sexy, in a way few of their British counterparts are (Padre Mary's attractiveness is important to the plot precisely because it is implicated in her apparent inefficacy). Sonny Dewey, the protagonist of *The Apostle*,[27] does not have quite the same allure but he is another charismatic physical presence. Deposed from leadership of his Texas megachurch, he beats up the man who has pushed him out and with whom his wife is having an affair, fakes his own death and starts afresh in Louisiana. He defends his new

---

[23] Paraphrase of Clint Eastwood in *Pale Rider*, dir. Clint Eastwood, 1985.
[24] Robert Duvall in *The Apostle*, dir. Robert Duvall, 1997.
[25] Dir. Clint Eastwood, 1985.
[26] *Elmer Gantry*, dir. Richard Brooks, 1960.
[27] *The Apostle*.

church in a fist fight with the unnamed racist 'Troublemaker',[28] who is later converted through Sonny's personal ministry. Sonny's power to reach out to this young man stems in part from his violence: when he says 'I was a worse sinner than you were', this is no mere pious truism. Another minister with considerable physical efficacy is portrayed in a recent biopic, *Machine Gun Preacher*.[29] Sam Childers is an American missionary worker in Southern Sudan.[30] He overcomes opposition to the construction of an orphanage and rescues children kidnapped by the Lord's Resistance Army.

The capacity of these figures to channel *spiritual* power is ambiguous. A question left open by *Elmer Gantry* is whether Elmer's revivalist effects are solely the product of showmanship, or may be something more.[31] Sonny Dewey in *The Apostle*, by contrast, is portrayed as a man who prays with his whole being, and whose prayers appear to be answered. At the level of changing the world about them, though, in their physical power, all of these media ministers are unquestionably high in efficacy.

What they are not is unquestionably benign. The Preacher is at best an example of Walter Wink's 'myth of redemptive violence':[32] his victims are clearly labelled evildoers, but he does a good deal more slaying than generally thought compatible with the clerical vocation. Gantry has a licentious past, and is to *some* degree motivated by greed and fame. Dewey ends *The Apostle* incarcerated for murder. Childers is a former bike gang member who at length resorts to bloodshed, becoming a 'machine gun preacher' to secure the release of kidnapped children. In diametric contrast with their British counterparts, these are ministers whose power to disrupt and challenge is palpable, even if they would not normally be invited to be present in our lives because of their gentleness and ministry of presence.

A different, but equally instructive, portrayal of the minister as efficacious but malign is found in films from Soviet-era Russia. In *The Feast of St Jorgen*,[33] two escaped convicts hiding in a church are able to observe how the priests enrich themselves at the expense of the people. In other films, such as the different animated versions of *The Tale of the Priest and of His*

---

28 Played by Billy Bob Thornton.
29 *Machine Gun Preacher*, dir. Marc Forster, 2011.
30 Played by Gerard Butler.
31 See also Steve Martin as the Preacher in *Leap of Faith*, dir. Richard Pearse (1992).
32 See Walter Wink, *Engaging the Powers: Discernment and Resistance in a World of Domination* (Minneapolis, MN: Fortress, 1992); *The Powers That Be: Theology for a New Millennium* (New York: Galilee Doubleday, 1998); and Jolyon Mitchell, *Media Violence and Christian Ethics* (Cambridge: Cambridge University Press, 2007).
33 *The Feast of St Jorgen*, dir. Protazanov Prazdnik, 1930.

Worker Balda,[34] based on an 1830 poem by Alexander Pushkin, priests are represented as lazy, dishonest and exploitative.

Benign and effectual: confessors, exorcists and sleuths

Mr President . . . you're just a boy from my church.[35]

(Father Tom Cavanaugh)

In the name of the Father, the Son and the Holy Spirit, I say to you, Go![36]

(Father Merrin)

Two highly efficacious American ministers make important cameo appearances in major TV series. Pastor Isaiah Easton,[37] the leader of a large Chicago church, is courted for his political influence by gubernatorial candidate Peter Florrick in the American political and legal drama, *The Good Wife*.[38] Father Tom Cavanaugh ministers to President Josiah Bartlet in *The West Wing*.[39] Both are ministers of unquestioned efficacy, loci of spiritual power, who shape the world around them.

Where they differ from the Preacher, Sonny Dewey, Gantry and Childers is that they are also portrayed as benign. Cavanaugh is deeply stamped with moral authority (this character is as much the creation of the veteran actor Karl Malden as of scriptwriter Aaron Sorkin). His role is to hear Bartlet's confession after the latter has lacked the moral and spiritual courage to pardon a condemned murderer. Easton, likewise, though Florrick seeks to draw him into the world of political horse-trading, persists in playing a primarily spiritual and pastoral role, encouraging Florrick to repentance.

Another group of ministers portrayed as having high efficacy *and* high benignity is represented by the exorcists. The original of the genre, Father Damien Karras in *The Exorcist*,[40] allows the evil spirit Pazuzu into

---

[34] *The Tale of the Priest and of His Worker Balda* was produced in 1934, directed by Michael Tsekhanovsky; then in 1940, dir. Panteleimon Sazanov; 1956, dir. Anatoly Karanovich; and 1973, dir. Inessa Kovlevskaya.

[35] Paraphrase of Karl Malden in 'Take This Sabbath Day', *The West Wing*, series 1, episode 14, NBC, 9 February 2000.

[36] Paraphrase of Max von Sydow in *The Exorcist*, dir. William Friedkin, 1973.

[37] Gbenga Akinnagbe in *The Good Wife*, series 2, episode 7, CBS, 16 November 2010.

[38] CBS, 2009 – present.

[39] NBC, 1999–2006.

[40] Jason Miller in *The Exorcist*, dir. William Friedkin, 1974.

himself and then defenestrates himself before Pazuzu can carry out his malign purposes. He is the screen pattern for many others, such as Father Andrew Kiernan in *Stigmata*[41] and Father Kovak in *End of Days*,[42] priests low in the hierarchy, often not holding parochial appointments, loyal to the Church but outside its institutional embrace. Through courage and faith they enable good to triumph over evil, often suffering or dying in the process.

Closely related to Hollywood exorcists are the ministers portrayed in some local West African films. Typically ministers of independent Charismatic churches, they bear symbols of wealth and power such as mobile phones and computers, as well as large black leather-covered Bibles. They confront priests of traditional religions, portrayed as fraudulent and malign.[43] There is often an interesting three-way contrast between the malign and efficacious traditional priest, the benign and ultimately *more* efficacious Pentecostalist minister, and the benign but ineffectual minister of a church with roots in the colonial period. The drama, however, is in the conflict between the first two. In the final scene of the Nigerian film *Magic Money*, the Christian pastor and African traditional priest cry out for the help of their respective Gods.[44] They both dance on the spot and gesticulate aggressively; at length the traditional priest is laid low, overwhelmed by the more powerful force called upon by the Christian pastor. In the video drama *Namisha*, a devotee of the evil spirit Obadzen hurls curses depicted as circles of light thrown towards the protagonist, a pastor; the pastor responds with more powerful prayers, accompanied by shafts of light bursting from him and knocking out his opponent.[45]

The last group of high-efficacy / high-benignity ministers consists of clerical detectives. Father Brown and Sidney Chambers, as we saw earlier, fit the English pattern of unquestionable benignity, but they are successful in what they attempt. Sidney, unusual among English portrayals of ministry, has physicality and sex appeal: the viewer sees a war wound on his well-muscled back; flashbacks show him as a tank officer in the

[41] Gabriel Burne, *Stigmata*, dir. Rupert Wainwright, 1999.

[42] Rod Steiger, *End of Days*, dir. Peter Hyams, 1999.

[43] Mitchell, 'Popularity of West African Video Film'. See also Birgit Meyer, *Sensational Movies: Video, Vision, and Christianity in Ghana* (Berkeley and Los Angeles: University of California Press, 2015).

[44] Jolyon Mitchell, 'From Morality Tales to Horror Movies', in Peter Horsfield, Mary E. Hess and Adán M. Medrano, *Belief in Media: Cultural Perspectives on Media and Christianity* (Aldershot: Ashgate, 2004), p. 112 (pp. 107–20).

[45] Mitchell, 'From Morality Tales to Horror Movies', p. 112.

Second World War. Father Brown is as physically unthreatening as Adam Smallbone, but like Chambers he always gets his man.

At the overlap between exorcists and detectives is the British TV horror drama *Midwinter of the Spirit*,[46] based on the book by Phil Rickman. Revd Merrily Watkins, a vicar and single mother, has, in her capacity as Deliverance Minister for the Diocese of Hereford, the job of 'ghostbusting for Jesus', as her daughter puts it. She faces evil both criminal and supernatural. She too is on the side of right; her life and ministry have integrity; but she does get the job done.

Ineffectual and malign: evil vicars

Fascists wear dark-coloured uniforms and order people around. Priests, however, . . .[47]

(Father Ted)

We may be evil, but we're still vicars despite everything, and we're back.[48]

(Evil Vicar)

The bottom-left quadrant, ministers with both low efficacy and low benignity, is the preserve of oddballs and caricatures, the Jungian shadow of ministry. Their significance inheres in their atypicality.

Bernice Woodall[49] is spectacularly malign, and so ineffectual that in the end she is kidnapped by the grotesque Papa Lazarou to join his collection of wives. Father Jack, the oldest of the three priests in *Father Ted* (1995–8), is violent and wholly bent on gross self-gratification. Ted himself has a liminal benignity – clearly venal, but at some level longing for purity – and his ineffectuality is the bedrock of the comedy. Like the characters in *All Gas and Gaiters*, however, Jack, Ted and Dougal exist in a closed clerical world and seldom minister to anyone. The ground zero of Evil Vicars is the character who appears once, memorably, in *That Mitchell and Webb Look*, asserting: 'I stand with two thousand years of darkness and bafflement and hunger behind me.'[50] Outraged by their 'half-arsed musings

---

[46] *Midwinter of the Spirit*, ITV, 2015.

[47] Paraphrase of Dermot John Morgan in 'Are You Right, There, Father Ted?', *Father Ted*, series 3, episode 1, Channel 4, 13 March 1998.

[48] Paraphrase of Robert Mitchell in *That Mitchell and Webb Look*, series 1, episode 3, BBC2, 28 September 2006.

[49] Reece Shearsmith, *The League of Gentleman*, BBC2, 1999–2002.

[50] Robert Mitchell in *That Mitchell and Webb Look*, series 1, episode 3, BBC2, 28 September 2006.

on the divine' he chases an enquiring couple out of his church and then calls plaintively after them, 'At least leave a quid for the upkeep.' This perfection in wicked media ministers is, in the snippet of his ministry we witness, entirely lacking benignity *and* efficacy.

One other non-benign, non-efficacious minister is worth mentioning: the incumbent of the Church of England parish of Downton, in *Downton Abbey*.[51] What is interesting about this minister is that he is almost never portrayed. He is not involved in the management of Downton Cottage Hospital; he does not, as many of his contemporaries actually did, lead the War Memorial committee. Indeed, at the instance of producers any reference to religion, which would have pervaded an upper-class household of the period, is completely absent. To preserve historical accuracy, the family is never depicted at the start of a meal, when grace would have been said; they never go to church except to get married.

Defying the paradigm: martyrs, holy fools and healers

If power is the most important thing, then there's no place for love. That might be true, but I don't think I can live in such a world.[52]

(*Father Gabriel*)

God seems so very remote . . . I feel so helpless.[53]

(*Pastor Tomas Ericsson*)

Some screen portrayals of ministry do not obviously fit the matrix of benignity and efficacy. Screen martyrdoms represent one such genre.[54] Martyrs have power, but not efficacy: their ministry derives strength not from what the minister does but from what others do to him. Father Gabriel, the Jesuit missionary in *The Mission*,[55] is shot by Portuguese soldiers; Archbishop Thomas Becket, in *Becket*,[56] defies royal authority and meets a violent end on the long swords of four helmeted knights. Óscar

51 *Downton Abbey*, ITV, 2010–15.
52 Paraphrase of Jeremy Irons in *The Mission*, dir. Roland Joffé, 1986.
53 Gunnar Björnstrand, *Winter Light*, dir. Ingmar Bergman, 1963.
54 See Jolyon Mitchell, 'Filming the Ends of Martyrdom', in Dominic Janes and Alex Houen, eds, *Martyrdom and Terrorism: Pre-Modern to Contemporary Perspectives* (Oxford: Oxford University Press), pp. 271–90.
55 Jeremy Irons, *The Mission*.
56 Richard Burton, *Becket*, dir. Peter Glenville, 1964.

Romero, in the biopic *Romero*,[57] is assassinated while celebrating Mass.[58] Physical power is with the killers; but in the longer term, the deep and enduring impact is that of the martyrs. Although *The Mission* ends shortly after the martyrdom of the fictional Father Gabriel, the final scene shows a party of determined children departing upriver with the purpose of renewing his work. Both biopics, *Becket* and *Romero*, without devoting much screen time to the influence of their protagonists after death, imply that their power survives and is if anything increased by their martyrdom.

Russian portrayals of ministry under communism, as we have seen, were of priests exercising a negative efficacy. Soon after the end of the Soviet era, though, the wounded healer and the holy fool, both enduring figures in classic Russian literature, began to appear more commonly in Russian cinema. One of the most popular recent Russian films is *The Island*,[59] depicting a group of Orthodox monks. The central figure, Father Anatoly,[60] is portrayed as a man in search of personal forgiveness, having been forced to shoot his captain during the Second World War. While this inner war rages, others come to his cell looking for advice, healing or holiness. Before his death Father Anatoly is reconciled on several different levels. This film touched a nerve in Russia. Churches used it in the same way churches in North America used *The Passion of the Christ*:[61] viewers at special screenings were encouraged to take off their hats and pray. Father Anatoly has power, both in the world of the film, and in the real world where the film is viewed; but it is a power of innerness and renunciation.

This kind of soft ministerial power is portrayed in several critically acclaimed films of the last half-century. The protagonist of Bergman's *Winter Light* is a doubt-ridden pastor,[62] who blames himself for the suicide of one of his parishioners. Although this is arguably a film about a *loss* of faith, there is a power in Pastor Tomas Ericsson's authentic vulnerability to doubt, ultimately recognized in the final scene as Christ-like. In Hitchcock's *I Confess*[63] the priest, at great personal cost, refuses to divulge the secrets of the

---

[57] Raul Julia, *Romero*, dir. John Duigan, 1989.

[58] For more on Romero, and other films about martyrs, see Theresa Sanders, *Celluloid Saints: Images of Sanctity in Film* (Macon, GA: Mercer University Press, 2002), especially pp. 50–4.

[59] *The Island*, dir. Pavel Lungin, 2006.

[60] Played by Pavel Mamonov, who became a popular speaker on monasticism and spirituality in Russia.

[61] *The Passion of the Christ*, dir. Mel Gibson, 2003.

[62] *Winter Light*, dir. Ingmar Bergman, 1963. This is one of Bergman's 'Trilogy of Faith' films (though perhaps better titled as 'Trilogy of Doubt'), which also includes *Through a Glass Darkly* (1961) and *The Silence* (1963).

[63] *I Confess*, dir. Alfred Hitchcock, 1952.

confessional. In Bresson's *Diary of a Country Priest*[64] the priest ignores his own declining health to care for his parishioners: even if 'God is no torturer', his gentle restraint embodies another famous line from the film: 'All is grace.'

Continuities and contrasts

He's got a nice smile. Haven't you, Henry? Smile nicely, Henry.[65]
(Bishop Cuthbert, of Archdeacon Blunt)

Just mind your own business or I'm gonna kick your ass . . .[66]
(Sonny Dewey)

The most obvious preliminary conclusion is that there is great variety in screen portrayal of ministry (see Fig. 1). In the same way that clerical roles have evolved, so too have screen portrayals.[67] Nevertheless, some examples do not fit the taxonomy adopted at the start of this chapter. Even those that do fit cover all four quadrants. There seems to be no trend.

Is there, however, something systematic going on? While no typology is complete and no analysis without exceptions, the argument here is that there is. Many of the portrayals surveyed, though superficially different, have structural similarities. A large proportion can be seen as attempts to negotiate with the quality of ministry identified at the outset: its potentially disturbing mixture of intimacy and power.

This is not to attribute conscious agency.[68] Just as patriotic films respond to moments of national danger without explicitly planning to do so, screen portrayals of ministry may respond in related ways to the same elements in ministry without an anti-clerical conspiracy. It is hard, however, not to notice a frequently recurring pattern. Some portrayals take the edge off the disturbing power of ministry by portraying the minister as ineffectual. Others have the same effect by allowing the minister efficacy but portraying him or her as malign, thus keeping ministry at arm's length. Yet others acknowledge the distinctive power of ministry, but portray it as not directed at *us*. There appear to be, beneath the contrasts, considerable continuities.

---

[64] *Diary of a Country Priest*, dir. Robert Bresson, 1951.
[65] Paraphrase of William Mervyn, 'The Bishop Gets the Sack', *All Gas and Gaiters*, series 1, episode 1, BBC1, 31 January 1967.
[66] Paraphrase of Robert Duvall in *The Apostle*.
[67] See Martyn Percy, *Clergy: The Origin of the Species* (London: Bloomsbury/Continuum, 2006).
[68] At least, not in every case: the Soviet-era films clearly *do* have an intentional anti-clerical stance.

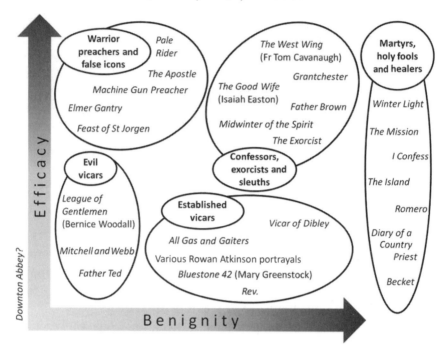

Figure 1 Variety in screen portrayal of Christian ministry

What hath Canterbury to do with Washington?

Being by God's Ordinance . . . Supreme Governor of the Church . . . We hold it most agreeable to this Our Kingly Office . . . to conserve and maintain the Church committed to Our Charge.[69]

Congress shall make no law respecting an establishment of religion.[70]

To begin exploring these continuities it will be helpful to compare screen portrayals of ministry on different sides of the Atlantic. As we have seen, they are superficially very different. British ministers are benign but ineffectual; Americans have efficacy but less benignity. The contrasts between Sonny Dewey and Adam Smallbone, between Clint Eastwood and Dawn French, must, however, be seen in context.

---

[69] 'His Majesty's Declaration' – preamble to the Anglican 'Articles of Religion', in *The Book of Common Prayer* (Oxford: Oxford University Press, 1969), p. 690.

[70] *Constitution of the United States*, First Amendment: <http://www.archives.gov/exhibits/charters/bill_of_rights_transcript.html> (accessed 30 November 2015).

If the stereotype of ministry in the UK is the Church of England vicar, it is worth noting that the Church of England is the state Church, officiating at significant national occasions and contributing to legislative processes, with its Supreme Governor also the constitutional head of state and commander-in-chief. Like the Church of Scotland, it owns some of the oldest and most imposing buildings in the country. Churches both established and independent together have a large impact on the world around them through food banks, employment and immigration centres, education and so on. In short, churches in the UK have significant efficacy. Why, then, are their ministers portrayed as ineffectual?

It may be that screenwriters perceive churches to be in terminal and rapid decline, ministers little more than the band playing on the *Titanic* as it sinks. The contention of this chapter, however, is that some at least of these narratives are driven by contemporary rather than historical perceptions, and function to defuse the potentially challenging elements of ministry. This would explain the persistent portrayal of inefficacy. So deeply imbedded is the Church in the English state that to question its benignity may be to question the benignity of the nation. This rootedness of ministerial benignity is well illustrated by Mitchell and Webb's Evil Vicar, one of 'the incredibly horrible and twisted people who are still unaccountably vicars'.[71] The key word is 'unaccountably'; for an *evil* vicar is an oxymoron. In the context of the UK it is problematic, then, to portray ministers as people we can keep at arm's length: they're just so darned benign. Hence their portrayal as ineffectual.

This inefficacy of British screen ministers, however, invites reflection. *Rev.* was welcomed for its realism: a *Daily Telegraph* interview with Tom Hollander (who plays Adam Smallbone), headlined 'a realistic and very funny new comedy', described the show as 'the antidote to *The Vicar of Dibley*', and quoted Hollander thus: 'we're trying to depict a real world'.[72] In reality, though, *Rev.* is just as unrealistic as *Dibley*. Bryony Taylor, who also welcomes *Rev.* as a 'revolution', says of Adam Smallbone, 'he constantly fails to carry out his ideas'.[73] Most ministers, however, *do* achieve many of their goals. Revd Richard Coles, often cited as a source of *vérité* for the writers of *Rev.*, is himself extremely efficacious, leading a flourishing

---

71 Robert Mitchell in *That Mitchell and Webb Look*, series 1, episode 3, BBC2, 28 September 2006.
72 Olly Grant, 'Rev: a realistic and very funny new comedy from BBC Two', *Daily Telegraph*, 25 June 2010: <http://www.telegraph.co.uk/culture/tvandradio/7855091/Rev-a-realistic-and-very-funny-new-comedy-from-BBC-Two.html> (accessed 30 November 2015).
73 Bryony Taylor, *More TV Vicar? Christians on the Telly: The Good, the Bad and the Quirky* (London: Darton, Longman & Todd, 2015).

parish church and practising a popular media ministry. He may not be typical of the way most ministers are efficacious, but his efficacy is closer to the norm than Adam Smallbone's. Few churches have such small and fissiparous congregations. At the most basic level, church closures are rare.[74] *Rev.*, then, far from being a revolutionary portrayal of ministry in the UK is a humorous restatement for our times of a vision of ministry which is reassuring but inaccurate: the low-efficacy, high-benignity Established Vicar.

This portrayal, however, does not suit the United States. A key difference between the USA and the UK is the separation of state and church. Thus it is much more open to an American to question the benignity of ministry without questioning the benignity of the nation. Moreover, for reasons that may not be unrelated, religion is a stronger force in the lives of more people in the USA than in the UK. With the passing of the Established Church after the American Revolution, 'religion was made part of the turbulent culture of the market'.[75] Even today, for many Americans 'God and Country' is still a motivating phrase;[76] but there is no particularly warm place in the national heart for God's ministers. As Deborah Whitehead puts it, Protestantism in the independent United States made 'the most successful ministers popular celebrities'; but ministry also 'became subject to the same kinds of suspicions and doubts that were endemic to a highly competitive and entrepreneurial economy'.[77] Ministry in the United States shares in the efficacy of capitalism – and that is something which it *is* hard to question. But ministry is, by the same token, much more plausibly portrayed as malign.

---

[74] The fate of Adam Smallbone's church at the end of series 3 befalls less than 0.2 per cent of churches per year (there are approximately 12,600 parishes, and 'around 20 to 25' close in any given year – as some parishes have more than one church, the closure rate of 0.2 per cent is if anything an overstatement. See <https://www.churchofengland.org/more/policy-and-thinking/research-and-statistics> and <https://www.churchofengland.org/more/parish-reorganisation-and-closed-church-buildings/closed-churches> (accessed 13 October 2018)). To put this in context, the long-term trend in pub closures from 1980 to 2013 is over 1 per cent per year, and in the last seven years of that period, after the introduction of the ban on smoking, the rate increased to almost 3 per cent per year. See Christopher Snowdon, *Closing Time: Who's Killing the British Pub?* (London: Institute of Economic Affairs, 2014): <http://www.iea.org.uk/sites/default/files/publications/files/Briefing_Closing%20time_web.pdf> (accessed 30 November 2015). Since 2010, 600 police stations have also closed: <https://www.thetimes.co.uk/article/600-police-stations-shut-in-eight-years-nvjdjwmwj> (accessed 13 October 2018).

[75] Deborah Whitehead, personal email to authors, 3 November 2015.

[76] See, e.g., *American Sniper*, dir. Clint Eastwood, 2014.

[77] Deborah Whitehead, personal email to authors, 3 November 2015.

Thus what at first appear as systematically contrasting portrayals are in important respects continuous. Both sets of portrayals have the potential to blunt the edge of ministry's threat to enter lives and the challenge to look at the world differently. Each does it in a way that makes sense in its cultural setting. The established vicar becomes safe by being denied prophetic efficacy. The warrior preacher is kept at arm's length by being denied benignity. Of course, it bears repeating that no hypothesis explains *everything*. Audiences can accept, negotiate with or resist the perceived dominant meaning of a screen drama. But it is hard not to see a common representative pattern emerging here, working out differently in different contexts.

Changing the target

What of ministers in the top right of the paradigm: efficacious *and* benign? What is noteworthy here is who is ministered *to*. Isaiah Easton ministers to the future Governor of Illinois.[78] Father Tom Cavanaugh ministers to the commander-in-chief of the world's largest army.[79] Father Brown and Sidney Chambers thwart criminals. The ministry of screen exorcists is the overcoming of evil spirits. All these ministers are benign; all are efficacious; but their efficacy is not directed at the viewer. They challenge and disturb; but they challenge and disturb the other, not the audience. Such is the indirect skill of drama. Audiences, however, interact and interpret drama creatively and in unexpected ways. One person's stereotypical malign religious leader can become another's saintly minister. Skilled screenwriters consistently play with audience expectations. Here the example of Yussef Hasan,[80] Adam Smallbone's Muslim counterpart in *Rev.*, is instructive. Hasan is a British screen minister portrayed with efficacy and benignity: his felicitous mixture of street wisdom and Ancient Wisdom, and his ability to raise money from his congregation, are admirable. Again, though, the object of his ministry is not the viewer.[81]

---

[78] CBS, *The Good Wife* (2009 – present).
[79] NBC, *The West Wing* (1999–2006).
[80] Kayvan Novak, *Rev.*, series 3, episode 1, BBC2, 24 March 2014.
[81] Naturally, to say this is, to some extent, to impute assumptions to the show and its viewers, but given that Christians are over-represented among the latter, these are almost certainly easy to defend. Moreover, the narrative does not invite the viewer to see Yussef Hasan from the point of view of those to whom he ministers – the narrative focus is on his relationship with Adam.

Real ministry

Most of these varied screen portrayals of ministry do one of three things: minimize efficacy; minimize benignity; change the target. All three types distance viewers from the risk that ministry might be both gentle enough to invite into their living rooms, and prophetic enough to disturb and challenge. Sometimes, as in the case of Soviet-era films, this stems from a conscious intent to neutralize ministry. For the most part there is no conspiracy: some of the most powerful screen portrayals (in *The Apostle*, for example) are highly sympathetic to religion. The structural consistency of these portrayals, however, is striking.

There are some strong and complex screen portrayals of ministry that don't fit the pattern, mostly in art-house or church-backed cinema.[82] Here we may see a distinctively Christian kind of ministry: what St Paul might have felt called to when Christ told him, 'My grace is sufficient for you, for power is made perfect in weakness.'[83] A recurring trope is the minister who changes lives in the long term almost despite his or her own doing, through vulnerability and authenticity. Adam Smallbone at his best has something of this power too.

Even this image, however, is not typical of most ministry. It is often at the edge of the screen where one finds the combination of the mostly benign with the fairly efficacious that in reality typifies much professional ministry today. The most realistic minister in contemporary British media is not even on screen at all: Revd Alan Franks, Vicar of St Stephen's, Ambridge.[84] Not without flaws, he is fundamentally well intentioned: he gets things done, and has a habit of upsetting the expectations of his parishioners in ways that work for their good. Revd Paul Coates,[85] a minor character in *Broadchurch*, is another good example. After serving an episode as a suspect, he broadens out to play the role of confidant and encourager, drawing the community together for mourning and healing, which actually is the stock in trade of much contemporary ministry. We glimpse Tom Hereward, Trixie Franklin's sometime fiancé in *Call the Midwife*,[86] as a

---

82 See *Romero* discussed earlier, the somewhat slow *Entertaining Angels: The Dorothy Day Story* (dir. Michael Ray Rhodes, 1996), and the more recent and powerful mainline *Selma* (dir. Ava DuVernay, 2014) portraying the civil rights work of Dr Martin Luther King Jr, all of which reflect in different ways the historical realities of ministries that were both benign and efficacious.

83 2 Corinthians 12.9 NRSV.

84 John Telfer in *The Archers*, BBC Radio 4.

85 Arthur Darvill, *Broadchurch*, ITV, 2013–15.

86 BBC, 2012–18; Jack Ashton plays Tom Hereward in 35 episodes from 2014 to 2018.

kind clergyman who gets things done, commended by his bishop for good work in a hard parish.

Such portrayals are rare, however. For the most part, screen portrayals of ministry offer the viewer ways to conceive ministry that allow its potential for intimacy and prophetic power to remain unthreatening. While portrayals have inevitably evolved over the last five decades, it remains a comparative rarity to encounter crafted and engaging fictional screen dramas that could be described as celebrating the ministry of reconciliation, peace-making or prophetic challenge.

Part 2

MODELS, METHODS AND RESOURCES

9

Global and ecumenical models of ministry

IAN S. MARKHAM

We all live in limited worlds. It is so easy for us to assume that our normal is the normal for everyone else. From expectations about meals and hot showers to assumptions about authority and structure, we think of every subject in certain ways. When it comes to the topic of ministry, it is important for us to locate the challenges of ministry in a more global and ecumenical context.

Starting with the global

It is Philip Jenkins who has made global ministry a major theme of his work. No longer, argues Jenkins, can we think of Christianity as a Euro-American project; instead it is increasingly African and Asian. He puts it as follows:

> Christianity has in very recent times ceased to be a Euro-American religion and is becoming thoroughly global. In 1900, 83 percent of the world's Christians lived in Europe and North America. In 2050, 72 percent of Christians will live in Africa, Asia, and Latin America, and a sizable share of the remainder will have roots in one or more of those continents. In 1900, the overwhelming majority of Christians were non-Latino whites; in 2050, non-Latino whites will constitute only a small subset of Christians. If we imagine a typical Christian back in 1900, we might think of a German or an American; in 2050, we should rather turn to a Ugandan, a Brazilian, or a Filipino.[1]

Now there is some dispute about the numbers. However, for our purposes we simply need to establish that ministry is a global operation, and that is undoubtedly the case.

---

[1] Philip Jenkins, *The Next Christendom: The Coming of Global Christianity* (New York: Oxford University Press, 2014). ProQuest ebrary. Web. 7 July 2016.

Increasingly, practical theologians in the two-thirds developing world are developing their own distinctive account of ministry. And there are three themes which are coming to the fore. The first is that context is central, and a local theology, which combines the insights of the Christian tradition with the best of local practices, is essential. The Nigerian theologian Cajetan Ebuziem has made this argument very elegantly. In a substantial study on ministry among the Igbo culture of Nigeria, Ebuziem makes the case that you need a creative interchange between Christian theology and local customs. And the result can be very healthy. Ebuziem is worth quoting at length:

> The impact of this local theology on Igbo culture is not only experienced in these changes, they are also felt in other avenues which are the task of local theology in its service to the local community – integration, maintenance of stability, and transformation. For instance, everyone is integrated in the local church in Igboland both indigenes and strangers. No segregation based on any ideology whether of class, sex, race, clan, or disability exists in the Igbo local church. Unlike in the past when caste systems were very strong and certain people were segregated in the church based on such beliefs, now the tide is turning. Disparate from the past when polygamous marriages were dealt with differently in a more dogmatic approach, nowadays polygamous marriages wherever they still exist, enjoy a more pragmatic and reconciliatory approach ... In the past, inter-denominational marriages were frowned at, but today mixed marriages are not uncommon. In the past, based on concentric circles and strict interpretation of extended family relations, inter-tribal or inter-ethnic marriages were discouraged, but today based on more extensive application of extended family system and the brotherhood and sisterhood of all humanity, such lines are no longer drawn. In the past it was difficult for a first born son, only son, or daughter to respond to God's call to the priesthood or religious life due to cultural implications; today the number of priests and religious within this bracket may outweigh others. All these are symbolic of the fact that the integrative, transformative task of Igbo local theology upon Igbo culture is very strong. The Igbo local theology has impacted the Igbo culture in stabilizing its institutional values to withstand the test of time and outside forces.[2]

The local theology develops a constructive atmosphere. It enables a diversity of practice to be tolerated. It creates a more stable church which is less likely to be subject to schism. And it confronts new problems that

---

[2]   Cajetan E. Ebuziem, *Bible and Theology in Africa: Doing Ministry in the Igbo Context. Towards an Emerging Model and Method for the Church in Africa* (New York: Peter Lang, 2011), p. 231. ProQuest ebrary. Web. 7 July 2016.

have not been a major part of the conversation in the Euro-American Church.

The second major theme is that apologetics and pastoral ministry must take into account the traditional indigenous beliefs. It was when I was in Tanzania leading a conference for local clergy at Msalato Theological College in Dodoma that I became aware of this reality. As we were thinking about the arguments for faith, I paused and simply asked the gathered group of clergy, 'So tell me, do you ever doubt your faith?' I was curious to see if Richard Dawkins had penetrated eastern Africa. After a few moments of silence, finally, one local pastor said, 'Sure'. 'So sometimes you are not sure about the existence of God?' I asked. They looked at me incredulously: 'No way. Of course God is there.' The pastor added, 'No, the problem is the other spirits, the power of the curse – sometimes I doubt whether Jesus is strong enough to counteract them.'

In the setting of Tanzania, the spiritual and the physical are intertwined. People are happy to use cell phones, go to a Western doctor, and appreciate the Internet, but at the same time these priests (almost all of whom are farmers), who live very closely to nature and the seasons, see the spiritually infused nature of reality. Even as cell phones and sophisticated medicine comes to Tanzania, the awareness of reality as infused with spirits is pervasive.

This is probably the greatest area of debate among African and Asian theologians. In respect of a vast array of topics, from ancestor veneration to witchcraft, there are difficult and challenging issues. The South African practical theologian, Matsobane J. Manala, has offered a very compelling analysis of the challenge. Manala explains in some detail the worldview. There are two categories of witches – day witches and night witches. The day witch is an ordinary person who learns the practice of witchcraft and then uses the acquired power for evil ends. Night witches do not need magical potions. They have considerable powers: they can cause infertility and strike a person down with a serious illness; they can enter closed huts; they can even turn a person into a zombie; and they have a close relationship with animals, especially the hyena. The worldview then gets more complicated when one factors in the sorcerer or sorceress. These are people who combine the use of magic with the cooperation of evil spirits. Then there is the witch doctor (perhaps more helpfully described as a 'traditional diviner-doctor', who has special magical powers that can be used to heal people. Manala explains:

> The so-called witch doctor is therefore engaged and involved in the broad task of resolving health/illness issues, as well as in predicting the future in

order to bring transformation that will improve the conditions of individuals within black African communities. The traditional healer (witch doctor) also has as task and responsibility the healing of relationships, that is between fellow humans, people and their ancestors, people and nature spirits, and between people and the environment. The name 'witch doctor' does not therefore convey the full spectrum of the role and function of the traditional medicine man/woman-diviner.[3]

This is a complicated worldview. The Bible includes plenty of exorcisms of demons and unclean spirits. How exactly to relate to these beliefs is a real challenge for many African theologians.

The third major theme is that the range and type of pastoral problems can vary considerably. It is important to avoid crass generalizations that imply that problems of poverty are only found in developing countries and problems of affluence are only found in first-world countries. The truth is that the Global South has growing concentrations of affluence with the associated first-world problems; and Euro-America has plenty of persons in poverty. Yet it is also true that the socio-economic context in which one is working does have a profound impact on the challenge of ministry. Again Matsobane J. Manala provides a helpful case study. HIV & AIDS is a worldwide crisis. However, when it comes to pastoral care in South Africa, it is important to recognize the distinctive context. Consider the case of Bryan, who has AIDS:

> Bryan was kept in isolation and visitors wore a mask, gown and gloves. I was warned not to touch Bryan, not to sit on his bed, not to be near him if he should sneeze as he had a parasitic infection of the lungs and not to eat anything he might give me in the way of chocolates or fruit. I was afraid, insecure and very anxious. The sister in charge told me that Bryan was twenty-four years old, was rapidly losing weight and had been in bed for a month. He had been a rather up and coming accountant having just finished all his studies at the university and was working in a good firm in the city. So far he had refused all contact with the pastoral care department saying that he did not want to talk to any strangers or people from the church.[4]

---

[3] Matsobane J. Manala, 'Witchcraft and Its Impact on Black African Christians: A Lacuna in the Ministry of the Hervormde Kerk in Suidelike Afrika', *Hervormde Teologiese Studies / Theological Studies*, vol. 60 (4) (2004), pp. 1491–1511.

[4] Matsobane J. Manala, 'An Afro-Christian Ministry to People Living with HIV/Aids in South Africa', in *Hervormde Teologiese Studies / Theological Studies*, vol. 61 (3) (2005), p. 902. Manala takes the story of Bryan from E. Ward, 'Enabling Lay Pastoral Care and Counselling of People Living with Aids: Clinical Pastoral Education as a Training Ground', in *Bulletin for Contextual Theology in Africa*, vol. 7 (1) (2000), p. 26.

This tragic case raises several questions. It is likely that Bryan is suffering from depression and therefore some medication might help. But more importantly, and this is Manala's point, the lack of community is crippling any chance of Bryan having a 'healthy' end to his life or perhaps even recovery. Pastoral care in the South African context requires the recognition that participation in and connection to community is vital. It is deeply South African. So Manala explains that when community has disappeared (perhaps for reasons of shame or embarrassment), the Church must step in. Manala writes:

> The church should be concretely there for, loving to and enthusiastic about people living with HIV/Aids. The church's ministry to people living with HIV/Aids should indeed be based upon the ministry of presence . . . This is quite necessary as healing in Africa is essentially a communal matter. Masenya states: 'Because a human being is only a human being because of other human beings, Aids victims cannot heal in isolation'. [5]

There is deep in the culture of South Africa a need for humans to be connected as they struggle with illness. The Western concept of the individual is not part of their worldview. There is much less interest in privacy. Therefore, a different model of pastoral care is needed.

These three themes provide a glimpse into the difference that a global sensitivity makes. More could be written about the insights being learned from cultures where Christians are in a small minority (for example, Pakistan). Comparative global ministry models need to be developed. This is a growing potential edge for ministry studies. However, the task of this chapter is to now turn to ecumenical differences in ministry.

The ecumenical dimension

When we think of ministry, it is the Roman Catholic Church that in so many ways dominates the field. Other traditions have no choice but to be in dialogue with the conceptual clarity of the Roman Catholic Church. The Roman Catholic Church teaches that God always intended 'representatives' of Christ (to allude to John Henry Newman's phrase).[6] These are

---

[5] Manala, 'An Afro-Christian Ministry', p. 907. The quote from Masenya is from Masenya (Ngwan'a Mphaphlele), 'The Bible, HIV/Aids and African-South African Women: A Bosadi (Womanhood) Perspective', *Studia Historiae Ecclesiasticae*, vol. 31 (1) (2005), p. 192.

[6] See J. H. Newman, 'The Christian Ministry', in *Parochial and Plain Sermons* (London: 1880), p. 304. Newman is here reflecting on the issue of authority and writes, 'the only question being, where there is reason for thinking that Christ has, in matter of fact, left representatives behind him'.

the apostles, from whom came the tradition of the bishops, who impart the power of Christ to subsequent generations through the priests of the Church. Plenty of defenders of this position are to be found. Aidan Nichols sets out some of the assumptions needed to be made when he writes:

> If we accept the notion of a development of doctrine, whereby some features of Catholic faith, ethics and worship are regarded as legitimate outgrowths from New Testament origins, then we commit ourselves to what may be termed a 'hermeneutic of recognition', whereby we who share the developed consciousness of the later Church come to the evidences of the earliest Church *in positive expectation of finding* the seeds from which the great tree of the *Catholica* has grown.[7]

Therefore, the argument goes, trusting that what is true of us now has its roots in what was originally required of us, we can then expect to find that Jesus Christ really did intend to create an apostolic priesthood. Nichols goes on to set out the argument for the three orders of ministry – bishops, priests and deacons. He argues that

> in the apostles, the Lord Jesus left to his community a ministry, for the purposes of sanctifying, teaching and governing it. The apostles are to pre-side over the worship that belongs to the new Covenant, and especially its Eucharistic meal-sacrifice, they are to proclaim the Word as Jesus' envoys; and they are to provide discipline for the community, to rule the new Israel. Such a summary of what apostles are for is arrived at by grouping together material about the Twelve, on the one hand, and about the apostleship in general on the other.[8]

Nichols then works through the history of the Church, arguing at every stage that the tradition affirms the structure and develops the complex sense of the priestly vocation. He concludes his study with a list of nine elements that form the pattern of the priestly life. These are:

1 evangelizing the unconverted;
2 teaching sound doctrine in faith and morals to the converted;
3 forming others to be apostolic;
4 celebrating the sacraments, and other rites of the Church;
5 in particular, by the celebration of Penance and the Eucharist, bringing the Paschal Mystery to bear on the lives of the faithful, who die to sin, and live with Christ to God;

---

[7] Aidan Nichols OP, *Holy Order: Apostolic Priesthood from the New Testament to the Second Vatican Council* (Dublin: Veritas Publications, 1990).
[8] Nichols, *Holy Order*, p. 31.

6 in the Mass, but also in the divine Office, acting as intercessor for the Church, and for all creation;

7 in union with the bishop, and, ultimately, with the pope, to build up, as pastor, the communion of the Church, gathering the faithful and opening them to the fullness of the Church's life;

8 visiting, and so counselling and encouraging, individual members of the Church community – especially the sick and the poor;

9 overseeing the community's wider attempt to meet the needs of its members, and of the wider realm in which their lives are set. (Here the priest will naturally find himself in relation to the deacon.)[9]

As Nichols himself goes on to note, these nine elements divide into three sets of three – the first three are the prophetic office of the priest; the second three are the priestly office; and the last three are the pastoral office.

In the Appendix of his book, Nichols goes on to explain why Roman Catholics should not open the sacrament of ordination to the priesthood to women and why there are strong arguments for celibacy. The arguments are theological. Indeed, for Nichols, these questions should never be located in the context of sociological considerations, such as the decline in the numbers of vocations to seminary or the tragedy of clergy sexual abuse of minors.

In contrast, Donald Cozzens has made the sociological data about the challenges facing the Roman Catholic priesthood central. He sees the predominance of gay men in the priesthood,[10] the declining respect for the role of the priest, and the exposure of clergy misconduct with minors as an opportunity. The crisis that is shaping the Church is the dark night of St John of the Cross. It is a moment when the soul of the Church can be renewed. Cozzens sets out his understanding when he writes:

> For the neo-conservative Catholic, any dark night the priest might be suffering was traced to the Church's infidelity to the pre-conciliar structures and practices that resonated with such surety and clarity amidst the social chaos and moral relativity of modernity. For other Catholics, however, and for most priests, I believe, the dark night was the work of the Spirit, leading priests through dark valleys only to bring them to a point where they could see new horizons. The darkness was necessary to bring about a

---

9 Nichols, *Holy Order*, p. 143.

10 Estimates vary considerably. James G. Wolf, writing in 1989, suggested that 48.5 per cent of priests and 55.1 per cent of seminarians were gay. See James G. Wolf (ed.), *Gay Priests* (San Francisco, CA: Harper & Row, 1989), pp. 59–60. Wolf does admit his numbers are highly impressionistic.

conversation of mind and heart, to effect a new way of seeing and listening, an *aggiornamento*.[11]

Cozzens see the way forward in a partnership between priest and people. This will involve a changed ecclesiology that celebrates the ministries of all God's people. He sees a healthier partnership between those who are ordained and those who are lay.

Cozzens' picture of a church in crisis has been challenged by those who are more theologically conservative. Probably the most helpful study is by Stephen J. Rossetti. Based on two studies, one in 2004 of 1,242 priests and the other in 2009 of 2,482, it argues that Roman Catholic priests are healthier, more balanced and happier than the laity. John L. Allen Jr in the Foreword offers the following summary:

Rossetti debunks a whole series of stereotypes:

- Although many observers assume that relationships between bishops and priests have been fatally ruptured, three-quarters of priests in the United States say they have a good relationship with their bishop and approve of his leadership.
- Many people presume that the sexual abuse crisis was caused in part by the celibacy requirement, assuming that it must breed an unhealthy degree of repression. In truth, Rossetti finds, a positive view of celibacy is strongly correlated with the psychological health of priests; the more content they are with celibacy, the better adjusted they're likely to be.
- In contrast to assumptions that priests are often lonely and struggle to form healthy friendships, Rossetti's data show that most priests have strong relationships both with other priests and with laity. In fact, the strength of a priest's human friendships turns out to be among the best predictors of the quality of his spiritual life.[12]

While Rossetti has a very positive view of the status quo and Cozzens has a much more negative assessment of our moment, there is a way in which they are both capturing the complexity of the moment. Rossetti is looking at priests who are currently in ministry who find their lives very fulfilling: it is indeed a privilege to care for the people of God in sacraments and service. Cozzens is looking at the data coming from seminaries, where vocations are declining, and from the macro-data about perceptions of the Church, where the child abuse scandal did deep damage. Taken together,

---

[11] Donald B. Cozzens, *The Changing Face of the Priesthood: A Reflection on the Priest's Crisis of Soul* (Collegeville, MN: Liturgical Press, 2000), p. 131.
[12] John L. Allen, 'Foreword', in Stephen J. Rossetti, *Why Priests Are Happy: A Study of the Psychological and Spiritual Health of Priests* (Notre Dame, IN: Ave Maria Press, 2011).

one probably has a fairly accurate picture of the Church. Priests are enjoying their work; they are also very aware of the perceptions of their role and their work in the wider society.

With the Reformation, we see the emergence of Protestant denominations. And we find different models and accounts of ministry emerging. Three major concerns with the Roman Catholic account emerged. The first was the relationship of the priest to Scripture. For those committed to *sola scriptura* (by Scripture alone), there was a concern that this picture of a person set apart from the rest of the congregation was not biblical. If the Bible is the supreme authority for the Church, then we must follow the biblical pattern of governance. The biblical pattern, they argued, does not talk about an 'apostolic succession' or a particular person who has the authority and ability to deliver the eucharistic prayer such that bread and wine become the body and blood of our Lord. The second difficulty was the 'semi-superstitious' aspects of Catholic theology. It was David Hume who talked about the pernicious influence of the theology of priesthood on society when he wrote:

My first reflection is, That superstition is favourable to priestly power, and enthusiasm not less or rather more contrary to it, than sound reason and philosophy. As superstition is founded on fear, sorrow, and a depression of spirits, it represents the man to himself in such despicable colours, that he appears unworthy, in his own eyes, of approaching the divine presence, and naturally has recourse to any other person, whose sanctity of life, or, perhaps, impudence and cunning, have made him be supposed more favoured by the Divinity. To him the superstitious entrust their devotions: To his care they recommend their prayers, petitions, and sacrifices: And by his means, they hope to render their addresses acceptable to their incensed Deity. Hence the origin of PRIESTS, who may justly be regarded as invention of a timorous and abject superstition, which, ever diffident of itself, dares not offer up its own devotions, but ignorantly thinks to recommend itself to the Divinity, by the mediation of his supposed friends and servants. As superstition is a considerable ingredient in almost all religions, even the most fanatical; there being nothing but philosophy able entirely to conquer these unaccountable terrors; hence it proceeds, that in almost every sect of religion there are priests to be found: But the stronger mixture there is of superstition, the higher is the authority of the priesthood.[13]

---

[13] David Hume, 'Essay X: Of Superstition and Enthusiasm', from *Essays Moral, Political, and Literary* (1742–54) found at <http://www.english.upenn.edu/~mgamer/Etexts/hume.super stition.html> (accessed 7 July 2016).

Now although the Reformers and their successors would not have contrasted the superstitious affirmation of priesthood with the need for reason and philosophy, they would have argued that the Roman Catholic Church was confusing service to the Church with superstitious claims about their powers. Many Protestant accounts of ministry, therefore, tend to stress the duties of preaching and service, rather than a particular role in respect to sacraments. The third area is inclusion. The Roman Catholic emphasis on a priesthood that is limited to men who are celibate was increasingly seen as unreasonable and unjustifiable. For many Protestant denominations, the patriarchy of the Bible and the tradition is a major factor in the exclusion of women. St Paul's affirmation that 'there is no longer Jew or Greek, there is no longer slave or free, there is no longer male and female; for all of you are one in Christ Jesus' (Galatians 3.28 NRSV) affirms a radical equality in the Church that makes exclusion and discrimination unacceptable.

The result of these three concerns is that there is much greater emphasis on the connections between ordained ministry and the people of God. The Presbyterian Church USA and the United Methodist Church (USA) provide two good illustrations of this connection. So *The Book of Order of the Presbyterian Church USA* states:

> All ministry in the church is a gift from Jesus Christ. Members and officers alike serve mutually under the mandate of Christ who is chief minister of all ... One responsibility of membership in the church is the election of officers who are ordained to fulfill particular functions. The existence of these offices in no way diminishes the importance of all members to the total ministry of the church. These ordained officers differ from other members in function only ... when women and men, by God's providence and gracious gifts, are called by the church to undertake particular forms of ministry, the church shall help them to interpret their call and to be sensitive to the judgments and needs of others.[14]

The Book of Discipline of the United Methodist Church, the book of law for this denomination, offers a similar statement:

> Ministry in the Christian Church is derived from the ministry of Christ, who calls all persons to receive God's gift of salvation and follow in the way

---

[14] Virginia Samuel Cetuk, *What to Expect in Seminary: Theological Education and Spiritual Formation* (Nashville, TN: Abingdon Press, 1998), p. 59. It is worth noting that the Presbyterian Church USA (PCUSA) now uses the title 'teaching elders' for what were previously called 'ministers of the word and sacrament'. There are therefore both 'teaching elders' and 'ruling elders'.

of love and service. The whole church receives and accepts this call, and all Christians participate in this continuing ministry. Within the church community, there are persons whose gifts, evidence of God's grace, and promise of future usefulness are affirmed by the community, and who respond to God's call by offering themselves in leadership as ordained ministers.[15]

The precise difference that ordination makes is a matter of much debate among these different traditions. The Baptist or Congregationalist polity tends to see a difference only in terms of role; apart from that, ordination makes very little difference. Anglicans, however, do want to retain something of the Catholic sense of being set apart to be granted by God's grace the ability to serve the people of God in a distinctively sacramental way. Some traditions are in-between these two positions. Methodism, for example, is interesting. The United Methodist Church describes the difference between elders (i.e. ministers or pastors) and deacons in the following way. Elders are called to preach and teach the word of God, administer the sacraments, order the Church for its mission and service, and administer the discipline of the Church.[16] Deacons are 'called to lead in service, word, compassion, and justice and equip others for this ministry through teaching, proclamation, and worship and [to] assist elders in the administration of the sacraments'.[17] There are clear hints here of the traditional Roman Catholic division between a priest and a deacon.

One last ecumenical theme around ministry needs discussing. It is the Presbyterian Church (USA) that has made the language of covenant central to its understanding of ministry. The key phrase is 'covenant relationship'. So Christians' relationship to God is important, along with the relationship with each other. When the Presbyterian Church talks about training for ordination, the denomination stresses that there are three partners in the covenant relationship. These are the 'individual under care', the session of the congregation (this is the leadership team of the congregation) and the presbytery of which the congregation belongs (a presbytery is the group of local elders and ministers in that area). The picture that emerges is an interconnected one. If one aspires to leadership, one does so with the leadership of a congregation and with the leadership of the local churches. And all these parties have certain roles and duties that they must fulfil in respect of each other.

---

[15] Samuel Cetuk, *What to Expect in Seminary*, pp. 59–60.
[16] *The Book of Discipline of the United Methodist Church* (2012), 303.2.
[17] *Book of Discipline*, 303.2.

Conclusion

Looking at ministry from a global and ecumenical perspective, one's view of ministry changes. Any simplistic model and all major generalizations crumble when one stands back and sees the diversity of approaches and issues in our world. Ministry is hard. The global dimension is primarily a challenge to practice; the ecumenical dimension is primarily a challenge to theology. Both dimensions make us aware of the complexity of ministry in the modern world.

10

Clerical and lay models of ministry

ANDREW TODD

Introduction

The World Council of Churches (WCC) document, *Baptism, Eucharist, and Ministry*, says this of ministry:

> The word *ministry* in its broadest sense denotes the service to which the whole people of God is called, whether as individuals, as a local community, or as the universal Church. Ministry or ministries can also denote the particular institutional forms this service may take.[1]

The breadth of the understanding of 'service' in this quotation is made clear in an earlier paragraph:

> All members are called to discover, with the help of the community, the gifts they have received and to use them for the building up of the Church and for the service of the world to which the Church is sent.[2]

Ministry, although it includes the work of the building up of the Church, is primarily 'service of the world'. It is, therefore, the outworking of a mission in which members of the Church 'seek relevant forms of witness and service in each situation', as they 'bring to the world a foretaste of the joy and glory of God's kingdom'.[3]

In this model the role of the ordained is to carry a particular authority and responsibility for acting as a focus of the unity of the Church, 'pointing to its fundamental dependence on Jesus Christ'.[4] As the report continues: 'The ministry of such persons, who since very early times have been ordained, is constitutive for the life and witness of the Church.'[5]

---

[1] World Council of Churches (WCC) (1982), *Baptism, Eucharist, and Ministry* (Geneva: World Council of Churches), p. 21.
[2] WCC, *Baptism, Eucharist, and Ministry*, p. 20.
[3] WCC, *Baptism, Eucharist, and Ministry*, p. 20.
[4] WCC, *Baptism, Eucharist, and Ministry*, p. 21.
[5] WCC, *Baptism, Eucharist, and Ministry*, p. 21.

This casts the ordained, or more widely all those who exercise a public ministry, as those who enable the ministry of the whole Church and all its members.

This represents, of course, only one model of ministry; albeit one which continues to command ecumenical assent, and to be formative of particular denominational positions, including Anglican ones. However, even taking into account its particularity (as a product of a particular socio-historical context), it gives rise to some useful questions for this chapter. These questions will be asked of a range of clerical and lay models of ministry:

- How far do models of ministry focus on the 'building up of the Church'; how far on the 'service of the world'?
- How far do such models focus on the ministry of the 'whole people of God'; how far on the ministry of the ordained?
- How far do such models focus on the relationship between the ministry of the ordained and that of the laity (and is the former seen as 'constitutive' of the latter)?

Baptism, Eucharist, and Ministry also serves to dispel an unhelpful and false distinction that sometimes colours conversations about ministry, the laity and the ordained. The report makes clear that lay people do exercise ministry, and that their ministry is the primary understanding of the ministry of the Church. This dispels the notion that in contrast to the ministry of the ordained, the Christian life of the laity is best characterized as discipleship. Rather, discipleship is the continuing learning and formation of all church members (including the ordained) that incorporates them in the body of Christ and equips them for ministry. Thus, 'baptism is a sign and seal of our common discipleship'.[6] And baptism 'looks towards a growth into the measure of the stature of the fullness of Christ (Eph. 4.13)'.[7] That growth in, and as, the body of Christ is then linked to the call to 'confess and serve'.[8] All are called, as disciples, to participate in the ministry of the Church.

This gives rise to a further question to be asked of perspectives on ministry:

- How do clerical and lay models perceive the relationship between ministry and discipleship?

---

[6] WCC, *Baptism, Eucharist, and Ministry*, p. 3.
[7] WCC, *Baptism, Eucharist, and Ministry*, p. 3.
[8] WCC, *Baptism, Eucharist, and Ministry*, p. 3.

The questions will be applied in the chapter first to a range of prominent statements (clerical and lay) that demonstrate the dynamics of contemporary thinking about ministry (including a dominant consensus in Anglican thinking and voices that run counter to that). The chapter will then explore the extent to which core theological statements are mirrored by the actual practice of ministry. Chaplaincy will be used as the particular test case of ministry practice, for three reasons: first, because chaplaincy has both a theoretical and practical emphasis on service of the world; second, because chaplaincy exhibits an interesting relationship between those who are ordained (or authorized) and those who are lay; and third, because chaplaincy provides the opportunity to consider how well an emphasis on service (including lay service) is respected and integrated within the wider Church.

A new clerical consensus – the ordained as enablers of the body of Christ

The first shift that should be noted in relation to clerical perspectives on ministry is the rewriting of the theoretical relationship between the ordained and the laity. In an earlier work I discussed some features of this shift.[9] These included a recognition of the end of any sense that Christendom was a reality. This involved redefining a notion of community, from one that was coterminous with the boundaries of a parish (in which the ordained exercised ministry to all) to one which differentiated between church and wider community (so that ordained and laity might minister together both within the church community and to the wider one).[10] A corresponding change of emphasis was in relation to apostolicity, from a particular stress on historical continuity (the apostolic succession)[11] to a more equal stress on continuity and on being sent out. This dual emphasis, seen for example in the House of Bishops statement *Eucharistic Presidency*,[12] was, I argued, rooted in a wider ecumenical debate.[13]

The shift was underpinned by a theological move from a primarily Christological approach to a Trinitarian one, of which Robin Greenwood

---

9   A. Todd (2002), 'Of Presbyters and Priests: An Anglican View', in P. Luscombe and E. Shreeve (eds), *What Is a Minister?* (Peterborough: Epworth Press), pp. 104–16.
10   Todd, 'Of Presbyters and Priests', pp. 105–6.
11   See R. C. Moberly (1897), *Ministerial Priesthood* (London: John Murray).
12   House of Bishops (1997), *Eucharistic Presidency* (London: Church House Publishing).
13   Todd, 'Of Presbyters and Priests', pp. 106–8.

was a key proponent.[14] I previously characterized this move as being from a transactional theology (related to receiving salvation in Christ) to a relational one (involving participation in the body of Christ).[15] It was accompanied by a changing theology of the Eucharist and of priesthood – in interaction with each other. This is signalled by a shift in language about the role of the priest in the Eucharist, from that of 'celebrant' (who thus represents the worshippers) to that of 'president'. In the latter model the priest gathers and enables the eucharistic community, to which he or she belongs.[16] Transition is also signalled by a changing use of liturgical space with altars brought forward and priests facing west, symbolizing their role of gathering the community.

Crucially, this changes the understanding of how the ordained are 'set apart' for their ministry.[17] The change is from seeing the ordained as set apart *from* the laity, to being set apart *within* the *laos*. The first perspective is detected in the report *The Priesthood of the Ordained Ministry*, which concluded of the ordained priesthood that:

> Its priesthood is not simply derived from the priestliness of the whole community. Rather, the common priesthood of the community and the special priesthood of the ordained ministry are both derived from the priesthood of Christ. Bishops and presbyters do not participate in a greater degree in the priesthood of Christ; they participate in a different way ... Thus theirs is not a magnified form of the common priesthood; the difference is this, that their ministry is an appointed means through which Christ makes his priesthood present and effective to his people.[18]

The second perspective is to be found in the Anglican-Reformed report, *God's Reign and Our Unity*:

> 'Priests' exercise their priestly ministry neither apart from the priesthood of the whole body, nor by derivation from the priesthood of the whole body, but by virtue of their participation, in company with the whole body, in the priestly ministry of the risen Christ, and as leaders, examples and enablers for the priestly ministry of the whole body in virtue of the special calling and equipment given them in ordination.[19]

---

[14] R. Greenwood (1994), *Transforming Priesthood: A New Theology of Mission and Ministry* (London: SPCK).

[15] Todd, 'Of Presbyters and Priests', pp. 108–10.

[16] Greenwood, *Transforming Priesthood*, ch. 6.

[17] This change is identified in Todd, 'Of Presbyters and Priests', pp. 110–12.

[18] Board for Mission and Unity (1986), *Priesthood of the Ordained Ministry* (London: Board for Mission and Unity).

[19] Quoted in House of Bishops, *Eucharistic Presidency*, p. 30.

This appears to hold the balance between the ministry of the ordained and that of the laity, or indeed the Church as a whole. The particular aspect of the shift of thinking that emphasizes this has to do with the way in which Christ's priesthood is made 'present and effective'. In the earlier view the ordained are an 'appointed means' through which this priesthood is made effective to Christ's people – the undifferentiated community that is both the Church and society. In the later view, the whole body exercises the priestly ministry of Christ, by implication, to the world.

Collaborative ministry for building up the Church?

This understanding of core perspectives on ministry involving both ordained and laity needs to be further interrogated. Steven Croft's significant work, *Ministry in Three Dimensions*, provides an interesting and more fully developed clerical perspective on the ordained–laity dynamic and the emergence of what is known as collaborative ministry.[20] Croft's major perspectives are, for example, captured in a triangular diagram that summarizes the dimensions of ministry:

- *episcope* or leadership and oversight ministries: enabling others and connecting different communities;
- priestly or presbyteral ministry: sustaining communities in mission;
- evangelism or diaconal ministries: working outside the churches to pioneer fresh expressions.[21]

The element of service, and of enabling the service of the laity, appears to be rather minimal here. The explicitly outward-facing dimensions are almost entirely about witness, rather than service. This is exacerbated by the combination of diaconal ministry with evangelism, and the specific focus of this in Fresh Expressions. Although 'fresh expressions of church' are characterized in part by serving those outside the Church and entering into their context,[22] they are more usually directed by the drive to nurture discipleship and form church. Further confirmation of the lack of attention to the Church serving the world is provided by the Anglican Church's limited provision for a real diaconal ministry that might enable and focus such service.

---

[20] S. J. L. Croft (2008), *Ministry in Three Dimensions: Ordination and Leadership in the Local Church* (London: Darton, Longman & Todd).

[21] Croft, *Ministry in Three Dimensions*, p. 207.

[22] <http://freshexpressions.org.uk/about/what-is-a-fresh-expression/> (accessed 2 October 2018).

Why service is so downplayed will become clearer through consideration of chaplaincy. But there are some clues within Croft's work itself. There is, for example, a recognition that new models of ministry are connected with changing patterns of deployment of the clergy.[23] This includes fewer stipendiary clergy. It is clear that a significant impetus of the development of collaborative ministry is to sustain a public, or authorized, ministry that will continue to build up the Church. Add to this a concern about decline in numbers of those attending churches Sunday by Sunday, and it becomes clear that the combined emphasis on ministry that sustains the gathered life of the Church, and on an engagement with the world characterized by witness and mission, makes good sense. A dominant emphasis in changing patterns of ministry is on sustaining not only what the gathered Church does, but also the numbers of those involved and the income they provide (as far as is possible). These factors too are recognized by Croft, in his discussion of the 'end of Christendom' and its impact on ministry.[24] In this scenario, open-ended service of the world (that does not appear to contribute directly to the activity of, or numbers involved in, or income of, the gathered church) can look like a luxury. Or as I have not infrequently heard senior Anglican church leaders put it, it's not 'core business'.

Reflecting on the dimensions of the clerical consensus found in Croft's *Ministry in Three Dimensions*, in the light of the questions derived at the beginning of the chapter from *Baptism, Eucharist, and Ministry*, suggests the following conclusions. In mainstream Anglican clerical models of ministry there is a much greater emphasis on 'building up of the Church' than on the 'service of the world'. This includes an understanding of discipleship being primarily about participation in the life of the Church (rather than its being a preparation for service). The corresponding understanding of the ministry of the 'whole people of God', and its relationship to the ministry of the ordained, is that while it is enabled by the ordained to a greater extent than previously, the main reason for nurturing lay ministry is to sustain the life of the gathered church in the face of a decline both in clergy numbers and those attending regularly. This could easily feel like a new collaborative clericalism, if that were the whole picture.

Two further observations might usefully be made. One is the irony of this perspective – that the proposal of greater lay involvement in authorized ministries, while lay people have engaged with it, has been a significantly clerical concept. Its proponents have been mostly ordained. This

---

[23] Croft, *Ministry in Three Dimensions*, pp. 11–12.

[24] Croft, *Ministry in Three Dimensions*, pp. 5–9.

perhaps underlines the notion that the move has been rather more of an extension of clericalism than a move to encourage the ministry of the whole people of God.

The second observation concerns the place that service does have within this picture. While it does seem that service is often directed by the aspiration of building the gathered church (as in the specific example of Fresh Expressions), it is not the case that serving the world has no perceived value in its own right. Croft includes in his book, in an Appendix, a summary chart of 'ministry in three dimensions' unchanged from the earlier edition of the book. In this chart, 'diakonia' includes the following:

- simple hidden, practical acts of service;
- service to the community . . .
- serving and being served.[25]

However, because of the practical emphasis not on diaconal, but on priestly ministry, the service offered to the world is significantly in and through the gathered life of the church. In practice the earlier picture of the ordained offering pastoral care to a stable congregation[26] continues to be offered within the context of a somewhat diminished congregational life (albeit with some lay involvement in that work), rather than being extended through the ministry of the laity beyond the confines of the gathered church – with notable exceptions discussed below.

A counter voice – a broader vision for lay ministry

As already suggested, despite the clerical consensus that tends to co-opt the laity into shoring up the gathered church, there are significant counter voices which suggest a different picture. One such lay voice is that of Ruth Etchells, notably expressed in her Archbishop of Canterbury's Lent book, *Set My People Free: A Lay Challenge to the Churches.*[27] This is a bold plea for rebalancing the dynamic between the life and ministry of the institutional Church and the wider ministry of the laity. Thus Etchells talks of lay people who:

> Have recognised that to be 'lay' for God is a calling: it is not the negative state of 'not being ordained', but the active state of living the secular life to

---

[25] Croft, *Ministry in Three Dimensions*, p. 211.
[26] Croft, *Ministry in Three Dimensions*, pp. 3–5.
[27] R. Etchells (1995), *Set My People Free: A Lay Challenge to the Churches* (London: Fount/ HarperCollins).

the glory of God, in the name and the power of God, because it is a place – perhaps *the* place – where God is at work. To be called to full-time active lay service in the secular world is to be called to live fully in that world, to be at ease with it, to know its idioms and assumptions, to engage in its affairs and its arguments, its hopes and distresses, because one's *centre* is there.[28]

This re-centring is at the heart of the book:

> Throughout this book I have urged that the way forward for the church, if she is to seize the moment of hunger in the nation, is through her laity, at work in the world as much as, if not more than, within the institutional church. And I have argued that the church must wake up, free herself from that accumulation of fine webbing that holds her down, her inward-looking attitudes which limit and frustrate her lay people, and not only free them but encourage and empower them to the work of heroic service in the world which is their proper calling.[29]

Etchells' voice has a clear theology that locates the presence and action of God in the world, and the primary ministry of the laity, and therefore of the whole people of God, also in the world, acting in cooperation with God. This is a wholehearted, post-Christendom theology, in keeping with the concept of *missio Dei*; the belief that mission is first and foremost what God does, and that the Church discerns and participates in that mission.[30] In this understanding mission is not constrained by, or entirely dependent on, the Church. And the extent to which the Church is missional is measured not by the sustainability of its gathered life, but by its contextual engagement, in witness and service, in the world.

Etchells offers then a model of ministry very much in keeping with *Baptism, Eucharist, and Ministry*. In this picture, ministry that builds up the Church is for the sake of the larger purpose of serving the world. The ministry of the ordained enables, and is constitutive of, the ministry of the whole people of God. Furthermore, as the genre of the book demonstrates (a Lent book designed to stimulate learning and reflection), discipleship is directed towards discovering the calling of the whole people of God.

There are various contexts in which to test the extent to which prominent clerical and lay voices, such as those of Croft and Etchells, meet responses from other, less prominent voices. For example, one could consider current moves towards greater social action in churches of different traditions.

---

[28] Etchells, *Set My People Free*, pp. 58–9; italics in original.
[29] Etchells, *Set My People Free*, p. 177.
[30] D. Bosch (1991), *Transforming Mission: Paradigm Shifts in Theology of Mission* (Maryknoll, NY: Orbis Books).

This chapter, however, will use chaplaincy as its worked example. As indicated above, chaplaincy has both a theoretical and practical emphasis on service of the world; it also exhibits an interesting relationship between those who are ordained (or authorized) and those who are lay; and it provides the opportunity to consider how well an emphasis on service (including lay service) is respected and integrated within the wider Church.

Chaplaincy – the people of God serving the world?

Service within a clerical paradigm – lay voices valuing the religious professional

Throughout the research on chaplaincy carried out by the Cardiff Centre for Chaplaincy Studies,[31] service is placed first in models of chaplaincy, as pastoral care is identified as the primary purpose of chaplaincy; witness is placed second, as chaplains talk of waiting for those they serve to raise the question of faith or religion. It is, of course, possible to have that emphasis in chaplaincy ministry on service but for that ministry to remain within a clerical paradigm. This is in keeping with the Anglican origins of modern chaplaincy, which envisaged it as the extension of parochial ministry to those who were prevented from having a direct connection with a parish church (because they were constrained by being in hospital, by residential education, by military service or by being in prison).

Interestingly, there is a significant lay voice that values this clerical model of service. In research carried out in prisons,[32] the lay voices of prisoners spoke of the primary value of this service: 'For the majority of prisoners interviewed and spoken with, regardless of whether they were of a particular faith or no faith, the overwhelming value of prison chaplaincy lay in its provision of a distinctive pastoral care and support service'.[33]

And the lay voices of prison staff expressed similar views:

Prison officers, like governors, seemed to value similar areas of contribution to prisoners, but from a slightly different perspective. The overwhelming value of the prison chaplain for the prison officer lay in their pastoral

---

[31] <http://www.stpadarns.ac.uk/?page_id=155>.

[32] A. Todd and L. Tipton (2011), *The Role and Contribution of a Multi-faith Prison Chaplaincy to the Contemporary Prison Service*: <http://orca.cf.ac.uk/29120/1/Chaplaincy%20Report%20Final%20Draft%20%283%29.pdf> (accessed 2 October 2018).

[33] Todd and Tipton, *Role and Contribution*, p. 29.

role – in particular the chaplain's availability and ability to do what was commonly described as the 'touchy-feely' stuff.[34]

As the report indicates, the clerical model was perceived to have changed. Chaplains were seen to be more professional. And they were recognized as being multifaith. But this represents a new clericalism, not to any great extent a vision of lay service. Interestingly this implies that the role of the significant number of lay volunteers (some 7,000 in England and Wales, compared with between 700 and 800 chaplains)[35] is largely invisible to prisoners and staff.

More recent research in the field of mental health offers a similar picture. In a piece of research that was specifically designed to look at how chaplains, other staff, service users and carers could produce chaplaincy or spiritual care together, one of the distinctive voices was that which spoke of the value of the chaplain being a religious professional. That included being a 'man of God', being a church leader with spiritual training (which might or might not involve ordination) and having a well-developed spiritual life.[36]

In these perspectives from those lay people who use, or work with, chaplains, the value of them offering service to their clients (prisoners or patients) is clear. But equally clear is that this is valued as a professional service. In this sense chaplains, in offering service, continue to do so as representatives of their faith communities. Christian chaplains represent the Church. And in so far as they nurture discipleship in service users, this is directed largely at their personal spiritual journey rather than explicitly at preparing them to serve alongside chaplains. These voices do not speak of clergy enabling laity; and the very real role played by volunteers (including in some cases prisoners and service users) is largely invisible.

Clerical and lay voices speaking of shared service

Other voices in chaplaincy, however, do speak of a broader vision of service. These are apparent in a piece of research done for the Church of England that involved case-studies of chaplaincies in different settings.[37] In

---

[34] Todd and Tipton, *Role and Contribution*, p. 31.

[35] Todd and Tipton, *Role and Contribution*, p. 9.

[36] J. Raffay, E. Wood and A. Todd (2016), 'Service User Views of Spiritual and Pastoral Care (Chaplaincy) in NHS Mental Health Services: A Co-produced Constructivist Grounded Theory Investigation', *BMC Psychiatry* 16.200: <https://bmcpsychiatry.biomedcentral.com/articles/10.1186/s12888-016-0903-9> (accessed 2 October 2018).

[37] A. Todd, V. Slater and S. Dunlop (2014), *The Church of England's Involvement in Chaplaincy: Research Report for the Church of England's Mission and Public Affairs Council:*

that research the numbers of lay volunteers that emerged through a quantitative study (utilizing the usual Church of England methods of reporting numbers of those in ministry) was minimal. The report discusses how and why this represents a significant underestimate of the numbers involved.[38]

However, the qualitative evidence made it clear that in a range of chaplaincy settings there was a significant model of chaplaincy that involved a lead chaplain (usually ordained) enabling significant teams of volunteers (most of whom were lay). Examples included an industrial mission group with 40 volunteers (matched by some 14 other such teams in the region). The (Anglican-ordained) director of this ecumenical group observed a 'huge energy' of people coming forward wanting to do chaplaincy and requesting training and support.[39] Other lead chaplains spoke similarly of the interest in volunteering, of the vital role of volunteers and of their role in enabling this model of chaplaincy. Lay volunteers spoke too of their enthusiasm for being involved in chaplaincy, for example as they got alongside people in the workplace and supported them in their work. One such volunteer chaplain to a busy shopping centre spoke both of this enthusiasm and of the invisibility of the role:

> I think what I found about chaplaincy is that when I started it, I'd never heard of it, and then you find that there are all sorts of chaplains in all sorts of places doing quiet work, and basically nobody else has heard about it either, but the work is amazing, but nobody has heard about it, that's what I'd say about chaplaincy. It's very quiet and underneath.[40]

In this context, therefore, both clerical and lay voices spoke of a shared ministry of both service and witness in the world, enabled by collaborative working between lay and ordained. Furthermore, when probed, chaplains spoke of this in terms of discipleship. Lay chaplains were seen as living out their discipleship through their ministry as chaplains in secular places.

The question remains, however, as to how far this model represents an enabling of the witness and service of the whole people of God in the world. However, the same research offers signs that chaplaincy does stretch beyond co-opting lay volunteers into a professional model of ministry. Workplace chaplains, in particular, spoke of their work with lay Christians in the context of their everyday work:

<http://orca.cf.ac.uk/62257/1/Todd%2C%20Slater%20%26%20Dunlop%202014%20Report%20on%20Church%20of%20England%20Chaplaincy.pdf> (accessed 2 October 2018).

[38] Todd, Slater and Dunlop, *Involvement in Chaplaincy*, pp. 19–20.
[39] Todd, Slater and Dunlop, *Involvement in Chaplaincy*, p. 19.
[40] Todd, Slater and Dunlop, *Involvement in Chaplaincy*, p. 23.

This was about: 'discussion meetings with Christians at work about issues like "management", "failure", "honesty"'; 'holding on to values of disciples in the workplace'; 'chaplaincy helps Christians to integrate their faith and work lives – discipling them to become mature Christians'.[41]

Reception of chaplaincy voices and models of ministry – under the radar

There is evidence here that chaplaincy can represent a practical outworking of a model of mission and ministry envisaged in the WCC report *Baptism, Eucharist, and Ministry* and by Ruth Etchells in *Set My People Free*. However, the research for the Church of England also revealed that this chaplaincy model did not always connect well with other approaches to being the Church, and in particular with the gathered life of the Church. The following represents a number of chaplaincy voices expressing this:

> Chaplains often spoke about how the local church not only did not engage with the work of chaplaincy, but in many cases seemed to be unaware of it. One volunteer police chaplain said, 'I suppose the frustrating bit is the lack of interest within the churches . . . You just wish they would see it as an integral part of church life, I suppose, or what the church does' . . . One volunteer workplace chaplain said, 'I don't think the church sees us.' In this case, she was speaking specifically about how the local church does not see chaplaincy as part of its mission. Indeed, when asked how the church could better support chaplains, by far the most frequent response was, 'by acknowledging that we exist' . . . one Licensed Lay Minister explained to us that her parish church is not interested in the work she does as a volunteer police chaplain.[42]

These voices are mirrored by those of the organizational Church, particularly in the expressed hope that chaplaincy might be able to demonstrate its 'impact'. This is a well-known demand on chaplains from the secular organizations they serve, but it is also a key church interest. This was part of the conversation with the research steering group for the Church of England research, not least in relation to the Church of England's Quinquennial Goals.[43] While there was productive conversation around chaplaincy contributing to 'the common good' and about its development of models

---

[41] Todd, Slater and Dunlop, *Involvement in Chaplaincy*, p. 33.
[42] Todd, Slater and Dunlop, *Involvement in Chaplaincy*, p. 25.
[43] The three goals are:
> to promote resourceful communities infused with the values of God's kingdom and, particularly at a time of economic hardship in society, to enhance the capacity and commitment of the Church both to stand alongside people facing unemployment and financial insecurity;

of ministry that supported that, and to some extent around chaplains enabling spiritual growth, a significant proportion of the conversation was about the difficulty of demonstrating that chaplaincy contributed to the numerical (as well as spiritual) growth of the Church.

This matches the church concern, identified above in relation to Croft's *Ministry in Three Dimensions*, about whether open-ended service of the world contributes to the sustainability of church life, particularly in terms of congregational numbers and associated income. The fact that chaplaincy's experience of its ministry of service is undervalued by other parts of the Church underlines how much the question of sustainability is a driving agenda in discussions of ministry. And chaplaincy's difficulty in demonstrating its contribution to this sustainability remains a stumbling block to the wider Church in its recognition of the value of chaplaincy.

Conclusion: the full extent of lay ministry constrained by the concern for sustainability

This chapter has proposed that contemporary perspectives on ministry, rooted in ecumenical debate and agreement, envisage a dynamic between the ministry of the ordained and the ministry of the lay in which the former enable the latter. In the most developed version of the model, ministry is exercised by the whole people of God, not only to build up the Church but also crucially to serve the world.

In considering prominent perspectives within the debate about ministry, especially in the Anglican Church, the chapter suggested that there might be a clerical consensus in which collaborative ministry remained more of an extended clericalism than an enabling of witness and service of the laity in their daily lives. This was further marked by an emphasis on discipleship that focused on participation in the gathered church rather than on preparation for service and witness in secular places. It was further suggested that the most significant driver in this constraint of the vision of lay ministry was the concern to sustain the life of the institutional Church, its historic patterns of ministry, its congregational numbers and its income.

---

to seek sustained numerical and spiritual growth in the Church of England over the next quinquennium and beyond;

to reshape, re-imagine and re-energise ministry in the Church of England so that it is equipped both to grow the church in every community and contribute to 'the common good'.

(GS MISC 995)

The chapter did indicate that there were significant counter voices that held to the bigger vision of the extent and purpose of lay ministry, notably the lay voice of Ruth Etchells in *Set My People Free*. In order to understand how such a prominent voice might work in practice, and how that practice might be received by the wider Church, the chapter offered the case-study of chaplaincy.

Evidence from chaplaincy research was deployed in order to show that chaplains were certainly engaged in service of the world, as well as witness. However, some research (from prisons and the field of mental health) suggested that this service might remain (in lay eyes) within a clerical paradigm (where users valued chaplains as religious professionals). Other research suggested that lay people were both involved in, and enabled by, chaplaincy. A particular model was highlighted in which ordained and lay worked together in a range of settings to offer public service and witness. And, in workplace chaplaincy, chaplains seemed to be supporting and shaping the participation of lay Christians in the world of work. These models were advocated by both ordained and lay chaplains.

However, research indicates that chaplaincy receives a mixed reception within the wider Church. This is perceived by chaplains as a lack of visibility, and is also shown by a concern on the part of the organizational Church that chaplaincy should demonstrate its impact on church life (including on numerical growth). This seemed to confirm that realizing a full vision of a ministry of witness and service exercised by the whole people of God continues to be constrained by the concern for the sustainability of the gathered life of the Church, and the direction of authorized ministry and discipleship to this end.

11

Non-parochial forms of ministry

CHRIS SWIFT

Introduction

It is indicative of the normative influence of the parish setting that this chapter groups together all other forms of recognized Christian ministry. Like many chaplains, I am asked time and again 'Where's your church?' To the extent that the public thinks about clergy at all, it is clear that we are supposed to be in an ecclesiastical building serving the needs of the parish. It follows that forms of ministry which depart from this model are diffuse and poorly understood. Even taking chaplaincy as the most common form of alternative public ministries, the numbers, diversity and location of those involved are quite staggering. To quote one report: 'Chaplains are everywhere.'[1]

Despite their ubiquity chaplaincies and ministry beyond the parish are hidden aspects of the Church's mission. For example, much of the data about the activities of ministers in hospitals and elsewhere never finds its way into the statistics which describe the work of the Church. 'Beyond the parish' is a shadow economy of spiritual care which appears to fluctuate in significance but is never accorded the status of the ministry which the Church funds. When I once made the observation, at a meeting to review a diocesan annual report, 'There's no mention of chaplaincy in this', I was told instantly: 'We don't pay for it.' In all sorts of ways chaplaincy and other ministries outside the parish seldom surface in mainstream church discussions.[2] This is a pity, not least because such ministries lie at points of pressing concern in our society: places where young people face mortal danger in foreign lands; where life-and-death medical decisions are a daily

---

[1] B. Ryan, *A Very Modern Ministry: Chaplaincy in the UK*, London, Theos, 2015, p. 6.
[2] The General Synod (GS) of the Church of England has received briefing papers and held debates about chaplaincies from time to time; for example, 'Hospital Healthcare Chaplaincy: Briefing Paper from the Hospital Chaplaincies Council', GS 1609 2006 (Feb.), pp. 249–66.

occurrence; and where some of our most vulnerable citizens are kept in secure accommodation.

The task of writing about the immense range of ministry exercised beyond the parish is daunting. No one is qualified to write it or possesses the knowledge needed to do it justice. Over the past 25 years I have ministered in part-time prison chaplaincy, been involved in the education of armed-forces chaplains, and spent two decades working in healthcare chaplaincy. Yet I am aware of so many other areas of ministry about which I know very little. It is helpful that in recent years the amount of publication about non-parochial ministry has grown, enabling second-hand insights to be developed.

The experience of observation and ministry in various institutions has taught me both the challenges and beneficial contributions available to chaplaincy. The nature of these contributions varies as the different theological facets of ministry are engaged by the unique nature of each institution. For the military this might revolve around morale; for healthcare mortality and suffering; in the penal system, restorative justice; in education growth and character; in industry the care of workers; and in the arts creativity as an expression of the sacred.

Looking back into the earliest publications by chaplains, many may find the following observation to be surprisingly contemporary:

> Part of this ministry will be pastoral work, continuing the work of parish priests among their church members. But very many of those whom [the chaplain] meets will be people who are out of touch with the Church, and even unsympathetic towards it.[3]

This statement was published in 1946. Many church leaders of today might look back enviously at a time of full churches; strong community spirit; and numbers of church baptisms, weddings and funerals that would make today's statistics pale into insignificance. Yet Wall, a hospital chaplain working in London immediately after the Second World War, writes of the frequent experience of meeting those distanced from the Church and unsympathetic towards it. Of course there is much that could be argued about this, especially when religion might have been felt to be an imposition rather than a choice. The unsympathetic responses Wall perceived came almost certainly from people who had experience of a Christian community. Nevertheless, it suggests that the care provided by ministers

---

[3] B. A. Wall, *Visiting the Hospital: A Practical Handbook for Hospital Chaplains and Clergy Who Visit Hospitals*, London, A. R. Mowbray & Co., 1946, p. 10.

to the unchurched and the anti-church has a longer history than many might imagine.

Secular ministers

In its original sense the secular clergy were those who 'operated out in the world'[4] as opposed to those who lived, prayed and worked in monasteries. In the medieval period they had a 'dual religious and worldly status'[5] which saw them involved with ecclesiastical institutions of law and education as well as in parishes. We would be unlikely (by contemporary standards) to think of these clergy as secular but I would suggest that the boundaries of this understanding have shifted rather than dissolved. Today it is ministers working in settings whose culture may seem antithetical to religion – such as major shopping centres – who might be regarded as secular ministers. They continue the tradition of holding dual status, albeit in new and challenging ways. Secularism has acquired a different meaning, and ministers immersed in public institutions may feel inherent tensions in their identity and role.

The Church of England's Fresh Expressions website offers a definition of pioneer ministry (one category of alternative ministries), but even here the task of coherent description is challenging. Writing about the development of pioneer ministry, Ross and Baker recognize the elusive nature of its definition, concluding that: 'There is something intriguing and wonderful about the mystery of it.'[6] Perhaps there is some truth that in the age of social media and the constant flux of discussion it is difficult to fix a description for something so emergent and fluid. However, while the mystery may be wonderful, the lack of clarity presents several problems. Without a shared understanding it is difficult for such ministries to be accurately perceived or analysed. This in turn may weaken the ability of the wider Church to identify and value (and continue, in some instances, to fund) what is intended. Simultaneously it inhibits the ability of both the churched and unchurched world to understand the role of pioneer ministers, and the ministers themselves may find that a lack of coherence leads to unhelpful tensions in their self-understanding and relations with their colleagues.

---

[4] Hugh M. Thomas, *The Secular Clergy in England, 1066–1216*, Oxford, Oxford University Press, 2014, p. 5.
[5] Thomas, *Secular Clergy*, p. 5.
[6] Cathy Ross and Jonny Baker, *The Pioneer Gift: Explorations in Mission*, Norwich, Canterbury Press, 2014, p. 3.

While newer forms of ministry outside the parish model may suffer from their novelty, there are non-parochial roles with much longer histories to sustain their identity. Chaplains are the most notable group, yet even here the variety of chaplaincies and differences in theological outlook pose problems for a clear definition. One researcher has provided a definition as follows: 'Chaplaincy is a practice of care involving the intentional recognition and articulation of the sacred by nominated individuals authorised for this task in secular situations.'[7] Such a definition will be heard in different ways by those engaged in chaplaincy. For example, while care may be the dominant element of chaplaincy in some places, the word needs to be capacious enough to include a practice of leadership (military); a practice of restoration (penal); and a practice of development (education). In forms of ministry such as street pastors and some pioneer ministries, recognition of the sacred may be less explicit and the provision of practical service as an expression of Christian vocation more pronounced. However, in all these cases the religious mandate of those involved is evident and any expression of spiritual enquiry by service users will be met with an articulation of the sacred.

A factor affecting all areas of ministry beyond the parish is the state of religious literacy in the wider population.[8] It is often assumed that a decline in acceptance of Christian teaching and participation in church life is a modern phenomenon in Western societies. This has been subject to a great deal of critique and debate in recent years, with public surveys suggesting an inexorable decline in knowledge about the basic teachings of the Christian faith. Inevitably this is itself a complex subject of study with distinctions between the religious knowledge of devotees and the knowledge of those who study and seek to understand religions (with some individuals engaged in both areas). What is important with regard to the varieties of ministry is the role chaplains and others can play in recognizing and interpreting religious and spiritual experiences. As Moore argues, 'Religion remains one of the most misunderstood and misrepresented dimensions of human experience.'[9] In order for public places to

---

[7] Mark Cobb, Chris Swift and Andrew Todd, 'Introduction to Chaplaincy Studies', in C. Swift, A. Todd and M. Cobb (eds), *A Handbook of Chaplaincy Studies: Understanding Spiritual Care in Public Places*, Farnham, Ashgate, 2015, p. 2.

[8] Diane L. Moore, 'Diminishing Religious Literacy: Methodological Assumptions and Analytical Frameworks for Promoting the Public Understanding of Religion', in Adam Dinham and Matthew Francis (eds), *Religious Literacy in Policy and Practice*, Bristol, Policy Press, 2016, p. 27.

[9] Moore, 'Diminishing Religious Literacy', p. 37.

handle this complexity safely and constructively, the role of ministers can be a crucial contribution.

Most of those ministering beyond the parish are reminded when they are commissioned or authorized that the mission of the Church is to continue the work of Christ in the world. For those with a theological understanding which affirms the presence of Christ as ubiquitous, it follows that the location and shape of ministry is as extensive as the varieties of human community.[10] In addressing the experience of chaplaincy and other ministries as 'presence' (see below), the risks and rewards of such a broad approach will be debated. However, it is true that ministers are today very widely scattered across society. On any given day there are clergy and ministers alongside military special forces; in prisons; courts; supermarkets; community centres; factories; hospitals; hospices; universities; schools; in attendance on the head of state and in the House of Commons. All of these are served by chaplains or other forms of authorized ministers.

Although developing from a low base, the interest in chaplaincy has grown in a number of directions since the start of the century, ranging from new postgraduate courses (at Cardiff; Leeds; Glasgow) to an exponential rise in journal articles and books. While still a largely hidden economy of pastoral care, secular ministry has become a new focus for research and study. One of the challenges for chaplaincy, even when this approach is valued, is to relate the organizational value of the service to budgets and staffing levels. The least precise and most complex task of the NHS England chaplaincy guidance review in 2015 was to crystallize the criteria for the chaplains' staffing calculation.

This introduction has raised the challenge of providing a definition for the variety of ministries present in the UK today. The simplest way to do this is to say that what follows concerns authorized ministers who are not parish clergy, or clergy ministering in ecclesiastical structures (e.g. archdeacons). However, this negative description fails to do justice to the positive characteristics of those called to minister in a diverse range of communities. I would suggest that chaplains and those tasked with ministry in chiefly secular settings are there to foster, embody and express Christian ministry in a manner appropriate to their context. They are also deployed theologians: people authorized to keep in constant perspective the pastoral needs of those in their care and to strive to recognize God's presence in the world. At the same time a common characteristic among

---

[10] This approach is described in the description of Jenny's ministry in Victoria Slater, *Chaplaincy Ministry and the Mission of the Church*, London, SCM Press, 2015, pp. 43f.

this group of ministers is a sense of distance from the institutional Church. This is not a universal phenomenon but one which recurs when a group of chaplains meet and share their experiences.[11]

Key features

Context

Perhaps the most notable characteristic of the context of ministries beyond the parish church is social pluralism. Across the NHS, and in education, the justice system and the military, institutions have been marked by growing diversity. Religion is one aspect of this but so too are human sexuality, ethnicity, gender equality and the abolition of a compulsory retirement age. Non-religious beliefs now find equal protection in law,[12] and organizations are beginning to come to grips with the implications of this for chaplaincy and spiritual care. After over 450 years of almost exclusively Anglican chaplaincy, the period between 1970 and 2020 is witnessing a ranging from ecumenical chaplaincy to multifaith chaplaincy to meeting the needs of those with non-religious spiritualities. This is a dizzying pace of change after centuries of apparent uniformity. In turn this reflects a society where traditional dichotomies are being eroded and new freedoms have been granted to those whose experience was silenced and denied. In England and Wales the marriage of same-sex couples became legal in 2014 and there is increasing public support for the needs of transgender people, notably around the implications for how people are treated within gender-segregated establishments.[13]

Some analysis of the Church of England's behaviour in this process of change has suggested a strategic retreat which has enabled the retention of influence. It is suggested that the Established Church has seen the writing on the wall and, rather than attempt to resist the reality of change, it has stepped into the role of diversification management. While this may seem constructive, the argument goes that brokerage is a powerful tool and one where the Church of England can open and close doors depending on the

---

[11] This was a significant theme in a chaplaincy consultation held at St George's House, Windsor, in October 2015. The chaplains involved came from both the public services and commercial settings, but the sense of distance from a parish-focused Church was a consistent experience.
[12] Equality Act 2010.
[13] K. Marlow, B. Winder and H. J. Elliott, 'Working with Transgendered Sex Offenders: Prison Staff Experiences', *Journal of Forensic Practice* 17, no. 3 (2015): 241–54.

forms of religion it favours.[14] The risk is that this focuses on constructive relations between faith leaders rather than the needs and preferences of the laity. However, an alternative perspective might suggest that the role of the Church of England, as an institution concerned with the spiritual needs of the whole community, has naturally led to the inclusion of faith representatives when the limitations of the Anglican clergy to meet universal need have been recognized. Hence chaplains have been at the forefront of promoting change fulfilling an Anglican vocation to serve a community rather than (solely) a congregation. Where ministers have been freed from the need to focus large amounts of their time and energy on fostering a gathered community of worship, the opportunity to be in the thick of social change and personal need has brought its own rewards. Chaplains have become adept at speaking into situations, and establishing a valued presence, avoiding more normative forms of church which tend to speak out of their own territory into the wider community. Chaplains and other ministers are embedded apologists[15] for a spirituality which continues to find resonance – if not outright assent – in the realm of the secular. This naturally leads into the second key feature of extra-parochial ministry: presence.

Presence

The concept of presence as an essential characteristic of chaplaincy has long been recognized. Peter Speck's landmark *Being There* suggests attendance as a key feature of caring for the sick, but it also provides an in-depth exploration of what goes on when the minister is present with patients and medical staff.[16] More recently Winnie Fallers Sullivan has also focused on the idea of presence in her consideration of chaplaincies and the law in the USA. However, presence has been criticized when it has been presented as 'loitering with intent': a passive readiness to minister which appears lacking in strategic insight or a concern with outcomes. The question naturally arises: 'What would change if chaplaincy was absent?' It may be that the traditional notion of loitering was invested in a sense of supernatural guidance: God will lead me to be where I need to be at that moment. However, in a large teaching hospital or in a military theatre of operation, should chaplains believe that drifting around will eventually snag them in the

---

[14] James Arthur Beckford and Sophie Gilliat-Ray, *The Church of England and Other Faiths in a Multi-faith Society*, Coventry: University of Warwick, Department of Sociology, 1996, p. 512.
[15] Mark Newitt, 'New Directions in Hospital Chaplaincy: Chaplains – the Church's Embedded Apologists?' *Theology* 117, no. 6 (2014): 417–25.
[16] Peter Speck, *Being There: Pastoral Care in Times of Illness*, London, SPCK, 1988.

right place? Among the gifts ministers have at their disposal are planning, intention, prioritization and thoughtful reflection. It is more than happenstance that leads a chaplain to be in the right place at the right time. In a hospital, the way nursing staff understand the role and contribution of the chaplain is essential for receiving effective referrals and being available to support patients. For this to happen chaplains need to invest their time in nurse training and education, and take the opportunity to speak with staff and widen the appreciation of how spiritual care can help their patients. Rather than an evasion of the 'real' work of pastoral care, an investment in reflection, thought and planning promotes a fairer distribution of the chaplain's time and talents. In turn this addresses questions about equity and equality, moving towards a position in which patients and staff all have an equal awareness of, and opportunity to access, the skills offered by the chaplain. For chaplaincy to be meaningful in modern institutions there needs to be both planned presence and reflective engagement.

For Fallers Sullivan and the British theologian Linda Woodhead, the development of chaplaincy has achieved a workable presence for spirituality and religion in surprisingly irreligious places. Chaplaincy is a way of presenting religion for 'the whole of society, rather than just for "religious people"'.[17] As I have observed, chaplains have made a quite remarkable journey over a relatively short period of time, moving through ecumenical diversification and multifaith working, and now incorporating humanist practitioners into the role. They have paid close attention to the evolving needs of the communities they serve and the political drivers of the organizations in which they work. Presence has not been passive. Some may argue that progressive accommodation has distorted the religious credentials of chaplains. However, others attest to a continuous dialogue between the chaplains' experience and the religious traditions they inhabit. The complexity of this is not without cost for the individual chaplain, and those who wish to defend the purity of their religious belief may find it especially difficult. In her report on healthcare chaplaincy and the Church of England, Dame Janet Trotter and her colleagues wrestled with the dichotomy experienced by chaplains conversant in their faith tradition yet dealing every day in the idioms of the NHS. The report stated that the Church of England:

> must help equip chaplains to learn to speak the languages of the NHS and of
> the church with equal fluency and to maintain the constant tension (which so

---

[17] L. Woodhead, 'Introduction', in Swift, Todd and Cobb (eds), *Handbook of Chaplaincy Studies*, p. xxi.

many chaplains reported to be at the heart of their lives and work) between Christian vocation and NHS employment. This is a necessity if chaplains are to be effective advocates for the interests of patients, both in the NHS and in the wider community context.[18]

Not everyone is suited to bilingualism. The challenge it presents spans the contexts of chaplaincy, from the military to commerce. In every instance there is the risk that the chaplain will avoid difficult conversations and speaking truth to power. The ambiguity of the role has been represented in literature and popular culture as alternately complicit and faithfully resistant.[19] The position of the chaplain offers both possibilities, and ensuring 'equal fluency' is an ongoing task that requires an investment of time and energy. The position of ministers beyond the parish is often described as liminal – caught between two or more worlds. This suggests that presence is not a passive state but a continual striving betwixt and between, working to sustain balance and keeping the different belongings of chaplains in creative tension. For example, the responsibilities of military chaplains mean that they are 'in some sense non-state actors within a state operation'.[20] A similar point is made by Gilliat-Ray and co-authors from the perspective of prisoners being highly alert to the 'tensions chaplains must face between being key-carrying servants of the state, and members of a shared religious community'.[21] The discomfort and difficulty for chaplains holding this position, in ever more defined and specialist environments, is telling. At the same time it has been suggested that experiencing liminality when ministering to people in different liminal states (e.g. dying) may be a unique tool in the care the chaplain provides.[22] Even so, it is logical to suggest that the unique position of the chaplain, and the stress it creates, warrants strategic support if chaplains are not to suffer ill health as a consequence. The presence of stress linked to uncertainty of role has

---

[18] Church of England, *Health Care Chaplaincy and the Church of England: A Review of the Work of the Hospital Chaplaincies Council*, London, Hospital Chaplaincies Council, 2011, p. 33.

[19] Winnifred Fallers Sullivan, *A Ministry of Presence: Chaplaincy, Spiritual Care, and the Law*, Chicago, University of Chicago Press, 2014, p. 6.

[20] A. Todd and C. Butler, 'Moral Engagements: Morality, Mission and Military Chaplaincy', in A. Todd, ed., *Military Chaplaincy in Contention: Chaplains, Churches and the Morality of Conflict*, Farnham, Ashgate, 2013, p. 153.

[21] Mansur Ali, Stephen Pattison and Sophie Gilliat-Ray (eds), *Understanding Muslim Chaplaincy*, Farnham, Ashgate, 2013, p. 133.

[22] M. Paterson, 'Supervision, Support and Self Practice', in Swift, Todd and Cobb (eds), *Handbook of Chaplaincy Studies*.

been demonstrated in hospice chaplaincy[23] and it may be assumed that it is present in varying degrees in a wide range of ministries.

Studying chaplaincy

There are a wealth of ways in which ministries beyond the parish can be studied. While this may also be true of local churches and their clergy, the location of chaplaincies and other types of ministry provide even more avenues of enquiry. At present there is no specific chaplaincy research methodology. The absence of such an agreed tool raises a number of questions. While it is useful and often enriching to adopt the techniques of other disciplines, it also means that the values and epistemologies of those fields influence the ways in which practice is observed and analysed. No method is neutral. Traditionally, practical theology has been employed to study chaplaincy, which itself draws on the methodologies of other disciplines. Often those writing practical theology are aware of these limitations and this mitigates some of the ways in which findings are shaped by research methods. Stephen Pattison has been a figure within this tradition and one able to question and query the role of chaplaincy,[24] including the risk that ministers adopt too readily the values and practices of the institutions where they operate. However, there is a fine balance to hold here as religious particularity has been a vehicle of excuse for disengagement from the core business of the places where ministry takes place.[25] Chaplains are contaminated by the context of their ministry – but they are also an ingredient of change if they are skilfully embedded in the organizations they serve.

There is little in the way of systematic evidence about the publication of data which investigates the efficacy of chaplaincy. Most notably Harriet Mowat found scant data of any significance to elucidate the benefit of chaplaincy spiritual care to patients. Much of what has been written amounts to practitioners' opinion which, valuable as it is, comes far down the pecking order of what the NHS considers to be evidence from which to build policy or develop action plans. However, I would suggest that

---

[23] Mari Lloyd Williams, Michael Wright, Mark Cobb and Chris Shiels, 'A Prospective Study of the Roles, Responsibilities and Stresses of Chaplains Working within a Hospice', *Palliative Medicine* 18, no. 7 (2004): 638–45.

[24] Stephen Pattison, 'Chaplaincy as Public Theology: A Reflective Exploration', *Health and Social Care Chaplaincy* 3, no. 2 (2015): 110–28.

[25] Christopher Swift, *Hospital Chaplaincy in the Twenty-first Century: The Crisis of Spiritual Care on the NHS*, Farnham, Ashgate, 2014, p. 36.

chaplaincy is witnessing a shift towards the next stage of research and evidence – the detailed study of individual practice. From auto-ethnographic research[26] to the publication of case studies,[27] there is now considerably more material available describing what chaplains do. There is a growing interest in theological reflection and forms of writing which enable ministers to develop greater insight into their practice.[28] All this is still largely from the perspective of the practitioner, but it nevertheless creates a body of description and analysis which begins to locate the nature and practice of ministry.

There is a temptation when studying chaplaincy to see large-scale statistical data as the panacea for the uncertainty of a service set within the cost–benefit rhetoric of public finance or, indeed, ministry operating in commercial or charitable enterprises. At the same time, critics of public funding for chaplaincy have been similarly looking for data which demonstrates a lack of impact or value. In both cases this desire, however reasonable, faces a multitude of practical challenges. Chaplaincy departments and services are small – even minuscule – compared with other aspects of a public institution. Furthermore, the practice of chaplaincy is spread widely, meaning it is difficult to isolate a concentrated area of practice with more promise of generating statistical difference. It is hard to think of another profession in healthcare whose scope of practice is as dispersed and variable as that of the chaplain. Ministry happens before birth, throughout life, and into advanced old age. It is potentially available to every patient, with every clinical condition, from any and every background of religious faith, culture and belief. Achieving the kind of standardization of factors influencing the effects and outcomes of ministry in this situation is very challenging. It has also been noted that there are limitations for 'large-scale statistical analysis when decoupled from more fine-grain studies'.[29] At present the exploration of fine-grain evidence in ministry beyond the parish offers the best way forward, building a picture of the range, variety and essential similarities of religious and spiritual care.

---

26 Swift, *Hospital Chaplaincy*, pp. 101–30.
27 G. Fitchett and S. Nolan, *Spiritual Care in Practice: Case Studies in Healthcare Chaplaincy*, London, Jessica Kingsley, 2015.
28 Heather Walton, *Writing Methods in Theological Reflection*, London, SCM Press, 2014.
29 P. Kevern and W. McSherry, 'The Study of Chaplaincy: Methods and Materials', in C. Swift, A. Todd and M. Cobb (eds), *A Handbook of Chaplaincy Studies: Understanding Spiritual Care in Public Places*, Farnham, Ashgate, 2015, p. 52.

Conclusion

In this chapter I have attempted to convey an impression of the diversity of ministries which are practised apart from the traditional roles of parish clergy and lay leaders. I have also suggested why these ministries are valuable and how they provide a potentially enriching bridge between secular contexts and religious communities. Chaplains and other ministers are equipped to be translators of experience and knowledge often shattered by life experiences, organizational misunderstandings, and even antipathy between the Church and the world. As such they can provide an essential function in the meeting of the sacred and the secular, interpreting the one to the other. This is not exclusively a verbal exercise but one made possible by the minister's familiarity with liturgy and ritual. Where organizations respond to death and loss, the mimetic skills of the chaplain do much to acknowledge and give expression to the unspeakable. As human beings seek to find meaning for themselves when undergoing extraordinary events, ministers can enable actions which sustain the person even if they do not resolve the crisis.[30] While this may rely to an extent on skills used by other groups (e.g. active listening), the dimension of belief is both an implicit and explicit framework for pastoral encounters.[31] Despite the relatively small number of people engaged with these kinds of ministry, the task of researching what happens in chaplaincy and other sectors is highly complex. Even when religion is not mentioned, do those who talk to minsters outside a church building react in some way to their ontological identity and religious associations? Given the range of variables involved in teasing out this question, a large number of subjects as well as highly detailed analysis of individual interactions would be needed. Yet it is a reasonable hypothesis that the identity of minsters and their unique collection of skills engender encounters that are unusual and potentially creative. This relates not least to the questions of meaning and purpose inherent in human identity.

Ministers in non-parochial settings can appear to belong to a messy category. They mostly lack the legal framework provided by the parish and as a consequence enjoy some freedom but also suffer from a lack of

---

[30] Hille Haker, 'Narrative Ethics in Health Care Chaplaincy', in Walter Moczynski, Hille Haker and Katrin Bentele (eds), *Medical Ethics in Health Care Chaplaincy*, Münster, Lit Verlag, 2009.

[31] Sylvia Collins-Mayo, Andrew King and Lee Jones, *Faith in Action: Street Pastors Kingston Social and Spiritual Impact Project*, London, Kingston University, 2012.

coherence.[32] Perhaps this is partly why they never quite come into focus in the eyes of the Church. For those who continue to care about the Christian faith, its place in society, and the role of chaplaincy and other such ministries, this is a pity. There is a wealth of learning to be shared and spiritual insight to be gained. Hopefully, as the profile of this wide variety of ministries continues to rise, there will be a growing appreciation of why this is important for both the Church and the world.

---

[32] F. Cranmer, 'Chaplaincy and the Law', in Swift, Todd and Cobb (eds), *Handbook of Chaplaincy Studies*, pp. 79–95.

12

A collaboratively shaped ministry for the coming Church

STEPHEN PICKARD

Introduction

There is no doubt that in the last half of the twentieth century the concept of ministry underwent a transformation. No longer does the term 'ministry' simply refer to those who have been ordained in the Church of God. The undeniable fact is that the term 'ministry' now includes the ministries of the whole people of God. As a result today we are familiar with references to the 'common' or 'corporate' ministries of the Church, 'ecclesial' ministries, and ministries of the 'whole people of God'. And these ministries continue to expand in the quest for fresh expressions of being the Church in the contemporary world. Diversification and multiplication of ministries is a feature of the ecclesial landscape. But such welcome developments can easily obscure more fundamental issues for the Church's ministry; principally to what extent ministry per se can remain a genuine 'ministry of the gospel'. For good theological and practical reasons the answer to this question is, I believe, closely tied to the capacity of the Church to generate a collaboratively shaped ministry. In what follows I examine some aspects of this matter and its implications for teaching ministry, and the Church's practice of ministry in the service of mission.[1]

A Christian future for the Church's ministry

'Does the Church's ministry have a *Christian* future?' This somewhat provocative question is the underlying concern of the exploration of

---

[1] This chapter draws upon my earlier work, *Theological Foundations for Collaborative Ministry* (Farnham: Ashgate, 2009). See also David Robertson, *Collaborative Ministry: What It Is, How It Works and Why* (Oxford: Bible Reading Fellowship, 2007) for an enquiry into the practical applications of collaborative ministry.

ministry that follows. My thesis is quite simple: that in order for the Church's ministry to remain firmly Christian and authentically catholic (as a ministry of the whole Church of God), it has to be unashamedly and consistently collaborative, not only in style but more fundamentally in substance. In short a collaboratively shaped ministry is an imperative of the gospel of God and is the foundation for a genuinely Christian future for the Church's ministry. This has implications for the teaching of ministry in theological and seminary settings, and for the Church's mission and engagement with the world, as I hope to show in this chapter.

A collaboratively shaped ministry presupposes, indeed requires, a collaboratively shaped Church. As soon as I speak of a collaboratively shaped Church it is clear what kind of challenge lies before us on the matter of the doctrine and practice of ministry. Highly individualized Western societies, where autonomy is prized above all else, are hardly the breeding grounds for a communitarian culture and cooperative ethos. Indeed this is a rarity and when it does occur – for example in some business or corporate activities – it is usually driven by utilitarian and pragmatic concerns with maximizing market outcomes. In other cultures and societies, where there is a deeper recognition of the connectedness between people and the innate reliance people have upon one another for the achievement of anything worthwhile, the environment seems more fertile for a more collaborative Church and ministry. Yet even in such contexts there are significant factors that thwart the flowering of a collaborative approach to ministry. For example, in communitarian societies which remain stubbornly hierarchical, the importance of the religious ruler ought never to be underestimated. What can result is a truncated version of collaboration where all share in serving the interests of the one in authority.

Thus we have to reckon with two realities that exist in tension. On the one hand collaboration and its cousin, cooperation, appear deeply encoded into human society. Yet on the other hand competition in many and various guises (from culture to culture and person to person) is a powerful driver for human life and achievement. The philosopher Raimo Tuomela captures the tension well when he states: 'Cooperation seems to be innate, a coevolutionary adaptation based on group selection, the basic reason for this being that human beings have evolved in a group context'.[2] However, he also notes the fact that people seem disposed to 'defect, act competitively, or even act aggressively'. The result is that we live in constant tension

---

[2] Raimo Tuomela, *The Philosophy of Sociality: The Shared Point of View* (Oxford: Oxford University Press, 2007), p. 150.

between these two elemental drives. In the life of the Church we see all too clearly the influence of the competitive spirit between churches, within churches, and among leaders and the ministries of the body of Christ.

The prevailing cultural values have a far greater impact on our religious life and forms of ministry than most of us either realize or care to know. Even more troubling are the remarkable ways in which competition and misuse of power can acquire religious legitimation. Divine sanction of competition establishes the conditions for unfettered misuse of power in the supposed interests of a higher good. With a long-running rupture between clergy and laity, and the all-pervasive influence of Western individualism, it is axiomatic that competition rather than cooperation will be the basic default when it comes to the ministries of the body of Christ. In one sense the problem is not new. Paul's letters to the Corinthians would be a good place to start to see how competition endangers the cooperative venture in ministry (e.g. 1 Corinthians 1.11–17). It is no surprise that the apostle regularly appealed to the idea of being 'partners' in the gospel.

In the light of the foregoing the question with which I began, 'Does the Church's ministry have a *Christian* future?', commends itself as a critical question for the Church to wrestle with. This is all the more so today when the emphasis is increasingly on a 'mission-shaped Church'. Gearing the Church up for the challenges of new engagement and witness to the gospel in the world is of course exactly what we ought to be working hard at. The horizon of mission and the coming kingdom does embody a future-oriented eschatological dimension. All much needed. But how does all this actually work? Too often in my experience the mission enterprise (and I use that word advisedly) takes a programmatic turn with attendant focus on innovation, restructure and rationalizing of resources. However, such missional moves are little match for an essentially non-collaborative culture. As the best in the business and corporate world know, culture eats strategy for breakfast. The result is that energy is often dissipated and lethargy takes over. Clearly we must work harder and smarter with new and brighter programmes.

But what if the secret of a mission-shaped Church lies in a collaboratively shaped ministry? And if this is true, how might that impact on the teaching of ministry in seminaries, the Church's ministry and its mission in the world? In other words a mission-shaped Church might require a collaboratively shaped mission, and a collaboratively shaped mission might require a ministry that is truly collaborative and thus reflective of the character of the God who gave it birth. To reiterate, a collaborative ministry may just be an imperative of the gospel. Moreover, if ministry is to remain Christian in any meaningful sense it will have to feel and look collaborative, and be practised in a genuinely collaborative manner. If such a ministry was in evidence, the Church's prophetic witness would be greatly enhanced.

Collaboration as a gospel imperative

The proposals and claims I have made so far clearly require some theological rationale. The following text offers an important clue.[3] The apostle Paul writes: 'we, who are many, are one body in Christ, and individually we are members one of another' (Romans 12.5 nrsv). The text is familiar enough. The apostle appeals to the metaphor of the body to encourage the members of the young church at Rome to work together. He wants to help them understand that in the community of Jesus each has a part to play and each has different gifts and graces. The intention is not so much ranking or weighing the gifts (in proportion to a quantum of faith) but acknowledging that the charismata are diverse and distributed among the many members of the ecclesial body. From the apostle's point of view cooperation is a fundamental feature of ministry in the kingdom of God. We may readily agree that this is a good idea, and no doubt all those in Christian ministry aspire to such an ideal.

Certainly in chapter 12 of Romans the apostle recommends a team approach to ministry and mission. Shared power and collaborative practice seems like a gospel imperative. The Holy Spirit is the baptizer, endowing the people of God with gifts and power for ministry. This Spirit is no respecter of position or privilege. We can imagine what it means to be members of the same body. We belong to families, networks of friends, work associates. And in the Christian community we talk much of being the body of Christ and embrace the organic image of the apostle. Just as a body has arms and legs, eyes and mouth, so in the body of Christ there are diverse parts and different gifts, and we share the common charismata of the Spirit. None of us owns our gifts; they are gifts! God is the giver. For

---

[3] This discussion is also developed in Stephen Pickard, 'The Collaborative Character of Christian Ministry', *Expository Times*, vol. 121, no. 9, 2010, pp. 429–36. I am also indebted to the insightful discussion by Bernard Wannenwetsch, '"Members of One Another": Charis, Ministry and Representation: A Politico-Ecclesial Reading of Romans 12', in C. Bartholomew et al. (eds), *A Royal Priesthood: The Use of the Bible Ethically and Politically: A Dialogue with Oliver O'Donovan*, vol. 3 (Carlisle: Paternoster; Grand Rapids, MI: Zondervan, 2002), pp. 196–224.

this same reason everyone ought to act in faith and embrace the God who gives gifts and calls us to break the tapes of yesterday – 'I can't do it', or 'I'm not good enough', or 'Leave it to me, you fools', or 'I'll show them how to do it', or 'They might have a gift, but mine is more important and they will just have to learn that the hard way'. Perhaps we need a conversion to enter into the meaning of the metaphor of the body of Christ and shared ministry for mission.

But what about the unusual words tacked on by Paul: 'and you are individually members of one another'? How can I be a member *of someone else*? The apostle's metaphor of the body breaks down.[4] How do we hear this? Perhaps we hear this as a summons for the people and leaders of a congregation to actively play their part? Maybe we hear it as a call for everyone to accept their assigned role and fulfil their ministry? It also includes allowing others to be part of the community, to have a task, role and place according to their baptismal calling. However, the apostle seems to be going further. He is saying that as individuals in the body, each of us is a member of someone else. How is this the case? The apostle's main burden is to convince the church that its members need to learn to recognize the ministry of others. Even the ministries we exercise are to be bent or inclined towards the ministries of others. Indeed we belong to the other! This is startling and is it not a little intrusive? The apostle is ascribing to others the dignity of becoming part of ourselves: 'each member belongs to all the others'. Here is a radical doctrine of ministry for mission. Learning to accept the ministry of the other *towards* myself is risky and often resisted. Not only am I to see myself as belonging to someone else; my ministry also belongs to and bends towards another. In this way the other has a claim upon me. The emphasis is not on the membership of *the other person* in the body – for example, to accept this whether we like them or not or have regard for their gifts – but something more radical. Rather our ministry is tied up with the ministry of others. The ministries are bound together.

The ministries we exercise can only be ministries of the gospel of Christ as they function in relation to others. It is as if the ministries give life to each other. Furthermore the ministry I exercise only has life as it belongs to the ministry of others. The accent is thus not on ownership of ministries but on truly shared visions of ministry for the common good. And this includes representative leadership in the threefold order of bishops, priests and deacons. My ministry is called forth by the ministries of others. In this

---

[4]   Wannenwetsch, '"Members of One Another"', p. 210.

way the ministries of the ecclesial body animate each other. There are no autonomous and self-perpetuating ministries. Our life is not only hid in Christ; our ministries are hid in Christ *and in each other*. And in the body of Christ all the ministries are interdependent. All act upon one another as if *each were not their own*; not self-constituting but constituted both *from* and *towards* each other. Such features of properly ordered ministries belong to a collaborative ethos and practice. Ministry as a collaborative and coordinating activity of the Church is, upon this account, a condition of it being a ministry ordered according to the gospel.

There is of course much more that needs to be said about how such a collaborative approach to ministry reaches deep into the doctrine of God. The relationship between the doctrine of the triune God and ministry has been a strong feature of contemporary discussions of ministry.[5] Space does not permit me to develop this. However, what I have tried to show in the discussion on Romans chapter 12 is that the roots of collaboration are to be located in a particular theological anthropology. This argument needs to be extended to show that the ontology of being members 'one of another' only has weight because it is grounded in the character of God as seen in the life of Israel, Jesus and the life of the Spirit. It is not a task that can be undertaken within the constraints of this chapter.

Fostering collaborative ministry

What shifts are required in the Church's practice of ministry that will positively foster a collaborative approach to ministry? The answer to this question ought to have a direct impact on the agenda for teaching and training for ministry in the Church, and of course professional development for the Church's leadership. I believe the most fundamental issue concerns the capacity of the Church to foster a more integrative approach to the theology and practice of ministry.[6]

From fragmentation to integration

As already noted above, the prevailing culture of the individual skews human activity away from connection and integration and towards fragmentation and dissipation of energy. The environment is not conducive

---

5 For an excellent overview see Don Saines, 'Wider, Broader, Richer: Trinitarian Theology and Ministerial Order', *Anglican Theological Review*, vol. 92, no. 3, Summer 2010, pp. 511–35.

6 For an extended discussion of these moves see Stephen Pickard, 'A Christian Future for the Church's Ministry: Some Critical Moves', *Ecclesiology*, vol. 8, no. 1, 2012, pp. 33–53.

to collaborative practices. The fragmentation can be observed in the long-standing split between clergy and laity which can be traced to conflicts in local churches from the late first century. Clement of Rome, writing to the church at Corinth in the late first century, offers an example. In his attempt to deal with conflict between presbyters and other church members, and establish some well-ordered relationships, Clement managed to cement a division between priesthood and laity (*anthropos laikos*).[7] Later Tertullian, writing in the early years of the third century, was the first Western theologian to distinguish the *ordo* of the clergy from the *plebs* – what we call laity or *laos*.[8] Certainly by the time of Cyprian in the fourth century the lines had been firmly established between clerical and lay life. From this early period tensions between the two would become a feature of the Church's ordering of its life.

Notwithstanding the ancient roots of the split between clergy and laity, the modern Western preoccupation with the individual, and the more recent emphasis on professionalism, performance and success, ensures that the rupture between clergy and laity continues to deepen.[9] A counter rhetoric about collaboration is powerless to dislodge an all-pervading culture of self-interest. The various solutions offered to heal this open wound between clergy and laity usually involve diminishing either one or the other. Moreover, within a culture of individualism the increasing diversity of the ministries of the body of Christ can easily operate in an uncoordinated and incoherent manner. Under these conditions fragmentation increases rather than abates. The future of a ministry that is Christian will be one that strives for the integration of the ministries of the people of God; that does not play one off against the other; that does not exalt one ministry by diminishing the other. For the Church to pursue such a ministry will require wisdom and resilience born of a prophetic calling.

The problem of the relationship between clerical and lay ministries has not been confined to any one ecclesial tradition.[10] Over the last two

---

[7] Alexandre Faivre, *The Emergence of the Laity in the Early Church*, trans. David Smith (New York: Paulist Press, 1990), pp. 18–19.

[8] Alan Hayes, 'Christian Ministry in Three Cities of the Western Empire', in Richard Longenecker (ed.), *Community Formation in the Early Church and in the Church Today* (Peabody, MA: Hendrickson, 2002), p. 140. Only a few years earlier in 177 at Lyons, in a letter transcribed by Eusebius, there is no such distinction between clergy and laity. Rather the *kleros* ('allotted portion'), as 'class' or 'order', refers to the martyrs. See Hayes, 'Christian Ministry', p. 133.

[9] For a recent discussion of the problem of professionalism and the clergy see David Heywood, *Reimagining Ministry* (London: SCM Press, 2011), especially pp. 2–14.

[10] For further discussion see Pickard, *Theological Foundations for Collaborative Ministry*, ch. 2.

decades there have been a number of attempts to develop more integrative accounts of the ministries of the Church. In the Roman Catholic tradition Edward Hahnenberg offered a relational account of the ministries.[11] In the Anglican tradition Robin Greenwood's *Transforming Priesthood* (1994) was an important and influential attempt to address the question of the relation between lay and clerical orders.[12] His work was indebted to the emergence of Trinitarian thinking in relation to the doctrine of the Church and ministry. He developed this further in *Parish Priests: For the Sake of the Kingdom*[13] wherein his debt to a relational ontology of ministry is further honed. Greenwood proposes a relational priesthood where the parish priest as *navigator* is set 'within the *communion* of all'.[14] For Christopher Cocksworth and Rosalind Brown,[15] 'Presbyters are not a caste outside the *laos*, they are a category within the *laos*. They are members of the *laos* who are placed in a particular pastoral relation to other members of the *laos*'.[16] This emphasis upon the presbyter's particular placement among the people leads the authors to state that 'presbyters are defined by their relationship to other members of the *laos*'.[17] Following the lead of R. C. Moberly in *Ministerial Priesthood* a century earlier, the authors refer to this relationship in terms of an 'intense "for-other-ness"'.[18] Underlying this is the fact that 'Christian identity is fundamentally relational'.

In an ecclesial environment which displays a greater self-consciousness regarding mission, it is vital that more energy and investment is directed to a more integrative approach to ministries of the Church in the teaching and practice of ministry. This of course raises a question about the kinds of moves associated with a more integrative account of ministry. I believe there are a number of related shifts that are constitutive of more integrative and hence collaborative ministerial practices.

---

[11] Edward Hahnenberg, *Ministries: A Relational Approach* (New York: Crossroad, 2003). Compare Kenan Osborne, 'Envisioning a Theology of Ordained and Lay Ministry', in Susan Wood (ed.), *Ordering the Baptismal Priesthood: Theologies of Lay and Ordained Ministry* (Collegeville, MN: Liturgical Press, 2003), p. 220.

[12] Robin Greenwood, *Transforming Priesthood: A New Theology of Mission and Ministry* (London: SPCK, 1994); *Transforming Church: Liberating Structures for Ministry* (London: SPCK, 2002).

[13] Robin Greenwood, *Parish Priests: For the Sake of the Kingdom* (London: SPCK, 2009).

[14] Greenwood, *Parish Priests*, p. 98.

[15] Christopher Cocksworth and Rosalind Brown, *Being a Priest Today: Exploring Priestly Identity* (Norwich: Canterbury Press, 2002).

[16] Cocksworth and Brown, *Being a Priest Today*, p. 15.

[17] Cocksworth and Brown, *Being a Priest Today*, p. 15.

[18] Cocksworth and Brown, *Being a Priest Today*, pp. 8, 20.

From competition to cooperation

Most obviously from what has been said above, ministry needs to be regarded and practised in a cooperative rather than a competitive spirit. The ministries of the body of Christ will only have a Christian future as they focus on the 'we-mode' cooperative venture rather than prevailing 'I-mode' competitive practices.

From skills and competencies to character

The future shape of Christian ministry will necessarily have a heavy emphasis on virtue and character.[19] I say 'necessarily' because it is not possible to move in the direction of integration and organic networked ministry and cooperative ventures if the people involved are not the kinds of people who know how to work openly and joyfully with others in a higher task. In a fragmented, competitive, mechanistic environment questions of character and virtue will always be trumped by skills and competencies. Easily overlooked is the fact that innovation requires collaborative practices from emotionally intelligent agents as much if not more than highly skilled competent people. The emphasis upon skills and competences needs to be balanced by attention to matters of character and the nurture of wisdom.[20] Clearly this has implications for the teaching of ministry, formation, preparation for leadership and ongoing professional development.

From structure to energy

The shift to more integrative, cooperative and character-focused ministry provides conditions essential for the recovery of energy. In changing times when the Church is aware that the old is passing away and new ministerial challenges have to be faced in order to witness to the gospel, the danger is always one of reverting to solutions focused on new structures. Little if any attention is devoted to the sources of energy. Structure and energy are co-related such that with a new structure or an evolving structure for mission comes an equal and critical need to rediscover the energy for the work of ministry. What are the things that give life and energy to ministry; to those in ministry of one kind or another; and especially to those in holy orders? What are the sources, and how does it work practically and

---

[19] See, for example, David Brooks, *The Road to Character* (New York: Penguin, Random House, 2015).

[20] See Stephen Pickard, 'The Content of Theological Education', in Tom Frame (ed.), *Called to Minister: Vocational Discernment in the Contemporary Church* (Canberra: Barton Books, 2009), pp. 93–109.

theologically? In terms of ministry the great need is to shift the emphasis from structure to energy: while not forgetting structure, to realize the energy potential for longevity and growth in wisdom. The collaborative ideal in ministry is a way of releasing fresh energy. How and why this is the case is a critical issue for us today. A question arises in this regard: is the life I am living the life that wants to live in me?[21] This is a question about where energy comes from for personal and social engagements. Such questions that press in on ministry today cannot be answered or solved without reorientation to a collaborative ministry that involves greater integration, cooperation, character and recovery of energy. What will be the result of such a reorientation? I believe it will signal a move from an emphasis upon servant ministry to a ministry marked by friendship.

From servant to friend

Can or ought friendship function as a paradigm for collaborative ministry? Should we heed the wisdom of those who see the dangers for responsible ministry of being a friend; or those who dismiss friendship as too fragile to bear the weight of gospel ministry? There are some serious problems in too ready a dismissal of the category of friendship for ministry. Most obviously, friendship would seem to be one of the most natural and important ingredients for a truly collaborative ministry. If the truth of our lives in Christ is that we are inescapably 'one of another' then friendship is encoded into our life together. Indeed friendship is the form of our 'mode of togetherness' or of 'we-mode cooperation'. All those well-loved phrases about interdependence and mutuality require high-quality relations. Often we professionalize the relationships – sometimes for very good reason – but often this simply masks our failure to appreciate how to be a friend within relationships of unequal power relations. This raises some questions about different kinds of friendship; different kinds of relationships in which friendship occurs.

The issue of friendship has deeper theological veins which ought not be neglected. For example, where the foundation for formal ministry has a strong Christological focus the 'stand-alone' nature of ordained ministry – with an associated 'over-againstness' – more easily generates a natural 'pastoral distancing' from the people of God. In this case friendship is hardly a category that commends itself. For some it is a matter of more formal distancing as a matter of principle, while for others I have heard it said that

---

21 Parker J. Palmer, *Let Your Life Speak: Listening for the Voice of Vocation* (San Francisco, CA: Jossey-Bass, John Wiley and Sons, 2000), ch. 1.

friendship is a fragile thing and not a sound basis for the work of the gospel which requires 'partnership'. Apparently partnership and friendship are not companion concepts. In those ministries that owe more to an emphasis upon the Spirit the category of friendship may seem more congenial. However, often the idea of 'everyone a friend' can mask other dynamics to do with the misuse of power. It seems that friendship cannot be easily dismissed from a discussion of collaborative ministry precisely because the ministry I am speaking of is *Christian* and is intended to serve the gospel of the kingdom.

Certainly we cannot ignore the fact that being a friend is exactly what Jesus seemed to encourage among the first disciples. Indeed in Jesus' farewell discourses he no longer calls his disciples servants but friends (John 15.15). This descriptor is associated with living in the joy of ministry (John 15.11). Jürgen Moltmann has captured the dynamic well: 'Through the death of their friend the disciples become his friends forever. On their side they remain in the circle of his friendship when they keep his commandments and become friends *of one another*' (my italics).[22] In this dying for the disciples 'out of divine joy' and 'for those who are his ... the relationship of servants to God, the Lord, comes to an end. Through the friendship of Jesus the disciples become the free friends of God'.[23] Although it is not strictly speaking an equal relationship, nonetheless it is one of mutuality.

Friendship is not a simple matter. Friendship can be genuine and mutual notwithstanding differences between people regarding authority and responsibility. Friendship is not friendship if one person controls, dominates or is sublimated to the other. Furthermore, the more intimate the friendship, the more each person begins to recognize the remarkable otherness and mystery of the other; what one theologian has aptly termed the 'unreachable height' of the other.[24] This occurs in a shared and collaborative ministry precisely because it is based on trust and true friendship.

This means that the real art and challenge of ministry that is collaborative is to live as 'one of another' in friendship within differing levels of formal and public authority. This requires spiritual maturity. Within a differentiated structure of authority friendship takes new and demanding

---

[22] Jürgen Moltmann, *The Church in the Power of the Spirit* (London: SCM Press, 1977), p. 117.
[23] Moltmann, *Church in the Power of the Spirit*, p. 118.
[24] See the discussion in Daniel Hardy, 'Christian Affirmation and the Structure of Personal Life', in Thomas F. Torrance (ed.), *Belief in Science and Christian Life: The Relevance of Michael Polanyi's Thought for Christian Faith and Life* (Edinburgh: The Handsel Press, 1980), pp. 71–90; this reference p. 87.

forms but it is not for that reason something to be avoided. The reason is clear: it is an imperative of the gospel of Jesus. It points to the fact that friendship as well as grace is a costly thing involving humility and respect for others, particularly those who have less authority and power than oneself.

I have wondered if servant leadership discourse is a more comfortable way of depicting collaborative ministry. It certainly appears more humble and self-effacing and seems to avoid some of the dangers observed in the appeal to friendship. And there is no doubt that the New Testament in general and Jesus' ministry in particular was deeply informed by the servant/slave paradigm. Yet the servant-leader approach to ministry, linked as it often is to self-emptying and diminishment, can produce unhealthy consequences, particularly for women and marginalized groups, and perpetuate a servant–master dichotomy.[25]

Apostolic life is not exhausted by the category of servant and, as we have observed above, Jesus called his disciples friends. The category of friendship is thus not an optional extra but theologically encoded into any ministry that actualizes the gospel of Christ. Ministry as friendship means 'being fully engaged with God, others, and one's self'.[26] It is a key category for an ecclesiology of ministry that seeks a more open, integrated, cooperative and energetic discipleship for the whole people of God.[27] Perhaps friendship and servanthood are companion categories for ministry and leadership. As such they are given in and with each other. They are not simply different options that present themselves for appropriation. Nor are they simply complementary forms of ministry. Rather they inhere in each other; they too are 'one of another'. Together friendship and servanthood make ministry what it is and inform the manner in which it is undertaken. This means ministry that is genuinely Christian is forever a fragile and suffering ministry that lives by trust and joy. It is the way in which Christian disciples learn how much indeed they are 'one of another', faithfully following the pioneer ministry of Jesus Christ.

Briefly stated, the above moves involve a shift from fragmentation to integration; from competition to cooperation; from skills to character; from structure to energy; from servant to friend. Such moves are interdependent and belong to a more general shift towards a more collaborative

---

[25] See for example the critique of the servant paradigm by Edward Zaragoza, *No Longer Servants but Friends: A Theology of Ordained Ministry* (Nashville, TN: Abingdon Press, 1999), pp. 32–7.

[26] Zaragoza, *No Longer Servants*, p. 83.

[27] For a recent exposition of friendship in this context see Steve Summers, *Friendship: Exploring Its Implications for the Church in Postmodernity* (London and New York: T&T Clark, 2009).

ecclesial ministry that is rooted in the Spirit that makes us 'members one of another' (Romans 12.5).

Prospects for teaching collaborative ministry

The foregoing discussion clearly has relevance to what (and how) ministry is taught in seminaries, and other sites for ministerial and theological education. The first thing to note about the teaching of ministry is the sheer diversity across the churches of contexts and arrangements for teaching; preparation for ministry; and ongoing professional development. While traditional residential seminary models are a feature of ministry training across the globe, increasingly this is being complemented by various combinations of non-residential programmes; distance education and local formation models; and on-the-job mission training types of situations. Inevitably, local context and resources dictate what model is deployed.[28]

The second thing to note is that underlying this emergent variety in modes of ministry training and theological education lie some unresolved tensions. For example in a brief article in the *Journal of Anglican Studies* in 2005, the former Archbishop of Canterbury, Rowan Williams, referred to 'an uncomfortable awareness that theological education in the [Anglican] communion was uneven and increasingly polarised'.[29] Williams contrasted the older churches' 'Divinity School' – with its accent on academic learning topped up with professional training – with the younger, under-resourced churches' focus on the 'Bible School', where attention to basic Bible knowledge and practical skills was paramount. At the time, Williams' comments resonated with my own observations of theological education in the Anglican Communion. I had suggested that theological education had become, if it wasn't before, a contested site in Anglican identity: 'Theological institutions, precisely because they have such potential impact on the shape of such national [Anglican] identity, become sites of contest'.[30] The dispute about theological education centres around its purpose. Are such institutions 'fundamentally training institutes for

---

[28] See the discussion of theological education across the Anglican Communion in the *Journal of Anglican Studies*, vol. 6, no. 1, June 2008; Ross Kinsler (ed.), *Diversified Theological Education: Equipping All God's People* (Pasadena, CA: William Carey International University Press, 2008).

[29] Rowan Williams, 'Theological Education in the Anglican Communion', *Journal of Anglican Studies*, vol. 3, no. 2, 2005, pp. 237–9; this reference p. 237.

[30] Stephen Pickard, 'National Anglican Identity Formation Project', *Journal of Anglican Studies*, vol. 6, no. 1, 2008, pp. 7–16.

ordained and/or lay mission fieldwork? Or are they places for more rigorous theological reflection to build an informed and intelligent engagement of the church with society?'[31] In my view there has been a discernible move towards the former and an increasing impatience if not suspicion of the latter. The tensions involved in such shifts are reflected in the differing emphases placed upon skills, competencies and character attributes in ministry preparation; and in the relationship between spiritual formation and community compared to academic and scholarly engagements. The tensions come to the fore in the emergence of what might be termed a discipleship paradigm for Christian ministry.[32]

The third thing to note is that no matter what church or ministry training context we are considering, or how the tension between academy and training model is being resolved, nonetheless the horizon of mission has become the backdrop for the teaching of teaching. It would be difficult to find an institution of theological education and ministerial formation across the Christian churches that is not trying to reinvent itself with a missiological trajectory. We might go so far as to say that the future capacity to enhance the mission of God in the world is directly related to the task of theological education. On this account, theological education is not an undertaking that is self-serving and hermetically sealed from the wider Church and society; nor is it restricted to those who are preparing for or are in holy orders. Rather, theological education is an agent of mission pointing to the coming kingdom; a task in progress as the Church prays: 'Your kingdom come, your will be done on earth as it is in heaven.'

What about collaborative ministry? I would surmise that, like the mission orientation for ministry and theological education, collaboration is becoming an increasingly significant focus or horizon for the teaching of ministry. A collaborative ministry for mission is the emerging paradigm for teaching ministry. This is not surprising given the remarkable development of the ministries of the whole people of God from the mid twentieth century. This is reflected in the way ministry training and theological education has broken the traditional mould of being for men in seminaries, and accordingly embraced women as well as men; lay as well as ordained.[33] The discovery (or rediscovery) of the common ministry of the baptized has of course raised further questions about the relations between

---

[31] Pickard, 'National Anglican Identity Formation Project', p. 14.
[32] See for example, 'Intentional Discipleship and Disciple-Making', unpublished paper prepared by Anglican Communion Office, 2015, as a background paper for Anglican Consultative Council 16.
[33] See Pickard, 'Content of Theological Education', pp. 93–109.

such general ministries and the traditional ordered ministries for which the churches – in various ways – have ordained certain people. In fact the accent on collaborative ministry has provoked further critical reflection on the coherence and rationale for traditional ordered ministries. It challenges the professionalization ethos for ministry. I suspect that further critical reflection is required on such matters. The nature and character of Christian ministry remains a contested site; a deed in progress; a place for continuing innovation. A collaboratively shaped ministry will increasingly move from being an add-on subject as such and become a fundamental frame in which Christian ministry is conducted and taught.

Collaboration and the cure of souls (cura animarum)

We may be surprised and encouraged to find a theology of collaboration embedded, at least in embryo, in the 1662 Book of Common Prayer. Its origin is in Thomas Cranmer's Second Collect for Good Friday in the 1549 Prayer Book. This prayer stresses the vocation and ministry of all the faithful:

> Almighty and everlasting God, by whose Spirit the whole body of the Church is governed and sanctified; Receive our supplications and prayers, which we offer before thee for all estates of men (*sic*) in thy holy Church, that *every member* of the same, in his (*sic*) *vocation and ministry*, may truly serve thee; through our Lord and Saviour Jesus Christ, who liveth and reigneth with thee, and in the unity of the same Spirit, ever one God, world without end. Amen [my italics].

The collect presumes that all members of the Church have a vocation and ministry. The reference to 'vocation and ministry' was added in the 1549 Prayer Book and points to Lutheran influence. In this collect ministry is not restricted to the ordained; it is an inclusive term. It points to a profound mutuality in ministry wherein each ministry bestows life and energy on other ministries. This theology of ministry resonates with the apostle's words: 'So in Christ we who are many from one body, and individually members of one another.' The Reformation reconstruction of an ancient catholic collect in terms of a broader understanding of ministry is a reminder that the equally ancient idea of delegation of responsibility for the 'cure of souls' to a priest takes place within a broader framework for ministry. Such a 'cure' is in fact a representative ministry (not a vicarious one), and exactly how that responsibility is entered into in relation to the whole body of Christ remains a work in progress and one subject to critical re-examination as new situations and challenges arise.

It seems that a collaborative approach to Christian ministry is not only a useful practical way of getting things done to advance the kingdom of God but also an imperative of the gospel that the Church bears witness to. Collaborative ministry is 'first nature'; the most natural pattern of practice for the ministries of the body of Christ. The Church's ministry will have a genuinely Christian future only to the extent that it undertakes a critical reappraisal. I have suggested in this chapter some lines of enquiry which might assist such a review. In this respect I note that the phrase *ecclesia semper reformanda* (the Church is always to be reformed) also applies to ministry: *ministeria semper reformanda*. This will require a new baptism for ministry for 'unless a grain of wheat falls into the earth and dies, it remains just a single grain; but if it dies, it bears much fruit' (John 12.24 NRSV).

13

Psychotherapy and ministry

ROBERT ROBERTS AND RYAN WEST

Early Christian ministry among rivals

Christian ministry grew up in a Hellenized, pluralistic world of soul-therapies, philosophies of life with associated practices that claimed to cure you of your anxieties, your self-defeating behaviours, your dysfunctional relationships, and confusions in your self-understanding. Stoicism, Epicureanism, Scepticism, (neo)-Platonism, Cynicism and other philosophies of life were schools of disciplined, guided self-transformation that would put you in touch with your true nature and shape you into the person you were meant to be. Consider Stoicism and Epicureanism as just two selected examples.

The Stoics would tell you that you are essentially a rational creature placed in an orderly, rational universe, and that your problems stem from your belief that what you call misfortune (illness, death, injury, ostracism, poverty and the like) is evil and bad for you. This false belief is embodied in your emotional reactions to such events in your life – for example, anger, anxiety, grief, terror and despair. These psychological sources of misery are false value-judgements that enshrine your failure to see the big picture, the ultimately harmonious way that all such events fit into the orderly ongoing of the universe – the will of God. Your emotions are symptoms of the myopia begotten of your seeing the world from the private vantage point of your own little life. To be a calm, rational, ideally formed, healthy and happy human being is to conform your mind to the mind (that is, the rational order) of the universe by learning to see all the events in your life, including the ones that you used to regard as misfortunes, as simply small contributions to the great harmonious rationality of the universe. The virtue you acquire by such discipline is *apatheia* – not what we would call apathy, exactly, but the emotional serenity of seeing the world from a God's-eye viewpoint. You are a being who is capable of adopting the viewpoint of the universe. That is your essential nature, so that when you shape yourself, by long cognitive and behavioural discipline of your mind/heart, in such a way that you track perfectly the mind of the universe, then you become what you were meant to be, a child of God.

The Epicureans had a different take on human nature. According to their psychotherapy, you are essentially a centre for conscious pleasure and your proper destiny is to live as pleasantly as possible. Your troubles in life come from two basic sources: fear of death and misunderstanding of how to maximize pleasure. We fear many things and our fears are our misery, but behind them all is the fear of death, and behind the fear of death is the belief in God. So one part of the Epicurean therapy is to teach you a new theology: the gods don't care about you; they have no interest in what you do or don't do. Another part is to realize that there's nothing to fear about death. You should memorize and tell yourself again and again that *where I am, death is not; and where death is, I am not; therefore death is nothing to me.* Also, you seek pleasure in counterproductive ways: by falling in love, by eating and drinking too much and insisting on luxuries, by seeking power for yourself. The remedy for the miseries that such activities bring on is to keep your aspirations low and simple: learn to enjoy simple, easily acquired food and drink and consume them in moderation; eschew personal power and fame and pursue low-profile friendships; avoid falling in love. This revision of your tastes from the extravagant to the simple is Epicurean virtue and the path to a meaningful, fulfilled and happy life.

Two excellent sources of information on these ancient psychotherapies are Pierre Hadot, *Philosophy as a Way of Life* (Blackwell, 1995) and Martha Nussbaum, *The Therapy of Desire* (Princeton University Press, 1994).

The ministry of the early Church arose among this welter of competing therapies and offered yet a different – indeed, *very* different – understanding of human nature, ideal of its proper functioning, explanation of the nature and sources of human misery and dysfunction, and ways to recovery. It proposed that human beings are, most fundamentally, *children*, where to be a child is to belong to somebody who loves and cherishes you and expects to exercise benevolent supervision over you, and expects you to return his love, within your limited capacities, by loving obedience to his supervision. Thus, in the Christian therapy human nature is defined as essentially related, in very 'personal' ways, to the divine. Being human is no more thinkable apart from God than being a child is from parenthood. Human nature is not divorceable from God, and divorce is the basic nature and source of human dysfunction and misery.

The theological term for this divorce from God is 'sin', sin being disobedience and lovelessness. The prescription for recovery is even more distinctive: God has reconciled the world to himself in the life, death and resurrection of Jesus Christ, who is the incarnation of the Second Person of the divine Trinity. The Son, representing all the other, wayward and self-divorced children, has taken their dysfunction on himself, and proleptically reconciled them to God, healing their fundamental disorder. The pastor-therapist practises his or her therapy by proclaiming this event of healing and overseeing its assimilation by the patients. The assimilation is fostered by various practices such as the preaching and hearing of God's word, prayer, fasting and other renunciation, study and discussion of God's word, and service to those in need. The practices are meant to assimilate, instantiate and bring into the actual personality of the patients the healing that has already been accomplished by the Son. The traits of character that are to emerge from this therapy are faith, hope, love, compassion, humility, gratitude, forgivingness, forbearance, generosity, perseverance, boldness and truthfulness, among others. These virtues are the foundation of proper psychological functioning according to the Christian framework. Each of these Christian virtues is distinct from any possible non-Christian counterpart virtue (say, Stoic generosity or Socratic humility) by its reference to God the Father and the Son's work on his behalf and on behalf of the Church.

Contemporary therapies in Christian perspective

One might think that in the contemporary world of scientific psychology psychotherapy would have settled down to a single consensus on the four elements of a psychotherapy: the view of human nature and of the character of psychological dysfunction, an ideal of psychological well-being or mental health, and the right way to bring people from dysfunction to proper function. But a perusal of the table of contents of the latest (10th) edition of Raymond Corsini's (now with Danny Wedding) *Current Psychotherapies* (Cengage Learning, 2014) reveals that psychotherapy is as pluralistic as ever, with chapters on psychoanalytic (Freudian), Adlerian, client-centred (Rogerian), rational emotive (Albert Ellis), cognitive, behavioural, gestalt, and several other 'models'. Something similar can be observed in Siang-Yang Tan's *Counseling and Psychotherapy: A Christian Perspective* (Baker Academic, 2011), which surveys ten psychotherapies and offers a Christian perspective on each one. Here we will again describe just two out of the many rival therapies.

Client-centred or Rogerian psychotherapy says that most of the common psychological problems that people face, such as obsessive-compulsive disorder, anxiety, eating disorders, post-traumatic stress disorder, problem and pathological gambling, depression, suicidal tendencies, medication adherence in schizophrenia, and the sorts of tendencies that land people in the correctional or criminal justice system[1] can be addressed by a psychotherapist who listens empathically as the client talks about his or her problems. The therapist wants to convey to the sufferer a total unreserved acceptance, an 'unconditional positive regard' that (without being explicit) communicates to the client: you can drop all artificiality and simply be yourself in my presence. The theory behind this practice is that our psychological problems stem from a lack of congruence between our self as it originally and deeply and individually is, and the self that we have built up in response to social expectations. This latter, artificial self is the one that we try to present to the world, and it may well be our self as we ourselves currently understand and feel it, despite the misfit and falsity of it. We have this artificial self because our parents, our friends, our workplace, our university, the advertisers, our society, have implicitly laid down some conditions of worth – conditions that we have to meet to be accepted and successful as we desire to be. We must be slim, beautiful, young-looking, productive, clever, independent, gregarious or whatever. These conditions of worth have been imposed on us without regard to our 'organismic valuing process' – our natural and individual way of valuing. Down deep we may not care to be productive, clever and independent, but since we want to be accepted and successful, we not only conform externally to these conditions of our worth but also 'introject' them – internalize them as our own – so that they become part of our self-understanding. And because of the persisting discrepancy between our original natural self and this artificially imposed and introjected social self, we are deeply dissatisfied with ourselves, and our dissatisfactions come out in the emotions and behaviours of various disorders like the ones listed at the beginning of this paragraph.

When our problems become intolerable, we may go to a therapist for help. If the client-centred therapist is congruent enough to give us the feeling that we can really reveal ourselves without being judged or condemned – that no matter what we reveal, he or she will listen with genuine, accepting, warm, empathic, personal interest – then we may begin to get in touch with our

---

[1] Siang-Yang Tan (2011), *Counseling and Psychotherapy: A Christian Perspective* (Grand Rapids, MI: Baker Academic), p. 143.

organismic valuing process and to dissociate from the artificial social accretions that we have, until now, taken to be our real self and values. Thus liberated from our introjected self, our psychological problems will tend to fall away.

The four dimensions of client-centred psychotherapy are these:

1 True human nature is the organismic valuing process: each of us is an individual with our own dispositions of valuing, with a need for our own special values to be satisfied.

2 The basis of the various kinds of psychological dysfunction is the inauthenticity that we exemplify when our deep valuing needs are at odds with our way of living and thinking and feeling.

3 The aim of proper human development, and thus of therapy, is the virtue of congruence: that we be in touch with our organismic valuing process so that the values we think and feel that we espouse are really *our own* values.

4 The prescription for making the transition from incongruence to congruence and well-being is an encounter with the unconditional positive regard of a congruent person who enters with empathic understanding into our internal frame of reference as we talk through our problems.

Theologians have sometimes suggested that this schema is a sketch of the Christian gospel and a road map for ministry,[2] and for a while in the twentieth century it was very influential among pastors.[3] According to this interpretation, incongruence is what the Church has called sin; the organismic valuing process is the *imago dei* (the image of God in the human person); introjected conditions of worth is the orientation towards justification by works; and the communication of unconditional positive regard by a congruent therapist is redemption. Rogers' theory and practice have been attractive to some pastors because unconditional positive empathic regard resembles, in some ways, the non-judgemental attitude commanded in the Sermon on the Mount and the gracious non-self-regarding love commanded in 1 Corinthians 13. But in the Christian tradition, the non-judgemental attitude crucially presupposes the pervasiveness of sin, and the love that Paul commends is in imitation of God's love. Neither sin nor God has any place in Rogers' philosophy of life, and these omissions make all the concepts of his psychotherapy work together in

---

[2] See T. Oden (1978), 'The Theology of Carl Rogers', in *Kerygma and Counseling: Toward a Covenant Ontology for Secular Psychotherapy* (New York: Harper & Row), pp. 83–113.

[3] See E. Brooks Holifield (2005), *A History of Pastoral Care in America: From Salvation to Self-Realization* (Eugene, OR: Wipf & Stock).

a way very different from and incompatible with Christian theology and ministry. The Rogerian philosophy tends to promote a rather narcissistic preoccupation with one's own needs rather than a loving willingness to put the neighbour's interests before one's own (Phil. 2.3–4), and if anyone is worshipped in the Rogerian scheme, it is the self.[4]

The mistake here is to confuse distant analogies with identities. Sin *is* no doubt a lack of congruence – of the sinner's will with the will of God, of the sinner's mode of existence with his or her proper nature – and sanctification is the corresponding approximation to congruence. The pastor may find helpful Rogers' stress on empathic listening if he or she disregards the theory behind it – though one hardly needs the encouragement of Rogers or any psychotherapist to see the pastoral value of empathic listening. As we will see, the empathic listening of the client-centred therapist is in fact effective in resolving the kind of problems for which people seek therapy.

Our second example of a modern psychotherapy is the rational emotive therapy of Albert Ellis. RET or REBT (rational emotive behaviour therapy) is a major variant of cognitive, or cognitive-behavioural, therapy. It stands in pretty stark contrast with client-centred therapy. Whereas Rogers tries to empathize his clients out of their problems, Ellis tries to argue them out of their problems. Ellis thinks empathy is overrated, and is more likely to make fun of his clients' foibles and bad mental habits, calling them by funny names like 'awfulizing', 'musturbation', 'catastrophizing' and 'can't-stand-it-itis', though he does think it's important for the therapist to have a good relationship with the client. Rogers is not interested in conveying his theory to the client, and certainly doesn't explain it to the client in the therapy session; indeed, the theory, if communicated, might be taken to lay another 'condition of worth' on the client. By contrast, Ellis is happy to make a discussion of RET's rationale a part of therapy sessions; he wants clients to think about, and treat themselves, in terms of RET's theory of therapeutic change. What is that theory?

According to RET, dysfunctional emotions such as depression, anxiety, crippling guilt, shame, resentment and anger, along with their behavioural manifestations and the consequences these have for relationships with others and the effects of these bad relationships on one's happiness, result from irrational beliefs. So the right way to address all of these kinds of psychological dysfunction is to attack the irrational beliefs and to help the client think rationally. Common sense may tell us that we get angry because people do

---

4   See Paul Vitz (1995), *Psychology as Religion: The Cult of Self-Worship* (Grand Rapids, MI: Eerdmans).

bad things to us or neglect to do the things they ought, that we feel ashamed because of our failures and defects, that we are anxious because of all the bad things that might happen to us, that we feel guilty because of all the bad things we have done, and so forth for all the emotions that disrupt our lives and lead to behaviour that makes us unhappy. According to RET this 'common sense' is itself distorted thinking. The truth is that emotions do not arise directly in response to situations and circumstances, but are always mediated by what we *believe* about those situations.

For example, if you feel ashamed of yourself because your father was a great man and you're reaching middle age and are still trying to find your 'calling' in life, Ellis will attack your belief that you 'must' equal your father in career success. If you're depressed because your husband is such a nag and won't stop regardless of what you do, Ellis will try to show you that there are lots of worse things than a nagging husband, and your catastrophizing over his demands is due to your can't-stand-it-itis – your belief that it's terrible and intolerable to have a nagging husband. If you feel anxious because your wife seems to have lost interest in you and has inadvertently left little clues in her belongings that she's seeing someone else, Ellis will try to disabuse you of the belief that it would be 'awful' to be abandoned for another man. And if you're quite cut up because you want to be a faithful disciple of Jesus Christ and find yourself backsliding again and again, Ellis will try to convince you that your belief that your fulfilment as a person depends on your being perfect as your heavenly Father is perfect is irrational.

The last example raises red flags for the Christian. Ellis's general strategy with beliefs that lead to 'down' emotions is: lower your standards; lower standards are more rational. Be content with a career inferior to your father's; don't insist on having a perfect husband; having an adulterous wife is nothing to get upset about. We think that Christianity prescribes something more paradoxical: we *are* called to be perfect as our heavenly Father is perfect; but we are also reconciled to God in spite of our imperfections by our perfect Lord Jesus Christ of whose body we are now members by his grace. Simply to lower our standards, to make do with something less because high aspirations cause pain, is what the Church has come to call 'spiritual sloth'. It is, by Christian lights, not irrational to desire perfection, but part of what it is to be faithful. Ellis is a pragmatic hedonist. He thinks the purpose of life is to live as long and pleasantly as possible, and that beliefs that tend to generate emotional pain are to be unmasked as irrational. Some Christian beliefs do generate emotional pain for sinners like us, and we don't conclude that they are irrational.

It's hard to object to rationality, but the point to see is that the word can be used to foist an agenda. When it comes to ethics and spirituality, rationality becomes a contested concept. What counts as rational from a hedonist's perspective may typify irrationality from a Christian's, and vice versa. It is possible, perhaps, to imagine a Christian rational therapy, a therapy governed by a distinctively Christian concept of rationality.[5]

The effectiveness of psychotherapy

Abundant evidence suggests that psychotherapies are effective against the kinds of problems that draw people to therapists. About every decade since 1978, Allen Bergin and Michael Lambert[6] have published a meta-analytical study of the literature reporting outcome studies for the various psychotherapies. Their studies have consistently shown that the therapies are effective. Lambert summarizes:

> Providers as well as patients can be assured that a broad range of therapies, when offered by skillful, wise, and stable therapists, are likely to result in appreciable gains for the client, including a return to normal functioning . . .

In some kinds of case, psychotherapy is more effective than medication:

> Only 25% of depressed psychotherapy patients relapse, while 50% of those who receive antidepressant medication do so.[7]

At the same time, the studies seem to show that there is surprisingly little difference in effectiveness among the various therapies:

> Although research continues to support the efficacy of those therapies that have been rigorously tested, differences in outcome between various forms of therapy are not as pronounced as might have been expected or hoped for. Behavioral therapy, cognitive therapy, and eclectic mixtures of these methods have shown marginally superior outcomes to traditional verbal therapies in several studies on specific disorders, but this is by no means the general case. When this superiority is evidenced, the results are often

---

5   A more detailed account of client-centred and rational emotive therapy, as well as four other contemporary therapies, with extensive Christian evaluation, can be found in Robert Roberts, *Taking the Word to Heart: Self and Other in an Age of Therapies* (Grand Rapids, MI: Eerdmans, 1995).
6   Most recently, Lambert alone: see Michael Lambert (2013), 'The Efficacy and Effectiveness of Psychotherapy', in *Bergin and Garfield's Handbook of Psychotherapy and Behavior Change*, 6th edn (Somerset, NJ: John Wiley & Sons), pp. 169–218.
7   Lambert, 'Efficacy and Effectiveness', p. 205.

diminished by the extent to which researchers do not enthusiastically and carefully implement alternative treatments.[8]

This is a surprising result because, as our examples of both modern and ancient psychotherapies have illustrated, the therapies differ rather starkly in their explanations of psychological dysfunction and the strategies, based on those explanations, for restoring proper function. They can't all be right about the basis of our problems, and yet the therapeutic strategies based on their theories all seem to work, and work with roughly equal success. The studies are all about modern psychotherapies, of course, but they lead us to speculate that probably the Stoic, neo-Platonic, Epicurean and Sceptic therapies also worked pretty well.

How can the therapies be so conceptually and strategically diverse, and yet resemble one another so much in effect? The answer that seems to be emerging is that their effectiveness is due, not so much to the theory and the related specifics of treatment, as to factors that are common to all or many of the therapies. Lambert comments on one of the most important common factors:

> Positive affective relationships and positive interpersonal encounters, that characterize most psychotherapy and are common across therapies, still loom large as stimulators of patient improvement. It should come as no surprise that helping others deal with depression, anxiety, confusion, inadequacy, and inner conflicts, as well as helping them form viable relationships and meaningful directions for their lives, can be greatly facilitated in a therapeutic relationship that is characterized by trust, understanding, acceptance, kindness, warmth, and human consideration.[9]

What do we mean by saying that a therapy 'works'? What 'effect' is in question in the 'effectiveness' of psychotherapies? Effectiveness in this context is success in correcting or mitigating the psychological problems for which people seek therapy. Just to have a distinct name for it, let us call this 'therapeutic effectiveness'. It's the kind that is being measured in the many outcome studies that Bergin and Lambert aggregated.

A literature arose in the last half of the twentieth century that complained about another kind of effect that some psychotherapy has on people. We have noted, in considering our examples of psychotherapies, old and new, that they are contestable philosophies of life. Each one that we looked at promotes a particular understanding of human nature

---

[8] Lambert, 'Efficacy and Effectiveness', p. 205.
[9] Lambert, 'Efficacy and Effectiveness', p. 206.

and (sometimes) the nature of the universe, along with a conception of well-being, of virtue, of the good life for a human being. The Stoics taught that people are rational centres of consciousness capable of conforming their minds to the rational order of the universe, and that well-being for us is *apatheia* – freedom from emotional disturbance. Epicurus taught that we are centres of pleasure and pain, that the gods have no interest in us, and that the good life is the maximization of pleasure and minimization of pain. Rogers taught that we are highly individualistic valuers in a world very apt to impose its values on us, that we are prone to cooperate by introjecting those alien values, and that our well-being consists in congruence between our living (feeling, thinking, acting) and our own organismic valuing process. And Ellis taught that we are beings whose emotions are driven by our beliefs, and that well-being is having only rational beliefs – that is, ones that are compatible with a long and pleasant life. And that literature that arose in the last half of the twentieth century pointed out that psychotherapy is very effective at worming whatever philosophy of life it's promoting into the hearts and minds of people who come into contact with it. Roberts sums up some of that literature:

> Among the pernicious traits that various therapies are accused of fostering are 'narcissism' (an inordinate preoccupation with one's own feelings, experiences, and satisfactions, and in particular one's self-esteem; and a corresponding neglect of duties and what is outside the self), individualism (an undervaluing of community, of social interdependence and bearing one another's burdens), consumerism (a traditionless, empty self that needs to be 'filled up' with things and experiences), emotivism (thinking oneself to be the source of one's values), egoism (making self-interest one's chief motive), instrumentalism (seeing one's behavior towards others as chiefly a means of shaping or controlling them), victimism (the inclination to blame others, or social forces, for one's problems), irresponsibilism (the belief that nobody is responsible for anything), and atheism.[10]

Let us call this kind of effectiveness 'spiritual effectiveness'. So psychotherapies have two kinds of effectiveness: they tend to help people with the problems that drive them to therapy, and they tend to affect their spiritual understanding of themselves, of other people and the meaning of their life.[11]

---

[10] Robert Roberts (2001), 'Psychotherapy and Christian Ministry', *Word and World* 21, p. 44.

[11] A sampling of the moral and spiritual critique of psychotherapies includes Philip Rieff (1966), *The Triumph of the Therapeutic: Uses of Faith after Freud* (New York: Harper & Row); Christopher Lasch (1979), *The Culture of Narcissism: American Life in an Age of Diminishing Expectations* (New York: W. W. Norton); Alasdair MacIntyre (2007 (1981)), *After Virtue: A*

Pastoral response

If a positive affective relationship and interpersonal encounter with a therapist who inspires trust by manifesting understanding, acceptance, kindness and warmth loom large as factors in the effectiveness of therapy, the professional therapist will have in principle no edge on the pastor as counsellor in one important dimension of therapeutic effectiveness. Other common factors are the client's natural support system (family, friends, church), the client's character (self-discipline, powers of insight, emotional dispositions), the client's perception of the therapist as an expert, the client's expectation of being helped, the client's own articulation of his or her problem, wise advice from the therapist and the very fact that the client has taken enough responsibility for his or her problem to ask for help. These and other common factors, too, seem within reach of the pastor–parishioner relationship or, more likely, the professional Christian counsellor or even the lay Christian counsellor.[12] The pastor will of course be concerned not to do his or her parishioner spiritual harm, and will indeed be eager to contribute something positive to the parishioner's spiritual development. We take the remainder of this essay to sketch a psychotherapy that would tend to have a distinctively Christian spiritual effectiveness.

The most developed psychology/spirituality in the New Testament is found in the letters of the apostle Paul (treating what is Pauline as including Colossians and Ephesians). In a number of his letters Paul develops a conception of the good and spiritually healthy human life as turning on accessing and actualizing a personality that has been created for and in believers by virtue of the incarnation, death and resurrection of Jesus Christ. 'For we are his workmanship, created in Christ Jesus for good [actions], which God prepared beforehand, that we should walk in them' (Eph. 2.10).[13] This personality, which exists in the believer (or the believer exists in) whether or not he or she manifests it in individual behaviour and attitude, is called the new self (or nature, or humanity:

Study in Moral Theory, 3rd edn (London: Duckworth); Robert Bellah (1985), *Habits of the Heart: Individualism and Commitment in American Life* (New York: Harper & Row); Paul Vitz (1995), *Psychology as Religion: The Cult of Self-Worship* (Grand Rapids, MI: Eerdmans); and Philip Cushman (1995), *Constructing the Self, Constructing America: A Cultural History of Psychotherapy* (Boston, MA: Addison-Wesley).

[12] Tan, *Counseling and Psychotherapy*, pp. 399–400.

[13] Unless otherwise noted, all Scripture quotations in this chapter are taken from the Revised Standard Version (RSV).

anthropos, Eph. 2.15; Col. 3.10) and is characterized by a set of virtues: hope (Rom. 5.5), love (Gal. 5.22), peace (1 Cor. 13.4), patience (Col. 3.12), kindness (Gal. 5.22), faithfulness (Gal. 5.22), gentleness (Col. 3.12), self-control (Gal. 5.22), humility (Eph. 4.2) and others. We give just one reference for each virtue; there are many others.

The new self stands in contrast and opposition to a dysfunctional personality that Paul names the flesh (Rom. 7.5; 8.9; 13.14), or body of sin (Rom. 6.6), or old self (Rom. 6.6; Eph. 4.22; Col. 3.9). This self, Paul tells us, died with Jesus Christ on the cross (Rom. 6.6); for us it was buried with Christ by baptism (Rom. 6.4). The old self too is characterized by a set of concerns, desires, behaviours, and patterns of thought and emotion: greed (Col. 3.5), malice (Rom. 1.29), envy (Gal. 5.20, 26), strife (2 Cor. 12.20), deceit (Rom. 1.29), gossip (Rom. 1.29; 2 Cor. 12.20), slander (Rom. 1.30), enmity to God (Rom. 1.30), insolence (Rom. 1.30), arrogance (Rom. 1.30), pretentiousness or pride (Rom. 1.30), jealousy (2 Cor. 12.20), anger (Gal. 5.19) and many others. Paul's message to the believers on whom he is practising his special brand of psychotherapy is that the personality expressed in these behaviours and emotions – the old self – is dead, having been put to death with Christ on the cross.

But it is evident that while it is dead it is not gone; and though believers are in possession of the new self, they very often fail to manifest it in actual emotion and action. The Christian life is standardly a battle for the supremacy of the new self over the old. Paul's words for this battle strongly suggest that the people whose healing is in question are active participants in the process by which the new self comes to dominate and replace the old, but several of the dozen or so verbs that denote this species of action indicate a kind of letting or allowing. He speaks of *yielding* our members to God as instruments of righteousness rather than to sin as instruments of wickedness (Rom. 6.13). '*Let* the peace of Christ rule in your hearts' (Col. 3.15) and '*let* the word of Christ dwell in you richly' (Col. 3.16). He also uses the more active metaphor 'walk': 'We were buried therefore with him by baptism into death, so that as Christ was raised from the dead by the glory of the Father, we too might walk in newness of life' (Rom. 6.4; see Gal. 5.16; Eph. 5.8; Col. 2.6). He uses clothing metaphors: we are to 'take off' our old self and 'put on' our new one, as though the new self is there like a garment to don when we will (Eph. 4.22–24). A violent metaphor is that of slaughter: 'If by the Spirit you kill the deeds of the body, you will live' (Rom. 8.13b, my translation; see Col. 3.5). And finally, there are the attention verbs, 'consider', 'set the mind on', 'give thanks' and 'rejoice':

So you also must consider yourselves dead to sin and alive to God in Christ Jesus.

(Rom. 6.11)

Those who live according to the flesh set their minds on the things of the flesh, but those who live according to the Spirit set their minds on the things of the Spirit.

(Rom. 8.5)

Give thanks in all circumstances . . .

(1 Thess. 5.18)

Rejoice in the Lord always . . .

(Phil. 4.4)

The therapy we envisage has two major parts. The Pauline therapist will seek to help the suffering Christian make connections between his or her presenting problem and the traits of the old self. Some of these connections will be quite direct (anger, for example), while others may be indirect (the emotional consequences of greed). The 'theory' of Pauline psychotherapy will be a rich conceptual fabric connecting the threads of the vices that Paul mentions with the psychological difficulties that drive people to therapy. To mitigate the apparent judgemental harshness of some of the Pauline language, the therapist will point out that sin is not just an individual thing, but an oceanic ethos in which we live and move and have our being. We're all in this together, but in the Church we've been given the blessing of new life in Christ.

The second major part of Pauline therapy will be a battery of ways that the sufferer, as a member of the body of Christ, implements access to the new self. The dozen or so Pauline verbs will guide the construction of this battery, and the whole battery will be persistently conceptualized in terms of the old self and the new self in Christ. So the sufferer will be constantly reminded that his or her life is parasitic on that of the living Lord. For example, one mode of access is indicated by the metaphor of walking (*peripatein*). This is one of the most 'behavioural' of the Pauline concepts, suggesting that one way to put on the new self is simply to *act as though* the new self is one's actual self. A principle of behaviour therapy is that proper motivation and emotion *follow* behaviour suggestive of them. The pastor or Christian counsellor might enter into a contract with the sufferer for such behaviour. Another strategy is suggested by the notion of *setting one's mind on* (*phronein*) the things of the Spirit of Christ: for example, and perhaps in connection with the behavioural contract, the counsellor assigns the reading of a spiritual biography, or fellowship with a parishioner who is more advanced in the Christian life.[14]

---

[14] We've been able to sketch Pauline therapy only in the barest outline. For a much fuller account, from which some of this final section is derived, see the chapter by Robert Roberts: 'Outline of Pauline Psychotherapy', in Mark McMinn and Timothy Phillips (eds) (2001), *Care for the Soul: Exploring the Intersection of Theology and Psychology* (Downers Grove, IL: IVP), pp. 134–63.

14

Leadership studies and ministry

KEITH LAMDIN

The Church's engagement with leadership studies and training

Although people have thought and written about leadership from the days of Aristotle, the fascination with the subject as a distinct focus of study and training became an established area after the Second World War. In the UK, in the early days, one of the most influential writers and teachers was John Adair,[1] who famously taught that leaders have to attend to the **task**, to the **individual** needs of the people led, as well as to the maintenance of the **group**. These three concerns need to be kept in mind all the time. This threefold focus has remained a constant teaching tool for over 50 years.

Leadership has been studied through a number of lenses – philosophical, sociological, theological – although much of the contemporary academic literature comes from the business schools and reflects, more generally, studies of practice. Many of these have become best-sellers in the airport lounges inhabited by leaders of multinational companies and are referenced throughout this chapter.[2] There has also been discussion about the relationship between what we call 'organizations' and 'institutions'. My own view is that we use 'organization' when we think of behaviour and structures, and we use 'institution(al)' when we are thinking about some of the assumptions and values embedded in any organization.

---

[1] John Adair has published many books. See for example *How to Grow Leaders: The Seven Key Principles of Effective Leadership Development* (2005), Kogan Page, London; or *The Inspirational Leader: How to Motivate, Encourage and Achieve Success* (2003), Kogan Page, London.

[2] R. Bolden, B. Hawkins, J. Gosling, S. Taylor (2011), *Exploring Leadership: Individual, Organizational, and Societal Perspectives*, Oxford University Press, Oxford; B. Carroll, J. Ford, S. Taylor (2015), *Leadership, Contemporary Critical Perspectives*, Sage, London; S. Western (2013), *Leadership: A Critical Text* (2nd edn), Sage, London.

A very crude distinction has been made between managing and leading. Managing is seen as the capacity of an organization to deliver effectively its chosen objectives. Leading is seen as the ability to realize that objectives need changing and to persuade members of the organization to be content to change them. Leadership as an idea has flourished in a world that is seen to be in a state of rapid and unending change. Driven mainly by scientific enquiry and technological developments, human life is thought to be changing all the time. Solutions and objectives that worked last year no longer do. Leaders, realizing that old solutions no longer work, dream up new ones and persuade people to change.[3]

In more recent years the global context and the sense of ever-increasing change has cemented 'leadership' and 'change' together.[4] Whether you are running a business or a local church many of the issues are the same. Change is all around, and rather than it being thought of as decay, it is promoted as innovative, exciting and full of potential. What is more, change is here to stay and unstoppable, whether it be technology, social media, the ebb and flow of global markets, or the ways in which women and men understand themselves. In such turmoil of change, leadership is now spoken about as the distinctive capacity to read the current context, be ahead of the game, and shape a vision that inspires people to create a new future. This would be as much in the mind of a newly enthroned bishop as of a new cabinet minister, head teacher, vicar or chief executive. They might use different words but the ideas would be the same. A bishop might express his or her understanding of leadership as: 'How can I ensure that this diocese is infused with vision for the Kingdom and is alert to reality, finely honed to adapt to change, well managed so that the stewardship of resource, physical and human, is best used to meet the challenges of the gospel?'

---

[3] There is an assumption here that leadership implies seniority in the organization – leadership is the same as being in charge. However, it is worth noting the important work by Donna Ladkin who distinguishes between being in charge, which she calls headship, and leadership, which needs to be active at every level of the organization and not just in senior positions. See D. Ladkin (2015), 'Leadership, Management and Headship: Power, Emotion and Authority', in *Leadership: Contemporary Critical Perspectives*, Sage, London.

[4] R. E. Quinn (1996), *Deep Change: Discovering the Leader Within*, Jossey-Bass, San Francisco; J. P. Kotter (1996), *Leading Change*, Harvard Business School Press, Boston; P. Senge et al. (1999), *The Dance of Change: The Challenges of Sustaining Momentum in Learning Organisations*, Nicholas Brealey, London.

Leadership – religious and secular

Many of the current narratives about leadership are shaped in the worlds of industry, commerce and the free market, areas of life that are distinctly secular. For commercial organizations to thrive and survive, they need to be adept at finding their place in the market, and winning and keeping customers and turning in a profit. Even the language of servant leadership,[5] which undoubtedly has its origins deep in the Judeo-Christian tradition, is used to justify a leadership set of behaviours that delivers a workforce that is motivated and successful, and can show benefit on 'the bottom line'.

This religious–secular dialogue has been taken up in several ways. In the first place, the leaders of secular organizations who have happened to be practising Christians have wanted to bring their secular practices into the life of the Church. Their experience of church has been so frustrating that they think it needs simple, decent management practices brought to bear to make it a better environment.[6] Some of them have made substantial donations and set up trusts to sponsor learning about leadership from their world of commerce and industry. They have thought that the churches would be better equipped to be obedient to the gospel imperative if they were willing to learn from the 'secular'. They understand that the Church may have eternal purposes within the providence of God, but see it as a human organization or institution, which needs to be respected and effective when measured by contemporary standards of leadership, management, capability and success. 'What is the good of a church which is failing?' they might say. And when asked what they mean by 'failing' they would point to lack of vision, poor administration, falling church attendance in a population that is growing, as well as a mindless belief that if people keep on doing what they have been doing for the last generation then God will bless it. Doing the same thing and expecting different outcomes, they say, is one of the signs of madness.

At the same time, there has been a growing number of church leaders who have in their own way looked over the wall at the secular world, and wanted to adopt many of these leadership learnings. They have seen the Church as an organization that needs to thrive in the marketplace of diverse religious and spiritual consuming.[7] Such adoption and baptizing

---

5   See the Robert E. Greenleaf Center for Servant Leadership: <https://www.greenleaf.org/>.
6   This has been the driving energy behind organizations such as Modem: <http://www.modemuk.org>, and the Foundation for Church Leadership; see also <www.teal.org.uk>.
7   For a fascinating study of the churches in America see J. Micklethwait and A. Wooldridge (2009), *God Is Back: How the Global Rise of Faith Is Changing the World*, Penguin, London.

of the secular has been easiest in the religious contexts of the United States, where the growth of the megachurches has required levels of sophistication in leadership and management not often needed in the local church in the United Kingdom. This new church world is coloured by the need for vision, strategic plans and success criteria that stand some chance of being measured. These church leaders know that in their congregations are many senior executives from the world of business, and they talk with them and learn from them. They recruit them to their boards, councils and fundraising activities, and seek advice from them as they structure and lead their churches. They find the secular measures of success easy to translate into church measures: numbers of new converts, growth in commitment and discipleship, and financial security. One of the most obvious examples would be the work of Bill Hybels[8] at the Willow Creek Community Church in South Barrington, Chicago. His passion for leadership has developed the worldwide Global Leadership Summit, two days of teaching in which international teachers such as Jim Collins, Patrick Lencioni, Garry Hamel, Condoleezza Rice, Bill George, William Ury, Jack Welsh and Michael Porter, to name but a few, are welcomed unashamedly because of what the churches can learn from the world. To quote from Bill Hybels: 'When leaders get better, everybody wins.'

A similar approach has often been adopted by those who have taken up chaplaincy roles in schools, hospitals, industry and the military. They have been able to watch and be involved in organizations which have been seeking to adapt to the current changes, which are as much cultural as technical. They have often had to develop patterns of leadership and organizational life that meet the requirements of the organization in which they are embedded. They have been able to discern both the values and the deficits of contemporary leadership development.

Inevitably, not all church people are happy to perform this rather wholesale adoption of the secular.[9] Some argue that the 'world' with its

---

[8] See B. Hybels (2002), *Courageous Leadership*, Zondervan, Grand Rapids; B. Hybels (2008), *Axiom: Powerful Leadership Proverbs*, Zondervan, Grand Rapids. See also R. Higginson (1996), *Transforming Leadership: A Christian Approach to Leadership*, SPCK, London; and the books published under the sponsorship of Modem and edited by John Nelson: *Leading, Managing, Ministering*, Canterbury Press, Norwich (1999) and *How to Become a Creative Church Leader*, Canterbury Press, Norwich (2008).

[9] S. Pattison, 'Management and Pastoral Theology', in J. Woodward and S. Pattison (2000), *The Blackwell Reader in Pastoral and Practical Theology*, Blackwell, Oxford; S. Pattison (2007), *The Challenge of Practical Theology: Selected Essays*, Jessica Kingsley, London; see especially chapters 5–8 in which there is a sustained critique of the ideology of contemporary management language and its impact on pastoral organizations.

organizational understanding is inevitably tainted by the fallen nature of humankind and needs to be treated with a great deal of care. While they acknowledge that many things change in life, they are not persuaded that the roots and experiences of human life change very much. Some theologians from the academy, which has been equally infected with 'secular' disciplines, are heard to regret the bureaucratization of the Church, and its apparent reliance on 'management speak'. People from this perspective often draw and emphasize the difference between a voluntary organization like the Church and the 'employment world' of business organizations. They indicate that the Church needs 'non business' methods of leadership. Others choose to focus rather on the language of 'formation' as showing a distinct difference from the business language of training and competency. A fascinating study by the psycho-historian Nick Duffell[10] explores the impact of boarding schools on leaders – and most of the leaders in the Church of England until very recently came from that stream of formation. In his Preface he introduces some of the key behaviours that result from early separation from parents: 'A tendency to overvalue work or achievements, a lack of empathy, an inability to grieve, and so on'.[11] There is always the fear that if the Church takes in behaviours and attitudes from the world, the purity of the Church is at risk.

Sometimes the response is defensive, fearing seduction by the world. But at other times and from other theological perspectives there has been a desire to critique the ways of the world in the light of kingdom values.[12] It is argued that it is proper to expect the Church to be a 'place' where alternative values to competition and the market shape not only personal life and discipleship but organizational life as well. People talk about 'an Acts chapter 2 Church' – shaped by values that are so different from the values of the world that they are 'counter-cultural'. For example, a dominant metaphor for the Church has been the family. Although it is reasonable to think of a family as a kind of organization, the language of the market, with its employers and employees, competition, market share, contracts and marketing, does not transfer to the culture of family life where the

---

[10] N. Duffell (2014), *Wounded Leaders: British Elitism and the Entitlement Illusion*, Lone Arrow Press, London.

[11] Duffell, *Wounded Leaders*, p. ii.

[12] See especially H. Nouwen (1989), *In the Name of Jesus: Reflections on Christian Leadership*, Darton, Longman & Todd, London; and G. A. Arbuckle (1993), *Refounding the Church: Dissent for Leadership*, Geoffrey Chapman, London. See also J. Lewis-Anthony (2013), *You Are the Messiah and I Should Know: Why Leadership Is a Myth (and Probably a Heresy)*, Bloomsbury, London.

more dominant language is of development, community, fidelity and love. Another example is the use by the Church of the language of the body, based on the use of it by Paul (1 Cor. 12.12ff.). The more we learn about the way the body works and its capacity to manage itself with endless feedback loops of nerves and chemicals, the less sense it makes to think of a top-down model, with the brain in control as the chief executive of the organization. Such discussion about being 'in the world but not of it' has been at the heart of all theological and missiological debates in every age. On the whole it is fair to say that people from this different point of view may not have a radically different set of ideas about what a well-led church would look like. But they do bring an instinctive scepticism to everything that comes from the 'world'.

Alongside those who adopt the ways of the world, and those who are inherently sceptical, a third response has emerged more recently. Rather than treating the 'world' as either the place of all wisdom or of all threat, this new approach seeks to meet the 'world' on a more equal footing. It searches the Judeo-Christian traditions and Scriptures, as well as those of other faiths, for learning on leadership that might not be found anywhere in the secular discourses. All the world's religious texts carry stories and wisdom about leadership garnered over millennia of experience and reflection. An obvious example of this would be the identification of servant leadership from within the Hebrew and Christian Scriptures. Another would be the growing interest in the ancient idea of wisdom. Moreover, as the Western world has moved towards more postmodern sympathies, there seems to be much more common ground in which joint explorations about the nature of spiritual leadership and leadership character bring people from church and society together on more equal footings. Critical to this approach is the expectation that the world can learn from the Church and vice versa. It is no longer a case of one-way traffic.[13]

Within this long history of Christian leadership the significance of St Benedict[14] can hardly be overstated. While there are obvious differences between an abbot in a monastery many hundreds of years ago and a chief executive in today's world, there are also strong resonances. Benedict advises listening to the youngest brother under his charge and caring for

---

[13] The General Synod report, *Nurturing and Discerning Senior Leaders* (GS Misc 2026), offers an interesting window into this way of thinking, although while many secular leadership trainers are listed, there is not a single theologian.

[14] Dermot Tredget (2002), '"The Rule of Benedict" and Its Relevance to the World of Work', *Journal of Managerial Psychology*, vol. 17, no. 3, pp. 219–29.

the honest ordering of life. The Church is not the only place where a recovery of monastic practices have borne fruit in discussions about leadership.

Jesus and leadership

Nestling within this third response is the idea that we should be able to learn about leadership from a study of the example and teaching of Jesus. His explicit teaching about leadership is found in his response to the mother of James and John in which he distances himself from the hierarchy, power and control of the world's leaders of his time and introduces the innovative concept of leadership for service (Mark 10.35–45; Matt. 20.20–28; Luke 22.24–27). This has given rise to the teaching of servant leadership as a specifically Christian theory and practice. It is adopted by those who want to see the Church as a counter-cultural expression of human community and action. Not surprisingly it has not often been the focus of writers who prefer the language of God as King, and Christ as King of Kings. These writers are more comfortable with the secular control-and-command structures.[15] They tend to reinterpret the servant language as the language of humility without abdicating the power of position. Perhaps they do not agree that this is expressly what Jesus is calling for. Their ready alternative is to champion the example of Jesus. Here an emphasis is placed on his calling of disciples and his clarity of vision and purpose. New emphasis is placed on his emotional and spiritual intelligence. His team leadership is shown to be exemplary. It is said that Jesus 'intentionally utilized leadership techniques which we can study, practice, and master'.[16] However, little mention is made of the fact that it would be risky to claim that the disciples were 'on message', as they often did not understand what he was talking about. And all his chosen trained disciples ran away when Jesus was arrested, and they seemed lost until after the gift of the Spirit at Pentecost. Nor is much attention drawn to the differing contexts of culture and history, or to the role of Jesus' revolutionary replacing of the old with the new Israel. It is worth bearing in mind that not many church leaders have the same task as Jesus, who had the distinctive vocation as the founder of a new and radical interpretation of the faith of the people of

---

[15] J. Adair (2001), *The Leadership of Jesus: And Its Legacy Today*, Canterbury Press, Norwich; K. Blanchard and P. Hodges (2008), *Lead Like Jesus: Lessons from the Greatest Leadership Role Model of All Time*, Thomas Nelson, Nashville.

[16] B. Perkins (2000), *Awaken the Leader Within: How the Wisdom of Jesus Can Unleash Your Potential*, Zondervan, Grand Rapids, p. 16; A. Watson (2009), *The Fourfold Leadership of Jesus*, Bible Reading Fellowship, Abingdon.

Israel at the time he lived. Seldom is such revolution the calling of today's church leaders.

Leadership gift or skill and the place of training?

Leadership discussions have ventured into the territory of competency, as has the whole area of ministerial training. At one end of the spectrum have been those who see all leadership within the Christian churches as a matter of calling and gifting. For instance, a situation arises, and from among the disciples of Jesus emerges a person who may feel called to respond and who may have natural gifts. Such gifts are enlarged with the spiritual gift of leadership that Paul talks of in his letters. Here, one is not selected and trained against a designated set of criteria; rather one is inspired, called and obedient. The Charismatic movement in more modern times exemplifies this attitude. Here in prayer and laying on of hands spiritual gifts are sought, prayed for and given, just as the tongues were on the day of Pentecost so that people could hear the message in their own languages. Such an attitude to gifting is also found in the Society of Friends where every person attending worship may be called upon to offer a ministry. It is also the culture of the contemplative where

> the grace of salvation, the grace of Christian wholeness that flowers in silence, dispels this illusion of separation. For when the mind is brought to stillness, and all our strategies of acquisition are dropped, a deeper truth presents itself: we are and always have been one with God and we are all one in God.[17]

It is within this cluster of approaches that metaphors for leadership might be taken from the creative arts, where alongside the need for skill and practice comes something else – the moment of creativity, the 'something out of nothing' that draws attention to the divine. It might be the idea of containment that speaks of a conversation with a therapist in which the therapist holds the narrative of the client and allows a reframing and a detoxifying. It might be a movement away from rational and technical language into the language of poetry, dreams, liturgy and ritual – a language that in the end has no words, or strategic plans, or measurable targets, but only praise and wonder. To pick up the words of Charles Wesley: 'Lost in wonder, love and praise', it could be argued that the core leadership development need is in the leadership of worship rather than in strategic management.

---

[17] Martin Laird (2006), *Into the Silent Land: The Practice of Contemplation*, Darton, Longman & Todd, London, p. 16.

At the other end of the spectrum are those who believe it is right to identify and list the core skills that leaders seem to have shown in the past. An interesting piece of work[18] was done among religious communities in the USA. First every abbot and prior was asked to name the five religious superiors from across the country who they thought were the best. There turned out to be remarkable agreement among those who were canvassed, and a list of about ten superiors, both men and women, were selected for in-depth interviews. They were asked to talk about critical incidents in their time as leaders and how they had handled them. The researchers worked through the narratives and drew out common strands of behaviour, as well as of attitude. This was worked into a set of competencies that might be looked for in the process of discernment when a new election was required. Such a point of view informs the discussions about criteria for bishops' advisors when potential ordinands are being interviewed. Competencies have also increasingly been used to identify the kinds of things to look for in identifying potential bishops, archdeacons and deans, and this view lies at the heart of the contemporary senior leadership endorsed and funded by the Church of England Commissioners.

An obvious criticism of the production of such a list is that it is thought to be possible to tick each box of a competency but still know that there is something missing, a quality in a leader that hasn't yet been discerned. In more recent leadership literature this aspect has been put down to character, and there is a growing awareness that character takes time to develop. In the churches we have often used the word 'formation' and see this as the necessary connection between these competencies and sustained faithful living. The view is often expressed that this way of life not only cannot be 'reduced' to a competency statement but also cannot be described in anything other than vague metaphors. Historically such a view has allowed all sorts of appointments to be made on the basis of the old school tie or friendship bonds. Such behaviour is seen to fly in the face of giving people equal chances to apply and be interviewed for leadership positions.

In the secular world there is talk about the difference between so-called 'hard' and 'soft' skills. A hard skill might be the ability to give a good talk to a group of colleagues, or to read a set of financial reports, whereas things like empathy and emotional intelligence are thought of as softer skills that are much less easy to measure. However, the competency world looks for

---

[18] D. J. Nygren and others (1992), *The Leadership Competency Assessment of Leaders of Religious Orders in the Roman Catholic Church*, The Cheswick Centre, Rockville.

measures of some kind, some assessment of whether a person has got 'it' or not, based on a collection of evidence.

The most striking example of this approach in the Church in recent years has been its approach to the issues of abuse and what is known as **safeguarding**. A tour of the safeguarding pages on the Church of England's website reveals that they are matched by those of other denominations. No one pretends any longer that the churches have good records on the issue of child and vulnerable adult abuse. Nor does anybody pretend that churches are not natural places for abusers to begin their work of grooming. So, in the light of historical abuse and the deep belief that these kinds of things should never be allowed in the Church, a small industry has grown up. In the Church of England every licensed person has to attend a set of modules with specified learning outcomes. Modules have been written, documents are produced and compulsory training programmes are delivered in every diocese. There are five full-time staff members employed in the national Church and many others in dioceses. The Theological Advisory Group of the House of Bishops has produced a report seeking to give missional and theological support. All this may be necessary to interrupt the natural tendency of the Church to protect its own, and it may be that in five to ten years we will have found a balance which continues to be passionate about the need to provide safety and, at the same time, to be less risk-averse. The problem from a theological point of view is that with every module attended, and every trace of evidence collated and recorded, there remains the possibility of evil, and the real chance that people with evil intent will find their way. It may just be the case that learning about evil is more important than managing evidence trails.[19]

Training leaders

Finally, it is worth noting the development of ideas about the most effective educational methods for training leaders that have been adopted. The early training decisions were to organize residential intensive leadership programmes, some of which were internal to organizations and delivered in their own training centres, while others were developed 'off site' to bring leaders from different organizations together. Most of these were offered

---

[19] A study about the way in which kind people, such as nurses, may end up behaving badly in hospital wards is a very good comparative study for understanding those who, called to be loving leaders in the Church, may end up being cruel and abusive; see J. Ballatt and P. Campling (2011), *Intelligent Kindness: Reforming the Culture of Healthcare*, RCPsych Publications, London.

in specialist colleges or training schools and often built relationships with universities which were able to provide master's degrees in leadership, business administration and so on. This residential mindset has been fundamental to the training of clergy, although not clergy in senior roles until very recently.

However, it was soon noted that the transfer of learning from the academy or training centre to the workplace was seldom easy, and thereafter 'work-placed learning' became more usual, often blended with more traditional learning. Ministerial training has taken similar paths with its new focus on context and placement, although it has retained its preoccupation with full-time residential training. At the same time, experiential methods became more significant than classroom lecturing, with role play, simulation and case study being familiar methods in use. The development of peer-group learning, often known as 'action learning', and work-based coaching or mentoring also became more important. Accompanying such methods has been the development of the collection of feedback from peers, reports and managers, which soon became known as '360 degree' feedback. These practices rooted the learning in the contexts of leaders in training.

There are basically two points of view in shaping educational design. The first of these, influenced by a sense of competency framework, starts with a sense of what is to be learned. An Oxford diocesan clergy leadership programme[20] had, as one of its declared outcomes, clergy who were more able to lead change in collaborative ways from a servant heart. So the programme design was shaped to deliver those outcomes. Within this perspective it is more possible to design assessment methods to see whether or not the programme has actually delivered the promised or hoped-for outcomes. This kind of perspective is more obvious when shaped by an institution's needs. For instance, the Church of England now sets out very specific learning outcomes at each stage in the discernment and training of clergy, and in the newly developed senior leader training programmes.

An alternative outlook sits much more loosely to prescribed outcomes while often being very clear about educational design strategies. Such programmes often work when people from different organizations and leadership responsibilities come together. For instance, the Voyage programme organized by the Diocese of Bristol brought together clergy from very different parochial contexts and an equal number of lay people exercising

---

[20] A. J. Berry (2007), *Developing Servant Leaders*, research paper 1 from the Foundation for Church Leadership; copy available at Sarum College Library.

their leadership in their workplaces. Each participant was invited to work out his or her own learning outcomes through a process of discernment and development. What has become known as 'self-managed learning'[21] is an important aspect of this kind of leadership development. As far as assessment is concerned, responsibility lies with the person, with the organization that may have funded the learning and with the training agency in a collaborative process.

Most contemporary training in leadership sits somewhere between these two perspectives. There is a general sense, which of course needs to be open to critical enquiry, of what leadership is about. There is also a much clearer sense that each person is shaped by his or her own story, that each context makes different demands, and at the same time there are educational methods which honour both diversity of person and context and a common horizon of leadership.[22]

The Church of England's commitment to senior leadership development sets out values that underpin its designs:

1 Leadership development is a process not an event; the programmes are designed to be a catalyst for an on-going development journey, rather than a short-term series of episodic events.
2 The approach to the design and the delivery of all modules reflects the principles of adult learning:

- participants are all at different points and on different paths on their own journey – some activities will therefore be more/less helpful for each individual;
- learning comes from the group – everyone is someone we can learn from and who can learn from us;
- learning is interpersonal – it requires safety, dialogue, confidentiality;
- learning is owned by individuals – it is an active process which requires engagement and commitment;
- learning is change – it requires willingness to shift how we think, feel and behave;
- learning requires reflection and integration – quiet space to consolidate learning and make decisions.[23]

---

[21] I. Cunningham (1999), *The Wisdom of Strategic Learning: The Self-Managed Learning Solution*, Gower, London.
[22] R. Goffee and G. Jones (2006), *Why Should Anybody Be Led by You? What It Takes to Be an Authentic Leader*, Harvard Business School Press, Boston.
[23] GS Misc 2026.

Conclusion

There have always been questions about the cost of leadership develop-ment and its effectiveness. This has been especially true in the Church where there have been few measures that enable adequate assessment of outcomes. How would we know when a church leader has improved as a result of a bespoke leadership programme? What kind of evidence would we look for? How are we to know whether all the money spent in our churches on leadership development has produced any changes, and would those changes have happened in any case? If God loves the Church, will God not raise up and gift people with the leadership we need? These questions are hard to answer at the moment but perhaps point the way to the next phase of our thinking about leadership in the Church.

15

Digital media for ministry: key concepts and core convictions

KYLE OLIVER AND LISA KIMBALL

Like many churches and para-church ministries, the Center for the Ministry of Teaching (CMT) found itself at a crossroads by the end of the twenty-first century's first decade. Founded in 1984 by Professor of Christian Education and Pastoral Theology Locke Bowman at Virginia Theological Seminary (VTS), the centre had once been at the forefront of faith formation ministry in the Episcopal Church and of educational technology at the largest seminary of the Anglican Communion. Our centre created the flagship curriculum for children and youth in the Episcopal Church. We offered Sunday school teacher training, a mail-order video-borrowing programme, a large and current collection of Christian education curricula, and consulting services in a cosy and welcoming space on the VTS campus just a stone's throw away from Washington DC.

But the nature of society and hence ministry had of late been changing rapidly, and the centre had not adapted to this new context. Our physical collection no longer drew steady numbers of patrons to our building – partly because of traffic congestion inside the Capital Beltway, but mostly because publishers no longer needed centres like ours to get their curriculum samples in front of religious educators. And these days there are a lot fewer of those, especially full-time faith formation ministers with formal training at the helm of vibrant programmes in stable churches. In short, the 'programme era' of congregation-based, school-patterned faith formation was coming to an end. To borrow language used by the start-up community, it was time for our centre to pivot.[1]

Lisa[2] became director of the centre in 2009 and quickly discerned that God was doing a new thing at Virginia Seminary. She knew that

---

[1] Eric Ries, 'The Lean Startup Methodology', *The Lean Startup*, <theleanstartup.com/principles>.

[2] She and co-author Kyle will refer to themselves in the third person as needed for clarity. While

technology would need to be a part of it, notwithstanding the school's historic commitment to residential formation. She initiated third-party audits of the seminary's information and educational technology infrastructure, helping the school begin to realize there was a difference. She also invited media-savvy theological educators[3] to campus to challenge the seminary community to think differently and to help the CMT convene a mutual learning and training event for ministry practitioners keen to do things differently.

This latter constituency formed the nucleus of what we have come to call the e-Formation Learning Community, a highly participatory community of practice[4] focused on training and inspiration for ministry in a digital age. The 2012 e-Formation Learning Exchange was the first event 'on the job' for Kyle, whom Lisa had just hired as the centre's first digital missioner and learning lab coordinator. Thus began the centre's 'digital mission', an endeavour both (1) to bring the CMT's ministry of training and resource curation up to date with respect to digital media, and (2) to convene conversations and experiences for ministers of all types wishing to understand and practise culturally savvy ministry in contexts deeply shaped by digital media.

The purpose of this chapter is to introduce key concepts and core convictions in the field we have come to know as **digital media for ministry** (aka 'digital ministry', 'digital media ministry', 'new media ministry', etc.). In the process, we will introduce some of the seminal works in this new and fast-changing area of practical theology, with an emphasis on the *practical*. (The task of Chapter 16 will be to construct a series of best practices from ministry case-studies and to articulate our vision for church leader formation in this vital area of ministerial practice.) Many of the authors and practitioners we will introduce have become friends and colleagues. Our relationships with them have confirmed what we had always suspected: they have largely arrived at their status as respected authorities not through writing theology per se but through active participation as reflective ministry practitioners online.

---

we want to avoid a purely 'show and tell' chapter, we have yet to identify a better way to frame our work than by telling the story of our transformation in the midst of it.

[3] Mary Hess, author of *Engaging Technology in Theological Education: All That We Can't Leave Behind* (Lanham, MD: Sheed & Ward, 2005); and Julie Lytle, author of *Faith Formation 4.0: Introducing an Ecology of Faith in a Digital Age* (New York: Morehouse, 2013).

[4] See Elisabeth Kimball and Kyle Oliver, 'Communities of (Digital) Practice: Preparing Religious Leaders for Lively Online Engagement', *Religious Education Association Annual Conference*, Boston, MA, 2013, <bit.ly/ComDigiPrac>.

Thus, the best advice we can give anyone wishing to use digital media for ministry is not 'Read their books' or 'Read our chapters in *this* book.' It's this: get online, connect with people in your community, and bring your good ministry instincts and practices with you.

Digital literacy

In their seminal pastoral letter on the US economy, the United States Catholic bishops defined basic social justice as demanding 'that people be assured a minimum level of participation in the economy'.[5] This same impulse to encourage full societal participation – here not just as a right but also as a responsibility – leads us to teach digital literacy and hold it up as a prerequisite for twenty-first-century ministry.[6] Without addressing the Church directly, Cassie Hague and Sarah Payton's definition makes it very clear why Christians should care about digital literacy:

> To be digitally literate is to have access to a broad range of practices and cultural resources that you are able to apply to digital tools. It is the ability to *make and share meaning in different modes and formats; to create, collaborate and communicate effectively* and to understand how and when digital technologies can best be used to support these processes.[7]

What is Christian ministry if not the making and sharing of meaning in a collaborative way with a community of fellow Jesus-followers and an intention to raise up new ones? We do it not just by breaking bread but by caring for one another, not just by giving or listening to sermons but by serving in the streets. These activities are not limited to the church building or even to in-person expression and reflection between believers. It is incumbent upon ministers of all kinds to be able to engage in meaning-making activities with the people we serve – or hope to serve. To engage authentically requires language proficiency, as the apostles discovered on the day of Pentecost.

Sociologists are telling us that technology plays a big role in how people make and share meaning today. Lee Rainie of Pew Research and

---

5   'Economic Justice for All: Pastoral Letter on Catholic Social Teaching and the U.S. Economy', *United States Conference of Catholic Bishops*, 1986, <bit.ly/USCCBjustice>: viii.

6   On digital literacy barriers to participation, see also Henry Jenkins, *Confronting the Challenges of Participatory Culture: Media Education for the 21st Century* (Cambridge, MA: MIT, 2009): 15–27.

7   Cassie Hague and Sarah Payton, 'Digital Literacy across the Curriculum: A Futurelab Handbook', *Future Lab (National Foundation for Educational Research)*, 2010, <bit.ly/DigiLitFuture>: 4. Emphasis added.

Barry Wellman of the University of Toronto's NetLab have coined the term 'networked individualism' to describe a 'new social operating system . . . in contrast to the longstanding . . . system formed around large hierarchical bureaucracies and small, densely knit groups such as households, communities, and workgroups'.[8] People are connecting on social networks and sharing far more than pictures of dogs in costumes. They're sharing their passions, their anxieties, their hopes for a life and a world transformed. And they're engaging in dialogue about them with people they love and with people they've not yet met.

Reports of communities' demise at the hands of these forces are highly exaggerated, if not dead wrong. Here again, Rainie and Wellman:

> A key reason why these kinds of networks function effectively is that social networks are large and diversified thanks to the way people use technology. To some critics, this seems to be a problem. They express concern that technology creates social isolation, as people rely on tech-based communication rather than richer face-to-face encounters. We find a different story . . . Rather than the internet or mobile phones luring people away from in-person contact, extensive internet use is associated with larger, more diverse, and growing networks. For example, one study of internet users shows that between 2002 and 2007, there was an increase of more than one-third in the number of friends seen in person weekly.[9]

For facilitators of relationships, the threefold revolution *Networked* describes (social networks, broadband internet, mobile technology) presents a wealth of opportunities. The Church now has a plausible means of connecting with many more people (and kinds of people) with a much richer range of stories and invitations than in the days of phonebook and newspaper advertising and the expectation that people (already) interested in their faith would come to the local church building for answers.

For example, a priest of Kyle's acquaintance spends more time at the local coffee shop than in his office at the church. He does so to help members of the wider community associate a human face with the church he serves. Employees and regulars at the coffee shop know he's the local Episcopal priest, whether he has his collar on or not. When Kyle asked him how his parishioners find him, he pulled out his smartphone and said, 'They know how to get in touch with me.' And in the meantime his laptop allows him to go about his business of sermon writing, meeting planning

---

[8]   Lee Rainie and Barry Wellman, *Networked: The New Social Operating System* (Cambridge, MA: MIT, 2014): 340 (Kindle location).

[9]   Rainie and Wellman, *Networked*: 469 (Kindle location).

or whatever else is on the day's agenda. There's an added resonance to this story if we consider that his answer is, in a way, not just instrumentalist but ontological. Yes, his phone is a communications tool. But it is also an icon pointing to an interesting reality, as we will see in the next section.

In the case of our ministry of faith formation resourcing and consultation, the CMT's new literacies have connected us with a wider constituency than ever before, and at a time when Christian educators are trying to make sense of how things are changing in their field. We have been able to listen deeply to voices expressing not just shame and regret about the state of Christian formation but also sober realism and a Spirit-filled hope that new models are emerging. Our expertise has shifted from our previous role as static knowledge keepers towards a new role as dynamic conversation partners. When several colleagues suggested, in person and online,[10] that adult formation might be dead because people are too busy to attend additional weekly programming, we worked with colleagues to develop and pilot a model[11] that depends less on in-person attendance. We used digital media both to spread the word about what we were up to and as the gathering places for leaders and participants to experience and reflect on this new approach. That the media played both roles is not a coincidence.

Digital tools *and* digital spaces

Church communicators extraordinaire Jim Naughton and Rebecca Wilson begin a section of their recent book with a pithy point about place: 'Willie Sutton supposedly said that he robbed banks because that was where the money was. Social media is where the people are.'[12] It's true to say that Facebook had, as of this writing, about 1.5 billion users, that is, 1.5 billion people using this particular communication tool. But it's also true to say that 1.5 billion people spent time *on/in/at* Facebook, like they might spend time *on* the job, *in* a coffee shop or *at* home. We don't use these prepositions with nearly the same frequency when talking about broadcast

---

[10] Episcopal Church in Minnesota, 'The Rev. LeeAnne Watkins: The Way We Do Formation Is Not Working', *Episcopal Story Project*, 16 February 2012, <bit.ly/FormationStory>.

[11] We call it 'hybrid faith formation'. See Day Smith Pritchartt, 'Shutting Down the Sunday School', *Key Resources*, 14 January 2014, <bit.ly/SundayShutdown>; and Kyle Matthew Oliver, 'Expanding Faith Formation Reach with Hybrid Networks', *Key Resources*, 10 December 2013, <bit.ly/HybridNetworks>.

[12] Jim Naughton and Rebecca Wilson, *Speaking Faithfully: Communications as Evangelism in a Noisy World* (New York: Morehouse, 2012): 692 (Kindle location).

media like television, radio or print. That's because online platforms enable interactive encounter and exchange with others.[13] As such, we can't seem to help but describe them not just as tools but as *environments*, analogous to the physical spaces where we gather to live, learn and love.

Like cities, regions and nations, these spaces have their own cultures. A significant part of digital literacy for ministers, then, is developing the skills to be culturally conversant in the digital spaces where our people spend so much of their time. This prospect can be intimidating, given the high rate of change and growth online (new tools and environments are launched every day) and the barriers to participation on each (the impenetrability of text message shorthand[14] and the notation conventions of Twitter to the uninitiated being two oft-cited examples). Each social network has its own dialect and etiquette, its own patterns of interaction, distinctive feel and flavour. It feels like a lot to learn.

If fact, if we consider some analogous in-person examples of culture-oriented ministry skills, we should positively *expect* that being formed for effective ministry in digital spaces would be challenging. Kyle, an upper-middle-class white man from the American Midwest, recently moved to a working-class Latino neighbourhood in New York City. To expect to communicate and relate effectively with his neighbours upon first arrival would be crazy. The same is true when we arrive in a new digital place, particularly if the people we meet there have backgrounds very different from our own.

We believe that learning to participate in meaningful, authentic ways within and between cultures has always been an essential, and probably underemphasized, ministry skill. We've tended to prefer honing our skills as curators of a dominant church culture (for example, how much of our catechesis involves teaching newcomers denominational terminology for the people, places and things our churches care about?). In a sense, then, the urgency of digital literacy work for ministers is simply a special case of a broader trend: our flattening, diversifying, reconfiguring and reconnecting world is calling ministers home to the art of translation, interpretation and belonging across boundaries. The Spirit is once again reminding us of our responsibility to be 'a light to the nations'. Our more provincial mindsets and patterns have proven indeed to be 'too light a thing' (Isaiah 49.6 NRSV).

---

[13] Lytle stresses that interactivity is the mark of this fourth era of communication and faith formation (after oral, written and mass-mediated). See Lytle, *Faith Formation 4.0*: ch. 4.

[14] I.e. 'txtspk'. See Elizabeth Drescher, *Tweet If You ♥ Jesus: Practicing Church in the Digital Reformation* (New York: Morehouse, 2011): 916–71 (Kindle locations).

This analogy is helpful in setting an agenda for digital media ministry formation (as we will do in Chapter 16). To the extent that social networking platforms are *tools*, we need to know how to use them effectively. There is a fundamental irreducibility to the matter of *technique* in this work; we can never fully get away from the 'how-to' question. However, since these platforms are also *spaces*, a better way of conceiving this work is the notion of pastoral *presence*. When we show up as reflective practitioners, prepared to participate fully according to the cultural patterns we encounter, we make ourselves available to the Spirit of God already working within them (this is one answer to the 'why' question). We engage in ethnography as pastoral practice.[15] If we are attentive, our theological reflection about the spaces can and should guide our development as savvy users of the tools. However, as we mentioned above, just as there are often cultural barriers to entry in neighbourhoods and other communities (appropriate language and dialect, knowledge of local customs and traditions), most of these tools have some barriers to entry as well, barriers that for many people can be overcome with a little how-to training. So even if technique is not our *primary* concern, it must often be our *first* concern.

Our thinking here is aided by Meredith Gould's essential handbook *The Social Media Gospel: Sharing the Good News in New Ways*. A sociologist by training and communications practitioner and consultant by profession, Gould realizes that the most significant matters she can discuss are why to choose to be present in particular online spaces. Her adaptation of Teresa of Avila's 'Christ Has No Body' prayer ('Christ Has No Online Presence but Yours') declares this work essential and holy.[16] Her most important chapter, 'Virtual Community Is Real Community', emphasizes that deep, focused, supportive conversation about faith happens online as meaningfully as in person, albeit according to an accelerated timetable.[17]

Gould's *Social Media Gospel* wisely focuses on the big picture: theological, sociological and especially strategic communication themes. That's partly because she knows these issues often go unexplored, and partly because printed 'how-to' books age badly in the era of weekly software updates. She does include a certain amount of how-to as well, particularly about writing online[18] – a skill that transcends any particular platform.

---

[15] Mary Clark Moschella, *Ethnography as a Pastoral Practice* (Cleveland, OH: Pilgrim Press, 2008).

[16] Meredith Gould, *The Social Media Gospel: Sharing the Good News in New Ways*, 2nd edn (Collegeville, MN: Liturgical Press, 2015): 9.

[17] Gould, *Social Media Gospel*: 30–1.

[18] Gould, *Social Media Gospel*: 121–4.

However, it is possible to 'get in the weeds' with Gould, to dive into matters of technique and tactics, and that is by following and/or participating in the weekly Twitter chat (and weeklong learning community) that she founded, using the Twitter hashtag #chsocm (CHurch SOCial Media).

Her experience matches our own in the Center for the Ministry of Teaching. The people we serve have certainly read with interest the books we share with them, including Naughton and Wilson's *Speaking Faithfully*, Gould's *Social Media Gospel* and Lytle's *Faith Formation 4.0*. But they have responded much more vigorously to *opportunities to practise* digital media for ministry in community – especially in person. A yearly e-Formation Conference and regular regional 'boot camps' have become our most vigorously sought-after offerings; we've increased the frequency and scale of these events despite the considerable effort they require to produce because people say this kind of programming is exactly what their professional development needs have led them to at this moment. The chance to dip a toe in the water and connect with others doing likewise has been a powerful motivator. In a recent planning conversation, our colleague John Roberto identified the optimal approach to this kind of training: 'We combine theory and practice, offering concrete examples and the chance for well-supported hands-on learning.' Naughton himself recently put it this way: '[T]here are a few things worth reading, but learning by doing is key.'[19]

Integrated digital practice

Thus far, we have discussed two main principles: (1) that digital media literacy is vital for faith communities' ongoing participation in society, and (2) that the media themselves are both new tools for communication and new spaces in which to offer our pastoral and missional presence. While we have introduced Gould's observation that there's not much different about so-called 'virtual' community and real community, and Rainie and Wellman's conclusion that the two ultimately support each other, there is more to be said about their (inter)relationship. Lutheran pastor Keith Anderson recently said it.

Allow us to make a bold prediction. When practical theologians interested in ministry and technology look back on the first few decades of the twenty-first century, they will talk about the time before and the time after Anderson's *The Digital Cathedral: Networked Ministry in a Wireless World.*

---

[19] On Twitter, of course: <https://twitter.com/JimNaught/status/667448226698493952>.

In this 2015 collection of ministry field reporting, Anderson developed a compelling and relevant metaphor to elucidate the following principle: digital spaces and practices infuse or supplement physical spaces and practices. (In another ten years, we might hasten to add 'and vice versa'.)

Anderson was certainly not the first or only digital ministry practitioner to free us from the paradigm of 'virtual' ministry in a separate 'cyberspace'.[20] Before Gould's work discussed above, Elizabeth Drescher's analysis of our modern cultural 'habitus' in *Tweet If You ♥ Jesus* stressed that our patterns of life use technology to *integrate*, rather than separate, the various spheres of our lives.[21] So Anderson's non-binary conception was already instilled into the minds of those active in conversations about digital media ministry. What's so helpful about *Digital Cathedral* is that it teaches the idea of digital integration with an appeal to a deeply entrenched and familiar community ministry model: the cathedral.

A cathedral is connected to its neighbourhood or village by an intricate and essential web of relational, cultural and physical connections.[22] Cathedrals blur the line between member and non-member, believer and non-believer, sacred and secular. Cathedrals cannot help but have 'roots' in the community. They offer a very old and very flexible way of being church, a way of being church that will become more and more essential as the cultural patterns created by the Baby Boom (which gave birth to the 'programme' era of church) continue to wane. Cathedrals create a public space for honest theological reflection and conversation. So does the Web.[23]

Anderson believes digitally integrated models of networked ministry can help any faith community embrace the faith- and community-forming practices of cathedrals. Mobile and social technology make possible cathedrals' way of being church in the neighbourhood without the instant recognition that comes with buildings so large that surrounding neighbourhoods are often named for them. One such church is Humble Walk, a Lutheran mission congregation in the West End of St Paul, Minnesota. Humble Walk doesn't have a building; the members meet in community

[20] Keith Anderson, *The Digital Cathedral: Networked Ministry in a Wireless World* (New York: Morehouse, 2015): 1381–2 (Kindle locations).

[21] Elizabeth Drescher, *Tweet If You ♥ Jesus: Practicing Church in the Digital Reformation* (New York: Morehouse, 2011): 231–84 (Kindle locations).

[22] Anderson showed a fascinating map of the waterworks of Canterbury Cathedral circa 1167 to make this point when he spoke at e-Formation 2015. See slides 6–7 at <bit.ly/KeithAndersonSlides>.

[23] Anderson, *Digital Cathedral*: 267–71 (Kindle locations).

spaces and keep organized about the wheres and whens with help from a simple website and an active Facebook group. Here's what Anderson noticed when he caught up with Humble Walk:

> I realized that, without a building, experiencing Humble Walk was, indeed, a walk. Embedded in the life of the West End, the people of the church had literally made their entire neighborhood their cathedral. West Seventh Street, the main road in this part of town, is their nave. The side streets are the ambulatories. And the shrines, well, the shrines are everywhere – in parks and bus stops, coffee shops and pubs, churches and community gathering spaces, homes and apartments . . . These are not episodic forays into the neighborhood, or trendy ways of doing ministry. They reflect a deeply held understanding of sacred space with strong roots throughout the Christian tradition . . . Humble Walk's distributed ministry presence and practice is a reminder that sacred space is everywhere, if we can remember to see and treat it that way.[24]

Notice that this passage makes no explicit mention of digital technology. We think that's a feature of Anderson's thinking, not a bug. We did some digital digging and discovered that digital practice indeed 'goes without saying' for Humble Walk. Pastor Jodi Houge posts to Twitter and Facebook when she's heading to a community demonstration, but those posts are pointers to something else. On the other hand, sometimes her pastoral care for her community comes in the very form of a Facebook post: deeply meaningful music and a deeply adorable hamster video made recent appearances in response to hardship. Sometimes the Humble Walk website and social media presence are for telling you where to meet up. Other times they are the meetup. And sometimes the meetup creates the very narrative that populates a post that draws another newcomer into the networked ministry.

We see many parallels to this line of thinking in our work at the Center for the Ministry of Teaching. A member of our team who joined us after serving full time in a congregation reflected:

> At first it was hard for me to understand the impact I was having here. But as I watched our website's subscriber lists[25] grow, I realized we're providing resources and nourishment for hundreds of people several times a week. It's like they're our congregation.

Indeed, after almost four years of 'digital mission', we can picture the digital cathedral that is a spiritual home to the primary community we serve: the

---

24 Anderson, *Digital Cathedral*: 594–608 (Kindle locations).
25 He co-edits our website buildfaith.org.

network of Episcopal and ecumenical faith-formation ministers serving congregations, dioceses, schools, camps, publishing companies, nursing homes and more. You might say that we help shepherd a segment of this cathedral network: we plan periodic in-person gatherings for worship and learning. We offer weekly drop-in office hours on campus and online. We work to foster community among the participants in our network between gatherings. We collaborate with others who serve this network, attending their events and contributing to the conversations they host. We're not competing with other organizations for members. We are collaborating with colleagues to support and grow the wider network.

The architecture of this digital cathedral comprises not just the buildings we ministers work from and the physical places where we gather the flock in person, but the Facebook groups, email lists, Twitter feeds, Pinterest boards, podcast channels, video conferences and other media spaces where we come together, build and grow. Like the digital cathedrals Anderson describes, the network we are a part of doesn't think of itself as digital or physical – it goes without saying that we're both.[26] And like the construction of a cathedral, our work of building will never be finished.

The point is, digital presence and digital practice can and should be seamlessly integrated components of any ministry. This approach allows us to be more public, present, playful ministers, like Kyle's friend who has made Starbucks his office. *The Digital Cathedral* invited us into an era in which we think less about the technology and more about the ministry. Ironically, it has taken the digital networking revolution to remind us that networked ministry has been the predominant model since Jesus, Paul and others set this ragtag project in motion.

Digitally integrated reflection

Anderson's integrated vision for digital media ministry practice suggests an approach to learning to do it better. Just as the binary between physical and virtual is collapsing in an era of integrated digital communication, so too is the distinction between sacred and secular proving unhelpful in the post-Constantinian societies in which most ministers in the Global North serve. The simple fact is that there is no longer much cultural pressure to religiously affiliate, and increasing numbers of people are choosing not

---

[26] Though we rely heavily on the digital because we are physically located across several continents.

to.[27] Thus, serving our current constituencies (who nevertheless participate in this secularizing culture) and especially reaching the growing numbers of un- and de-churched individuals is going to require some serious communications savvy. The Church cannot and should not do it alone. Thankfully, excellent resources exist to help us – if, Gould points out, 'everyone agrees not to freak out about terms like "consumer" or "target audience" or "brand."'[28]

In other words, we need an integrated model of reflection to inform our practice. No area of knowledge should be off limits, but all of what we say and do should conform to our belief in a loving God who comes to us in Christ to free us from sin and draw us closer to himself and each other. This brings us to our final core conviction: Ministers should bring the knowledge of digital media experts into mutual conversation with the wisdom of Christian theological values. The risks are significant if we omit either end of the spectrum. Without learning from professionals in digital communications theory and practice, we are likely to miss key insights about how to connect with new and different people or how to connect more deeply with certain of them. Ministers should seek to be good stewards of their time, money and energy by putting such insights to work. But if we do not stay grounded in our theological formation, we are likely to lose touch with the reasons we are using these tools in the first place or to use them in ways unfaithful to the God who calls us.

A tremendous well of inspiration and guidance for this work of balanced and integrated reflection comes to us from Roman Catholicism. Catholic leaders have carefully considered these questions in the twentieth and twenty-first centuries. Daniella Zsupan-Jerome weaves a masterful narrative through the relevant church teaching documents in *Connected toward Communion: The Church and Social Communication in the Digital Age*. She points out that, since as early as 1963 (in *Inter Mirifica: The Decree on Mass Media*), the Catholic Church has sought to balance a spirit of openness and positivity towards media production and consumption[29] with the need to form a critical Christian consciousness with respect to their message and

---

[27] In the American context, the non-religiously affiliated are growing as a percentage of the population and becoming less religious in their practice. See Gregory A. Smith et al., 'U.S. Public Becoming Less Religious', *Pew Research Center*, 3 November 2015: <http://www.pew forum.org/2015/11/03/u-s-public-becoming-less-religious/>.

[28] Gould, *Social Media Gospel*: 48.

[29] Daniella Zsupan-Jerome, *Connected toward Communion: The Church and Social Communication in the Digital Age* (Collegeville, MN: Liturgical Press, 2014): 488.

means of distribution.[30] For anyone wishing to dive deeply into the theology of social communication, we heartily recommend Zsupan-Jerome's work as well as the New Media Project's series of theological essays.[31]

In some straightforward cases, the work of mutual conversation between theology and digital media theory and practice is a matter of pure translation – perhaps substituting business world jargon ('target audience') with church-world jargon ('congregant').[32] At other times, the intersection of ideas leads to more ambiguous situations, and in these cases it is good to have a framework guiding our process. Our default framework is that of practical theologian Richard Osmer, who outlines a cyclical process he calls 'the four core tasks of theological interpretation':

1 *The descriptive-empirical task.* Gathering information that helps us discern patterns and dynamics in particular episodes, situations or contexts.
2 *The interpretative task.* Drawing on theories of the arts and sciences to better understand and explain why these patterns and dynamics are occurring.
3 *The normative task.* Using theological concepts to interpret particular episodes, situations or contexts, constructing ethical norms to guide our responses, and learning from 'good practice'.
4 *The pragmatic task.* Determining strategies of action that will influence situations in ways that are desirable and entering into a reflective conversation with the 'talk back' emerging when they are enacted.[33]

The extensive business and communications literature has much to offer us to inform the second and fourth tasks. Our theological traditions animate the third task. Thus, in moving from one stage of the process to the next (or from the final stage back to the beginning), we often see the richness of the interplay at work.

Let's consider a hypothetical example. Say we have been tasked with improving an online platform for delivering religious news and spiritual reflections. Perhaps our review of the data (task 1) shows us that many readers view just a single page and then leave the site (in web analytics, the percentage of visits like this is known as the 'bounce rate'). In interpreting

---

[30] Zsupan-Jerome, *Connected toward Communion*: 669.
[31] Available at <http://www.cpx.cts.edu/newmedia/findings/essays>.
[32] Gould, *Social Media Gospel*, 49. Also throughout in David Meerman Scott, *The New Rules of Marketing and PR*, 5th edn (New York: Wiley, 2015).
[33] Richard Osmer, *Practical Theology: An Introduction* (Grand Rapids, MI: Eerdmans, 2008): 4. Italicized emphasis his, bold emphasis ours.

this data (task 2), we might determine that the content is not serving our readers well. On the other hand, we might discover that the problem is being exacerbated by the website's navigation. Perhaps there are inadequate invitations to explore more content beyond what brought the reader to the site in the first place.

Before jumping directly to a strategy (task 4, in this case probably a change in editorial philosophy or an overhaul of the site's navigation), we would do well to ask some theologically normative questions (task 3): how are these reflections contributing to the spiritual growth of our readers? How are these news items inviting deeper faith engagement? Does our content have a sense of progression? Does one piece build upon another, reflecting our belief that 'the glory of God is man fully alive'[34] and that learning is therefore an expression of becoming more fully alive? How would we like our site to fit in with our readers' other spiritual practices? And with their other media consumption practices? What does it mean to be a person of prayer? And to be an engaged citizen?

With answers to these kinds of questions in mind, we are better equipped to make good decisions about ongoing strategy (task 4). For example, one way to lower bounce rates is to employ an 'infinite scroll' browsing feature, in which one item leads directly into the next. If you've ever found yourself wondering why you just spent 45 minutes on Facebook instead of the five you'd intended, you've experienced the effectiveness of this technique. There is no invitation or prompt to stop using the platform. Of course, this technique works for social networking companies who want to maximize the amount of time users spend logged on to the platform (and scrolling past a paid advertisement every ten items or so).

However, such a practice does not stand up well to our normative task. If cultivating the spiritual life is mostly about making intentional choices about how we spend our time, it seems unwise to play on the power of unintended momentum or to manipulate our visitors. If we honour the agency of a disciple on a spiritual journey, providing more relevant follow-up content is probably better than a chronological feed. Perhaps a better site design would be to suggest a couple of related articles for follow-up. Even better, we could stop suggesting articles after the second or third click, or even borrow from Google's 'empty inbox' message and tell them to go enjoy their day (or go love and serve the Lord). Obviously, there's no right answer of how to proceed, but we would argue there is a right method. Many technically effective approaches will also be spiritually edifying. Just

---

[34] Popularized translation of St Irenaeus' 'Gloria Dei est vivens homo.'

as preachers are encouraged to hold a Bible in one hand and a newspaper in the other, digital media ministry practitioners need to stay connected to the timely techniques of 'new media gurus' and the timeless truth we have received from the saints.

Before bringing this section, and chapter, to a close, we would be remiss if we didn't tell one last story from our direct experience in the Center for the Ministry of Teaching. In the first year of our offering e-Formation as a fully fledged conference, we didn't really know who we needed (and could afford!) as a keynoter. We had a sense that we wanted a tech innovator, someone splashy from outside the church world who would – we hoped – 'get' the Church well enough to say something that would resonate theologically. We were hoping to hear some 'theories from the arts and sciences' that would provide grist for the practical theological mill in our context. We approached media outlets in Metro Washington, found someone who was interested, and held our breath.

What we weren't expecting was to have a church outsider[35] explain the Church better than we could have. Sarah Lumbard was then vice president (VP) of content strategy and operations for National Public Radio (NPR). She began her talk with a playful joke about how NPR is 'competing for habit' (like the Church is) and that, every year, its audience gets one year older (like the Church's does). This is gonna be fine, we thought. And then she said this:

> The digital world is an extension of our physical world. And everything that we expect of people in the physical world is true in the digital world, and it brings us the same joy. You need trust in this world. That's everything friendship and community is built on, and that's all we're talking about here. Trust is created by being active, being present, being yourself. And when you break it – and you can do that digitally – it's hard to rebuild. But we already knew that.[36]

If all this sounds familiar, then we know you didn't just skip to the end of the chapter. It's true: we learned as much about being the Church in an era of digital mediation from a VP at NPR as we have from the many gifted practical theologians we have cited in this chapter. Sometimes it's a lot of work to bring the tech experts and the faith experts into conversation together, and other times we're already on the same wavelength.

---

[35] In fairness, she did tell us that she grew up Episcopalian but no longer really practised.

[36] Kyle Oliver, 'NPR Exec to Church Educators: "Be Present, Be Active, Be Yourself" Online', *Virginia Theological Seminary*, 7 June 2013: <http://www.vts.edu/podium/default.aspx?t=204&nid=859770&sdb=1>.

Our goal in this chapter has been to introduce you to some widely read and broadly useful resources for shaping your practice of digital media ministry. Most of these resources are from our American context, though we believe much of their guidance will translate well throughout the Global North and – to an extent that may surprise you if you live in the Global North – in the Global South as well. We are even more confident that our four general principles will prove sturdy almost everywhere, particularly as mobile technology continues to spread and mature and as existing demographic trends continue:

1 **Digital literacy** is becoming an essential part of ministry formation [because . . .]
2 pervasive **digital tools** are also populous **digital spaces**, spaces where our presence as ministers is welcome and needed, [and yet . . .]
3 the physical and digital spheres are increasingly enmeshed, calling for an **integrated practice** of networked ministry, [in which . . .]
4 the Christian tradition and digital media expertise inform one another in our processes of **integrated reflection** (and further action).

With this road map of the digital media for ministry landscape in place, we are ready for Chapter 16, in which we present some of our favourite case studies and vignettes, share best practices gleaned from this learning and develop a vision for the formation of digitally literate twenty-first-century ministers.

16

Digital media for ministry: portraits, practices and potential

KYLE OLIVER AND LISA KIMBALL

As we complete this manuscript, we are in the midst of preparations for the fifth e-Formation Conference, a gathering of church leaders learning to better integrate technology in their ministry. (See Chapter 15 for an introduction to the event and, more importantly, for an explication of the concepts and convictions underlying this work.) When we review feedback from previous conferences, we see a consistent pattern in what participants tell us they appreciate about it: they love the networking. They love the practicality. They love – to use the words they usually choose – 'seeing what others are doing'.

As educators, we find this trend fairly unsurprising. Researchers know that of all the learning we hope our students will achieve, the most difficult of all is **transfer**. Transfer is taking information or skills from one domain and applying them to another.[1] So it is not enough for us to teach people particular software skills or particular ways of reconceptualizing minis-try in digitally mediated contexts.[2] We have to help them encounter and reflect upon concrete examples of those skills or reconceptualizations in action in everyday ministries.

Describing such examples of digital media ministry in action is one of two purposes for this chapter. We begin with short portraits of col-leagues and associates exercising their ministries. These lightweight digital case studies[3] will allow us to reflect on the craft of using digital media

---

[1] For an older but accessible and sturdy literature review in transfer of learning and transfer of training, see Bhawani Shankar Subedi, 'Emerging Trends of Research on Transfer of Learning', *International Education Journal*, vol. 5, no. 4 (2004): 591–9.

[2] Just as it is insufficient to teach seminarians the tools of scholarly biblical exegesis without helping them to develop a framework for applying those skills and to practise them in a more pastoral context.

[3] For an example of theological educators using case study methodologies inspired by Harvard Business School, see Auburn Theological Seminary's Case Study Initiative in partnership

for ministry and generalize some practices that should transfer to other settings. In the second part of the chapter we will zoom out from local practices to sketch a more general framework for the 'digital formation'[4] of ministry leaders in training – both in formal and informal settings throughout the Church.

Case studies in digital media ministry

Building on strengths

It has become common practice in church settings in North America to adopt the methods of community organizers. For example, Episcopal Relief and Development regularly both uses and teaches a model called Asset-Based Community Development, which attempts wherever possible to identify, affirm and build on local strengths. This method of working suits the organization's mission 'to assist individuals and whole communities to believe in themselves . . . [and] to break through traditional hierarchical perceptions of power and cycles of dependence reinforced by an overemphasis on outside solutions and outside funds'.[5] We believe analogous issues are at play with respect to faith groups' preparation for digital media ministry. Many would prefer to rely on interventions from outside experts (web designers, communications consultants, freelance social media managers, etc.) and to do as little internal work as possible. Still others use the lack of financial resources to pay for such assistance as an excuse not to do the work at all. While we encourage communities to get the help they need, we also believe that claiming ownership of the sustainable day-to-day practice of this ministry is essential to its flourishing *in situ*. Moreover, the actual barrier to entry is much lower than generally perceived. The tools and approaches do not need to be particularly sophisticated or high-tech to be effective. Thus, we too seek to help communities identify the assets already present in their local contexts and to build on those strengths.

---

with Harvard's Pluralism Project: <http://www.auburnseminary.org/casestudy>. We use 'case study' here in the less formal sense of an action research vignette. We will describe the context and practices of digital media ministry colleagues and attempt to identify emerging best practices.

4   To borrow from the name of a 2013–14 programme founded at General Theological Seminary by Colin Chapman and Joseph Peters-Mathews.

5   'Asset-Based Community Development', *Episcopal Relief and Development: Healing a Hurting World*, accessed 29 February 2016, <bit.ly/ERDassets>.

One group of colleagues who needed very little help from us in building an incredibly effective and authentic digital media ministry is the
Society of St John the Evangelist (SSJE). Located just off Harvard Square
in Cambridge, Massachusetts, this order of Episcopal monks knew what
they had to share: monastic wisdom. They are well-known, trusted stewards and teachers of the Christian spiritual traditions that have come down
to the modern Church through monastic communities. Nonetheless, the
SSJE brothers find themselves caught in a ministry conundrum: on the one
hand, they believe these practices are essential and life-giving and wish to
share them with as many individuals and faith communities as possible.
On the other hand, the mostly introverted brothers are vowed to settled
patterns of Benedictine living, and there are only 24 hours in a day. To
accept every teaching invitation from around the Episcopal Church would,
ironically, rob the brothers of the very thing they're being asked to share.

Thus, Jamie Coats, director of Friends of SSJE, working with production assistance from editor and designer Conor Byrne, set out to build on
the strength of this community (briefly, 'teaching spiritual wisdom') using
appropriate social media tools to reach the brothers' desired audiences.
SSJE began using their 'Brother, Give Us a Word' daily email meditation
as the launching point for more embodied teaching. In Lent of 2013, they
released short videos in the daily emails, each one elaborating the theme
of 'Praying Our Lives'. These were honest and accessible explications of
prayer practices both ancient and modern and also served to humanize
the brothers for viewers who had perhaps never met a monk. The most
popular videos were seen thousands of times, and subsequent SSJE Lenten
programmes have exhibited broader viewership, more substantive participant contributions and increasing pedagogical sophistication.[6] SSJE
has since added a complementary social media offering during Advent, a
global Advent calendar crowdsourced via photo-sharing apps.

There is much to admire about how Coats and his colleagues went
about their work. It's true that, looking back on that first year's videos,
we notice plenty of flaws: in audio and video quality, in how the series
was promoted, in the spoken contributions from the brothers themselves
(several of whom were not yet used to being on camera). However, SSJE
did not let a desire for high production values get in the way of releasing
something that was usable. Not surprisingly, the act of creating new videos
with continuous feedback has given the community increasing confidence

---

[6] Full disclosure: we have partnered with SSJE in promoting and, more recently, developing
these resources.

and skill. Another strong aspect of this project is the excellent fit between the (relatively unchanging) *message* of the brothers and the *method* (informal teaching) and *media* they chose to carry that message. Video-sharing tools make a great informal teaching platform, as the Khan Academy has certainly demonstrated in a more secular vein. Similarly, social media apps like Instagram and Pinterest are a brilliant venue for updating the visual and tactile experience of keeping an Advent calendar in the company of a (here very large) community of faith. The case of SSJE helps us identify the first of many principles we will share in this chapter: Use technology for what it's good at to help you do what you're good at. Doing so is an exercise in Christian discernment; the goal is to interpret how God is already working to empower particular ministries and to deploy digital resources in service of that mission.

Marrying digital and physical

There's a complementary principle lying in wait when digital media ministry has a more local scope, one that builds on the central observation of Keith Anderson's *The Digital Cathedral.*[7] We noticed it (and many of the best practices that follow) in the midst of our hybrid faith-formation cohort programme,[8] in which participating congregational and judicatory ministers launched hybrid[9] learning initiatives in their local faith communities while networked to each other (and us) for support and reflection. Three of our colleagues were particularly adept at taking the general model we had proposed – gather a small group to meet once per month in person and to connect weekly online for learning at home – and coordinating the work of its component parts.

In the case of First Presbyterian Church of Libertyville, Illinois, a suburb of Chicago, associate pastor Roberta Dodds Ingersoll realized digital tools could complement an existing church network, extend its reach, and

---

[7] Namely, that physical and digital connections and practices form an integrated whole for ministry in networked, post-programme era churches and communities. Keith Anderson, *The Digital Cathedral: Networked Ministry in a Wireless World* (New York: Morehouse, 2015).

[8] For a broad introduction, see Day Smith Pritchartt, 'Shutting Down the Sunday School', *Key Resources*, 14 January 2014, <bit.ly/SundayShutdown>; and Kyle Matthew Oliver, 'Expanding Faith Formation Reach with Hybrid Networks', *Key Resources*, 10 December 2013, <bit.ly/ HybridNetworks>. For a thorough report of the first year's experience, see Elisabeth Kimball and Kyle Oliver, 'Communities of (Digital) Practice: Preparing Religious Leaders for Lively Online Engagement', *Religious Education Association Annual Conference*, Boston, MA, 2013, <bit.ly/ComDigiPrac>.

[9] 'Hybrid' in the sense that some of the learning happens in person at church and some outside of church via connected learning online.

strengthen community within it. Club M.O.M. (Meeting Other Moms) is 'a parenting group that welcomes mothers of young children' one weekday morning per month. It was working well, but of course it excluded most mothers who work outside the home. So rather than create a new hybrid faith formation group from scratch, Ingersoll worked to digitally connect the Club M.O.M. regulars – both to each other and to moms who *couldn't* usually make the meetings. She then focused on bringing more faith formational content and activities to this newly expanded group. We realize this isn't an idea of earth-shattering originality, but for us it served as a good reminder that existing programmes and relationships benefit from digital connection. We don't always need to launch something entirely new when we seek to expand our ministries into the online space.

At St Paul's Episcopal Church in Kansas City, associate rector Megan Castellan sought to raise the profile of newly launched family faith formation initiative The S.P.O.T. (St Paul's Online Theology) with the wider congregation. To do so, she focused the group's early in-person gathering time on creating a physical artefact of their online learning. The banner they created became a sort of icon, offering a glimpse into learning that would otherwise have gone unseen most Sunday mornings. Another such icon was employed by cohort member Day Smith Pritchartt of St Andrew's Episcopal Church in Arlington, Virginia. Her group rehearsed and performed a theatrical production at the church that served as the culmination of a hybrid learning unit in which the families of the parish studied God's promises to Abraham. Again, networked learning outside of church came together to form a sign that could be seen *at* church. We were thus reminded that the complementarity of physical and digital goes both ways; sometimes an online learning initiative needs its own physical representation or avatar.[10]

Avoiding assumptions, bringing individuals along

Many experienced ministers remind us of the importance in our work of what amounts to informal ethnography.[11] While it is helpful to learn about

---

[10] An avatar is usually a digital representation of a person's identity online, but our usage here inverts that pattern in the light of the increasing integration of these spheres. For another playful example of a digital initiative celebrated in person, see Kyle Matthew Oliver, 'Digital Ministry Field Notes: Dedicating a Parish Resource Center', *Key Resources*, 8 September 2014, <bit.ly/parishcenter>.

[11] See, for example, Mary Clark Moschella, *Ethnography as a Pastoral Practice: An Introduction* (Cleveland, OH: Pilgrim, 2008). See also the primacy for Osmer of the descriptive-empirical task (Richard Osmer, *Practical Theology: An Introduction* (Grand Rapids, MI:

general digital ministry principles and review aggregate research about people's online behaviour,[12] nothing substitutes for knowing your people and how they live their everyday lives. Avoid making assumptions about how the people you are connecting want to communicate; it's much better to ask them proactively.[13] Consider, for example, the following humorous exchange, in which Kyle and one of his Digital Media for Ministry students talk about some unexpected behaviour at a local congregation:

STUDENT: I really like the idea of using social media more in my ministry, but I don't think it will work at my home parish, because most people aren't on Facebook.

KYLE: What church is that?

STUDENT: [Redacted] Episcopal Church in [Redacted] Maryland.

KYLE: Oh, because they're all spies!

STUDENT: Uh, yeah. How did you know that?

He knew that because we have many colleagues in Metro Washington DC, so this was not our first encounter with a church whose location practically guarantees drawing many members who work for US intelligence agencies.[14] Indeed, another colleague in a similar situation told us flat out that Facebook would not be an option for her hybrid learning initiative because too many of her parishioners were – for, um, professional reasons – not allowed to use social networking tools. In these two cases, the aggregate national data about demographics and online behaviour is simply wrong at the local level. In such a situation, more private, anonymous, or one-way 'hubs' of digital communication become better options than a group. Other churchgoers are simply tired of particular tools. Day Smith Pritchartt chose a blog to disseminate activities to her Faith at

---

Eerdmans, 2008): 4) and Leonora Tubbs Tisdale's brilliant *Preaching as Local Theology and Folk Art* (Minneapolis, MN: Fortress, 1997).

[12] In the US context, the Pew Internet and American Life Project (<www.pewinternet.org>) is an invaluable source of reliable data. In the UK see 'Home internet and social media usage', *Office of National Statistics*, accessed 4 March 2016, <http://bit.ly/OffcNatlStats>.

[13] This same principle is increasing the effectiveness of marketing communications in the business and non-profit worlds. See David Meerman Scott, *The New Rules of Marketing and PR*, 5th edn (Hoboken, NJ: Wiley, 2015). (Kyle has served as manuscript editor for all five editions of the book.) This desire to avoid guessing people's likely behaviour and instead incorporate their continuous feedback also forms the core of the so-called Lean Startup methodology (build, measure, learn). See Kyle Matthew Oliver, 'A Prototyping Mindset for Ministry', *Key Resources*, 3 November 2015, <bit.ly/ProtoMin>. A colleague in our recent study of theological educators teaching digital media put it this way: 'the literacy of the twenty-first century is the ability to learn, to unlearn, and to learn again.'

[14] Though of course few of those members can, as they say, 'confirm or deny' this.

Home participants because they just didn't want to connect via Facebook. The cost of this choice was a much lower likelihood of online interaction between families, since comments on the blog are public and deep conversation is therefore significantly harder to foster. The benefit of the choice was that it honoured group members' agency and avoided alienating participants from the beginning.

A second aspect of bringing people along and building buy-in from participants is even more 'local'. Experienced ministers know that untargeted calls to action have always been less effective than direct invitations. We are all more likely to respond to the shepherd who 'calls us each by name,' whether that person happens to be the Good Shepherd, our parish pastor, or a volunteer asking us to attend next month's silent auction for charity. Bring people along on social media through a combination of 'broadcast' and 'narrowcast': both public posting and direct contact. Our friend and colleague Anthony Guillén is the master of this approach. Anthony needs to be direct, because his job as Latino/Hispanic Missioner for the Episcopal Church means he is organizing ministry leaders throughout North, Central and South America. If Anthony only used his office's social media channels in broadcast mode, it would be easy for him to fall 'out of sight, out of mind'. Instead, he tags[15] key individuals he hopes will see and share his public updates. He uses back channels like email and texting if he believes his messages aren't getting through to his colleagues, or if tagging isn't appropriate.[16] Most importantly, he cultivates genuine friendships and prayerful collaborations that build his social capital and make it much more likely that his direct outreach will be trusted and bear fruit. Know that the more targeted your online outreach becomes, the more likely it is to be considered 'spam' if it lacks the proper relational context between sender and receiver. Anthony's success building an international coalition for Episcopal Latino/Hispanic Ministry demonstrates how digitally enriched organizational communication is more interpersonal craft than data-driven science.

---

[15] Tagging is a directed mode of contact available on most social media channels in which authors of public content select and name certain people they want to be sure will see this content. Those users then get a special notification, greatly increasing their likelihood of engagement.

[16] To give a couple of obvious examples, one would not want to publicly tag individuals in announcements for something like an Alcoholics Anonymous meeting or weight-loss club. As always, direct address in a public setting can become manipulative or shaming if we don't keep context and privacy in mind.

The importance (and risk) of choice

We believe that, by helping ministers optimize the use of digital resources and platforms, our colleague John Roberto has done more to advance high-quality, forward-thinking Christian formation in US Roman Catholic and Protestant churches than any other active religious educator. Of the many gifts he has given the thousands of leaders he has trained in twenty-first-century faith formation, perhaps the greatest is the curator's mindset. John consistently points out that we now have more than enough resources to support connected, semi-autonomous faith learning based in (but not limited to) the context of congregational life. Most of these resources are free, are available and shareable online, and are easily adapted to a variety of denominational contexts. John is himself a master curator, and he generously shares his extensive library of recommendations at curatingfaithformation.com. We concur with his belief that ministers today need to worry much less about creating educational content and much more about how to engage participants with the content that already exists.

The core assumption in this paradigm shift is that learners – both adults and children – do best when they have some agency in the learning process: 'Time and again, research has shown that the more educators give students choice, control, challenge, and collaborative opportunities, the more motivation and engagement are likely to rise.'[17] Thus, offering participants in connected faith learning a selection of activities is key; since when we don't have a 'captive audience', we are under more pressure to help our students self-motivate. The experience of the hybrid faith formation ministers we've worked with suggests that balance between freedom and structure is important to this work. Participants like having a choice, but when they feel overwhelmed by the number of choices they've been given, they report being *less* likely to actually do any activity.[18] Indeed, this is why curation is such a significant digital media ministry skill; it narrows down

---

[17] Eric Toshalis and Michael J. Nakkula, 'Motivation, Engagement, and Student Voice', *Jobs for the Future Project*, April 2012, <bit.ly/StudentMotiv>: 27. We often also hear appeals to varied learning styles as another reason to offer a variety of activities. This guidance can be helpful if we bear in mind that learning styles are *preferences* individuals develop rather than rigid and determinative limitations on how learning can happen for them. For a very short and accessible introduction to the limitations of learning styles theory, see Nancy Chick, 'Learning Styles', *Vanderbilt University Center for Teaching*, accessed 6 March 2016, <bit.ly/VandyLearningStyles>.

[18] Psychologist Barry Schwartz called this phenomenon 'the paradox of choice' in his book of same name (New York: HarperCollins, 2009). We experienced it most profoundly in this context through feedback about an excellent resource from Vibrant Faith Ministries called *Vibrant Faith at Home* (vibrantfaithathome.org). Ministers consistently reported that families

the seemingly limitless options the internet provides. For a nice example of manageable choice in a digital lesson meant to be done by families at home, see Day Smith Pritchartt's 'God's Promises'.[19]

Investing in community

We regularly begin our training events with a brief video that efficiently describes the 'new media ecology' in which today's ministers work. In it, Lee Rainie of the Pew Internet Project addresses a common critique: 'People are using these [social networking] technologies to do something profoundly human: they're connecting with other people and sharing their stories. *So they're not hooked on their gadgets – they're hooked on each other.*'[20] The word choice of 'hooked on' gestures to the common observation that technology can create addictive patterns in our day-to-day behaviour. But we hasten to point out that faith communities have good reason to expect our people to be 'hooked on each other': we believe community and relationship are basic human needs and one of the most powerful ways to experience the love of God. Conceived in this light, the digital connections that bind Christians one to another represent one of the many ways in which we comprise the mystical Body of Christ.

Thus, we conclude this first section on wise practices by sharing and discussing what may be the most important and reassuring data from the evaluations of our 2014 and 2015 hybrid faith-formation cohorts:

Q: What kept you motivated to participate in the cohort?

A: The others in the group. I wanted to know what they were up to and what they were thinking about.

A: The messages and questions I got from fellow cohort members. I wanted to find out what happened with them!

A: [I]nformal conversations were so supportive.

A: The ongoing posts with ideas and, when needed, prayer support.

A: Knowing that there was a community of people in the cohort available for support was quite helpful.

A: I felt connected and motivated thru the conversations on FB [Facebook] that I had with a few people.

---

would not do an activity if they were simply sent to the website (which contains hundreds of activities) but would do so if given a single activity or very short list to choose from.

[19] Day Smith Pritchartt, 'God's Promises', *St. Andrew's FISH: Families Integrating Sunday and Home*, 30 September 2014, <bit.ly/PromisesAbraham>.

[20] Lee Rainie, 'Networked: The New Social Operating System', *Pew Research Center* (YouTube), 24 May 2012, <bit.ly/NetworkedVideo>, emphasis added.

A: I liked the Facebook connections, and honestly a big part of that was becoming FB friends with many folks in the group. Suddenly their work and interests began to appear in my newsfeed, and I would end up being inspired and intrigued frequently!

Even in a professional development context that could easily have taken an instrumentalist tone ('Just teach me how to use these tools!'), our participants told us again and again that the best part of their connected learning experience was, in fact, *the connections*. Relationships, much more so than the content and skills, were what ultimately resonated most strongly. This is as it should be as we endeavour to continue in the apostles' teaching and fellowship, and if anything that is more true when we gather or connect to grow disciples in congregations and other faith communities today.

Every case we have studied has shown us that the best thing you can do to use technology effectively in your setting is to invest in community. Help people get to know one another, so they'll keep coming back each week for ongoing encounter. Help them get comfortable sharing and being vulnerable, within the limitations of whatever digital tool is helping facilitate this essential communication. Help them take ownership of their own ongoing connection and participation, so facilitators can become less like camp counsellors and more like fellow disciples and peer mentors. Help them create and share their own resources, insights and experiences, following Jesus in distinct and authentic ways and turning outward with curiosity and a desire to serve. The stronger the community of faith, the more the details of the technology will seem to fall away. We move from being 'hooked on' each other by means of digital media to being a part of each other by means of the Holy Spirit.

A vision for digital literacy formation for faith leaders

In the light of what we have learned in this chapter and in Chapter 15, we will close by sharing our vision for how church leaders – lay and ordained, staff and volunteers, technophobic and technophilic – should be formed for this significant aspect of twenty-first-century ministry. As we have throughout, we will make steady use of examples and principles gleaned from our own practice and that of our colleagues. We do this not because we think we have all the answers (we don't), nor because we want to be the only ones involved in providing these opportunities (we aren't and could never be). Rather, we believe we have stumbled upon some emerging models that seem to be working well in our context and would likely work well for others.

A formation ecology

Inspired by an approach to formation that goes back to Maria Harris's seminal *Fashion Me a People*[21] and has been rearticulated today by our colleagues Julie Lytle[22] and John Roberto,[23] we want to think about the systems of preparation for digital media ministry as a networked ecology of hands-on training, contextual practice and theological reflection in community.[24]

This ecology has three characteristics we believe to be essential to its success. First, it has a wide scope of inclusion. There are a lot of potential participants in this network, and diversity within it is a positive and indeed essential thing. For example, geographical diversity serves several important functions. In the US context, the well-known adoption curve[25] for most digital media tools means that urban areas along the North American coasts can serve as 'test markets' for various digitally mediated faith activities. By the time tools are widely adopted in other areas, participants in the network can either describe (early adopters) or learn about (late adopters) models that seem to be working well.

On the other hand, geographical diversity can also turn traditional power dynamics and stereotypes on their head. Leaders from Province 9 of the Episcopal Church (which comprises the Dioceses of Colombia, the Dominican Republic, Central Ecuador, Litoral Ecuador, Honduras, Puerto Rico and Venezuela) have been key innovators in using social networking, mobile media, and hybrid pedagogies for learning and communication in faith settings. The geographic distribution and limited financial resources in this province have driven some of this innovation by necessity, but more important have been the creativity and skill of digital missioners like our friends Edgar Giraldo and Pablo Velazquez. We envisage, and see glimpses of, a digital literacy formation ecology that is not just geographically

---

[21] Harris sees religious education as the integrated work of an entire community engaged together in the mission of the people of God (proclamation, prayer, service, teaching and fellowship) rather than some sequence of age-segregated, schooling-model programmes. This is, of course, a very old way of understanding Christian formation. See Maria Harris, *Fashion Me a People: Curriculum in the Church* (Louisville, KY: Westminster John Knox Press, 1989).

[22] See Julie Lytle, *Faith Formation 4.0: Introducing an Ecology of Faith in a Digital Age* (New York: Morehouse, 2013): ch. 6.

[23] See John Roberto, 'A Vision of 21st Century Faith Formation', *Lifelong Faith Journal* 7, no. 2 (Summer 2013): 3–25.

[24] From the 'secular' education world, we are inspired by the communities of practice literature and have described our work elsewhere with respect to its central tenets. See Kimball and Oliver, 'Communities of (Digital) Practice': 2–4.

[25] See Everett M. Rogers, *Diffusion of Innovations*, 5th edn (New York: Free Press, 2003): 11–38.

diverse but also racially, culturally, economically, and ecumenically diverse. So much of the lack of diversity in our Episcopal Church contexts has to do with the segregation of neighbourhoods. We believe it is not just possible but essential that our digital networking for digital formation contribute to the work of dismantling this legacy.

A second, and related, characteristic of our proposed learning ecology is a combination of low- and high-barrier activities. We need low-barrier activities because many churches – including the ones most in need of digital formation – cannot afford to devote financial and human resources to anything else. A church with very part-time or completely non-stipendiary staff members is unlikely to convince them to attend an event like our e-Formation Conference, or to have room in the budget to support such participation. For these churches, free training that does not ask leaders to travel too far or devote too much time is an essential first step. On the other hand, a church that has existing digital media ministries in place but would like to grow their sophistication and impact probably needs a higher-barrier experience, one that asks for a sustained commitment to experimentation and evaluation among a team of leaders. 'Commitment converts', as one of Kyle's mentors likes to say. Finding the right balance between ease of access and transformative challenge requires careful discernment and practice.

Finally, we believe it is essential for teaching and training networks in digital media for ministry to include both gathered (preferably in-person) opportunities and sustained connected learning in context. Just as faith formation happens most effectively in the home, formation for digital media ministry happens most effectively in the local faith community context. Flying off to a national conference or intensive course once per year isn't likely to bear much fruit unless leaders also have access to both an ongoing peer community and – obviously and even more importantly – to the community of disciples their new efforts are designed to serve in the first place. Leaders need to be able to try things out, get a feel for what works, let go of what doesn't, and adjust the path forward. The extended learning community can provide essential support and mutual mentoring during these moments of reflection and course adjustment.

However, we don't think networked learning reaches its full effect unless participants do have the opportunity to gather (preferably in person) from time to time. Online and asynchronous[26] relationships can be incred-

---

[26] I.e. not occurring at predetermined or regular intervals. Participants communicate at will and independent of one another.

ibly strong, meaningful and supportive, as we have discussed. And yet we know that ministry colleagues are energized and empowered when they come together. The in-person aspect of network participation is especially important for the portion of participants who are anxious about using technology tools on their own. We believe part of the draw of hands-on, in-person training is that it allows these participants to build confidence, particularly confidence that they will be able to sustain connections to people who can help them in the future.

Sample learning outcomes

In some sense, the desired learning outcomes for participants in a digital media ministry formation ecology should be as diverse as those participants. Indeed, an ecology is powerful precisely because it offers different opportunities for those with different needs. And yet there are undeniably universal knowledge and skills for this work that can and do transfer when leaders are properly supported. These broad categories should include at least the following:

- **Maintaining an online presence.** Through practice, feedback and instruction in the norms and patterns of digital culture, leaders learn to participate in online communities in ways that are authentic, responsive and appropriate to the ministry context. As with all socialization, this is largely a matter of learning to understand how one's behaviour is received and interpreted by others. With increasing experience, individuals learn to distinguish between their personal presence and that of the organization they represent.
- **Gathering and connecting with an audience or community.** As we discussed above, bringing others along is essential if digital media ministries are to flourish. Leaders need to be able to assess the communications needs and digital habits of the people they serve to determine the best way to share religious, spiritual, and organizational messages and encourage growing relationships. Requisite skills vary but include writing for the web, organizing contact lists, creating images and video, and managing project calendars.
- **Evaluating new tools with respect to communication and learning goals.** A challenging aspect of digital media ministry is that the *media* are always changing, even if the basic *message* and even *methods* for communicating it haven't. Leaders need to keep up with the big picture in social and mobile communication to help communities decide which platforms and approaches to embrace, which to ignore for now, and

which to let go of – all based on critical criteria derived from community objectives.

- **Fashioning a 'digital rule of life'.** Although not everyone will relate to this traditional monastic language for the rhythms of prayer, work, study and rest that shape our days, anyone who wants to serve effectively online needs a plan for staying motivated, setting boundaries, managing information overload and avoiding burnout. This too will be a work in progress for all of us, but those who develop some experience and critical techniques will also be able to help guide others.[27]

We very nearly added a fifth item to this list. It may not be strictly essential, but our experience suggests it is life-giving. We believe that to flourish with others online means wanting to be there, and a facility with fun and play in the online space can greatly support this desire. Having fun together is part of the culture of almost any successful online community,[28] just like it should be part of any church. We therefore believe that part of any one minister's 'digital formation' should be the opportunity to find a little corner of the internet that feeds and sustains him or her. We are right to seek and expect to receive living water and the bread of life in the midst of online community. But there's nothing wrong with also looking for some healthy laughs.

Types of learning activities

Allow us a brief summary of the chapter before we bring it to a close. We began with case studies, but we hope the reader found in them not just examples of promising ministry practices but also some demographic portraits of audiences for digital formation. We have spoken about congregational leaders, judicatory leaders, denominational leaders and parachurch organizational leaders. Some are lay people, some are clergy. Some are volunteers, though most are ministry professionals. In short, we believe all ministers need training in digital media for ministry, because all ministers can benefit from these tools and practices. In today's mission and ministry contexts – even in rural areas, even in developing countries, even where church members are ageing rapidly or have primarily low incomes – basic digital literacy is essential for church leaders. We think not teaching it is

---

[27] For a field report on some of our thinking in this area, see Kyle Oliver, 'An "Infomagical" Week of Doing More with Less', *e-Formation*, 5 February 2016, <bit.ly/InfoRule>. For enumerations of sample principles for digital rules of life, see especially Drescher, *Tweet If You ♥ Jesus*: ch. 9; and Anderson, *Digital Cathedral*: ch. 12. For a sample digital rule of life course assignment, see Kyle's most recent Digital Media for Ministry syllabus at <bit.ly/RCL524>.

[28] OK, maybe not LinkedIn, but perhaps we just haven't found the fun places there.

like not teaching preaching or pastoral care. Therefore we have described a formation ecosystem that is diverse, accessible, flexible and adaptable; that takes advantage of digital interactions and pedagogies but does not rely on them completely or treat them as possessing saving power; that invites participation and trusts that God will provide richly for those who prepare room in their hearts, minds and schedules. And not wanting to put media before message, we have described some of what we hope participants in such a system will learn.

Our final challenge and invitation is this: start or continue learning together. There are countless ways to do so, though we will name our four favourites. Find some partners and an internet connection, reserve a room or a URL, and start practising. Maybe you need a teacher, or maybe you're already prepared to be one. Maybe both are true. The two of us and the colleagues and networks we have introduced you to are both models and potential conversation partners. But there are almost surely others in your networks asking these same questions. Find them and try out some or all of the following:

- **Small groups to support daily practice.** The biggest barrier to change in any professional practice is a lack of external accountability. Convene a group online (or some combination of online and in person) for regular learning, check-in and support. You could start by reading together one of the books we introduced in Chapter 15. If you still feel like you are pooling more ignorance than gaining insight, try asking a more experienced mentor to help facilitate or at least point you in the right direction. Nothing will help you develop as a leader of online community better than being a participant in online community.

- **Seminary courses for ministry trainees and lifelong learners.** There are multiple schools of thought about teaching practical leadership skills in theological education. We belong firmly to the school that says we do our students a disservice if we use the immense challenge of this task as an excuse to abdicate the responsibility. If you're a student in seminary or other ministry training program that doesn't teach digital literacy as a stand-alone course or across the curriculum, ask for an opportunity to create an independent study, a series of alternate assignments[29] or a standalone course – or seek these out at a partner

---

[29] For a preliminary report on a research project incorporating digital literacy assignments into a Hebrew Bible course, see Judy Fentress-Williams and Stacy Williams-Duncan, 'Everything Is a Remix: Using Digital Storytelling to Re-engage Oral Texts', *The Vanderbilt Divinity Program in Theology and Practice*, 3–5 June 2015, <bit.ly/BibleRemix>. Kyle served as the

institution. For a richer experience, open the course up to practising ministers as well.[30]

- **Day(s)-long intensive gatherings for training and inspiration.** One advantage of seminary courses over networked online learning for ministers is that seminary education tends to correspond with a time in life set aside for focused study and deep learning. One way to hold such a space in the midst of the busy life of full-time ministry is to set aside a day or more for exclusive focus on digital media ministry formation.[31] Make it as practical as you can, and try to focus some of the content on providing concrete next steps.[32]

- **Project-based learning with experienced mentors.** One great thing about digital media ministries is that they create lots of digital artefacts: websites, posts with comment threads, images and video, web conference recordings, e-newsletter issues, etc. That means getting contextual feedback from mentors is surprisingly easy. Groups like the Mozilla Foundation, DIY.org and the Cities of Learning Project have turned that insight into programmes of digital literacy micro-credentialing.[33] We think this approach sets a fantastic example for church leaders. But whether or not you're earning a badge, consider sending off an artefact to a more experienced mentor next time you think you could benefit from some feedback.

As a dismissal and (we hope) a blessing, we leave you with our Collect for Interactive Communication,[34] inspired by Lytle's *Faith Formation 4.0*. May prayers like it be ever on our lips as we seek and serve Christ in the twenty-first century and beyond.

---

video training consultant to Fentress-Williams' students, and the resources he developed are available at <bit.ly/eform15story> and <bit.ly/easyvideoVTS>.

[30] Kyle's January 2016 offering of Digital Media for Ministry was greatly enhanced by the presence of 'continuing education' students. They brought concrete knowledge of current local ministry contexts that full-time seminarians sometimes understandably lack.

[31] Obviously, our main attempt to do so is our three-day e-Formation Conference. But we have developed a regional 'bootcamp' model as well, intended for ministers who can't afford the travel and that much time away. Read more at <bit.ly/eformBootcamps>.

[32] Which is, of course, what we're trying to model in this conclusion.

[33] See Kyle Oliver, 'Digital Badges Could Document, Motivate Faith Learning', *e-Formation*, 5 August 2015, <bit.ly/DigitalBadges>. We are piloting a series of digital media ministry badges as part of our e-Formation Learning Community.

[34] Kyle Oliver, 'Collects for Communication', *Key Resources*, 1 November 2013, <bit.ly/CommsCollects>.

Loving God, your triune life shows us that there is no unity without diversity, no centre without an encircling dance: Strengthen our mutual connections, that we may bear one another's burdens and celebrate the joys of our shared abundant life in you; in the name of the One who calls us each by name. Amen.

Part 3

MINISTRY IN CHRISTIAN TRADITION

17

Scripture and ministry

HYWEL CLIFFORD

The sacred texts of Christianity – the Bible or Holy Scripture – play a central role in the daily life of the world's most populous religion. Without a doubt, their interpretation in the history of Christianity has been controversial. The quincentenary in 1992 of Christopher Columbus's discovery of the New World in 1492 was a reminder of the complex legacy of a period when European powers tried, with mixed motives, to be the voice of God in distant lands 'that have not heard of my fame or seen my glory'. Another quincentenary was the commemoration in 2017 of Martin Luther's protest in 1517, in the manner of a prophet like Isaiah (with whom he identified himself, according to *Table Talk*), against the abuses of the late-medieval Church that precipitated the fracturing of Christian Europe. Looking further forward, 2054 will provide occasion for a millennial anniversary: the Great Schism of 1054 that divided Christendom into East and West over Christology (and much else), a doctrine rooted in the portrayal of Jesus Christ in Scripture. There have been moves to heal this ecclesiastical wound, as also the wounds of colonialism and Catholic and Protestant division. Not everything, however, about the interpretation of Scripture in the history of Christianity has been without benefit: theological dispute is sometimes necessary.

But there is another story that Christians tell from day to day in many local contexts across the world: Scripture nourishes faith like no other texts because its texts proclaim God's redemptive purposes. This has been the quieter and more dependable constant in the history of Christianity, and there is no reason to suppose, thankfully, that it will change. It is therefore essential that those preparing for, or who are already active in, public Christian ministry, know and appreciate how Scripture functions in theology and practice. When Scripture is read, they and their congregations should not 'keep listening, but . . . not comprehend' but be equipped to participate in God's redemptive purposes, so that the Church might be 'a light to the nations'. The book of Isaiah, called 'a fifth evangelist' in early

Church writings (and the source of the quotations above: see 66.19; 6.9; 42.6; 49.6), will largely guide us. In this essay Scripture is viewed through five prisms: revelation, worship, ministry, mission and education. It is, after all, important to situate Scripture in a broad framework given its many and varied roles. Each section contains foundational principles, key pointers, and pitfalls to avoid.

Scripture and revelation: 'Hear . . . listen . . . for the LORD has spoken' (Isa. 1.2)[1]

The Church has always given prominence to Scripture when laying out the main areas and points of Christian theology and practice. This may be seen in all sorts of Christian literature, whether concerned with doctrine, liturgy, ethics or pastoral care. This is because it is through Scripture that we learn of God's redemptive purposes. This is another way of saying that Christianity is a 'revealed religion'; that is, it is not based on human reason alone, even if reason may be used to explain and account for Christian faith. The prominence of Scripture is illustrated by the instructional genre known as 'catechism' (typically in question and answer format) traditionally used in the preparation of candidates for the sacrament of baptism. The *Catechism of the Catholic Church* places its discussion of Scripture in the context of God's revelation: the human desire for God, how God comes to meet humanity, and the human response to this revelation; only then is there discussion of the creed, the sacraments, vocation and prayer. *The Longer Catechism of the Orthodox, Catholic, Eastern Church*, structured around the three Christian virtues of faith, hope and love, also starts with revelation, by considering Scripture in the context of the knowledge of God and Church tradition, much like its Catholic equivalent. The classic Protestant catechisms (e.g. Lutheran, Genevan, Heidelberg, Westminster) all make Scripture their principal reference point in itemising how Christians should live in faithful obedience to God; they, too, articulate this with a robust doctrine of divine revelation.[2]

It is not that there are no major differences between these catechisms; a good number stem from historic disputes. Is Scripture sufficient in and of itself for learning about God's redemptive purposes; or is it part of ongoing revelation (within 'tradition') of which the Church is the guardian?

---

[1] All Scripture quotations in this chapter are taken from the New Revised Standard Version (NRSV).

[2] The texts of these catechisms are available online.

Should the canon of Scripture include the Apocrypha/Deutero-Canon; if so, in what way? How can Scripture be interpreted in ways that are neither institutionally authoritarian nor individualistically anarchic? These are important questions. But there are deeper similarities between the catechisms. They all agree about revelation as such: 'the LORD has spoken' (Isa. 1.2). This may be seen from different angles. Scripture possesses a sanctified authority because its ultimate author is God. That its texts were 'inspired' – the Holy Spirit enlivened and steered their human authors' responses to revelation, while not overriding their minds – gives them unique qualities.[3] Moreover, Scripture plays a unique role in the revelation of God. There are many ways through which God may be perceived (e.g. the splendour of the natural world, the delight of a newborn child, and acts of sacrificial love) but Scripture teaches us things we would not otherwise know, such as the divine assessment of the human condition, and the divine promise to bless all nations. Furthermore, Scripture witnesses to the triune action of the one God: its texts have a united purpose in referring to the activity of God the Father (e.g. John 5.17–18), the Son (e.g. Matt. 16.16) and the Holy Spirit (e.g. Mark 12.36).[4] Some key pointers emerge from this:

- It is essential in public ministry to attend to the primary subject of Scripture: God's redemptive purposes. Its texts are neither a repository of incidental detail from antiquity nor an encyclopaedia for all branches of knowledge. Rather, from the Old Testament through to the New Testament, God's redemptive purposes are revealed to be no less than the healing and renewal of the broken relationships between God and humanity and between human beings, and all that is implied in the love of God, and of our neighbour as ourselves.
- Scripture reveals the actions of the triune God. This helps to explain the unique contribution of Christianity in a world of many religions. The incarnation of God in Jesus Christ ('the Word became flesh', John 1.14), and the translation of divinely inspired Scripture into many languages beyond their original composition in Hebrew, Aramaic and Greek, illustrates the rich understanding of revelation in Christianity. This understanding is neither as strictly textual nor confined to one

---

[3] The famous Scripture text on this (2 Tim. 3.16) has as its context instruction about ministerial formation and the functions of *hiera grammata* 'sacred writings' or *graphē* 'scripture' which serve that end.

[4] For a recent account of Scripture as 'Trinitarian discourse' see K. J. Vanhoozer, 'Holy Scripture', in M. Allen, S. R. Swain (eds), *Christian Dogmatics: Reformed Theology for the Church Catholic* (Grand Rapids, MI: Baker Academic, 2016), 41–56.

language as some views of the Hebrew Torah in Judaism, or the Arabic Qur'an in Islam.[5]

- Reflection on the texts of Scripture in their breadth and depth is part of the lifeblood of public ministry during all stages of formation and growth. In services of ordination texts from Scripture are customarily read to remind listeners of revelation as a basic aspect of calling and vocation (e.g. Jer. 1.4–10; Acts 9.1–19). Isaiah's response to the divine call was unusually enthusiastic: 'Here am I; send me!' (Isa. 6.8). Learning from Scripture in public and private worship is, accordingly, a hallmark of practices and patterns that guide and sustain the vision for ministry.

There are pitfalls to avoid. The best known in the modern world are fundamentalist and liberal approaches. The former identifies revelation with Scripture too uncritically in order to defend divine truth. The human facets of Scripture (e.g. context, genre, language) are acknowledged less, and in consequence the interpretation of Scripture is narrowed too sharply. The latter distances Scripture from revelation too critically in order to honour human experience. The divine facets of Scripture (e.g. sacred wisdom, prophetic oracle, apostolic witness) are revered less, and in consequence the illumination of Scripture is lost.[6] The challenge, as with Christology, is to hold together the divine and the human – not one at the expense of the other. That requires an understanding of history as the setting for revelation: God acts with redemptive purpose by both communicating clearly and by addressing the human context. To quote from Isaiah: 'my word . . . that goes out from my mouth . . . shall accomplish that which

---

[5]   This does not preclude fruitful inter-religious interpretations of the same and different religious texts. See J. D. Levenson, *The Hebrew Bible, the Old Testament, and Historical Criticism: Jews and Christians in Biblical Studies* (Louisville, KY: Westminster John Knox Press, 1993); D. Ford, 'An Interfaith Wisdom: Scriptural Reasoning between Jews, Christians and Muslims', in *Christian Wisdom: Desiring God and Learning in Love* (Cambridge: Cambridge University Press, 2007), 273–303; M. Z. Cohen, A. Berlin (eds), *Interpreting Scriptures in Judaism, Christianity, and Islam: Overlapping Inquiries* (Cambridge: Cambridge University Press, 2016).

[6]   This contrast makes use of the popular reception of approaches that have their own pedigree in modernity. See H. A. Harris, *Fundamentalism and Evangelicals* (Oxford: Oxford University Press, 1998), ch. 3; M. D. Chapman, 'Liberal Readings of the Bible and Their Conservative Responses', in J. Riches (ed.), *The New Cambridge History of the Bible: From 1750 to the Present* (Cambridge: Cambridge University Press, 2015), 208–19. It is important to note that the former has 'right' and 'left' versions (so must be distinguished from Christian 'fundamentals') just as the latter connotes more broadly a humane spirit as well as a non-traditionalist stance.

I purpose, and succeed in the thing for which I sent it' (Isa. 55.11). This reassuring promise is addressed to those languishing in exile for whom the cycle of food production from sowing to eating – made possible by rain from heaven – is a picture of revelation through Scripture. It is proclaimed 'in the world' in the context of human experience, but it is, ultimately and wonderfully, not entirely 'of the world'.[7]

Scripture and worship: 'the seraph touched my mouth' (Isa. 6.7)

If the previous section was in effect creedal then this next section is about contemplation. The choice of the word 'contemplation' is deliberate: the attitude to Scripture that characterizes a worshipping congregation distinguishes it from other settings (e.g. home, office, school). It is not that these settings are entirely distinct (worship guides the whole of life), but if gathered worship is about joining corporately 'with angels, and with archangels, and with all the company of heaven' (Eucharistic Prayer) then it is essential to be receptive to this remarkable reality of which Scripture speaks. In this setting, the contemplation of *Immanuel* 'God with us' (Isa. 7.14; 8.8, 10; cf. Matt. 1.23) – focused reflection on God's redemptive purposes – is the appropriate response. Scripture also directs and nourishes a spiritually broken, needy and hungry congregation: our horizons are lifted higher than our many human concerns towards 'the high and lofty one who inhabits eternity, whose name is Holy'. This is because God dwells 'with those who are contrite and humble in spirit' and revives 'the spirit of the humble' and 'the heart of the contrite', rather than the proud and arrogant (Isa. 57.15; 2.10–17). If being receptive and responsive to Scripture is one core component of worship, Scripture also teaches and interprets the sacrament of Holy Communion, the other core component through which that brokenness, need and hunger is met: a vivid sign and symbol of

---

[7] This need not be inimical to 'critical' methods used to analyse the historical contexts in which Scripture emerged. There is, however, a variety of views on how their use affects biblical authority and theology generally. See J. Barton, *People of the Book? The Authority of the Bible in Christianity*, rev. edn (London: SPCK, 1993); D. P. Bechard (ed., trans.), *The Scripture Documents: An Anthology of Official Catholic Teachings* (Collegeville, MN: Liturgical Press, 2002); V. Bacote, L. C. Miguelez, D. L. Okholm (eds), *Evangelicals and Scripture: Tradition, Authority and Hermeneutics* (Downers Grove, IL: IVP, 2004). A recent inter-religious collection is M. Z. Brettler, P. Enns, D. J. Harrington, *The Bible and the Believer: How to Read the Bible Critically and Religiously* (New York and Oxford: Oxford University Press, 2013). See also below under 'Scripture and education'.

Christ, by whose bruises 'we are healed' (Isa. 53.5). Contemplation of this reality is, again, the appropriate response.[8]

Liturgical forms and orders of service typically contain scriptural content that links local congregations to the universal Church, however fixed or free those forms and orders are; whether or not, for instance, a lectionary is used. It is, however, in the preaching of Scripture that those in public ministry are especially conscious of their responsibility as servants of God. This is because preaching, which may be seen as a microcosm of ministry, is about the reality of which Scripture speaks, albeit conveyed in the preacher's own words. It is a spiritual and creative task that requires the preacher to choose words carefully, not least because reactions to preaching within just one congregation are often many and varied. There are, however, encouragements to hand. Scripture offers examples of how preaching can be done (e.g. exposition, reflection, proclamation) such that a sermon or talk need not be a straitjacket that constrains the preacher or bores listeners to sleep. It may also be helpful to think of preaching as a task that (to repeat two adjectives used above) is both spiritual and creative. For instance, the exiles in Babylon were addressed by ancient tradition in a way that brought it to life in the present: 'From this time forward I make you hear new things, hidden things that you have not known' (Isa. 48.6). The 'new' was not novelty for its own sake but the reapplication of the narrative of redemption from slavery in Egypt to their lives in Babylon, even if the contexts differed. Here was a precedent for New Testament writers of the first century, when God's redemptive purposes, now revealed in Christ, came to fuller prominence as a major hallmark of Christian faith. Some key pointers emerge from this:

- Those who preach Scripture are as much members of the worshipping community as their listeners. They are not exempt from the humbling that worship brings about when coming face to face with the God who is 'holy, holy, holy' (Isa. 6.3). Isaiah was deeply aware of this communal dimension: 'I am a man of unclean lips, and I live among a people of unclean lips; yet my eyes have seen the King, the LORD of hosts' (6.5).

---

[8] On listening to Scripture liturgically and spiritually, see J. Daniélou, *The Bible and the Liturgy* (London: Darton, Longman & Todd, 1960; original 1951); P. Adam, *Hearing God's Words: Exploring Biblical Spirituality* (Downers Grove, IL; Leicester: IVP, 2004). On Scripture and the Eucharist, see G. W. Bromiley, *Sacramental Teaching and Practice in the Reformation Churches* (Grand Rapids, MI: Eerdmans, 1957); V. Boland, T. McCarthy (eds), *The Word Is Flesh and Blood: The Eucharist and Sacred Scripture* (Dublin: Dominican Publications, 2012); P. Gooder, M. Perham, *Echoing the Word: The Bible in the Eucharist* (London: SPCK, 2013).

He was told that his lips had been cleansed, which was necessary for his role as a prophet who was commissioned to preach. But it was through divine encounter – as a worshipper – that he was able to step forward with confidence (6.6–8).

- The preaching of Scripture calls for faithfulness, which depends on the formation and growth in virtue of the preacher's character. This does not mean 'cut glass' perfection: a survey of the all-too human figures in Scripture that God used shouts the opposite. Indeed, the call to faithfulness and virtue only makes sense as something that can be answered (or avoided) over time. If formation and growth do take place then the spiritual task of preaching becomes humanly possible – even if the content of the preaching is demanding, as well as hopeful – as Isaiah discovered (Isa. 6.9–13; cf. Mark 4.1–34).

- Scripture shows that preaching is a task in which creativity is welcome. The forms of literature in Scripture that, in their effects, 'convince, rebuke, and encourage' (2 Tim. 4.2) are many and varied: law, proverb, oracle, parable, letter. There are examples in Scripture of what is akin to the modern sermon – the book of Acts is full of early apostolic preaching – but there is no good reason to be rigid about form or structure. It is the scriptural content, in the context of worship and formation in faithfulness and virtue, which matter most of all.

There are pitfalls to avoid. This may be framed as follows: the tendency in planning church services either to make too little or to make too much of Scripture. The former risks being so taken up with a liturgical form that little space and time is given to the congregation to be receptive and responsive; a few minutes of reflection on Scripture risks downplaying the importance of its instruction for Christian faith and life. The latter can be so taken up with the exposition of the detail of Scripture that little space and time is given for other aspects of worship (e.g. praise, prayer, community); too much explanation of Scripture within a set amount of time overwhelms the listener. This caricature is merely intended to encourage reflection on the place of Scripture in worship; after all, the balance may tip in many different directions for good reason, depending on the service or setting (e.g. wedding, funeral, home-group Bible study). But the central point stands: Scripture is a core component of worship because its sacred texts reveal God's redemptive purposes. Those tasked with public ministry are responsible for the stewardship of that component, whether in planning a church service or more obviously in preaching. The preaching of Scripture is not an end in and of itself – worship is our final purpose

(Isa. 66.18–20; Rev. 7.9) – but its immediate aim is to minister to others in the service of God, to which we now turn.

Scripture and ministry: 'he will faithfully bring forth justice' (Isa. 42.3)

If the previous section was about contemplation then this next and central section is about context. A notable feature of Scripture, compared with other ancient literature, is the way that its texts reflect diverse periods in sequence – from creation through to new creation – via the Egyptian, Assyrian, Babylonian, Persian, Greek and Roman periods. This is no accident: in addressing the comings and goings of history, Scripture claims divine sovereignty over that history. The book of Isaiah echoes this: its texts arguably contain oracles that refer to all of those periods (explicitly three, e.g. Isa. 10.5; 39.1; 45.1); and one of its major theological themes is kingship: God enthroned (6.1; 37.16; 40.22; 52.7; 66.1). But this is no heavenly power-trip: divine rule is exercised through service marked by justice and compassion. This is beautifully displayed in its portrait of the divinely commissioned servant figure, which begins as a royal ideal, and then moves through suffering to final vindication (11.1–9; 42.1–4; 49.1–7; 50.4–9; 52.13—53.13). Here is a model that is neither overbearing in its strength (although the proud and brutal are humbled) nor undone by its gentleness (which is not a sign of weakness but of tender care). This model, according to New Testament texts, was integral to Jesus Christ's understanding of ministry. That understanding was fed by various scriptural strands; Isaiah attests to many of them: the legal, priestly, wise and prophetic – as well as the royal. A fuller scriptural account of ministry would include passages from New Testament letters (e.g. on 'gifts' and 'roles'; see Rom. 12.6–8; 1 Cor. 12.4–11; Eph. 4.11–12; 1 Tim. 3.1–13).

This scriptural diversity may be applied to a specific issue in ministry: suffering. There is no account of its origin in Scripture. The primal episodes of Genesis are potent and far-reaching in their portrayal of the human condition, but its influential texts do not appear to explain why evil, and the suffering that ensued, was a reality that could be chosen in God's 'very good' creation. That said, theological accounts of suffering (e.g. sin, retribution, lament) are prominent in Scripture. Its writers did not always invoke these, but sometimes cast this issue in almost natural terms: suffering is a part of the lot of human experience in a dynamic and unstable world, whether due to disaster, accident or human folly. Then again, other passages portray suffering in redemptive terms: the discipline of testing and character formation, sacrifice on behalf of another, or vindication through death and resurrection.[9] These three accounts – the theological, natural and redemptive – are evident in Isaiah. The Assyrians faced retribution for violent expansionism that brought about the downfall of God's people, Israel (Isa. 11.24–25). King Hezekiah seemingly acted with human folly in opening up the royal treasury to a Babylonian delegation (39.1–4). And though the servant figure 'made his grave with the wicked' it is also said that 'he shall see light' and make intercession for 'transgressors' (53.9, 11–12). This range of responses, which are diverse due to the varied contexts they address, is a reminder of the importance of interpretative wisdom when using Scripture in ministry. In the face of suffering, silence is sometimes forced upon us; at other times, Scripture provides insight and hope. Some key pointers emerge from this:

- Scripture contains rich resources for helping those in public ministry with their sense of purpose. God is portrayed as the cosmic king whose rule is marked by justice and compassion. This is significant in a world in which power is often used and abused at the expense of others. Isaiah's contemporary, Micah (whose book has oracles in common with Isaiah), expressed this memorably: 'He has told you, O mortal, what is good; and what does the LORD require of you but to do justice, and to love kindness, and to walk humbly with your God? (Mic. 6.8; cf. Matt. 23.23).
- Jesus Christ is the model minister because in him all the offices of Scripture (e.g. prophet, priest, king) combine uniquely. His identity and status as the ideal servant is illustrated in the New Testament (e.g. Matt. 12.15–21). Disciples of Christ – among whom minsters in the Church are more obviously public representatives – are called to follow his example. Since he exemplified divine justice and compassion in his ministry these hallmarks should be characteristic of all ministry in the Church, even if gifts and roles (ordained or lay) differ in nature and activity.
- Scripture must be read with interpretative wisdom when it is applied to specific issues in ministry. The diversity of Scripture is a reminder of this, given the range of its own historical contexts and the multiple issues

---

9   This range has been expressed as follows: 'the Bible does not claim that *all* suffering is the will of God or that *no* suffering is the will of God. Or, that *all* suffering is due to sin or that *no* suffering is due to sin. Or, that *all* suffering is bad and to be avoided at all costs or that *no* suffering is bad.' T. E. Fretheim, 'To Say Something – about God, Evil, and Suffering', *Word and World* 19/4 (1999), 345–50.

that its texts address in different ways. The range of scriptural responses to suffering is but one example among many others (e.g. work, money, relationships). That said, interpretative wisdom, which requires discipline, imagination and virtue, takes time to grow and develop.[10]

There are pitfalls to avoid. On the one hand, there is a tendency among some to use Scripture in blunt ways that are insensitive to the multiple factors at play in ministerial situations. On the other hand, there is an opposite tendency among others to ignore Scripture, as if its ancient texts have little or no real connection to issues in modern life. The former type of minister may well be motivated by good intentions, whereas the latter may well have tried and all but given up! There is a middle way between these extremes that combines Christian wisdom and faithfulness, but it depends upon a willingness to attend to both the complexity of life and the theological convictions in Scripture that remain true in spite of new circumstances.[11] The issue of suffering again serves as an example, not least because it is relevant to us all. It is an exercise of interpretative wisdom to recognize that people suffer in various ways in different contexts, and that there is no single answer for responding to all of those situations equally; the writers of Scripture knew this very well. At the same time, while death – our ultimate and personal enemy – ends all suffering, both as the consequence of each kind of suffering and in its final attempt to thwart God's redemptive purposes, death is not the victor. Jesus Christ has gone ahead of us all, as the 'suffering servant' who modelled a life of ministry to others in the service of God, and then enjoyed vindication beyond death and resurrection.

Scripture and mission: 'new heavens . . . new earth' (Isa. 65.17)

If the previous section was about context then this next section about mission concerns the largest context of all: creation. Scripture is framed by the excitement of new life that is declared 'very good' and the vision of a renewed world in which communion with God, squandered in Eden, will be restored. Similarly, just as God said 'Let there be light' at creation

---

[10] The role of the virtues in reading Scripture is explored in R. Briggs, *Reading the Bible Wisely* (London: SPCK, 2003). See also below under 'Scripture and education'.

[11] For discussions of the use of Scripture in ministry see P. H. Ballard, S. R. Holmes, W. Elkins (eds), *The Bible in Pastoral Practice: Readings in the Place and Function of Scripture in the Church* (London: Darton, Longman & Todd, 2005); S. Pattison, M. Cooling, T. Cooling, *Using the Bible in Christian Ministry: The Workbook* (London: Darton, Longman & Todd, 2007).

(Gen. 1.3; cf. 1.31), so the apocalyptic vision revealed by Jesus Christ promises servants of God that 'the Lord God will be their light' (Rev. 1.1; 22:5; cf. 2 Cor. 4:6). In-between this beginning and end are the visions of the book of Isaiah, which anticipate both cosmic renewal and the calling of people from all lands to worship together (Isa. 65.17–25; 66.18–23). It is often thought that ancient Israelites were concerned with their own status as the chosen people of God, but their vocation was to serve the world as 'a priestly kingdom and a holy nation' (Exod. 19.5). This scope is resumed and developed in the book of Isaiah, whose famous words about ideal service express it as follows: 'a light to the nations' (Isa. 42.6; 49.6). Those passages indicate that the distinction between Israel and the nations was neither fixed nor final. An appreciation of this illuminates other parts of the Old Testament (e.g. Zech. 8.20–23; Jonah 4.9–11; Joel 2.28–29) which, in New Testament perspective, show that what was germinal in ancient Israel had its flowering in the early Christian movement. It is the Church of both Jew and Gentile – a restored and unified humanity (1 Cor. 10.32; Eph. 2.11–22; 1 Pet. 2.9–10) – that is God's instrument of mission in the world.[12]

The scope of mission is worth dwelling on for a moment. Its basis is found in the distinctive theology of Scripture: the activity of the one God's redemptive purposes for the world – a theology that distinguishes its thought from ancient polytheism. The other gods of antiquity were often satirized as nothing but material idols (e.g. Isa. 44.9–20; cf. Wisd. 13—14; Lett. Jer. 6.16, 23, 29; 1 Cor. 8.4). This claim was rooted in a conviction about the living God who creates and sustains all things. Not to worship the creator God was to settle for less than silver, let alone gold. This is a powerful theology: it offers a causal origin of all things; it generates a unified and coherent worldview; and it warns us that it is possible for us to lower our horizons in settling for a narrow worldview.[13] Expressed positively, the scope of mission helps to explain why the Church, from its inception, has had an international outlook; and why the Church is often at the forefront of peace-making between individuals, groups or nations.

---

[12] On this trajectory in the book of Isaiah, and beyond, see H. G. M. Williamson, *Variations on a Theme: King, Messiah and Servant in the Book of Isaiah* (Carlisle: Paternoster, 1998), 123–4, 144–5.

[13] At this juncture Christianity shows itself to be a religious philosophy that may be critically compared with other ancient (and modern) worldviews. See G. E. Karamanolis, *The Philosophy of Early Christianity* (Durham: Acumen, 2013). This pursuit can quickly become apologetic: see W. L. Craig, J. P. Moreland, *Philosophical Foundations for a Christian Worldview* (Downers Grove, IL: IVP, 2003), Part IV.

In his earthly ministry and mission, Jesus called those who worked for this peace 'blessed' (Matt. 5.9; cf. Rom. 12.18). Whatever characterizes people as individuals – be it gender, status, language or nationality – is not unimportant. But God's redemptive purposes for the world are such that none of these are barriers to becoming 'the children of God', offspring of the living God of all creation; and nor should they be barriers within Christian community. Some key pointers emerge from this:

- Scripture generates a broad vision. This is all too easy to lose when we associate the Church with a particular nation, language or group. Jokes such as 'God is . . .' (my nationality), 'God speaks . . .' (my language) and 'God prefers . . .' (my group) can be comical, but the darker versions of these natural instincts are an aberration of the vision of God's redemptive purposes for the world. This criticism, which applies in principle to denominationalism, does not derive from a naive ecumenism but the belief that the Church is the creation of the one God. Simply put: it does not belong to any of us (John 17.20–23; Eph. 1.20–23; 2.11–22; 4.4–6).

- We are called in Scripture to bear witness to God's redemptive purposes for the world. The notion of 'witness' is especially valuable. Scripture is itself a collection of witnesses – an anthology of sacred texts – about God's words and works. More than this, though, witness is not about the success or otherwise of those in public ministry, because the final focus is not on us as individuals, ordained or not. But there is a responsibility placed on us all: to bear witness to God, whose redemptive activity in Christ for the world is the message of Christian mission. It is indeed a joy both to discover and to participate in God's redemptive purposes.

- The writers of Scripture were realistic about the challenges of mission. Isaiah was initially given a difficult message to proclaim: it addressed the proud attitude of the people with whom he also identified (Isa. 6.9–13; cf. 3.8; 5.18–23). And yet, other oracles in the book are nothing short of glorious (e.g. 40.1–11; 61.1–4). Jesus also experienced challenge (e.g. Luke 4.16–30; John 4.39–42), as did the early apostles (e.g. Acts 17.32–34). But the final word was, is and will always be hopeful, because it is God's mission. How important it is, therefore, to hold the horizon high: to keep alive in our minds and hearts the scriptural vision of God's redemptive purposes for the world.

There are pitfalls to avoid. On the one hand, there is a tendency for us to narrow our vision. This can be done in numerous ways; some have already been identified. Others might be to insist on a particular church practice (e.g. clerical clothing, sermon length, music style) at the expense of mission. On the other hand, there is a tendency for us to broaden our vision so much that the content of the Christian faith is diluted. This, too, can happen in various ways. There are so many causes with which the Church can associate itself while forgetting what is central to Christianity. Some arguably grow out of Scripture (e.g. environmental stewardship) whereas others are hotly disputed because of their clear discontinuity with Scripture in its ancient Jewish and Christian settings (e.g. non-heterosexual marriage). It is not a question of finding a balance between extremes, as if a little of every venture produces faithful service. Rather, the calling on those in public ministry, supported by the Church at large, is to get to grips with what is distinctive about Christianity, and to identify with and live in the light of its message. In terms of Scripture and mission, it is the proclamation of God's redemptive purposes for the world. The gospel of Jesus Christ, in other words, is the wellspring of the Christian life. This is the theological drama of Scripture that has inspired, and continues to inspire, faithful public ministry. Once this is realized and acted out, only then will the Church have a fruitful impact in wider society and culture.[14]

Scripture and education: 'to listen as those who are taught' (Isa. 50.4)

If we arrived in the previous section at what is distinctive about Christianity then this fifth and final section has a complementary educational focus. The history of Christianity has a strong culture of learning because of the major role its sacred texts have played in institutions (e.g. Church, university) that built on the use of texts in preceding institutions (i.e. Temple, synagogue). This culture of learning has had a major impact. For instance, the writings of Augustine, which are infused with Scripture, influenced European society in many areas (e.g. philosophy, psychology, politics), as well as articulating Christian theology and practice.[15] Some of the finest literature, art and music ever produced shows the influence of Scripture:

---

[14] On Scripture and mission in general, see D. Senior, C. Stuhlmueller, *The Biblical Foundations for Mission* (London: SCM Press, 1983); C. J. H. Wright, *The Mission of God: Unlocking the Bible's Grand Narrative* (Nottingham: IVP, 2006); P. Hoggarth et al. (eds), *Bible in Mission* (Oxford: Regnum Books International, 2013).

[15] Augustine was instrumental in integrating Scripture into an early *artes liberales* 'liberal arts' model of *paideia* 'education' for those without a sophisticated 'secular' education (e.g. *De doctrina Christiana*, 1–2). See F. M. Young, 'Interpretation of Scripture', in S. A. Harvey, D. G. Hunter (eds), *The Oxford Handbook of Early Christian Studies* (Oxford: Oxford University Press, 2008), 851.

allusions in Shakespeare's plays; scenes in the High Renaissance frescos of the Sistine Chapel in Rome; and the texts of the sacred music of Bach, Handel, Haydn and Mozart. The embedding, explicitly and implicitly, of scriptural motifs in popular culture is another marker of influence. Some of the reasons for this culture of learning have been explored so far: Scripture is a textual means for the revelation of God's redemptive purposes; it is a core component in worship; it is a rich resource that needs interpretative wisdom in ministry; and it provides an all-encompassing vision for the distinctive mission of the Church in the world. This section – that Scripture is the curriculum of Christianity – invites some comments of a more exegetical nature.

Isaiah chapter 40 may be used to illustrate the kinds of ideas that need considering. They may be labelled as follows: context, canon, creed, community and culture. The chapter, which famously begins 'Comfort, O comfort my people, says your God' (Isa. 40.1), has as its context the restoration to their homeland of the Judean exiles in Babylon. The British Museum in London houses the Cyrus Cylinder, a small barrel inscription that describes Cyrus the Great's successful conquering of Babylon; although the oracles in Isaiah attribute this to the Lord (44.24—45.7).[16] The command to 'prepare the way of the LORD', which refers to God's return as king to Jerusalem (40.3–5; cf. 52.7), is later quoted in the opening of Mark's Gospel about the arrival of Jesus Christ, the Son of God, whose ministry ushered in the kingdom of God (Mark 1.1–3). This, together with the chapter's general theology – the divine court (Isa. 40.3, 6), the critique of idolatry (40.18–20) and the incomparability of the creator God (40.21–26) – were beliefs that continued as hallmarks of Christian theology, which the creeds of the Church articulate in summary form. The community in exile that struggled to trust a God who seemed absent were reassured by divine justice ('she has served her term', 40.2) and compassion ('they shall run and not be weary . . . walk and not faint', 40.31). There is, then, a poetic vision in Isaiah 40 that contains contours of the Christian faith. It went on to inspire musical culture: 'Every valley' (40.4) is the scriptural title of the first tenor aria in Handel's *Messiah* (1742).[17] Some key pointers emerge from this:

---

[16] For further discussion of this, and many archaeological finds in relation to the Bible, a useful primer is C. E. Fant, M. G. Reddish, *Lost Treasures of the Bible: Understanding the Bible through Archaeological Artifacts in World Museums* (Grand Rapids, MI; Cambridge: Eerdmans, 2008).

[17] On the latter dimension see S. S. Long, J. F. A. Sawyer, *The Bible in Music: A Dictionary of Songs, Works, and More* (Lanham, MD: Rowman & Littlefield, 2015); T. K. Beal (ed.), *The Oxford Encyclopaedia of the Bible and the Arts* (New York: Oxford University Press, 2015). See

- Learning the texts of Scripture requires a knowledge of their ancient context, composition and message. Numerous resources are available to help in this. The following types of literature are recommended: a Bible dictionary or encyclopaedia, a Bible atlas, commentaries on biblical books, and introductions to canonical sections (e.g. Prophets, Gospels). This is assisted by digital media: software (e.g. Logos, Accordance) and online (e.g. bibleodyssey.org, biblehub.com). This learning includes 'critical' methods for the analysis of Scripture as a collection of ancient texts.[18]

- Learning about Scripture is an invitation to delve into not only their ancient context but also the rich tapestry of the history of their inter-pretation: Christianity in its early, medieval, Reformation, modern and global phases and varieties. This is very important because readers of Scripture are often unaware of the origins of their own ideas about its texts; that is, in interpretations often bound up with the concerns of a particular denomination and its traditions.[19]

- Learning about Scripture is not only a question of acquiring knowledge of its texts, but also a question of considering how they apply in the life of faith. Major areas were addressed above (i.e. worship, ministry, mission) within which a range of specific issues and skills find their place (e.g. social justice, pastoral care, the arts). This often ends up hav-ing a double aspect in practice: the application of Scripture both in the Church and in wider society, notably in contemporary concerns that affect everyone (e.g. trade, migration, violence, climate).

There are pitfalls to avoid. On the one hand, there is a tendency to approach Scripture as an anthology of influential ideas from antiquity that merely satisfies intellectual curiosity. On the other hand, there is a tendency to be so concerned to relate Scripture to contemporary society that its ancient texts are read in ways that their authors would have neither intended nor agreed with. The good version of each approach has admirable motiva-tions and strengths – accurate knowledge and ministerial relevance – but

---

also M. A. Beavis, M. J. Gilmour (eds), *Dictionary of the Bible and Western Culture* (Sheffield: Sheffield Phoenix Press, 2012).

[18] On 'critical methods' see D. R. Law, *Historical Critical Method: A Guide for the Perplexed* (London: T&T Clark, 2012). On these, and much more, see J. Barton (ed.), *The Cambridge Companion to Biblical Interpretation* (Cambridge: Cambridge University Press, 1998).

[19] See S. L. McKenzie (ed.), *The Oxford Encyclopedia of Biblical Interpretation*, 2 vols (New York: Oxford University Press, 2013); D. K. McKim (ed.), *Historical Handbook of Major Biblical Interpreters* (Downers Grove, IL; Leicester: IVP, 1988); J. C. Paget et al. (eds), *The New Cambridge History of the Bible*, 4 vols (Cambridge: Cambridge University Press, 2012–16).

both are needed to ensure that ministry to others remains faithful to God, and so that the whole person is addressed by Scripture. To take again the example of Isaiah 40: to focus solely on the philosophical legacy of its monotheism ('To whom then will you liken God . . .?', Isa. 40.18) would be to miss the impassioned pleading and tenderness of its divine voice; similarly, to focus on its message of redemption as a platform for any sort of political or social liberation would be to miss its probing moral challenge about idolatry that had led to exile in Babylon in the first place. This discussion of Scripture and education therefore points to the necessity of both scientific discipline and artful finesse when approaching Scripture. This is what was described above, in the central section, as interpretative wisdom, a phrase that usefully describes all good approaches to Scripture.

There are countless ways in which 'Scripture and ministry' may be discussed because Scripture plays a central role in the world's most populous religion. Here it has been viewed through five prisms: revelation (creed), worship (contemplation), ministry (context), mission (creation) and education (curriculum). The central and final sections provided an opportunity to present a model for approaching Scripture. What has emerged, in addition to the exegetical content (i.e. context, canon, creed, community, culture) and other aspects (e.g. faithfulness, virtue), is the importance of interpretative wisdom. This is a useful catch-all phrase for all good approaches to Scripture. It highlights the sacred text itself: that Scripture needs to be learned and interpreted. It also highlights the practical importance of a pastoral outlook at the heart of ministry to others in the service of God. This has been explicit and implicit throughout, in considering ways in which Scripture functions in theology and practice for those preparing for, or who are already active in, public Christian ministry.

18

Liturgy and ministry

JAMES FARWELL

A theological account of the relationship between liturgy and ministry properly begins with an account of each term in its Christian context and usage. As it turns out, liturgy and ministry are the same business, seen from different perspectives. Only when the referents of the two terms are clear does the relationship between liturgy and ministry come into view, and only then can the significance and purpose of orders of ministry that have typified the organization of churches in various ways be understood.

Liturgy as Christ and the liturgy of the Church

'Liturgy' is a term derived from Greek (*leitourgia*) and particularly relevant to a Greco-Roman context, where it referred to a public act undertaken, often by a wealthy citizen, for the life and good order of the polis. For example, a Roman citizen's donation towards the construction of, say, a road or an aqueduct from which the citizenry as a whole would benefit would be a liturgical act. By extension the term 'liturgy' came to be used for a *cultic* act – a more religious sense of the term, with the caveat that in the context of Athens and later Rome, the distinction that moderns make between 'religious' activity and other activity is not very illuminating. At any rate, the term *leitourgia* appears once in the Septuagint to refer to the worship of the Temple and is picked up for the same purpose in Christian Scriptures; therein, and subsequently, Christians appropriated the term for their own public worship, although it is not the only term they used. The crucial point here is that, contrary to a common definition of the term 'liturgy' in a number of modern churches as a 'work of the people', the more precise definition is that a liturgy is a work *for* the people; an action – a cultic/ritual action in its developing usage – that is for the sake of recipients beyond the original agent of the act.

With this in mind, what is the meaning of 'liturgy' in a Christian context, if a liturgy is a work *for* a people? Theologically speaking, the answer can only be that the liturgy is *Christ himself.* Jesus Christ is God's liturgy for the sake of the world; that is, Jesus' life, death and resurrection are God's work for the sake of the world's renovation, liberation, redemption, flourishing. (Of course, the precise nature of the world's need and the corresponding salvific outcome of this liturgy that is Jesus Christ has been expressed in diverse ways by Christians and takes one to matters of theological anthropology, soteriology and eschatology.) As Robert Taft notes: 'According to the New Testament, it is *this* Incarnate Lord and savior in his self-giving, reconciling obedience to the will of the Father that for the followers of Jesus is the new liturgy.'[1]

If the theologically primary referent of 'liturgy' is the action of God in Christ, then to be the Church – to be *in Christ* – is to be joined to this work of kenotic self-giving, to incarnate it as the body of Christ in the world. Again, Taft:

> *Christian liturgy in the Pauline sense is this same reality, Jesus Christ in us.* Our liturgy, our service, is to be drawn into him, who is our incarnate salvation, and to live out his life, the same pattern he has exemplified for us.[2]

What do we mean, then, when we refer to the services of worship in which we engage as 'liturgies'? Christian liturgical worship is that act of thanksgiving and supplication, of proclamation and grateful response, by which Christians join themselves to the one liturgy who is Jesus Christ. In worship, the living Word and Way, the crucified and risen Lord, is the One in whom God addresses the Church through and in Scripture, who draws us into Christ's kenotic death and thus into the hope of his resurrection by baptism,[3] who makes himself present in the eating and drinking of eucharistic bread and wine. The liturgy, in this sense of a service of worship, is, in ritualized form,

> the saving deeds of God in the actions of those men and women who would live in him. Its purpose, to . . . return to the Pauline theology of liturgy with which we began, is to turn you and me into the same reality. The purpose of baptism is to make us cleansing waters and healing and strengthening oil; the purpose of Eucharist is not to change bread and wine, but to change you

---

[1] Robert Taft, 'What Does Liturgy Do? Toward a Soteriology of Liturgical Celebration: Some Theses', excerpted in *Primary Sources of Liturgical Theology*, Dwight Vogel, ed. (Collegeville: Liturgical Press, 2000), 140.

[2] Taft, 'What Does Liturgy Do?', 140.

[3] Romans 6.3–4.

and me: through baptism and Eucharist it is *we* who are to become Christ to one another, and a sign to the world that has yet to hear his name.[4]

That the eucharistic liturgy is a privileged, ritualized way the Church joins itself to Christ is a theme prominent in early Christian preaching and catechesis. Augustine serves as a notable example:

> So if it's you that are the Body of Christ and its members, it's the mystery meaning you that has been placed on the table of the Lord: what you receive is the mystery that means you. It is to what you are that you reply *AMEN* . . . When you were baptized it is as though you were mixed into the dough . . . It's the same thing with the wine . . . That too is how the Lord Christ signified us, how he wished us to belong to him, how he consecrated the Sacrament of our peace and unity on his table.[5]

Corollary to the way of thinking outlined here – of Christ as the one Liturgy of God to whom Christians join themselves in worship, by which they are to become his continuing liturgy in the world – is the affirmation of Christ as Priest; more specifically, the one who is both priest and the end of 'priesthood' in the sense that no further priestly act is necessary to join people to God, save Christ himself. For Christians, priesthood is a multivalent symbol that Jesus at once occupies solely, opens up to those who worship him, and abolishes. One sees all these senses of Christ's priesthood across Scripture. In the Gospel of John, Jesus is presented as the one true Passover Lamb but also as priest, as he prays for his disciples; in Hebrews, he is presented as High Priest and one who brings the purpose of priestly sacrifice to its *telos*; for the writer of Ephesians, he makes of his own self the sacrificial offering to God on our behalf. But we must, at this point, hold further reflection on priesthood; it falls to us first to speak of the meaning of 'ministry' and its connection to liturgy.

Ministry as Christ and the ministry of the Church

It is an ongoing theological and pastoral challenge in the modern era to prevent the reduction of ministry in the minds of many to a professional vocation to which some commit themselves – leading the life of a congregation or other ecclesial body as an ordained person – as one among a number of 'serving' professions. Yet the instinct to group this profession with 'service' is right-minded; the term 'minister' derives from the

---

4 Taft, 'What Does Liturgy Do?', 143–4.
5 Augustine, Sermon no. 272 in *The Works of St. Augustine*, vol. III/7, trans. Edmund Hill (New Rochelle: New City Press, 1993), 300–1.

Latin that means 'to serve'. But ministry is a description of the work of the whole Church; and, even more primarily, this service is a sharing in the identity and work of Jesus Christ himself, who, 'taking the form of a servant' (a permutation of *doulos*, which could be translated more strongly as 'slave'), humbled himself and gave his life for the world, even to the point of death.[6] In the majority of places where English translations of the Christian Scriptures use 'minister', the term being translated is some permutation of *diakonia*, service, and it is clear that this servant ministry is first that of Jesus Christ; and second, it is the work of the Church as his 'body'. Jesus came 'not to be served but to serve, and to give his life as a ransom for many', while those who are his disciples are to take on the servant life as their own, as he both taught[7] and modelled,[8] and by that pattern of life they themselves are blessed.[9]

What emerges, then, at the centre of a theological account of ministry is a pattern much like what we saw with the meaning of liturgy, where 'liturgy' referred first to the work of God in Christ; and second to the worship by which the Christian assembly joins itself to their Lord's purposes. First, and primarily, when we refer to 'ministry' we are referring to a comprehensive term that gathers up the entire life of Jesus: his pastoral and prophetic teaching, his healing, his blessing of those on the margins, and his death itself, which consummates that life of blessing and lifting up human persons, is a *service* to the world. This is the *ministry* of Jesus Christ; the work of the Church is to join itself to that ministry, in imitation of its Lord, marking its identity as Christ's 'body' in the world, and recognizing, in the resurrection of Jesus, the ratification, the triumph and the power of that form of life as divinely ordained.

The holographic relationship between Christ, liturgy, ministry and the Church

With these corollary patterns identified, one can perhaps best describe the relationship between liturgy and ministry as holographic. In ordinary perception, one can stand before an object and see the aspect of it immediately open to one's view, but cannot see its other aspects – its reverse side, for example – unless one walks around the object and views it from that side.

---

6 Philippians 2.5–11 RSV.
7 Mark 10.42–44 RSV.
8 John 13.2–16.
9 John 13.17.

One's mind supplies the confidence on the basis of accumulated experience that there is another side, or other sides, and even supplies some reasonable assumptions of how the other side might look, on the basis of the
side one can see. Standing before a hologram, however, one sees the particular aspect of the projected object that is in the foreground of one's view;
but one can also see all other parts of the object in their relationship to
the aspect that is in the foreground of one's perspective. One sees all sides,
all aspects of the one object *at once*, in their global and organically seamless
relationship to one another.

So it is that the relationship between liturgy and ministry, along with
their relationship to 'Christ' and 'Church' as well, are seen rightly as holographic. When one looks at the liturgy of the Church, its ritually scripted
performance of gratitude, proclamation and grateful response, one is also
seeing the world as God is bringing it into being through Christ;[10] and one
is seeing Christ himself, and the pattern of his ministry that is, first and
foremost, his lived-out ministry to the world, the very pattern into which
the world is being called for the sake of its own flourishing. When one looks
at the ministry of Christ, one is seeing the liturgy that he *was* and is, the
work for the world that he offered, the liturgy that his whole life constituted.
Christ's liturgy, his work for the world, was his servant life; the Church's life
is the service that Christ embodied, as his disciples; the liturgy is the Church
practising the dispositions of such a life, in the mode of gratitude and worship.[11] No matter what one's angle of view on the theological hologram of
Christ, liturgy and ministry, one sees the organic and inextricable connection of each to the other and to the world. They are all one reality: God's
action for the flourishing of the world, embodied and brought to pass in
and through Christ, God's liturgy for the world, which is the Church's own
ministry to carry forward in the world as its own liturgy-as-life, given by
grace, continuously renewed by the Spirit, and celebrated ever anew in its
liturgy-as-worship, as the eschatological sacrament of the whole world's
transformation as kingdom of God.

It is in this connection that we can revisit the notion of 'priesthood',
introduced earlier, as belonging first and primarily to Christ and *eo ipso*
to the whole Church, the whole corpus of all the baptized. Christ's work,
as noted in Hebrews 8.6 – his *ministry* as it appears in most English translations – is here, in the Greek, not his *diakonias* but his *leitourgias*. Here,

---

[10] Aidan Kavanagh, *On Liturgical Theology* (Collegeville: Liturgical Press, 1984), 46.
[11] Don E. Saliers, *Worship as Theology: Foretaste of Glory Divine* (Nashville: Abingdon Press, 1994), 146–8.

the reference is to the work of the temple priest. Before speaking of priesthood as an office and order of ministry in the narrow sense, one anchors priesthood firmly in the ministry of Christ, the life, death and resurrection of Christ as priest. God's work in Christ, God's liturgy for the world, is a priestly work, restoring the relationship between people and God analogously to the way the priest did so in the Temple in the rituals of atonement. From this foundation – Christ as our One Priest – one can then speak of the priesthood as belonging to the whole Church, all the baptized, to the extent that they are *in Christ* and carry on his ministry of reconciliation. The holographic relationship between liturgy and ministry, then, turns out to include 'priesthood' as well. Why then do we refer to a *particular office* within the Church as priestly – and some others as episcopal or diaconal – and why are they exercised as liturgical roles in the worship of the assembly?

Liturgy, ministry and the emergence of ecclesial orders

The answer to that question requires first that we consider the foundation that is laid by joining the first major ecclesiological motif – the notion of the Church as a priestly people in union with Christ, whose union is enacted and celebrated in liturgical worship – to a second major motif: that the Church carries on its work in a differentiated unity, a practice of various gifts, skills and roles. The Church is the 'body of Christ' and, like a body, it has many parts, each of which plays a role that serves the organic unity and work of the whole.[12] One can restate these two motifs as a unity in this way: the ministry of Christ our Priest, his life-as-liturgy for the world's benefit, is celebrated and carried on by his priestly people, joining themselves to that ministry in the intentional activity of worship, becoming there through liturgical formation the body of Christ that carries on his work through the various gifts given to its members. Coming together in worship, their primary act of thanksgiving to God, the various members join themselves to God's ongoing liturgy, God's mission: the salvation and transformation of the world in Christ.

While all the roles and parts played in this mission by members of the body of Christ have their purpose, some roles emerge as characteristic of the work of the Church as a whole,[13] or signal the spirit in which all the Church's ministry is done: in particular, oversight (*episcope*) and service

---

[12]   1 Corinthians 12.1–31.
[13]   Ephesians 4.11–12.

(*diakonia*). The history and biblical accounts of such roles, in detail, are addressed elsewhere in this volume. For our purposes, we note that oversight of the Church, upbuilding its faith in Christ and formation especially through teaching and liturgical leadership and also pastoral care, was originally linked to apostolic authority, those who were *sent by Christ himself*, whose later institutional descendants many Christians call 'bishops'; and those apostolic leaders were joined by 'deacons' (the relevant term, again, is *diakonia*), charged with service to the vulnerable – particularly widows, orphans and the poor – work that was *deeply connected to Christ's own teaching and his healing activity* among the marginalized of his day.

The New Testament goes into some detail, though not as much as we might like, about how these constitutive ecclesial marks of oversight and service took shape in particular roles that individuals played within the Church's worship and life. But by the late first or very early second century, for example from letters traditionally attributed to Clement of Rome, and a short while later in documents of other regions, bishops and deacons appear to be already distinct roles, and 'presbyters' or other elders in faith have developed to assist the bishops and extend their oversight. As time passes, these roles developed into 'orders' of ministry, including the 'priestly' order. 'Priests' eventually became the term used for what the New Testament mostly calls 'presbyters' through an accident of translation, although the distinction between bishops and presbyters is, in the New Testament, not always sharp. Over a much longer period, as the Church became as much an institution as a community, particularly after the time of Constantine, these orders collected administrative as well as liturgical and pastoral dimensions to their work. But theologically, it remains important to keep clear about the fact that these roles are, first and foremost, the work of particular persons (whose call to these roles are discerned in various ways over history) to support the work of the whole *Church* in union with Christ, *especially in their leadership of the liturgical assembly*. The faith that the bishop guards and teaches, especially as he or she presides over the liturgical gathering of the assembly, and the service that the deacon both practises and signifies in the same assembly, are fundamental to the life of the Church and its adoption by God in Christ. The basic ecclesial unit of both liturgy and ministry is the *assembly of the baptized*, whose life is centred in the worship of God that forms them continuously to be the body of Christ not only when gathered in assembly but also when dispersed in the world, in proclamation and service that embody God's reconciliation in Christ, according to their various gifts. This proclamation and service, symbolized by the leadership of the bishop (and by the priests who extend the bishop's ministry in the local congregations) and of the deacon, is, quite simply, what it means to be Church. This basic understanding was central to the ecumenical liturgical movement in the twentieth century and animates the liturgical theology of the churches, both catholic and reformed, that make up the majority of Christians today. The theology also appears in the major churches of the Eastern rite, albeit in an idiom somewhat different than the Western.

An ecumenically important word here on terminology: there is an ecumenical convergence around the theology of orders expressed here that goes beyond titles. While this chapter uses the terms that dominate in Christianity – 'bishop,' 'priest' and 'deacon' – as a function of the sheer number of Christians in particular families of the faith, the ministries of apostolic oversight, pastoral congregational leadership in continuity with that oversight, and service are present in churches that do not use those terms. Ever since the promulgation of the ecumenical document *Baptism, Eucharist, and Ministry* (*BEM*),[14] we have recognized that apostolicity and service take a number of specific forms and names across Christianity, and although the terms used here have some weight of history, other terms for these orders of ministry are used. What is important, to understand ministry and its relationship to liturgy, is to appreciate the central and constitutive status of certain characteristics of the Church, and to recognize and respect those in one another, however particular churches organize and title them.

Bishops, priests and deacons in the liturgy: living, breathing sacraments

It was noted above that the orders of ministry, these particular roles and offices of bishop, priest and deacon, are both signifying the nature of the Church's ministry as the body of Christ and enacting their purposes *especially* when they are practising their roles in the liturgical assembly. Of course, the Church does its work through its members dispersed in the world, but the Church's members, with all their gifts, assembled in worship, is the primary mode of the Church's existence. If the work of God in Christ is indeed reconciliation between God and humanity and, *eo ipso*, the reconciliation of members one with another is rooted in God, then the assembly's worship, *consenting to being addressed by God* in the breaking open of Word and breaking of Bread, and *addressing God* in praise and prayer – being in relationship in worship face to face, as it were – is

---

[14] *Baptism, Eucharist, and Ministry* (Geneva: World Council of Churches, 1982), sects II–IV.

central. The orders of ministry that point most directly to the constitutive work of the assembly as a whole, then – proclamation of Christ's ministry of reconciliation and embodiment of the character of that ministry as service – are naturally the leaders of the liturgical assembly and signify those constitutive characteristics of the Church at the moment of its most important and central activity: being in relation to God in worship. The bishop, priest and deacon are doing their most essential work when exercising their gifts and the orders to which they have been called when they do their work in support of the eucharistic assembly. The intrinsic relationship between the orders and the enactment of the Church's identity in the eucharistic assembly is remarkably clear, as John Klentos has observed, in the Byzantine rites for ordination in which the liturgical language by which bishops and priests were ordained was almost entirely focused on their function within the liturgical assembly; and in which persons of all three orders were ordained at a moment within the eucharistic liturgy that corresponded to the actual function that person would play within the liturgy.[15] Klentos sees there the 'nexus of liturgy and ecclesiology', the way in which these rites enact a theology of the Church 'by which "the Church is *informed* of her cosmic and eschatological vocation, *receives* the power to fulfill it, and thus truly [*becomes*] what she is – the sacrament, in Christ, of the new creation"'.[16]

What instincts are at work in the content and structure of these old rites of ordination that help us articulate the meaning of orders today? That is, if the Church in its liturgy is the sacrament of the new creation reconciled to God in Christ, how is it that *ordination* to these particular ministries, exercised especially in the leadership of the Church's liturgy, comes to be known in many Christian churches as itself 'sacramental'? Theologically speaking, we might turn again to the metaphor of the hologram. When looking at the Church as liturgical assembly, we said, one is seeing the ministry of Christ in liturgical form, the world being reconciled to God, which is God's own liturgy for the sake of the world. Walk around our metaphorical hologram to look directly at the particular orders of ministry that lead the Church's liturgical worship, and one sees in particular persons the

---

[15] John Klentos, 'Byzantine Ordination Prayers: From Text to Theology', in *Studia Liturgica Diversa: Essays in Honor of Paul Bradshaw*, Maxwell E. Johnson and L. Edward Phillips, eds (Portland: Pastoral Press, 2004), 153–61.

[16] Klentos, 'Byzantine Ordination Prayers', 153–4. Klentos is quoting Alexander Schmemann and exemplifying his method. See Schmemann, 'Liturgy and Theology', in *Liturgy and Tradition: Theological Reflections of Alexander Schmemann*, Thomas Fisch, ed. (Crestwood: St Vladimir's Press, 1990), 57.

characteristics of the Church overall in its reconciling ministry in Christ: the chief characteristics of loving oversight, proclamation and service that mark the Church and its characteristics as the body of Christ. The particular orders are, at one and the same time, servants of the liturgical actions of the Church as sacrament and sacraments to the Church of its own very identity. Put differently, as the world, ideally, looks to the Church and sees in its life and worship the reality of God's liturgy reconciling the world through the ministry of Christ, so the Church looks to those who lead its worship and sees in them the characteristics of the Church as a whole.

That, then, is the paradox of the orders of ministry in their liturgical leadership, and the source of simultaneous reference to the Church as a whole and the ordained minsters within it as 'sacraments'. When members of the Church, gathered around the Book, the Font and the Table, look to the leaders in their midst – leading the assembly's worship, proclaiming the Word, serving the world in prayer for its needs, offering thanksgiving and petition over bread and wine, breaking bread and pouring wine in which the Church will know its Lord in the holy meal – what they see, *if indeed they understand rightly*, is themselves: proclaimers of the Word, servants of the world, themselves broken and poured out for the world's sake in unity with their Lord whose own life was the true pattern and enactment of this divine ministry. As sacraments are material symbolic crystallizations in a particular place, time and thing of something that is of universal soteriological significance, so it is that the ordained ministers are living, breathing material symbols of the genesis of the Church in Christ's work of reconciliation that is ultimately, and finally, God's own work.

Sacraments nested within sacraments: the spirituality of ordained ministry follows from its nature, then, as a sacrament (the orders themselves) of a sacrament (the Church) of the Sacrament (Christ) of God's *leitourgia*, God's loving and healing of the world and its relationship to God. The work of those ordained ministers, then, is marked by *humility*, as the work is ultimately to serve the Church's mission and ministry; *joyful confidence* that, despite the shortcomings and failings of the Church to be fully itself, many though they are, the work and mission to which they testify is ultimately God's, and God's to guarantee; and *deep and daily prayer* to be strengthened and accompanied by God in this ministry, as there is no work of greater importance and gravity than to animate continually the worship of the liturgical assembly through Christ, the one who 'loved us and gave himself up for us, a fragrant offering and sacrifice to God'.[17]

---

[17] Ephesians 5.2 RSV.

19

Missiology and ministry

ROBERT HEANEY

Missiology

Missiology is a cross-disciplinary field of study focused on the practice and theologizing of those who believe that what they say and what they do is, in some sense, a response to or participation in a divine 'sentness'. Missiologists may study the history of missionary migration in different eras. Missiologists may propose theological theses for Christian mission. Missiologists may examine the linguistic issues at stake in the various contextualizations of theology across cultures. Missiologists may be involved in analysing and strategizing for church growth. Missiologists may compare the outreach of distinct religions and cultures. Missiologists may engage with critical theories in a bid to uncover injustice and/or establish more just mission structures and practices. The guild of missiologists includes, therefore, scholars, practitioners and activists influenced by and contributing to diverse fields such as history, anthropology, sociology, psychology, linguistics, biblical studies, religious studies, theological studies, ethics and critical theory.

The sentness (*missio*) of mission may be understood in distinct and interrelated ways expressed in terms of calling, vocation, evangelization, inculturation, contextualization, humanization, development, prophecy, liberation, decolonization and/or dialogue. This sentness is Christian because it draws from a theological reservoir of images and commitments including eternal processions, divine missions, revelation, redemption, salvation, grace, incarnation, kingdom of God and mission of God that coalesces in the person of Jesus Christ. Justifying a particular point of departure for the study of mission might be seen as an impossible task given the inherent plurality of the subject matter, the many disciplines that contribute to the field, and the diversity of theological and ecumenical sources drawn upon. The present volume, however, deals with ministry. That is to say, whatever else is in view here the focus is better Christian practice. Beginning with missionary practice this chapter will set out the importance of a *critical* and *constructive* approach to mission that might nourish ministry.

A critical approach to the practice of Christian mission does not ignore experience, missionary malpractice, or criticisms from recipients of missionary endeavours. On the contrary, a critical missiology directly examines malpractice and critique. If, as will be seen, mission theology cannot be abandoned without abandoning the very message of the gospel then a critical approach to missiology cannot end in deconstruction. A constructive move must also be made. Consequently, this chapter will begin to outline a particular approach to missiology and how that approach might resource ministry.

A critical turn: missionary practice

The field of missiology, the practice of missionaries and Christian theologies of mission are contested and, at times, controversial. There is no shortage of literature criticizing the practice of foreign missionaries as they migrated from powerful imperial centres to places far beyond the imperial metropoles. The relationships missionaries benefited from or brokered with those in political power are central to the criticisms of mission practice, at least since Christianity moved from a Jewish to a Greco-Roman milieu.[1] Since Christianity's expansion in relation to the Roman Empire, Christian mission would often mean a movement 'from the superior to the inferior'.[2] At the close of the fifteenth century the so-called Age of Discovery was as much an age of European colonization and Christian expansionism as it was an age of subjugation and slavery. The Christian nations of Spain and Portugal extended programmes of colonization while at the same time purporting to expand programmes of christianization.[3] Yet, perhaps even more castigated than these eras of mission is the period of the modern missionary movement. The movement emerges in the aftermath of the Enlightenment and centres not on government-sponsored

---

[1] It should be noted that this criticism may depend upon undervaluing the equally important story of the eastern migration of Christianity. If this is the case, instead of simply criticizing 'western' mission, the criticism also adds to a Eurocentric narrative frame. See the Introduction in Peter C. Phan, ed., *Christianities in Asia* (Malden, MA: Wiley-Blackwell, 2011), 1–6.

[2] David Bosch, *Transforming Mission: Paradigm Shifts in Theology of Mission* (Maryknoll, NY: Orbis Books, 1991), 193.

[3] Bosch, *Transforming*, 190–4, 226–30.

missions but on the voluntary society within a British empire.[4] Six criticisms are often made of the modern missionary movement. Paternalistic missionary interest overlapped with colonial interest. Missionaries justified imperialism, promoted acculturation, practised racism, disparaged traditional practice and exacerbated societal divisions.[5]

Gayatri Spivak describes British expansion in India as 'giving Christianity with one hand and ensuring military superiority with the other'.[6] The first criticism of Christian mission is that missionary interest often overlapped with colonial interest and that this compromised the gospel. Crucial to such a criticism is that the nature and means of imperial expansion influenced understandings of Christian mission as an expansionist endeavour relying on the agency of Europeans and European colonizers. R. S. Sugirtharajah argues that in British missionary circles it was this broader imperial expansion that set the scene for a rediscovery in the eighteenth century of the 'unfashionable' text of Matthew 28.19.[7] The missionary Johannes Rebmann would do more than discern a divine expansionist commission. In the light of 30 years spent working in the absence of European political governance, he reflected in 1856 that 'where the power of a Christian nation ceased to be felt, there is also the boundary, set by Providence, to missionary labour'.[8]

The first criticism takes for granted that imperialism is a sin and thus treats with suspicion relationships between missionary and imperialist practice. Such an assessment of imperialism is contested. The second criticism points to the explicit theological justification for empire and its missional benefits that some missionaries and Christian leaders provided. Appeal is made to providence as causing, or allowing, colonial expansion, thus providing opportunity for moral renascence. Both themes are present in the writings of Bishop Charles Blomfield as he argues for the establishment of a colonial bishoprics fund. In 1840, as Bishop of London, he claims that such a fund would

> cause the reformed Episcopal Church to be recognised, by all the nations of the earth, as the stronghold of pure religion, and the legitimate dispenser

---

[4] Bosch, *Transforming*, 280.

[5] See Robert S. Heaney, *From Historical to Critical Post-Colonial Theology: The Contribution of John S. Mbiti and Jesse N. K. Mugambi* (Eugene, OR: Pickwick, 2015), 31–61.

[6] Gayatri Chakravorty Spivak, *A Critique of Postcolonial Reason: Toward a History of the Vanishing Present* (Cambridge, MA: Harvard University Press, 1999), 216.

[7] Heaney, *Historical*, 214.

[8] Cited by Robert W. Strayer, *The Making of Missionary Communities in East Africa: Anglicans and Africans in Colonial Kenya, 1875–1935* (London: Heinemann, 1978), 33.

of its means of grace: and will be a chosen instrument in the hands of God for purifying and restoring the other branches of Christ's Holy Catholic church.[9]

In the first edition of *The Colonial Church Chronicle* (1847), colonialism is considered the means through which British Christianity can universalize its values and Anglicanism can demonstrate its catholicity.[10] A hundred years later, when it appeared that an imperial Christian America was replacing an imperial Christian Britain, the general secretary of the Church Missionary Society would propose a 'theology of imperialism'. Max Warren justified empire in terms of providence, vocation, order and greater good.[11]

It is the case that tension did at times exist between colonialists and missionaries, and sometimes missionaries opposed colonial lifestyles and policies. Despite this, Elizabeth Isichei writes, 'It has been suggested that both mission and imperialism rest on the same postulate: the superiority of one's own culture to that of the other.'[12] A third criticism, therefore, of mission practice is that missionaries often imposed foreign cultures on converts. This could take place through Western missionary endeavour internationally but it could also take place on the 'home mission field'. The 1819 Civilization Fund Act in the USA made funds available to missionaries for the purpose of educating Native peoples in 'the habits of civilization'.[13] These funds made such missionaries the 'de facto arm of the US government's civilization project throughout the nineteenth century'.[14] The policy to 'civilize' by providing both 'the Bible and the plough' would eventually lead to the forcible removal of children to residential schools. Proselytization, through education into European

[9] Rowan Strong, *Anglicanism and the British Empire c.1700–1850* (Oxford: Oxford University Press, 2007), 200.

[10] N.a., 'Extension of the Reformed Catholic Church', *Colonial Church Chronicle* (July 1847 – June 1848), 3–5.

[11] M. A. C. Warren, *Caesar the Beloved Enemy: Three Studies in the Relation of Church and State* (London: SCM Press, 1955). See Robert S. Heaney, 'Coloniality and Theological Method in Africa', *Journal of Anglican Studies* 7:1 (2009): 55–65.

[12] Elizabeth Isichei, *A History of Christianity in Africa: From Antiquity to the Present* (London: SPCK, 1995), 92.

[13] L. Daniel Hawk and Richard L. Twiss, 'From Good: "The Only Good Indian Is a Dead Indian" to Better: "Kill the Indian and Save the Man" to Best: "Old Things Pass Away and All Things Become White!": An American Hermeneutic of Colonization', in Kay Higuera Smith, Jayachitra Lalitha and L. Daniel Hawk, eds, *Evangelical Postcolonial Conversations: Global Awakenings in Theology and Praxis* (Downers Grove, IL: IVP, 2014), 47–60 at 47–8.

[14] Hawk and Twiss, 'Good', 52.

mores, was the end aimed for and often resulted in the imposition of a 'consciousness that negates and denies the lived reality – hence the identity and value – of indigenous people'.[15] The imposition of, for example, individualism, dualism and futurism was seen by missionaries as the introduction of a Christian and biblical worldview.[16]

Fourth, racism, predicated upon practices of expansionism, militates against claims for the beneficence or benignity of mission. 'Lightness' and 'darkness' and 'lightness' in preference to 'darkness' could function in nineteenth-century missionary literature as signifiers not only for the nature of sin but also for the nature of some races purportedly sunk deeper into sin than others.[17] Whiteness is given 'formative power'.[18] The history of the modern missionary movement is, it seems, replete with stories of local theological leadership being suppressed and displaced. It is such racism that provokes, from especially the late nineteenth century, the emergence of locally or independently initiated churches as one potent, practical and grounded response.[19] Such initiatives are concerned not only with theological voice but also with the theological importance of place, land and geography. They signify, in part, a more holistic participation in God's mission, resisting practice that 'imagines Christian identity floating above land, landscape, animals, place, and space'.[20]

All mission depends upon dialogue. The explicit proclamation of the gospel of Jesus Christ by evangelists in places where the Church does not exist depends upon pre-Christian traditions and philosophy. Yet, a fifth criticism of the modern missionary movement is that it often resulted in the disparagement of traditional belief and practice. A twentieth-century missionary to Kenya reflected that 'the spiritual beliefs of the African' were 'superstition rather than religion'. She adjudged God in African thought to be 'a power which must be propitiated' and that 'Fear . . . is the motive inspiring all their spiritual beliefs.'[21] John S. Mbiti identifies a 'bulldozer mentality' among many missionaries who assumed that African traditions

---

[15] Hawk and Twiss, 'Good', 57.

[16] Heaney, *Historical*, 48–50.

[17] Myra Rutherdale, *Women and the White Man's God* (Vancouver: University of British Columbia Press, 2002), 29.

[18] Willie James Jennings, *The Christian Imagination: Theology and the Origins of Race* (New Haven, CT and London: Yale University Press, 2010), 290.

[19] Robert Edgar, 'New Religious Movements', in Norman Etherington, ed., *Missions and Empire* (Oxford: Oxford University Press, 2005), 216–37.

[20] Jennings, *Christian*, 293.

[21] Cited in Heaney, *Historical*, 44.

were demonic and needed to be 'swept aside'.[22] Given this, pre-Christian theology and practice was seen to be a great danger and standing in opposition to the Christian gospel. Traditional pre-Christian thought and practice was a danger to the purity of the gospel and the integrity of an emerging Church.

Evangelization often results in an explicit distinction between those who are part of the body of Christ and those who are not. A sixth criticism of missionary practice is, therefore, that it provokes or exacerbates societal divisions. In some contexts this did not only mean an apparent disparity between those who had access to divine blessing and those who did not. It could also mean converts gaining more access to education and promotion within colonial structures.[23] Further societal division was evidenced with the importation not only of the Church of Christ but also of denominations. Indeed, denominations sometimes negotiated together over access to certain areas and peoples, creating, quite literally, a denominational tribalism. By the fourth decade of the nineteenth century, in the face of rationalism and liberalism, denominationalism was often an embedded reality in foreign missionary strategy, so much so that particular theological emphases within church traditions hardened and cooperation abated.[24]

Criticism of missionaries and Christian mission past and present cannot and must not be avoided. Equally, the recognition of criticism and malpractice cannot result in mission isolationism or reductionism. For even in the face of colonialism, imperialism, acculturation, racism, subjugation and division, many have joyfully welcomed Jesus Christ. Not a Jesus of empire but a Jesus despised by empire. Not a Jesus dependent on foreign culture but a Jesus present in the particularity of land, language and culture. Not a white Jesus but a black Jesus. Even at this juncture, therefore, one might already see that a constructive turn will include mission theology that stresses participation over expansion (*contra* colonialism and imperialism), contextualization over assimilation (*contra* acculturation and subjugation) and ecumenism over confessionalism (*contra* racism and divisiveness).

---

[22] John S. Mbiti, 'Confessing Christ in a Multi-Faith Context, with Two Examples from Africa', *Metanoia* 4:3–4 (1994): 138–45.

[23] See Jane Tschurenev, 'Incorporation and Differentiation: Popular Education and the Imperial Civilizing Mission in Early Nineteenth Century India', in Carey A. Watt and Michael Mann, eds, *Civilizing Missions in Colonial and Postcolonial South Asia: From Improvement to Development* (London: Anthem Press, 2011), 93–124.

[24] Bosch, *Transforming*, 329–34.

A constructive (re)turn: the *missio Dei*

This chapter has considered mission 'from below', beginning not with the Bible, theology or a narrative of historical westward expansion, but with key criticisms of modern practice.[25] The purpose of this section is to consider the importance of a shift to mission of God (*missio Dei*) language as one broad theological response to criticisms of modern mission and to begin to assess to what extent such an emphasis might resource a theology of mission that is participationist, contextualist and ecumenical. As will be seen presently, a participationist approach has implications for understandings of human agency, and contextualization means a more expansive view of the work of the Spirit of Christ in the world which, in turn, leads to a capacious ecumenism.

The mid-twentieth century was a turbulent time for much of the world. That turbulence, especially in the wake of two world wars, had Christians in both the Global North and the Global South questioning the vaunted expansion of European and American 'progress'. Reflecting this reaction against expansionism, the 1952 International Missionary Council sought to stress the primary agency of God in mission. Summing up the significance of this meeting David Bosch writes, 'There is church because there is mission, not vice versa . . . To participate in mission is to participate in the movement of God's love toward people, since God is a fountain of sending love.'[26] While the term has been at times adopted with vague definitions and imprecise implications, at its best *missio Dei* theology declares that mission is at the heart of a Christian vision of God. In other words, mission does not belong primarily to a theology of the Church, humanity or salvation; neither does it belong primarily in the realm of pastoral, practical or political theology. Rather, to speak of mission is to speak of God. Mission is thus not a consequent of the doctrine of God. It is part of the doctrine of God. This emphasis, though beginning with conciliar Protestants, has spread to influence Roman Catholic and Orthodox thinking, as well as the broader constituencies of world Protestantism. Famously, the Second Vatican Council document, *Ad Gentes*, declared that, 'The pilgrim Church is missionary by her very nature' because 'it is from the mission of the Son and the mission of the Holy Spirit that she draws her origin, in accordance

---

[25] See Heaney, *Historical*, 200–18.
[26] Bosch, *Transforming*, 390.

with the decree of God the Father'.[27] *Missio Dei* theology, or at least the adoption of the term, has become an important way for post-colonial Christians to talk about mission.

While the language of the *missio Dei* has been widely accepted and widely used, it has also caused controversy. Two distinct understandings, referred to here as inculturationist and institutionalist, resource distinct understandings of ministry. To develop a theology of the *missio Dei* with an emphasis on inculturation is to take a position that emphasizes God's work in all cultures. God is at work among all people in all places at all times. The mission of God is present in all cultures and the Spirit of God is at work in all religions. The mission is God's. It is not dependent upon the work, presence or even distinct existence of the Church. To the extent that the Church is a discrete body it is 'a pointer' to how God reaches out to the world, and one agent for the 'humanization' of society. A call to repentance and conversion could be seen as evidence of imperialistic proselytism. Indeed, in its most radical form it is believed that the existence of an institutionally organized Church can stand in the way of the mission of God. Such a view, present in ecumenical conversations especially in the 1960s, saw mission no longer as pointing the world to the true God through Christ and Church but pointing people to true humanity through processes of humanization (for example, healthcare, welfare, politics and education).[28]

An institutionalist emphasis sees the Church as central to the mission of God. It is God's sovereign choice to make a people that experience and testify to re-creation through the work of Christ. This community becomes and makes visible, in history, the new creation of God. Its most radical form can be stated plainly: outside the Church there is no salvation. Thus, Christian ministry must include the development of the Church as theologically bounded and guarded from worldly influences that would pollute her testimony and integrity. The primary movement in mission is, then, from God to the Church. If there is movement beyond the Church it is through the institution extending itself outwards into the world in welcoming the children of the world into the shelter of the Church through God's grace received in word and sacrament. While the kingdom of God and the Church are not necessarily coterminous, it is difficult to conceive of one without the other. From this perspective it is argued that an inculturated approach ultimately embeds the very thing *missio Dei* theology

---

[27] Second Vatican Council, *Ad Gentes* (*On the Mission Activity of the Church*): <http://www.vatican.va/archive/hist_councils/ii_vatican_council/documents/vat-ii_decree_19651207_ad-gentes_en.html> (accessed 21 January 2016).

[28] Bosch, *Transforming*, 381–9.

sought to displace in the mid-twentieth century. That is to say, an inculturated emphasis promotes a bloated sense of human agency because of a 'secularization' or 'horizontalization' of mission.[29] In contrast, an institutionalist approach defines mission in relation to God's work of new creation in and through the Church. The call of mission is, first, for the Church to demonstrate in its life the overflowing grace of God. This grace, second, overflows into the surrounding context through the commissioned and dispersed congregation.

Lesslie Newbigin highlights the danger of polarized notions of the *missio Dei* when he defines as monstrosities both an 'unchurchly mission' and an 'unmissionary Church'.[30] An inculturated approach, focused on the work of the Spirit of God beyond the Church, can tend towards an 'unchurchly mission'. An institutionalist approach, emphasizing mission as a second or secondary move of the Church, can tend towards an 'unmissionary Church'. The Church's identity and the Church's work cannot be separated. The Church is the community that has met the risen Christ. The Church is the reconciled community of God. The Church is the new creation made visible in history. The Church is the communitarian embodiment of God's mission in God's world. Thus, God's community, striving and straining towards ecumenical unity, in declaring the risen Christ, working for reconciliation and bringing new life to the world, is being the Church. The Church is outward-turning life and love, or it is not God's community.[31] Yet, as the Church remains central, so the Lord remains sovereign. Thus, the concept and practice of ecumenism is expanded beyond tradition and denomination to the work of God in God's world (*oikoumenē*).

John the Baptist warned his hearers, 'Bear fruits worthy of repentance. Do not begin to say to yourselves, "We have Abraham as our ancestor"; for I tell you, God is able from these stones to raise up children to Abraham' (Luke 3.8 NRSV). The same Spirit that brings to birth the Church is the same Spirit that judges the Church and the same Spirit that is at work drawing all people to Christ even where there is apparently no church presence. Mission is not, then, contingent upon the needs or resources of a particular community or culture, nor is it exhausted by the final realization of God's reign. On the contrary, the Church is contingent upon its witness to the risen Christ, and mission is God's eternal nature, forever

---

[29] Bosch, *Transforming*, 392.
[30] Lesslie Newbigin, *The Household of God: Lectures in the Nature of the Church* (London: SCM Press, 1953), 147–8.
[31] John G. Flett, *The Witness of God: The Trinity, Missio Dei, Karl Barth, and the Nature of Christian Community* (Grand Rapids, MI: Eerdmans, 2010), 293; see 287–98.

drawing creation deeper into divine love. Mission does not exist simply because of want and wealth. Mission does not exist simply because of historical, sociological or economic circumstances. It is not contingent upon circumstance or organization. Mission is not an answer to decline nor an opportunity to expand. It is not the clamour for the freshest branding of church foisted upon unsuspecting communities by this year's celebrated sage. It is the eternal being of God. It is the eternal invitation to fellowship. It is creation's eternal response, 'Worthy is the Lamb that was slaughtered to receive power and wealth and wisdom and might and honour and glory and blessing!' (Rev. 5.12). This worshipful response as participation in the reconciliation wrought by God in Christ is a living relationship ever infused by the Spirit, turning humans to the Lord, which is always and simultaneously a turning outwards to others.[32]

> Mission is the abundant fellowship of active participation in the very glory that is the life of God from and to all eternity. It is life in the community of reconciliation moving out in solidarity with the world in the active knowledge that God died for it, too. It is the response of doxology as we follow the Spirit's lead as captives in the train of the living glorious Lord, the lamb that was slain.[33]

Missiologically shaped ministry

It has been argued that a stress on the *missio Dei* means a participationist understanding of Christian mission that displaces bloated notions of human agency. A balance between inculturationist and institutionalist understandings, centred on the work of the Spirit of Christ, means the Church practises ministries of contextualization that do not deny the mission of God beyond the Church. A recognition that the Church is the fruit of God's mission in reconciling the world to God's self fuels ongoing work for the highest degree of visible unity possible and results in an expansive ecumenism. By way of conclusion, this final section will begin to illustrate why such a participationist, contextualist and ecumenical understanding of mission has particular implications for ministries of worship, formation and reconciliation.

Mission begins with God, is entered into through doxology and finds its end in God's reconciliation of all things to God's self (1 Corinthians 15.28; Colossians 1.20). In the congregation, this doxological and eschatological

---

[32] See Flett, *Witness*, 287–90.
[33] Flett, *Witness*, 297–8.

movement centres on the resurrected Christ's movement out into the world. Mission is not, therefore, a consequent of the Church's existence. It is the means by which the Church exists. As a result, human agency is put in its rightful place as dependent upon the grace of God and as a response to the grace of God. Worship, as submission to the lordship of Christ, as discernment of the presence of Christ in the world and as a participation in Christ's risen life, is itself a sending out of the Church to the world. The Church as the community that meets the risen Christ, seeks the risen Christ and witnesses to the risen Christ is a community that is outward-turning. A missiologically shaped ministry will, therefore, counter liturgical and sacramental thought and practice that tends towards a distinction between the existence of the Church and the outreach of the Church. It will instead frame word and sacrament as participation in the outward-moving life of Christ. A missiologically shaped ministry, baptized in prayer, renews a Christian vision so that believers might begin to see the 'God infested' nature of the world.[34] The liturgical heart of Christian mission beats in particular communities and particular settings. Indeed, worship that is testimony to God declares both the catholicity of faith (the Church is a fellowship that transcends time and space) and the contextualism of grace (people experience God's presence in their lives at a particular time and place). That is to say, mission cannot be reduced to the neighbourhood at the expense of the nations. Catholicity and contextualism means that Christian formation is necessarily intercultural.

Practices of contextualization that seek to hold together both the divine sovereignty of the Spirit of Christ and the divine mission active through the Church will depend on processes of formation that nourish spiritual discernment across differences. The idea that intercultural theologizing is a specialism must now be left behind. Rather, such work is inherent to discipleship in a missiologically shaped ministry. The discerning of the mission of God, emerging from prayer, is neither subjective nor denominational. The God of creation and creatures, wholly other in eternal love, calls us to God's self through fellowship with the Son in community with others. A critical and constructive theology of mission invites, therefore, formation in an ecumenism not limited to denominational boundaries, and calls for a more expansive Christian discipleship across cultures and religions.[35] Because the Spirit of Christ is at work in God's world,

---

[34] Marilyn McCord Adams, 'Prayer as the "Lifeline of Theology"', *Anglican Theological Review* 98:2 (2016): 271–83 at 275.

[35] For one important model see Cathy Ross and Stephen Bevans, eds, *Mission on the Road to Emmaus: Constants, Context and Prophetic Dialogue* (London: SCM Press, 2015).

theologizing that equips believers to understand the significance of culture is needed alongside practical means to 'read' cultural phenomena. Cross-cultural voices, texts and partnerships beyond the formative and dominant cultures and voices of a given congregation become part of how believers understand and practise formation.[36] In terms of the formation process for full-time and/or ordained ministers, such intercultural theology becomes necessary to sustain any claims that the theology in, for example, degree programmes is critical and that students actually understand the reconciling mission to which the Church is called.

The mission of God in Christ reconciles God's creation to God's self. The Church is the reconciled and reconciling body of Christ (Romans 5; 2 Corinthians 5.19). The call of the Church is to witness to God's reconciliation. While reconciliation is an act of God, the Church is called to this mission as the embodiment of God's reconciliation. Indeed, the message and practice of reconciliation, in a world of seemingly insatiable brutality, may be the most compelling way of expressing the mission of God. At personal, cultural and political levels the Church is called into reconciling practices.[37] Such reconciling practices, whether within families or communities, between oppressors and oppressed, across violent political divides, is complicated not least because the Church has been complicit in violence and has not always been a just arbiter. Reconciling practices are, therefore, as much about 'inreach' as they are about outreach. Reconciling practices are about the Church witnessing to God's reconciliation in the ways it laments for its own failures and in the ways it struggles to be more just in its dealings. This also occurs through the ways in which the Church humbly reaches out to the wider society in providing particular philosophical and religious analyses of conflict, space for difficult conversations and models for good disagreement, all undergirded by a prophetic impulse that because God wills peace it is possible.

In conclusion, mission is not accidental to the Church's existence. If it is understood or practised in such terms, the Church's ministry is in danger of being determined by the fortunes and vicissitudes of history. If it is understood or practised in such terms, ministerial practice becomes malpractice. A critical approach to mission seeks to identify such malpractice

---

[36] For some resources see, for example, Gerald O. West, ed., *Reading Other-Wise: Socially Engaged Biblical Scholars Reading with Their Local Communities* (Atlanta, GA: Society of Biblical Literature, 2007); Kathryn Tanner, *Theories of Culture: A New Agenda for Theology* (Minneapolis, MN: Fortress Press, 1997).

[37] Stephen B. Bevans and Roger P. Schroeder, *Constants in Context: A Theology of Mission for Today* (New York: Orbis Books, 2006), 390–4.

not only as it exists in historical and contemporary mission practice, but also in historical and contemporary theology:

> missiology acts as a gadfly in the house of theology, creating unrest and resisting complacency, opposing every ecclesiastical impulse to self-preservation, every desire to stay what we are, every inclination toward provincialism and parochialism, every fragmentation of humanity into regional or ideological blocs, every exploitation of some sectors of humanity by the powerful, every religious, ideological, or cultural imperialism, and every exaltation of the self-sufficiency of the individual over other people or other parts of creation.[38]

Yet, the critical turn in missiology is not an end in itself. It is done in the service of a renewal of mission that begins with a refreshed vision of God. God is missionary, therefore the Church of God is missionary.[39] Mission is the mode of the Church's existence. The Church's life is a life that is joined to the life of Christ. As God in God's being is eternal, outward-moving love, so the Church, joined to God in the life of Christ, exists in outward, boundary-crossing movement to the world. Ministry, defined missiologically, is the reception and proclamation of that profoundest of all messages: God is love.

---

[38] Bosch, *Transforming*, 496.
[39] Flett, *Witness*, 208.

20

Ethics and ministry: witness or solidarity?

ROBIN GILL

Introduction

A number of commentators on contemporary (present-day) Christianity in the Western world have argued that over the last half-century many denominations have become increasingly polarized on ethical issues concerned with sexuality or the status of life. Although the question of the justifiability of warfare, for example, has divided churchgoers throughout Christian history – a radical minority of denominational churchgoers, as well as some sectarian groups such as Quakers and Anabaptists, have followed Tertullian in being thoroughgoing pacifists and thus at odds with the majority, who have followed Augustine and are not – cultural changes since the mid-1960s on sexuality, abortion, capital punishment and euthanasia do seem to have particularly polarized Christians across denominations throughout Western society.

Using data from the *World Values Survey* in the 1980s, the American sociologist Ronald Inglehart showed clearly that attitudes towards homosexuality were already polarized between age groups within most of the Western countries studied.[1] Aggregating data, he found that whereas some three-quarters of respondents aged 65 or over thought that homosexuality could 'never' be justified, this dropped to exactly half of those aged 35–44, and to less than two-fifths of those aged 18–24. Since many congregations were and remain elderly it seemed likely that the attitudes of church people towards homosexuality were, even then, increasingly at odds with those of younger people. Five years later, Leslie Francis and William Kay confirmed from their extensive data that less than a third of British Anglican teenagers who went regularly to church thought that homosexuality was 'wrong'.[2]

---

[1] Ronald Inglehart (1990), *Culture Shift in Advanced Industrial Society* (Princeton, NJ: Princeton University Press).

[2] Leslie J. Francis and William K. Kay (1995), *Teenage Religion and Values* (Leominster: Gracewing / Fowler Wright).

The British sociologist Callum Brown has concluded (as did Inglehart) that this 'cultural shift' represents a radical process of secularization.[3] Indeed, for Brown, secularization fully emerges in the mid-1960s as a direct result of this cultural shift. The British theologian and sociologist Linda Woodhead and the journalist Andrew Brown are not persuaded that this cultural shift results in secularization as such, but they do see it as a real threat to the social relevance of the Church of England today.[4]

This evidence presents a serious ethical challenge to Christian ministers in the contemporary Western world. Given that attitudes to sexuality and status-of-life issues have been changing radically for half a century in the general population, how should ministers across denominations respond? To put this too bluntly, should they actively combat these changes, hoping that they are reversible (at least among the faithful), or should they re-examine traditional ethical teaching within their own denominations?

For Catholic priests in the Western world this is not simply an academic question. The papal encyclical *Humanae Vitae* (1968) decided not to change Catholic teaching prohibiting the use of hormonal or barrier means of contraception, even within marriage. This prohibition remains the official teaching for Catholic laypeople. Yet from population statistics across the West it is clear that most married Catholics of child-bearing age do not follow this official teaching. It also seems likely that many Catholic parish priests have become loath even to preach about this teaching. In other words, the official prohibition of hormonal or barrier means of contraception has become irrelevant both to wider society *and* to many churchgoing Catholics.

Ministers in Methodist, Anglican and Presbyterian churches in a number of Western countries have also experienced increasing ethical polarization on the legitimacy of homosexual practice and same-sex marriage. For example, bishops within the Church of England were highly involved six decades ago in effecting changes in English and Welsh legislation decriminalizing homosexuality and suicide, abolishing capital punishment, legalising induced abortion and liberalizing divorce.[5] However, recently they have opposed English legislation on same-sex marriage, required gay candidates to be abstinent if they wish to be ordained, and opposed attempts

---

3   Callum Brown (2001), *The Death of Christian Britain* (London: Routledge); Callum Brown and Michael Snape (eds) (2010), *Secularisation in the Christian World* (Farnham: Ashgate).
4   Linda Woodhead and Andrew Brown (2016), *That Was the Church That Was: How the Church of England Lost the English People* (London: Bloomsbury).
5   See Robin Gill (2013), *Society Shaped by Theology: Sociological Theology, vol. 3* (Farnham: Ashgate, 2013).

to legalize physician-assisted euthanasia – despite clear support for voluntary euthanasia among assiduous Anglican churchgoers.[6] Here too ethical polarization is present *within* denominations and not simply between
churches and society.

Witness or solidarity?

There are various ways of depicting the opposite perspectives of this
polarization. Some have used Ernst Troeltsch's contrast between inclusive
churches and exclusive sects. In terms of ministry this would imply that
ministry within churches is socially inclusive, mirroring cultural shifts in
society at large and seeking to nuance or deepen them, rather than simply
oppose them. In contrast, ministry within exclusive sects makes a sharp
distinction between Christians and non-Christians, between believers
and non-believers, and between Christian and secular values. However,
in practice, denominations do not readily divide discretely into either
churches or sects. Aspects of some churches can appear highly sectarian,
and some sects have become remarkably inclusive (for example, modern
Quakers). As a result, sociologists of religion are now generally loath to
adopt Troeltsch's typology wholesale. In any case the term 'sectarian' in the
hands of theologians too easily becomes a weapon.

Those who follow Reinhold Niebuhr are more likely to use the terms
'realist' and 'non-realist' to depict the opposite perspectives of this polarization. The realists are those who take the world and its concerns seriously, while the non-realists are those who do not. For postmodernists
(unknown, of course, to Niebuhr) non-realism often appears especially
attractive. Once the assumptions of the Enlightenment have been dismissed and there is no longer thought to be a single rational discourse,
Christian ministers are free to espouse their own narrative and attempt
to out-narrate secular narratives. Meanwhile Christian realists continue to
take various secular and religious narratives seriously while, once more,
seeking to nuance or deepen them. Yet the term 'realist' on its own may
also become a weapon – especially if its opposite is labelled as 'fantasist' or
(using Niebuhr's term) 'utopian'.

David Horrell's *Solidarity and Difference: A Contemporary Reading of
Paul's Ethics* offers another (better, I believe) way to depict the difference
between these two perspectives – using the term 'solidarity' borrowed from

---

[6] Again see Gill, *Society Shaped by Theology*.

social ethics and contrasting it with 'difference'.[7] Horrell argues at length that both perspectives can be found (in an uneasy tension) within Paul's letters, so it is unsurprising that they remain a feature of contemporary Christian ministry. Horrell also argues that they address rather different audiences and that some common ground can be found between them. Nevertheless, tension between them is likely to remain. My suggestion is to use the more biblical and ethical term 'witness' rather than 'difference' in the context of ministry – in the early Church the Greek word *martus* (witness) soon came to signify a saintly person murdered for witnessing to the faith.

Horrell recognizes that the witness perspective is dominant in Paul's letters, but he also sees important evidence of a solidarity perspective:

> First, we have seen the prominence of the outsiders, or (more positively) of seeking to do good to all people . . . [with] injunctions to act with consideration towards 'all people' throughout Paul's letters – 1 Thessalonians (3.12; 5.15), Galatians (6.10), 1 Corinthians (10.32 [cf. 1.22]), Romans (12.17–18) and Philippians (4.5) – [which] indicates that this moral responsibility is, in Paul's view, incumbent on all Christians, whatever their specific situation and whether or not they appear to be suffering from the abuse of outsiders . . . Secondly, it is apparent that the appeal to do good to all means specifically acting in a way which all will acknowledge and recognise as good . . . Thirdly, beyond the sense that the knowledge of right and wrong is shared in common, Paul also indicates that non-Christians can and do act in accordance with these insights [e.g. Romans 13.1–4].[8]

These three points apply to all Christians but it is not difficult to see that they also apply very specifically to Christian ministers. Herein lies the tension in Horrell's account: Christians are simultaneously enjoined to recognize moral goodness in non-Christians *and* to give witness to the particularity of the Incarnation.

Applying this tension to the contemporary situation, Horrell offers the German philosopher Jürgen Habermas as an example at the very edge of the first (solidarity) perspective, and the American theologian Stanley Hauerwas as an example of the second (witness) perspective. It is true that Habermas has made much use of the concept of solidarity (along with the Kantian axiom of universalizability) and, in the last two decades, shown increasing admiration for some faith-based moral perspectives. Yet it

---

[7] David G. Horrell (2016 (2005)), *Solidarity and Difference: A Contemporary Reading of Paul's Ethics*, 2nd edn (London: Bloomsbury T&T Clark).
[8] Horrell, *Solidarity and Difference*, pp. 294–5.

would be difficult to see Habermas as a theologian. My suggestion here is to take the Dominican Edward Schillebeeckx as a more appropriate theological example, along with Robin Lovin and Lisa Sowle Cahill. Hauerwas, on the other hand, represents an obvious choice of the witness perspective in Christian ethics for both of us, as does his Mennonite mentor John Howard Yoder and the Anglican John Milbank.

One further suggestion beyond Horrell: these two ethical perspectives – witness and solidarity – can be analysed at three different levels in the context of Christian ministry: (1) moral decisions about particular issues; (2) moral virtues differently understood and valued; (3) moral theological justifications viewed alongside purely secular justifications.

Witness ministry: strengths and weaknesses

In one of his most popular and trenchant books, *Resident Aliens*, Stanley Hauerwas, together with William Willimon, wrote as follows about Christian ministry:

> Being a minister (like a pastor) is not a vocation merely to help people. We are called to help people 'in the name of Jesus.' And that's the rub. In fact, we are *not* called to help people. We are called to follow Jesus, in whose service we learn who we are and how we are to help and be helped. Jesus, in texts like his Sermon on the Mount, robs us of our attempts to do something worthwhile for the world, something 'effective' that yields results as an end in itself. His is an ethic built not upon helping people or even upon results, certainly not upon helping folk to be a bit better adjusted within an occupied Judea. His actions are based upon his account of how God is 'kind to the ungrateful and the selfish,' making the sun to rise on the good and the bad. We are called to 'be perfect' even as our Heavenly Father is.[9]

The term 'resident aliens' depicts Christians and their ministers as distinct from society at large and at considerable odds with it. The subtitles on the cover conveyed this clearly: 'Life in the Christian Colony' and 'A provocative Christian assessment of culture and ministry for people who know that something is wrong'. Of course the paragraph above contains qualifying words that also leave some room for solidarity: the word 'merely' in the first sentence; 'as an end in itself' in the fifth; and 'within an occupied Judea' in the sixth sentence. Yet the overall force of the third sentence and most of the fifth and sixth sentences supports the notion of 'resident aliens'

---

[9] Stanley Hauerwas and William Willimon (1989), *Resident Aliens: Life in the Christian Colony* (Nashville, TN: Abingdon Press), p. 121.

as a distinct and separate 'Christian colony' living apart from society at large. This is both its strength and its weakness. Christian ministry is very distinctive in Hauerwas's account, but it is also divisive and idealistic.

Twelve years later Hauerwas, now writing on his own, made much less use of such terms as 'resident aliens' and 'Christian colony', preferring, instead, the term 'witness':

> Does the truth of Christian convictions depend on the faithfulness of the church and, if so, how do we determine what would constitute faithfulness? Am I suggesting that the ability of the church to be or not to be nonviolent is constitutive for understanding what it might mean to claim that Christian convictions are true? Do I think the truthfulness of Christian witness is compromised when Christians accept the practices of the 'culture of death' – abortion, suicide, capital punishment, and war? Yes! On every count, the answer is 'Yes'.[10]

This more recent version of Christian witness is open to adoption by individual Christians across denominations, but it becomes much more problematic if it is applied to Christian ministry. Taking the first of my three levels – moral decisions about particular issues – it is quite difficult to identify any denomination that would support wholesale condemnation of all four of the particular issues that he itemizes here, namely abortion, suicide, capital punishment and war. Hauerwas follows the radical pacifist position of his mentor John Howard Yoder and is followed in turn by John Milbank (albeit with important theological differences between Hauerwas and Milbank). Yet while Catholic priests, for example, might condemn specific recourses to war, they have seldom adopted thoroughgoing pacifism. In addition, papal opposition to capital punishment is very recent and, at most, qualified.[11] Church of England bishops, as already mentioned, acted to decriminalize suicide, abolish capital punishment *and* legalize induced abortion. Free Church denominations have long had individual ministers who are radical pacifists but it is exceedingly rare for them to become a majority within their own denominations. American Southern Baptist ministers would probably be very reluctant to support the abolition of capital punishment.

More support might be garnered at the second and third levels for, say, Christian 'faithfulness', but even the way that Hauerwas proposes this

---

[10] Stanley Hauerwas (2001), *With the Grain of the Universe: The Church's Witness and Natural Theology* (Grand Rapids, MI: Brazos and London: SCM Press), p. 231.
[11] E. C. Brugger (2014), *Capital Punishment and Roman Catholic Moral Tradition*, 2nd edn (Notre Dame, IN: University of Notre Dame Press).

suggests doubt in his mind about Christian unanimity once 'faithfulness' is actually defined. If the term 'non-violence' were actually to be adopted by Christian chaplains to the armed forces, say, at most it could only be an eschatological aspiration and not the thoroughgoing practice of non-violence that Hauerwas champions. Some feminists have also argued that Hauerwas's critique of violence tends to have a male focus upon war and to neglect domestic violence.[12]

Hauerwas's critics also argue that he exaggerates both the secularity of society at large and the moral distinctiveness of Christian ministry within that society. Nicholas Healy, for example, writes as follows:

> Ethnographic descriptions of congregations indicate how unlikely it is that more than a relative few would be able to present to those outside the kind of clear alternative identity and way of life Hauerwas demands. Rather, each congregation and each congregation's members bring diverse kinds of non-Christian-specific influence to bear upon their identities in complex and confused ways. This probably ubiquitous phenomenon puts sharply in question the heavy reliance upon the theory of Christian formation through church practices that lies at the heart of Hauerwas's account of the nature and function of the church . . . they cast doubt on the church's ability to function as an effective witness to Jesus by the specific means of embodying his story in its own identity; and they raise some significant theological questions about the membership of the church.[13]

Solidarity ministry: strengths and weaknesses

Hauerwas is emphatically a Protestant theologian; however, his emphasis upon Christian distinctiveness and witness (with Christian ministry being a part of that distinctiveness/witness) shows some parallel with an emphatically Tridentine understanding of priesthood, albeit with priests being understood in that as ontologically distinct. Edward Schillebeeckx became a sharp critic of Tridentine priesthood with the publication first in Dutch and then in English of his seminal book *Ministry: A Case for Change*.[14] Five years after his death and on the centenary of his birth, the publication of

---

[12] Linda Woodhead (2000), 'Can Women Love Stanley Hauerwas? Pursuing an Embodied Theology', in M. T. Nation and S. Wells (eds), *Faithfulness and Fortitude: In Conversation with the Theological Ethics of Stanley Hauerwas* (Edinburgh: T&T Clark), pp. 161–88.

[13] Nicholas M. Healy (2014), *Hauerwas: A (Very) Critical Introduction* (Grand Rapids, MI: Eerdmans), pp. 101–2: see also Robin Gill (2012), *Theology in a Social Context: Sociological Theology, vol. 1* (Farnham: Ashgate), pp. 207ff.

[14] Edward Schillebeeckx (1981), *Ministry: A Case for Change* (London: SCM Press).

the 11 volumes of *The Collected Works of Edward Schillebeeckx* stirred up new interest in this extraordinary theologian.[15] Tracking the changes that he made over the course of his long academic career, it is possible to see how *Ministry: A Case for Change* marks a decisive shift in his thought. Here he moved away from any concept of ministry as a separate way of being, bestowed by episcopal authority, and towards a contextual understanding of ministry that derives its authority from the local communities that it serves:

> I see the first requirement for the functioning of the ministry not primarily as a personnel plan or the recruiting of 'vocations', of ministers who, having secured the 'power of ordination', only need to wait for employment from the 'powers above'. I certainly see the need to develop a short-term pastoral plan for particular situations. In ecclesial terms: what must happen here, within this local pastoral unit, for the building up of a living community of men and women? In specific terms this means: what is the particular contribution of perhaps a small Christian grass roots community in the building up of a life of solidarity which is of a pluralist kind (and which sooner or later will feel the need to use the word 'God')? The more time goes on, the more this is the particular situation of a Christian community . . . The agenda of a Christian community, the questions with which it should be concerned, are here for the most part dictated by the world itself.[16]

In sharp contrast to Hauerwas, Schillebeeckx used socio-historical methods as an essential part of his theological investigation of ministry, saw Christian ministry as being in solidarity with both church communities and wider society, and argued that the latter should dictate the agenda for the former. There is an element of 'witness' here, as his parenthesis above shows, but it is not the strident witness of Hauerwas. Solidarity is uppermost for Schillebeeckx.

In his critique of individualistic and sacerdotal understandings of (Tridentine) priesthood, Schillebeeckx traced their origins to Roman imperial power and authority and contrasted them with the less differentiated and communal models of ministry present within the New Testament. He also concluded that 'both priestly celibacy and women [excluded from] the ministry seem to me at root to be of a pseudo-doctrinal kind' and indeed 'a hindrance' to the Church.[17] Most offensive of all to the Vatican, he suggested that, in the absence of ordained priests, lay leaders of local

---

[15] E. Schillebeeckx (2014), *The Collected Works of Edward Schillebeeckx*, ed. T. Schoof and C. Sterkens, 11 vols (London: Bloomsbury T&T Clark).

[16] Schillebeeckx, *Ministry*, p. 135.

[17] Schillebeeckx, *Ministry*, p. 98.

church communities should be allowed 'to preside over a community and thus over its eucharist'.[18]

Schillebeeckx did not give extended attention to the ethical implications of his concept of ministry. This is highly significant. Whereas a witness perspective in ministry readily polarizes people on moral decisions about particular issues, a solidarity perspective may be more reluctant to do so, precisely because polarization can run counter to solidarity. But he did offer a number of hints at my other two levels. For example, this is how he depicted the 'diaconal task of a Christian education' – a depiction that contrasts sharply with Hauerwas's notion of 'resident aliens' in 'a Christian colony':

> Here the building up of a community, as a catalyst in a pluralist society, is experienced as a growth process which takes its secular, human starting point in Christian participation in the various forms of communal life which already exist outside the church, in the neighbourhood of the pastoral unit. In this way it is possible to avoid the formation of a ghetto or too much looking inwards. Thus, there should be critical Christian solidarity with the work of social restructuring which is already present, political involvement.[19]

If Schillebeeckx offered only hints about this, the feminist Catholic theologian Lisa Sowle Cahill has given the general ethical implications of such Christian solidarity considerable attention. In her significant recent study *Global Justice, Christology and Christian Ethics*, she sets out her agenda firmly in terms of solidarity with society at large and extends her discussion of Christian ethics to inter-religious cooperation:

> Global realities of human inequality, poverty, violence, and ecological destruction call for a twenty-first-century Christian response that can link the power of the gospel to cross-cultural and interreligious cooperation for change. The aims of this book are to give biblical and theological reasons for Christian commitment to justice, to show why just action is necessarily a criterion of authentic Christian theology, and to give grounds for Christian hope that change in violent structures is really possible. The premise of this work is that religious experience of God carries a moral way of life as its equally original counterpart. This is because inclusive community with other human beings is a constitutive dimension of community with God. 'Love the Lord your God with your whole heart, mind, and soul; and your neighbor as yourself' (Mark 12.28–34). Love God *and* neighbor – not God, *then* neighbor. To experience salvation is to have one's life completely reoriented

---

[18] Schillebeeckx, *Ministry*, p. 139.
[19] Schillebeeckx, *Ministry*, p. 136.

in relation to God and simultaneously, integrally, in relation to other human beings. Authentic religious experience – salvation – is inherently transformative and political. Reconciled human relations are lenses through which we glimpse the goodness and power of God.[20]

The strength of this solidarity perspective in ministry and Christian discipleship is that it involves a serious engagement with other disciplines and a frank recognition of both the enduring Christian values in society at large and the limitations of socially constrained churches. However, its weakness, as the Methodist theologian Robin Lovin frankly recognizes, is that it 'is reduced to saying what everyone already believes' and, as a result, its inadequacy 'becomes more apparent over time, as beliefs change and what inspires one generation loses credibility with the next'.[21]

Lovin, building upon the work of Reinhold Niebuhr, has done more than any other theologian to foster a realist or solidarity perspective within Christian ethics. He identified different layers of realism within Niebuhr's writings – political, ethical and theological – in his book *Reinhold Niebuhr and Christian Realism*.[22] And he has extended this exploration beyond Niebuhr in *Christian Realism and the New Realities*, arguing that:

> For most of the twentieth century, [Christian realists] were at least united by common enemies, antirealist movements of nationalism, revolution, or totalitarianism that sought to resolve the tensions of modern life by bringing private choices under public control and obliterating the distinctions between the various spheres that make up modern society. In recent years, the family has become more fractious, and the more susceptible to persuasion by those who insist that some members of the family do not really belong to it at all. Old aunts whisper in the corners that Niebuhrian realists are really secular liberals, or that a theology of the spheres and orders is nothing but theocracy under another name.[23]

These polarized ethical perspectives – witness and solidarity – do seem currently to be enmeshed in mutual and internal criticisms within Christian ethics with little prospect of them being resolved. They present contemporary Christian ministry with an obvious dilemma: which

---

[20] Lisa Sowle Cahill (2013), *Global Justice, Christology and Christian Ethics* (Cambridge and New York: Cambridge University Press), p. 1.

[21] Robin W. Lovin (2003), 'Reinhold Niebuhr in Contemporary Scholarship: A Review Essay', *Journal of Religious Ethics* 31.3, pp. 489–505, here 499.

[22] Robin W. Lovin (1995), *Reinhold Niebuhr and Christian Realism* (New York and Cambridge: Cambridge University Press).

[23] Robin W. Lovin (2008), *Christian Realism and the New Realities* (New York and Cambridge: Cambridge University Press), p. 82.

is finally to be relied upon to guide the actual practice of ministry? Or are both perspectives in tension needed within churches?

Concluding comments

It is at this point that identifying different audiences or contexts might help to offer some resolution. Returning to David Horrell, he argues that there are some points of contact between these two perspectives and he claims that both (in tension) are indeed finally needed to represent Christian discipleship adequately in any age or society. More specifically he sees Hauerwas and Habermas as addressing very different audiences:

> Hauerwas's overriding concern is to spell out *for the Church* what the Christian tradition should mean in practice, calling in effect for Christians to be shaped by their own story and not that of liberal democracy and thus to be faithful witnesses. In doing so, he does not take his task to be one of reflecting on what kind of moral framework might be necessary for various groups and traditions (including those that Christians represent) to negotiate their claims and counterclaims in the public sphere . . . Habermas's key concern, on the other hand, is precisely to theorise the kind of morality necessary for the regulation of the public space in which conflict of interest and conviction, often arising from commitments to different ways of life, must be resolved. He recognises that specific traditions and forms of life are crucial for people's identity and ethical convictions, but equally insists that tradition-specific justifications cannot suffice to validate a norm in the public sphere of modern, plural, secular societies.[24]

Now *if* both of these tasks are considered important for Christian ministry, they may need to be handled rather differently (and perhaps by different ministers) depending upon which audience is addressed. Hauerwas's idealistic witness perspective may well be important for a purely ecclesial context. His earliest writings largely ignored this context and were more concerned to engage with philosophers such as Iris Murdoch. But mid-career he became convinced that belonging to a church congregation (which he had not done previously) and focusing upon Scripture and theology were much more fundamental to his understanding of Christian ethics than engaging with philosophers such as Murdoch. Given a radical focus upon ecclesial context, this makes sense. In contrast, Schillebeeckx started life in a traditional Catholic ecclesial context and then, also mid-career, became convinced through his engagement with Vatican II that this

---

[24] Horrell, *Solidarity and Difference*, pp. 86–7.

ecclesial context needed radical reformation, looking beyond itself in solidarity with the needs of society at large.

There is clearly an uneasy tension between these two approaches, yet Horrell argues at length that both are present in Paul's letters. He does indeed concede that Paul's emphasis is primarily upon the witness perspective, yet (as already noted) he sees evidence of the solidarity perspective in Paul as well. Similarly, I have suggested that elements of witness can be found in Schillebeeckx, as can elements of solidarity in Hauerwas. When writing they were, however, addressing very different ecclesial contexts. Both Ernst Troeltsch and F. D. Maurice before him argued that churches and sects each have strengths and weaknesses. As a result they both concluded that churches and sects, in tension and in combination, offer together a more adequate representation of Christianity than they could separately. Perhaps something like that is also true of Christian ministry. Both ethical perspectives on ministry may need to be heard within Christian denominations in any age if believers are to be encouraged by their ministers to be holy *and* to address the needs of wider society. For this to happen, the ethical tension in ministry might well be a necessary and enduring theological tension.

21

Politics and ministry

SUSANNA SNYDER

Politics. Activism. Social justice. Words that send shivers up the spines of many ministers. Religion and politics have been unhappy bedfellows at best, and made for a deadly chemical reaction at worst. People are coming to church for relationship with Jesus, not for more of the same struggles they find outside its walls. And anyway, we do not have time as we need to focus on worship, evangelism and Christian education. Christian ministers should therefore avoid politics at all costs – talking about it, practising it, encouraging it – and concentrate rather on deepening the spiritual lives of their congregations. If only they could. Christian ministry is inherently political, and Christian ministers are called to engage with politics at local, national and global levels as an intrinsic aspect of their vocation. Leading a religious community – whether in a lay or ordained capacity – and fostering spiritual growth and discipleship requires political reflection and political activity. As Mahatma Gandhi is reputed to have said, 'Those who say religion has nothing to do with politics do not know what religion is.' In the light of this, this chapter seeks to explore the following questions: what do we mean by politics, and how should Christian ministry interact with the political? What could ministers learn from political theory and political theology that might enhance their understanding and practice in whatever context they find themselves working? First, though, I will make the case that Jesus was committed to transformative politics and that Christian ministry today involves following his example.

Jesus was political

Jesus was political, and he was not the first among the people of God to be so. In his seminal work, *The Politics of Jesus*, Mennonite theologian John Howard Yoder argued that Jesus, embodying and developing the prophetic tradition found in the Hebrew Bible, challenged the authorities of his day and sought to establish a kingdom that provided an alternative to existing earthly kingdoms.[1] Jesus' kingdom grew out of the suffering servant tradition in the Hebrew Bible – 'He was despised and rejected by others; a man of suffering . . . he was wounded for our transgressions, crushed for our iniquities' (Isa. 53.3–5 NRSV) – and it was based on humility and non-violence.[2] Jesus contested the political powers of the day by refusing to play by the rules they set – rules rooted in the interconnected practices of violence, military might, avarice and wealth, and entrenched hierarchies of power – and this ultimately led to his death. Challenging what Walter Wink has described as the 'Domination System' or 'Powers-that-Be', he rejected all forms of injustice and exploitation and called prophetically for economic and social equality. He ate with sinners and tax collectors, and engaged with women, Gentiles, and lepers deemed to be impure. He stated that 'You cannot serve God and wealth' (Matt. 6.24 NRSV); and in the Beatitudes, he dared to claim that peacemakers and the persecuted were blessed rather than the powerful and wealthy (Matt. 5.3–12).[3] In his living and dying, Jesus personified a politics of liberation that challenges oppression and takes the side of those left behind and excluded.[4] He sought to establish a 'kin-dom' of equals rather than a business-as-usual monarchical system.[5] If Jesus was political in this way, it follows that the Church should also be political. By political, I am here talking about *political* with a lower case 'p', meaning 'the use of structural power to organize a society or community of people' and engagement in transformative action to alter or shift power structures.[6]

---

[1] John Howard Yoder (1994 (1972)), *The Politics of Jesus*, 2nd edn (Grand Rapids, MI: Eerdmans).

[2] Walter Brueggemann (2004–7), 'Scripture: Old Testament', in Peter Scott and William T. Cavanaugh (eds), *The Blackwell Companion to Political Theology* (Oxford: Blackwell), 7–20, here 9.

[3] Walter Wink (2000 (1998)), *The Powers That Be: Theology for a New Millennium* (New York: Galilee Doubleday).

[4] Ched Myers (1988), *Binding the Strong Man: A Political Reading of Mark's Story of Jesus* (Maryknoll, NY: Orbis Books).

[5] Ada María Isasi Díaz introduced the term 'kin-dom' to challenge the patriarchal notion of kingdom. See her 1998 article, 'Solidarity: Love of Neighbor in the 21st Century', in Susan Brooke Thistlethwaite and Mary Potter Engels (eds), *Lift Every Voice: Constructing Christian Theologies from the Underside*, rev. edn (Maryknoll, NY: Orbis Books), 30–9.

[6] Peter Scott and William T. Cavanaugh (2004–7) (eds), *The Blackwell Companion to Political Theology* (Oxford: Blackwell), 2.

The political landscape and the Church – contours and interactions

So, how is the Church – and consequently, how are Christian ministers – to engage politically? In order to grapple with this question, it is first necessary to understand our political context and to consider some frameworks for engaging with it. This is where political theory (study of the concepts, principles and institutions that provide the foundation for political life) and political theology (reflection on the relationship of Christian life to political matters) come in: the former helps us to understand the contours of our political system and environment, and the latter offers us possible frameworks for relating to and acting within these.

Contours of contemporary political landscapes

A foundational element of the contemporary political landscape is that we inhabit a global system of nation states. While various societies use power to structure themselves differently – for example, there are tribal structures in some locales that shape the daily lives of people there – most of us reading this are likely to be living in a political environment defined by being a nation state. It is assumed that territory (land, geographical unit), sovereignty (power, government) and a people (culture, language, religion) coincide.[7] Those with rights to participate in the life of a particular nation state are citizens of that nation, and they are able to vote and afforded the protection of the state. In theory, each nation state is equal in international law and has sovereignty over its own territory and domestic affairs.

While some nation states are organized and governed through military dictatorship, theocracy or other means, many – including all states in the West – operate, at least in theory, as liberal democracies. Liberal democracy is a term used to describe a political system predicated on the individual rights of every citizen within that nation. What precisely is meant by this term and when liberalism came into being are both contested. However, between the 1930s and 1950s, liberalism came 'to be viewed through a wide-angle lens, as a politico-intellectual tradition centred on individual freedom in the context of constitutional government'.[8] Or, as Elizabeth Phillips puts it, liberalism has become associated with democracy, freedom,

---

7   Charles Westin (1999), 'Regional Analysis of Refugee Movements: Origins and Response', in Alastair Ager (ed.), *Refugees: Perspectives on the Experience of Forced Migration* (London and New York: Continuum), 41.

8   Duncan Bell, 'What Is Liberalism?', *Political Theory* 42(6) (2014), 699.

reason and progress.[9] John Locke (1632–1704) is regarded as the founding father of this system, and Immanuel Kant (1724–1804), John Stuart Mill (1806–73) and John Rawls (1921–2002) are also associated with its development. Rawls explored the concept of justice within liberal democracies, arguing that justice was fairness. He asserted that all individuals had a claim to equal basic liberties as free and equal persons, and that as a result, two principles of justice – liberty and difference – were crucial. In other words, there should be equal access to opportunity and where there was not, there should be minimization of social and economic inequality – that is, differences should most benefit the least advantaged members of society.[10] Liberal democracy has come to be seen by many as synonymous with Western civilization rooted in a Christian heritage.[11]

We cannot grasp our current political landscape, however, until we understand the extent to which liberal democracy has become tied up with globalized neoliberal capitalism. Neoliberalism refers to a minimal state and deregulated market, and revolves around the free movement of goods and capital across borders. It emphasizes competition as the way for individuals to prosper and thrive, and its watchwords are laissez-faire, 'trickle-down', free markets, privatization and big business. It is often contrasted with what is known as controlled capitalism – which was the main approach in the West from the Second World War until the 1980s – where the state takes more of a role in stimulating the economy and in providing a social safety net. The development of neoliberalism is intimately intertwined with globalization processes – meaning the intensifying of 'networks' and 'flows' of capital, goods, information, technology, companies, brands, images, governance mechanisms and human beings across the world during the last 60 years that has led to greater connectivity among peoples as well as entrenchment of local identities in response.[12] These processes are, in turn, complexly interwoven with new forms of empire. While formal colonialism may have declined during the second half of the

---

[9] Elizabeth Phillips (2012), *Political Theology: A Guide for the Perplexed* (London and New York: T&T Clark), 109.

[10] John Rawls' major works include *A Theory of Justice* (Cambridge, MA: Harvard University Press, 2005 (1971)) and *Justice as Fairness: A Restatement*, 2nd edn (Cambridge, MA: Harvard University Press, 2001).

[11] Bell, 'What Is Liberalism?', 704.

[12] See Frank J. Lechner and John Boli (eds) (2008), *The Globalization Reader*, 3rd edn (Oxford: Blackwell); Manuel Castells (2000), *The Rise of the Network Society: The Information Age: Economy, Society and Culture*, vol. 1, 2nd edn (Oxford: Blackwell); and Arun Appadurai (1996), *Modernity at Large: Cultural Dimensions of Globalization* (Minneapolis, MN: University of Minnesota Press).

twentieth century, its legacy is woven into the warp and weft of Western societies. New transnational corporate forces are creating a 'new imperial form of sovereignty' which is decentralized and deterritorialized and 'wields enormous powers of oppression and destruction'. Michael Hardt and Antonio Negri present a stark warning: 'Empire is materializing before our very eyes.'[13] In addition, nations including the United States, Russia, the UK and China exercise military power (through direct intervention and arms sales) and economic intervention (through trade agreements, loans, etc.) far beyond their own borders and with far-reaching effects. Joerg Rieger employs the language of 'postcolonial empire' to signify these dynamics.[14]

Fissures are increasingly apparent within the liberal democratic nation-state system. International migration has increased significantly during the last 60 years, leading scholars to label our era as an 'age of migration'.[15] With the criss-crossing of borders has come increasing diversity within nation states in terms of nationality, religion, culture, language and racial/ethnic identity. Debate among political theorists and politicians in Western societies surrounding citizenship, belonging, identity, multiculturalism, pluralism and cosmopolitanism has accompanied these shifts. Communitarians, such as Michael Walzer, argue that citizens have a primary responsibility to those within their own communities – to fellow citizens of their own nation – particularly in relation to security and welfare, and argue for closed borders in relation to migration, and a prioritizing of 'our' needs. Ethics 'begins at home'.[16] Walzer suggests the need for '*communities of character*, historically stable, ongoing associations of men and women with some special commitment to one another and some special sense of their common life', and explains why:

> The primary good that we distribute to one another is membership in some human community. And what we do with regard to membership structures all our other distributive choices: it determines with whom we make those

---

[13] Michael Hardt and Antonio Negri (2001), *Empire* (Cambridge, MA: Harvard University Press), xi–xv, 205.

[14] Joerg Rieger (2007), *Christ and Empire: From Paul to Postcolonial Times* (Minneapolis, MN: Fortress Press), ch. 7.

[15] Stephen Castles and Mark J. Miller (2009), *The Age of Migration: International Population Movements in the Modern World*, 4th edn (New York and London: Guilford Press).

[16] See William O'Neill (2016), 'The Place of Displacement: The Ethics of Migration in the United States', in Agnes Brazal and María Teresa Davíla (eds), *Living with(out) Borders: Catholic Theological Ethics on the Migration of Peoples* (Maryknoll, NY: Orbis Books), 68.

choices, from whom we require obedience and collect taxes, to whom we allocate goods and services.[17]

Communitarian voices have risen in volume and number in recent decades, and in the public square often claim justification on the grounds of limited socio-economic resources and/or security and terrorism. Turning to the internal landscape of a nation state, communitarian approaches value different communities – defined by themselves or others on the grounds of work, class, region, religion, culture and so on – building up their own distinct traditions, character and virtues; engaging with civil society as part of their group; and determining socio-political rights and responsibilities from this perspective.[18]

Cosmopolitanism, by contrast, is a perspective that sees all human beings as belonging to a single community with a shared moral understanding. Scholars such as Seyla Benhabib argue for open borders on the grounds of global citizenship, and believe that it is possible to state universally that being human is what engenders human rights – they should therefore be equally available to all.[19] Paul Gilroy advocates a cosmopolitan convivial culture or 'conviviality', meaning 'the processes of cohabitation and interaction that have made multiculture an ordinary feature of social life in Britain's urban areas and in postcolonial cities elsewhere', and for a 'planetary human-ism' in contrast to the dominant 'us' and 'them' mentality.[20] Advocates of pluralism and multiculturalism argue that the existence of multiple distinctive cultures within a single nation state is positive and mutually enriching, and point out the need for specific groups to have specific rights in order to ensure equality. Group-specific rights, they suggest, can address existing injustices and imbalances brought about by racism, sexism, hetero-sexism, ableism, ageism, classism and religious discrimination.[21]

---

[17] Michael Walzer (1984), *Spheres of Justice: A Defense of Pluralism and Equality* (New York: Basic Books), 62, 31. See also Alasdair MacIntyre (1981), *After Virtue: A Study in Moral Theory* (London: Duckworth).

[18] See Luke Bretherton (2010), *Christianity and Contemporary Politics* (Malden, MA, and Oxford: Wiley-Blackwell), 32–3, for a discussion of the communitarian turn in British politics.

[19] Seyla Benhabib (2004), *The Rights of Others: Aliens, Residents and Citizens* (Cambridge: Cambridge University Press). See also Joseph Carens (2013), *The Ethics of Immigration* (Oxford: Oxford University Press) and Kwame Anthony Appiah (2007), *Cosmopolitanism: Ethics in a World of Strangers* (London: Penguin).

[20] Paul Gilroy (2005), *Postcolonial Melancholia* (New York: Columbia University Press), xv.

[21] Texts on multiculturalism include Will Kymlicka (2001), *Politics in the Vernacular: Nationalism, Multiculturalism and Citizenship* (Oxford: Oxford University Press) and Tariq Modood (2005), *Multicultural Politics: Racism, Ethnicity and Muslims in Britain* (Edinburgh: Edinburgh University Press).

What these and other scholars have sought to make clear is that the current neoliberal democratic nation-state system benefits some far more
than others. While some reap ever-increasing profits, the gap between rich
and poor grows within and between countries, and billions of people –
particularly those in the Global South – are struggling for basic resources.
In the Global North, the division between those who have prospered from
neoliberal globalization and those left behind, not least those in former
manufacturing regions, has become increasingly apparent. Food poverty,
unemployment, homelessness and lack of access to healthcare and education are some of the manifestations of economic inequality. For theologian
Gustavo Gutiérrez, the current situation represents a 'dehumanization of the
economy', and Daniel Groody refers to the idolization of capital as 'money-
theism'.[22] Economic inequality intersects with other forms of exclusion
along lines of race/ethnicity, gender, sexuality, class, dis/ability, age and
religion within the neoliberal democratic system. Paul Gilroy, Cornell
West, Audre Lorde and Michelle Alexander, among others, have exposed
the pernicious ongoing effects of racism. Writing about the United States,
West notes the 'unprecedented levels of unregulated and unrestrained
violence' directed at Black people, and Alexander has analysed the racism
inherent in the criminal justice and prison system – understanding it to
be a new form of the segregationist Jim Crow laws.[23] Increasingly, scholars and activists are pointing to the problems caused by the intersectional
nature of exclusion – meaning the ways in which different aspects of identity intersect to intensify and exacerbate dynamics of exclusion.[24] What is
more, patterns of domination are connected with increasing ecological
devastation: it tends to be nations, communities, groups and individuals

---

[22] Gustavo Gutiérrez (2003), 'The Situation and Tasks of Liberation Theology Today' (trans.
J. B. Nickoloff), in Joerg Rieger (ed.), *Opting for the Margins: Postmodernity and Liberation
in Christian Theology* (Oxford: Oxford University Press), 100; Daniel Groody (2007),
Globalization, Spirituality, and Justice: Navigating the Path to Peace (Maryknoll, NY: Orbis
Books), 22–3.

[23] Cornel West (2001), *Race Matters*, new edn (New York: Vintage); Michelle Alexander (2012),
The New Jim Crow: Mass Incarceration in the Age of Colorblindness, rev. edn (New York: New
Press); Paul Gilroy (2002 (1987)); *There Ain't No Black in the Union Jack: The Cultural Politics
of Race and Nation* (London: Routledge); Audre Lorde (2007), *Sister Outsider: Essays and
Speeches* (Berkeley, CA: Crossing Press).

[24] Kimberlé Crenshaw introduced the concept of intersectionality in 'Demarginalizing the
Intersection of Race and Sex: A Black Feminist Critique of Antidiscrimination Doctrine,
Feminist Theory, and Antiracist Politics', *University of Chicago Legal Forum* 140 (1989),
139–67.

that are already marginalized that experience the worst effects of environmental disaster and degradation, and climate change.[25]

For those who find themselves outside the nation-state system entirely rather than at the bottom of the social ladder within a nation state, the consequences can be worse still. Giorgio Agamben has described refugees as 'bare humanity', recognizing that full humanity is associated with being a full political participant within a polity, and Hannah Arendt has similarly pointed out how 'loss of home and political status' effectively means 'expulsion from humanity altogether'. The 'alien' is 'a frightening symbol of difference'.[26] The experience of millions of stateless people in the world, many of whom are Palestinian, is defined by the nation-state system: lack of recognition as people with a nation-state identity undergirds the violation of human rights they experience.

For these and other reasons, some political and cultural theorists and activists now suggest that the system of liberal democracy is effectively broken: at local, national and global levels human beings do not have an equal say or access to participation in the democratic process and economic prosperity. If the world is run for the benefit of existing elites, they argue, it is not engendering progress, freedom or justice for all. Among them are Romand Coles who advocates 'radical democracy' and J. K. Gibson-Graham who sees hope through a feminist post-capitalist politics.[27] Both scholar-activists stress the importance of revitalizing politics at the local level – through community organizing and everyday political action – arguing that only then can societies become truly democratic, as the local democratic process can inform wider, national political debates and activity.

A final aspect of the political landscape that it is important to consider when reflecting on Christian ministry and politics is where it lies on the continuum between religiously justified or rooted state, secularism and post-secularism. It is widely argued in the West that we are no longer living in an era of Christendom, but rather – and particularly, in Europe – that we live in post-secular societies. While the idea that societies had become secular (unconnected with the religious or spiritual) was popular during

---

25 See Vandana Shiva (2005), *Earth Democracy: Justice, Sustainability and Peace* (Boston, MA: South End Press).

26 Giorgio Agamben (1998), *Homo Sacer: Sovereign Power and Bare Life*, trans. D. Heller-Roazen (Stanford, CA: Stanford University Press); Hannah Arendt (1951), *The Origins of Totalitarianism* (San Diego, CA: Harcourt Brace Jovanovich), 290.

27 Romand Coles (2005), *Beyond Gated Politics: Reflections for the Possibility of Democracy* (Minneapolis: University of Minnesota Press); J. K. Gibson-Graham (2006), *A Postcapitalist Politics* (Minneapolis: University of Minnesota Press).

the second half of the twentieth century, many scholars now contest this notion, preferring the term 'post-secularism' to capture the new and multiple ways in which religion and spirituality are resurging in deinstitutionalized ways, and to recognize the increasing salience of and consciousness about religion in the public square.[28] The relationship between the political authority and religion is not always as obvious as it may appear. In the UK, while the Church of England is an established Church, religion plays far less obvious a role in politics than it does, say, in the United States, where there is official separation of church and state. The first amendment to the constitution states, 'Congress shall make no law respecting an establishment of religion, or prohibiting the free exercise thereof.'[29]

Interactions between church and political authorities – political-theological frameworks[30]

If the contours of our political landscape inevitably shape the ways in which ministers engage with it, so too does our answer to this question: Can earthly political authority be divinely ordained and in tune with the way of Jesus Christ – can we work with it – or is it always hopelessly flawed, and something that Christians will have to stand in opposition to? Christians have been debating the answer to this question since the first century, and their struggles and conclusions can help us to think through our own position today.

Early followers of Jesus sat in an uncomfortable relationship with the authorities of their day. They inhabited the margins of society, and were tolerated at best, often persecuted and occasionally martyred. As the writer of the second-century *Epistle to Diognetus* wrote of their status:

> For Christians cannot be distinguished from the rest of the human race by country or language or customs . . . They live in their own countries, but only as aliens. They have a share in everything as citizens, and endure everything as foreigners.[31]

---

[28] The term 'post-secularism' was popularized by Jürgen Habermas. See 'Notes on a Post-Secular Society', <http://www.signandsight.com/features/1714.html> (accessed 23 February 2016). For further discussion, see Mika Lassander Nynäs and Terhi Utriainen (eds) (2015), *Post-Secular Society* (New Brunswick, NJ and London: Transaction Publishers); and Rodney Stark (1999), 'Secularization, R.I.P.', *Sociology of Religion* 60.3: 249–73.

[29] See <https://www.law.cornell.edu/constitution/first_amendment> (accessed 23 February 2016).

[30] I am indebted to the survey of much of the following material offered by Phillips in *Political Theology*. Her book is essential reading for those in ministry.

[31] *Epistle to Diognetus*, in J. Philip Wogaman and Douglas Strong (eds) (1996), *Readings in Christian Ethics: A Historical Sourcebook* (Louisville, KY: Westminster John Knox Press), 17.

With the conversion of Constantine in the fourth century, Christianity's relationship with politics was transformed as it became allied and intertwined with power. Christianity gave symbolic and ritual power to the imperial state, and received economic, political and social power in return. In 413–26, by which time the Roman Empire was in decline, Augustine of Hippo wrote *De Civitate Dei* – or 'City of God' – in which he described two cities representing different ways of being political in the world. This text has become a seminal work in political theology. The city of God was worthy and virtuous, characterized by love, peace, justice, service of one another and divine worship, while the earthly city was sinful, being motivated by self-love and characterized by violence.[32] For Augustine, the city of God and earthly city were co-mingled within society: state and Church – or the secular and sacred – did not have separate spheres.[33] Due to the Fall and the sinfulness of the earthly city, Augustine believed that government was a necessity and should be respected.

Theologians in the centuries following Augustine, from Thomas Aquinas to John Calvin, continued to explore the purpose and potential of earthly government, and the ways in which Christians should engage with it. While men wrote most of the texts on these issues that have survived, Christian women were also politically active in both overt and indirect ways. Catherine of Siena, fourteenth-century mystic and scholastic theologian, represents one extraordinary example. She travelled and wrote letters to ruling authorities, working for an end to ecclesial schism and the return of the papacy from Avignon to Rome, as well as being appointed as an ambassador to bring about peace among feuding Italian city states.[34]

Returning to the contemporary context, consideration of three broad approaches to the state, government and political authority advocated by different theologians may be helpful to ministers thinking about their own engagement with politics. While some theologians are in agreement with the operation, laws and policies of a particular state, the majority tend to believe that current political realities, relationships and power do not represent the kind of politics that should ideally characterize the kingdom of God. How, though, do they suggest that Christians should address this disconnect? One framework, which has been adopted by many, including usually historic mainstream denominations, involves working

---

[32] Augustine, *City of God*; Phillips, *Political Theology*, 254.
[33] See Phillips, *Political Theology*, 25–6; William Cavanaugh (2011), *Migrations of the Holy: God, State, and the Political Meaning of the Church* (Grand Rapids, MI: Eerdmans), 57–8.
[34] Don Brophy (2010), *Catherine of Siena: A Passionate Life* (New York: BlueBridge).

within the system. This approach can be labelled Christian liberalism, and involves transforming but not removing or radically altering current structures. Liberal democratic power can and should be wielded for the common good. Phillips argues that this type of approach characterized the first generation of political theologians that emerged in the 1960s, including Jürgen Moltmann and Johann Baptist Metz – when political theology emerged as a distinct theological sub-discipline – and it has resonance too with numerous earlier figures. Dietrich Bonhoeffer understood Jesus to be 'Lord of all government and Head of the Church', and the Barmen Declaration, written by Karl Barth and the Confessing Church in protest against the Nazi-supported German Christian movement, stated: 'We reject the false doctrine that there could be areas of our life in which we would not belong to Jesus Christ but to other lords.'[35] These statements reflect the idea expressed in Romans 13.1–7 (ESV) that God ordained governments with authority to exercise earthly rule:

> Let every person be subject to the governing authorities. For there is no authority except from God, and those that exist have been instituted by God. Therefore whoever resists the authorities resists what God has appointed, and those who resist will incur judgment.

Walter Rauschenbusch, in works including *A Theology for the Social Gospel* (1907) and *Christianizing the Social Order* (1912), wrote out of his belief that human societies and structures could be saved and that it was crucial to work with them: the idea that Christianity should engage with social and political structures to counter structural sin and bring about the 'kingdom of God' lay at the heart of what was known as the Social Gospel Movement.[36] More pessimistically, Reinhold Niebuhr saw absolute good and evil as impossible, and as a result, government was necessary and moral compromises would sometimes need to be made by governments in pursuit of the common good. He advocated for Christian realism and for the necessity of earthly political authority: 'Man's capacity for justice makes democracy possible; but man's inclination to injustice makes democracy necessary.'[37] Eric Gregory has argued that we need liberal democratic government because of sin, and that the role of the Church is to try to ensure

---

[35] See Phillips, *Political Theology*, 42, 68–9.

[36] J. Philip Wogaman (2000), *Christian Perspectives on Politics*, rev. edn (Louisville, KY: Westminster John Knox Press), 137. See Gary Dorrien (2008), *Social Ethics in the Making: Interpreting an American Tradition* (Oxford: Wiley-Blackwell), ch. 2.

[37] Reinhold Niebuhr (1945), *The Children of Light and the Children of Darkness* (London: Nisbet & Co.), ix; Reinhold Niebuhr (1953), *Christian Realism and Political Problems* (London: Faber & Faber).

that we structure our politics according to the ways of neighbour love: he advocates an 'Augustinian civic virtue' as an 'ambitious political practice' that promotes a more just, egalitarian and charitable society.[38] While some Christians who adopt this framework have argued for the reform of the current system towards the left, others such as Michael Novak are right-leaning or neoconservative in their approach, arguing for a liberalism based on small government and capitalist structures – especially limited government interference in economic and moral spheres. Novak sees capitalism as a spiritual achievement and of intrinsic spiritual value, embodying the grace and creativity of God.[39]

A second approach to contemporary politics can be described as Church as revolutionary.[40] Theologians reflecting on politics from this perspective see the needs of the poor and oppressed as being primary, and they challenge secular and ecclesial political structures and practices that inhibit the flourishing of marginalized groups. Wogaman contrasts revolution with reformism, recognizing that reformers suggest that the system is 'fundamentally sound' and just needs improvement. By contrast:

> The call for revolution addresses the need for total, systemic change. It implies that the whole social order is fundamentally, if not irredeemably, flawed . . . Those who have held power must be dethroned. The powerless must be empowered – or rather, they must, through revolution, empower themselves.[41]

Christians can participate in existing political structures, but as current forms of liberal democratic power tend to serve the needs of existing elites, they do so with a view to overthrowing them for the benefit of those with no power. If Christians do nothing to challenge the unjust status quo, they are complicit in oppression. Those adopting this approach see evil as existing within institutions and systems – sin is often structural rather than simply personal. Liberation theology, which emerged in Latin America in the late 1960s and is associated with figures such as Gustavo Gutiérrez and Leonardo and Clodovis Boff, sought to address the oppression faced

---

[38] Eric Gregory (2008), *Politics and the Order of Love: An Augustinian Ethic of Democratic Citizenship* (Chicago, IL and London: University of Chicago Press), 8; Phillips, *Political Theology*, 123.

[39] Michael Novak (1982), *The Spirit of Democratic Capitalism* (New York: American Enterprise Institute/Simon & Schuster).

[40] Wogaman suggests that the call to revolution has characterized much liberation theology; see *Christian Perspectives*, 86.

[41] Wogaman, *Christian Perspectives*, 86.

by the majority of the poor in their continent.[42] Their work exemplifies this approach. Simultaneously, in the United States, James Cone wrote *Black Theology, Black Power* (1969), and *God of the Oppressed*, in which he prophetically challenged the oppression of Black people in US society and churches, stating 'Jesus is Black' because God stands with the oppressed:

> He is the political God, the Protector of the poor and the Establisher of the right for those who are oppressed. To know him is to experience his acts in the concrete affairs and relationships of people, liberating the weak and the helpless from pain and humiliation . . . Theology is always a word about the liberation of the oppressed and humiliated. It is a word of judgment for the oppressors and the rulers.[43]

Liberative theologies that are intentionally crafted from within and in response to particular contexts and experiences have burgeoned in the decades following the 1970s – even if the connection of early liberation theologies with Marxism and a concrete political project is less clear – and these now include ecofeminist, womanist, Mujerista, Dalit, African, Minjung and Queer theologies.[44] God is in and with the experience of those who are oppressed, and it is their voices that should be heard first when enacting the political. Post-colonial theologies challenge the foundations of Western states as inherently imperial and imbued with inequitable power hierarchies.[45]

A third and increasingly prevalent approach is to view the Church as alternative political authority – or what Arne Rasmussen has described as the move towards a 'theological politics'.[46] According to theologians who hold this view, the role of the Church is essentially to be the Church. Rejecting a distinction between the sacred and secular, they have sought

---

[42] See Gustavo Gutiérrez (1974), *A Theology of Liberation* (London: SCM Press); Leonardo Boff and Clodovis Boff (1987), *Introducing Liberation Theology* (Maryknoll, NY: Orbis Books).

[43] James H. Cone (1997), *Black Theology, Black Power* (Maryknoll, NY: Orbis Books); James H. Cone (1977), *God of the Oppressed* (London: SPCK), 62, 82; James H. Cone (2011), *The Cross and the Lynching Tree* (Maryknoll, NY: Orbis).

[44] See for example Kwok Pui-lan (ed.) (2010), *Hope Abundant: Third World and Indigenous Women's Theology* (Maryknoll, NY: Orbis Books); Stacey Floyd-Thomas (ed.) (2006), *Deeper Shades of Purple: Womanism in Religion and Society* (New York: New York University Press); and Patrick Cheng (2011), *Radical Love: Introduction to Queer Theology* (New York: Seabury Press).

[45] See for example Kwok Pui-lan (2005), *Postcolonial Imagination and Feminist Theology* (Louisville, KY: Westminster John Knox Press); and Rieger, *Christ and Empire*.

[46] Arne Rasmussen (1995), *The Church as Polis: From Political Theology to Theological Politics as Exemplified by Jürgen Moltmann and Stanley Hauerwas* (Notre Dame, IN: University of Notre Dame Press). See Phillips, *Political Theology*, 50–4.

to argue that the theological is the underlying reality or framework that should define all else – including the political. The Radical Orthodoxy movement, led by John Milbank, Graham Ward and Catherine Pickstock, has exemplified this approach, arguing that modern forms of democracy need to be informed by pre-modern ideas which were inherently theological. Far from being service agencies or a critical friend to the state, Radical Orthodoxy critiques the very project of liberal democracy. Oliver O'Donovan – a post-liberal theologian – has argued that Jesus is monarch over all and that 'the Gospel of the Kingdom offers liberation to an imprisoned political culture'.[47] Christendom, for O'Donovan, reflects structural recognition by the state of the mission of the Church, and he argues that king (centralized political authority) and prophets (dissenting voices) offer the best hope for a flourishing society. Again, he draws upon pre-modern sources – including the history of Israel – to argue for the authority of the Church. Stanley Hauerwas, also a post-liberal theologian, argues that the Church needs to be a 'community of character' – a community that is formed by a Christian narrative and which practises virtues.[48] For Hauerwas, the Church is an alternative polity not beholden to the nation state, and thus the most political act the Church can undertake is to be the Church. The Church needs to be a counter-authority that refuses to confirm the assumptions and norms of liberal societies. He writes, 'If the church is in fact a community determined by a counter-story to the story that we story ourselves, I have suggested that the church cannot help but appear as a counterpolitics to the politics of the world.'[49] As Bretherton summarizes, these theologians all 'envisage different aspects of Christian worship as a counter-performance of social and political relationships to those conditioned by the modern state and the capitalist economy'.[50]

Given such different possibilities for approaching engagement with the political, an important question for ministers to consider is: how do I, and how do we as a congregation or Christian community, understand and inhabit our relationship with politics and government? Do we want to

---

[47] Oliver O'Donovan (1996), *Desire of Nations: Rediscovering the Roots of Political Theology* (Cambridge: Cambridge University Press), 119. Phillips describes post-liberal theology as 'calling into question modernity's public/private dualism'. *Political Theology*, 52.

[48] Stanley Hauerwas (1981), *A Community of Character: Toward a Constructive Christian Ethics* (Notre Dame, IN: Notre Dame University Press).

[49] Stanley Hauerwas (2004), *Performing the Faith: Bonhoeffer and the Practice of Nonviolence* (London: SPCK), 149.

[50] Bretherton, *Christianity and Politics*, 17; see also Phillips, *Political Theology*, 50–4.

work within the existing liberal democratic system, or do we feel that it is fundamentally flawed? Where do I understand power to lie? Do I see the Church as an institution that operates within a liberal democratic system, or does it stand outside it and/or prior to it? Denominations have different histories of relating to state, government and power, and it is therefore also valuable for ministers to understand and reflect on the particular Christian tradition within which they are answering these questions.

Practising politics

There is, though, a general consensus that Christians need to act and be in a way that improves or challenges the current liberal democratic system and its effects – even if it is not agreed by Christians about what changes need to take place or how they are to be brought about. In this section, I would like to move from the theoretical and general to the practical and specific. Given all of this, how can and should we act? Politics can be practised at local, national and international levels, and in a host of different ways, and Christian communities are increasingly joining with other faith-based organizations and non-profit partners to tackle various issues, from poverty, homelessness and exclusion of migrants to mass incarceration and the death penalty. Some issues may resonate or be more pressing in one context or another (although it is important to recognize that oppression tends to be intersectional and multifaceted), and the passion of a minister, congregation or local community may direct political energy in a particular direction or through a particular kind of activity. Indeed, Bretherton argues that explorations of the relationship between Christianity and politics can never be definitive because of the need to be responsive to and improvise faithfully within a particular context.[51] In this section, all I hope to do is outline briefly a few possibilities for consideration – possibilities that go beyond the middle-class chequebook activism or 'slacktivism' that has become increasingly common, where some engage with socio-political concerns at a distance from the safety of the couch.

It is important to recognize, first, that worship and prayer – activities that lie at the heart of church life – are themselves inherently political. Through the liturgical life of a Christian community – and particularly in listening to the word of God, and sharing together in the Eucharist – we are formed by a narrative and tradition that interrogates politics-as-usual. We

---

[51] Bretherton, *Christianity and Politics*, 21.

are kneaded, moulded, converted by a story in which the weak are made strong, the poor and powerless and peacemakers are blessed, and all are equal and included in the hope that God has for human flourishing. This should have consequences for how we live when we are sent out into the world beyond the church doors. William Cavanaugh has written of the power of the Eucharist as an ecclesial response to the use of torture as a means of ensuring social control in Chile during the Pinochet regime. He argues that the 'church does not simply perform the Eucharist, the Eucharist performs the church', and builds a social body – the body of Christ – which, in the case of Chile, was able to stand against a regime that fragmented society through fear of the pain of torture.[52] In relation to immigration, the Eucharist similarly represents a powerful embodying of an alternative political reality – a borderless body of Christ in which all are welcome equally and fully – to that in which we dwell currently.[53] Intercession is about inviting God to work within us to act to bring about hopeful transformation, and lamentation, an often neglected mode of prayer, enables us to look at and feel keenly social and political ills and the suffering they cause – which can be an act of solidarity and a spur to a resistive response.

Beyond the context of worship – walking out in the streets if you like – service provision (or what might historically have been called undertaking works of charity or mercy) often represents an important first political response for Christian communities. It involves addressing the needs of those among us or who dwell within our broader community who have been marginalized by current political realities. Night shelters offering a meal and a place to sleep for those who are homeless, as well as food banks that provide basic provisions for those who would otherwise go hungry, are familiar examples. Church members have been involved in running English language classes for asylum seekers; visiting people in prison; supporting those who are ageing with companionship; and offering sanctuary to irregular migrants facing deportation. Much of this kind of ministry involves being alongside – befriending, getting to know, chatting with – and this points to the fact that listening can in and of itself be a political act. Listening to those who are usually denied a

---

[52] William Cavanaugh (1998), *Torture and Eucharist: Theology, Politics, and the Body of Christ* (Malden, MA: Blackwell), 235.

[53] See *One Border, One Body: Immigration and the Eucharist*, director, John Carlos Frey; executive producer, Daniel G. Groody (Gatekeeper Films, 2008); and Kristine Suna-Koro (2014), 'The Sign of Unity and the Bond of Charity: On the Eucharist as a "Taskmaster" in the Context of Migration', *Dialog* 53.2 (June), 138–48.

voice in society can be powerful and lead to change. Nelle Morton talked of empowering 'one another by hearing the other to speech', and Lynne Westfield has shown how the hospitality offered by African American women to one other – in the Dear Sisters Literary Group – was a practice that fostered socio-political resilience.[54] Bretherton values listening as '*the* constitutive political act' and 'a primary form of faithful witness to the Christ-event within political life'.[55] While he suggests that political listening primarily takes place through listening to the word of God, listening to 'others in order to hear them as neighbors' is also crucial and requires hard, intentional work.[56] Listening desires to see what is really going on – to understand from the inside – and the kind of service that emerges from listening is not about 'us' helping 'them', but involves rather humility and deep solidarity (a sense of being united in interests or aims).[57]

Christians are called to engage in other levels of political response that involve partnership building, strategizing and engagement with political power structures – activities that may be less familiar and comfortable for many ministers. Often, these activities emerge from pastoral encounters or service, as we come to realize that those are important but limited band-aid responses and that deeper, structural change is required to address systemic problems. Advocacy in solidarity with those who are experiencing oppression and on issues from limiting global plastic use through to national health policy or local welfare services cuts is crucial. Christian ministry can involve signing petitions, writing to MPs or representatives, making a case at a meeting with policy-makers and compiling or supporting reports. We are called to raise awareness about pressing issues and injustices through sermons, cell-group topics, Lenten activities and congregational newsletters. The simple act of encouraging people to vote in general and local elections, and referenda – to exercise this democratic right – is an often-overlooked ministerial task. Protest activism – by which I mean attending or organizing protests – is another way in which

---

[54] Nelle Morton, 'The Journey Is Home': <http://actsofhope.blogspot.co.uk/2007/08/hearing-to-speech.html>; N. Lynne Westfield (2001), *Dear Sisters: A Womanist Practice of Hospitality* (Cleveland, OH: Pilgrim Press).

[55] Bretherton, *Christianity and Politics*, 100–1.

[56] Bretherton, *Christianity and Politics*, 102. Bretherton is primarily talking about structured listening undertaken in the context of community organizing, but his insights also have relevance to the spontaneous or one-off pastoral encounter.

[57] See Joerg Rieger and Kwok Pui-lan (2012), *Occupy Religion: Theology of the Multitude* (Lanham, MD: Rowman & Littlefield), on the concept of 'deep solidarity'.

ministers can exercise their political voice. Christians have held up plac-ards and shouted out against the death penalty in the United States, immi-gration detention, racist police shootings, inequitable international trade agreements, military intervention and the Iraq War, among many other – including local – issues.[58]

A response that is gaining momentum in many contexts today – and often with faith-based organizations, including churches and Christian minis-ters, playing a crucial part – is community organizing. The community-organizing movement is widely regarded as having been founded by Saul Alinsky (1909–72) in the United States in the 1930s, and developed through his work with the Industrial Areas Foundation (IAF). Broad-based community organizing is a process through which local commun-ities come together to identify issues of shared concern to them, and develop their own leadership capacity and strategies to find solutions. It is about building power and mobilizing resources among a range of people with a common interest/problem necessitating change, and doing this through building an organization that is constantly growing and developing. Decisions about actions are democratic, and attending to the democratic process within the organization is a crucial part of the work. Solutions often involve negotiating with, or confronting, those in power through non-violent direct action or shaming to effect change. Issues tackled need to be 'immediate, specific, and winnable issues' as small victories are crucial to sustain engagement and motivation. Bretherton argues that faith communities, including churches, have much to learn from community organizing's practice of 'consociational democracy' – meaning 'a mutual fellowship between distinct institutions or groups who are federated together for a common purpose'.[59] Informal groups that seek to build their own power and strategies for effecting change also exist and employ a variety of political responses. In a world where divisions within and between societies are glaring, the importance of ministers participating in and generating difficult, honest and respectful con-versations between those with different experiences and views in local communities and congregations – and acting with others to respond to the needs that arise out of these – cannot be overstated.

---

[58] See for example Keith Hebden (2017), *Re-enchanting the Activist: Spirituality and Social Change* (London: Jessica Kingsley).

[59] For an introduction to community organizing in relation to faith-based organizations, see Luke Bretherton (2014), *Resurrecting Democracy: Faith, Citizenship, and the Politics of a Common Life* (Cambridge: Cambridge University Press), 6.

A concluding thought – the political is the spiritual

Wogaman writes bluntly: the effect of politics 'upon human life and con-duct and well–being can scarcely be exaggerated'.[60] Human flourishing is what Christian ministry is about, and flourishing involves the creation of right relationships with God and human beings – something that cannot be brought about in isolation from the political sphere. More than this, though, the political can be a place of intense, vibrant, challenging and life-giving encounter with God, and a space of profound spiritual growth. There is, then, no conflict or contradiction for ministers in attending to both the spiritual and the socio-political lives of members of their com-munity. In our own encounters with injustice and with others directly affected by it, and through our efforts to counter it, we can be broken open, transformed and drawn into a sense of oneness with others and the divine.

---

[60] Wogaman, *Christian Perspectives*, 7.

22

An ecumenical theology of ministry

ROBIN GREENWOOD

Outlining my practice of enquiry

In considering ministry today, there are prior fundamental questions about ecclesial identity: how to become Church in given contexts as a sign and foretaste of the triune God's desire for the final beatitude of all creation.[1] Discerning the Spirit's prompting on how to be Church is always a view from a point; we are earthed in God's presence within places, times, narratives and relationships and through attending to the insights within traditions of the contexts, churches and theologies with which we have engaged.[2] Although some of the avenues briefly explored in this overview arise from dialogue with those in churches very different from my own, I write as an Anglican priest and educator, deeply rooted in a eucharistically focused ecclesiology for the sake of God's kingdom.

This chapter on theologies of ministry recognizes the tension between a number of influences and pressures/demands/needs; these include contemporary theological reflection; the corporate task of sharing in God's mission to heal the world and individual human lives; the proclamation of the gospel; the credibility of churches; and the need to move away from maintaining outworn ministerial patterns.[3] Although those exercising regional oversight make available resources for the pastoral counselling of

---

[1] Robin Greenwood, *Transforming Priesthood: A New Theology of Mission and Ministry*, London, SPCK (1994), 2001; and Stephen Pickard, *Seeking the Church: An Introduction to Ecclesiology*, London, SCM Press, 2012.

[2] Emmanuel Y. Lartey, *Pastoral Theology in an Intercultural World*, Peterborough, Epworth Press, 2006; Angie Pears, *Doing Contextual Theology*, London, Routledge, 2010; Louise J. Lawrence, *The Word in Place: Reading the New Testament in Contemporary Contexts*, London, SPCK, 2009; and John Inge, *A Christian Theology of Place*, Farnham, Ashgate, 2003.

[3] Malcolm Grundy, *Leadership and Oversight: New Models for Episcopal Ministry*, London, Mowbray, 2011; Nicholas M. Healy, *Church, World and the Christian Life: Practical-Prophetic Ecclesiology*, Cambridge, Cambridge University Press, 2000; and Pete Ward (ed.), *Perspectives on Ecclesiology and Ethnography*, Grand Rapids, MI, Eerdmans, 2012.

local leaders brought to a personal crisis at the sharp end of dysfunctional systems, a commitment to finding the necessary innovative resources is rare.[4]

In the following sections I offer my reading of three overlapping aspects of contemporary ecumenical and international ecclesiological discourse; in each case I shall briefly indicate leading implications for ministerial theology and practice.[5]

The three aspects of being Church I identify are a deliberate corporate calling to, *first*, discern, demonstrate and participate in God's work in the world, *second*, as ministries that evoke, lead and sustain worship, community and identity, and *third*, as a reflective practice of curating spaces for transformation.

Ministry as discernment, demonstration and participation in God's work in the world

Church as embodiment of divine abundance

Arising within the context of a precarious time for the corporate practice of Christian faith, Vatican II's *Ad Gentes* statement, that by its very nature the entire Church is missionary, has become iconic for ecumenical ecclesiology and theologies of ministry.[6] Recent decades of ecclesiological theory-practice have opened the possibility of a radically new settlement for churches between the roles of 'clergy' and 'laity', women and men, adults and children. At this present moment three highly influential statements continue the exploration of mission as the central paradigm in ecclesiology: *Together towards Life,*[7] *The Cape Town Commitment*[8]

---

[4] The particular challenges of strategic innovation require more complex approaches than merely agreeing group aspiration and even appointing leaders of change. See, for example, Vijay Govindarajan and Chris Trimble, *The Other Side of Innovation: Solving the Executive Challenge*, Boston, MA, Harvard Business Review Press, 2010.

[5] James Nieman and Roger Haight SJ, 'On the Dynamic Relation between Ecclesiology and Congregational Studies', in Christian B. Scharen (ed.), *Explorations in Ecclesiology and Ethnography*, Grand Rapids, MI, Eerdmans, 2012, pp. 9–33.

[6] Second Vatican Council, *Decree Ad Gentes: On the Mission Activity of the Church* (Vatican Press, 1965), at <http://www.vatican.va/archive/hist_councils/ii_vatican_council/documents/vat-ii_decree_19651207_ad-gentes_en.html>.

[7] World Council of Churches (WCC), *Together towards Life: Mission and Evangelism in Changing Landscapes*, Geneva, WCC, 2012.

[8] *The Cape Town Commitment: A Confession of Faith and a Call to Action* (Lausanne Movement, 2011), at <http://www.lausanne.org/contnt/ctc/ctcommitment>.

and Pope Francis's *Apostolic Exhortation on the Proclamation of the Gospel in Today's World.*[9] Vibrant themes in these documents include the following: God invites us to draw all into the triune life and to witness to the abundance and loving purposes of God for the fulfilment of all creation; all baptized Christians have a vocation to be missional disciples; the Holy Spirit enables the Church to reveal the availability of God's love and grace; Christians are called to share God's compassion for the foreigner, the hungry, the fatherless, the widows and all pushed to the margins; and that joy, boldness and hope are characteristics of a missionary Church.[10]

Within the past half-century the movement towards an eschatological, ecclesiological and ministerial vision is exemplified in the work of countless individual scholars and practitioners. Notably, the late Anglican ecclesiologist Daniel W. Hardy explored the dynamics of divine glory and blessing 'which expand the possibilities, implicit in all the universe, for spatio-temporal diversity and dynamic unity' and the unique ordering of human beings and societies that suit them to participating in the activity of the Trinitarian God for the 'unfolding "economy" of the cosmos'.[11]

Paul Lakeland SJ, building on the insights of Vatican II, challenged all within the communion of the People of God to become contemplatively and actively engaged in the challenges of society and culture.[12] He offered a vision of Christian women and men reading the signs of the times, struggling against all that constricts human freedom to know themselves as God's loving creation, and challenging the individualism of capitalism and dehumanizing tendencies of globalization by living reflectively and accountably within the world and in partnership with other world religions. For this he was convinced the Church as institution would need to be radically reformed, recalling the mark of the early Church that all are God's people and all are 'heirs according to the promise', so although some may be called to particular roles, this does not imply their greater or lesser significance.[13]

---

[9] Pope Francis, *The Joy of the Gospel: Apostolic Exhortation of the Holy Father Francis, Evangelii Gaudium*, Nairobi, Pauline Publications, 2013.

[10] See *International Review of Mission* 104.2 (401) (November 2015).

[11] Daniel W. Hardy, *God's Ways with the World: Thinking and Practising Christian Faith*, Edinburgh, T&T Clark, 1996, pp. 148–50.

[12] Paul Lakeland, *The Liberation of the Laity: In Search of an Accountable Church*, New York / London, Continuum, 2003, pp. 220–85.

[13] See also William E. Diehl, *Ministry in Daily Life: A Practical Guide for Congregations*, Herndon, VA, Alban Institute, 1996.

Church: corporate and personal sign of God's reign

The New Testament reveals the kingdom of God as a liberating mode of relationship demonstrated in healing, resurrection, acceptance, abundance and love, justice and peace for all. The contemporary removal of gender as a bar to public ministry is a sign of the coming kingdom, in the face of centuries of patriarchal relationships, diminution of women, and wide disregard of lay people and children. There is much to celebrate after years of often painful pioneering. But still many women suffer through being measured by themselves and others against ecclesiological landscapes created by men. The journey is just beginning that seeks justice for women and all others who are routinely marginalized. However, there is much to celebrate in the prophetic ministry of women, ordained and in leadership, and as writers, musicians and artists. In Letty Russell's terms these display 'an inclusive community, as a round table, as a place of love, care, respect and sacrifice'. This vision is advocated by Elizabeth Behr Sigel as

> the supreme reality of the mind of God: a community of faith, hope and love, of men and women, of mysterious human persons, unutterably equal yet different, made in the image and reflecting the glory of God, the Three in One.[14]

A. Theodore Eastman distilled a fourfold interlocking paradigm of baptism as Death and Resurrection (living from the centrality of God's operative grace), Incorporation (the provision of divine power to overcome self-centredness), Commissioning (the pledge to follow and obey Christ in the world) and Inaugurated Eschatology (the initiation of a journey rather than a completed transformation).[15] He states:

> The ministry of lay persons is to represent Christ and his Church; to bear witness to him wherever they may be; and, according to the gifts given them, to carry on Christ's work of reconciliation in the world; and to take their place in the life, worship and governance of the Church.[16]

During my incumbency of a Leeds outer estates parish, this analysis, combined with Schillebeeckx's insights on baptism as ordering for ministry, inspired many experiments in collaborative ministry, notably the reordering of the worship space, the widespread provision of spiritual

---

[14] Letty M. Russell, 'Hot-house Ecclesiology: A Feminist Interpretation of the Church', *Ecumenical Review* 53.1 (2001), pp. 48–56. See Eleni Kasselouri-Hatzivassiliadi, 'Mission, Gender and Theological Education', *International Review of Mission* 104.1 (April 2015), p. 37.

[15] A. Theodore Eastman, *The Baptizing Community: Christian Initiation and the Local Congregation*, New York, Seabury Press, 1982.

[16] Eastman, *Baptizing Community*, p. 35.

accompaniment, small task-groups to take forward the mission vision of the Church Council, process learning for those preparing for baptism, confirmation and sharing in the Eucharist, and close contact with agencies dedicated to building capacity in the neighbourhood.

Illustrations of pioneer ministry within this framework must include the patient, incarnational approach of William Vanstone. After years as a reflective parish priest on a new housing estate, he articulates the struggle to know honestly the meaning of God's glory and love in the seemingly unimportant detail of ordinary human situations. His mystical under-standing of nurturing a corporate Christian ministry that inhabited but transcended practical service resonates in his hymn 'Morning Glory, Starlit Sky', which includes the description of God as 'bound in setting others free, poor in making many rich, and weak in giving power to be'.[17]

Ann Morisy links ministries of pastoral care with discipleship to combat injustice and serve the basic needs of localities with 'apt liturgy'.[18] 'Tentmaking', after the example of St Paul, often called self-supporting ministry, has assumed a highly significant place within Anglican provision of deacons and priests in recent decades. Although initially its undergird-ing perspective was of Christians prophetically active in the world,[19] it is probably fair to suggest that the agenda for non-stipendiary clergy to offer a prophetic encouragement to churches to prioritize agency for the king-dom has been diluted by the gap in sacramental priestly provision caused by the diminishing availability of stipendiary clergy. Steven Croft led the reinterpretation of the diaconal ministry, as not just an apprenticeship to priesthood, but a dimension of the whole Church's serving ministry, car-ried by a few as an invitation to all in discovering how to collaborate with God for the world's healing.[20]

Becoming missional disciples

Graham Tomlin has helpfully summarized Christian priestly communities as vital agencies for the final blessing of all creation. His theology-practice

---

[17] W. H. Vanstone, *Love's Endeavour, Love's Expense: The Response of Being to the Love of God*, London, Darton, Longman & Todd (1977) 1991, p. 119. Reproduced by kind permission.

[18] Ann Morisy, *Beyond the Good Samaritan: Community Ministry and Mission*, London, Mowbray, 1997, p. 49.

[19] James M. M. Francis and Leslie J. Francis (eds), *Tentmaking: Perspectives on Self-Supporting Ministry*, Leominster, Gracewing, 1998.

[20] Steven Croft, *Ministry in Three Dimensions: Ordination and Leadership in the Local Church*, London, Darton, Longman & Todd, 1999 (2012), pp. 67–82.

of a spreading circle of God's blessing 'from the Church, to the nations, to the whole earth itself'[21] has the following main elements:

1 Christ involves the Church and all humanity, as a corporate priesthood, in blessing creation towards its final flourishing;
2 as those who bless human beings remain integral parts of the created order, all humans have the dignity of being called and given grace to bless creation to its fulfilment;
3 embedded in humanity, the Church, in its frailty, is called to make creative connections with others in their difference;
4 the Church's vocation is to evoke and support this blessing of creation by all humanity, and personally and communally to be witnesses and agents of the gospel of reconciliation within the praise of the Father;
5 ordained priests are primarily identified by their baptism; their main task is to develop Christian communities of those who are the Church in working in various ways for the coming of God's kingdom;
6 all of this is to be lived in joyful communion with Christ and creation to the glory of God.

Ministry to evoke, lead and resource Christian worship, community and identity

Formed through intimacy with the triune God

Ministries of reciprocity and generativity arise from an attitude of dismantling rather than defending, responding to the desiring God who is a 'ceaseless outgoing and return'.[22] 'The invitation to be truly participative within the life of God Godself'[23] is incompatible with a distant patriarchal monologue. Sarah Coakley represents the Holy Spirit as revealing the mystery of the Trinity as infinite tenderness. Here is a lively resource for the recasting of gender, the reordered practice of mutually animating Christian community, and a serious but joyful searching for the flourishing of all creation. Recovering relational ways of being Church requires awareness of at least the following elements: ourselves in our present circumstances, Church as lived in its practices, Church for the formation

[21] Graham Tomlin, *The Widening Circle: Priesthood as God's Way of Blessing the World*, London, SPCK, 2014. See especially Tomlin's summing up of his argument on pp. 156–8.
[22] Sarah Coakley, 'God and Gender: How Theology Can Find a Way Out of the Impasse', *ABC Religion and Ethics*, 8 March 2012, p. 4.
[23] Sarah Coakley, *God, Sexuality, and the Self: An Essay 'On the Trinity'*, Cambridge, Cambridge University Press, 2013, p. 299.

of desire, Church as called to unity, holiness, catholicity and apostolicity, searched and sustained by the Holy Spirit, and ordered in love.[24]

Although precisely how its significance should be understood is much contested, a renaissance of the Christian doctrine of God as Trinity, combined with an eschatological approach to mission,[25] especially since the 1990s, has illuminated the theology-practice of mission, liturgy and ministry.[26] A wide range of ecumenical scholars have supported churches in recovering from a doctrine of God for too long dominated by a philosophical, juridical, static and impassible approach, and embracing one more influenced by scriptural, covenantal and graceful relationship. Notably, John Zizioulas recalled God as Being-in-communion, inviting humanity to know its true self in free communion with God.[27]

A triune God, revealed in Jesus' constant invitation to intimate relation, and richly crystallized in terms of interpersonal, *perichoretic* difference-in-relation, implies a communal discipleship in which there are no permanent structures of subordination, but rather, overlapping patterns of mutual relationship. Although this can only ever be considered in analogical terms, such a link between Trinitarian theology and ecclesiology has met with profound misgivings in some quarters as mere idealism, because everyday human communities engage in conflictual and often unresolved disagreement. However, in my experiences of leadership, actively fostering an ecclesiology echoing Trinitarian relating, it has been precisely an accessible articulation of an intra-Trinitarian culture that has both inspired and corrected congregational life in times of trauma and threatened disintegration.[28] In the past quarter-century the development of ecclesiology as rooted in the renewal of a social Trinitarianism, linked with the renewal of the perception of all God's people sharing in God's

---

[24] Robin Greenwood, *Being Church: The Formation of Christian Community*, London, SPCK, 2013, pp. 1–9.

[25] Coakley, *God, Sexuality, and the Self*; Ruth C. Duck and Patricia Wilson-Kastner, *Praising God: The Trinity in Christian Worship*, Louisville, KY, Westminster John Knox Press, 1999; Stephen Pickard, *Seeking the Church: An Introduction to Ecclesiology*, London, SCM Press, 2012, ch. 4, p. 81ff. Note the groundbreaking work of Karl Barth and Eberhard Jüngel, Colin Gunton, Sarah Coakley, Jürgen Moltmann, James B. Torrance, Elizabeth Johnson, Miroslav Volf, John D. Zizioulas, Catherine LaCugna and Mary C. Grey.

[26] British Council of Churches (BCC), *The Forgotten Trinity: The Report of the BCC Study Commission on Trinitarian Doctrine Today*, 3 vols, London, BCC, 1989–91.

[27] John D. Zizioulas, *Being as Communion: Studies in Personhood and Church*, Crestwood, NY, St Vladimir's Seminary Press, 1985. J. B. Torrance in his Didsbury Lectures succinctly summarizes and draws out the significance of the BCC report on the Trinity in *Worship, Community, and the God of Grace*, Carlisle, Paternoster, 1996, pp. 24–31.

[28] Greenwood, *Being Church*, pp. 17–19.

mission in the world, has generated a variety of practical expressions across the Anglican Communion. Notably, the movement has been identified in the UK, Australia and New Zealand as 'Local or Shared Ministry' and often in North America as 'Total Ministry'. Frequently a pragmatic diocesan response to shrinking clergy numbers, its deep roots lay in articulating and fostering the notion of local churches in mission, through the recognition of the baptismal vocation of all and a vital renewal of the identity of the particular call of those ordained. At the time of writing, this impetus seems often to be seen as a distraction from a commitment to growing churches rather than an essential element in releasing fresh energy and support for the vocations and ministries of all.[29]

Daniel W. Hardy and David F. Ford, both leading Anglican scholars, have consistently supported churches in countering frustration by offering an ecclesiology rooted in glory, praise and the dialogical engagement of the triune God with all creation. They explored basic existence and a Christian understanding of evil, suffering and death and God's activity in the world in terms of praise and blessing, 'a form of causality that is effective but is in accordance with the respect God has for creation'.[30] Ford has drawn out the notion of every person, regardless of his or her role within the faith community, and within work and wider society, as in some way exercising 'leadership'. This resonates with many contemporary organizational theories of leadership as participation.[31] He takes as the touchstone for developing this theme the Genesis 12.1–3 account of Abraham responding to the challenge of God to travel within the promise of receiving a blessing in order to be a blessing and bless others. Although God is the chief source of blessing, often blessing comes to us from other people and often through chains of person-to-person blessing, through teachers, books or the Internet. In order that they may bless wisely, Ford suggests that all who are included in this corporate ministry of 'leadership' within faith communities need to be formed in four aspects of theology: first, to be wise interpreters of Scripture; second, to engage with God in prayer; third, to

---

[29] See Robin Greenwood, *Practising Community: The Task of the Local Church*, London, SPCK, 1996; Robin Greenwood, *Transforming Church: Liberating Structures for Ministry*, London, SPCK, 2002; and Robin Greenwood and Caroline Pascoe, *Local Ministry: Process, Story and Meaning*, London, SPCK, 2006, especially pp. 1–17.

[30] Daniel W. Hardy and David F. Ford, *Living in Praise: Worshipping and Knowing God*, London, Darton, Longman & Todd, 2005, p. 103.

[31] E.g. Bill Torbert and Associates, *Action Inquiry: The Secret of Timely and Transforming Leadership*, San Francisco, CA, Berrett-Koehler, 2004; Judi Marshall, Gill Coleman and Peter Reason (eds), *Leadership for Sustainability: An Action Research Approach*, Sheffield, Greenleaf, 2011.

engage in new developments within the world's life, in order that their capacity for discernment, judgement, decision-making, and creative and intelligent thinking might be fully stretched. Fourth, the 'leader' has to be able to communicate effectively, and so far as possible to listen attentively and to speak and write well.[32] Ford develops this formation in terms of friendship (across different and deeply held convictions), Scripture (as a place of being present to God and one another in mutual discovery) and organization (in the sphere of education and public understanding), and all 'for the sake of God and God's good purposes'.[33] My own development of ministry as blessing, as an antidote to fear, deficit anxiety and pathos, taking a Participatory Action Research approach, indicates how the corporate mission and ministry of local churches can be renewed through evoking a conversational and respectful ethos.[34]

Sharing responsibility

Stephen Pickard's account of theoretical-practical approaches to ministry that are fragmentary, mechanistic and competitive, and over-focused on the servanthood (but with scant reference to friendship) of a dedicated few, reflects monist concepts of God that inhibit rather than release energy. He argues that sustained ecclesial heresies become refracted in inadequate ministerial values and practices.[35] Although since the middle of the last century the rhetoric of communion, participation and co-responsibility has been a leading theme in theologies of ministry, benignly patronizing practice is not difficult to find. Among the many contributory factors in this scenario, I would identify the common clerical experience of being overwhelmed by clusters of irreconcilable demands and the absence of a continuity of approach so that a culture of shared responsibility does not become embedded. What is required is a move from an obsession with expertise to the fostering of a spirit of relatedness rooted in the total working of God. In his assessment of the contribution of the Local Shared Ministry movement to ecclesiological discourse and practice, Hardy relates ministry to Church as a

---

[32] David F. Ford, 'What Is Required of a Religious Leader Today?', lecture at the Institute of Shariah Studies, Muscat, Oman, 20 April 2009, in *A Muscat Manifesto: Seeking Inter-Faith Wisdom*, University of Cambridge and Kalam Research and Media, Knowledge Village, Dubai, 2009, pp. 19–27.

[33] Ford, 'What Is Required of a Religious Leader Today?', p. 27.

[34] Robin Greenwood, *Sharing God's Blessing: How to Renew the Local Church*, London, SPCK, 2016.

[35] Pickard, *Seeking the Church*, ch. 3.

corporate vision of the intensive identity of the holy God, of the God whose 'being is law to his working', and who is always active in gathering his people, whose 'nature is always to have mercy', whose care reaches into the whole of their lives . . . redirecting the course of their lives and giving them – by his Spirit – the promise of fulfilment in God's kingdom, and whose just and compassionate care in its full extent is actually mapped out onto the Church in its mission, [bringing] the world to the kingdom of God.[36]

In his panoramic *Theological Foundations for Ministry*, Ray S. Anderson, searching for 'the fundamental paradigm of ministry', turned to the 'foundational work of God himself in establishing a ministry of revelation and reconciliation in the world'.[37] He raised the profile of baptism as 'the qualifying act of consecration and ordination for ministry and mission; each baptized believer is "ordained" into the apostolic, charismatic, and sacrificial ministry of the Church'.[38] In the final decades of the twentieth century Edmund Flood OSB reimagined bishops, pastors and laity sharing responsibility as 'Church' together, as Christ's body for the transformation of the locality and the world. Rooted in reflection on power given by the Spirit in the New Testament, he asked radical questions about who can be regarded as a minister and what evolution of the parish would be ideal and possible in the coming years.[39] Contemporary enquiry demonstrates that the innovative initiative required to move from a culture of dependency requires a difficult, deliberate departure from 'business as usual'.[40] Churches can learn with community developers and educationalists to invest in local key ministries of strategic development; they can trust and support localities in networking, collaborative leadership, hospitality, and the wisdom to reinterpret ancient truths as emergent and fluid rather than static, in a culture that encourages questions and challenges, rather than importing external expertise and 'solutions'.[41]

---

[36] Daniel W. Hardy, 'Afterword', in Greenwood and Pascoe (eds), *Local Ministry*, pp. 136–7. See the essays in Julie Gittoes, Brutus Green and James Heard (eds), *Generous Ecclesiology: Church, World and the Kingdom of God*, London, SCM Press, 2013.

[37] Raymond S. Anderson (ed.), *Theological Foundations for Ministry: Selected Readings for a Theology of the Church in Ministry*, Edinburgh, T&T Clark, 1979 (1999), p. 3.

[38] Anderson, *Theological Foundations*, p. 256.

[39] Edmund Flood OSB, *The Laity Today and Tomorrow: A Report on the New Consciousness of Lay Catholics and How It Might Change the Face of Tomorrow's Church*, Mahwah, NJ, Paulist Press, 1987.

[40] Vijay Govindarajan and Chris Trimble, *The Other Side of Innovation: Solving the Execution Challenge*, Boston, MA, Harvard Business Review Press, 2010.

[41] Sheryl A. Kujawa-Holbrook and Fredrica Harris Thompsett, *Born of Water, Born of Spirit: Supporting the Ministry of the Baptized in Small Congregations*, Herndon, VA, The Alban Institute, 2010, p. 47.

Resourcing and leading

What does it mean for a church leader to be 'in charge' of the local mission and to preside within the eucharistic liturgy without diminishing others through accruing to oneself an imbalance of power? Stephen Pickard has rigorously examined the theological foundations of a collaborative approach to ministry, noting the volume of ecumenical discourse on an integrative approach to the relationship between ordained and lay ministries. He remains dissatisfied with current attempts to express this ministerial dynamic in ways that deeply recognize ministerial interconnectedness that is an authentic expression of being ordered together (Romans 12.5) in the economy of God, the transforming gospel of Christ and a spirit-led ecclesiology.[42] Readers of this chapter will vary widely in the way they would articulate and inhabit the unresolved balance between the role of all the faithful and those called into ordained and licensed roles. Provocatively, I have chosen to embed the vital work of overseeing, resourcing, ordering together, gathering and representing within the matrix of ministries that constitute the People of God. In times when churches were actively supported by government and clergy held respected status, metaphors for priesthood included shepherd, parent, gardener and servant. In practice a significant element of the commissioned public role of clergy is to take sacramental leadership and act as a bridge with society. But within a reciprocal ecclesiology, generative metaphors for clergy will include navigating, overseeing, narrating, interpreting, releasing, encouraging and presiding.[43]

Ministry to curate spaces for transformation

Growing in faith and wisdom

A Church characterized more by attentive conversation than by adversarial discussion has become a significant thread in the formation of Christian community.[44] Anne E. Streaty and Maisha I. Handy, for instance, in the context of female mentoring as gift-exchange, write of 'conversations of hope' as 'healing spaces'. 'Whether in the company of females only or with both females and males, the shared narrative becomes the means by which wisdom seekers gain new insights into their lives and envision new

---

[42] Stephen Pickard, *Theological Foundations for Collaborative Ministry*, Farnham, Ashgate, 2009.

[43] The Church of England, *Eucharistic Presidency. A Theological Statement by the House of Bishops of the General Synod*, GS 1248, London, Church House Publishing, 1997.

[44] It has educational and community development parallels in the work of Parker Palmer and Margaret Wheatley.

or renewed direction.'[45] Joanna Collicutt, an Anglican priest and facilitator of spirituality, locates formation within both the belief that every Christian is called to minister and the conviction that personal and communal transformation belong within the context of the transformation of the whole created order (Romans 8.19–21).[46] This is the Holy Spirit, working uniquely with each part of creation, 'marked definitively by the radical transformation of a group of cowering wretches into articulate and bold witnesses to Jesus at the first Pentecost'.[47] The Spirit never frees us beyond our own disposition and cooperation, nor does it recognize or foster an elite spiritual group. As all may be said to have a unique calling, all may participate in the formation of corporate Christian character, according to our contexts and personalities. Formation is essentially to be drawn to Christ, see God's glory and so become part of God's good pleasure – in other words, to be blessed and bound with the cosmos for beatitude.

Making Christ known and attractive to others

The once popular discourse of ideal 'models' of Church and ministry[48] can now seem too mechanical and formulaic. Dialoguing with Alastair McIntyre's *After Virtue*[49] and with Gerard Mannion's *Ecclesiology and Postmodernity*,[50] I am drawn to the development of a 'virtue ecclesiology'. By this I mean a synthesis of the core practices of the local church and the virtues required to support them. Rather than setting up familiar dynamics of suspicion between local community and institution (e.g. diocese), a creative path opens through expecting and deliberately embedding the same values and practices at every point in the ecclesial and ministerial landscape.[51]

A notable indicator of a virtue ecclesiology is recognizable in the teaching and pastoral ministry of Pope Francis. In *On the Joy of Evangelism*, he invites churches to worship and follow a God of mercy and tenderness, and within that culture, advocates detailed practices of forming Christians

---

[45] Anne E. Streaty Wimberly and Maisha I. Handy, 'Conversations on Word and Deed', in Anne E. Streaty Wimberley and Evelyn L. Parker (eds), *In Search of Wisdom: Faith Formation in the Black Church*, Nashville, TN, Abingdon Press, 2002.

[46] Joanna Collicutt, *The Psychology of Christian Character Formation*, London, SCM Press, 2015, pp. 3–12.

[47] Collicutt, *Psychology of Christian Character Formation*, p. 4.

[48] See especially Avery Dulles, *Models of the Church*, New York, Image Books / Doubleday, 1978 (2002).

[49] Alasdair McIntyre, *After Virtue: A Study in Moral Theory*, 3rd edn, London, Bloomsbury, 2011.

[50] Gerard Mannion, *Ecclesiology and Postmodernity: Questions for the Church in Our Time*, Collegeville, MN, Michael Glazier/Liturgical Press, 2007.

[51] Greenwood, *Being Church*, especially ch. 6, p. 68ff.

generally as missional disciples. Varying patterns of a renewed monastic movement are practised in Christian community living, as a way of knowing Christ and making Christ known – practice ministries of hospitality, mutual disciplining, celebrating the Eucharist with a physically communal emphasis, encouraging dynamic practices in Bible study, teaching contemplative prayer, seeking greater intimacy with God, and serving one another, the neighbourhood and society.[52]

Reflecting on the significance of the WCC policy statement on mission and evangelism, *Together towards Life*,[53] Kirsteen Kim, referring to the era of Paul and the first apostles, portrays an international movement in which Christians and churches are experiencing a new dynamism of the Spirit. Kim calls for a prophetic boldness in ministries of evangelism, underpinned by pneumatology. Going beyond urgent strategies for church growth, recalling that only God's Spirit creates new life, she advocates a perspective among Christians that imagines evangelism as a spirituality, filled with God's love for those who do not know him, present with people in their own contexts, meeting God who has preceded us and active wherever the fullness of life is affirmed. She concludes that practising evangelism is a sign that we love our neighbours and that in sharing the source of our blessing we deconstruct colonial habits of creating dependency in those we seek to serve.

Imaginative practice

Imagination needs to take its place alongside inherited knowledge, insist Michael Frost and Alan Hirsch. They provoke inherited churches radically to recalibrate the practice of local churches and leaders through moving beyond serving the needs of existing Christians and growing through making disciples.[54] An excellent example of a practical resource for drawing people into discipleship is provided by Sara Savage and Eolene Boyd-Macmillan.[55] They write from a standpoint that honours and wishes to enhance both pioneer and traditional ministry and brings into partnership Scripture, theology, spirituality, theories and practices for community

---

[52] Greenwood, *Being Church*, ch. 10, pp. 112ff.

[53] Kirsteen Kim, '*Together towards Life* and the Mission Studies Curriculum', *International Review of Mission* 104.1 (April 2015), pp. 98–117.

[54] Michael Frost and Alan Hirsch, *The Shaping of Things to Come: Innovation and Mission for the 21st Century Church*, Erina, NSW, Strand (2003), 2007.

[55] Sara Savage and Eolene Boyd-Macmillan, *The Human Face of Church: A Social Psychology and Pastoral Theology Resource for Pioneer and Traditional Ministry*, Norwich, Canterbury Press, 2007.

dynamics, conflict management, human emotions, and sharing in God's mission in the world. Rooted in the loving presence of God in people's lives, the workbook offers resources for nurturing confident Christian community, ministry and maturity in human persons and relations. Its practice assumes that good theology and good humanity will travel together. The undergirding theology, implicit in the workbook, has the key elements of God's holiness known through the presence of Jesus Christ, healthy human relating, transformational learning, reflection on images of God, review and revision of practice, and self-aware leadership.

The 2012 Church of England Common Awards process for reimagining ministerial formation assumed the need for a holistic set of virtues and practices. A review of David Heywood's *Reimagining Ministry* emphasized the urgency for altering inherited patterns of both training for ministry and ministry itself in a Church and educational system characterized by inertia.[56] In my experience within local churches the most transformational learning processes draw out maturity in the whole selves of people and collect all ages together in ways that are counter-cultural in a consumerist and individualist society.[57] Invigorating practices, either in a single large church or in a group of churches include a leader with long experience in educational design who can train and coach others, an emphasis on reflection on experience, accepting all that people bring, and linking learning with worship and communal values and practices.

Christian A. B. Scharen and Eileen R. Campbell-Reed have presented the fruits of a five-year theoretical and story-based project on projecting how ministry could embody pastoral imagination. They conclude that, formed over time through ministerial experience, pastoral imagination is 'an individual's capacity for seeing a situation of ministry in all its holy and relational depths, and responding with wise and fitting judgement and action'.[58] What is clear is the need for all in ministry to learn pastoral imagination. This requires approaches to ministry formation that are integrative, embodied and relational, and centred on integrated teaching that articulates the challenges of the practice of ministry today. This requires immersion in both the daily practice of ministry over time and critical

---

[56] Simon Martin, 'Review of David Heywood's *Reimagining Ministry*' (SCM), *Journal of the Rural Theology Association* 10.1 (2011), pp. 91–2.

[57] Robin Greenwood and Sue Hart, *Being God's People: The Confirmation and Discipleship Handbook*, London, SPCK, 2011.

[58] Christian A. B. Scharen and Eileen R. Campbell-Reed, *Learning Pastoral Imagination: A Five-Year Report on How New Ministers Learn in Practice*, Auburn Studies 21, New York, Auburn Theological Seminary, 2016.

unforeseen moments that may arise from crisis or calamity. Further, this approach requires opportunities for both apprenticeship and mentors with capacity for offering relational wisdom through shared reflection and making sense of a situation. Its capacity for working with complexity arises through the intersection of social and personal forces of injustice and it is a crucial learning environment for preparing to inhabit ministry as a spiritual practice, opening up self and community to the presence and power of God.

Conclusion

This chapter has mapped three interconnected elements of a contemporary ecumenical missiology: a deliberate corporate calling to, *first*, discern, demonstrate and participate in God's work in the world, *second*, as ministries that evoke, lead and sustain worship, community and identity, and *third*, as a reflective practice of curating spaces for transformation.

Notable illustrations of the theology-practice of ministry have not emerged as having a coherence that can be reduced to a disparate list of activities. They include: the recognition and encouragement of baptized women and men dispersed in the everyday world as contemplative activists for the kingdom, a critical engagement between theological and human disciplines, movements towards a collegial patterning of Church that bypasses previous polarities of gender or commissioning, a kinesthetic and holistic approach to the architecture and performance of liturgy and presentation of learning, an increasing coherence (personally and institutionally) between outward and inward responses to the loving invitation of the triune God, responding to urgent pressure for innovation, not as a programmatic or anxious strategy but through open conversational processes, and a move towards leadership as a sharing of *episkopé*, fostering a culture of Trinitarian relating. All of these together are signs of the Holy Spirit summoning churches to courageous imagination and effective missional discipleship to be a communication of the gospel in a transitional and challenging time.

No one can safely predict the future of the inherited churches and the contours of their ministries. At a time of acute uncertainty and attendant anxiety, the most reliable path for reaching forward to a renewed theory-practice approach to Christian ministry is a fulsome engagement with the glory, abundance and blessing of the triune God and that God's call and gift which enables events of church to make spontaneous responses of participation in seeking the world's fulfilment.

Part 4

STYLES OF CHRISTIAN MINISTRY

23

Roman Catholic pastoral theology

TOM HUGHSON

Pastoral horizon

'Standing before you I tremble somewhat with emotion but am humbly resolute in my purpose to proclaim a twofold celebration: a diocesan synod for the city of Rome, and a general council for the universal Church.'[1] With these words on 25 January 1959 Pope John XXIII startled everyone, not least his own Curia.[2] Logistical and substantive preparations preceded his 11 October 1962 convoking of the Second Vatican Council. He intended a 'pastoral' council modelled on Christ the Good Shepherd (Latin: *pastor*), rather than a doctrinal council devoted to confuting errors and determining an orthodox formulation of faith.[3] The unprecedented conciliar orientation with an accent on ecumenism and dialogue is less surprising when set against the background of the First and Second World Wars.

The First World War ended not only the nineteenth-century ideal of progress through the expanding scope of scientific and technological reason, but also the universally normative status of Western Christendom. In both world wars Christians on both sides recited the Our Father and, with the exception of the Filioque among the Orthodox and non-creedal belief among Baptists, professed the same Niceno-Constantinopolitan Creed. Catholics, in armed forces on conflicting sides, for example, went to the same type of Latin Masses. Without resorting to a retrospective and

---

[1] Pope John XXIII, online only in the original Italian at <http://w2.vatican.va/content/john-xxiii/it/homilies/1959/documents/hf_j-xxiii_hom_19590125.html>. In English, Giuseppe Alberigo, trans. Matthew Sherry, *A Brief History of Vatican II* (Maryknoll, NY: Orbis Books, 2006), 1.

[2] See Giuseppe Alberigo gen. ed., Joseph Komonchak English version ed., *The History of Vatican II*, vols 1–5 (Maryknoll, NY: Orbis Books, 1995–2006) and John W. O'Malley, *What Happened at Vatican II* (Cambridge, MA: The Belknap Press of Harvard University Press, 2008).

[3] Giuseppe Alberigo, 'Preparing for What Kind of Council?', *The History of Vatican II*, vol. 1, 501–8 at 503.

dubious moral equivalence of both sides in both wars it still seems undeniable that the wars doubled the scandal of Christianity divided into competing churches. Twentieth-century Christianity did not present to the
world a hopeful, credible witness to one Lord, one Spirit and one gospel.

The World Council of Churches (1948–) may be understood as an
Orthodox and Protestant answer, Vatican II (1962–5) as a later Catholic
response. Not the revealed content but faith as a way of life was the primary pastoral, spiritual and theological challenge for the council. The pastoral council took up the task. More than 2,500 bishops met and invoked
the blessing of the Holy Spirit in solemn assemblies during four consecu-
tive autumns. There were disagreements over what it meant to be pastoral. A minority, led by Roman curial officials, insisted on continuing the
nineteenth-century papacy's assertion of church doctrine in the teeth of a
misguided modernity. The majority, from an international variety of
perspectives, grasped that communication of the gospel involved taking
account of the hearers and of the modern world, assessed as not altogether
without some truth, value and beneficial achievements. The latter approach,
more in line with the pastoral intent of John XXIII's distinction between
the doctrines of faith and their formulation, came to prevail.

The Constitution on the Sacred Liturgy (*Sacrosanctum concilium*),
the first and least controversial among the documents, was approved
on 3 December 1963.[4] It initiated a liturgical renewal that immediately
affected everyday parish life except in nations under communist rule.
Renewal pruned accretions in favour of a 'noble simplicity' in structure,
movements and prayers.[5] Gerald A. Arbuckle, on behalf of social anthropology, not traditionalism, criticizes this norm as a Roman ideal imposing
a classicist idea of culture on the Church. African and Polynesian cultures
on the other hand appreciate 'colorful symbolic repetitions'.[6] Rational
criteria and transparency congruent with Western modernity governed
renewal. Arbuckle's critique could be applied by interpreting declining
attendance in the West as a sign of postmodern movement past modern renewal. Yet local churches in Africa have found ways to incorporate

---

[4] All conciliar texts are available at <http://www.vatican.va/archive/hist_councils/ii_vatican_
council/index.htm>.

[5] Second Vatican Council, Constitution on the Sacred Liturgy, *Sacrosanctum concilium*,
<http://www.vatican.va/archive/hist_councils/ii_vatican_council/documents/vat-ii_
const_19631204_sacrosanctum-concilium_en.html>, no. 34.

[6] Gerald A. Arbuckle SM, *Culture, Inculturation, and Theologians: A Postmodern Critique*, with
Foreword by Anthony Gittens CSSp (Collegeville, MN: Liturgical Press, A Michael Glazier
Book, 2010), Kindle edition, ch. 8, location 3263.

repetitive symbolism. Eastern Catholic churches have retained colourful, symbolic repetitions. The traditional Roman structure joins a liturgy of the word based in synagogue practice to a liturgy of the Eucharist recalling the Last Supper. Arbuckle's postmodern interpretations of lived faith, ministry and governance bring pastoral/practical theology into a thought-provoking consultation with anthropology.

The controverted text of the Pastoral Constitution on the Church in the Modern World (*Gaudium et spes*) finally found approval on the last day of voting, 7 December 1965. Its dialogical approach extended the renewed pastoral vision and practice to the Church–world relation. The pastoral orientation did not override a searching fidelity to divine revelation from the Father, enabled by the Spirit and centred in Christ as mediated by Scripture and Tradition.[7] Attention to God was at the centre of the council whose pastoral nature was for the sake of deepened communion with the Trinity. The 21 November 1964 Dogmatic Constitution on the Church (*Lumen gentium*) and the 18 November 1965 Dogmatic Constitution on Divine Revelation (*Dei verbum*) could not have been doctrinally richer had the purpose of the council been doctrinal.

Lumen gentium taught the Trinitarian ecclesiology that in Chapter Two affirmed the constitutive presence of baptismal discipleship. Chapter Three reaffirmed divinely instituted service by bishops as successors to the apostles both of whose collegiality rebalanced Petrine primacy. *Dei verbum* interpreted revelation as God's self-revelation, subsumed the propositional model of revelation, and enlarged the role of Scripture in the daily life, ministry and practice of the Church.[8] The momentous conciliar event altered personal, structural and doctrinal characteristics put in place by the counter-Reformation Council of Trent (1545–63) and fortified by the counter-Liberalism of the First Vatican Council (1869–70).

The council professed and Catholics believe that the Holy Spirit was active during the council at the basis of graced human freedom struggling within and among episcopal and expert minds, consciences and hearts.[9] Many bishops reported that their common active presence in the council

---

[7] For pastoral-theological appropriation of *Dei verbum* see Clare Watkins, 'Texts and Practices: An Ecclesiology of *Traditio* for Practical Theology', in James Sweeney, Gemma Simmonds and David Lonsdale, eds, *Keeping Faith in Practice: Aspects of Catholic Pastoral Theology* (London: SCM Press, 2010), 163–78.

[8] See Avery Dulles, *Models of Revelation* (Garden City, NY: Doubleday, 1983) and Christophe Theobald, 'The Church under the Word of God', *History of Vatican II*, vol. 5, 275–372.

[9] For a pneumatological perspective see Thomas Hughson SJ, 'Interpreting Vatican II: "A New Pentecost"', *Theological Studies* 69, 1 (2008): 3–37.

awakened an experience of conversion to a reformed institutional and personal way of being dialogical Catholics. A strong theological case can be made that reception of Vatican II likewise has been tantamount to conversion in laity and clergy.[10] Collectively and singly, all 16 Vatican II documents bring reform, better enabling fulfilment of the universal call to lives with the Father, through Christ and in the Spirit by way of revelation/ faith, hope and charity. The overall tendency in the documents, not only *Gaudium et spes*, is in that sense pastoral and has become the lived, ecumenical, inter-religious horizon within which Catholic pastoral/practical theologians are conceiving ministry and theology.

A tension

Nevertheless, a pronounced tension is internal to Catholic pastoral/practical theology too. Two conciliar documents addressed priestly ministry, the 28 October 1965 Decree on Priestly Training (*Optatam totius*) and the 7 December 1965 Decree on the Ministry and Life of Priests (*Presbyterium ordinis*). They do not altogether escape an earlier narrowness.[11] Even the post-conciliar *New Catholic Encyclopedia* featured an entry on pastoral theology adverting to patristic authors but still attached to an idea of pastoral theology revolving around how to apply theological content 'to the daily ministry of the priest'.[12] A few years ago the editor of a periodical put it clearly: '"[p]astoral theology" includes everything connected with the priestly ministry to the faithful; it is a practical science which tries to apply the revealed truths of our faith, and the directives of the Magisterium, to the problems of daily living.'[13] Such an approach approximates what Protestant theologians criticized as the 'clerical paradigm' in Protestant theology.[14]

---

[10] See Ormond Rush, 'Ecclesial Conversion after Vatican II: Renewing the "Face of the Church" to Reflect the "Genuine Face of God", *Theological Studies* 74 (2013), 785–803.

[11] A question for conciliar history and hermeneutics is: how did conciliar discussions and debates pertaining to *Lumen gentium* intersect with, or not, the commissions preparing *Optatam totius* and *Presbyterium ordinis*?

[12] J. H. Brennan, 'Pastoral Theology', in *New Catholic Encyclopedia: Volume X, Mos to Pat*, editorial staff, Catholic University of America (Palatine, IL: Jack Heraghty & Associates, 1981; original 1967), 1080–4 at 1080, col. 2.

[13] Kenneth Baker SJ, 'What Does It Mean to Be "Pastoral"?', *Homiletic and Pastoral Review*, 26 November 2012: <http://www.hprweb.com/2012/11/editorial-what-does-it-mean-to-be-pastoral/>.

[14] See Bonnie J. Miller-McLemore, 'The "Clerical Paradigm": A Fallacy of Misplaced Concreteness?', *International Journal of Practical Theology* 11 (2007): 19–38.

Trent had reformed clerical education.[15] Continuing a medieval direction, the sacrament of Orders revolved around priestly ministry in parishes, most frequently Mass and the Sacrament of Penance, with less frequent administration of Baptism, Marriage and the Sacrament of the Sick. Confirmation was reserved to bishops. Conferred participation in Christ's power (with perfunctory invoking of the Spirit) to consecrate the bread and wine and to forgive sins expressed the core of priestly ministry.[16] While valid, this concept of ministry, as Edward Schillebeeckx and others have shown, narrowed its scope in defence against the Reformers' rejection of any hierarchy. The effect was to separate priesthood from prophetic and leadership dimensions and from universal (all the baptized) ministry. This was the clerical paradigm in ministry and theology insofar as its pastoral implications touched ministry.

Vatican II broke through the paradigm. Historically conscious systematic theologians have variously explored the breakthrough.[17] In Catholic circumstances the clerical paradigm overlooks Vatican II's ecclesiology. A renewed pastoral theology, focused on the primacy of baptized discipleship, better curates conciliar reform.[18] English-speaking pastoral/practical theologians, with attention to induction, have been considering concrete actualizing of conciliar potential on ministry.

Complete renunciation of the paradigm has attracted Protestant and Catholic theologians.[19] Such a peremptory move, however, discounts Bonnie Miller-McLemore's argument against wholesale rejection of the focus of the older pastoral theology on preparing seminarians for ordained ministry.[20] Likewise, and agreeing with the primacy of universal ministry, I do not see a compelling reason why pastoral/practical theology has to abandon theological interest in rethinking, resituating and renewing theology in anticipation of ordained ministry. Funnelling advances from a

---

[15] See John W. O'Malley, *Trent: What Happened at the Council* (Cambridge, MA: The Belknap Press of Harvard University Press, 2013). Canon 18 mandated diocesan seminaries, especially for poor boys, to replace haphazard parish apprenticeships, 212.

[16] Edward Schillebeeckx, trans. John Bowden, 3rd edn, *The Church with a Human Face: A New and Expanded Theology of Ministry* (New York: Crossroad, 1988).

[17] See David N. Powers, 'Order', in Francis Schüssler Fiorenza and John P. Galvin, eds, 2nd edn, *Systematic Theology: Roman Catholic Perspectives* (Minneapolis, MN: Fortress, 2011), 567–82.

[18] Kathleen A. Cahalen, 'Pastoral Theology or Practical Theology? Limits and Possibilities', in Sweeney et al., eds, *Keeping Faith in Practice*, 99–116.

[19] Many struggle with the paradigm, but Henri Jérôme Gagey renounces it in 'Pastoral Theology as a Theological Project', in Sweeney et al., eds, *Keeping Faith in Practice*, 80–98. Gagey conceives practical theology as a project, not a discipline, an approach suited to fostering collaboration.

[20] Miller-McLemore, '"Clerical Paradigm"'.

revised pastoral/practical theology into education for ordination would serve the People of God.

Middling through and then some

Receiving Vatican II has involved cooperative praxis. Liturgical renewal has touched cooperation between clergy and laity in worship that embodies conciliar themes. Liturgy in Christ has mediated, middled, chiefly between the divine and the human but also between conciliar content and worshippers. The latter middling can be understood in the light of Bernard Lonergan's analysis of meaning. There is a kind of meaning that Lonergan calls 'effective' because it aims towards effects. It guides practice and cooperation by directing, requesting, commanding, planning and organizing activities in economic, political and technological spheres.[21] Effective meaning differs from the cognitive function of meaning. Cognitive consciousness attends to experience, and seeks hypotheses, surmises, explanatory ideas, interpretations and theories. It comes to fulfilment in freedom's most fulfilling act, love. A third function of meaning constitutes a person's, group's or society's way of being and acting. The accumulating impact of a person's or a society's freedom is exercised in value-judgements, in adopting ideas, judgements and decisions that shape from within a person's, group's or society's priorities in organization, structures and culture. Liturgical renewal has been something very like the effective function of conciliar meaning.

Renewal proceeds not by people's first comprehending the cognitive content in *Dei verbum* and *Lumen gentium*, then, second, putting it into liturgical action. Instead, churchgoers learn renewal by speaking and hearing vernacular prayers and enacting new gestures like the handshake of peace in a revised physical environment. Designing and executing architectural modifications in parish churches and diocesan cathedrals also effectively realizes liturgical meaning as do new church buildings. Liturgical renewal has been the most familiar, direct, widespread and primary effective function of faith renewed by Vatican II meanings. Reception of liturgical revisions for 50 years has been an effective function of conciliar meaning leading to constitutive meaning in the everyday life of Catholics.

Another way of middling through effective meaning has been afoot as well. Institutional adaptations in some theological education have

---

[21] Bernard Lonergan, *Method in Theology* (New York: Seabury Press, 1979; originally Herder & Herder, 1972).

appropriated conciliar meanings that broke from the clerical paradigm. The effective function of meaning guided initiatives like the following. In 1963, moved also by pre-conciliar ideas outside the clerical paradigm, Marquette University in Milwaukee, USA, began to offer the first PhD programme in the USA designed for lay theologians. In 1964 Loyola University-Chicago inaugurated the Institute of Pastoral Studies for clergy and laity.[22] Corporate memberships in ecumenical consortia – e.g. Regis College in the Toronto School of Theology, Heythrop College in the University of London, Catholic Theological Union in Chicago, the Jesuit School of Theology at Berkeley/Santa Clara in the Graduate Theological Union, the Boston College School of Theology, and in Dublin the Milltown Institute of Theology and Philosophy – opened MDiv programmes to men and women looking towards either further academic theology or lay ecclesial ministry. Graduate study in theology for clergy and laity together likewise became available in Belgium at KU Leuven. The Ateneo de Manila in the Philippines offers advanced degrees to those preparing for ordained ministry and to those preparing for lay ecclesial ministry. Since the early 1970s the Gregorian University in Rome has had programmes in advanced theological studies for lay women and men alongside seminarians. It might seem that liturgical renewal plus institutional adaptations were the day's work in effective meaning, after which the evening has arrived when the (pastoral-theological) owl of Minerva can take to wing in the cognitive meaning of systematic theology.

Meanings and discipleship

However, on two counts the Hegelian trope would not be correct. Another kind of day's work had been under way that combined effective, cognitive and constitutive meanings. First, in Latin America post-conciliar Catholic pastoral ministry and theology were redefined by the 1968 Puebla meeting of Latin American bishops, Gustavo Gutiérrez's ensuing *The Theology of Liberation*, and liberation theology.[23] The option for the poor and the commitment to justice were effective meaning. Liberationist critique of systemic injustice was cognitive and constitutive meaning, shaping personal stances and social movements. Cognitive meaning on the public ministry of Christ and the primacy of discipleship infused the *praxis* of

---

[22] Cahalen, 'Pastoral Theology or Practical Theology?', 101–2.
[23] Pontifical Council for Justice and Peace, English trans. Libreria Editrice Vaticana, US Conference of Catholic Bishops (USCCB), *Compendium of the Social Doctrine of the Church* (Washington, DC: USCCB Publishing, 2005).

integral liberation. The option for the poor was constitutive meaning for *comunidades de base*. Despite early interventions by the Congregation for the Doctrine of Faith, the option for and hermeneutical privilege of the poor have spread around the world. The *Compendium of the Social Doctrine of the Church*, unlike the US bishops' document, *Economic Justice for All*, interpreted the option as primarily a preferential love for the poor without saying social justice.[24]

Second, renewal of cognitive meaning in pastoral theology began with Karl Rahner in 1968. He and others produced the 2,000-page *Handbuch der Pastoraltheologie*.[25] Rahner cooperated with US Dominican Daniel Morrissey on the English version of *A Theology of Pastoral Action*, and wanted the book to contribute to renewal of pastoral theology.[26] From a perspective in the German tradition of philosophical and theological speculation, Rahner extolled such a theology as one which, in its characteristic preoccupation with action, practice and efficacy, suited the English-speaking world of Anglo-Saxon thought. He took account of Vatican II's universal call to holiness and recognized that faith lived in discipleship takes place within the ongoing, interactive life of the whole Church. Accordingly he conceived pastoral theology as 'a theology of the Church in action, and of action in the Church . . . a *concrete, existential ecclesiology*' that was a *locus theologicus*.[27]

Did his gaze pass too quickly over interest in action by the Belgian, French and Italian bishops and *periti* whose prominent roles in the council carried familiarity with creative pre-conciliar pastoral initiatives and reflection? The thought of Flemish Dominican Edward Schillebeeckx, for example, was influential during the council and remains a major if not yet thoroughly assimilated influence for an historically and socially conscious theology of

---

[24] Pontifical Council for Justice and Peace, *Compendium of the Social Doctrine of the Church*, 182; and USCCB, *Economic Justice for All*, 1986, in David O'Brien and Thomas A. Shannon, eds, *Catholic Social Thought: The Documentary Heritage*, 13th printing (Maryknoll, NY: Orbis Books, 2005), 572–680.

[25] Franz Xavier Arnold, Karl Rahner, Viktor Schurr, Leonhard M. Weber, Ferdinand Klostermann, *Handbuch der Pastoraltheologie: Praktische Theologie der Kirche in ihrer Gegenwart*, rev. edn, vols 1–5 (Freiburg: Herder, 1970–2; 1st edn, 1968). Volume 5 is *Lexikon der Praktische Theologie*, ed. Ferdinand Klostermann, Karl Rahner and Hansjörg Schild. Note the use of both *Pastoraltheologie* and *Praktische Theologie*. In Chapter 14 of *Method in Theology* Bernard Lonergan footnoted this massive opus as an exemplar of the crowning theological specialty, communications.

[26] Karl Rahner, with Daniel Morrissey, trans. W. O'Hara, *A Theology of Pastoral Action* (New York: Herder & Herder, 1968), the English version of Rahner's contribution to Volume 1, Part 2, of *Handbuch der Pastoraltheologie*.

[27] Rahner, Morrissey, *A Theology of Pastoral Action*, 25.

ministry. The overlooked pre- and post-conciliar pastoral theology of French Dominican Pierre-André Liégé recently has come to English-speaking attention.[28] Italian cleric Pietro Pavan spoke constructively in the commission out of which came the Declaration on Religious Liberty (*Dignitatis humanae*) influenced by John Courtney Murray.

Rahner, Yves Congar, Edward Schillebeeckx and Pierre-André Liégé already had broadened their perspectives beyond the clerical paradigm. Rahner recognized the charism of each member of the faithful – not only the clergy, hierarchy and religious – to live and contribute to the Church from a unique reception of the gospel. That lived faith was a *locus theologicus* for pastoral theology. His reflection nevertheless did not fully escape the orbit of the clerical paradigm. His proposal did not explicitly consider theology, pastoral or otherwise, as a contribution from lay theologians. Congar had been a preponderant influence on the council's theology of the laity. Schillebeeckx in the 1980s undertook a methodologically exemplary *ressourcement* of ministry that traced its understandings from the New Testament through and after Vatican II. It reinterpreted the Tridentine image of priestly ministry.

Arguably the universal (all the baptized) call to holiness is the hallmark of Vatican II. Pastoral/practical theology, broadened beyond the clerical paradigm, considers the universal call in discipleship, and in lay ecclesial ministries. The universality of discipleship reframes all ministry in light of Baptism/Confirmation not first by reference to the sacrament of Orders. Adopting the more academic definition, practical theology, does not evade commitment to discipleship. Kathleen A. Cahalen states, '[t]he basic task that orients practical theology is to promote discipleship . . . supporting and sustaining lived discipleship.'[29] Miller-McLemore divides 'person and pathos-centered' pastoral theology in seminaries from a more comprehensive, process-oriented practical theology focused on academic study that is 'integrative, concerned about broader issues of ministry, discipleship, and formation, pastoral theology.'[30] The frequently combined

---

[28] See Pierre-André Liégé OP, trans. A. Manson, *What Is Christian Life?*, volume 56 in the *Twentieth Century Encyclopedia of Catholicism* (New York: Hawthorn Books, 1961); and Nicholas Bradbury, with Foreword by Timothy Radcliffe OP, *Practical Theology and Pierre-André Liégé: Radical Dominican and Vatican II Pioneer* (Farnham: Ashgate, 2015).

[29] Kathleen A. Cahalen and John R. Nieman, 'Mapping the Field of Practical Theology', ch. 3 in Dorothy Bass and Craig Dykstra, eds, *For Life Abundant: Practical Theology, Theological Education, and Christian Ministry* (Grand Rapids, MI: Eerdmans, 2008), Kindle edition, locations 716–969 at 762.

[30] Bonnie J. Miller-McLemore, 'Five Misunderstandings about Practical Theology', *International Journal of Practical Theology* 16, 1 (2012): 5–26 at 17–18. See the mainly Protestant *Blackwell*

'pastoral/practical' adjective for 'theology' signals respect for a complex situation not resolvable by systematic theology because Christian discipleship is an experienced way of life, a whole comprising beliefs, practices, attitudes and values interacting with an influential historical context.[31] Understanding that totality requires broadening two millennia of interdisciplinary dialogue with philosophy and history to include social-scientific studies of contemporary lived faith.[32]

Characteristics and contributions

In the view of David McLoughlin and Gemma Simmonds Catholic pastoral theology has four characteristics in an ecumenical spirit: (1) attention to the essential kerygma of the Church renewed by conciliar *ressourcement* of Scripture and Tradition, especially in *Dei verbum* and *Lumen gentium*; (2) correlations of Church and world, Christ and society, gospel and daily life, guided by *Gaudium et spes*;[33] (3) exploration of lived pastoral experiences in the Church, particularly in the area of Catholic social teaching; (4) modes of enabling movement from the above three to decision and action.

The two authors see six sources for Catholic contributions to an ecumenical pastoral theology: (1) a wide range of institutional resources; (2) Catholic social teaching; (3) the international and national area of pastoral adaptation and application; (4) a heritage of voluntary, lay movements such as the Catholic Workers; (5) a tradition of the works and spiritualities of religious congregations in mission and ministry; (6) post-conciliar renewal in spirituality and ecotheology. This is an instructive scan of the territory.[34] It could include a seventh source: the advent of and pastoral practice in lay ecclesial ministries. Lay ecclesial ministries are mainly

---

Reader in Pastoral and Practical Theology, and the invitation from Stephen Pattison to which Sweeney et al., eds, *Keeping Faith in Practice*, and Claire E. Wolfteich, ed., *Invitation to Practical Theology: Catholic Voices and Visions* (New York: Paulist Press, 2014), respond.

[31] Nicholas Healy, 'Ecclesiology and Practical Theology', in Sweeney et al., eds, *Keeping Faith in Practice*, 117–30 at 117.

[32] See for example Jerome P. Baggett, *Sense of the Faithful: How American Catholics Live Their Faith* (New York: Oxford University Press, 2009); Gerald A. Arbuckle, *Catholic Identity or Identities? Refounding Ministries in Chaotic Times* (Collegeville, MN: Liturgical Press, 2013). On Catholic identity, see also William V. D'Antonio, James D. Davidson, Dean R. Hoge and Mary I. Gautier, *American Catholics Today: New Realities of Their Faith and Their Church* (Lanham, MD: Rowman & Littlefield, 2007).

[33] The next section discusses the method of correlation.

[34] David McLoughlin and Gemma Simmonds CJ, 'Pastoral and Practical Theology in Britain and Ireland – A Catholic Perspective', in Sweeney et al., eds, *Keeping Faith in Practice*, 26–42.

internal activities for the good of the Church rather than modes of witness in society.[35] In post-conciliar Catholicism, notes Donna M. Eschenauer, 'Thousands of laypeople have answered a call to serve the church. This call is rooted in a serious recognition of one's baptismal vocation to carry on the mission of Jesus Christ.'[36] Response to this call typifies 'a population of laypeople who carry out such roles as pastoral associate, parish catechetical leader, director of youth ministry, school principal, director of music and liturgy, RCIA director, and so on'.[37] Accompanying these professionally prepared, salaried lay ministers are a greater number of volunteers. The lived faith and practice of both groups fall within the scope of pastoral theology. Has renewed pastoral theology followed up John Paul II's *Christifideles laici* on how lay ecclesial ministries intersect with the lay apostolate?[38]

Still another way to think about Catholic traits and contributions has to do with key questions. Cahalen raises several that are existentially salient at this time in the USA. How are we to do ministry in clustered parishes? What are ministers doing about declining rates of attendance at liturgy? What are the most effective methods of catechesis in the post-denominational situation today?[39] An added question arises from a sociological finding that US parishioners of all theological stripes want a role in parish decision-making while a younger generation of priests formed in the cultic model of priesthood accords that less significance. What changes will serve discipleship? Pastoral theology engaging the above queries serves the People of God.

A prior pastoral/practical question deals with God. Where is God in this time of our world's crying needs?[40] Is God absent or present? The liturgical

---

[35] See the United States Conference of Catholic Bishops, *Lay Ecclesial Ministry: The State of the Questions* (Washington, DC: United States Catholic Conference, 1999), and *Co-Workers in the Vineyard of the Lord: A Resource for Guiding the Development of Lay Ecclesial Ministry* (2005), <http://www.usccb.org/upload/co-workers-vineyard-lay-ecclesial-ministry-2005.pdf>; Bishop Matthew H. Clark, *Forward in Hope: Saying Amen to Lay Ecclesial Ministry* (Notre Dame, IN: Ave Maria Press, 2009); and Donna M. Eschenauer and Harold Daly Horell, eds, *Reflections on Renewal: Lay Ecclesial Ministry and the Church* (Collegeville, MN: Liturgical Press, A Michael Glazier Book, 2011).

[36] Donna M. Eschenauer, 'Introduction: The Fordham University Convocation', in Eschenauer and Horell, eds, *Reflections on Renewal*, xv–xxi at xvi.

[37] H. Richard McCord, 'The Development of Lay Ecclesial Ministry in the United States', in Eschenauer and Horell, eds, *Reflections on Renewal*, 3–10 at 3.

[38] John Paul II, *Christifideles Laici: On the Vocation and Mission of the Lay Faithful*, at <http://w2.vatican.va/content/john-paul-ii/en/apost_exhortations/documents/hf_jp-ii_exh_30121988_christifideles-laici.html>.

[39] Cahalen, 'Pastoral Theology or Practical Theology?'

[40] See Michael Kirwan SJ, 'Reading the Signs of the Times', in Sweeney et al., eds, *Keeping Faith*

life of Catholicism concentrates Christian apprehension of God's immanence in the world as Creator and Saviour. Universal divine immanence
through the self-giving of uncreated grace presupposes the logically prior
Creator–creature relationship that Thomas Aquinas among others has
adumbrated.[41] Water, palms and ashes, beeswax candles, bread and wine,
verbal vows, oil, medicine, physical assistance are historically embedded while belonging in the physical cosmos that the Father through the
Word and with the Spirit has created and still does create. The ineradic-
able immanent transcendence or transcendent immanence of the Creator
in the cosmos is the condition for the possibility of universal redemptive
grace and sacramental mediation.

Sacraments and sacramentals bring water, wine, palm branches, ashes,
beeswax and all of nature into worship of God. Aquinas, relying on yet
transforming Aristotle, expounded observable water, bees, trees, wheat,
grapes, and those enjoying their use, through properties, natures and existence dependent on the Creator. Divine immanence in physical creation
undergirds the realm of reverent practice known as 'sacramentals', along
with the corporal works of mercy and social justice seeking physical and
social conditions for the flourishing of humanity and creation. Reclaiming
divine creational immanence would assist pastoral/practical theology in
opening up a way of discipleship determined neither by reverting to what
is thought to be an undifferentiated, medieval, pre-modern sacred–secular
whole, nor at the other extreme by unilaterally siding with the sacred in a
postmodern antithesis to the secular.

The question of how

I'd like to close by commenting on why in pastoral theology the method
of *ressourcement* may be more helpful than the method of correlation.
The first point has to do with correlation. How fixed on the method of
correlation is pastoral/practical theology? The second concerns *ressourcement*. Correlation puts two kinds of content in dialogue so that theology
does not proceed in ignorance of what other disciplines have to say about
the context and content of a Christian way of life. It prevents unexamined pre-commitment to Barthian or von Balthasarian monologue to the
modern world in contravention of the dialogical approach of *Gaudium*

---

in *Practice*, 49–63; and Clare Watkins, 'Texts and Practices: An Ecclesiology of *Traditio* for
Practical Theology', in Sweeney et al., eds, *Keeping Faith in Practice*, 163–78.

[41] See chapters and sources in Aquinas, in Harm Goris, Herwi Rikhof and Henk Schoot, eds,
Divine Transcendence and Immanence in the Work of Thomas Aquinas (Leuven: Peeters, 2009).

et spes. However, correlation is not the last word. As Watkins points out, dealing with a gap between 'theological tradition' and the 'concrete situation' builds on disparate, abstracted, objectified realms of 'experience' and of 'tradition' put into 'dialogue' as if the former were not already in contact with and formed by the latter.[42]

Robert Doran and Neil Ormerod, drawing on Lonergan, also have pointed out objections to a correlational method.[43] Lonergan distinguished general from special categories in theology. General categories are also in use by other fields while special categories are unique to theology. Conceiving their relationship as correlation fails to state the enlightening primacy of revelation and faith in relation with knowledge from other disciplines. That is, the method of correlation lacks an explicit normative commitment to the primacy of special categories from revelation and the gift of faith. Consequently, the method of correlation is not specifically theological. Treating special categories with uniquely theological content as if on a par with non-theological content in general categories is reductive. Then, for example, social-scientific findings not only partially interpret but also determine the meaning of revealed content. The logic of correlation equates the epistemological significance of both sides, thereby removing the divine novelty in revelation. Still, faith enables theologians often to overcome that logic.

Schillebeeckx's method in *ressourcement* is not correlational but distinguishes and relates.[44] So systematic (theoretical) and pastoral/practical (practical) theologies are distinct but related to each other on a middle ground between sameness and difference. Lonergan does something similar in *Method in Theology* by distinguishing and relating systematics and communications. Finally, books by authors such as Bernard Cooke, Thomas O'Meara, Kenan B. Osborne, Susan K. Wood and David N. Powers, Schillebeeckx's *The Human Face of the Church* prominent among them, exemplify *ressourcement* on ministry in the Church.[45] They re-source discussion of ministry by returning to New Testament and traditional sources

---

[42] See Watkins's revelation-centred ecclesiology in 'Texts and Practices', 163–5.

[43] Lonergan, *Method in Theology*, 281–93; Robert M. Doran, *Theology and the Dialectics of History* (Toronto: University of Toronto Press, 1990), 115–19; Neil Ormerod, 'Quarrels with the Method of Correlation', *Theological Studies* 57 (1996): 707–19; and Robert Doran, *What Is Systematic Theology?* (Toronto: University of Toronto Press, 2005), ch. 5.

[44] Martin Poulsom SDB, 'The Place of Praxis in the Theology of Edward Schillebeeckx', in Sweeney et al., eds, *Keeping Faith in Practice*, 131–47. See Marguerite Thabit Abdul-Masih on the validity or not of a hermeneutic of experience in *Edward Schillebeeckx and Hans Frei: A Conversation on Method and Christology* (Waterloo, ON: Wilfrid Laurier Press, 2001).

[45] See the Select Bibliography in Powers, 'Order', 582.

in church history. Doing so recapitulates the influential pre-conciliar *ressourcement* and puts their work in line with *Dei verbum* on Scripture and Tradition.[46] Catholic pastoral/practical theology in an ecumenical spirit similarly benefits if continuing a recourse to Scripture and Tradition on the contextual meaning and practice of 'pastoral' and 'disciple'.

---

[46] Andrew Purves, *Pastoral Theology in the Classical Tradition* (Louisville, KY: Westminster John Knox Press, 2001), makes an ecumenical start.

24

Pentecostal-style ministries

BENJAMIN McNAIR SCOTT

In such a short chapter there is little chance to do justice to the numerous ministries that help constitute the Pentecostal–Charismatic movement (PCM). However, I trust this guide will provide an insight into theologies and practices that are found among Pentecostal-style ministries. After an introductory section on the history of the PCM, I will touch upon Pentecostal emphases and hallmarks of Pentecostal–Charismatic worship, before outlining a common theology of ministry and giving examples of past and present influential Pentecostal–Charismatic leaders. After this I will focus in large part on the theology and methods of the healing and deliverance ministry which has been a core feature of the PCM. In many cases they are styles of ministry that I have encountered first-hand through my own involvement in the PCM both in England and abroad.

Introducing Pentecostalism and the Charismatic movement

At the beginning of the twentieth century a movement emerged that changed the landscape of Christianity. The story of the beginnings of Pentecostalism has been told numerous times – the events associated with Charles Parham's Bible school in Topeka, Kansas, at the turn of the twentieth century, when Agnes Ozman received the 'baptism in Spirit' evidenced by speaking in other tongues after Parham prayed for her with the laying on of hands; and then more significantly with the African American William Seymour's meetings at Azusa Street in Los Angeles (1906–15). Azusa became a place of pilgrimage for dried-out ministers who returned to their respective homelands or places of mission with the 'blessing', and so Pentecostalism spread; missionaries were sent out from Asuza announcing the 'full gospel' – an integral part being that Christ was not only the Saviour but also the baptizer in Holy Spirit – and the flames went further afield.[1]

---

[1]   See Robert Owens and Gary McGee in their respective essays on the beginning of Pentecostalism (ch. 3) and the global expansion of it (ch. 4) in V. Synan (ed.), *The Century of*

To begin with, the 'fire fell' within existing churches; a famous example in Britain was an Anglican church in Sunderland headed by the Reverend Alexander Boddy (1854–1930). Yet, given the controversial nature of the Pentecostal experience associated with speaking in other tongues, Christians of all stripes were suspicious and some even denounced the movement as satanic. Many 'Spirit-baptized' Christians were forced out of their existing denominations, and a sense of 'us' and 'them' began to dominate. Numerous Pentecostal churches were started, most prominent of which in the UK were the Assemblies of God, Elim and the Apostolic Faith Church. In the USA, the Assemblies of God, the Pentecostal Church of God and the Foursquare Gospel Church quickly gained prominence. For many Pentecostals, most denominational churches were 'dead' and people were to be called out of them; the common mainstream perspective was that these Pentecostals were fanatical and even deceived.

Although there were some notable exceptions, the general attitude towards Pentecostals for the first half of the century was one of disdain. The tide began to turn, though, in the 1950s. The late missionary bishop, Lesslie Newbigin (1909–98), in his prophetic work *The Household of God*, first published in 1953,[2] identified three distinctive streams in the Church catholic that were essential to the nature of the Church and had their origins within the initial community of Christ. These were the Catholic, the Protestant and the Pentecostal. His was a radical approach as it gave weight to the burgeoning Pentecostal movement that was spreading like wildfire across the globe.

It was during the 1950s that Pentecostalism began to re-emerge in the older denominations. Within 20 years there were numerous denominationally faithful Roman Catholics, Anglicans, Presbyterians and Baptists, all declaring that they had been baptized in the Spirit and were manifesting the same spiritual gifts/charisms written about by the apostle Paul in 1 Corinthians 12.[3] This embracing of Pentecostalism by the denominations

---

the Holy Spirit: 100 Years of Pentecostal and Charismatic Renewal, 1901–2001 (Nashville, TN: Thomas Nelson, 2001).

[2] Lesslie Newbigin, *The Household of God: Lectures in the Nature of the Church* (London: SCM Press, 1953).

[3] The relevant section is verses 7–10: 'Now to each one the manifestation of the Spirit is given for the common good. To one there is given through the Spirit a message of wisdom, to another a message of knowledge by means of the same Spirit, to another faith by the same Spirit, to another gifts of healing by that one Spirit, to another miraculous powers, to another prophecy, to another distinguishing between spirits, to another speaking in different kinds of tongues, and to still another the interpretation of tongues.' (Unless otherwise noted, all Scripture quotations in this chapter are taken from the New International Version (NIV).)

has become known as the Charismatic movement. Alongside this impact upon the denominations at a local level, there were increasingly positive notes being made about it by senior figures within the historic churches. Pentecostalism was gaining in respectability. This may well have been due in part to the fact that many who headed up the Charismatic movement were well-educated and often respected clerics within their denomination; furthermore, they tended to utilize the gifts in ways which fitted into their denominational liturgies and services. Scholarship started to emerge that gave credence to Charismatic convictions.[4] Today there are Pentecostal scholarly journals, and the scope of the movement's influence can be seen in the way that churches from a multiplicity of denominations use the theologically Charismatic Evangelical course, Alpha, to both lead people to faith and catechize Christians.

By all accounts the speed and size of growth of this movement is unparalleled in world Christianity:

> The Pentecostal and Charismatic movements in all their multifaceted variety constitute the fastest growing group of churches within Christianity today. According to some often-quoted estimates there are over five hundred million adherents worldwide, found in almost every country in the world.[5]

This number can be classified into three distinct groups:[6]

1 Historic Pentecostal denominations such as the Assemblies of God, Elim, Church of God in Christ. These are those churches begun prior to 1950 which were connected with Charles Parham and the later Asuza Street revival, emphasizing 'tongues' as the sign of being baptized in the Spirit.
2 Historic denominational Charismatic – those who believe in the ongoing charisms and ministries of the Spirit found in the older churches such as within the Roman Catholic, Orthodox, Anglican and Baptist churches since 1950. To begin with, they tended to embrace speaking in tongues as the sign of being Spirit-baptized.
3 Independent Charismatic (IC) and Modern Independent Pentecostal (MIP) – for example, the Vineyard Church and New Frontiers would

---

4   Some notable examples were George Eldon Ladd's theology of the kingdom and James Dunn's work on the Spirit in the New Testament.
5   A. Anderson, *An Introduction to Pentecostalism: Global Charismatic Christianity* (Cambridge: Cambridge University Press, 2004), p. 1.
6   As I have done elsewhere in more detail; see B. G. McNair Scott, *Apostles Today: Making Sense of Contemporary Charismatic Apostolates. A Historical and Theological Appraisal* (Eugene, OR: Pickwick, 2014), 5–7. For a different classification that divides up PCM groups into three waves, see David B. Barrett, 'Worldwide', ch. 15 in Synan (ed.), *Century*.

be described as IC, and the Redeemed Christian Church of God as MIP. These are churches that have started post-1950 and which embrace Pentecostal gifts and ministries. The Independent Charismatics do not necessarily advocate speaking in tongues as the sign of being baptized in the Spirit, nor do they necessarily hold that event as occurring subsequent to conversion, unlike the Modern Independent Pentecostals. Within this milieu has been the emergence of 'apostolic networks'.

All of these are committed to certain facets of Pentecostal theology that came to the fore in early Pentecostalism. It is to these aspects that I now turn.

Pentecostal emphases

The Pentecostal movement has been marked by its emphasis on the person and work of the Holy Spirit in the life of the believer and in the community of the Church. To all Pentecostals, of whatever shade, there is a unanimous belief that the signs that marked the initial Christian community as recorded in the book of Acts and referred to in the Epistles are to be expected today. Whether it be the nine gifts of the Spirit written about in 1 Corinthians 12, or the ministries of the ascended Christ mentioned in Ephesians 4,[7] there is an expectation that these were not done away with in the first century: they are to continue until the Parousia. The experiential awareness of the Spirit and his charisms should be part and parcel of every Christian's experience in the here and now. They were never meant to be the preserve of the chosen few, but are for the whole Church.

This belief sets Pentecostals apart from ecclesial traditions that linked the miraculous charisms of the Spirit to godliness, whereby these gifts were only given to those individuals particularly marked by holiness. It also differentiated them from the popular Conservative Evangelical view that held that most of the charisms mentioned in 1 Corinthians 12 were done away with in the first century; this view is popularly known as cessationism and is alive and well in sectors of Evangelicalism today.

According to Spittler there are five implicit values that govern Pentecostal spirituality: the importance of personal experience; the importance of oral tradition; spontaneity; otherworldliness; and commitment to biblical

---

[7]   The relevant verses are 11 and 12: 'So Christ himself gave the apostles, the prophets, the evangelists, the pastors and teachers, to equip his people for works of service, so that the body of Christ may be built up'.

authority.[8] Although Spittler is indeed correct about biblical authority, there is no set Pentecostal–Charismatic view on Scripture. Nevertheless, the fact that Pentecostalism was born in an Evangelical culture that accepted Scripture as painting reality as the way it is and was wary of liberal interpretations, Pentecostals naturally assumed that the worldview of the New Testament was how things are. The usual Evangelical Protestant perspective of the supremacy of Scripture and the need to check all doctrines with it was carried over into Pentecostalism.

Within the Charismatic movement, due to its broad churchmanship there has been more diversity regarding approaches to Scripture, depending on which evangelical worldview one was convinced by – there are Pentecostal–Charismatic inerrantists[9] and those who see Scripture as divinely inspired but not necessarily without error in whatever it touches upon. There are Charismatic Roman Catholics who see Scripture in the same way that their Church does. However, across the spectrum Pentecostals and Charismatics tend to be united in having a high view of Scripture.

The usual Protestant suspicion regarding tradition also seeped into the early Pentecostal movement. Terminology or ideas that were not clearly evident from Scripture were questioned. For that reason, particularly in the United States, there was a reappraisal of orthodox doctrines concerning the Trinity, and there was the emergence of 'Oneness Pentecostals'. Nevertheless, most Pentecostal and Charismatic groups, aside from the Oneness churches, have adopted an orthodox view of the Trinity. Furthermore, most Pentecostal groups are Christocentric and have a strong pneumatology. There was a notable complaint in the late 1970s and early 1980s that there was not enough focus on the Father in Charismatic/Pentecostal circles – the Charismatic theologian and church leader Tom Smail (1928–2012) wrote a book called *The Forgotten Father* to highlight and correct this deficiency.[10] This lack of emphasis seems now to be on the decline with a renewed focus on the Father, which has been particularly prominent within groups impacted by the Toronto Airport Fellowship, home of the 'Toronto blessing'.[11]

---

[8] R. P. Spittler, 'Spirituality, Pentecostal and Charismatic', in S. M. Burgess (ed.), *The New International Dictionary of Pentecostal and Charismatic Movements*, rev. edn (Grand Rapids, MI: Zondervan, 2002), pp. 1097–9.

[9] The belief that the Bible in its original manuscripts is without error.

[10] Thomas A. Smail, *The Forgotten Father* (Grand Rapids, MI: Eerdmans, 1981).

[11] This was a term used to describe the revival and phenomena associated with this 'outpouring' which many described as a move of the Spirit; like Azusa its impact was felt around the world

Pentecostals will often pride themselves on being both word and Spirit Christians – firmly rooted in the Apostles' Doctrine as found in the Bible (see Acts 2.42), yet open to the miraculous workings of the Holy Spirit. In this they see themselves as being true successors to the early Christian community. Nevertheless, the usual differences of opinion on eschatology, church government and most secondary doctrines are commonplace within the PCM.

Hallmarks of Pentecostal and Charismatic groups – style of worship

Despite the differences outlined above, there are usually tell-tale signs of a Pentecostal–Charismatic group. One of these is their form of worship.

'The experience of divine presence is foundational to Pentecostal-charismatic spirituality.'[12] There is therefore an expectation in the context of worship that God will manifest his presence in felt ways, often through the exercise of the charismata (spiritual gifts). It is here that Pentecostals expect to hear from God or experience God in profound, life-changing ways. Pentecostal worship is usually both exuberant and hallmarked by the raising of hands during sung worship; in some contexts there is dancing and banner waving too. The main exhortation is to worship God with one's whole being. Another feature in some Pentecostal gatherings is 'singing in the Spirit'; this is where the congregation are invited to sing out in 'tongues'. It is unintelligible, but many see it as an expression of Spirit-inspired worship.

Some caricatures of Pentecostalism present it as opposed to any form of liturgical and ritual worship as these tend to involve planning and take away from being open to the spontaneity of the Spirit. In this there is a notable affinity with Quakerism; although there is some truth to this picture in certain Pentecostal circles, the opposition to rituals is far from universal. The burgeoning Charismatic movement within Catholicism that has incorporated this spontaneity within the liturgical setting of the Mass is a clear rebuff to this caricature, as are the ways in which the other older churches incorporated the PCM.

---

with ministers travelling to Toronto to receive the 'blessing' and impart it to people back in their home churches. Others denounced it as demonic.

[12] M. Lindhardt, 'Introduction', in M. Lindhardt (ed.), *Practicing the Faith: The Ritual Life of Pentecostal-Charismatic Christians* (New York and Oxford: Berghahn Books, 2011), p. 8.

Pentecostal theology of ministry

As Anderson and other scholars have pointed out, it is very difficult to point to a definitive Pentecostal theology as there is much variation; the same is true in regards to the movement's theology of ministry. However, I believe there are certain facets that are shared across the spectrum of Pentecostalism, whether classical or neo.

The first is that the ascended Christ gives charismatic ministries to the Church. These are usually identified as constituting the 'fivefold ministry' and are listed in Ephesians 4.11 as apostles, prophets, pastors, teachers and evangelists. Pentecostals and Charismatics often differ among themselves on the exact nature of each of these gifts of ministry – particularly as regards apostles and prophets – but they are convinced that Christ is still giving them. If someone is called to any of these ministries or any other ministry in the body of Christ, that person needs to be empowered by the Spirit. It is expected that all Spirit-filled or Spirit-baptized members will manifest spiritual gifts; usually attention is drawn towards the various charisms mentioned in 1 Corinthians 12.

Second, the purpose of these gifts is twofold – first to build up the Church so that it reaches maturity. As Paul states in Ephesians 4:11–13:

> So Christ himself gave the apostles, the prophets, the evangelists, the pastors and teachers, to equip his people for works of service, so that the body of Christ may be built up until we all reach unity in the faith and in the knowledge of the Son of God and become mature, attaining to the whole measure of the fullness of Christ.

A similar sentiment regarding the benefit given to the church community by spiritual gifts is present in 1 Corinthians 12:7: 'Now to each one the manifestation of the Spirit is given for the common good.' Second, the gifts of the Spirit and the ministries of the ascended Christ are to enable the Church to bear witness to the salvation and lordship of Jesus in accordance with the purpose of the empowering of the Spirit: 'But you will receive power when the Holy Spirit comes on you; and you will be my witnesses' (Acts 1.8).

Pentecostal ministry – examples from the past and present

The Pentecostal and Charismatic movements have a rich history of characters from a variety of backgrounds. Already there are a number of leaders to whom current Pentecostals wistfully look back. Numerous hagiographical accounts of their deeds and ministry style have been recounted.

Some of the early celebrities of Pentecostalism are figures such as John G. Lake (1870–1935), Smith Wigglesworth (1859–1947), Aimee Semple McPherson (1890–1944) and Maria Woodworth Etter (1844–1924).

Later figures who have joined these Pentecostal legends include Kathryn Kuhlman (1907–76), T. L. Osborne (1923–2013), Oral Roberts (1918–2009) and John Wimber (1934–97). In the main these individuals continued in the American Revivalist 'platform minister' approach familiarized through Evangelical ministers such as Charles Finney (1792–1875) and D. L. Moody (1837–99). All of their ministries were associated with healing and unusual miracles, including in some cases raising people from the dead. Many current prominent Pentecostal–Charismatic ministers seek to emulate the way in which these people ministered.

Pentecostal–Charismatic ministers have been quick to utilize modern forms of communication, whether it be radio, TV, Internet or podcasts, to propagate the gospel. As a result numerous ministers have achieved an international sphere of influence. Figures such as Benny Hinn (1952–) and Reinhard Bonnke (1940–) have been notably prolific.

Healing and deliverance in Pentecostal–Charismatic ministry – the theology

It is undeniable that one of the reasons why Pentecostal–Charismatic Christianity has grown so significantly is its insistence that Jesus Christ still heals today, that the miracles recounted in the Gospels are not parables but are instructive for how Jesus heals and can even be seen as a model for how Christians are to minister Christ's healing. They hold that Christ's charge to the Twelve to 'heal the sick' and 'drive out demons' (Matthew 10.8) is still relevant for today. The focus on this 'worldly' dimension has been criticized by certain Evangelical groups who see it as a move away from eternal matters; nevertheless, defenders of Pentecostalism have pointed out that this is easy to say from a well-fed Western perspective, but for those who are struggling with ill health and who do not have a national healthcare system such as that in the UK, the promise of healing is immensely attractive and a necessity for survival. Furthermore, Pentecostals often call people to repentance and to believe in Jesus so as to be saved from hell, and that is seen as the most important healing and deliverance.

There are pockets of Pentecostalism that are exploring and advocating a holistic approach to healing, in that they see Christ's healing applying to the whole of the cosmos as well as to the individual; some Pentecostal revivalists seek city-wide and societal transformation. However, it is usually the case that focus has been given to the individual seeking healing. The healing being sought is not necessarily bodily healing, and may be relief from emotional or perceived spiritual forces.

The high view and often literal interpretation of the Gospels has led Pentecostals to take the worldview of the New Testament very seriously. As a result it is common for them to believe that spiritual beings such as angels and demons are part of the created universe. From this, there has been an expectation that confrontations with spiritual evil are part and parcel of Christian ministry, as it was for Jesus in the Gospels, and for the early Church as recorded in Acts. Yet there is an assurance that Spirit-filled Christians come from a position of power over evil forces. Pentecostals are convinced that Jesus Christ is Lord, and that demonic forces have to bend the knee to the exalted King.

Alongside unclean spirits being confronted and expelled, there is a similar line taken on sickness. Jesus Christ came to liberate humanity – spirit, soul and body. A common view within Pentecostal–Charismatic circles is that just as Jesus bore our sins in his body on the cross, so he took upon himself our sicknesses, and it was by his stripes that we were healed. Although this belief did not originate with the Pentecostals – we see it, for example, in a number of writers associated with the 'faith cure' or 'healing' movement[13] – it has raised its head most prominently within Pentecostalism.

There are many Pentecostals and Charismatics who are reluctant to tie in healing to the atonement; their emphasis is more upon the charism of healing, and the presence of the Spirit, to bring wholeness to sick bodies and minds. The prayer 'Come, Holy Spirit' is often used to invoke the healing presence of Jesus.[14] There has been disagreement among Pentecostals about the satanic nature of sickness. Some see all sickness as satanic in origin and therefore believe that the demon behind it needs to be expelled; others have made a clear demarcation between sickness and demonic activity: some cases of sickness may well be demonic, but others merely a result of living in a fallen world.

A popular view within Pentecostal–Charismatic circles is that there can be blocks to the healing or deliverance of an individual believer. This is usually tied to sins that the believer has not repented of – whether it be unforgiveness or some other besetting sin, particularly involvement in the

---

[13] See Anderson, *Introduction to Pentecostalism*, 30–3.
[14] This prayer was frequently used by John Wimber and through his mentorship has gained prominence within Anglican Charismatic circles, particularly through the influence of Bishop David Pytches (1931–) and the New Wine network that he instigated.

occult. Some link a lack of healing to 'ancestral sins' or 'curses'. It is within this context that faith is often seen as vital – whether it is the faith of the one praying or the one seeking healing and deliverance.[15] There is often a tension between some Pentecostals who believe every sickness can and should be healed in the here and now because God wills perfect health, and those who allow for an element of mystery to why some are not healed.

Deliverance from evil spirits is understandably a contentious issue. Some Pentecostals see all sorts of sins as being the domain of demons and believe prayers of deliverance are needed, whether by the one who is demonized or the one ministering deliverance. Other Pentecostals believe that all sins have a spirit counterpart; therefore there are spirits of witchcraft, adultery and even homosexuality.[16] Yet others are very suspicious of this kind of talk and see it as an unbalanced view of the Christian's battle against the world, the flesh and the devil, and one which unnecessarily transfers the fight against the flesh to the demonic.

There has also been disagreement among Pentecostals about whether Spirit-filled Christians can be inhabited by a demon. There have been those, such as Derek Prince (1915–2003), who were insistent that Christians can indeed have a demon. Others see this view as damaging and unbiblical; this is the official position of the Assemblies of God, for example. Also in some Pentecostal circles believers avoid using the term 'exorcism' due to an association of that word with 'people using ancestral powers';[17] as a result they prefer the term 'deliverance'.

Healing and deliverance ministry – the methods

Pentecostals and Charismatics claim that acts of healing and deliverance can happen in many different contexts: in one-on-one meetings; through anointing with oil by church leaders; within church services; at crusades and large platform gatherings; even while out and about within the normal

---

[15] Influential authors exploring these themes are Francis MacNutt (1925–) and Derek Prince (1915–2003).

[16] Historically Pentecostalism has seen any expression of homosexuality as sinful. The majority of Pentecostal–Charismatic churches still take this line. However, there are exceptions; for example, The Fellowship of Reconciling Pentecostals International.

[17] J. Brown, 'Pentecostalism and Deliverance or Exorcism? Narratives from the Beneficiaries and Benefactors (*sic*) in Lagos, Nigeria', p. 15. Paper presented at the Nigeria Pentecostal and Charismatic Research Conference, 12–13 December 2011: <http://www.academia.edu/5210947/PENTECOSTALISM_AND_DELIVERANCE_OR_EXORCISM_NARRATIVES_FROM_THE_BENEFICIARIES_AND_BENAFACTORS_IN_LAGOS_NIGERIA> (accessed 14 April 2016).

daily routine of working life. Nowhere is beyond the reach of Christ the Healer.

There is a great variety of styles in the Pentecostal–Charismatic world when it comes to healing and deliverance.[18] For example, the Catholic Charismatic movement has often focused on the healing and delivering power of Christ in the Mass and has encouraged Catholics to receive Christ's healing when partaking of the elements.[19] The idea of being healed at the Lord's Table has also emerged in some Pentecostal churches as well, and I heard a prominent Elim Pentecostal minister speak of the Eucharist as a 'divine encounter', encouraging Christians to expect to encounter God when they partake.

Some Charismatic groups have delved into healing ministry through prayers of repentance on behalf of those in one's family tree.[20] There is also a large body of Charismatic literature advocating inner healing – healing of the emotions and memories. In this type of ministry Jesus is invited into the memory that has caused such pain, and people have recounted how they have seen Christ and heard him speak, bringing closure and healing.[21] Some Charismatics are wary of this practice and argue that we are not to go digging up the past, but rather stand firm on the truths of our identity in Christ which assert that 'the old man' is dead and has been buried and does not need healing; believers are therefore encouraged to meditate on these truths and allow them to set them free.[22]

What is common among healing and deliverance ministers is the belief that they should be under the guidance of the Spirit, submitted to Christ and open to manifesting the charisms of the Spirit to bring Christ's wholeness. In this regard the various charisms, mentioned in 1 Corinthians 12, that bring healing and deliverance are drawn attention to – such as the 'discerning of spirits' (this is often interpreted as giving the minister divine insight to identify what type of spirit may be oppressing an afflicted person); the 'gifts of healing'; the 'working of miracles'; 'words

---

18 For numerous case studies and examples across the continents and denominations, see C. G. Brown (ed.), *Global Pentecostal and Charismatic Healing* (New York: Oxford University Press, 2011).

19 See Robert Degrandis, *Healing through the Mass*, rev. edn (Totowa, NJ: Catholic Book Publishing Corp, 1994).

20 I have encountered this approach most often in Roman Catholic Charismatic settings, but Charismatic Anglicans Michael Mitton and Russ Parker have also promoted it; Dr Kenneth McAll (1910–2001) was the pioneer of this ministry.

21 John (1930–2018) and Paula (1931–2012) Sandford were renowned and influential authors and practitioners of this style of ministry.

22 This is a view advocated by the Charismatic leader, Colin Urquhart (1940–).

of wisdom' and 'words of knowledge'. Even 'tongues' and 'interpretations of tongues' and 'prophecy' are also seen as being able to be vehicles of God's grace of healing.[23]

Prominent healing evangelists, across the denominations, who minister healing will also tend to engage in deliverance ministry, and there is an evident overlap between the methods used. In the healing ministry there are differing prayers and actions that are commonly utilized; for example, petitionary prayers asking God or Jesus to heal an individual; and prayers of command where the sickness is rebuked in the name of Jesus and proc- lamations of wholeness are made, such as 'Be healed in Jesus' name.' Often these differing forms of prayer are accompanied by the laying on of hands to the sick person's body. If this is being done in the context of a large gathering, the minister may tell those present to lay their own hands on the afflicted area and repeat a prayer of petition or command. There is often a reliance on 'words of knowledge' (equated with the charism mentioned in 1 Corinthians 12) where the minister announces what he or she perceives God is doing; once these messages are given, the leader might invite those to whom that 'word' applies to come to the front and be prayed for.

Many of the above 'healing' techniques are replicated where deliverance is involved. However, in this arena there seems to be more diversity. In some African Pentecostal groups there have been some appalling abuses of this ministry – particularly when witchcraft has been suspected. Several doc- umentaries and journalists have highlighted how innocent children have been branded witches and have undergone inhumane 'exorcisms' involv- ing physical hardships.[24] The more balanced Pentecostal and Charismatic methods of deliverance are very different.

Some deliverance ministers will seek to minister deliverance in the same way as healing, that is, through prayers of command. In this approach they will usually speak directly to the spirit and command it to leave the per- son in the name of Jesus Christ. Some will lay on hands while praying this prayer, while others are wary of any 'spiritual transference' and will avoid touching the demonized person. The use of anointed handkerchiefs or other sanctified objects by the 'servant of God' may be a feature here; these are sometimes placed upon the demonized or sick individual in the belief that the 'anointing' will bring wholeness.

---

[23] For a full discussion of these various charisms see Mark Stibbe, *Know Your Spiritual Gifts: How to Minister in the Power of the Spirit* (London: Marshall Pickering, 2000).

[24] See BBC online article at <https://www.bbc.co.uk/news/resources/idt-sh/nigeria_children_ witchcraft>.

The most colourful forms of Pentecostal deliverance ministry occur in Africa. In countries, such as Nigeria, where Independent Pentecostal–Charismatic churches have grown exponentially, deliverance has been a key ingredient. In this context, believers may use unusual methods which many other Pentecostals see as unscriptural; for example, the afflicted person is encouraged to jump over a fire while the other members of the congregation repeat after the pastor, 'Fire, fire . . .'; or a troubled individual may speak his or her problems into water, which is then carried in a bucket to the pastor's office for his sacrificial prayers.[25]

A belief that has been common in some circles, particularly due to the ministry of Derek Prince, is that the expulsion of the demon from the human body is made evident through a manifestation such as coughing or vomiting. Other Charismatic ministers do not draw attention to this at all, and instead say that the focus is on faith and trusting that Jesus has liberated you, once you have followed the steps of repentance and faith. There is no focus on physical manifestations or even a belief that they will occur at all. This is a view I have encountered in the ministry of the influential ex-Anglican, now Apostle in the Kingdom Faith network, Colin Urquhart.

Another feature that has differed widely between Pentecostal–Charismatic groups has been their approach to spiritual warfare. The belief in Satan and the demonic seems nigh on universal among them, but exactly how these evil forces are to be fought against has not been universally agreed. Some groups have argued that spiritual warfare occurs through the preaching of the gospel and the prayers of God's people. Other groups have engaged in what has become known as 'spiritual mapping'. In this approach, intercessors or prophets or apostles are given revelation about the particular 'strongholds' that are preventing a certain community or ethnic group from believing in Jesus Christ, and then specific intercession is made: forms of repentance are enacted and prayers of command are prayed which are believed to change the spiritual atmosphere so that more people in those communities will embrace the Christian faith.[26]

In typical Pentecostal gatherings or revivals or missions, great emphasis is placed on the main platform minister. There is an expectation that God will use his servant to speak in God's name and operate in the charisms of the Spirit for the benefit of those gathered. Often people will come to these gatherings because of the reputation of the man or woman of God

---

[25] For a fuller description of these and other methods see Brown, 'Pentecostalism and Deliverance or Exorcism?', pp. 40–5.

[26] This was an idea popularized by Charismatic leaders such as John Dawson and Peter Wagner (1930–2016).

and a belief that God will meet people's needs by his Spirit through the 'anointed' minister. This format is remarkably consistent around the globe.

There is usually a set pattern within such gatherings. Aside from the usual sung worship, there is an exhortation to believe in God's ability and desire to address the particular need one is facing. Faith is encouraged through preaching from the Bible or testimonies, then the minister might ask afflicted people to perform some action that they could not do before they attended for healing, and if they can do this they are to come to the front and testify to their miracle. Another frequent occurrence is what is known as 'words of knowledge', whereby the minister will declare what he or she believes God is up to at that moment;[27] for example, the minister will announce that 'God is healing those with chronic fatigue syndrome right now', and those who believe they have been healed of that particular problem are invited to come to the front of the assembly to testify to their miracle. This is very much the method that Benny Hinn uses.

Throughout its history, Pentecostalism has followed on from the Faith-Cure movement and drawn attention to the 'prayer of faith' and the role of church leaders in ministering healing within the local church context. Focus has been put on the following verses from the epistle of James:

> Is anyone among you sick? Let them call the elders of the church to pray over them and anoint them with oil in the name of the Lord. And the prayer offered in faith will make the sick person well; the Lord will raise them up. If they have sinned, they will be forgiven. Therefore confess your sins to each other and pray for each other so that you may be healed. The prayer of a righteous person is powerful and effective.
>
> (James 5.14–16)

As a result it has been common practice for congregants to approach their church leaders in a state of penitence, and look to them to pray the 'prayer of faith' and anoint them with oil, so that they might be healed.

Although Pentecostalism has a rich history of ministers who purport to perform healing miracles in the name of Christ, it has also encouraged the belief that ordinary lay Spirit-filled Christians can be conduits of God's healing and delivering power. Kenneth Hagin (1917–2003) and others have written and preached about the 'believer's authority' to heal the sick and liberate the demonized.[28] Unlike the older denominations that have specific orders for exorcists – such as the Roman Catholic and Anglican

---

[27] This style of ministry was particularly associated with Kathryn Kuhlman and John Wimber; it is prominent in the ministry of Randy Clark of Global Awakening (1952–) today.

[28] Frances (1916–2009) and Charles Hunter (1920–2010) were prolific in this regard.

churches – Pentecostals tend to highlight the biblical assertion that it is ordinary believers who 'cast out demons . . . speak in new tongues . . . lay their hands on the sick [so that] they will recover' (Mark 16.17–18 NRSV). John Wimber was particularly determined to empower all Christians to 'have a go'. Many Charismatic churches were influenced by Wimber's approach and have trained up 'prayer ministers' who are on hand to pray for members of the congregation after or during the service, believing that God will speak prophetically through them, or minister healing or deliverance through them.

Bill Johnson (1951–) appears to have succeeded John Wimber as a charismatic leader with a very large appeal to Charismatics of all stripes.[29] His church, Bethel Church in Redding, California, has become a mecca for Christians of all denominations who are eager to learn from and be empowered to practise charisms, both within their church contexts and missionally. Bethel is very welcoming to all Christians; the evident desire at the heart of this church is for the universal Church to be instrumental in bringing 'heaven to earth'.

Generally, Pentecostals and Charismatics view healing as a charism of the Holy Spirit which are his to decide when and where they operate. Therefore, there is a stress on the need to listen to the promptings of the Spirit and only do what 'you see the Father doing'.[30] Alongside this has been the emphasis on faith – with some holding that sometimes a miracle can be initiated purely by the faith of the seeker. For both of these models Pentecostals look to the example of healings and deliverances in the Gospels and in the book of Acts. There we see cases where Jesus initiated healing,[31] and other instances where healing was requested of Jesus, causing him to respond according to the recipient's faith.[32] The weight placed on faith has often been a source of contention and even damage, where some individuals have been blamed for their continuing sickness due to their unbelief. However, many leading Pentecostal–Charismatic leaders have spoken out against this abuse.[33]

---

[29] Johnson is a much sought-after speaker internationally and has written numerous bestselling books.

[30] This relates to Jesus' confession in John 5.19 where he declares that he does nothing except what he sees the Father doing. Charismatic ministers see Jesus as their role model and attempt to imitate his methods.

[31] For example, John 5.1–9.

[32] For example, Mark 5.25–34.

[33] A renowned rebuke was Charles Farah's book, *Faith or Presumption: From the Pinnacle of the Temple* (Plainfield, NJ: Bridge Logos, 1979).

As is clear, Pentecostals and Charismatics do not limit the charisms to either revival/mission gatherings or even church services; there is an expectation that these gifts can be used in other settings as well. Therefore, exercise of healing and deliverance gifts may occur within one's daily sphere of work. John Wimber used to say that 'the meat is in the streets', emphasizing that the work of God was intended to be carried out not in safe church gatherings but in the context of mission.[34] With this in mind, various Charismatic Christians have set up special 'prayer rooms', do 'healing on the streets',[35] organize and lead Charismatic retreats, and hold counselling sessions, as well as being open to God moving in their day-to-day lives whatever the situation, trusting that God will bring healing and deliverance in each of these contexts.

The Pentecostal–Charismatic world is highly diverse, and core shared convictions regarding Christ's ongoing healing and deliverance ministry through the Church have been incarnated in the various cultures and denominations that it finds itself in, resulting in different styles of ministry. Nevertheless, the overriding belief is that Christians are engaged in a war against spiritual forces who are intent on distorting and destroying God's work,[36] particularly humanity which is made in God's image. Alongside this is the conviction that Christ is victor, and that the Church, as his body, in obedience to him is to be empowered by his Spirit and utilize his gifts to come to full maturity, as well as witness to his salvific kingship and demonstrate it through healing and deliverance.

Oft-quoted Pentecostal–Charismatic scriptures include the following:

You will receive power when the Holy Spirit comes on you.

(Acts 1.8)

He will baptize you with the Holy Spirit . . .

(Matthew 3.11)

They will speak in new tongues . . . lay their hands on the sick, and they will recover.

(Mark 16.17–18 NRSV)

---

[34] Mark Stibbe has written a book called *Prophetic Evangelism: When God Speaks to Those Who Don't Know Him* (Milton Keynes: Authentic, 2004) that seeks to build on this idea of using the gifts in mission contexts.

[35] An initiative that involves praying for the sick on the high street; see <https://www.healingon-thestreets.com>.

[36] The Scripture passages often quoted in this regard are John 10.10 and Ephesians 6.11–12.

Where the Spirit of the Lord is, there is freedom.

(2 Corinthians 3.17 NRSV)

To each one the manifestation of the Spirit is given.

(1 Corinthians 12.7)

God anointed Jesus of Nazareth with the Holy Spirit and with power . . . he went about doing good and healing all who were oppressed by the devil.

(Acts 10.38 NRSV)

The thief comes only to steal and kill and destroy; I have come that they may have life, and have it to the full.

(John 10.10)

'When he ascended on high he made captivity itself a captive; he gave gifts to his people' . . . The gifts he gave were that some would be apostles, some prophets, some evangelists, some pastors and teachers . . . until all of us come to the unity of the faith and of the knowledge of the Son of God, to maturity, to the measure of the full stature of Christ.

(Ephesians 4.8, 11, 13 NRSV)

Jesus Christ is the same yesterday and today and for ever.

(Hebrews 13.8 NRSV)

For our struggle is not against flesh and blood, but against the rulers, against the authorities, against the powers of this dark world and against the spiritual forces of evil in the heavenly realms.

(Ephesians 6.12)

At the name of Jesus every knee should bow . . .

(Philippians 2.10)

There is salvation in no one else, for there is no other name under heaven given among mortals by which we must be saved.

(Acts 4.12 NRSV)

25

Anglican theologies of ministry

TESS KUIN LAWTON

This chapter considers the theology of ministry in the context of Protestant and Anglican pastoral theology. Pastoral theology is a recent development in the field of practical theology and focuses particularly on pastoral care, homiletics and ethics. More recently, pastoral theology has started to work within a specific dialectic between what Martyn Percy has called 'the external phenomena of ministry and the internal realities of ministering', or the relationship between 'ontology and functionality'. My own work has looked at the relationship between systematic theology and practical theology and I have suggested that the history of Anglican ecclesiology offers the earliest typology of this method of doing theology. In the field of ministry, the Church of England has always held together three approaches: that of being the Church *in this place* (the parochial system), a continuing Catholic tradition of priesthood, and the Reformed understanding of priesthood as ministry. With this in mind, I shall be looking at three of the classic interlocuters of pastoral theology in order to explore their ideas and explain how they fit into the wider picture of Anglican practical theology. This chapter, then, will use an investigation into Anglican practical theology as a framework and then consider the work of Karl Barth (1930s), Michael Ramsey (1970s) and Gordon Oliver (2000s) within this context.

Anglican practical theology

'Practical theology' is a term which emerged in the German Protestant tradition as part of the academic theological curriculum in the late eighteenth century. It was the German Reformed theologian Schleiermacher (1768–1834) who defined the modern understanding of practical theology, which he saw as a set of techniques for governing and perfecting the Church, the 'crown' of a theological 'tree' whose roots were in philosophical exploration. Many people prefer the term 'pastoral theology' to describe the theological activity that undergirds and accompanies pastoral care. Of those theologians I shall be looking at, only Gordon Oliver self-consciously uses the term 'pastoral theology' and Karl Barth formed much of his own theology in direct opposition to the nineteenth-century liberalism embodied by Schleiermacher. Practical theology has tended to be preferred as a term that *includes* pastoral theology within the mainstream Reformed tradition. Scotland, for example, has had university departments of practical theology since the middle of the twentieth century. In England and Wales, practical theology was almost unknown and only came into the universities in the 1960s as 'pastoral studies'.

I would argue that practical theology is the Church of England's 'way of *doing* theology' (so, it's methodology). It is a very particular kind of practical theology; namely one which includes and builds upon a history of Anglican tradition and ecclesiology. Practical theology was defined by Browning in 1991 as 'the social and intellectual context in which theology is brought into conversation with the vision implicit in pastoral practice itself and with the normative interpretations of the faith handed down in the tradition of the Church'. Practical theology looks at doctrines of the Church and its ministry and 'refracts' them through the prism of a contextual hermeneutic.[1]

The ecclesiology of the Church of England is a complex matter, understood best (I would argue) through its history as well as through its official documents and liturgy. There are various strands of theology present. My intention has been to demonstrate that in the context of English history and society, Anglican theology has always been practical theology. It is therefore this contextual and historical hermeneutic which is offered by Anglican theology as a compatible methodological approach. Theology in process. An 'ongoing dialectic' between ontology and function. Thus, methodology, theology and ecclesiology are all interconnected; and the reconciling, dialogical ecclesiology of the Church of England is about living faithfully in accordance with both the gospel and the traditions of the Church.

There is a debate within the Church of England about whether it has any distinctive doctrines of its own. It sees itself as standing within a continuity of tradition and not as a separate confessional Church. When its history is considered, it seems obvious that the Church of England holds in balance both Catholic and Reformed traditions. I argue that there is such a thing as a distinctive Anglican theology and that it is best understood as

---

[1] Martyn Percy (2006), *Engaging with Contemporary Culture: Christianity and the Concrete Church* (Aldershot: Ashgate).

one of the earliest kinds of practical theology. Practical theology finds an historical home in the Church of England.

The word 'Anglican' is first found in the 1215 Magna Carta and later in the 1534 Act of Supremacy as part of the Latin term *Ecclesia Anglicana*, used simply to describe the whole of the Church as it was found in England. Of course, even before the Reformation there would have been different ways of being a church, depending on the people who had brought Christianity to any particular part of England. There is a temptation to think that the Church before the Reformation was in some way monolithic, which of course it was not.[2] So, *Ecclesia Anglicana*, as used in 1215, was already describing a broad range of liturgical practices and theological understanding.

'Anglican' appears as an adjective from 1650, although, like the term 'the Church of England', it simply distinguished the English Church and its members from other national churches and from the Roman Catholic Church. Indeed, the Church of England does not use the term 'Anglican' in any of its formal expressions of identity (e.g. the Declaration of Assent and the Thirty-Nine Articles). 'Anglicanism' was first used by J. H. Newman in 1838, as distinct from 'Protestantism'. Later he wrote: 'Anglicanism claimed to hold that the Church of England was nothing else than a continuation in this country of that one Church of which in old times Athanasius and Augustine were members.' As I hope to argue in this chapter, one essential aspect of 'Anglican' theology and ecclesiology is that it does indeed see itself as standing within a continuity of tradition and not as a separate, confessional Church. Since the first colonial churches became independent provinces (e.g. the American Episcopal Church, whose first bishop, Samuel Seabury, was consecrated in 1776 by the Scottish Episcopalians) and following the first Lambeth Conference in 1867, it appears from ad hoc usage that the term 'Anglican' could mean any type of Christianity which owes its origins to the Church of England and is in communion with the Archbishop of Canterbury. Hence why I have suggested that one important aspect of Anglicanism is that it is a synonym for 'the Church in this place'.

The birth of the Church of England is traced to the sixteenth century and the monarch of England, Henry VIII (1509–47). However, its establishment and development took place largely during the reign of Elizabeth I (1558–1603). When Henry VIII first sought to draw clear lines of control

---

[2] See Eamon Duffy (1992), *The Stripping of the Altars: Traditional Religion in England 1400–1580* (New Haven, CT: Yale University Press), particularly ch. 5.

over the Church in England, he was doing so against both the power of the pope and the influence of the new Reformers: he did not want to establish a new Church. Pope Leo X had granted him the title *fidei defensor* in 1521 in recognition of his book *Assertio Septem Sacramentorum* (Defence of the Seven Sacraments). This was also known as the 'Henrician Affirmation' and was seen as an important statement of opposition to the early stages of the Protestant Reformation, particularly the ideas of Martin Luther.[3] Although the doctrine of the reformed English Church was not regarded as differing in essentials from that of the other Reformed churches, 'the English Reformers were selective in what they adopted: justification by faith but not Luther's sacramental doctrine', for example.[4] The reforms during Henry VIII's reign seemed continually to chart a middle way between Rome and the Reformers. As Richard Rex notes in his *Henry VIII and the English Reformation*:

> the silent majority in rural England did not veer violently from one eccle-siastical allegiance to another as the Reformation followed its chequered course, but continued doggedly in the midstream of Christian tradition, holding as fast as possible to the central truths and continuities of practice.[5]

The Elizabethan Church was keenly involved in doctrinal debates but Elizabeth I was concerned particularly with national cohesion and consensus and allowed space for a wide range of theological opinion in what has been called a *via media*: establishing the foundations of comprehensiveness, tolerance and flexibility. The modifications of the Elizabethan Prayer Book, away from that approved in 1552, did 'seem designed to soften its more starkly Protestant features', and at the same time the reintroduction of vestments, of prayers for the dead, of saints' days and a wording at the Eucharist which allowed a Catholic interpretation of the Real Presence had a similar effect.[6] In this, Elizabeth may have been demonstrating 'typical English ambiguity', following in the footsteps of her father, Henry VIII, whose 'Ten Articles' (1536) are described as 'deliberately ambiguous' and 'sublimely imprecise' by John Schofield in his 2006 book, *Philip Melanchthon and the English Reformation*.[7] Elizabeth's Archbishop of Canterbury was

---

[3] See Paul Avis (2007), *The Identity of Anglicanism: Essentials of Anglican Ecclesiology* (London: Continuum), p. 168.

[4] Paul Avis (2002), *Anglicanism and the Christian Church: Theological Resources in Historical Perspective*, 2nd edn (Edinburgh: T&T Clark), p. 21.

[5] Richard Rex (1993), *Henry VIII and the English Reformation* (Basingstoke: Macmillan), p. 35.

[6] Duffy, *Stripping of the Altars*, p. 567.

[7] John Schofield (2006), *Philip Melanchthon and the English Reformation* (Aldershot and Burlington, VT: Ashgate).

Matthew Parker, a moderate theologian who was in charge of the revisions made to the Book of Common Prayer during Elizabeth's reign. The revisions clearly demonstrate a desire to tread a *via media* between the Reformed and Catholic churches; for example, Parker dropped the prayers against the Pope during the Litany. Parker was friends with Martin Bucer, the Strasbourg Reformer who had been corresponding with Cranmer since 1537 and the Regius Professor of Divinity at Cambridge. Bucer's writings were an important source of liturgical revision for Parker, and Bucer himself wrote a treatise of *applied* theology in 1550 (as a gift for Edward VI). In this treatise, he set out 'his mature vision of Christian Discipleship within a loving, responsible *respublica*'. Despite its publication in Latin, with French and German translations in the years immediately following it, this 'seminal treatise' was only fully translated into English in 1960.[8] This would represent the first ever example of practical theology in the Church of England. Avis argues that it is possible to identify two types of Roman Catholicism in the sixteenth century – conciliar and monarchical.[9] The Church in England went on to adopt a conciliar ecclesiology, despite the monarch's position as the supreme head of the Church. Thus, rather than being merely the result of political expediency, the Church of England can be seen as 'a distinctive inculturated expression of the Western Catholic Church, shaped by the conciliar and reforming movements of the late Middle Ages and early modern period'.[10] The Church of England, from its inception, saw itself as the Church *in* England; standing firmly within the continuity of tradition and charting a middle way between the Reformers of Europe and the authority of the Pope in Rome.

The context and background for Anglican theologians in the sixteenth century was often that of a practical (usually polemical) response to distinct problems as well as the attempt to define 'the very essence of Christianity', in common with so many other theologians of the period. Richard Hooker's *Laws of Ecclesiastical Polity* is still seen as the bedrock of Anglican theology and, as he interacted with both the leaders of the Roman Catholic Church and the great Reformers, he was the first to consciously argue for a 'Via Media'.[11] In Book III he was reluctant to attack Rome: 'Notwithstanding so far as lawfully we may, we have held and do hold fellowship with them . . . we gladly acknowledge them to be of the

---

[8] See *Oxford Dictionary of National Biography*. <oxforddnb.com>.
[9] Avis, *Identity of Anglicanism*.
[10] Avis, *Identity of Anglicanism*, p. 168.
[11] Book III, i, 4.

family of Jesus Christ.'[12] On the other hand, he also held John Calvin in the deepest respect and honour.

However, Hooker was uncomfortable when some radical English Protestants claimed that matters of discipline and government were 'matters necessary to salvation and of faith'. This doctrine followed inevitably from the Puritan view of Scripture as the absolute authority for prescribing conduct in every area of life, and made polity equal to faith. Hooker argues that Scripture cannot be understood entirely in terms of revelation. There are the 'essentials' of Christian faith (those things necessary to salvation) and the *adiaphora* or accessories to the Christian faith. These are the areas where the Elizabethan Church decided to exercise reticence and restraint (a phrase coined by Avis). For those matters on which Scripture is silent, the other two legs of Hooker's metaphor of a 'three-legged stool' must be used to work out the particulars. For Hooker, matters of church order depended on reason rather than divine injunction. His three-legged stool meant that the Church in England would always rest on 'Scripture, Reason and Tradition' and with it he was able to work out which supernatural (positive) laws were immutable (such as the sacraments) and which were mutable because their 'matter' alters with the circumstances (in Hooker's time, this would include the outward government of the Church). This was not seen as a radical new theology but simply a 'method' which could be applied to contested issues of the day. It was a method to distinguish issues of faith from issues of order, issues of doctrine from issues of polity. Avis describes this *via media* not as a bland compromise but as a struggle for survival: 'following the middle way was like walking a tightrope over an abyss.'[13] The ideal of moderation was not a lazy, relaxed alternative but an escape route passionately pursued. At the time of the Restoration, Joseph Glanville claimed: 'we are freed from the idolatries, superstition and corruption of the Roman Church on the one hand; and clear from the vanities and enthusiasms that have overspread some Protestant churches on the other.'[14]

Protestant theology of ministry: Karl Barth (1886–1968)

Karl Barth was understood to be one of the twentieth century's greatest systematic theologians, even during his lifetime. He held academic positions

---

[12]   Book III i, 10: I, p. 347.
[13]   Avis, *Anglicanism and the Christian Church*, p. 62.
[14]   J. Walsh, C. Haydon and S. Taylor (eds) (1993), *The Church of England c.1689–1833: From Toleration to Tractarianism* (Cambridge: Cambridge University Press), p. 58.

at Bern, Göttingen, Münster and Bonn, leaving Germany in 1935, after he refused to sign his commitment to the National Socialist Party, and returning to the University of Basel in Switzerland. He was not simply an academic, however, and his early training as a pastor in the Swiss Reformed Church informed much of his theology. It was this connection with his congregation which contributed to his rejection of the Protestant liberal theology in which he was first trained and which had become characteristic of nineteenth-century European Protestantism. He was also influenced by the biblical realism movement which writers like Kierkegaard were heading. However, it is impossible to fully understand Barth's theology without contextualizing him as a pastor and theologian writing at the time of both the first and second world wars. The support of many of his teachers and colleagues for the First World War led Barth to dwell on the dangers of liberal theology in identifying itself too closely with human expressions of the divine nature through culture and the arts – something which they believed they were defending by going to war. Their 1914 'Manifesto of the Ninety-Three German Intellectuals to the Civilized World' included the signature of his former teacher, Adolf von Harnack. Barth's work could not be labelled simply within the category of conservative theology of the time. Indeed, he seems to have understood his theology as dialectical (part of the dialectical theology movement, including Brunner and Bultmann), with a particular emphasis on the nature of divine truth as a paradox of both judgement and grace. He reaffirmed, above all, the sovereignty of God and the 'infinite qualitative distinction between God and mankind'. His most famous works are his commentary on the Epistle to the Romans and the 14-volume set (13 plus an index) of *Church Dogmatics* – the write-up of his classroom notes on dogmatic theology. The *Church Dogmatics* address four major doctrines: revelation, God, creation, and atonement or reconciliation.

Barth's writings on ministry are drawn together from a variety of different sources by Ray S. Anderson in his collected work, *Theological Foundations for Ministry* (T&T Clark, 1979/2000). As one might expect, Barth believes that 'the enquiry and doctrine of theology' are an essential element of ministry. Indeed, despite his fame as an academic, he argues that 'theological studies are not an end in themselves but, rather, functions of the community and especially of its *ministerium Verbi Divini*'.[15]

---

[15] Ray S. Anderson (ed.) (1979/2000), *Theological Foundations for Ministry: Selected Readings for a Theology of the Church in Ministry* (Edinburgh: T&T Clark), p. 46. All page references come from Anderson (2000) but are quotations directly from Barth's *Church Dogmatics*.

For Barth, theology is 'committed directly to the community' and in particular to those within it who are responsible for counselling, teaching and preaching. In this way, theology is the backbone of the local Christian community or 'the Church in this place'. For Barth, Christians have a duty to be theologically literate because this will 'lead them to face squarely the question of the proper relation of their human speech with the Word of God'.[16] Theology is therefore the only chance that humans have of understanding what their relationship with God should be. Barth makes a clear distinction between God and humans: 'even the most able speech of the most living faith is a human work'.[17] Humans can never understand God, except through God's own reaching down to them through grace. The purpose of ministry is to help others to 'respond to God's word'[18] through counselling, preaching and teaching. Human endeavour, through theological study, interprets the witnesses to God (the Bible) but it can never interpret the Word itself (Christ). In this respect, the best that ministers can do is to confirm and announce God's word itself.[19] Barth understands the Church as 'a community . . . destined and commissioned to proclaim the work and word of God in the world'.[20]

While Barth's theological emphasis on the sovereignty of God and preaching the word seems to be all-encompassing, he does talk about church growth in his section on the 'Growth of the Community'.[21] He does so by first considering the parables in the Gospels where Jesus talks about seeds and growth, and his conclusion is that while the '*communio sanctorum*' must grow,

> it can never be healthy if the Church seeks to grow only . . . with a view to the greatest possible number of adherents . . . this cannot become an end in itself. It knows of only one end in itself – the proclamation of the kingdom of God.[22]

The community grows 'up into Him who is the Head – Christ' and only because of him does the Church grow at all: 'His being is its being'.[23] It grows out of Christ and therefore in him. 'It accomplishes its own

---

[16] Anderson, *Theological Foundations*, p. 46.
[17] Anderson, *Theological Foundations*, p. 45.
[18] Anderson, *Theological Foundations*, p. 31.
[19] Anderson, *Theological Foundations*, p. 31.
[20] Anderson, *Theological Foundations*, p. 51.
[21] *Church Dogmatics* (hereafter abbreviated as *CD*) IV/2, in Anderson, *Theological Foundations*, pp. 641–76.
[22] Anderson, *Theological Foundations*, p. 265.
[23] Anderson, *Theological Foundations*, pp. 281, 282.

growth – in virtue of His real presence.'[24] There are echoes of Anglican ecclesiology, as well as an eschatological sense of the Church, when Barth talks of the '*communio sanctorum* as a provisional representation of the new humanity in the midst of the old'.[25] All this is done within the context of the Church as also being the '*communio peccatorum*', participants in the transgression and fall of humankind. Barth's emphasis is always on the omnipotent grace of God and the response of gratitude which is the proper response of humans to God. The Church is understood as made up of human weakness, and the preservation of the Church takes place because of Christ and in defiance of human sin. Barth warns of the twin dangers of 'alienation and self-glorification'. The one comes about when the Church is too outward-facing and listens too carefully to the world, the other when the Church starts to rely on itself ('self-assertion') rather than relying on the grace of God. Barth reiterates the idea that 'Christ is the community . . . but the community is not Christ, nor is it the Kingdom of God.'[26] The Church is always in danger of 'making itself like the world' by losing its focus on Christ. This is not to say that Barth does not believe that the Church is ultimately 'the Community for the World' but that he is always warning of the possibility of 'too close conformity to the world' if it starts to see itself as 'existing for its own sake'.[27]

Barth's theological outlook for mission is that the Church is 'called and appointed to the active service of God. Within the limits of its creaturely capacity and ability it is ordained and summoned to co-operate with Him in His work'.[28] The Church exists *for* the world, but must never conform *to* the world. Mission and discipleship are united, and Barth spends large sections of theological reflection considering the biblical references to the disciples as 'light of the world' and 'salt of the earth' and 'the good seed sown in the field.'[29] His work is profoundly, foundationally concerned with the word: made flesh, in Jesus Christ and preached, as the Living Word. There are no details here as to how the priest or minister is supposed to be involved 'in the world and for the world'. There is no discussion of how Christians should be involved with the homeless or refugees, no description of soup kitchens or charity fundraising drives. His work is systematic and theological.

---

[24] Anderson, *Theological Foundations*, p. 283.
[25] Anderson, *Theological Foundations*, p. 260.
[26] Anderson, *Theological Foundations*, p. 293.
[27] *CD* IV/3, as quoted in Anderson, *Theological Foundations*, p. 258.
[28] Anderson, *Theological Foundations*, p. 512.
[29] Anderson, *Theological Foundations*, pp. 500ff.

Yet, while it may not be practical, there is a deeply pastoral approach which runs throughout his theology, as he considers the theology behind 'The Growth of the Community' and 'The Community for the World'. He even writes about 'The Event of Divine Worship' at some length;[30] and it is in this act that he sees the synthesis between the Church and the world. For here is an act which represents the 'inward life of Christians' and yet must always be 'a public act at the centre of the community'. Divine Service, as Barth calls it, 'becomes a witness to its own being' because 'it exists and acts prophetically in relation to the world'. Inwardly, for the community of Christians, it allows a 'common confession of the One who has brought them all together', but its object is that the word of God is 'proclaimed and published and taught and preached and heard', and Barth ties this in to the moral dimension of church law.[31] Acts of worship are times when members of the community rehearse the moral law by which they are to live. The wooden tablets of the Ten Commandments placed in English churches during the Reformation springs to mind.

There is, not surprisingly, no reference in Barth to the sacramental nature of worship, but there is absolutely no doubt that the entire event is focused on Christ, present and made real within the community in the word. Interestingly, in none of Barth's work on ministry is there any reference to the single focus of the pastor or minister. The only focus for him is the Sovereign God incarnate as the Word. The way in which this is made real to 'the community' and to 'the world' is through preaching. Those who are called to preach, to teach and to lead are those with theological training and aptitude; for preaching the word is the most important role of the priest.

Anglo-Catholic theology of ministry: Michael Ramsey (1904–88)

Arthur Michael Ramsey was an English Anglican bishop and the one hundredth Archbishop of Canterbury (1961–74). In one individual he reflected the breadth of the Anglican Church; his father was a Congregationalist and his mother a socialist and active supporter of the movement for women's suffrage, and he is often described as 'an Anglo-Catholic Nonconformist'. His father was an academic, and Michael Ramsey went on to combine the twin vocations of preacher and teacher,

---

[30] *CD* IV/2, in Anderson, *Theological Foundations*, pp. 695–710.
[31] Anderson, *Theological Foundations*, pp. 335, 336.

taking professorships in Durham and Cambridge. Unlike Barth, however, the latter half of his career was within the Church rather than the university. However, his academic credentials meant that the foundations of his pastoral books are self-consciously and systematically theological. One of the concepts that interested him particularly was the Orthodox concept of 'glory', which became the heart of his 1949 book, *The Glory of God and the Transfiguration of Christ*.[32] Perhaps with his atheist academic brother Frank in mind, he was also prepared to respect what he termed 'honest unbelief', and when Bishop John Robinson brought out his seminal book responding to the secular revolutions of the 1960s, *Honest to God* (SCM Press, 1963), Ramsey engaged with Robinson's ideas very seriously.

Unlike Barth, who includes sections on ministry within his overall systematic theology, Michael Ramsey writes very specifically on ministry in his classic work, *The Christian Priest Today*.[33] Published while he was Archbishop, it also draws on his early work as a lecturer to ordination candidates at the Bishop's Hostel in Lincoln and his retreat notes for ordinands while he was Bishop of Durham. Where Barth's focus is on the whole community (more in line with Luther's 'priesthood of all believers'), Ramsey's focus is on the priest, whose duty is simply 'to make God real to people'. Within the Church the role of the priest is to promise 'to be daily with God with the people on your heart'. The primary emphasis, for Ramsey, is on intercession; the priest as 'man of prayer'. After that, the priest is a 'minister of reconciliation' (confession and absolution), a 'man of the Eucharist' (for the liturgy belongs to all the people) and a teacher and preacher.[34]

In this small book, Ramsey is anxious to remind those called to the priesthood that they are 'pledged to be dedicated students of theology'. This study need not be 'vast in extent but it will be deep in its integrity, not in order that [the priest] may be erudite but in order that he may be simple'.[35] In this respect, both Protestant and Catholic theologies of ministry are clear: theology is a vitally important starting point for those in the Church. Not simply as part of training but as an ongoing heart of everything a minister may do. For Ramsey (for whom the priest is also intercessor and absolver), theology is about study but also rest and spiritual refreshment. In a practical way, he states clearly that priests need 'sabbatical periods for rest' and 'greater provision both for study and for silent

---

[32] Arthur Michael Ramsey (1949), *The Glory of God and the Transfiguration of Christ* (London: Longmans, Green).

[33] Michael Ramsey (1972, reissued 2009), *The Christian Priest Today* (London: SPCK).

[34] Ramsey, *Christian Priest*, pp. 7–11.

[35] Ramsey, *Christian Priest*, p. 7.

retreat'.[36] On a day-to-day basis, priests should incorporate a day of study into their working week. Interestingly, this emphasis on the theological underpinning of ministry is lost in more recent works, as we shall see. This means the loss not only of a theologically educated priesthood but also of a refreshed priesthood. In arguing for a day spent reading and thinking and writing each week, Ramsey is also arguing for something profound to sustain ministry; the 'living water' which hydrates the body and soul. 'Study gets very irksome if you think of it as adding more and more items of knowledge to your bag. Think of study rather as being refreshed from the deep, sparkling well of truth which is Christ himself'.[37]

As well as this, the priest is 'a man of prayer' because ordination is about the promise to be with God 'with the people on our heart'.[38] Ramsey commends the Daily Office because 'we need to soak ourselves in God's historic revelation and redemption'.[39] Prayer, for Ramsey, is how the transcendence of God 'is to be found in the midst of secular experience and not apart from it'.[40] Prayer is the overlap between sacred and secular. Intercession is the synthesis of the dialectic between Church and world which so exercised Barth. In prayer, we mediate the love of God, for 'nothing that is human and nothing that is created lies outside the compassion of God'.[41] In a similar note, he counsels priests to 'beware of attitudes which try to make God smaller than the God who has revealed himself to us in Jesus'.[42] Priests must lead worship at which they hear confession and pronounce absolution, but this worship is always still part of the world: 'Our concern as Christians is with a divine order embracing heaven and earth, and with its reflection in every part of human affairs'.[43] There are echoes here of the contemporary Anglo-Catholic principal of St Stephen's House, Robin Ward, who argues that worship is a 'priority of time over space restored': 'Liturgical living is an ethical critique of any conception of time which is not eschatological and any conception of space which is secular'.[44] The theology behind Ramsey's writing is evident, but, without referring to specific situations, he is able to give clear practical advice to those ordained leaders in the community. This is Anglican practical theology at its finest.

---

[36] Ramsey, *Christian Priest*, p. 3.
[37] Ramsey, *Christian Priest*, p. 56.
[38] Ramsey, *Christian Priest*, pp. 14–16.
[39] Ramsey, *Christian Priest*, p. 15.
[40] Ramsey, *Christian Priest*, p. 17.
[41] Ramsey, *Christian Priest*, p. 23.
[42] Ramsey, *Christian Priest*, p. 25.
[43] Ramsey, *Christian Priest*, p. 40.
[44] Robin Ward (2011), *On Christian Priesthood* (London: Continuum), pp. 22, 26.

In this vein, perhaps his most memorable chapters are on 'Humility' and on 'Sorrow and Joy'.

In the twenty-first century, a significant amount of pastoral theology concerns the mental health of the priest or minister. In *The Christian Priest Today* there is no direct reference to this, except for the need to create spiritual space and to spiritually sustain yourself. However, the two chapters on humility, sorrow and joy are full of deeply practical advice to help arm the priest against 'this present darkness' (Ephesians 6.12 NRSV). So good are they that I lift them out of the heart of his prose and reproduce them here as a list:

> Recapture the sense of wonder.
> Let the griefs, pains and humiliations which come to you help you to
>   be a little nearer to Christ crucified.
> Think far more often about heaven.
> Thank God, often and always.
> Take care to confess your sins.
> Accept humiliations.
> Use your sense of humour.
> Our Lord will be there with the words, 'Peace be unto you.'

The final emphasis which Ramsey offers his readers is that of obedience; again, an approach which is not reflected in more recent writings on ministry. 'We are servants, called upon to obey. Has not the idea of obedience as a Christian virtue rather slipped out of our contemporary religion?'[45] Ramsey argues that the obedience of the priest should be concerned chiefly with being 'ready for the comings of Christ'. This is connected to the 'power to deal with interruptions'. Using the Advent Gospel and referring to 'loins girded' and 'lamps burning', he warns priests not to be 'encumbered. Be ready to move rapidly and unexpectedly . . . think in terms of the will of God.' So, discipline is in obedience to the will of God, 'both in what we know already to be his will and in what may at any moment be his will'. The priest must recognize God in all things, and in those frustrating interruptions to the day you have planned, you 'must be ready for the comings of Christ'.[46]

Twenty-first-century theology of ministry: Gordon Oliver

Gordon Oliver is also a teacher, although he has less of an academic pedigree than the two previous theologians covered in this chapter. In itself,

---

[45] Ramsey, *Christian Priest*, p. 62.
[46] Ramsey, *Christian Priest*, p. 67.

this may be telling. The theology of ministry today is coming from ministry and training departments of dioceses rather than university departments of theology. However, the contemporary theology of ministry in
the Church of England is deeply rooted in extensive parish experience,
whereas the Protestant and Anglo-Catholic models we have considered
were much less so. Also of note is the fact that Oliver offers retreats and
spiritual direction. Again, this seems to inform a very pastoral theology of
ministry, rather than a theoretical one.

The modern approach to theology may be characterized as a 'postmodern' one, in which a systematic metanarrative is spurned in favour of pockets of local stories. Anglican theology is able to embrace this with little
difficulty; as we have seen from its history, it has always been a Church
'in this place'. However, putting Oliver's work in the context of Barth and
Ramsey leaves one hungry for a more developed theological framework,
as we shall see.

Gordon Oliver's 2012 book, *Ministry without Madness*, is recommended
by the former Bishop of Oxford, John Pritchard, as being 'off centre (or
ex-centric), rather than colluding with the wisdom of the age'.[47] It has a
very different feel from other books on priesthood, and from its reception
(for example at a Readers' Conference in Norwich) it seems to act as a
very useful way of opening up people's own stories in ministry. Oliver uses
the postmodern hermeneutical tool of individual narrative as a means of
drawing his readers in and allowing them to reflect on their own situation;
and this method of sharing the stories of others proves to be a very effective way of broadening our understanding of the realities of ministry today.
The methodology of *Ministry without Madness* is to take a single theme
('madness' or 'the foolishness of God') and fit his writing around it. While
I have purposefully not assigned a label of 'Protestant' or 'Catholic' to this
theology of ministry, the use of 'themes' in this way is more reminiscent of
the Protestant approach, and the lack of reference to sacraments as well as
to confession and absolution reinforces this impression. Certainly, in his
book, we return to an emphasis on the sovereignty of God and the grace of
God; but Oliver offers what Barth did not: in his chapters on 'called to be
human', 'called to serve', 'called to lead', he gives us the detail which readers
concerned with ministry will be hungry for. His list, at the beginning of
his book, about the 'madness' which ministers can sometimes feel (and
there is a lot of emphasis on 'feeling', which is in line with the postmodern

---

[47] John Pritchard, 'Foreword', in Gordon Oliver (2012), *Ministry without Madness* (London:
SPCK), pp. ix–x.

perspective) is clearly drawn from many years' experience and there is an important authenticity about this. The appearance of this list at the start of the book sets out the framework for Oliver's thesis, but what saves it from being a self-help manual is the focus he continually wants to draw us back to:

> If the kingdom of God that Jesus called for could be organized into existence by church committees and mission projects, the job would have been completed long ago! However, the gospel we commend is not primarily about how we resource church-based processes, but how we live Christ-centred lives.[48]

It is these lives that Oliver wants to use to inspire his readers, and we hear many stories of such priests in the daily life of parish ministry, providing a genuinely fascinating insight into what ministry is like in twenty-first-century Britain.

Oliver's chapter on holiness is (unexpectedly) a chapter about the 'renewal of all-member ministry', and he begins it with a powerful visual image of the Eucharist:

> I hold up the chalice and as we all join in words of praise to God, I can see a distorted reflection of myself in the silver, and God whispers to me, 'Always remember, Gordon, this is for you as well as for everybody else.'[49]

This is a different perspective on Barth's single-focus theology of the word for the whole community, and a new way of looking at the 'priesthood of all believers'. Oliver's subsequent theological refection on several key passages of the Bible sets the priest firmly with the rest of the congregation in the journey towards holiness and this is an emphasis that can be lacking in the Anglo-Catholic theology of ministry. With one eye firmly on Reformation history, this natural corrective of Protestant and Catholic within the Anglican Church is something precious.

However, I am not yet convinced that this approach offers us the kind of solid theological basis for priesthood which we continue to need for today. The recognition of the need for practical and pastoral training for ministry can mean that formation for priests and lay ministers does not have the theological underpinning it could have. The emphasis on 'pastoral theology' has led us to a contemporary vision that can sometimes place more emphasis on the 'clay jars' than on the 'treasure' inside them, as ministers are encouraged to find 'our strength in weakness'. This

---

[48] Oliver, *Ministry without Madness*, pp. 21–2.
[49] Oliver, *Ministry without Madness*, p. 35.

may be the result of a healthy shot of realism, or it may reflect a lack of confidence, indeed even victim mentality, among those called to lead the Church today. Postmodernism has led to a fractured and 'feeling-centred' approach to ministerial training which encourages us to consider our ministry as 'friendship with Jesus' and 'foolishness for God'. It seems that this is what practical Anglican theology has become – a kind of benign seminar resource for those in need of a bit of uplifting positivity. This is not the 'living water' which we should be drinking from on a daily basis and which should act as the backbone of everything we are. Oliver does talk a lot about prayer and that is a hugely important thing. The examples of priests in trouble that he offers us are full of people who pray every day; for their congregations, for their mission, for their vision. And he does not hide from talking about bishops having nervous breakdowns and clergy who miss funerals because they are drunk. This is eye-opening and refreshingly honest and is one of the real strengths of the book.

As a biblical study, there is also a lot to commend *Ministry without Madness*. Oliver has two really beautiful reflections on time and rest. Here he is at his pastoral best. But being pastoral is not the same as pastoral theology and there is a lot more that needs to be done with this Bible study before you could call it theology. This book is written from the heart of a very good spiritual director but it is wearing the emperor's clothes of a book of theology. It is not that; and by pretending to be so, it diminishes what is on offer in the twenty-first century for priests. It dumbs down what the clergy need. The call of clergy to be 'publicly and locally human' gives the author lots of opportunity to talk about Jesus and the Incarnation, but it does not give us the solid systematic foundations of Barth or Ramsey.

Pastoral theology is a branch of practical theology. All branches of theology, whether theoretical or practical, have as their purpose to make priests 'the ministers of Christ, and the dispensers of the mysteries of God' (1 Corinthians 4.1 DRB). Current explanations of pastoral theology suggest that it presupposes other branches, including moral, historical, liturgical and ecclesiastical, and applies these various conclusions to the priestly ministry. If the Church of England can indeed boast of being the earliest formation of practical theology, then it has solid foundations to offer a variety of theologies of ministry in the twenty-first century.

26

The parish church

ALAN BILLINGS

In 1988, the Centre for Explorations in Social Concern, an offshoot of the Grubb Institute, published a collection of essays entitled, *The Parish Church?* The question mark was significant. The essays were by academics and church leaders, sympathetic to the idea of the parish church, who were concerned that its relevance to the Church's mission and ministry in the late twentieth century was increasingly questioned. Society, critics said, was becoming too secular and fragmented for the idea of 'the parish church' to make sense.[1] More recently the questioning has intensified as churches have reacted to the decline in attendances; contemporary writers in mission and ecclesiology often declare themselves either 'for' or 'against' 'the parish'.[2] All of which begs the question: what is a 'parish church' and how is it different from other types of congregation? That leads to further questions: if parish churches were lost, what, if anything, would that mean for both Church and society? What exactly is at stake?

The 'parish' church

The term 'parish church' has both sociological and theological connotations. From a more *sociological* perspective, a contrast can be made between a 'parish' and an 'associational' or 'gathered' understanding or model of a church.

The traditional churches of the Church of England are 'parish churches', organized territorially. The congregations of parish churches think of themselves as having a responsibility before God for all who live or work in the parish. The vicar is appointed to the 'cure of souls', as set out in the

---

[1] Giles Ecclestone (ed.), *The Parish Church? Explorations in the Relationship of the Church and the World* (London and Oxford: Mowbray, 1988), p. 3.

[2] See, for example: Andrew Davison and Alison Milbank, *For the Parish: A Critique of Fresh Expressions* (London: SCM Press, 2010); Justin Lewis-Anthony, *If You Meet George Herbert on the Road, Kill Him: Radically Re-thinking Priestly Ministry* (London: Mowbray, 2009).

Ordinal in the Book of Common Prayer (BCP). Worshippers pray regularly for the well-being of the whole parish and they hold the church building in trust for present and future generations of parishioners, not just churchgoers. They join local organizations that work for the good of the community, and commit time, energy and money to them. The parish priest leads the way, getting involved as much as he or she can in the general life of the parish. This is partly a pastoral ministry and partly what Wesley Carr calls an 'interpretive' ministry: the priest is a 'local theologian', helping congregations make sense of their context from a Christian perspective and using those insights to identify and support what makes for the common good in the parish.[3] A similar understanding can also be found in churches that are not necessarily organized by parishes but nevertheless have the *mind* of the 'parish church'.

A parish church generally has an ecumenical spirit, cooperating with other Christian denominations and participating in the Week of Prayer for Christian Unity. Since the arrival in the UK of large numbers of people of other faiths, that spirit has also extended to them as well. The parish church supports interfaith activities and joins with other faith groups in making the parish a better place to live for all. If there is a church school, it willingly accepts children of other faiths and seeks to accommodate their religious and spiritual needs, something that those of other faiths recognize and value.[4]

A parish church seeks the common good by opening the church door to as many as possible, working for community cohesion and making significant contributions towards building local social capital.[5] It reflects the spirit of Jeremiah, who exhorted the Jews exiled in Babylon to seek the welfare of the city, in whose welfare they would find their own (Jeremiah 29.7).

The 'associational' church

An 'associational' or 'gathered' church has a different starting-point. It understands itself as a group of Christians called together to worship God, to build up one another in Christian faith and to be equipped as an effective instrument of evangelism. Teaching is of particular importance

---

3 Wesley Carr (ed.), *Say One for Me: The Church of England in the Next Decade* (London: SPCK, 1992), p. 114.
4 'Jewish Head, Muslim Pupils – but C of E School', headline in *The Guardian*, 12 October 2015.
5 Alan Billings, *God and Community Cohesion: Help or Hindrance?* (London: SPCK, 2009), pp. 36–9.

because associational congregations want to make clear the difference between those who are inside the Christian fellowship and those who are not, and also recognize that some aspects of Christian practice – such as prayer – are not easy and require explanation and support.[6]

While an associational church may encourage its members to involve themselves in non-church activities in their locality, the real test of their faithfulness to the gospel is how far they succeed in bringing at least some of those they meet into the fellowship. They may pray for the people living around them, but they will probably pray that they too may soon come to Christian faith. Many associational congregations could relocate to another part of town and would not feel that their essential mission and ministry had changed significantly; other groups in the area might not even notice they had gone.

Historically, associational congregations have arisen in order to serve the needs of particular social and status groups.[7] In England, the Established Church was perceived as the Church of the upper classes. As the Industrial Revolution gathered pace, working people sought churches where they were affirmed and encouraged rather than put in their place. The BCP Catechism – a series of questions and answers that children learned by rote as a preparation for confirmation – taught working-class children that they should obey all that are in authority, order themselves lowly and reverently to all their 'betters', and do their duty 'in that state of life, unto which it shall please God to call me'. These were not the sentiments of those who were shaping the politics of the working classes through the trade unions and labour movement. Many Nonconformist chapels – 'gathered' congregations – have their origins in the attempt by working people to shake off this understanding of a fixed social order with them permanently at the bottom. More recently, the UK's urban centres have seen the growth of Pentecostal churches that have done something similar for the aspirations of mainly black Christians from Africa and the Caribbean.

'Ideal types'

Of course, what is described above are what Weber called 'ideal types' – ideal in the sense that they describe what a parish or associational church would look like if it only had the attributions of the particular

---

6   T. M. Luhrmann, *When God Talks Back: Understanding the American Evangelical Relationship with God* (New York: Vintage, 2012), pp. 132–56.

7   David Martin, 'A Cross-Bench View of Associational Religion', in Ecclestone (ed.), *The Parish Church?*, p. 44.

type. But most congregations share at least some of the characteristics of the other type.[8] In the United States, for example, where the various denominations have always competed among themselves for members, 'associational' church life has been the norm.[9] However, these churches may also play significant roles within the community, and one reason for people joining a particular church might be its ministry beyond its membership.

If we allow that these descriptions identify some of the principal characteristics that mark off the parish and associational churches, we can begin to see why those that belong to more associational congregations think that churches that have the parish mindset are now failing. If the test of faithfulness is church growth, then parish churches by and large fail the test. Almost the only congregations that seem to be growing in Europe are those that resemble the associational model.[10]

This raises serious questions about the future of the parish church. Before turning directly to that, we need to expand further on the characteristics of the parish church and, in doing so, draw out how these churches understand themselves *theologically* and what they fear could be lost if a denomination such as the Church of England were to abandon the parish model and become an organization of associational churches.

Four characteristics of the Anglican parish church

Using the Church of England as a paradigm, we can identify four marks of a 'parish' church.

First, a parish church is a broad church. For most of its history, the Church of England has sought to include as many parishioners as possible. It has learned to tolerate a range of theological opinions, hence it is both catholic and reformed. This is summed up in the Preface to the 1662 Book of Common Prayer:

> It hath been the wisdom of the Church of England, ever since the first compiling of her Publick Liturgy, to keep the mean between two extremes, of too much stiffness in refusing, and of too much easiness in admitting any variation from it.

---

[8] Max Weber, *The Theory of Social and Economic Organization* (New York: Oxford University Press, 1947).

[9] Grace Davie, *Europe: The Exceptional Case: Parameters of Faith in the Modern World* (London: Darton, Longman & Todd, 2002), pp. 27–33.

[10] Linda Woodhead and Paul Heelas (eds), *Religion in Modern Times: An Interpretive Anthology* (Oxford: Blackwell, 2000), pp. 1–11.

In other words, the BCP, like the Church of England, was a compromise, a settlement, seeking to secure the maximum agreement between people who did not necessarily see eye to eye on either the finer points of doctrine or ways of worshipping.

This has not always been an easy position to hold. There have been times when one party or another has sought to push an agenda, sometimes with little regard to the religious sensibilities of others. In the late nineteenth and early twentieth century, for example, the High Church Party sorely tested the tolerance of other Anglicans as they became more ritualistic and moved closer to Roman Catholic practice and belief. From the 1960s, zealous liturgical reformers caused deep distress in many English breasts as they made it difficult for people to find churches using the King James Version of the Bible (1611) or BCP services.[11] Something similar may be happening in the early years of the twenty-first century as more clergy pursue strategies of church growth and show an impatience with the idea of the parish church.

For the parish church, however, it is theologically important to be as inclusive as possible. What these churches seek to do in their communal life is to exemplify the gospel promise that there can be reconciliation between people who are different. If the only kind of reconciliation is one that demands that one party capitulates to the other in matters of belief, that is hardly good news. Christ breaks down the dividing walls of hostility but not by expunging all difference (Ephesians 2.14–16).[12]

In contrast, associational churches tend to have a much sharper focus on what can and cannot be believed and are less willing to tolerate within the congregation other points of view. This has the effect of segregating the Christian congregation from the rest of the community and making a pastoral and interpretative ministry beyond the congregation much more difficult. For most of its history, however, the Church of England maintained a broad and tolerant approach and this seemed to suit most English people most of the time. On the whole, the English have not been a people much exercised with matters of doctrine.

Second, what did matter to parishioners was to have the means of sanctifying the ordinary experiences of life – birth, marriage and death – without too much fuss and in a place where, from time to time, they

---

[11] David Martin, *Christian Language and Its Mutations: Essays in Sociological Understanding* (Aldershot and Burlington, VT: Ashgate, 2002), pp. 127–34.

[12] A. Skevington Wood warns of the limits to 'pluriformity' in A. Skevington Wood, 'The Local Church', in Howard Belben (ed.), *Ministry in the Local Church* (London: Epworth, 1986), pp. 11–12.

could be reminded of something that transcended the ordinary.[13] Douglas Davies calls these 'occasional congregations'.[14] The parish church was where *rites de passage* were available to people, even if they rarely came to worship at other times. The church building was also accessible even if, like Philip Larkin, people only visited when they were sure nothing was going on.[15] Larkin is an example of those who are relatively unmoved by the liturgy or message of the Church, yet are drawn to 'sacred space' – the sacred space of the familiar parish churches and their graveyards.[16] The parish church enables this differential participation.[17]

Some Christians from more associational churches find this puzzling. For them, faith occupies a great deal of their waking life. They find it hard to believe that other Christians are not similarly consumed or that their neighbours could be thought of as Christian at all if they are only occasional attenders.[18] But the reality is that most people across the Western world live without constant reference to religion. This is not to say that religion can never be of importance to them. There are moments when they may look for some transcendent meaning in their lives, especially at those mundane yet significant points where people feel compelled to come together: at the birth of a child, at the joining of couples in marriage, at someone's passing from this life, or at a time of personal or community celebration or memorial – harvest-tide or Remembrance Sunday. The parish church might be a 'subdued presence' in their lives most of the time, but it remains one of the few institutions that continues to make available deep reservoirs of meaning.[19]

The capacity of the Church to play this role should not be overestimated, but neither should it be dismissed. From time to time we suddenly see manifested this latent capacity of the parish church to touch lives, not just of individuals but of whole communities. In 2002, for example, a school caretaker in the Cambridgeshire town of Soham murdered two

---

[13] Roger Scruton, *Our Church: A Personal History of the Church of England* (London: Atlantic, 2012), p. 93.

[14] Douglas Davies, 'Priests, Parish and People: Re-conceiving a Relationship', in Matthew Guest, Karin Tusting and Linda Woodhead (eds), *Congregational Studies in the UK: Christianity in a Post-Christian Context* (Aldershot: Ashgate, 2004), pp. 150–66.

[15] Philip Larkin, 'Church Going' (1954).

[16] Alan Billings, *Lost Church: Why We Must Find It Again* (London: SPCK, 2013), pp. 65–8.

[17] Timothy Jenkins, *Religion in English Everyday Life: An Ethnographic Approach* (New York and Oxford: Berghahn Books, 1999), p. 37.

[18] A sensitive account of this type of Christianity can be found in T. M. Luhrmann, *When God Talks Back: Understanding the American Evangelical Relationship with God* (New York: Vintage, 2012), pp. 300–25.

[19] Scruton, *Our Church*, p. 3.

schoolgirls. The tragedy stunned people across the country, though especially in Soham. The parish priest, the Revd Tim Alban Jones, facilitated people coming into the church to say prayers, light candles, lay flowers or just sit in silence. None of this would have been possible had there not been a parish church, willing to serve the people of Soham at times such as this, and recognized by people over many years as an appropriate place to go – a serious place on serious earth but also a place where they would feel comfortable. This is the local establishment of the Church of England without which the national establishment might not be possible.

This is also a role played by traditional liturgies and language. The familiar liturgies of the parish church can even help those who have no religious faith at all. Baroness Mary Warnock, the moral philosopher and atheist, has written about how she is helped by formal liturgy:

> Moreover, some people at least, though they do not believe in a personal God watching over them, nevertheless sometimes need to behave as if there were such a being; their emotion may be a sense of generalised gratitude, a generalised remorse, a generalised sense of pity and sorrow for the sufferings of others. For many such people, of whom I am one, the rituals and the metaphorical language of religion, their traditional religion, are the most accessible and the most fitting expression.[20]

This is not a retreat into fantasy or nostalgia. But it only works if the liturgies are the traditional forms of service that have become familiar through settled usage over many years and the language is elevated. This is why attempts to 'modernize' the Lord's Prayer resulted first in a time of confusion followed by the loss of the prayer altogether from people's personal religious resources, especially of those occasional worshippers.

Sometimes a parish church can play a role in changing the destiny of an entire nation. In Leipzig, in what was then the German Democratic Republic (DDR), the Nikolaikirche, an Evangelical-Lutheran parish church in the city centre, kept alive an alternative to the state's atheism and became a meeting place for those who longed for a different future. The Monday Demonstrations, which began at the church, contributed to the collapse of communist rule and the reintegration of the two Germanies. Again, this was only possible because the Nikolaikirche was a parish church, whose priest and congregation were willing for it to be used in this way and prepared to welcome people of many faiths and philosophies, and none. Some argue that parish churches hold memories of a more sacred past

---

[20] Mary Warnock, *Dishonest to God: On Keeping Religion Out of Politics* (London: Continuum, 2010), p. 160; cited in Billings, *Lost Church*, p. 26.

'vicariously' for their non-churchgoing neighbours to call upon as need-ed.[21] If the parish churches were lost, that would be a significant loss to the wider society.

Third, a parish church tends to be relatively non-judgemental about the lives of those to whom it ministers. This has two aspects. On the one hand it means that Christians in these congregations are likely to be less dog-matic and more open to possible re-evaluations of ethical positions where a reasoned case can be made. There has been a shift in opinion in recent decades on such matters as divorce, abortion, the place of women in soci-ety, and gay relationships. On the other hand, it has enabled such churches to affirm and support those whose lives are judged harshly by society because they fail some moral test or other. Parish churches are more will-ing to leave judgement to God, who alone knows the secrets of hearts. As a parish priest I recall a single mother's self-worth restored because she was able to bring her child for baptism at her parish church. Though not a churchgoer, she was able to 'do the right thing for my daughter', who could receive God's blessing like other children. Sacraments are a 'means of grace', though not always in the way churches intend.[22]

This tolerant attitude of the parish church is captured very well in the words of a hymn by F. W. Faber. God's judgement is contrasted with human judgement:

> There's a wideness in God's mercy
> like the wideness of the sea . . .
> But we make his love too narrow
> by false limits of our own;
> and we magnify his strictness
> with a zeal he will not own.

This contrasts with the moral certainties of many of the more associational churches and the very directive pastoring that can sometimes be a feature.

Fourth, a parish church rests on a particular theology that is often described as 'incarnational'.[23] This is a more complex idea than is some-times supposed. It assumes other doctrines – such as creation, redemption and the idea of the kingdom.

---

[21] Grace Davie, *Religion in Europe: A Memory Mutates* (Oxford: Oxford University Press, 2000), pp. 59, 81.

[22] Alan Billings, *Secular Lives, Sacred Hearts: The Role of the Church in a Time of No Religion* (London: SPCK, 2004), pp. 41–59.

[23] Anglican theologians who particularly developed the idea include Charles Gore, William Temple and Michael Ramsey.

Christianity understands the world as a creation. It is no accident but is brought into being by God, who finds it 'very good' (Genesis 1.31 NRSV). Yet the world is also 'fallen' and in need of redemption. However, because God loves the (fallen) world, he sent his Son, not to condemn it, but to save it (John 3.17). Christ, the incarnate Son of God, is present in the world for a purpose – to redeem it. Christianity is a religion of salvation.

Jesus in his ministry speaks about redemption in terms of God's kingdom breaking into this fallen world. When a sinner repents, or the sick are healed or the hungry fed, the kingdom comes. Christ's followers are taught to pray that the kingdom may come, and much of his teaching, especially the parables, is about how the coming of the kingdom is to be recognized and made real.

This goes to the heart of the Church's mission. As Christ was present in the world not to condemn but to redeem, so the Church must be deeply immersed in the life of the world, a world that is often hostile to the things of God, as a channel of God's redeeming grace. This is the high calling of the Christian Church: not only to proclaim the message of salvation but also to be a means of bringing God's grace to others – to individuals, but also to communities, by pointing to and forwarding the kingdom. This is a dynamic understanding of incarnation – engagement for a purpose, not simply presence. In this sense the Church is an extension of the Incarnation, and the parish church is its local embodiment.

One persistent danger for the parish church in seeking to fulfil this mission is that its members over-identify with the culture in which it is set and succumb too easily to the values of the world.[24] They have to work hard to ensure that their love of the world does not blind them to the need for redemption. They must seek at all times not to be shaped by the world's values but to be transformed by the constant renewal of their mind (Romans 12.2). For this reason, Christians live in the world but are never completely of it: they live as resident aliens.[25]

The criticism of the associational churches is that they often have a very negative view of 'the world' – of human life and culture outside the Christian fellowship. They stand in judgement over it, losing sight of

---

[24] This is Clifford Longley's criticism of the Protestant state churches; see 'The Ideological Corruption of a National Church', in Ecclestone (ed.), *The Parish Church?*, pp. 53–63.

[25] This theme is explored in the second-century anonymous *Epistle to Diognetus*, in *Early Christian Writings: The Apostolic Fathers*, trans. Maxwell Staniforth (Harmondsworth: Penguin, 1980), pp. 176–8. See also Stanley Hauerwas and William H. Willimon, *Resident Aliens: Life in the Christian Colony* (Nashville, TN: Abingdon Press, 2008).

the wideness of God's mercy and the Church's vocation as an instrument of God's grace.[26]

The changing context of the parish church

The parish churches of England have a long history. They developed from the early evangelization of the country in the Roman period. Initially, the spiritual needs of those in the countryside – which was most people – were met by priests who were sent out first from monasteries and then, by the Anglo-Saxon period, from minster churches.[27] Preaching crosses, where people would gather to hear the priests' sermons and receive their blessings, can still be seen in some parts of the country. But over time, people in each locality – the administrative term was *parochia* – wanted a building in which to gather, a sacred space of their own, funded through tithes, where they could pray and hear Mass said, have their children baptized, get married and, in the churchyard, finally be laid to rest. The church became, therefore, the church for that parish. In this way, the parish system developed organically within a society where Christian faith was simply taken for granted.[28] By the twelfth century Britain had become a land of parish churches and the ancient parish church still remains a significant part of the landscape in much of rural Britain. After the Reformation, the Church of England retained the idea of the parish church, as did the Church of Scotland and the Lutheran state churches of Scandinavia.

The parish priest's interactions with his parishioners were many and various. As well as taking services, he could be a schoolmaster, a magistrate, a giver of alms, a dispenser of medicine, and so on.[29] George Herbert (1593–1633), the priest-poet, described the role of the Anglican vicar in a short manual, *The Country Parson: His Character and Rule of Life*, which clergy used as a guide until the 1950s.[30] From the late eighteenth

---

[26] Davison and Milbank, *For the Parish*, pp. 64–92.

[27] N. J. G. Pounds, *A History of the English Parish: The Culture of Religion from Augustine to Victoria* (Cambridge: Cambridge University Press, 2000).

[28] After the Reformation, the state Church assumed – in the words of Richard Hooker in 'Of the Laws of Ecclesiastical Polity' (1594) – that there was not a member of the commonwealth that was not a member of the Church of England, nor a member of the Church of England that was not a member of the commonwealth.

[29] Anthony Russell, *The Clerical Profession* (London: SPCK, 1984).

[30] Alan Billings, *Making God Possible: The Task of Ordained Ministry Present and Future* (London: SPCK, 2010), pp. 55–76. Other influential training manuals were Peter Green, *The Town Parson* (London: Longmans, Green and Co., 1919), and Charles R. Forder, *The Parish Priest at Work: An Introduction to Systematic Pastoralia* (London: SPCK, 1945).

century onwards, Herbert's parson is a constant figure in English literature until well into the twentieth century: Henry Fielding, Jane Austen,
the Brontës, Anthony Trollope, George Eliot, George Orwell, P. D. James,
Joanna Trollope – all write about parish priests. One thing that Herbert
insisted on, which was not always practised, was residence: clergy had to
live among the people they served. This contrasted with Methodist ministers who were expected to be 'itinerant', preaching the message and moving
on, as their founder, John Wesley, had done.

However, as the organic society began to break down, somewhere in the
late eighteenth and early nineteenth century, and the population began
to move from agricultural labouring to work in the industrial towns,
churches became increasingly 'associational', defined as much by social
class as by theology.[31]

By the middle of the nineteenth century there were almost as many
people attending Nonconformist as Anglican parish churches. This was
the verdict of the 1851 (voluntary) religious census which found that
out of a total population of almost 18 million, only 10 million were in
churches of any denomination on census Sunday – just over 5 million
in Anglican churches and 4 million in other Protestant churches. There
were only 383,630 Roman Catholics; the period of Irish immigration had
not yet begun. These figures led to a spate of competitive church building
in the industrial cities where the major absences were assumed to be.[32]
Many of these churches were far bigger than any conceivable local demand
might warrant, something that threatened sustainability.[33]

With the rise of the Anglo-Catholic movement in the later Victorian
and Edwardian period, there was a renewed emphasis on parish ministry,
especially in the expanding industrial towns.[34] The slum priests were resident and deeply involved in all aspects of the life of their communities.
They were as interested in the direction of sewers as of souls. But while they
were respected, they proved unable to win over the working masses, in part
because their catholic ritual was resisted, in part because they were often
from a very different social class, patrician and authoritarian.[35]

---

[31] This is reflected in George Eliot's *Adam Bede* (1859).
[32] Owen Chadwick, *The Victorian Church, Part One 1829–1859* (London: SCM Press, 1971),
p. 365.
[33] Robin Gill, *The Myth of the Empty Church* (London: SCM Press, 1992).
[34] E. A. Down, 'The Tractarian Tradition', in N. P. Williams and Charles Harris (eds), *Northern
Catholicism: Centenary Studies in the Oxford and Parallel Movements* (London: SPCK, 1933),
pp. 263–89.
[35] Francis Penhale, *The Anglican Church Today: Catholics in Crisis* (London: Mowbray, 1986),
pp. 74–8.

A fresh invigoration of Anglican parish ministry came in the 1950s with the Parish and People movement (1949–2013), especially on the new housing estates. Again, the focus was on building Christian congregations that were immersed in the total life of the parish. The Parish Communion became the central service where the people of God gathered Sunday by Sunday to prepare themselves for building the kingdom of God through their secular activities during the working week.[36]

But this post-war confidence began to falter from the 1960s when numbers attending churches across the West began to slide, the United States being the great exception.[37] In Europe, the further north, the greater the collapse, nowhere more so than in Great Britain and Scandinavia.[38] Church attendance is now at historically low levels, though some of this decline is exaggerated by people attending less frequently.[39] What especially worries the churches is the age profile of attenders. Churches are ageing. If that trend does not stabilize or reverse, it is thought, the Church might not be able to replicate itself.[40] But this may be too hasty a judgement. The population is also ageing and churches seem particularly good at drawing in older age groups and better at maintaining numbers when so many voluntary bodies have collapsed. This is not an age of mass memberships.[41]

There is an exception to the statistics of decline and that is the growth of the Pentecostal and more Charismatic Evangelical congregations, though this makes little significant difference to the overall numerical decline. At the start of the new millennium, some sociologists routinely wrote about this decline as 'terminal' and saw the collapse of Western Christianity as the precursor to the eventual global disappearance of all religion.[42] That confidence in the demise of faith is more muted now – though, paradoxically, as Martyn Percy has noted, 'churches believe in

---

[36] The origins of this lie earlier. See Donald Gray, *Earth and Altar: The Evolution of the Parish Communion in the Church of England to 1945* (Norwich: Canterbury Press, for Alcuin Club, 1986).

[37] Peter Berger, Grace Davie and Effie Fokas, *Religious America, Secular Europe? A Theme and Variations* (Aldershot and Burlington, VT: Ashgate, 2008), pp. 9–21.

[38] Grace Davie, *Religion in Britain since 1945: Believing without Belonging* (Oxford: Blackwell, 1994), pp. 45–71.

[39] Martyn Percy, *Clergy: The Origin of Species* (London and New York: Continuum, 2006), p. 78.

[40] Steve Bruce, *God Is Dead: Secularization in the West* (Oxford: Blackwell, 2002); Callum G. Brown, *The Death of Christian Britain: Understanding Secularisation, 1800–2000* (London and New York: Routledge, 2001).

[41] Robert Putnam, *Bowling Alone: The Collapse and Revival of American Community* (London and New York: Simon & Schuster, 2000).

[42] This seems to be the view of Steve Bruce and Callum Brown.

the steady decrease of public faith almost more than any other group'.[43] Religion has turned out to be more resilient than anyone thought and has seen off one secular rival – communism. There is a global Islamic resurgence, post-communist Russia has seen a movement back to the Orthodox Church, and in parts of South America, Africa and Asia, Pentecostal forms of Christianity are flourishing.[44]

The parish church today

The context in which the parish church in England now finds itself is very different from even 50 years ago when most people would call themselves Christians. On the one hand, there are now substantial and growing numbers of adherents of other faiths, especially Muslims, while on the other, the British Social Attitudes Survey found that the number of people who profess 'no religion' has been steadily rising, from 31 per cent in 1983 to 51 per cent by 2009 – trends that are also borne out by the two national censuses of 2001 and 2011. But the greatest threat to the idea of the parish church comes from a lack of confidence within the Church itself.

Some argue that 'for 350 years the Church of England has been haunted by a pattern of parochial ministry which is based upon fantasy and has been untenable for more than 100 of those years'.[45] It was never possible, it is claimed, for the parish church or priest to function in the way Herbert commended, but even less so in a fragmented, highly mobile, non-religious and plural society. Others have become mesmerized by the statistics of decline and lost sight of the theological argument for the parish church. The authors of the influential report *Mission-shaped Church* (2004) argue that the Church has become over-reliant on one model of church, the parish church, and must diversify. In particular, it must shift the focus of congregations to that of 'growing' new Christians.[46] As a result of that report, many dioceses and parishes began to make church growth their primary, almost their only, objective.[47] This has affected all

---

[43] Percy, *Clergy*, p. 77.

[44] Peter L. Berger (ed.), *The Desecularization of the World: Resurgent Religion and World Politics* (Grand Rapids, MI: Eerdmans, 2005), pp. 1–18.

[45] Lewis-Anthony, *If You Meet George Herbert*, p. 1.

[46] *Mission-shaped Church: Church Planting and Fresh Expressions of Church in a Changing Context* (London: Church House Publishing, 2004); Steven Croft, *Ministry in Three Dimensions: Ordination and Leadership in the Local Church*, new edn (London: Darton, Longman & Todd, 2012), pp. 3–9.

[47] See David Goodhew (ed.), *Church Growth in Britain: 1980 to the Present* (London: Ashgate, 2015), ch. 1.

aspects of church life and work – from forms of worship to the type of commitment demanded of attenders.

The report encouraged the creation of other types of congregation outside the parochial system, known as 'fresh expressions'. The idea is to bring together like-minded people with little or no prior contact with the Church – they could be students or artists or ramblers – in non-church settings, such as cafés or community rooms, to form a new type of Christian congregation. One northern diocese has described this re-focusing very plainly in a diocesan 'vision statement': 'The Diocese of . . . is called to grow a sustainable network of Christ-like, lively and diverse Christian communities in every place which are effective in making disciples and seeking to transform our society and God's world.' There is no reference here to parish churches and existing structures but to the creation of 'diverse Christian communities' held together as a 'network' whose main responsibility is 'making disciples'. Some of these groups will be existing congregations, refocused on church growth, some will be church plants and some Fresh Expressions. The focus shifts from the traditional pastoral concerns of the parish church to that of church growth and, as it does so, it has the effect of devaluing the parish church and losing its incarnational and kingdom-focused theology.

Eventually, this will fundamentally change the nature of the Church of England and its relationship to the people of England. The new congregations and forms of church have little room for many of those who previously found a home in traditional parish churches. One of these, the philosopher Roger Scruton, describes his kind of Anglicanism, the traditional Anglicanism of the parish church, as 'a quiet, gentle, unassuming faith that makes room beneath its mantle for every form of hesitation'.[48] This is not the kind of faith that the movement for church growth easily recognizes. The 'occasional' congregations of Douglas Davies are similarly dismissed, as are those people whose faith flickers on and off like a badly wired lamp – as Sir Andrew Motion, the former poet laureate and occasional Anglican, once described his own faith.[49] By giving little priority to the traditional parish churches, the Church of England is turning away from a large swath of the population that still values its ministry, even if they do not always value weekly attendance. Some might regard that as reckless.

---

48 Scruton, *Our Church*, p. 185.
49 Andrew Motion, 'I've Seen the Light. And It Flickers On and Off', *The Times*, 18 December 2010.

Conclusion

The parish church is different from many of the other churches along the high street. It has an outward focus, seeking to find evidence of God already bringing in his kingdom in the parish and working to further what it glimpses, often alongside those of other faiths or none. It seeks to encompass as great a diversity of Christian belief as possible and to provide a home for those who struggle with faith or who only look to it on occasions of particular need. The fact that it is still the subject of debate so long after the publication of *The Parish Church?* in 1988 says something of its resilience and the value that many Christians and non-Christians see in it. But some of the Church's contemporary leaders are less convinced, and that may be the greatest threat to its survival.

27

Contested Church: mission-shaped, emerging and disputed

JUSTIN LEWIS-ANTHONY

The naming of parts

To-day we have naming of parts. Yesterday,
We had daily cleaning. And to-morrow morning,
We shall have what to do after firing. But to-day,
To-day we have naming of parts.

The problem described in Henry Reed's 'Naming of Parts' applies to the emerging patterns of ministry within the Church of England in particular, and the North Atlantic Church in general, over the last 15 years. There is an absolute lack of settled knowledge. Nomenclature is disputed. Processes are undecided. Contributory factors are controverted. There is a perennial, and perhaps convenient, confusion between normative and descriptive when it comes to narrating the history, describing the situation and prescribing the solution.

For example: what is 'Mission-shaped Church'? How does it relate to 'Fresh Expressions of Church' (and how does that relate to 'Fresh Expressions', *tout court*?). What is 'Emerging Church', in a British context, or in an American or Australian context? How is that different from 'Emergent Church'? Where is the place of kingdom or liberation theology? How do 'base communities' or 'new mission practices' or 'new monasticism' intersect with these groupings? Do they precede or prevent the virtues espoused by Mission-Shaped or Emerging Church?

In a restricted format such as this chapter we will be unable to address satisfactorily all these questions, let alone answer them. But the fact that it is possible, almost 30 years after the beginnings of Mission-Shaped and Emerging Church, to have such a variety of basic, Naming-of-Parts, questions warns us that explorations are provisional and contingent. In other words, your mileage may vary.

Having reminded ourselves of the partiality (in all senses of the word) of this process, let us begin at a beginning.

The history and future of evangelism

In 1988 the Lambeth Conference of the Anglican Communion, realizing that the world was changing, passed Resolution 43, in which the churches of the Communion, in cooperation with other churches, were enjoined to make the closing years of the millennium a 'Decade of Evangelism', with 'a renewed and united emphasis on making Christ known to the people of his world'.[1] In the Church of England, despite the enthusiastic and public support of George Carey, Archbishop of Canterbury, the resolution was not successful: 'virtually nothing happened.' A combination of complacency and 'cultural blindness' meant that a 'back to church' mentality prevailed.[2] Robert Warren, in a mid-decade survey, demonstrated that the importance of the Decade's goal had been realized by some: 'The Decade of Evangelism has made a tremendous difference to our church. It has put evangelism onto the agenda . . . We still can't do it; but it is on the agenda.'[3] Neither ecumenical initiatives nor the 'Springboard' project had any positive affect on church attendance figures.[4] The Decade did not have its intended consequences: using a range of six different performance indicators (usual Sunday attendance, Easter and Christmas communicants, enrolled members, baptisms and confirmations), the best performing diocese in England shrank by 11.69 per cent and the worst by 30.26 per cent.[5]

---

[1] Lambeth Conference, 'Resolution 43 – Decade of Evangelism', Lambeth Conference Resolutions Archive (London: Anglican Consultative Council, 14 August 1988), <http://www.anglicancommunion.org/media/127749/1988.pdf>. The year 1988 is an arbitrary date to begin this history: George Lings chooses 1984, based upon his own direct involvement with church planting in the Church of England, but also mentions 1980, 1960 and 1910: George Lings, 'A History of Fresh Expressions and Church Planting in the Church of England', in *Church Growth in Britain: 1980 to the Present*, ed. David Goodhew, Ashgate Contemporary Ecclesiology (Farnham and Burlington, VT: Ashgate, 2012), 161–78.

[2] Lings, 'A History', 167.

[3] A woman deacon at a 'typical urban "middle of the road" parish' quoted in Robert Warren, *Signs of Life: How Goes the Decade of Evangelism?* (London: Church House Publishing, 1995), 42.

[4] Leslie J. Francis and Carol Roberts, 'Growth or Decline in the Church of England during the Decade of Evangelism: Did the Churchmanship of the Bishop Matter?', *Journal of Contemporary Religion* 24, no. 1 (January 2009): 68–9; Warren, *Signs of Life*, 51–2.

[5] See Table 1 in Leslie J. Francis, Patrick Laycock and Andrew Village, 'Statistics for Evidence-Based Policy in the Church of England: Predicting Diocesan Performance', *Review of Religious Research* 52, no. 2 (December 2010): 212. See also the summary in Clive Field, 'Assessing

In the middle of the Decade a report was presented to the House of Bishops in an attempt to determine a structural and systematic approach to church growth. *Breaking New Ground*[6] (*BNG*) was not admired at the time; Nigel Scotland was particularly harsh in his condemnation:

> A more honest description of its contents would be 'Entrenched in the Old Ground'! Like many other Anglican papers and documents, the report is weak because it asks no serious questions about the validity and appropriateness of existing patterns of ministry, ecclesiastical structures or mission strategies of the Church of England.[7]

This criticism came from a group closely associated with New Wine, a movement, network, conference and worship-style franchise with its roots in the Charismatic renewal in the United States of the 1960s and its base in the 'Anglican Renewal' heartland of St Andrew's Church, Chorleywood. Therefore, it is not surprising that, when the Church of England looked to capitalize on the lessons learnt from the failure of the Decade of Evangelism and the lack of traction that *Breaking New Ground* had found, it would look to a number of people closely associated with New Wine to revise the earlier report.

Mission-Shaped Church (*MSC*) was presented to the General Synod at the February meeting in 2004.[8] Its authors made clear that the root of *MSC* was *Breaking New Ground*, the 'first formal document in which the Church of England owned "planting" as a missionary strategy'.[9] But *BNG* assumed that church planting was a 'supplementary strategy';[10] that was not possible in the changing context of the mission field of England in the twenty-first century: 'The nature of community has so changed . . . that no

---

the Decade of Evangelism', *British Religion in Numbers*, 2 March 2011, <www.brin.ac.uk/news/2011/assessing-the-decade-of-evangelism>.

6   Church of England Board of Mission, *Breaking New Ground: Church Planting in the Church of England* (London: Church House Publishing, 1994).

7   Nigel Scotland, *Recovering the Ground: Towards Radical Church Planting for the Church of England* (Chorleywood: Kingdom Power Trust, 1995), 12; quoted in Ian Bunting, 'Anglican Church Planting: Where Is the Problem?', *Anvil* 13, no. 2 (1996): 108.

8   Graham Cray and Mission and Public Affairs Council, *Mission-Shaped Church: Church Planting and Fresh Expressions of Church in a Changing Context* (London: Church House Publishing, 2004). It was later republished in an American edition as *Mission-Shaped Church: Church Planting and Fresh Expressions in a Changing Context*, 2nd edn, Mission-Shaped Series (New York: Seabury Books, 2010).

9   *MSC*, xi.

10 *BNG*, v; *MSC*, xi.

one strategy will be adequate to fulfil the Anglican incarnational principle in Britain today.'[11]

The report was strongly endorsed by the authorities of the Church. The Archbishop of Canterbury, Rowan Williams, wrote a Foreword, in which he commended the 'wealth of local detail and theological stimulus' that could be found in *MSC*. In General Synod debate he was more forceful: 'I don't want to get too apocalyptic about it, but the point is that God has opened for us a door of opportunity for the growth and maturation of our Church.'[12]

MSC required changes in the way the Church of England structured itself, and those changes (technically 'measures', with the force of law for the Established Church) were swiftly prepared and presented. On the very same afternoon that Synod voted on *MSC* it was asked to consider GS 1528, a report of the review of the Dioceses and Pastoral and Related Measures Working Group, who understood their task to be 'to determine what legislative framework might best facilitate the Church's response for the future; enabling speedy and flexible responsiveness yet ensuring reasonable good order and accountability'. That 'future' was already intimately bound up with the ecclesiology and assumptions of *MSC*:

> we sought to build on the best of the past Measures, and provide for a new single, coherent Measure . . . that we believe will facilitate the development of our 'mission- shaped' Church, take us with confidence 'for the future' and last effectively 'for the years'.[13]

By the end of the year, the national institutions of the Church were able to boast, in an advertising insert to The *Church Times*, that the report 'has sold around 15,000 copies in 11 months and its impact is already being seen in dioceses throughout the country'.[14]

---

[11] *MSC*, xi.

[12] Rowan Williams, 'General Synod: Archbishop Remarks in the Debate on the Mission-Shaped Church' (General Synod, London, 10 February 2004), <http://rowanwilliams.arch bishopofcanterbury.org/articles.php/1832/general-synod-archbishop-remarks-in-the-debate-on-the-mission-shaped-church>.

[13] Dioceses and Pastoral and Related Measures Working Group and Archbishops' Council, 'A Measure for Measures: In Mission and Ministry' (London: General Synod of the Church of England, February 2004), ix, x. GS 1528 is no longer archived on the Church of England's website, but is accessible through archive.org at <http://bit.ly/GS15282004>. The quotations in the second passage are allusions to Timothy Dudley-Smith's hymn 'Lord for the Years', which appeared to be a controlling trope for the report's compilers.

[14] 'In Review: Update from the National Church Institutions', *Church Times*, 3 December 2004, 17.

What was in *MSC* to cause this impact? Roland Riem provides an even-handed summary.[15] First, *MSC* wanted to address three cultural trends: a 'shift from neighbourhood to network', the development of consumerism, and 'the accelerating suspicion of institutional religion in a post-Christendom culture'.[16] Second, and in parallel, there are three ways forward: the Church will need a 'diversity of structure', a 'call to discipleship' and a renewed understanding of the 'process of engagement'.[17] In other words, the Church must move from 'where?' to 'how?' to 'be with people where they are, how they are'. The call to discipleship is vital, to counter the previous confusion between 'attendance' and 'discipleship'.[18] The process is part of an appropriate methodology for a 'missionary church', which includes 'double listening' and 'context shaping the church'.[19]

This latter point is important. If the Church is properly seated on the fundamental doctrines of Christianity, the Trinity and the Incarnation, then context will not impinge upon the values held by the Church. The medium, in this case, will not affect the message. Thus, says Riem, the properly mission-shaped Church will be 'focused on God the Trinity' and worship will be central to that understanding; it will be 'incarnational', shaping 'itself in relation to culture' and not to the preferences of those who lead it; it will be 'transformational', changed 'through the power of the gospel and the Holy Spirit'; it will be a disciple-making organization, based upon calling 'people to faith in Jesus Christ'; lastly, it will be 'relational', exercising a real hospitality.[20]

This is a complete and systematic revision of the Church of England's self-understanding and understanding of its relationship to the mission field of England. So complete, that George Lings expresses it in a somewhat totalitarian manner:

> We think **we have arrived at generic principles** lying behind the creation of all authentic expressions of church. Ignorance about how to start is now

---

[15] Roland Riem, 'Mission-Shaped Church: An Emerging Critique', *Ecclesiology* 3, no. 1 (September 2006): 125–39. Another good and balanced summary of *MSC* can be found in the work of the Doctrine Commission of the Anglican Church of Australia; see Michael Stead, 'Introducing Mission-Shaped Church', *St Mark's Review*, no. 200 (2006): 3–7.

[16] Riem, 'Emerging Critique', 126. The references to *MSC* are 1–8, 9–11 and 11–12.

[17] Riem, 'Emerging Critique', 127.

[18] *MSC*, 12, 33.

[19] *MSC*, ch. 6.

[20] Riem, 'Emerging Critique', 128.

culpable, re-inventing the wheel is now unnecessary and all churches may review their existence in this light.[21]

MSC may have developed from a revision of a church-planting report, but its intentions were much greater than that. Its subtitle tells us so: 'Church Planting and **Fresh Expressions** of Church in a Changing Context'. It is this latter concept which carried much of the practical load and received most of the practical resources in the following years. But what are 'fresh expressions' of church? Simply enough, to begin with, they were the 'variety of new forms of church in mission [that] were emerging or being put into practice'. They are both manifestations of church planting and also 'attempts to make a transition into a more mis- sionary form of church'.[22]

Perhaps it was the association of *MSC* with the New Wine movement which sparked the earliest critiques. Certainly, New Wine felt 'vindicated' by *MSC*. As John Coles, then vicar of St Barnabas's, Finchley, said in an interview with the *Church Times*: 'It [*MSC*] has given official permission to what we've already been doing, which is fantastic ... We can continue what we've been doing with greater confidence'. Graham Cray 'has been part of New Wine since it began'. This confidence meant that 'New Wine could be forgiven for believing it holds the future of the Church of England in its hands',[23] not necessarily something which would recommend either New Wine or *MSC* to those suspicious of it.

Perhaps it was the totalizing mood of *MSC*'s introduction to the wide Church which engendered misgivings. I recall being present at a diocesan synod for Canterbury Diocese where we were told, in no uncertain terms, that old expressions of church must continue, but new expressions were not optional.[24]

Certainly, criticism came soon and swift. One of the first was John Hull's theological response to the report.[25] He identified one of the most glaring weaknesses in the original report, its lack of a rigorous theological under- pinning to its recommendations: even though the report 'revolves' around

---

[21] George Lings and Bob Hopkins, *Mission-Shaped Church: The Inside and Outside View*, Encounters on the Edge 22 (Sheffield: The Church Army, 2004), 4, emphasis in the original. Riem hoped that this was 'slightly tongue in cheek', although with Lings's assertion that *MSC* was a 'Copernican revolution' and a 'divine process', I think we should take it at face value: Riem, 'Emerging Critique', 128; Lings and Hopkins, *MSC: Inside and Outside View*, 18, 4.

[22] From the 'Introduction', *MSC*, xi, xii.

[23] Malcolm Doney, 'On Earth as It Is in Heaven', *Church Times*, 30 July 2004, 14–15.

[24] I couldn't but help think of Jedi Master Yoda: 'Do. Or do not. There is no try.'

[25] John M. Hull, *Mission-Shaped Church: A Theological Response* (London: SCM Press, 2006).

fundamental concepts of 'church, mission and kingdom', these ideas are not 'adequately clarified'. For example, there is no distinction made between 'the church and the mission of God'. Also, *MSC* says that the purpose of church planting is in 'creating new communities of Christian faith as part of the mission of God to express God's kingdom in every geographic and cultural context'.[26] But this begs the question of whether the Church 'is the object of the mission or whether, on the other hand, the church is better regarded as a servant or instrument of the mission'. In other words, does the Church create itself by both participating in the mission and being the goal of the mission?[27]

Hull concludes with a devastating attack on the overreaching goals of *MSC*. Because it arose from a revision of a church-planting report, in a time of great urgency, it was led 'into a missiology too expansive for the task'. It attempted to camouflage this stretching with 'a slightly absurd series of metaphors', and a collapse into bathos: 'The report presents us with this vision of the whole creation moving on towards the freedom of the children of God, so to speak, and then produces nothing more than a demand for more café churches.'[28] Its ambition was greater than its abilities. This was something that Davison and Milbank also noted, with less generosity: '*Mission-shaped Church* is the least impressive theological publication from the Church of England that either of us can remember . . . Fresh Expression literature has hardly engaged with contemporary theology beyond the popular paperback.'[29]

Martyn Percy noted how reluctant some of the Fresh Expression proponents were to concretize their ideas: a fresh expression of what? Very rarely 'of the church'. Too often, the 'church' 'as an institution . . . emerges as the problem . . . with all its trappings, miscibility, complex structures and organizational baggage'.[30] The 'fresh expressions movement is a form of collusion with a contemporary cultural obsession with newness, alternatives and novelty'.[31] It proclaims its newness through the use of a missiological idea first described in middle of the twentieth century:

---

26 *MSC*, xii.
27 Hull, *MSC: Theological Response*, 1.
28 Hull, *MSC: Theological Response*, 35.
29 Andrew Davison and Alison Milbank, *For the Parish: A Critique of Fresh Expressions* (London: SCM Press, 2010), 225, 18.
30 Martyn Percy, 'Old Tricks for New Dogs? A Critique of Fresh Expressions', in *Evaluating Fresh Expressions: Explorations in Emerging Church: Responses to the Changing Face of Ecclesiology in the Church of England*, ed. Louise Nelstrop and Martyn Percy (Norwich: Canterbury Press, 2008), 28.
31 Percy, 'Old Tricks for New Dogs?', 29.

Donald McGavran's 'homogeneous unit principle' (HUP). McGavran argued that 'people become Christian fastest when least change of race or clan is involved'.[32] This became aphoristic: 'people like to become Christians without crossing racial, linguistic or class barriers.'[33] *MSC* quotes from McGavran (p. 108), and notes that his model is controversial, but continues to endorse it: according to Percy, 'there is no deep difference between the missiology that McGavran advocates and that of the fresh expressions movement.'[34] It is not hard to see why it is controversial when the consequences of the following are considered:

> It takes no great acumen to see that when marked differences of color, stature, income, cleanliness, and education are present, men understand the Gospel better when expounded by their own kind of people. They prefer to join churches whose members look, talk, and act like themselves.[35]

As Stanley Hauerwas points out, the churches of North Carolina have embraced the HUP enthusiastically, with the result that 'eleven o'clock on Sunday morning remains the most segregated hour' in the state. This is not problematic because it offends 'democratic egalitarian assumptions' (though it does), but because it prevents the Church from being/becoming the Church: congregations so constituted [are not the Church] 'gathered and therefore [are] not able to properly worship God'.[36]

As Percy puts it, the HUP was subsequently widely discredited by theologians, and also condemned by missiologists for its focus on pragmatism, and its willingness to sanction narrowly constituted groups (on the basis of age, gender, race, class, wealth, etc.) as 'church', which of course then legitimizes ageism, sexism, racism, classism and economic divisiveness.[37]

Finally, John Hull avers that *MSC*'s endorsement of McGavran's principle of homogeneity is the 'basic principle of apartheid'.[38]

---

[32] Donald A. McGavran, *The Bridges of God: A Study in the Strategy of Missions* (London: World Dominion Press, 1955), 23.

[33] Donald A. McGavran, *Understanding Church Growth*, 3rd edn (Grand Rapids, MI: Eerdmans, 1990), 163.

[34] Percy, 'Old Tricks for New Dogs?', n. 12, 206.

[35] McGavran, *Understanding Church Growth*, 167.

[36] Stanley Hauerwas, 'The Liturgical Shape of the Christian Life: Teaching Christian Ethics as Worship', in *In Good Company: The Church as Polis* (Notre Dame, IN: University of Notre Dame Press, 1995), 157.

[37] Martyn Percy, *Clergy: The Origin of Species* (London and New York: Continuum, 2006), p. 38.

[38] Hull, *MSC: Theological Response*, 14.

Emerging as emergent

'Emerging Church' (EC) emerged sometime between 1996 and 2006, according to John Drane. In the 1990s the term at least 'would have been unknown'. By 2006, when the *International Journal for the Study of the Christian Church* devoted an issue to the idea, it was 'impossible to go very far . . . without encountering both the word and the reality which it describes'.[39] The reality it describes is that of declining religious observance, along with an accompanying, although not necessarily causal, rise in 'spirituality'.[40] The word, however, is subject to definitional dispute: this is partly because the Church that is emerging is just that – it is 'a work in progress'.

On one hand EC can be shorthand for a genuine concern among leaders of traditional denominations to engage in a meaningful missional way with the changing culture, and as part of that engagement to ask fundamental questions about the nature of the Church as well as about an appropriate contextualization of Christian faith that will honour the tradition while also making the gospel accessible to otherwise unchurched people.[41]

In this way EC is another way of describing Mission-Shaped Church (MSC), and Drane makes that explicit connection. However, another, sterner use of EC comes from Christians 'who have become angry and disillusioned with their previous experience of church'. These refugees, predominantly from conservative, fundamentalist or Charismatic churches, establish their own 'faith communities', which are fiercely opposed to the 'larger tradition' and 'often highly critical of those who remain within what they regard as the spiritually bankrupt Establishment'.[42] Drane sees a territorial division into these two, broadly defined types: the UK, Australia and New Zealand for the former, and North America for the latter. This is partly due to the 'free-market Christianity' that is more ingrained in North America, but it is also due to the failure of the leaders of mainline denominations to deal with the culture of North American society, and to foster

---

[39] John Drane, 'The Emerging Church', *International Journal for the Study of the Christian Church* 6, no. 1 (March 2006): 3.

[40] Drane cites the depth study of religion and spirituality conducted by Heelas and Woodhead in Kendal, and the earlier, longitudinal study by Hay and Hunt of adult spirituality: Paul Heelas and Linda Woodhead, *The Spiritual Revolution: Why Religion Is Giving Way to Spirituality*, Religion in the Modern World (Malden, MA; Oxford: Blackwell, 2005); David Hay and Kate Hunt, *Understanding the Spirituality of People Who Don't Go to Church: A Report on the Findings of the Adults' Spirituality Project at the University of Nottingham* (Nottingham: University of Nottingham Press, 2000).

[41] Drane, 'The Emerging Church', 4.

[42] Drane, 'The Emerging Church', 4.

any rigorous 'active missional engagement' with it.[43] There is, inescapably, a strongly admonitory component to EC.

Gibbs and Bolger attempted to describe and explore what might be emerging from EC. Through fieldwork and interviews they decided that:

> Emerging churches are communities that practice the way of Jesus within postmodern cultures. This definition encompasses nine practices. Emerging churches (1) identify with the life of Jesus, (2) transform the secular realm, and (3) live highly communal lives. Because of these three activities, they (4) welcome the stranger, (5) serve with generosity, (6) participate as producers, (7) create as created beings, (8) lead as a body, and (9) take part in spiritual activities.[44]

It is hard to see that this might be distinctively *emerging* (as opposed to the sorts of things that every church community has always sought to do), with the simple exception of the explicit citing of the community within a *postmodern* culture. The problem is seen in the interview Gibbs and Bolger quote with Ben Edson of Sanctus1,[45] an EC in Manchester: 'emerging church for me is quite simply a church that is rooted in the emerging context and is exploring worship, mission, and community within that context.'[46]

In an attempt to break out of this deliberate definitional circularity, Scott Bader-Saye gives us a typology of EC, as it appeared in 2006. However, as he warns even then, the conversation is 'fluid', which is why he finds the assumptions of 'improvisation' to be a useful hermeneutic.[47] Bader-Saye gives us three main categories: Evangelical Pragmatists, Post-Evangelical Emergents and Mainline Missionals. The first is EC as style: 'these evangelicals imagine [that Christianity – with its unchanging core beliefs] can be re-packaged in new cultural forms without changing the content.' It is a marketing person's response to the crisis of commitment. 'Emerging' is synonymous with '"hip" or "cool"', and hip or cool can be sold. Post-Evangelical Emergents are more concerned with the impact of

---

[43] Drane, 'The Emerging Church', 4–5.

[44] This is McKnight's summary of Gibbs and Bolger: Scot McKnight, 'Five Emerging Streams', *Christianity Today*, February 2007; Eddie Gibbs and Ryan K. Bolger, *Emerging Churches: Creating Christian Community in Postmodern Cultures* (Grand Rapids, MI: Baker Academic, 2005), ch. 2.

[45] Sometimes I think 'postmodern' means 'refusing to acknowledge conventions of orthography'.

[46] Quoted by Gibbs and Bolger, *Emerging Churches*, 42.

[47] Scott Bader-Saye, 'Improvising Church: An Introduction to the Emerging Church Conversation', *International Journal for the Study of the Christian Church* 6, no. 1 (March 2006): 13.

postmodernism on the content of Christianity: 'These communities exhibit a spirit of inquiry about doctrinal questions and spiritual formation as well as a desire to move beyond the traditional liberal-conservative divide.' The Mainline Missionals demonstrate how EC is not limited to subcultures of Christianity, but may actually question the '"maintenance" mindset' of denominational churches. A 'discredited liberalism' is being left behind along with 'the remnants of civil religion' in order 'to establish creative, postliberal, missional communities'.[48] The groups developing under the umbrella of MSC belong to this category.

Bader-Saye's is not the only typology. Scot McKnight gives 'five streams' of EC.[49] First, it can be 'Prophetic (or at least provocative)', content to use language and expressions of language which might be offensive to those who already describe themselves as Christian. Second, it is 'Postmodern', not as a simple 'denial of truth', but revelling in 'the collapse of inherited metanarratives'. EC can minister *to, with* or *as* postmoderns. Third, EC is 'Praxis-oriented'. It is more interested in ecclesiology than in doctrine, and this is expressed by worship, a concern with orthopraxy and a missional orientation. Worship in the EC is 'creative, experiential, and sensory'. It wishes to question previous assumptions about right living: '*how a person lives* is more important than *what he or she believes*.'[50] Missional means participating in God's redemptive work in the world (Romans 8.18–27). Fourth, EC is 'Post-Evangelical', which means that EC is uninterested in systematic theology, because 'God didn't reveal a systematic theology but a storied narrative', and it is uninterested in the boundary issues of Evangelicalism and Neo-Evangelicalism:[51] 'the issue of who is in and who is out pains the emerging generation.' Fifth, EC is 'Political'. McKnight celebrates EC's reputation as a 'latte-drinking, backpack-lugging, Birkenstock-wearing group of 21st-century, left-wing, hippie wannabes'.

McKnight's piece is polemical, designed to shock his fellow travellers in the EC movement as much as those on the outside (see his first 'stream'). There are other typologies available, such as the sixfold model of John Williams,[52] or the fourfold model of Bretherton and Walker.[53] This latter,

---

[48] Bader-Saye, 'Improvising Church', 13, 14.
[49] McKnight, 'Five Emerging Streams'.
[50] Emphasis in original.
[51] McKnight's terms.
[52] John Williams, 'Twenty-First-Century Shapes of the Church?', *Theology* 114, no. 2 (March 2011): 108–19.
[53] Andrew Walker and Luke Bretherton, eds, *Remembering Our Future: Explorations in Deep Church*, Deep Church (London and Colorado Springs, CO: Paternoster, 2007).

as a part of a short-lived 'Deep Church' seminar movement, attempted to describe 'what it means to be church in the contemporary context'.[54]

First, there is the attempt to develop, nourish and sustain a Christian life and witness beyond the boundaries of a congregation or 'identifiable church tradition'. This is the place we meet the 'believing, not belonging' cohort, identified first by Grace Davie, which subsequently has become such a vital part of model ecclesiologies.[55] Davie's thesis is 'crucial' to understanding this group, whose faith 'may be sustained through art and cultural events, domestic practices or small groups, or participation in occasional events such as Greenbelt'. For Bretherton and Walker, this group represents EC.

Second, patterns of worship and fellowship outside existing, denomi-nationally determined patterns may be called fresh expressions of church.

Third, inherited forms of church life (patterns of worship and fellow-ship) may be renewed, into 'patterns of mission and church life appropriate to the contemporary context'. This may include the examples in *Mission-Shaped Church* which are denominationally situated, or it may include extra-denominational patterns which seek to recover forms of worship and fellowship from within the tradition (implying, but not specifically, that this stream is where we may find new monastic practices).

Fourth, there is an attempt to affirm the distinctiveness of Christian beliefs, practices and identities despite the challenge of declining numbers and a threatening wider culture.

Bradley Long labels these four streams as, respectively, 'Emerging', 'Fresh Expressions', 'Mission-Shaped' and 'Inherited'.[56] But, as we have seen all

---

[54] Andrew Walker and Luke Bretherton, 'Introduction: Why Deep Church?', in Walker and Bretherton (eds), *Remembering Our Future*, xvii.

[55] Davie's thesis, that what people believe and what people do about and with those beliefs exist in a profound imbalance, was first expressed in a journal article in 1990, and then became an important component of a general survey of the role of religion in modern Britain. However, in the second edition of her book, she has removed the meme from the subtitle, stating that the use of the idea has become problematic, in that it 'separates one kind of religiousness (belief) from another (belonging)' and does not acknowledge that both can be '"hard" or "soft"' (2015: p. 6). Grace Davie, 'Believing without Belonging: Is This the Future of Religion in Britain?', *Social Compass* 37, no. 4 (December 1990): 455–69; *Religion in Britain since 1945: Believing without Belonging*, Making Contemporary Britain (Oxford; Cambridge, MA: Blackwell, 1994); *Religion in Britain: A Persistent Paradox*, 2nd edn (Chichester: Wiley-Blackwell, 2015).

[56] Bradley Long, 'How Is Mission-Shaped Church Changing Church of England Missio-Ecclesiology in the Light of Classical Anglicanism?' (master's thesis, MF Norwegian School of Theology (Det teologiske Menighetsfakultet), 2011), 17–18, <http://hdl.handle.net/11250/161172>.

along, the typology is not hard and fast. Bretherton and Walker indicate that the four streams all flow into one another: that is, there is intersection and overlap between 'Emerging' and 'Fresh Expressions', if not between 'Inherited' and 'Emerging', and so on. But something of the difficulty of precision can be seen in Bretherton and Walker's thumbnail sketch of the third stream, which 'can include the kinds of *emerging churches ...* [in] ... '*Mission-shaped* Church', that is, *fresh expressions*'.[57] One stream contains three of the four!

EC in its American expression is controversial and fissiparous. EC can sometimes appear to be a tattooed, latte-drinking version of the battles between the Judean People's Front and the People's Front of Judea. Attempts are made to distinguish between 'emerging' and 'emergent', although, as Kimball and Hunt acknowledge, the terms are 'essentially synonymous in popular understanding'.[58] And yet these distinctions within EC are very important for its participants. Tony Jones, at one time National Coordinator for Emergent Village (one of the main, 'organized' expressions of EC in North America), once disputed the motivations for those who asked the very question:

> people are making a huge mistake, methinks, because they are perpetuating the very modern mistake of separation and fragmentation . . . Note well, O Definers, you may define me 'out' of emerging or evangelical or orthodoxy, but beware, it'll be you next. Drawing lines and defending borders never ends well for the line-drawers because before you know it, someone has drawn a line right behind your heels and, guess what, you're suddenly on the other side of the line with me.[59]

And yet, in his book published the same year, Jones gives some 'working definitions': 'Emergent' is understood as the 'specifically new forms of church life rising from the modern, American church of the twentieth century', specifically 'referring to the relational network which first formed in 1997; also known as Emergent Village'.[60] In other words, 'emergent' appears here to be functioning as a form of 'virtue-signalling': '"Emergent"

---

[57] Bretherton and Walker, 'Introduction: Why Deep Church?', xvii, emphasis added.

[58] Dan Kimball, *The Emerging Church: Vintage Christianity for New Generations* (Grand Rapids, MI: Zondervan, 2003); Stephen Hunt, 'The Emerging Church and Its Discontents', *Journal of Beliefs & Values* 29, no. 3 (December 2008): 288.

[59] Tony Jones, '"Emerging" vs. "Emergent"', *Theoblogy*, 15 April 2008, <www.patheos.com/blogs/tonyjones/2008/04/15/emerging-vs-emergent/>.

[60] Tony Jones, *The New Christians: Dispatches from the Emergent Frontier* (San Francisco, CA: Jossey-Bass, 2008), xix–xx.

is the sort of thing that I and my friends like and are.' It is reminiscent of Ben Edson's definition above.[61]

Another sign of EC's contested status is the frequency with which its opponents and supporters have announced, assumed or explained its death.[62]

Expedient fruit

We must remember, as Scot McKnight told us, EC is more concerned with orthopraxis that orthodoxy (even though that is disguised under definitional disputations): 'By their fruits (not their theology) you will know them.'[63] The disputes about form determining content, which are so important to Davison and Milbank, Bader-Saye, and Barbour and Toews,[64] are not important to the exponents of EC–MSC. For them, as Bader-Saye perceptively identifies, there is a pragmatic imperative about the need for EC–MSC. So, taking that imperative seriously, what are the fruits of EC–MSC?

To begin with, the fruit was all in the anticipation. Steven Croft's presentation to the General Synod of the Church of England put this excitement well: 'Fresh expressions of Church are beginning . . . There is a tremendous range and spectrum. I hear about new ventures every single week, beginning in all kinds of different ways and places. It is awesome, what is happening.'[65] But now, 10 years, 15 years, 30 years on from the beginnings of the idea, are we able to measure the mission-shaped Church?

George Lings's hard work in studying the reach and impact of Fresh Expressions in the United Kingdom demonstrates the difficulties involved:

---

[61] An excellent treatment of the history of Emerging/Emergent/Emergent Village is in Adam Sweatman's as yet unpublished paper: Adam Sweatman, 'A Generous Heterodoxy: Emergent Village and the Emerging Milieu' (A23–139 Emerging Church, Millennials, and Religion: What Is the Emerging Church? Definitions and Constructions, AAR/SBL, Atlanta, 23 November 2015). For a history of the difficulties within Emergent Village, see Travis I. Barbour and Nicholas E. Toews, 'The Emergent Church: A Methodological Critique', *Direction: A Mennonite Brethren Forum* 39, no. 1 (Spring 2010): 32–40.

[62] Url Scaramanga, 'R.I.P. Emerging Church', *Leadership Journal*, 19 September 2008, <www. christianitytoday.com/le/2008/september-online-only/rip-emerging-church.html>; Anthony Bradley, 'Farewell Emerging Church, 1989–2010', *WORLD*, 14 April 2010, <www.worldmag. com/2010/04/farewell_emerging_church_1989_2010>; Tony Jones, 'Where Is the Emerging Church?', *Theoblogy*, 13 April 2013, <www.patheos.com/blogs/tonyjones/2013/04/13/where-is-the-emerging-church/>.

[63] McKnight, 'Five Emerging Streams'.

[64] Davison and Milbank, *For the Parish*; Bader-Saye, 'Improvising Church'; Barbour and Toews, 'The Emergent Church'.

[65] Steven Croft, 'Presentation on the Work of Fresh Expressions', General Synod of the Church of England, London, 27 February 2007.

'We simply do not know the overall total number of fresh expressions of Church started since the report but estimates of over 1,000 do not appear fanciful.' Some dioceses seem to be particularly good at encouraging these projects: 'Several dioceses have records of up to 100 alleged examples', but Lings is honest enough to say, 'I am sure not all of these are fresh expressions in the terms described in *Mission-shaped Church*.'[66] Later, he reveals that he ought to be sure of his suspicion: '"annual Christmas tree lighting service" is an entry on a recent database that entertains me most and convinces me least.'[67] It is obvious that some Fresh Expressions are merely 're-badging existing activities'.[68] The Church Army's Report on Fresh Expressions noted the methodological difficulty in overcoming this (self-)evaluation: 'In nearly all cases we have only one data source, the nominated leader of the fxC [Fresh Expression of Church] . . . we usually speak to only one leader and have no way of testing the accuracy of their perceptions.'[69] In a report from the following year, the definitional difficulties were addressed in an admonishing register. One thousand cases for 'fxC' were presented, and yet 54 per cent had to be excluded because 'there was a serious definition of what counted' and these did not conform to that definition: 'the term was being misused and devalued. This careless, and sometimes devious, usage needs to stop. Only then can helpful and more realistic expectations be arrived at.'[70]

John Walker has demonstrated convincingly that MSC began from the wrong place. The British Social Attitudes surveys of 1991, 1998 and 2008 showed that 'the proportion of the non-churched was much smaller, and the proportion of church attenders much larger' than the MSC report estimated.[71] This, understandably, should properly have had an effect on the proposal set out in MSC: rather, it developed 'an inaccurate and misleading model drawn from research with a quite different purpose'.[72]

---

[66] Lings, 'A History', 175.

[67] Lings, 'A History', 177.

[68] Lings, 'A History', 176. Incidentally, Lings's 2010 article in the journal *Anvil*, despite its name, is exploring qualitative rather than quantitative methods of measurement: 'Evaluating Fresh Expressions of Church', *Anvil* 27, no. 1 (2010): 23–38.

[69] Church Army's Research Unit, 'An Analysis of Fresh Expressions of Church and Church Plants Begun in the Period 1992–2012', Church Growth Research Project (Sheffield: Church Army, October 2013), sect. 3.2.4 Singularity of source.

[70] George Lings and Church Army Research Unit, 'Evidence about Fresh Expressions of Church in the Church of England: Key Messages from Research across Ten Dioceses' (Sheffield: Church Army / Archbishops' Council, February 2014), para. 4.

[71] The tables of comparison, 7.7 and 7.8, are in John Walker, *Testing Fresh Expressions: Identity and Transformation*, Ashgate Contemporary Ecclesiology (Farnham; Burlington, VT: Ashgate, 2014), 120.

[72] Walker, *Testing Fresh Expressions*, 122.

An example is in Walker's examination of Messy Church, one of the freshest of fresh expressions.[73] Although Messy Church was purported to be a bridging mechanism to bring adults into an expression of Christian faith, 'the adult participants who were not members of the organizing team did not consider themselves to be attending a church, despite the name and the overt Christian content'. Messy Church was a 'community service provision', which meant that the attenders had no interest in 'building relationships within the Christian community running the service' and did not do so.[74] What Walker has determined as constitutive of 'constructing a new Christian identity', namely, 'questions of self-perception, the internalization of Christian tradition and participation in a Christian community', would not happen in this Messy fxC.[75]

The difficulties of moving beyond participating in an activity to keep the children happy, towards constructing a new Christian identity (for individuals and communities), is seen in the *Talking Jesus* project research. A total of 2,545 English adults, screened for representation by 'age, gender, region and socioeconomic grade', were questioned to determine what English adults know and believe about Jesus Christ.[76] Among that group, 'practising Christians' were identified,[77] and were asked about the influences that had led to their conversion. The two largest factors were growing up in a Christian family (41 per cent) and attending church services (28 per cent). Only 1 per cent had become practising Christians as a result of 'newer forms of church such as messy church or café church'. Even more traditional outreach programmes (such as 'parent and toddler group, food bank') had been the pathway into faith for only 5 per cent.[78] The relative low percentage of fXC practising Christians cannot be explained by the recent introduction of fxC either. As the discussion booklet published to accompany the data says:

---

[73] George Lings, ed., *Messy Church Theology: Exploring the Significance of Messy Church for the Wider Church* (Abingdon: Bible Reading Fellowship, 2013).

[74] Walker, *Testing Fresh Expressions*, 204.

[75] Walker, *Testing Fresh Expressions*, 204.

[76] Barna Group et al., *Perceptions of Jesus, Christians and Evangelism in England (Executive Report)* (London: Talking Jesus, 2015), 4, <http://talkingjesus.org/wp-content/uploads/2018/04/Perceptions-of-Jesus-Christians-and-Evangelism-Executive-Summary.pdf>.

[77] Defined as those who identify as 'Christian', but who also 'report praying, reading the Bible and attending a church service at least monthly (and often more frequently)'. This number was 1 in 6 of the self-identified Christians, which in turn, are about 57 per cent of the general population. In other words, 'practising Christians' make up 'about 9 per cent of the total adult population'. Barna Group et al., *Perceptions of Jesus*, 4.

[78] Barna Group et al., *Perceptions of Jesus*, 17. The survey asked about 'influences', a non-exclusive category, so it is possible that individual respondents appear in more than one category.

Our survey reveals that 93% of practising Christians came to faith more than 11 years ago – before fresh expressions of church such as Messy Church or Café Church had been established. How can we make use of these new forms of church to draw people towards Jesus?[79]

After 20, 30, 40 years of restructuring and reimagining the practical mission of the Church to participate in the *missio dei*, the question remains the same.

The 'neutral ground'

In 1936, in preparation for the 'World Conference on Faith and Order', Karl Barth produced a slim volume, a 'message' to the delegates, in which he discussed the impediments to church unity. He warns the delegates of two dangers. On one hand, we might claim to follow the dictates of individual conscience, and thereby 'substitute for the obedient mind and will . . . one or other of the many available historical or aesthetic interests'.[80] On the other hand, we might seek a 'neutral ground outside or above the churches'. In this space, we might think that we can discuss the problems of church fairly, rationally, objectively. Barth demurs:

> such inter- and supra-denominational movements as thus come into being are either ineffective because they do not seriously tackle the problems of the Church, of doctrine, or order and life, or they have an effect because they do take them seriously, and lo and behold, they are engaged in forming a church; a new church or church-like society comes into being, and neutrality is abandoned.

He concludes: 'Church work . . . must be done within the churches, in its proper Christian home, or it will not be done at all.'[81]

Barth notes that this is a painful, provisional position to take, but, for him, that is part of its utility *and* truthfulness. Any enquiry into the truth of Christ, and his lordship over the Church (and churches), cannot but demonstrate that the 'really decisive work [is not] an achievement of human power'.[82]

---

[79] Steve Clifford et al., *Talking Jesus: Perceptions of Jesus, Christians and Evangelism in England* (London: Talking Jesus, 2015), 23, <http://talkingjesus.org/wp-content/uploads/2018/04/Talking-Jesus.pdf>.
[80] Karl Barth, *The Church and the Churches* (Grand Rapids, MI: Eerdmans, 1936), 79.
[81] Barth, *The Church and the Churches*, 80.
[82] Barth, *The Church and the Churches*, 92.

28

New ministries – new ministers

TOM KEIGHLEY

In the country as a whole, though not everywhere to the same degree, the Church of England is facing a loss of membership and the attribution of its power and influence . . . The apparatus of its once central position remains, but emptied of power . . . The Church is not at the heart of their affairs [ordinary men and women] as once it was, despite popular attachment to it as an historical and picturesque institution.[1]

Introduction

The word 'new' has great attraction. It appears, for example, in marketing, in politics and in research, all suggesting that the 'something different' that has emerged is better than what has preceded it. To attach it to the terms 'ministry' and 'ministries' is to immediately assert a process of change; in other words, the nature of ministry and the ministries delivered in the Church of England are not static phenomena. This can be examined by reflecting on the last two centuries as key developments both reveal changes and, even more importantly, point up how the relevant decisions leading to changes were made and what effect they have had on the Church. The particular focus of this chapter will be the emergence of the worker priest (also incorporating titles such as self-supporting minister (SSM), minister in secular employment (MSE) and priests ordained to serve a local, defined community) but also the emergence of readers, of industrial mission, of chaplaincy and of women priests. Other formats of ministry have been considered elsewhere in this volume. However, all the ones mentioned here share a common heritage and similar trajectories of development and integration.

Lesley Paul, quoted above, was the author of one of a series of prescient studies in the 1960s and 1970s that pointed to the need for change

---

[1] L. Paul (1964), *The Deployment and the Payment of the Clergy*, London, Church Information Office.

in the Church of England, and change that needed to occur in a way that responded to cultural and societal developments of the era. It was not the first time in the last two centuries that such observations had been made. This points therefore to repeated and ongoing challenges facing the Church ecclesiologically. As the cultural and social changes of the nineteenth and twentieth century were played out, the Church struggled in its decision-making and policy development. From the perspective of the second decade of the twenty-first century, it is illuminating to compare modern demand for research and evidence to facilitate decision-making when compared to the historical process adopted by the Church. Developing an understanding of the emergence of new ministries and ministers will illuminate some of the events of the last two centuries and offer some suggestions about the facilitation of the emergence of new ministries and new types of minister in the future.

The nineteenth century

The Napoleonic Wars, the Great Reform Acts, the Crimean War, the expansion of empire, the reign of Queen Victoria, industrialization, compulsory education, steam trains, mass migrations, the development of science and the professions, are all events that in different ways characterize the nineteenth century. In the space of a hundred years England had been transformed from a mainly rural to a mainly urban society. From the church perspective, Trollope's *Barchester Towers*[2] holds many truths of a hierarchically structured system beholden to personal and historic patronage. Pounds[3] narrates the historical development of the parish for over 800 years, but as industrialization spread and population migration occurred, the system broke down in many ways. The rural parishes ceased being the centre of village life and town dwellers could find nowhere to worship. The creation of the Ecclesiastical Commissioners in 1835 resulted in the creation of 2,651 chapelries and 1,037 districts and parishes in the next hundred years.[4] This went hand in hand with a stripping out of clergy from cathedrals and pressuring those who held benefices to pay a more reasonable stipend. In consequence, by 1911 there were 22,000 clergy licensed in the Church of England. Further, such had been the pressure

---

[2]   A. Trollope (2013), *Barchester Chronicles*, e-artnow.
[3]   N. J. G. Pounds (2000), *A History of the English Parish Church: The Culture of Religion from Augustine to Victoria*, Cambridge, Cambridge University Press.
[4]   A. Jones (2000), *A Thousand Years of the English Parish: Medieval Patterns and Modern Interpretations*, Moreton-in-Marsh, Windrush Press.

that the historic providers of clergy had been unable to supply the required numbers and, in consequence, new colleges were established by dioceses around England to supplement the supply of men, for men they all were.

Another influence on the decision-making had been the possible disestablishment of the Church following the Great Reform Act of 1832. One response came from Thomas Arnold who wrote a pamphlet on the subject of the reform of the Church.[5] In a wide-ranging discussion, Arnold included some commentary on the wisdom of reviving other orders of ministry so as to enable the mostly unchurched populations of the expanding cities to be drawn into Anglican church life. Though his concerns about how to engage the lower classes in ministry were characteristic of his era, the pamphlet raised questions about the then current processes for selection and training of priests. The debate that followed drew in a number of prominent church people, especially William Hale[6] and Walter Hook,[7] and led ultimately to discussion about the priestly role at the Convocation of Canterbury in 1862 and again in 1884 and, in-between these events, at the Convocation of York in 1882. From this process emerged not a different role for ordained priests, but that of Readers and a very limited number of ordained deacons in employment. This was a key moment in the development of new roles. There was acknowledgement that the current provision was inadequate and that other roles needed to be developed. Further, that some of the shibboleths could be broken to the extent that not every minister needed to be ordained and that it was acceptable, at least for a deacon, to be ordained and to earn a living.

The wider implications of this would not be recognized widely in the Church of England for nearly 80 years.

Learning from the mission fields

David Bosch[8] noted that as well as promoting Christianity, missionary work was part of the imperial process, taking with it the implicit adoption of the home culture of the missionaries, whether the missionaries meant

---

[5] T. Arnold (1833), *Principles of Church Reform*, London, SPCK.

[6] W. H. Hale (1850), *The Duties of the Deacons and Priests in the Church of England Compared: With Suggestions for the Extension of the Order of Deacons and the Establishment of Sub-Deacons*, London, Francis and John Rivington.

[7] W. F. Hook (1851), *What Are the Best Means of Reclaiming Our Lost Population? A Report Presented to the Ruri-Decanal Chapter of Leeds from a Committee of That Body*, Leeds, Thomas Harrison.

[8] D. J. Bosch (1991), *Transforming Mission: Paradigm Shifts in Theology of Mission*, Maryknoll, NY, Orbis Books.

to or not. This included the fact that selection and preparation for the ordained ministry was limited to the sending church. The ordination of priests extended very slowly to the indigenous population, and only when models of church were ecclesiologically sufficiently similar to the home church. Eventually two figures emerged to challenge that position from their own experience of mission and were to go on, therefore, to challenge many assumptions about ordained ministry in Anglicanism. The first was Herbert Kelly, founder of the Society of Sacred Mission.[9] His experience of working with an expanding church in Japan led him to make radical proposals about how to combine full- and part-time ordained ministry and how to move on from parish-based systems to more local forms of Christian community. He was inspired to found Kelham Hall, the first centre to focus on the training of the 'ordinary' man, that is, not one with qualifications for graduate education, another significant development.

Kelly had been influenced by Roland Allen's 1912 publication, *Missionary Methods: St Paul's or Ours?*[10] Allen had worked in China from 1895 to 1903. He had reached similar conclusions to Kelly and had begun to believe that the only answer to the question of how to sustain a missionary church was to encourage the development of local pastors and to challenge the concept of full-time priests as the sole model of ordained priesthood. Allen was to spend much of the rest of his life pursuing this goal in different settings, but especially in the Church of England. The key note here is that it was mission that brought part-time ministry and MSEs on to the Church's agenda. The original impetus was mission overseas, not mission in the home country, a point that was to prove unhelpful over the next 70 years or so. The discussion was about how to take religion to other people and enable Christian communities to be self-sustaining, outside the traditional Church of England parish frameworks. The centre of the debate was the question as to whether or not the Church of England could tolerate, let alone welcome, an approach to being church that was not absolutely and only parish-based. This was a fundamental challenge to the received ecclesiology in which the role of the parish priest was normative and in which role the individual was paid a stipend.

Despite a harshly prophetic approach to the issue, both in terms of message and in the acerbic manner he generally chose to deliver it, Allen gained one very significant supporter for his ideas. F. R. Barry was in due

---

[9] H. H. Kelly (1916), 'The Pattern of the Early Church: The Formation of Ministry', *The East and the West* 14: 429–39.

[10] R. Allen (1912), *Missionary Methods – St Paul's or Ours?*, London, Robert Scott.

course to become Bishop of Southwell. He was aware of the response within the Church to Allen's badgering about the subject of MSEs. In his review of Allen's book, which appeared in *The Guardian* on 11 April 1930, he wrote:

> But I feel bound to record my own conviction that the case [made by Roland Allen] in its essentials is unanswerable . . . It cuts right down into our whole conception of the Christian life and the meaning of the church: that is, in the end, of the Incarnation.[11]

Not only is this the strongest possible statement of support, but it also emphasizes the nature of the theology that underpinned Allen's arguments. Allen's focus on the Incarnation was to establish one of the other key features of MSE ministry, namely a concern for the whole of God's creation that had become obscured by an unbalanced emphasis in church teaching on the redemptive message. It highlighted the nature of the selection process. Barry agrees with Allen that the Church no longer selected its leaders as the Church did in the New Testament and that selection had become based on social class and educational achievement rather than being determined by qualities identified and valued in a community setting. Barry's criticism of a sacrament-centred church dependent on the presence of an ordained minister, namely that it appeared to exclude other forms of being church and of sharing Christian community because a priest could not be provided, was exactly the point that Allen had been trying to make.

The charge of exclusivity and isolation was to resonate throughout the twentieth century as other groups took up the challenge of how to achieve inclusivity in the ordained ministry of the Church, and how to reach those who did not darken its portals.

Women, chaplaincy and homosexuality – foci of church life with unexpected outcomes

Debates about the ordination of women have been part of the Church of England's discussions since the 1920 Lambeth Conference. This preceded full emancipation for women and was part of the same social reawakening about the potential roles of women after their workplace experiences in the First World War. As the regard for authority diminished in the 1960s, so a number of ginger groups arose in the Church of England, parallel to

---

[11] F. R. Barry (1998), 'Who Are Fit Persons?', in *Tentmaking: Perspectives on Self-Supporting Ministry*, ed. J. M. M. Francis and L. J. Francis, Leominster, Gracewing: 77–80 at 78.

the pressure groups and the lobbying activities in public life. Two in particular seemed to have run alongside the development of MSE. One was concerned with the Sexual Offences Act of 1967. This Act legalized certain types of homosexual activity in the UK, and in 1969 the Committee for Homosexual Equality was formed, having as one of its key agenda items the Church of England's attitude to homosexuality. A second group concerned the ordination of women. In due course a group of women made sure that the issue about their ordination was debated regularly by the bishops from the 1960s onwards. This process of change in both initiatives shares many of the same staging-posts as MSE and offers insights into how the Church faces difficult decisions. It demonstrates that MSE was not the only process in the Church of England during this period to be the subject of a particular form of decision-making.

Another form of challenge to the Church in the UK during the 1960s was the Charismatic Renewal movement. This was part of a wider neo-Pentecostalist movement that manifested itself in several denominations and included developments like house churches and cell churches. Though the adherents of the Charismatic movement did not by and large leave a denomination, their methods of worship, types of leadership and focus on the Holy Spirit gave a very individualistic perspective to Christian living. In the 1960s this movement also created a focus on the type of organizational authority a church should adopt and, with its almost sectarian separation, experienced significant changes in leadership and styles of being church. This focus on individualism in society generally – identified by Marwick,[12] Mark Donnelly,[13] Howard Sounes[14] and Dominic Sandbrook[15] – pointed to a profound cultural change to which, as these authors noted in less than complimentary terms, the Church found only limited ways of responding; hence the start of a 60-year fall in church attendance.

An often less remarked-on area of development is that of chaplaincy. This had first come to prominence with the experience of chaplains in the military in two world wars, as well as the emergence of industrial chaplaincies. All were based on an understanding that significant parts

---

[12] A. Marwick (1998), *The Sixties: Cultural Revolution in Britain, France, Italy and United States, c.1958–c.1974*, Oxford, Oxford University Press.

[13] M. Donnelly (2005), *Sixties Britain: Culture, Society and Politics*, Harlow, Pearson Education.

[14] H. Sounes (2006), *Seventies: The Sights and Sounds of a Brilliant Decade*, London, Simon & Schuster.

[15] D. Sandbrook (2006), *White Heat: A History of Britain in the Swinging Sixties*, London, Little, Brown.

of the population were completely unchurched, and if they were ever to be exposed to Christianity in England, the Church would need to go to them. There had of course been chaplaincies in centres of education, but reaching men in particular required a form of priestly activity which was essentially non-parochial. As sectoral ministry developed, the emergence of chaplaincies in major institutions and in industry indicated that the shape of the Church was changing and becoming less geographic in definition and more associated with where people were during their work and leisure time. Implicit in this development was a change in the parameters of authority of a bishop: the chaplains were paid by employers and not the Church. This meant that while the bishops might license the position, they did not resource or determine the parameters of the role. The Church's role became permissive and enabling rather than instituting and resourcing. The challenge therefore was to achieve a balance between church-based life and service to Christians and others in their daily lives, which meant the places where individuals lived their daily life. The Church was revealed as being in flux and not only unclear about the social change issues but also uncertain how to devise a solution; it was being challenged both culturally and ecclesiologically.

Self-supporting ministry – an old 'New Expression'

While all the developments in church life described so far had a significant impact on ecclesiological practice, perhaps the one that incorporated and reflected the challenges of the change process most deeply was the ordination and licensing of ministers who were not stipended and whose focus was the world of work and not the parish; the workplace and not the residence. It was to involve women disproportionately, it was missionary and incarnational, and, perhaps most significantly, it was to result in a cadre of ordained ministers who would in time come to outnumber significantly the stipendiary ministry. The 1939–45 war caused a major hiatus in the thinking on, and discussion about, self-supporting ministry (SSM), long stimulated by Allen and Barry. As with the 1914–18 war, the Church had been reminded of how wide the rift was between itself and the mass of the people. The Church responded with the Commission on Evangelism, which produced the report *Towards the Conversion of England*[16] in 1945. It contained two adventurous recommendations:

---

[16] Archbishops' Commission on Evangelism (1945), *Towards the Conversion of England: Report of the Archbishops' Commission on Evangelism*, London: Press and Publications Board of the Church Assembly.

- in some circumstances a parish priest should be allowed to take a job in industry for a shorter or longer period;
- in exceptional circumstances an industrial worker should be ordained as a deacon or a priest, to remain in industry and exercise his ministry as an industrial worker (pp 64-5).[17]

These recommendations from the subcommittee, chaired by Mervyn Stockwood, mark a key step on the journey to the establishment of MSEs. It cannot be without significance that, as Bishop of Southwark, Stockwood was to oversee the innovatory changes in training for the priesthood that the committee anticipated.

Before that, however, there was a very small-scale attempt to generate an English worker-priest to parallel the developments in France and Germany. Mantle records how a 'large handful' of men in the 1950s who had been trained and ordained for parish ministry took up labouring occupations.[18] The initiative acted as a precursor to Stockwood's launch of the part-time training programme which came into existence under the aegis of an 'experiment' approved by the 1958 Lambeth Conference, with the severe rider that: 'Such provision [of SSMs] is not to be regarded as a substitute for the full-time ministry of the Church, but as an addition to it.'[19]

Stockwood initiated the programme and ordained the participants to engage in workplace ministry, even before the legal obstacles to ordained men earning a living had been lifted. This is indicative of the nature of episcopal decision-making: the bishop acting on his own authority. The independence of the decision, especially in respect of episcopal colleagues, meant that there was no strategic approach to this development. However, there was implicit agreement with it, as reflected in the number of courses that emerged in the next 20 years.

Having achieved this 'holy grail' of non-stipendiary ministry, the lack of planning, especially in how to integrate this new boy on the block into church life, was to have significant outcomes. The first was that the nature of the role was never clearly defined. Mantle captures the issue when he describes six outcomes:

Within the Church of England by the beginning of the 1970s, a variety of ministries had emerged, and may be delineated as follows:

---

[17] *Towards the Conversion of England*, pp. 64–5.
[18] J. Mantle (2000), *Britain's First Worker-Priests: Radical Ministry in a Post-War Setting*, London, SCM Press.
[19] Lambeth Conference (1958), *Resolution 89*, The Lambeth Conference. London.

(i) There was an 'original' group of worker-priests, 'priests turned workers' episcopally licensed, but in keeping with the French worker-priests wholly committed to a working-class milieu. Their story began in the late 1940s and early 1950s.

(ii) There were priests in secular middle-class and professional employment; some, though licensed to a parish, specifically sought to focus their ministry at work. They would eventually become known as Ministers in Secular Employment.

(iii) There were others who, though engaged in secular middle-class and professional employment, focussed their attention on the territorial parish, sometimes known after the Welsby Report (1968), as Auxiliary Parochial Ministers (APM). They might also, however, declare some ministry at work.

(iv) There was a growing number of clergy from the 1960s on who 'forsook' (to use Lloyd's term) the territorial parish and had effectively become worker-priests in the sense that they took on manual labour. Others took to teaching, social and administrative jobs. Many had 'had enough' of the institutional church, and their abandonment of the institution, sometimes temporary, can be seen as a form of protest.

(v) There also evolved a new category: Local Non-Stipendiary Ministers, who, with the support of their local territorial parish, i.e. their own congregation, were trained within their diocese to serve their own parish. The pioneer here was the Lincoln diocese (1978), but other dioceses followed, and while there was often ambiguity about a role sometimes indistinguishable from NSM generally, it was easy for cynics to claim that this time it really was 'clergy on the cheap'.

(vi) Last but not least, there were, as there had always been, forms of 'secular' ministry in universities, schools, hospitals, forces and industrial settings. This growing 'sector ministry' of 'chaplaincies', sometimes stipendiary, that is, paid for by the church, but sometimes employed by institutions themselves, meant that there were clergy who saw themselves, with some justification, as having a 'ministry at work'.[20]

This useful list reveals the diversity of roles recognized in this category. Combined, this list points to the Church having a remarkable missionary initiative under way as clergy accompany baptized Christians in the place where an increasing proportion of daily life is spent. No longer do people live and work in the same place; urban life has evolved. No longer do people work principally from 9 a.m. to 5 p.m.; the working day has now been defined by the Internet and the capacity of people to engage with

---

[20] Mantle, *Britain's First Worker-Priests*, pp. 243–4.

each other in numerous and evolving ways. Work is less labour-based and more intellectual. The parish is fixed and geographical, while the life of the laity is mobile, fluid and networked; herein lies the crunch issue.

Discussion

The ordination of women as priests and ultimately as bishops, the on-going struggle to come to terms with non-heterosexual relationships among Christians and in the wider society, and the emergence of self-supporting ministers as the numerically dominant element of the workforce (if ordained ministry can be described in such terms) have redefined the Church ecclesiologically. Socially, the Church has retained its geographic focus through parishes but is presented with an increasingly limited capacity to support such a model of church financially. This is reflected in the falling numbers of stipends available. The Church has failed to recognize that the SSM initiative of the last 55 years has been one of the greatest potential missionary initiatives available to it. The concern about keeping parishes going and providing services locally has obscured what might be described as one of the Holy Spirit's great offerings. The Church has been unable to pivot around to see the opportunities such vocations offer. The harsh words of the 1958 Lambeth Conference continue to res-onate: 'not to be regarded as a substitute for the full-time ministry of the Church'. Notions of being full-time, of being stipended (remunerated, paid) and located in a parish have dominated the debate down to the present. Some more rural dioceses have moved more rapidly to a non-stipended ordained ministry but still with the same focus of covering services in churches. The pace of even this limited change has been determined by the approach of the bishop. Just as Stockwood acted with-out constraints, even ignoring the legality of his actions, so bishops have determined the local approach.

This brief summary of some of the more significant changes over the last hundred years or so reflects strongly the episcopal style of different diocesans as they considered how to manage their responsibilities. The two great reality checks of the world wars, which demonstrated in the most public of manners how out of touch the Church was, did not result in any major change of direction. The initiatives of the last 30 years, no mat-ter how high-profile, have not had a significant impact on the slow fall in numbers in church. The need to study this has resulted in numerous reports and analyses of the church numbers. What has not developed in church circles is the need to be 'evidence-based' in its approach to decision-making. The anthropology of this points to a wish to avoid drilling down into matters and developing consistent resources and strategic approaches, and instead to achieve a compromise that keeps everyone on board. While the world has moved over to developing transformational and transactional patterns of leadership, the Church is still trapped in 'command and control' mentality.

In consequence, the Church has been caught on the back foot repeatedly in the light of fundamental social and cultural changes. The independence granted by the motor car, the shift from local work to commuting, the emergence of new patterns of sexuality and the acceptance of old ones, the reshaping of urban life and the nature of networked living rather than geographic communities; all have challenged the Church and the Church has been found wanting. The belief that the Church determines culture rather than being responsive to it has been a weakness. Appiah's work on perceived and received identify demonstrates how this can come about.[21] Assumed identities are meaningless unless confirmed by the community in which the individual exists. MSEs report this time and again as they are asked to explain what their church is doing and, when pointing out that they are part of that institution, are reminded that they are 'different'. As the cadre of SSMs is recognized as ordained but different, the Church still seems to be battling to integrate them into a model of service based on the need to ensure the survival of a nineteenth-century way of being church.

There is no question that ordained ministry in this setting of confusion and contradiction is stressful. The added tension between assumed and perceived identity simply adds to the inherent difficulties of undertaking the role. The nature of parochial twenty-first-century ministry seems to be coming to the end of a cycle of development which emerged in the early nineteenth century as the Church responded to the urbanization of the Industrial Revolution. Prior to that the prevailing model was of gentlemen priests who were either moneyed or engaging in approved activities with incomes, notably as school masters. Many were amateur academics and were part of wider learned societies. The priesthood was not a 'full-time' occupation. Making the occupation full-time changed the nature of ministry and set often undeliverable goals, with many of the roles now subsumed in social work and welfare provision in society. With the removal of those responsibilities was the opportunity to review the role, especially as newer forms of ordained ministry emerged. The research suggests that

---

[21] K. A. Appiah (2005), *The Ethics of Identity*, Oxford, Princeton University Press.

something of a crunch point is being approached when a Church has fewer resources for stipended ministry than before and a large proportion of its current ordained workforce is non-stipended. The implications of the change need a much clearer focus and a more corporate approach to the provision of ordained ministry. This will of course challenge the traditional freedoms of the diocesan bishops, but it is time that this too came under review as the shape of ministry as a whole changes.

To conclude, the opening quotation from Leslie Paul has turned out to be truly prophetic: numbers have continued to fall, the Church's influence in the public domain goes on waning, the structures remain but the power has evaporated, people no longer turn to the Church to determine their affairs, and popular attachment continues to diminish. If this is not the time to evaluate new ministries and new ministerial roles, it is difficult to know when it will be.

29

Critical paradigms of ministry

JOHN FITZMAURICE

'But he hasn't got anything on,' a little child said.[1]

Here's to the crazy ones. The misfits. The rebels. The troublemakers.
The round pegs in the square holes. The ones who see things differently.
They're not fond of rules. And they have no respect for the status quo.
You can quote them, disagree with them, glorify or vilify them. About
the only thing you can't do is ignore them. Because they change things.
They push the human race forward. And while some may see them as
the crazy ones, we see genius. Because the people who are crazy enough
to think they can change the world, are the ones who do.[2]

Who controls the discourse?

Who controls our discourse around ministry? Does it primarily belong
to those who are actively engaged in the tasks of ministry; does it belong
to those who are the recipients of that ministry; does it belong to the hierarchy of the Church; does it belong to the wider society in which ministry
takes place? There are, I suspect, many other constituencies which, it could
be argued, have a legitimate vested interest or indeed axe to grind in relation to the manner in which ministry is offered and the theoretical framework that informs it. Such concern, it's worth noting, is indicative of the
power of ministry as a human activity. It quickly becomes clear, then, that
there are significant issues of power and control that orbit around ministerial discourse, not least in their ability to shape the paradigms through
which ministry is enacted. What I hope to show in this essay is that should
any particular interest group or indeed individual achieve a disproportionate level of control or influence over the practice of ministry or the

---

[1] Hans Christian Anderson, 'The Emperor's New Clothes'.
[2] Rob Siltanen with the participation of Lee Clow (narrated by Steve Jobs), *ThinkDifferent*,
Apple Inc., 1997.

theoretical framework that informs it, the consequences are almost certainly deleterious for the performance of that ministry, and that it is only when the discourse around ministerial practice is liberated for the captivity of particular interest groups, particularly those who wish to use it for predetermined ends, and opened up to a wide range of dialogue partners that it can most truly flourish.

Key to understanding why this liberation is necessary, why critical paradigms need to be admitted to the conversation, is an understanding of the reality of 'groupthink'.

Groupthink

A number of years ago, in the depths of winter, I attended a day conference at Coventry Cathedral for those involved in church school education. We were welcomed by the then subdean, now Archbishop of Canterbury, Justin Welby. In his welcome Canon Welby, as he then was, said, 'As if to prove that committees make decisions that no sane individual ever would, the cathedral chapter have decided to have the boiler replaced . . . over the winter!' We shivered our way through the day. This is a classic example of the phenomenon of groupthink – when committees or groups of people make decisions that no one individual would ever make on their own. So why does this happen and why is it so potentially dangerous?

Irving Janis's pioneering work in the 1970s brought groupthink to wide public attention.[3] More recently, Harvard law professor and former administrator of the White House Office of Information and Regulatory Affairs Cass Sunstein and his co-author Reid Hastie have examined the destructive power of groupthink, its causes and how to counteract it.[4] They note that groups and teams, which are the ubiquitous norm in many work environments, have the effect of amplifying rather than correcting individual errors of judgement. The root cause of this is people's unwillingness to appear stupid, ignorant or antipathetic to the group – individuals become victim to their own inner dialogue which says, 'They're probably right.' This leads to what Sunstein and Hastie call the **cascade effect** where members of a group simply fall in behind what others think, abdicating their own inner convictions and insights. This is particularly

---

[3] I. Janis, *Groupthink: Psychological Studies of Policy Decisions and Fiascos*, 2nd edn, Orlando, FL: Houghton Mifflin, 1982.

[4] C. Sunstein and R. Hastie, *Wiser: Getting beyond Groupthink to Make Groups Smarter*, Boston, MA: Harvard Business Review Press, 2015.

the case if the person making the argument is a well-respected figure; he or she then occupies a role described as 'the surprising validator', for example the pivotal role played by Colin Powell in supporting the US invasion of Iraq in 2003. The consequence of all this is a hardening of positions in the groups concerned – diversity of opinion gives way to uniformity, however tenuously subscribed to, and dialogue gives way to monologue. Sunstein and Hastie note that while such processes undoubtedly create a greater unity within the group, and often an increase in confidence, this usually happens at the cost of accuracy.

The implications of this are far-reaching. As groups become less able to tolerate diversity internally, the only way that diversity can be expressed is by the formation of alternative groups, each containing only those who subscribe to the particular position of the group. The fragmenting effect of this within public, and indeed ecclesiological and ministerial, discourse should not be underestimated. Inevitably this leads to a polarization of positions which, as we have seen, is based on decreased accuracy of understanding the particular issue(s) in the group.

The culture that generally allows groupthink to thrive is that of 'happy talk'. Unconsciously, or even consciously, the group excludes any information that might challenge its unity and clarity of direction. Any such interventions are identified as negativity, which is seen to undermine the work of the group and can lead to the exclusion of the individual or groups of individuals who dare to speak out. How then do groups move out of this dysfunctional mode of working and into a more open, creative and truthful one? Sunstein and Hastie propose that the first question a group needs to ask itself is what information it needs to make the decision required of it – what and who does it need to hear? There is a real requirement for groups to consider all that information without favour or prejudgement, particularly in the case of emotive issues. Such an approach is a very different one from that of the compliant group member who under the influence of groupthink feels the requirement to sublimate his or her own opinion to that of the larger group. For Sunstein and Hastie, and this is critical, what is required is a change of group culture, whereby the good team player is seen as the person who provides the information that the group lacks. This is a significant insight with far-reaching implications for the way we make decisions as individuals, as communities, as organizations and in the public square. It also has implications for how we engage in discourse around pastoral and ministerial theology and practice.

Despite its unique character, the Church is not protected or excused from the influence of groupthink. Indeed perhaps the Church is even more subject to this dynamic, rooted as it is in a narrative of being a community of unity, love and peace, in which we are urged not to prefer our own wishes over those of others, and indeed of God. So, notwithstanding the methodological safeguards that I will explore below, the Church, and the way it does its business, is susceptible to groupthink as much as any other organization, if not more so. Add to this a dash of institutional panic about its future viability – a sense of being, as one bishop put it, in the 'last-chance saloon'[5] – and the temptation to collude with the loudest and strongest voices in the room is amplified. In such desperate and potentially time-sensitive situations critical voices, voices that challenge the status quo, are generally not welcome. Accuracy is sacrificed to strategic intentionality and quick wins – the pain must be stopped at all cost.

How can we better hear the marginal voices? What are the prophetic voices saying?

So how do we in the Church hear the voices that are seeking to give us the information our current discourse in general lacks? Whose are these voices and what are they saying?

One thing held in common by those who seek to challenge the current groupthink in the Church, and in its thinking about pastoral and ministerial theology, is that they are to some extent, though not exclusively, marginal to the life of the institution. Perhaps there is something about the margins that means it is easier not to get caught up in groupthink; perhaps the margins provide a perspective that makes it easier to identify the groupthink that enraptures those closer to the centre of power and responsibility; perhaps the margins are so dissociated and un-clubbable by nature that groupthink simply wouldn't work for those who operate out of its hinterland. Kenneth Leech suggests that the margins are not only the correct place *in* which to undertake Christian ministry, not least with those who have been pushed to the edge of society, but also *from* which to reflect on pastoral and ministerial theology.[6] It is not coincidental for Leech that Jesus undertook his most significant work, that of his Passion and resurrection, outside the city, in a marginal and liminal place.[7] This, he contends, is a vital corollary to the success-based paradigms and strategies that are so

---

5   See <https://www.virtueonline.org/bishop-pete-broadbent-church-england-near-last-chance-saloon>.

6   K. Leech, *The Sky Is Red: Discerning the Signs of the Times*, London: Darton, Longman & Todd, 1997.

7   K. Leech, *Doing Theology in Altab Ali Park*, London: Darton, Longman & Todd, 2006.

much part of the contemporary mainstream. For Leech, the priorities for ministry and for pastoral theology look very different from the margins.

While ministerially those margins are often demographic and/or related to financial or social deprivation, the critical paradigms that must inform our pastoral theology do not find their origins exclusively in such places. In order to get a sense of who these marginal voices are and what they might be saying to the Church, I am going to briefly examine four of them.

Justin Lewis-Anthony

Justin Lewis-Anthony is Deputy Director of the Anglican Centre in Rome. Before that, he was Dean of Students at Virginia Theological Seminary, having formerly been on the staff of a cathedral, and a parish priest. He is best known for two books that offer quite different critical perspectives on pastoral theology and ministerial practice: *If You Meet George Herbert on the Road, Kill Him*[8] and *You Are the Messiah and I Should Know*.[9]

In *If You Meet George Herbert on the Road, Kill Him*, Lewis-Anthony critiques the archetypical paradigms of Anglican priesthood derived from the ministry of George Herbert, as described in Herbert's book *The Country Parson*. Lewis-Anthony suggests with good reason that this model is still deeply ingrained in the unconscious, if not the conscious, expectations of Anglicans, clergy and laity alike, and goes on to suggest, however, that it is a deeply inappropriate model for the shape and demands of contemporary ministry. He reminds us that Herbert's ministry at Bremerton, a community of around 500 people, lasted only three years and was supported by two curates and a private income! He questions whether the vision of England portrayed by Herbert actually ever existed.

The gentrified functions of the late eighteenth- and early nineteenth-century clergy gave way to the professionalization of the clergy in the mid-to-late nineteenth century and ultimately to the identity crises that affected much of the Church's ministry a century later. Lewis-Anthony sums up the context of contemporary ordained ministry thus: 'The parson is no longer the gentleman of the parish; he is no longer the professional "person" of the parish, for the skill and knowledge which he possesses are no longer valued by a wider society.'[10]

---

[8] Justin Lewis-Anthony, *If You Meet George Herbert on the Road, Kill Him: Radically Rethinking Priestly Ministry*, London: Mowbray, 2009.

[9] Justin Lewis-Anthony, *You Are the Messiah and I Should Know: Why Leadership Is a Myth (and Probably a Heresy)*, London: Bloomsbury, 2013.

[10] Lewis-Anthony, *If You Meet George Herbert*, p. 45.

As if to compound this identity of alienation, Lewis-Anthony suggests that contemporary clergy are blighted by the 'cult of nice',[11] and he doesn't pull any punches in delineating its detrimental effect on clergy lives in terms of overwork and poor morale. He draws on the work of Yvonne Warren to note the deep external and internal conflicts that clergy are victim to, due largely to their adherence to this outmoded model of pastoral theology and ministerial practice, which not infrequently leads to burnout.

In terms of remedy, Lewis-Anthony prescribes a re-articulation of the purpose of ministry, drawing on the model of **witness**, **watchman** and **weaver**, as articulated by Rowan Williams in a profoundly influential lecture given in May 2004.[12] Pragmatically and in conclusion, Lewis-Anthony offers five pointers for the contemporary priest: know who you are, know what you are for, know who you are set over, know how to make decisions, know how to manage conflicts.

The continued confusion of identity in many clergy, both individually and collectively, validates Lewis-Anthony's examination and critique of the Herbertian paradigm, but this critique of inherited models is neatly balanced by his critique of some contemporary approaches to ministry in his book *You Are the Messiah and I Should Know* (Mowbray, 2013). This subsequent book examines the uncritical adoption in the Church of the language of leadership, and questions its appropriateness, going so far as to question whether or not it might represent a heresy.

In defining heresy, Lewis-Anthony draws on the work of Lester Kurtz, suggesting that a heretic has to be 'close enough to be threatening but distant enough to be considered in error'.[13] Lewis-Anthony poses two key questions: (1) why is leadership considered the panacea for all ills, and (2) is it something that should be encouraged and fostered in the Church? His starting point is that 'leadership' is a contested word with no agreed definition, and goes on to suggest that leadership is best understood as a myth. Lewis-Anthony contends that the myth of leadership, as with all contemporary myths, is created and sustained through the medium of cinema, his book being an extensive evaluation of the interrelation between cinema, leadership myth and ministerial practice. Given the

---

[11] Lewis-Anthony, *If You Meet George Herbert*, p. 48ff.

[12] 'The Christian Priest Today': <http://rowanwilliams.archbishopofcanterbury.org/articles.php/2097/the-christian-priest-today-lecture-on-the-occasion-of-the-150th-anniversary-of-ripon-college-cuddesd>.

[13] Lester R. Kurtz (1986), *The Politics of Heresy: The Modernist Crisis in Roman Catholicism*, Berkeley: University of California Press, 1986, quoted in Lewis-Anthony, *You Are the Messiah*, p. 258.

relative dominance of Hollywood in this myth-making process, the myths we are exposed to, more often than not, embody American values. The mode of leadership embodied in American cinema is that of the 'strong man', the personification of which, Lewis-Anthony suggests, is the actor John Wayne. This embodiment of leadership is founded on the promise and use of violence, hence Lewis-Anthony's concern that it is not an appropriate myth for a Christian context. This is most clearly manifest in a culture's practice of importing a 'leader' from outside the community in order to take control of the community and to drive it forward, in vision and mission. The inference of course being that the community itself is impotent and has no real, valid resources of its own with which to do this. Lewis-Anthony offers the general witness of Scripture along with the 2010 film *Of Gods and Men* – which tells the story of a community of French Cistercian monks captured and murdered in Algeria – as an anti-mythos, a model of embracing powerlessness as a mode of leadership rather than that of implied, or actual, violence.

In his Foreword to the book, Stanley Hauerwas notes that in the book of Acts the disciples chose the replacement to Judas by lot, and not by 'strong man' virtues. He writes:

> When 'leaders' are chosen by lot it is not the deficiencies of the community that makes leadership necessary, but rather a leader is needed to coordinate and give direction to the many gifts that constitute the life of the community. In such a community the 'leader' does not impose order on the community but rather the leader is an agent of memory to help the community not lose what makes them what they are.[14]

The two texts by Lewis-Anthony discussed above illustrate the importance and contribution of critical paradigms to pastoral theology and the practice of ministry. They challenge widely held preconceptions, both inherited and contemporary, and cause the Church to think deeply about the purpose, motivation and practice of its ministry.

Martyn Percy

It might be difficult to envisage Martyn Percy, Dean of Christ Church Cathedral, Oxford, and de facto master of the associated college of the university, and indeed chief editor of this volume, as marginal, but it is perhaps the fact that Percy has a foot in two camps that has allowed him to

---

14 S. Hauerwas, in Lewis-Anthony, *If You Meet George Herbert*, p. xi.

offer a particularly cogent and increasingly controversial analysis of the life of the Church. A recurring theme in Percy's work has been that of power in the Church,[15] with a particular focus on the dynamics of power around fundamentalism, the Pentecostal/Charismatic revival, and the bureaucratization of the Church and associated commodification of the gospel. In recent years he has been noted as a trenchant critic of the Reform and Renewal initiative (now rebranded Renewal and Reform) in the Church of England and has recently summarized his critique in a short paper, published on the website of Modern Church,[16] in which, drawing on the work of James Hopewell, he suggests that the reformers should first make an effort to understand the Church before they try to improve it. He writes:

> the primary problem with the proposed agenda is that the reformers don't seem to understand the subtle, rich nature of the church they seek to improve. They have set about proposals of alteration and transformation, yet with little evidence of having a deep and rich comprehension of the body they propose to reform.[17]

He addresses the dynamic of groupthink head on: 'Those querying the wisdom of colluding in a collective anxiety about the future, together with the ensuing "panic attack" consuming the resources of the body, are held to be dissenters or deviants.'[18]

Percy vigorously resists the reductionism that limits the Church to a mere organization, subject to the manipulations of contemporary business leadership and management ideology. He argues for a much deeper, embedded and implicit understanding of the Church and of religious practice than organizational theory will allow. He is strident in challenging the notion that the Church is, or can even be compared to, a membership-based organization such as the National Trust, despite the enthusiasm for some within the central institutions of the Church to make such comparisons. His approach recognizes that people express identity and belonging in complex ways, and that the journey of claiming identity and belonging is multifaceted – to define those on the periphery of the Church as somehow not real members is to misunderstand

---

[15] See M. Percy, *Power and the Church: Ecclesiology in an Age of Transition*, London: Cassell, 1998.
[16] M. Percy, 'On Not Rearranging the Deckchairs on the *Titanic*: A Commentary on Reform and Renewal in the Church of England': <https://modernchurch.org.uk/worship/prayer-liturgy/cremation-rite-for-unborn-children/send/32-articles/768-on-not-rearranging-the-deckchairs-on-the-titanic>.
[17] Percy, 'Not Rearranging', p. 3.
[18] Percy, 'Not Rearranging', p. 3.

the process of identity formation and of implicit theology and religion generally. Such an understanding of the Church does not easily lend itself to numerical auditing of usual Sunday adult attendance, because it's not always easy to define who belongs and who doesn't. Percy rejects this crude black-and-white approach; he says: 'The church is a body with a soul – a mystery; more than the sum of its parts. It's a social-transcendent reality; occupied with God, virtue and values.'[19]

So what in Percy's view is the root cause of the erroneous route marked out by Renewal and Reform? It is, in his words, the mistaken notion that 'impassioned fervour and spiritual zeal, linked with secular reasoning and business-think' can take the place of the theological building blocks of the Church; those determining the future polity of the Church are suffering a theological and ecclesiological amnesia that risks backfiring and, not-withstanding any short-term successes, causing long-term damage to the Church it professes to support: 'The builder that does not understand the material and structure of the house (of God), nor has any real appre-ciation for its evolved architecture, is likely, in attempting to improve the property, [to] commit unintentional vandalism.'[20]

But Percy's critique extends beyond the theological and ecclesiological – he asserts that the proposals lack emotional intelligence as well, mistaking 'reluctant cooperation for agreement . . . hesitant compliance with con-sent'.[21] Alongside this he also identifies Renewal and Reform as being an 'imposed vision', as opposed to one that seeks to bring people with it, or indeed emerged from the wider Church in the first place.

The consequences of this, according to Percy, is a 'zombie' Church, evac-uated of all its theological and spiritual riches. To avoid this, he suggests that Renewal and Reform be abandoned and that the Church re-engage with theology and the spiritual tradition to articulate a new vision. He asks: 'Is it really too much to ask for a vision from our leadership that is robustly intellectual, theological and spiritual?'[22]

Percy's criticism of Renewal and Reform is trenchant and is a classic example of why pastoral theology and ministerial practice, and those who shape it, need to hear the insights of the critical paradigms that supply the information the conversation is missing – the information that makes a fully informed decision possible.

---

19 Percy, 'Not Rearranging', p. 5.
20 Percy, 'Not Rearranging', p. 5.
21 Percy, 'Not Rearranging', p. 7.
22 Percy, 'Not Rearranging', p. 8.

Maggie Ross

Another voice that is trenchant, indeed frequently angry, and even polemical, is that of Maggie Ross. Ross differs from both Lewis-Anthony and Percy in that she neither is ordained nor holds any formal academic position. She has lived as a solitary for many years, first in the United States and latterly in the United Kingdom. Her book *Pillars of Flame*[23] is an examination of the relationship between power, priesthood and spiritual maturity.

Ross makes the case that true priesthood, Christ's priesthood, has been fatally compromised by its institutional expression in what she describes as 'the ordained secular power structure that currently organises the church'.[24] She recognizes that 'there are a few clergy of singular priestly holiness', but sees the majority as those whose 'dedication is rather to power and expediency'.[25] This is strong stuff, but she continues by asserting that ordination doesn't bestow priesthood, and that the 'hierarchical orders that exist in many Christian churches are true neither to the disclosure of Christ's humility nor to New Testament Christianity'.[26] Ross follows this assertion by questioning the motivation of candidates offering themselves for ordination, the notion of an internal sense of call which she suggests is a relatively new innovation in the Church's understanding of priesthood,[27] and the selection process itself which she deems too secular.[28] The increasing professionalism of the (stipendiary) clergy and with it, suggests Ross, the careerist mentality, alongside the exclusive right of the ordained to preside at the sacraments – thereby, in her eyes, turning them into magic rituals – has served to keep the majority of the Church spiritually immature and largely illiterate.

True priesthood, according to Ross, is rooted in an inner *kenosis* that seeks to imitate the kenosis of God. From this, Ross is happy to recognize, often flow ministerial prerogatives, but this priesthood and ministry are nothing to do with the power structures of ordination. The true priest is called to enter the depths of human pain and despair and, having met Christ there, for that is where Christ is to be found, is to witness to 'new

---

[23] M. Ross, *Pillars of Flame: Power, Priesthood and Spiritual Maturity*, New York: Harper & Row, 1988.
[24] Ross, *Pillars of Flame*, p. xiv.
[25] Ross, *Pillars of Flame*, p. xv.
[26] Ross, *Pillars of Flame*, p. 3.
[27] Ross, *Pillars of Flame*, p. 8.
[28] Ross, *Pillars of Flame*, p. 15.

life, hope and joy'.[29] The danger for Ross of the institutional priesthood is that its external demands and vanities are too great a distraction to allow the priest to have a rich enough inner life to truly engage with the kenosis to which Christ invites him or her.[30]

It's not clear, in Ross's demolition of the ordained ministerial priesthood, if she is espousing the priesthood of all believers, or simply a priesthood of those who have been called to (and achieved) a profound level of kenosis through solitude and silence. Her work is of interest because it is so angry, so polemical, and because of that it causes us to ask if it can legitimately be considered a critical paradigm to inform the practice of pastoral theology and ministry. Some may well argue that it is too subjective, too rant-like, but I would suggest that to exclude certain voices because they don't speak politely enough, or because their argument isn't entirely balanced, or simply because they don't entirely fit our mode of discourse, risks cutting us off from the very voices we need to hear. The Church so desperately needs to hear the passionate, the fiery, the subjective voices, as well as the more objective and closely argued.

Eugene Peterson and Wendell Berry

Finally, two gentler voices who nonetheless illustrate an important mode of critique – the farmer, activist and writer Wendell Berry, and the pastor and teacher Eugene Peterson.

The breadth of Berry's concerns is breathtaking – he is an astute critic of American life and culture. Some of his most powerful insights, however, come through his reflections on the life of faith gleaned through his work as a farmer, seeking to work with natural rhythms and processes rather than violently imposing on them. Berry's experience as a farmer has led him to an alternative epistemology. Matthew Bonzo and Michael Stevens write:

> Berry identifies the 'Sympathetic Mind' as 'the mind of our creatureliness' as well as 'the mind of our wholeness' and a 'preeminently faithful mind, taking knowingly and willingly the risks required by faith.' In opposition is the prideful blindness of the 'Rational Mind,' which 'is objective, analytical, and empirical; it makes itself up only by considering the facts; it pursues truth by experimentation; it is uncorrupted by preconception, received authority, religious belief, or feeling.'[31]

---

[29] Ross, *Pillars of Flame*, p. 38.
[30] Ross, *Pillars of Flame*, p. 83.
[31] J. M. Bonzo and M. R. Stevens, *Wendell Berry and the Cultivation of Life: A Reader's Guide*, Grand Rapids, MI: Brazos Press, 2008, p. 28.

Berry has been a huge influence on Eugene Peterson, whose writing on pastoral theology and spiritual practice are widely influential. Writing of Berry's influence Peterson says this:

> The importance of place is a recurrent theme – place embraced and loved, understood and honoured. Whenever Berry writes the word *farm*, I substitute *parish*; the sentence works for me every time . . . Parish work is every bit as physical as farm work. It is *these* people, at *this* time, under *these* conditions.[32]

He reminds us that growth is a biological, not an arithmetical, metaphor. Peterson illustrates how he embraces Berry's farming methodology and mindset in his pastoral work:

> It is not my task to impose a different way of life on these people in this place but to work with what is already there. There is a kind of modern farmer, Berry tells me, who is impatient with the actual conditions of any farm and brings in big equipment to eliminate what is distinctively local so that machines can do their work unimpeded by local quirks and idiosyncrasies. They treat the land not as a resource to be cared for but as loot . . . When I take up this attitude, I see the congregation as raw material to manufacture into an evangelism program, or a mission outreach, or a Christian Education learning center.[33]

He notes how counter-cultural such an approach is, and how his congregation have got so used to the imposition model that they think he's not being a proper pastor if he doesn't impose some new initiative on them. Peterson notes the risk of imposed strategies for the pastor as it becomes easy for the strategy to be more important that the person – how tempting it is to get frustrated with people because they are not what or who we want them to be! He quotes Thomas Merton in saying that pastors who don't accept their people as they are will never be able to guide them to who they ought to be. This working with the given, working with the grain of a particular congregation or individual, is intrinsic to the approach Peterson has learnt from Berry. He suggests that it is not possible or desirable to prejudge what Christ will call an individual or congregation to, that there is an implied humility required of the pastor in the face of almighty God; holiness can never be imposed externally by another, but rather emerges from within an individual or congregation. Peterson likens the way he understands his

---

[32] E. H. Peterson, *Under the Unpredictable Plant: An Exploration in Vocational Holiness*, Grand Rapids, MI: Eerdmans, 1992, p. 131.

[33] Peterson, *Unpredictable Plant*, p. 131.

congregation to the way Berry understands topsoil – ordinary, unobtrusive, rich in nutrients and potential, and frequently taken for granted.

So Eugene Peterson under the influence of Wendell Berry offers a powerful critique to the contemporary Church, with its rational, objective and empirical approaches. A critique that is distinctive in its linking of ministerial and agricultural practice. This is a vision of pastoral theology not often heard, but one that has much to offer and demands to be taken seriously. It is yet another piece of information that is lacking in most discourse about pastoral theology and ministerial practice.

Theological reflection as critical paradigm

We've looked at four vignettes of critical paradigms and seen how what they offer might be that piece of vital information that allows those making decisions about ministerial practice and policy, be it at national or local level, and those involved in grassroots ministry, to hear voices and see perspectives that add significant insight to the mainstream paradigms, thus avoiding the pitfalls and errors of mindless groupthink. However, I also want to suggest that that central activity to pastoral theology and ministerial practice, namely theological reflection, is in and of itself a critical paradigm – that pastoral theology at its best is a self-reflective critical paradigm.

Just because reflective practice has been systematized in recent years, we should not succumb to the delusion that it is something new – such methodology is as old as self-consciousness itself. What making it explicit does is to ensure that all the relevant information is assembled and considered prior to a decision being made. In the tasks of reflective observation on a critical incident, and subsequent situating of that reflective observation within some form of abstract conceptualization, there is an overriding expectation that all the voices, all the information needed to move to the next stage of active experimentation, will be summonsed and reviewed.[34] To exclude certain voices is simply not to do the activity properly. And yet because of the cyclical nature of theological reflection, when done comprehensively, any information missed the first time around the cycle can be picked up in subsequent iterations.

---

[34] See L. Green, *Let's Do Theology: A Pastoral Cycle Resource Book*, London: Mowbray, 1990; and P. Ballard and J. Pritchard, *Practical Theology in Action: Christian Thinking in the Service of Church and Society*, London: SPCK, 1996.

Conclusion: why critical paradigms are good for pastoral theology

How are we to exercise ministry to the best of our abilities as individuals, as communities and as a Church? We can only do so when we are in possession of as much of the relevant data as possible and we have a methodology to process it. Pastoral theology, no less than any other discipline, is subject to the inaccuracies and errors caused by groupthink and happy talk in the Church. In order for pastoral theology and ministerial practice to remain faithful it is vital that the voices that challenge the predominant paradigms, whatever they may be, are heard and encouraged, regardless of the cost. This will immeasurably enrich both our thinking about, and our practice of, ministry.

Part 5

ISSUES IN CHRISTIAN MINISTRY

30

The challenge of preaching

RUTHANNA HOOKE

The perennial challenge of preaching

Judging from job advertisements for ministers and priests, preaching is central to the ministerial vocation. Congregations often list compelling preaching as one of the principal abilities they seek in a new pastor. In some denominations the minister is given the title 'Preacher', signalling the centrality of preaching to the ministerial role. Even in liturgical traditions, in which the sermon is not the only or even the chief focal point of the liturgy, the task of preaching is considered a crucial part of the vocation of pastor.

These job advertisements also suggest that the task of preaching is difficult, that it can be hard to find someone who fulfils the demand for excellent preaching. Ministerial job descriptions emphasize this aspect of ministry in part because painful experience reveals that it is all too common for preachers to fall short of these ideals. The title of a recent collection of essays about preaching, *What's the Matter with Preaching Today?*, captures a widespread sense that preaching is not what it could be. The volume's title is a quote from Harry Emerson Fosdick in the early part of the twentieth century, suggesting that this concern about the quality of preaching is a matter of at least a hundred years' duration.[1]

The importance of preaching as an aspect of ministry, and the difficulty of preaching, are two sides of the same coin – what makes preaching difficult is also what makes it important. In this essay I will consider the perennial difficulties of preaching, and then focus attention on the challenges of preaching in the particular cultural context of consumer capitalism, a set of cultural forces that profoundly shapes preaching in North America, Europe and increasingly around the globe, and which poses unique challenges for preachers.

---

[1] Mike Graves, ed., *What's the Matter with Preaching Today?* (Louisville, KY: Westminster John Knox Press, 2004).

A perennial challenge in preaching is that of enculturating the gospel into the lives of present-day listeners, executing the hermeneutical task of linking the horizon of the Bible and the Christian tradition with the horizon of the listener's life-world. To many contemporary listeners, it is not self-evident that a two-thousand-year-old text, and the tradition springing from it, would speak so decisively to them as to transform their very existence, and yet this is the audacious claim of the Scripture and tradition of the Church, and the case which the preacher has to make. When the preacher preaches in the context of the liturgy, the liturgy itself assists in making this case and presenting this claim, and yet the crucial insight of the Protestant Reformers is that the liturgy itself, and the sacraments, require the proclamation of the gospel in order to make this claim convincingly.[2] The sermon is crucial in speaking the promise of the gospel clearly, and enabling this promise to touch the hearts of worshippers.

A further difficulty has to do with *how* preachers enculturate the promise of the gospel, namely, by passing it through the lens of their own personal existence. In liturgically oriented traditions, the liturgy is often largely set by denominational bodies. The sermon, however, is an unscripted moment; it is a moment in the liturgy when the preacher speaks her own words, not those inherited from the tradition, and seeks to show how these traditional forms ought to transform the lives of her hearers, by showing how they have first transformed *her*. The preacher's own life is a lens through which to view the gospel, and an example of how the gospel ought to shape the lives of listeners. In saying that they want strong and compelling preaching, it is in large part the preacher's personal connection to text and tradition that listeners long for. However, it is not easy for preachers to discern how to draw on the personal within their preaching. The debate in the field of homiletics over the appropriate use of personal stories in sermons is but the tip of the iceberg of this larger issue of how the preacher's personhood ought to figure in the sermon, since without our even speaking a word about ourselves, we are deeply involved in our preaching.[3] Indeed, even if we seek to hide aspects

---

[2] Luther, for instance, described preaching as 'the word [that] brings Christ to the folk and makes him known in their hearts, a thing they never understood from the sacrament'. In Karl Barth, *The Doctrine of the Word of God*, trans. G.T. Thomson (New York: Charles Scribner's Sons, 1936), 78.

[3] For the debate in homiletics concerning the role of the personal in preaching, see, among others, David Buttrick, *Homiletic: Moves and Structures* (Philadelphia, PA: Fortress Press,

of our personhood in preaching, that too is a personal statement in which we are implicated. Thus, preaching is inescapably personal.

This highly personal nature of preaching crystallizes one of the issues with which this volume is concerned – namely, the complex relationship between the subjective and objective dimensions of ministry. The minister is subject to the 'panopticon', a figure on public display at all times. Nowhere is this sense of being on display more pronounced than in preaching, because it is a moment of public manifestation of the preacher's faith and conviction. For this reason, there is inevitably tension between this public display and the subjective experience of ministry. The preacher seeks to symbolize as well as transmit the Christian tradition, but, as a fallible human individual, how can he do so adequately? More than this, how can or should the personal existence of the preacher be used as a lens through which to understand the gospel?

Despite the challenges of negotiating the hermeneutical gap between the world of the text and the world of the reader, the deeper difficulty of presenting the claims of the gospel has to do with the radically counter-cultural demands of the Scripture and tradition themselves, which have been a challenge to every age in which they have been preached. The proclamation that the same mind must be in us that is in Christ Jesus, who took on the form of a slave and died on the cross, will always be challenging. The demands of radical love, of the giving away of self and of life itself, are difficult for any culture to hear and accept.

Preaching in consumer culture: the challenge of commodification

In addition to the perennial challenges of preaching, there are particular challenges to preaching in contemporary times. It is instructive to compare the cultural situation of Christian proclamation now with that in nineteenth-century Denmark, in the time of Søren Kierkegaard. Kierkegaard fiercely criticized Christian preachers, arguing that their proclamation was undermined by 'the monstrous illusion we call Christendom . . . the illusion that in such a land as ours we are all Christians of a sort'.[4] The common assumption of the day that all people within a certain geographical

---

1987), 141–3; Anna Carter Florence, *Preaching as Testimony* (Louisville, KY: Westminster John Knox Press, 2007), xiii.

[4] Søren Kierkegaard, *The Point of View, Etc.: Including The Point of View for My Work as an Author, Two Notes about 'The Individual', and On My Work as an Author*, trans. Walter Lowrie (Oxford: Oxford University Press, 1939), 5–6.

area were Christians as a matter of course meant that Christianity itself had become a matter of habit and convention. Christian preachers had colluded with this illusion, presenting Christianity as a reasonable belief system, easily reconciled with secular culture. Writing pseudonymously as Johannes de Silentio, Kierkegaard ruthlessly mocks preachers who preach on the binding of Isaac without noting the nigh-impossibility of doing as Abraham did, and then are shocked when parents go home and murder their children. This 'profound, tragic, and comic misunderstanding' occurs because the preacher made the mistake that 'he did not know what he was saying'.[5] In domesticating the story of Abraham and Isaac so as to make it palatable to the Christendom of his time, the preacher utterly failed to capture its terror and difficulty, with tragic results. Kierkegaard maintains that the whole purpose of his authorship is to combat this dangerous propensity to make the demands of Christian faith easier than they really are; he seeks to reintroduce the difficulty of Christian faith into a culture that has cheapened and distorted it, 'to make it clear what the requirement of Christianity truly is – even though not one person should be induced to enter it'.[6]

The cultural conditions and thus the nature of the forces confronting Christian preaching have changed since Kierkegaard's time. North American and European churches no longer exist in Christendom, in which they can assume that all within a certain geographical area 'are Christians of a sort'; rather, Christians now live in religiously pluralist cultures. More than this, our cultural context is more radically shaped by consumer capitalism than was Kierkegaard's. Nevertheless, the challenge that Kierkegaard posed to preachers is just as trenchant in our own time, since the illusion of Christendom and the dynamics of consumerism function similarly, in that both dynamics foster a superficial rather than a deep engagement with religious faith. This shallow engagement with faith is one of the principal challenges of preaching in these times.

As Vincent Miller notes, consumerism fosters a superficial encounter with religious faith because consumerism shapes not so much our beliefs as how we engage these beliefs. Miller analyses these dynamics by drawing on Karl Marx's account of how commodification functions in capitalism: 'commodities appear on the scene, as if descended from heaven, cloaked in an aura of self-evident value, saying nothing about how, where, and by

---

[5] Søren Kierkegaard (Johannes de Silentio), *Fear and Trembling / Repetition*, ed. and trans. Howard V. Hong and Edna H. Hong (Princeton, NJ: Princeton University Press, 1983), 28, 29.

[6] Søren Kierkegaard, *On My Work as an Author*, in *The Point of View, Etc.*, 160.

whom they were produced.'[7] While Marx was chiefly concerned with the commodification of material goods, the expansion of consumer capitalism now encompasses cultural goods as well. We consume cultural objects in abstraction from their origins, the cultural associations and practices that give them meaning. Religion too becomes commodified, such that 'elements of religious traditions are fragmented into discrete, free-floating signifiers abstracted from their interconnections with other doctrines, symbols, and practices. This abstraction of elements from their traditions weakens their ability deeply to affect the concrete practice of daily life.'[8]

In consumer capitalism, it is not so much that we believe wrongly; it is that we engage religious beliefs and practices shallowly. As Miller states:

> The problem is not simply a clash of beliefs, values or cultures that pits consumerism against Christianity. Although very real conflicts in values exist, the problem is deeper and more subtle. Rather than a conflict between cultures, we face a cultural infrastructure that is capable of absorbing all other cultures as 'content' to be commodified, distributed, and consumed. This changes our relationship to religious beliefs and practices profoundly. They continue to be revered and celebrated, but are increasingly deprived of their ability to influence and shape our individual, interpersonal, and communal lives.[9]

We treat religious beliefs and practices as commodities from which we can pick and choose, divorced from their meanings within communities of practice. So, for instance, we hang Tibetan prayer flags in our homes without having any knowledge of the meaning of these symbols within Tibetan Buddhism; or we idolize Pope Francis as a religious celebrity, while paying scant attention to his teachings on matters such as climate change, global poverty and war. The prayer flags and the pope have become religious commodities to be selected or discarded according to our personal preferences; cut off from the institutional and communal settings in which they have meaning, they lose their power to form us deeply.

Both preachers and their hearers are deeply formed by the culture of commodification. It is not so much that consumer capitalism presents structures of meaning that compete with religion, as that consumer capitalism teaches us to approach religion as yet one more commodity that we can select or reject. In this context, preaching itself risks becoming a

---

[7] Vincent Miller, *Consuming Religion: Christian Faith and Practice in a Consumer Culture* (New York: Continuum, 2005), 3.

[8] Miller, *Consuming Religion*, 4.

[9] Miller, *Consuming Religion*, 179.

commodity to be consumed. From this stance a hearer may enjoy a sermon and may celebrate the preacher, but may still engage the sermon superficially and not be deeply formed by it. The preacher, for his part, may wonder why he feels that he has not really connected with the hearers such that their lives are transformed. Commodification renders religious beliefs and practices frictionless, such that it is difficult for sermons to gain traction in shaping hearers' lives. Given this challenging hearing environment, how can preachers and hearers best proclaim and respond to the gospel in preaching?

Preaching beyond commodification: a liturgical turn

In answer to this question, I propose that the cultural setting of consumer capitalism demands the foregrounding of the personal element of preaching, although this must be done in a way that takes account of how commodification functions, and thus how to counter it. As noted earlier, the question of how the personal ought to figure in preaching is a complex one, a crystallization of the difficult relationship between the subjective and objective dimensions of ministry. The pressures of commodification make it more important than ever to both theorize and practically incorporate the personal in preaching. To make this argument requires a further investigation of the role of preaching in its primary setting in the liturgy.

Miller turns to liturgy as a means of resisting commodification because he argues that an effective response to commodification does not lie primarily at the level of theological argumentation. Whatever theologically rich counter-narratives are offered to set against the ideologies of consumer capitalism, it is all too easy for these counter-narratives themselves to be co-opted by consumer culture. Indeed, market capitalism 'greets subversion and denunciation with mercantile enthusiasm', treating such critiques as yet one more product to sell.[10] Thus, the most effective way for those who wish to steward religious traditions to resist consumer culture is not principally at the level of beliefs, but at the level of practices. The liturgy, the Church's corporate worship, is its central practice, the practice in which it most clearly becomes and manifests what it is. As such, the liturgy of the Church is one of the most powerful practices the Church has at its disposal to challenge consumerism. In liturgy, we encounter our faith not primarily as a series of propositions, but as embodied actions. We *enact* the tenets of our faith – listening to the God who addresses us in his word,

---

[10] Miller, *Consuming Religion*, 179.

confessing sin and receiving forgiveness, being incorporated into God's very life in the Eucharist, united to one another in the body of Christ. In other words, liturgy shapes us powerfully because it engages us not solely at the level of our ideas but at the level of our bodies' performances.

The term 'performance', used to describe either liturgy or preaching, can be off-putting, as it seems to imply artifice and inauthenticity. However, there are at least two aspects of the concept of performance, as it is used in performance theory, which are helpful in understanding the ways the liturgy and preaching can resist the dynamics of commodification. First, performance refers to actions which are not spontaneously created by a subject, but are rather the repetition of a previously created script. Richard Schechner coined the term 'restored behaviour' to describe this quality of performance. Marvin Carlson notes that 'restored behavior emphasizes the process of repetition and the continued awareness of some "original" behavior, however distant or corrupted by myth or memory, which serves as a kind of grounding for the restoration'.[11] Second, the concept of performance suggests the ways that identities are constructed through restored behaviour, through the repetition of scripted actions and practices. As Judith Butler notes, the performance of the self proceeds by certain stylized, repeated and ritualized acts, out of which the self is produced. Performance thus has the power to shape and even produce the self. Butler uses Pierre Bourdieu's idea of **habitus** to emphasize the way repeated performance shapes our way of being in the world. Habitus, says Butler, is 'a tacit form of performativity, a citational claim lived and believed at the level of the body'.[12]

Not only in individual lives, but in communities also, practices of performance have the power to form selves shaped by a distinctive habitus. The liturgy is one of the primary places where the Church does this, where it 'performs' its founding narratives and doctrines, and thus both becomes and manifests what it is. Participants in the Eucharist engage in restored behaviour through repeating the script of the eucharistic prayers and actions, carrying forward the power of the originary event. In the performance of the Eucharist the Church repeats and manifests Christ's Incarnation; in the Eucharist the Word again becomes flesh and dwells among us. Through the repetition of this performance the habitus of participants, their way of being in the world, is shaped and transformed.

---

[11] Marvin Carlson, *Performance: A Critical Introduction*, 2nd edn (New York: Routledge, 2004), 47.

[12] Judith Butler, *Excitable Speech: A Politics of the Performative* (London: Routledge, 1997), 155.

William Cavanaugh, in his analysis of how the Church in Chile combated a repressive state regime, describes how the performative power of liturgy was a vital part of this struggle.[13] Cavanaugh argues that the state used torture as a way to conscript the bodies of its citizens into the performance of certain scripts. Torture invaded the bodies of citizens, reshaping them into docile victims of state control. For the Church to resist this control involved not only pronouncements but, more significantly, the induction of its members into bodily performances that shaped them according to a Christian imagination, rather than the imagination of the state. The primary performance of this Christian identity was the liturgy of the Eucharist, which transformed participants into the body of Christ, rather than being bodies under state control. Through participation in the Eucharist, participants were assimilated into Christ's incarnation, and specifically into Christ's self-sacrifice. As participants were conformed to his self-sacrifice, they became capable of offering themselves as sacrificial martyrs rather than victims of the state.

Cavanaugh's argument suggests how liturgy has the power to shape believers into identities that run counter to those offered by the surrounding culture, and thus is applicable in the context of consumer capitalism, where religious communities struggle to express different identities from those provided by the surrounding culture. Consumer capitalism does not invade and shape bodies through torture; rather, it colonizes their imagination and shapes their identities through subtler means. Liturgy, however, has the capacity to form participants into identities that resist the shaping power of consumerism. As Butler's and Cavanaugh's arguments demonstrate, liturgical practices form us powerfully because they are embodied. Our bodies do things in worship, and these acts, more than what we say we believe, shape us into the people we are. This emphasis on bodies is consonant with the Christian claim that God in Christ became flesh and dwelt among us, and thus that 'God saves humanity right in our very material actions and circumstances', that is, in our very bodies.[14] As Louis-Marie Chauvet expresses it, 'Faithful to its biblical roots, ecclesial tradition has attempted to discern what is most "spiritual" in God on the basis of what is most "corporeal" in us. This is especially the case in liturgy.'[15] It is above

---

[13] William T. Cavanaugh, *Torture and Eucharist: Theology, Politics, and the Body of Christ* (Malden, MA, and Oxford: Blackwell, 1998), 230.

[14] Bruce T. Morrill and Bernard Cooke, eds, *Bodies of Worship: Explorations in Theory and Practice* (Collegeville, MN: Liturgical Press, 1999), 3.

[15] Louis-Marie Chauvet, *Symbol and Sacrament: A Sacramental Reinterpretation of Christian Existence*, trans. P. Madigan and M. Beaumont (Collegeville, MN: Liturgical Press, 1995), 523.

all in our embodied experience that we are brought into relationship with God, for 'there is no disembodied realm where we are being saved'.[16]

Although this emphasis on the body as the locus of salvation is as old as Christianity itself, in recent scholarship in liturgical theology there has been an increased emphasis on bodies in worship, which is connected to a redefining of what makes for the sacramentality of worship. There has been 'a move away from thinking about the sacraments as objects that dispense grace to perceiving them as relational events, as personal encounters among God and people'.[17] The focus is less on the abstract principles involved in a material substance becoming sacred, and more on the relational encounter with God that takes place in the liturgy. One upshot of this shift has been to understand the whole of liturgy as sacramental, since all of it reveals and partakes of God's life. The sacramentality of liturgy cannot be reduced to one moment when a material object is transformed from profane to sacred; rather, the whole of liturgy is sacramental, as a progressive manifestation of the realities of Christ's saving work. Moreover, this focus on the sacredness of the entire liturgy, as an event of encounter with God, focuses attention on the bodies of participants who are involved in this encounter. It is in their bodies, at least as much as in the bread and wine, that the transforming power of grace is at work.

Sacramentality and the preaching body

One of the primary ways that liturgy focuses our attention on materiality is by fostering the sacramental imagination. As described by Richard McBrien, sacramentality is a way of seeing 'God in all things . . . the visible, the tangible, the finite, the historical – all these are actual or potential carriers of the divine presence'.[18] This sacramental imagination endows particular physical things with importance; they are not 'just symbols', because the material mediation itself matters. Hence sacraments function by 'tying the significance of symbols to their particularity'. The sacramental imagination runs directly counter to the dynamics of commodification, in which objects are sundered from the origins of their production. For the sacramental imagination, these origins matter; Miller suggests that in offering the bread and wine at the Eucharist, we consider the origins of these material objects: 'through your goodness we have this bread to offer,

---

16 Morrill and Cooke, eds, *Bodies of Worship*, 4.
17 Morrill and Cooke, eds, *Bodies of Worship*, 1.
18 Quoted in Miller, *Consuming Religion*, 189.

which earth has given and human hands have made. It will become for us the Bread of Life.' Hearing these words focuses our attention on the conditions under which these objects were produced, challenging us to ask pointed questions about these origins, such as: *which* part of the earth gave this bread? *Whose* hands made it into bread? In this way the sacramental imagination connects symbols with their materiality, countering the commodity fetish, in which things are conveyers of meaning and status separate from their particularity. Sacramentality challenges us to connect the meaning and sacredness of objects with their material conditions, not abstracted from them.

Since the whole of the liturgy is a sacramental encounter with God, the sacramental imagination attends not only to the materiality of the bread and wine, but perceives God's presence in *all* of the 'visible, tangible, finite, historical' parts of the liturgy, including the preaching event. Preaching, as part of a liturgy which is wholly sacramental, is itself sacramental, which means not only that it is an event of personal encounter with God, but also that this encounter occurs through material means. The sacramental imagination draws attention to the 'visible, tangible, finite, historical' aspects of preaching itself, the ways that God is made known through the particular. The particular material elements through which God reveals Godself in preaching are the words and the embodied existence of the preacher.

The sacramental imagination focuses on the particular materiality of sacramental objects; hence, in relation to preaching, such an imagination considers the preacher's speaking body not as an abstract body, but rather as a body embedded in its social location, the various political and economic relationships that influence it. Just as the sacramental imagination brings to awareness the material origins of the bread and wine, so too in preaching the origins of the preached word in the existence of the person preaching need to be made visible. Liturgy in general foregrounds the material particularity of bodies, and preaching does this in a powerful and exemplary way, precisely because it is the most personal moment of the liturgy, the moment when the particularity of one human person is brought to the fore. The listener's encounter with the particular humanity of the preacher creates friction, making it more difficult to receive the sermon as an abstract commodity.

It is crucial, therefore, for preaching to be grounded in the particular body and life-experience of the preacher. This does not mean a proliferation of personal stories; rather, it means that the preacher needs to make evident that he is personally involved in his preaching, that the sermon is of life-and-death importance and emerges from his whole life. This is accomplished not only by what the preacher *says*, but also how he *is* in preaching – specifically, whether he is present in a way that integrates body, mind and spirit. Are preachers present in such a way that their breath is flowing, that their voice is connected to the words they are speaking, and that their bodies are also integrated into and involved in this communication? Are they connected to their bodies' own knowledge of what they are saying, which may well go deeper than what their minds know? Do their voices and bodies manifest a passionate commitment to the truth of their message?

It is difficult to answer these questions, since we are not accustomed to relying upon the body's knowledge. The disconnection between mind and body is deeply embedded in Western culture. This dualism affects the ways that we engage knowledge or reflect upon our experience, despite the centrality of the Incarnation in Christian doctrine, which insists that we are saved in our bodily existence. Moreover, the Church tends to harbour suspicion about the body, viewing it as dangerous, unruly, possessed of desires which might disqualify it from the pulpit. For this reason preachers often manifest a disconnection between mind and body, preaching as though they did not have bodies, or were unaware of them. The layout of preaching, with the preacher partially hidden behind a pulpit, or obscured by amorphous robes, further operates to hide the preaching body. The recent tendency to use screens and projections in worship further attenuates the presence of the bodies of both preachers and hearers. Given all of this, to bring specific attention to the body in the act of preaching feels like breaking a taboo, encountering and pressing through potent internal and external resistance.

In this situation of resistance to the full integration of our bodies in preaching, the operations of commodification may be a perverse blessing in that they compel us to find solid ground that cannot be abstracted, and that in the end pushes us back to the body's reality and wisdom, as a firm landing place that resists abstraction. The preacher takes her stand in her body so as to speak from a place of a particular truth grounded in her material existence. This demands a total engagement of the preacher, which inevitably requires vulnerability. The sacramentality of preaching suggests that this vulnerability is intrinsic to proclamation. As the bread is taken and blessed, so too the particularity of the preacher is taken and blessed, so as to be broken open and shared, as the bread is broken and shared. To be broken open requires self-offering and sacrifice; all of this is implied in the call to the preacher to be fully present in preaching – in body, mind and spirit.

Strengthening communal agency in preaching

In the liturgy we become what we are – the body of Christ – and we do this not as individuals, but as a community. One of the difficulties of preaching is that it tends to undermine the communal nature of the liturgy. Preaching often feels like a solo performance – indeed, one reason many preachers dislike the word 'performance' to describe preaching is that it seems to privilege one person (the preacher's) actions, to put the preacher on a pedestal while rendering the hearers as passive recipients. The dynamics of consumerism magnify these tendencies; the passivity of hearers readily puts them into the position of being consumers of a spectacle or product rather than active co-creators of a communal event.

That preaching is a communal event, co-created by preacher and community, has been argued persuasively by many homileticians in recent years. Thomas Long describes the preacher as being sent to the Scripture 'on behalf of the community', rather than operating on one's own.[19] Leonora Tubbs Tisdale insists that preachers need to be as attentive to the congregational context of their preaching as they are to the Scripture text.[20] Fred Craddock describes the preacher as preaching not only *to* the community but *for* the community, putting into words the proclamation of the community.[21] These arguments indicate that the community is integral to preaching, not only as hearers but as creators of it.

In a culture shaped by consumerism, the active role of the community in the preaching event needs to be even more strongly emphasized. As Vincent Miller notes, one of the most powerful ways to resist the commodification of religion is to strengthen the agency of its adherents. Believers shaped by consumerism tend to see themselves as active agents of their beliefs in that they feel free to 'draw from traditions with little knowledge of their intrinsic logics and goals and without a sense of obligation for the preservation of traditions'.[22] Rather than exercising agency in this way, believers need to be authorized and encouraged to be agents of their traditions, seeing their applications and understandings of the faith as a contribution to a living tradition to which they are responsible. In the liturgy, this means establishing the congregation 'not as a group of passive consumers who are served

---

[19] Thomas G. Long, *The Witness of Preaching*, 2nd edn (Louisville, KY: Westminster John Knox Press, 2005), 7.

[20] Leonora Tubbs Tisdale, *Preaching as Local Theology and Folk Art* (Minneapolis, MN: Fortress Press, 1997), 33.

[21] Fred B. Craddock, *Preaching* (Nashville, TN: Abingdon Press, 1985), 26.

[22] Miller, *Consuming Religion*, 210.

by the celebrant but as active agents praying together the central prayer of the church'.[23] The same goals apply to preaching, although the impression of the sermon as a monologue makes this ideal of active communal engagement in the sermon difficult to achieve.

In practice, realizing this goal may mean adopting practices of conversational preaching, such as those proposed by Lucy Atkinson Rose and others, in which the sermon is imagined as a communal conversation gathered around God's word, in which all congregational voices are valued as participants in the sermon itself.[24] Other models of conversational preaching propose an active role for the community in the preparation of the sermon, perhaps through sessions of Scripture study which provide material for the sermon. These practices are a development of Tisdale's insistence that the preacher listen to the situation of the congregation as closely as she listens to Scripture texts. It is crucial, of course, that these participants understand themselves as agents of their traditions, and responsible to them, which suggests a need for catechesis in order for congregation members to take an active role in sermon creation.

The way that the preacher is present in her preaching can also open the sermon to the congregation. The preacher who practises her preaching as sacramental in a thick way, that is, in terms of the eucharistic arc of taking, blessing, breaking and giving, can be present in her preaching in such a way as to open herself and her sermon to the hearers. In particular, when the preacher practises the breaking open of the word as involving a breaking open of the self, the vulnerability of this act makes it evident that the preacher preaches in fundamental connection to the congregation, and not apart from it.

Conclusion

The cultural context of consumerism adds to the perennial challenges of preaching the particular challenge of the commodification of preaching itself. While there are aspects of the sermon that make it prone to commodification, such as the fact that it is a solo performance to a seemingly passive audience, there are also aspects of the sermon that make it a particularly powerful practice to offer resistance to these dynamics. In particular, the tensions between the subjective and objective dimensions

---

23 Miller, *Consuming Religion*, 214.
24 Lucy Atkinson Rose, *Sharing the Word: Preaching in the Roundtable Church* (Louisville, KY: Westminster John Knox Press, 1997), 89.

of ministry, the communal tradition and the personal instantiation of it, come to the fore in preaching and are often painfully felt by the preacher. However, it is precisely the creative inhabiting of these tensions that leads to a powerful counter-experience to that of commodification. The preacher who can instantiate, physically as well as spiritually, the intrinsic connection between the content of the sermon and its rootedness in his or her existence offers a practice that resists abstraction. Preaching that displays its origins in the particular embodied life of the preacher demands to be encountered not shallowly, as a commodity without a history, but deeply, as an event with thickness and integrity. Likewise, when the sermon is not a solo act but a communal performance in which the congregation participates, believers are formed into agents of a living tradition, rather than consumers.

Preaching has always been demanding, a difficult balancing of the personal and the public, the individual and the communal. Each era presents its own challenges for preaching; in this era, the culture of consumerism confronts preaching with particular challenges. However, if preaching in these times is more difficult than ever, it is also true that the need for and the promise of proclamation are greater than ever as well.

31

Ministry among other faith traditions

BONNIE EVANS-HILLS

To be a minister, whether it is, in Christian terms, as an ordained member of the clergy or as a lay person, whether it is formally recognized or something that happens along life's journey, to be a minister is to live a life of courageous, sacrificial love. There is nothing naive or trite in this statement, although it may sound so. Interpreting the Bible in a manner less literal but rather metaphorically, the priest of the Temple received the offerings of the faithful, took on their sin, cleansed and healed them, worshipped and glorified God on their behalf, taught wisdom and distributed alms to the poor. They were to be empty vessels, bearing the pain of the people and appealing to God on their behalf. Theirs were the hands that discerned dis-ease and healed, that made clean the darkened heart. They sanctified people and place. This is no mean task.

There are myriad models of ministry within the Christian tradition, some of which we may recognize within other faith traditions, and some which we may not translate in exactitude, but fulfil in spirit and intention. Rather than attempt any kind of exact comparison which could only prove disappointing, if not apologetic at best and offensive to other traditions at worst, it might prove more productive to provide examples of the individual ministry of those working within faith traditions other than our own. Within each there will be models we may recognize, and models which seem to hold a shadow of our own and yet be wholly different. Let it go without saying that each tradition will have exceptions to the ideal. There will be those whose exclusivist approach will prohibit the pastoral perspective intended in this chapter, and that will be as true of some of our Christian colleagues as those of other traditions.

The examples presented are intentionally positive, yet not without their limitations and tensions. It is hoped there is much that will be familiar within the story of each, something that begs the recognition of a trusted and trusting friend; someone with whom it is possible to wrestle to the depths of our seeking souls and emerge together with a more profound, wider grasp of the mysterious grandeur of the God of whom we are all Lovers. Can we find the face of God, and God's presence, in one another?

A chapter in the book *Engaging Islam from a Christian Perspective* explores the experience of a dialogue between Muslim scholars from Iran visiting Ampleforth Abbey in 2005, just after the 7/7 bombings in London.[1] Following several days of endeavouring to find common theological ground, it was the exploration of the love affair with God on the final day which brought coherence and concord. Participants realized that when speaking of their love of God, they were speaking the same language.

And this is the common thread running through those involved in ministry, and among the faithful, of all faiths. I would even hazard this to be true of those of the humanist or atheist conviction. Motivation to help the poor, feed the hungry, clothe the naked, heal the sick, all stem from a heart that loves fellow humanity, and finds sanctity within the human heart. Buddhism is considered to be a tradition without deity, without a concept of God, and yet Love, in the form of ecstatic joy, bliss, permeates that state of *ahimsa* – detachment. The Buddhist nun, Tenzin Palmo, describes moments of being overtaken by Love, the drive behind her determination to live as a recluse for 13 years in a cave in the Himalayas. Those choosing to live in solitude describe the full connection they are able to experience with the rest of creation that living among a crowd drowns out. It is a kind of intimacy, the intimacy of a wedded couple, the intimacy of the Beloved and the Lover in the language of religious mystics.

Palmo describes how this 'bliss' can have its own distractions:

> The only problem with bliss is that because it arouses such enormous pleasure, beyond anything on a worldly level, including sexual bliss, people cling to it and really want it and then it becomes another obstacle . . . It's only useful when it is used as a state of mind for understanding Emptiness – when that blissful mind is able to look into its own nature.[2]

Amid stories of saints with the ability to fly, withstand extreme temperatures or live without food is the story of the Buddha himself defrocking a monk for performing such public miracles. To him the only miracle that counted was the transformation of the human heart.[3] Even though this

---

[1] Bonnie Evans-Hills and Michael Rusk, *Engaging Islam from a Christian Perspective*, Peter Lang, New York, 2015, pp. 256–7.
[2] Vicki Mackenzie, *Cave in the Snow*, a biography of Tenzin Palmo, Bloomsbury, London, 1998, p. 113.
[3] Mackenzie, *Cave in the Snow*, p. 112.

state of bliss is a stumbling block if one seeks to remain there, it is also all the greater when brought about by connection to others. From her mountain retreat, where she could only be reached for three months out of the year, Palmo would write letters, receive visitors and read voraciously in order to support her correspondence. The simplicity of everyday tasks became meditation and service in themselves and a deep connection to humanity.

Later spending time in Assisi, Palmo lived in a convent, and studied and was inspired by the life of St Thérèse of Lisieux. She writes of Thérèse:

> She didn't perform any great miracles. She didn't have any great visions. She did something very simple, which we are all capable of doing – she changed her attitude. We cannot transform the world, but we can transform our mind. And when we transform our mind, lo and behold, the whole world is transformed![4]

Palmo, born Diane Perry, the daughter of a fishmonger in London's East End, has become a source of inspiration for many practising Buddhism in the West, and for many women. Prior to her 13 years in a Himalayan mountain cave, Palmo spent years in study and service of the local poor. She lived for a time as the only woman in a men's monastery. She has declared matter-of-factly that she had 'made a vow to attain Enlightenment in the female form – no matter how many lifetimes it takes'.[5] The Venerable Tenzin Palmo continues to be a strong advocate for women's ordination and the establishment of women's religious institutions in the Theravadan Buddhist tradition.

Women in ministry don't tend to set out to challenge or even break taboos surrounding gender; they merely seek to follow the path they believe they are meant to follow, to seek truth and to follow the Love that is buried in the hearts of each one of us. When man-made barriers get in the way, they will find a way to get past – as lovers will surpass any barrier to obtain the object of their love. The goal of these women of faith is not to shatter male tradition, but if that tradition gets in the way of their voca-tion, then shatter it they will. One of the more powerful books on ministry in different faith traditions has been *Faithfully Feminist: Jewish, Christian and Muslim Feminists on Why We Stay*. In the chapter 'Speaking Forward', Deonna Kelli Sayed writes:

---

[4]   Ani Tenzin Palmo, *Reflections on a Mountain Lake: Teachings on Practical Buddhism*, Snow Lion, New York, 2002, p. 53.
[5]   Mackenzie, *Cave in the Snow*, p. 5.

Feminism can be the political struggle against structural and patriarchal oppression, but it can also be the quiet personal choice to honor your faith – indeed, to fight for your place in it – and to carve out spaces for others to do so, as well.[6]

Much of this breaking of bonds asunder is not achieved by grand gestures, but by the patient unpicking of threads, often with the help of supportive male colleagues. For Tenzin Palmo it was done with the support of her guru, Khamtrul Rinpoche. At the 2012 Modern Church conference on Women and Religious Authority, Hamburg, imam Halima Krausen shared something of how she came to be accepted in her position as imam for German-speaking people at the Hamburg mosque. Krausen has studied and written widely on Islam, the Qur'an and the Hadith, and is considered a leading imam and faith leader among Muslims in Europe and the USA, as well as other parts of the Muslim world. She spent 12 years working alongside her predecessor at the mosque, stating that when the time came for him to retire, the congregations were used to her being in a position of authority and providing religious judgement. There were no issues made over her being a woman.

A predecessor to religious leadership of women among Muslims was Nusrat Amin of Isfahan in Iran. Born in 1886, she was supported and encouraged by her father in her pursuit of Islamic studies. He continued to fund her even after her marriage. Amin set up a school, or *madrasa*, for women in Isfahan which catered for a generation of thousands of Iranian women, and was revered and sought out by the leading clerics of the eventual Islamic Revolution. Her legacy is one of a wide number of women's colleges and universities, especially within the theological centres of Qum. It is fair to say there are as many women as men studying in the Shia centres of Iran, and also at the oldest university of Sunni traditions, al-Azhar in Egypt. Despite having their own, separate, women's campus, women also sit alongside men at the feet of top Islamic scholars giving lectures in the famous al-Azhar mosque, where anyone is free to join in. Men and women both ask questions and share in the discussions, as has been happening since 1961, breaking somewhat stereotypical assumptions of this being taboo.

Students of al-Azhar University come from all over the world. I am sure there are many other rigorous requirements, but it was said to me by one of their professors that the main entrance criterion is to have

---

[6]   Gina Messina-Dysert, Jennifer Zobair and Amy Levin, *Faithfully Feminist: Jewish, Christian, and Muslim Feminists on Why We Stay*, White Cloud Press, Ashland, OR, 2015, p. 7.

memorized the whole of the Holy Qur'an. To put this into perspective, there are a little over 77,000 words in the Holy Qur'an, and around 65,000 words in the four Gospels based on the Greek New Testament. In reality, the list of requirements on their website includes having memorized four *juz*. The Qur'an is divided into 30 sections, or *juz*, so this means memorizing about 9,000 words. Among the other requirements are a knowledge of Arabic, comparable to Greek for the Christian scholar, and demonstrable learning or skill in an area such as theology, jurisprudence or recitation. Having sat in some classes during a theological exchange for the Anglican Communion's al-Azhar Dialogue, I can attest that the feel is much like that of any Christian theological college: an amount of debate, an amount of naivety on the part of some younger students and a passion for learning.

Al-Azhar takes in students from a wide range of theological traditions. One of the more visual examples was provided at the women's campus. One of my hosts, a post-graduate student at the university, stood with me and pointed out the various manners of dress of both male and female students – but among the women the theological differences were more pronounced. There were those who wore the full *niqab*, or face veil and long black robes, some who wore long robes, others who wore what could be considered more fashionable clothing – a dress and trousers. All of them covered their hair, but some had colourful scarves tied in weird and wonderful ways, some had simple head-coverings, and others tied a smaller scarf behind their necks. I was told that those dressed in black and covering their faces had come under 'foreign' influence. At one point many Egyptians had gone to work in the Gulf for the oil industry and brought back these 'foreign' traditions. Some of the older women professors, with whom I was privileged to share in a seminar, did not cover their hair, or wore smaller head-coverings. While this difference was more pronounced among the women, there was also a range of dress among the male students, from those who were clean-shaven and wearing jeans to those with long beards and robes.

What this demonstrated was a range of theological traditions ranging from the more austere and pietist Salafi, to traditional Islam, and through to the mystic and Sufi traditions. Al-Azhar at that point, in 2009, was a model for how well the different traditions within Islam are able to work alongside one another, hold rigorous discourse and build community together as seekers of Truth. But there have since occurred the events of the Arab Spring, and the al-Azhar campuses were raided by army forces upon ousting the former president, Mursi. Al-Azhar has had a reputation of supporting both the government and the Muslim Brotherhood – possibly the result of what happens to most religious institutions trying to survive amid political upheavals. When there is such a range of ideologies within any institution, there are bound to be supporters of what are considered to be unhealthy beliefs, but it is their presence in such a rigorous academic context that enables critical challenge to happen.

The theological exchanges that had begun with the Anglican Communion through the auspices of the British Council and Foreign Office went into obvious decline during the upheavals in Egypt. But with the visit of the Grand Imam of al-Azhar to the Archbishop of Canterbury in July 2018, it is hoped further exchanges can take place.

Needless to say, the leadership among the Muslim community in the UK has benefited from al-Azhar education. Shaykh Ibrahim Mogra studied there, as did the late Sheikh Zaki Badawi, still affectionately remembered and held in high regard. What has made their contribution so invaluable within the UK has been their ability to maintain a traditional understanding and practice of Islam while relating effectively to British culture and context.

One of the things which has made al-Azhar so effective is the inclusion in its curriculum of theologies outside that of Islam. There is a programme for studying the Abrahamic faiths mentioned on its website, but a short trawl through the English library on campus also indicated an interest in European and Western thought. Much of the teaching I experienced was from an apologetics perspective, but there was strong similarity as a model with that of Christian apologetics.

Across the theological divide of Sunni and Shia, when the Rt Revd Michael Ipgrave visited the theological centres of Qum during his time as interfaith adviser to the Archbishop of Canterbury, he reports coming across one particularly enthusiastic fan of Richard Hooker, the sixteenth-century English priest and theologian. This Iranian scholar and cleric had translated all of Hooker's works into Farsi (Persian), and was looking forward to a good theological debate about Anglicanism.

And more recently, in the ancient Shia centre of learning in Najaf, Iraq, a new centre for the study of religions has opened.[7] This has been years in the planning with the help and support of the al-Khoei Foundation in London, and its director, Yousif al-Khoei. Yousif has continuously worked to bring together people of all faiths and none in a move towards greater understanding. He encourages young students as well as clerics of both

---

[7]   See <http://www.economist.com/blogs/erasmus/2015/12/religious-diplomacy-iraq>.

Sunni and Shia Islam. He has provided space for students of other faiths to do placements within his centre, and supported the ministry of many Christians – including myself. The Foundation works with Prince Hassan of Jordan and the Royal Institute for Inter-Faith Studies, as well as the Vatican and Lambeth Palace.

Seyed Yousif al-Khoei is reminiscent of others I have known following this same vocation, a belief in the peace of their homeland, the peace of the world, and the only authentic path in their faith has been to know and to love all peoples, of whatever tradition or nation, because this is what God is calling them to do. Much as was the case with the women mentioned previously, this path has not been without controversy. I once heard a priest involved in peace talks during the 'troubles' in Northern Ireland describe how, as difficult as it was to reach the hand of friendship across the divide, it was more difficult explaining what he was doing to the community behind him. Many considered him a traitor.

The 2010 film *Of Gods and Men*, about a group of monks in a monastery in Tibhirine in Algeria, depicts the story of how the monks befriended, cared for, helped, loved and lived alongside their Muslim neighbours. It was because of this friendship that they remained during the height of threat from terrorists, and were eventually killed by them. They studied the Holy Qur'an alongside the Bible, holding it to be vital to their ministry among their community. In the book *Christian Martyrs for a Muslim People*, the story of the abbot of the monastery, Father Christian de Chergé, is told. He had served in the French army during the Algerian revolution and had made friends with an Algerian policeman. One day his friend told him not to go into a certain area as there was a plot to have him killed. Father Christian discovered the next morning that his friend had been killed instead, because he had saved his life. Father Christian had then determined he would dedicate his life to the people of Algeria – because his Muslim friend had given his life that Father Christian might live. He acknowledged the sacrifice – martyrdom – his friend had taken on. And this is what led him to pre-emptive forgiveness for any terrorist that might take his life at some point in the future – saying they would meet as two happy thieves in paradise.[8]

There is a similar story from Syria and the monastery of Deir Mar Musa. The abbot of the monastery, Father Paolo Dall'Oglio, rebuilt the monastery in the 1980s from its abandoned ruins. One of the monks,

---

8   Martin McGee OSB, *Christian Martyrs for a Muslim People*, Paulist Press, Mahwah, NJ, 2008, p. 93.

Father Jihad, while in Rome studying towards ordination, came to speak at St Ethelburga's Centre for Peace and Reconciliation. He shared how the monastery was rebuilt with the help of their neighbours – 98 per cent Muslim. It was their Muslim neighbours who put in the running water and electricity, built the roads, looked after the crops and the goats, and their Muslim neighbours who shared daily prayers with them.

An Evangelical Christian pastor from Egypt once told me of how in a poverty-stricken area, known for its conservative radicalism, people had asked him to build a church. They believed the presence of Christians would lend a peaceful influence, and they themselves helped to build the church, supplying the electricity and water. During some of the violence of the Arab Spring, when Coptic churches were attacked, it was Muslim leaders and their followers who circled the churches for protection, and visited Christmas services in a show of solidarity and support for their Christian neighbours.

I myself have been at the receiving end of overwhelming hospitality on the part of Jewish communities and their leading rabbis. I have been invited to read the English translation of the Psalms during a service, to help in covering the Torah before it is returned to the tabernacle, and to light one of the candles of the menorah during Chanukah. Each of these gestures is a significant act of generous hospitality. The offer of participating in holy liturgy is not an invitation that is easily made, and I can think of few churches where this would happen so readily.

At one time I was made an honorary member of the Jewish Women Friends in Sussex, partly to enable me to attend the annual Passover meal held at the University of Sussex chaplaincy building. This group of women had come together from a generation of Jews who, following the Holocaust, did not want their children to stick out from the crowd. They knew they were Jewish, and that was about it. What drew them together was the desire to know something of their heritage and traditions, something their families had refrained from teaching them. Why was this, I asked myself. As I came to know more of the community, I realized that for each and every person there was some member, or many members, of her family who had been killed during the Holocaust. For each of them, it was not a distant but rather a living memory. They lived with the fear that such a thing could happen again – and the parents of these women had refrained from teaching them about their heritage in an effort to protect them, to keep from drawing attention to their 'difference'. This realization has made their hospitality all the more poignant for the necessary trust it implies.

That trust is also demonstrated in challenge. We can only challenge friends we trust well. One of the more significant challenges I have received was from the Liberal rabbi, Eli Tikvah Sarah. In a partnership, she once chastened me, stating that it was because of my bishops in the Church of England that she could not 'marry' her partner. Before the time of even civil partnerships, she was angry that, as a rabbi, she was prevented from calling her relationship a 'marriage' due to Anglican objection to the use of the term. She felt her personal life and her ministry were curtailed due to the actions of the Church. Of course the situation has now changed, but it is an indication of some of the tension surrounding equality legislation and exceptions provided for faith communities. When do the religious traditions and ideologies of one faith curtail the religious expression of others?

It was an Orthodox rabbi who shared with me that it is the role of a rabbi, as teacher, to study. It is his job to study, to read, to discuss, to discern. He is paid for the times he is unable to study, for when the people need his guidance. That love of study and scripture among rabbis, and the respect that learning has held within the Jewish community, was made apparent during a theological exchange at Leo Baeck College in London. A group of us Anglican ordinands were invited to spend several days with those studying to be ordained as rabbis. We were invited to participate in the daily Jewish prayers, learned something of scripture and even sat in the 'fishbowl' – a process for discussion whereby one person sits in the middle of a circle and the rest present questions around a theme or scriptural passage. All was good-natured and courteous, while at the same time a rigorous scrutiny.

That same theological scrutiny is utilized by a courageous group of women who struggle on a regular basis with the guards and conservative traditionalists of the Western Wall in Jerusalem in order to be able to read Torah and pray in the women's section; recently, for the first time, they have been able to bring a menorah to celebrate Chanukah. The Attorney General of Israel declared that every year the menorah in the men's section has been lit in a way that discriminates against women. The leader of Women of the Wall Nashot HaKotel[9] declared it a miracle that she and her companions were able to bring the menorah to the women's section. This group seeks for girls to be able to have Bat Mitzvah at the Wall, in the same way in which boys have been able to celebrate Bar Mitzvah. The women are often prevented from reading Torah – their scrolls are seized or spat at,

---

[9] See <http://womenofthewall.org.il>.

and objects are thrown at them from the men's section. Members are also arrested from time to time and on the receiving end of threats and violence from conservative Jewish women.

There is a cost to breaking boundaries.

My first experience of a Hindu temple was when I called in at my local temple in Portslade in Sussex. It is in what used to be an ordinary house on a residential street. The ground floor is used as a temple, and the upper rooms for meetings and meals. When I called in, one of the faithful was leaving following his devotions, and he ushered me inside to introduce me to the priest. The priest's English was scanty, but we managed to communicate – everyone else having left to head off to their jobs or carry on with the day. I just about managed to get through to him that I was there as a Christian (this was before I was ordained) and interested in building relations with him and with the temple. He was smiling shyly the whole time and really very pleased that I had come. As I left he insisted I take a supply of sweets and savouries back to my diocesan office to share around. These were viewed by my colleagues with a certain amount of suspicion – was this generous offering on the part of a priest of another religious tradition going to be seen as consuming the offering to other gods? It brought up questions of whether or not we were worshipping the same God.

I later lived in Leicester, working in a parish where there were a number of Hindu temples. The temple just a few doors down from the church was lively, with lots of people going in and out at all hours of the day and night. They often used our church hall for functions, and many of the Hindu faithful also came into our church to say prayers and light candles. The church was seen as a holy sanctuary, a place where prayers should be said. The priest, living on the temple premises, was also kept busy at all hours. English was a struggle for him, but he was gradually coming to grasp its use, and a younger generation of English-speaking priests were being encouraged. Their role is to be resident in the temple, to say the prayers, and to ensure the holiness of the temple, its surrounding area and the people who worship there.

A visit to India, and some of the temples in the south, brought me greater clarity and understanding. As part of a visit of church leaders from Leicester to the Church of South India, we were taken to various places, including rural Dalit villages. The temple of one village had been closed, and we asked why. We were told that when the Indian government had passed a law that anyone of any caste should be able to study for the priesthood and become a priest in a temple, one young Dalit man from the village had done just that. Upon his return to the village to become the local priest, someone took exception to a Dalit taking on this role and murdered him. Despite this, the temple remained open. But then a year later, as part of this same dispute, another murder took place. And so the authorities closed the temple. We were told that it is the role of the priest to ensure the goodness of a place, to ensure the security and well-being of the people. If there is something wrong, then the priest is held responsible. This was the price paid by one young Dalit for crossing cultural and traditional boundaries, despite the law of the land being in his favour.

As we were in the midst of closing several churches in Leicester, a city with a significant Hindu community, we pondered how these closures might be perceived. I had certainly been told by many Hindus that they felt the Church was abandoning them by closing.

There is something in all of these stories that as a Christian and as a priest I find deeply humbling. There is the sense that leaders or ministers within religious communities are the holders of the sanctity of people and place, and of the sacred journey all of us take in search of God, however we understand God to be.

On this journey, there is a holy compulsion to challenge traditions, to continually question their validity for changing contexts within life and the world, while not letting go of the essence that tradition stands for. This entails rigorous and thorough study, of our histories, developments of doctrines and of the workings of the human heart.

The cost of that journey is our lives, living a life of sacrifice that draws out fear as much as it inspires faith. We take on the people's sins, which means we see them. We hear the confessions and we offer forgiveness and cleansing. Sometimes that cleansing is to fall victim to the shame, frustration and even violence of others – especially those who cannot bear to see their own faults reflected back to them in the loving forgiveness of the priest or holy woman or man.

In the lives of those of faith and conviction who give all of themselves in the pursuit of understanding this thing we call God, perhaps there is room for understanding the concept of the priesthood of all believers in a wider sense. Can we allow ourselves to be loved by them? Can we love so unconditionally, so fully and so trustingly in return?

Come to him, a living stone, though rejected by mortals yet chosen and precious in God's sight, and like living stones, let yourselves be built into a

spiritual house; to be a holy priesthood, to offer spiritual sacrifices acceptable to God through Jesus Christ.

(1 Peter 2.4–5 <small>NRSV</small>)

As people of faith, people in search of God, people seeking to love those
around us, as commanded by Jesus, as commanded by human decency, we
take on the sins of the people, we cleanse and heal through loving forgiveness, we challenge the tyrant and wipe clean the suffering and the poor. We
break boundaries. We bless the land. We make the people holy.

32

Discrimination and ministry

IAN S. MARKHAM AND ALLISON ST LOUIS

It is ironic. When we think of ordained ministry in the Anglican tradition, our basic assumptions are that we are thinking of a priest or a deacon working with individuals to help them grow in the gospel. In our heads, we think of the obligation to preach the word, provide the sacraments and be pastorally present when things get hard. The individuals are rarely located in terms of gender, race and sexuality.

Yet Scripture almost always engages with human lives in community. So God calls Abraham to be the father of a nation (Genesis 12.2). God judges the nations when they oppress the poor in Damascus (Amos 1.3), Gaza (Amos 1.6), Tyre (Amos 1.9), Edom (Amos 1.11), Ammon (Amos 1.13), Moab (Amos 2.1), Judah (Amos 2.4) and Israel (Amos 2.6). When we encounter Jesus in the synagogue at the beginning of his ministry, he reads the words of Isaiah, which state: 'The Spirit of the Lord is upon me, because he has anointed me to bring good news to the poor. He has sent me to proclaim release to the captives and recovery of sight to the blind, to let the oppressed go free' (Luke 4.18).[1] Jesus has a gospel for the poor, for captives, for the blind and for the oppressed. Almost all of Paul's letters are addressed to entire churches. And in the book of Revelation, it is the seven churches that are addressed. While we minister to individuals, Scripture deals with communities.

We believe that all good ministry needs to recognize the corporate location of all human lives. The location includes gender, race, sexuality and socio-economic status. And we need to heed with some care the resounding message of Scripture that God takes a side. James Cone puts it with his customary clarity when he writes:

[I]n a racist society, God is never color-blind. To say God is color-blind is analogous to saying that God is blind to justice and injustice, to right and

---

[1] All Scripture quotations in this chapter are taken from the New Revised Standard Version (NRSV).

wrong, to good and evil. Certainly this is not the picture of God revealed in the Old and New Testaments. Yahweh takes sides . . . Jesus is not for *all*, but for the oppressed, the poor and unwanted of society, and against oppressors. The God of the biblical tradition is not uninvolved or neutral regarding human affairs; God is decidedly involved. God is active in human history, taking sides with the oppressed of the land. The meaning of this message for our contemporary situation is clear: the God of the oppressed takes sides with the black community. God is not color-blind in the black-white struggle, but has made an unqualified identification with blacks.[2]

Ministers cannot proclaim Scripture without recognizing that the social and political dimensions are a central part of the biblical witness.

In a short chapter, it is impossible for us to deal with all the complexities of our topics. We will explore briefly five major areas of discrimination: gender, race, sexuality, transgender and special needs. Then we shall offer two responses: the first is theological; and the second is congregational.

The challenge of discrimination

Starting then with sexism: the United Nations Entity for Gender Equality and the Empowerment of Women provides some disturbing data:

- Between 40 and 50 per cent of women in European Union countries experience unwanted sexual advances, physical contact or other forms of sexual harassment at work.
- Women and girls are 80 per cent of the estimated 800,000 people trafficked across national borders annually, with the majority (79 per cent) trafficked for sexual exploitation. Within countries, many more women and girls are trafficked, often for purposes of sexual exploitation or domestic servitude.
- In the United States, 83 per cent of girls aged 12 to 16 experienced some form of sexual harassment in public schools.[3]

And one recent and tragic development is the way in which women have been victims in war zones around the world:

- Conservative estimates suggest that 20,000 to 50,000 women were raped during the 1992–5 war in Bosnia and Herzegovina, while approximately

---

[2] James H. Cone, *A Black Theology of Liberation* (Maryknoll, NY: Orbis Books, 1990), p. 6.

[3] See <http://www.endvawnow.org/en/articles/299-fast-facts-statistics-on-violence-against-women-and-girls-.html> (accessed 8 July 2016).

250,000 to 500,000 women and girls were targeted in the 1994 Rwandan genocide.

- Between 50,000 and 64,000 women in camps for internally displaced people in Sierra Leone were sexually assaulted by combatants between 1991 and 2001.
- In eastern Democratic Republic of Congo, at least 200,000 cases of sexual violence, mostly involving women and girls, have been documented since 1996: the actual numbers are believed to be far higher.[4]

These statistics illustrate the deep-seated nature of patriarchy and sexism. Naturally, there has been progress. In 1893, New Zealand was the first country to give women the vote; the United Kingdom followed in 1918, with the United States passing a law two years later. Anglicans worldwide have been ordaining women to the priesthood since the early 1970s, although there are still some provinces that do not do so. At the level of attitudes, problems continue to abound. The 'glass ceiling' is a reality for women in the workplace: the most able do not get promoted, and there are plenty of women who are doing the same work as men for less. The flourishing pornography industry and the high incidence of rape and sexual harassment provide clear evidence of a continuing failure to live out the injunction of Paul that 'there is no longer male and female; for all of you are one in Christ Jesus' (Galatians 3.28).

It is important to stress that the Pauline affirmation for equality has tended to be overlooked by the Church. Instead the Bible was used to reinforce and justify patriarchy. From the statement that Eve was created first and was the one who tempted Adam to sin (see 1 Timothy 2.9–15) to the decision of Jesus to appoint only males to be his 12 disciples, women have been told that theologically women are second-class citizens.

Turning now to race, there is a sociological reality that must be faced. White brutality against the non-white is a deep pervasive reality. Over the course of 400 years, there were over 15 million non-white men, women and children who were treated as commodities and shipped abroad and sold in the marketplace. Even when slavery was made illegal in the United States, legal segregation became a reality. With the shameful illusion of 'separate but equal' facilities for blacks and whites, the Jim Crow laws mandated segregation of schools, transport, restrooms, restaurants, even drinking fountains. James Cone reflects on his own upbringing in the town of Bearden, Arkansas, when he writes:

---

4 See <http://www.endvawnow.org/en/articles/299-fast-facts-statistics-on-violence-against-women-and-girls-.html> (accessed 8 July 2016).

The presence of eight hundred whites made me realize, at an early age, that black existence cannot, indeed *must* not, be taken for granted. White people did everything within their power to define black reality, to tell us who we were – and their definition, of course, extended no further than their social, political, and economic interests. They tried to make us believe that God created black people to be white people's servants. We blacks, therefore, were *expected* to enjoy plowing their fields, cleaning their houses, mowing their lawns, and working in their sawmills. And when we showed signs of displeasure with our so-called elected and inferior status, they called us 'uppity niggers' and quickly attempted to put us in our 'place.'

To be put in one's place, as defined by white society, was a terrible reality for blacks in Bearden. It meant being beaten by the town cop and spending an inordinate length of time in a stinking jail. It meant attending 'separate but equal' schools, going to the balcony when attending a movie, and drinking water from a 'colored' fountain. It meant refusing to retaliate when called a nigger – unless you were prepared to leave town at the precise moment of your rebellion. You had no name except your first name or 'boy'; and if you were past the age of sixty-five, you might attain the dubious honor of being called 'uncle' or 'auntie.'[5]

The deprivations, in terms of education, opportunities and services, were considerable. However, more fundamentally, the damage to one's self-esteem and dignity was crippling.

It is true that segregation was made illegal with the passing of the Civil Rights Act of 1964. And it is true that the United States elected its first African American president with President Obama in 2008. Yet it sometimes feels as if America is still a long way from healthy and good 'race relations'. From January to July in 2016, 136 African Americans were killed by the police. Both minorities and the white majority know that racism is still very much part of the modern American experience. Most white people know some racists – often in their own families – and people from all minorities have had moments when they have experienced prejudice or exclusion simply because of the colour of their skin.

It needs to be recognized that biblical texts played a key role in the justification of slavery (Exodus 21.2–6; Ephesians 6.5; Titus 2.9; 1 Peter 2.18). In 1788 an Anglican priest, Raymond Harris, wrote a pamphlet entitled *Scriptural Researches on the Licitness of the Slave-Trade Shewing its conformity with the principles of Natural and Revealed Religion delineated in the*

---

5   James H. Cone, *God of the Oppressed* (Maryknoll, NY: Orbis Books, 1997), pp. 2–3.

Sacred Writings of the Word of God.[6] This pamphlet was a resolute defence of the divinely intended nature of the institution of slavery, where blacks are required to serve whites.

Turning now to sexuality, a major civil rights question for the churches has been the experience of the LGBTQI (lesbian, gay, bisexual, transgender, queer or questioning, and intersex) community. Being gay or lesbian is difficult. In 2011, the FBI in the United States reported that there were 1,572 hate crime incidents based on sexual orientation. The Orlando shooting at a gay club in 2016, where 49 people died, illustrates just how being gay can get you killed. It is also true that gay rights have come a long way over the last decade. Same-sex marriage has been available since 13 March 2014 in the UK. In the USA, the bans on same-sex marriage were ruled unconstitutional when the ruling in *Obergefell v Hodges* came down from the Supreme Court in 2015.

While gay rights have made particular progress in Europe and America, the picture is quite different in other parts of the world, especially in Africa and the Muslim world. In Africa, there has been a significant reaction. In Cameroon in 2005, a newspaper revealed that certain prominent and elite members of society were inducting young men into gay sex, which led to persecution of the gay community. Uganda is famous for the bill, submitted by David Bahati in 2009, which called for the death penalty in cases of 'aggravated homosexuality'. Robert Mugabe, the former president of Zimbabwe, has claimed that homosexuality is an 'immoral import'. A video of a gay wedding ceremony, which was probably a fake, provoked consternation in Morocco, Senegal, Nigeria and Malawi. It does look like Africa is in the grip of a significant homophobic reaction.

In a thoughtful co-written article by Awondo, Geschiere and Reid, the picture of a homophobic Africa and an enlightened West has been subject to appropriate critical scrutiny. First, they note that such a picture ignores the internal debates within Africa and the significant number of voices who are challenging laws against homosexuality. Second, a case can be made that the legacy of colonial powers is still an issue of major complexity. Most of the laws prohibiting homosexuality were put in place by the European colonial powers. In addition, in Uganda, for example, certain right-wing Christian groups are key agents in supporting and encouraging anti-homosexual legislation. Third, some scholars have expressed concern that the Western binary approach – you are either gay or straight – has

---

[6]   The text of his pamphlet is summarized in Ian S. Markham, *Do Morals Matter? A Guide to Contemporary Religious Ethics* (Oxford: Blackwell, 2007).

been very problematic in Africa. There is a whole trajectory of same-sex intimacy which did not have the connotations of definitive and sure identity. What was viewed as innocent has suddenly assumed more complex overtones. Finally, there are in every case other internal perceptions, unrelated to homosexuality, which are major factors in the reactions of these academics. So, in respect to Cameroon, for example, they write:

> Overall, what is particularly striking in the Cameroonian case is the quite specific image of the homosexual that was at the basis of the uproar. Both the lists and the attacks by the Yaounde archbishop and others targeted mainly *les Grands*, who are supposed to subject young men to humiliating same sex rituals. In this vision the link of homosexuality to witchcraft, as well as other forms of occult power and secret associations like Freemasonry and the Rosicrucians, is heavily emphasized.[7]

In other words, the issue of homosexuality is becoming part of a wider and more complex narrative about secret societies and potential exploitation.

While conceding these complexities, it is important to recognize that men and women whose only desire is to express their love in a sexually intimate way with a person of the same sex are often victims of abuse and frequently denied their fundamental human rights. Naturally, much of this antagonism is justified by the use of biblical texts (see Genesis 19.5; Leviticus 18.22; Leviticus 20.13; Deuteronomy 23.17; Romans 1.26–27). The Church has not been an ally of the LGBTQI community.

Before we leave the LGBTQI, it is necessary to pause and consider in particular those who have a transgender identity. In March 2016 the governor of North Carolina signed into law House Bill 2, the Public Facilities Privacy and Security Act. The key component was that people are required by law to use the bathroom based on their gender identity, which is given at birth. The underlying fear was that lots of men who had become women would be seeking to go into women's public toilets.

Ever since Bruce Jenner became Caitlyn Jenner, this topic has generated considerable attention. A person who is transgender is one whose sense of self does not fit the assigned sex given to them from birth. A person who is transsexual is a person who wants to undergo medical treatment and move from one gender to another. Getting a sense of the numbers who make up the transgender population is very difficult. The United States Census Bureau documents individuals who change their name. The results are interesting:

---

[7] Patrick Awondo, Peter Geschiere and Graeme Reid, 'Homophobic Africa? Toward a More Nuanced View', *African Studies Review*, vol. 55, issue 3 (December 2012), p. 152.

Since the Social Security Administration started in 1936, 135,367 people have changed their name to one of the opposite gender, and 30,006 also changed their sex accordingly, the study found. Of Americans who participated in the 2010 census, 89,667 had changed their names and 21,833 had also changed their sex.[8]

This probably underestimates the numbers partly because there was a requirement from 2002 to 2013 for the Social Security Administration to have proof that genital surgery had happened. So the Williams Institute study of 2011, using a survey instrument, estimated that 0.3 per cent of the population of the USA identified as transgender (700,000 adults). Given these numbers, the worry about predatory males in women's toilets seems misguided.

However, the experience of transsexual persons is hard. Mathias J. Wirth writes, 'A significant number of transsexuals, approximately thirty percent, are suicidal since they are frequently not integrated in society and are also more likely to experience isolation, unemployment, discrimination, and feelings of self-hatred.'[9] Wirth goes on to argue that the Christian fixed binary division between male and female is a key factor. He writes:

> According to the Judeo-Christian narrative of creation, God intended humans to be either male or female and assigned them the task of reproduction. Non-conformity with this strict binary concept of gender and sexual orientation which in itself is not conducive to natural reproduction appears to oppose the first book of Moses and its creation narrative. This religiously rooted gender belief was and still is of enormous importance in terms of gender thinking; although this thinking might be secularized in many contexts it still partially answers the question as to why there is noticeable and widespread refusal to deviate from established gender norms, as well as a marked hostility toward persons who are perceived as transgressing these very gender norms.[10]

Once again there is a significant theological difficulty that adds to the challenge for transgender people.

This section will conclude with the issue of discrimination against persons with special needs. The term 'special needs' arose in education, but it is increasingly helpful to describe all those who have a mental, emotional

---

8   Claire Cain Miller, 'The Search for the Best Estimate of the Transgender Population', *New York Times*, 8 June 2015.
9   Mathias J. Wirth, '"Living in a Shell of Something I'm Not": Transsexuality, Medical Ethics, and the Judeo-Christian Culture', *Journal of Religion and Health*, vol. 54 (2015), p. 1584.
10   Wirth, '"Living in a Shell"', p. 1584.

or physical disability. The numbers of people who suffer from some form of disability are considerable. The World Health Organization estimates that 600 million people worldwide have a significant disability. In the United States, 2.7 million people use a wheelchair; 1.8 million are blind or partially blind; 1 million are registered deaf; 14.3 million have a cognitive functioning limitation or an emotional or mental illness that inhibits daily activities.[11]

Such people are subjected to widespread prejudice. When they enter a restaurant, for example, they may provoke stares or the fear that they will make excessive noise. The resources needed to support them often create resentment in tax-paying able-bodied people. Accommodations to make their lives easier are subject to endless debate. It doesn't help that religious organizations were exempt from the requirements of the Americans with Disabilities Act (ADA).

Once again there is a theological dimension to this discrimination. Although it is true that we have Job and a crucified Jesus, it is also true that there are passages in Scripture that seem to imply strongly that health and being abled-bodied are blessings, and disease and disabilities are punishments for sin (see Deuteronomy 32.39; Exodus 15.26). God gives Miriam leprosy for daring to question her brother's credentials (Numbers 12.10). And the following Levitical text about the unclean and the Temple was used as grounds for the exclusion of persons with disabilities from ordination:

> The LORD spoke to Moses, saying: Speak to Aaron and say: No one of your offspring throughout their generations who has a blemish may approach to offer the food of his God. For no one who has a blemish shall draw near, one who is blind or lame, or one who has a mutilated face or a limb too long, or one who has a broken foot or a broken hand, or a hunchback, or a dwarf, or a man with a blemish in his eyes or an itching disease or scabs or crushed testicles. No descendant of Aaron the priest who has a blemish shall come near to offer the LORD's offerings by fire; since he has a blemish, he shall not come near to offer the food of his God. He may eat the food of his God, of the most holy as well as of the holy. But he shall not come near the curtain or approach the altar, because he has a blemish, that he may not profane my sanctuaries; for I am the LORD; I sanctify them.
>
> (Leviticus 21.16–23)

---

[11] For this data see Deborah Beth Creamer, *Disability and Christian Theology: Embodied Limits and Constructive Possibilities*, AAR Academy Series (New York: Oxford University Press, 2009). ProQuest ebrary. Web. 8 July 2016, p. 3.

It is important to note how every instance of discrimination has been reinforced by theological and biblical justifications. Therefore, in the last two sections of this chapter, we shall examine our theology and then our pastoral practice.

Theology and discrimination

We start with a simple axiom. The revelation of God in the eternal Word made flesh teaches us this: we are called into an abundant life (John 10.10), in a community witnessing to kingdom values (Luke 18.16). What we learn from Christ is that God wants love to overcome fear (1 John 4.18). Discrimination is grounded in fear. Those of us seeking to live under the reign of God are being invited into a community of love where discrimination is forbidden.

Sin, however, plagues us all. We are all still struggling with the temptation of abusing power, being suspicious of difference, and wanting to build barriers and walls. In addition, we do need to do some hard theological work. There are aspects of our tradition that have been oppressive. We need to find ways of reading those aspects so that they affirm the primary revelation of a community free from discrimination.

Good work in this area abounds. Space will not permit a sustained discussion. So we shall confine our observations to the identification of two very constructive trajectories. First, we have the emergence of identity theologies. These are theologies that take seriously as a theological resource the *experience* of women, of persons of colour, of lesbians and gays, of the transgender community, and of persons with special needs. The insights of feminist, black, and queer theologies need to be taken seriously by all ministers of the gospel. There is some exceptionally creative work available. For example, Deborah Creamer is advocating for a disability theology. And the primary theological question that is the focus of her work is the appropriate theological view of the body. In a situation which is polarized, she steps in and insists that it is wrong to see the perfect healthy body (the medical model) as the paradigm, and also wrong to see the disability as necessarily a good (the minority model). Although it is true that the medical model celebrates the gift of healthy embodiment, it also denigrates difference. And although it is true that disability can bring real insights and a unique perspective, the minority model overlooks the pain and suffering that is often part of the disability. So instead, Creamer suggests a view of body that is called 'embodied limits'. She writes:

This new model attends to human diversity by recognizing the prevalence of limits and by rejecting dualistic categories and negative valuations. The limits model highlights the fact that human limits need not (and perhaps ought not) be seen as negative or as something that is not or that cannot be done, and instead claims that limits are an important part of being human – a fact that is overlooked when we reflect on the human body as generic. The limits model also reminds us that 'normal' bodies are not as much the norm as we might think, and that it thus is inappropriate for an ideal or imaginary normative body to be the starting point for our theoretical or theological reflections.[12]

There are real insights here. We all have a body with limits. Creamer places all human beings on a spectrum of limitedness, and in so doing helps us see our sisters and brothers with special needs as kin rather than significantly different.

Creamer is just one illustration of what those in ministry can learn from this crucial identity theology. Comparable insights are found in all identity theologies. They are all seeking to challenge our theological paradigm so that we shift to really become the community that Jesus is inviting us to join.

Second, we need to recognize the depth and reality of sin. Traditionally, sin has been understood as primarily individual and often 'sexual' in nature. Thanks to the liberation theologians, we now talk about institutional sin and corporate sin. Prejudice is deeply ingrained in our history and in our language. We can sin without thinking about it. Ministers of the gospel should be suspicious of the current attack on all forms of 'political correctness'. Granted there are moments when discourse is examined so closely that a person can, for example, unknowingly move from making an innocent and positive generalization to being accused of racism. This is unhelpful. But political correctness does have a positive role. 'Herstory' instead of 'history' is an appropriate corrective to our perception of the past as an era dominated by men, where women were simply wives, sisters and mothers. It is wrong and cruel to assume that all Muslims are violent and all African Americans are thugs. This is sin. And it needs to be named as such. These sins are just as bad as (if not worse than) our obsession with 'immoral thoughts' about sexual intimacy.

However, this leaves us with a challenge. How does a minister of the gospel bring these insights to a congregation? How do we challenge discrimination when we find it? What should we do?

---

[12] Creamer, *Disability and Christian Theology*, p. 116.

Discrimination and leading a congregation

Ministers who commit to partnering with God in challenging prejudicial attitudes and discriminatory practices can expect to be transformed. At birth, each of us enters a cultural narrative that in theory affirms, but in practice negates, the declaration that all persons are created equal. Like the generations before us, each of us is assigned roles that, exercised without conscious intervention, perpetuate the notion that some persons are less capable, less worthy of love and less human than others. Embarking on a journey towards freedom from collusion with such an entrenched, multi-faceted and pernicious system begins, therefore, with the recognition and acceptance that ministers, as well as those we serve, have been shaped by that system.

Thankfully, as people of faith and as ministers of the gospel, we also have been gifted with, and shaped by, God's counter-narrative. This narrative teaches us that all of God's creation is good; that each person has inherent, God-given worth, and that God calls us to 'respect the dignity of every human being'.[13] Committing to living and leading from this narrative therefore requires a willingness to venture inward, perhaps to notice in ourselves that which we have come to deplore in others, perhaps to discover anew our radical dependence on God, and perhaps to trust more wholeheartedly in the Spirit's work in and among us. It also requires a willingness to journey with those who demand that we take an alternative route, those who complain that we are moving too quickly and those who contend that we are not moving quickly enough.

Prior to embarking on the journey, we will do well to anticipate some potential obstacles: we are beginning a marathon, not a sprint; the journey will be fraught with unknowns, and even some of our most trusted companions may decide to leave us on the way. In other words, this is not a journey for the fainthearted. So those of us who are faint of heart – and even the bold, confident and courageous among us – need to remember that ours is a response to God's call to partner with God in this ministry, not the other way around.

Because building a congregational culture which has zero tolerance for discriminatory practices is likely to be a gradual, lifelong process, it is paramount that spiritual leaders remain vigilant about, and consistently create space for, deepening our relationship with God. In addition to regular personal and corporate worship, Bible study and retreats, the gift of spiritual

---

[13] Episcopal Church, *The Book of Common Prayer and Administration of the Sacraments and Other Rites and Ceremonies of the Church* (New York: Church Publishing Inc., 1979), p. 417.

direction and friendship can inspire us to seek God's wisdom, strength and guidance; to notice the 'log in [our] own eye' (Luke 6.41) so that we can more clearly see how to lead others faithfully; and to reignite hope and courage when our spirits are low. Attending to our life with God also increases the likelihood that we will approach and engage this ministry from a loving, gracious and life-giving place. Failing to do so ensures that, in spite of well-intentioned efforts, we will become burned out, cynical and/or perpetrators who, in thought, word and deed, unwittingly victimize the perpetrators of discrimination – thereby perpetuating the cycle of discrimination and violence we have come to abhor.

There is another, fundamental reason for spiritual leaders who engage this ministry to tend to our relationship with God. In many churches, the counter-narrative of being intrinsically beloved of God co-exists with the narrative of needing to earn (God's) love. If the latter becomes the primary, even if unconscious, motivating force for challenging discrimination, both ministers and their congregations become vulnerable to being unduly distracted and buffeted by the howling winds of guilt and shame, approval and disapproval, hopelessness and powerlessness we are likely to encounter on the journey. If, on the other hand, we remain focused on the One 'who knit us together in our mother's womb' (see Psalm 139.13b), we become more deeply grounded in the love which can sustain us through the journey's ups and downs.

Trusting in our belovedness can also undergird our efforts to disentangle the notions of earning and being graced with God's love. Instead of becoming paralysed by the fear of making mistakes, of being labelled as insensitive or oversensitive, or of any of the other myriad of fears that assail us as we move into uncharted territory, we are empowered to move forward, confident that God loves us and has promised to never leave or forsake us. We also are empowered to redefine the criteria for the success of this ministry (for example, in terms of reporting progress in our church, we would hope to be able to say: 'The vestry engaged in a difficult conversation about our parish's tendency to keep women and minorities out of leadership positions in the church', in addition to – or even instead of: 'Since I became rector, our parish has grown to include 12 families of colour, 7 gay couples and 1 wheelchair-bound, female associate'!).

While showing up, being fully present, listening and receiving require a willingness to be vulnerable, our time with God and with a sturdy support system can be empowering, albeit at times disconcerting, reminders that we human beings are creatures, and God is creator. When the going gets tough, our interactions with our fellow travellers can be freeing, although humbling, reminders that we are not alone in our desire and efforts to confront discrimination. For instance, regular (bi-weekly or monthly) meetings with an accountability partner or coach as well as with a confidential, preferably diverse group of other spiritual leaders can be instrumental in overcoming the isolation and fear expressed so well by the prophet Elijah (1 Kings 19.14b). In such non-judgemental relationships, we can explore our own prejudices, examine our triggers, and become aware of our limits and blind spots. For instance, what thoughts and feelings arise as we reflect on the experience of an African American male parishioner who was pulled over by the police for driving a vehicle with a broken rear light? Or how might we feel if one of our children falls in love with and decides to marry someone of the same gender? As we pray and reflect in community, we can become increasingly aware of the ways in which we have been shaped by cultural standards of beauty, intelligence and worth, how those have impacted our ministerial identity and functions, and how we can co-create with God and others more life-giving ways of sharing the good news of God's love for all.

Processes which can be helpful in discerning both the timing and approach to this ministry in our particular context include studying the history of our congregation, learning its ways of dealing – or avoiding dealing with – discrimination, entering into dialogue with lay leaders and members of the congregation as well as of the wider community, and consulting with mentors who have experience in challenging congregations to deal with discrimination and interacting with persons and communities whose worldview, values and customs are distinctly different from ours. In the process, we can gain a keener understanding as well as a greater appreciation of how language shapes perception, reveals biases and perpetuates stereotypes.

Preaching, teaching and modelling that repeatedly remind members of our communities that they, as well as others, are inherently loved provide a foundation for exploring issues of discrimination. They will also sustain us on the road towards freedom from the paralysing shame and guilt that colour so many of our, and our congregations', relationships with those whom the larger culture deems 'other'. Likewise, offering workshops on learning how to let go of negative emotions can assist parishioners in getting unstuck while using their newfound energy to participate in creating a more just society.

In addition to preaching and teaching, hosting regular forums in which ministers, lay leaders and/or guest speakers clarify and/or reiterate God's counter-narrative for human communities is an essential step in supporting, including challenging, a congregation to confront discrimination. In creating a vision for their common life, both ministers and members may find it helpful to ask the following questions of themselves, of one another and as a community: what is my (our) understanding of God's counter-narrative? Are there parts of that narrative that I can embrace easily? Are there other parts I find it difficult to embrace? What do I believe about discrimination? What forces have shaped my current beliefs? Is what I believe congruent with my understanding of God's alternative vision for humanity? If not, how can I allow God to lead me to a place of greater congruence? What are the joys and the challenges of believing, as well as living from a belief, that all persons are: created by and for love; beloved of God; created equal? As a community of faith, what do we want to be known for regarding discrimination? The equality of all persons?

Some ministers and congregations may find it helpful to create a behavioural covenant. For example, covenanting to express curiosity instead of judgement about a person's off-colour remarks can help to lower defensiveness and increase the likelihood that the speaker will share his or her perspective, whether or not we agree with it. If we choose to share our differing perspective, that individual may be more open to listening, even if his or her opinion remains the same. At the same time, it is important for congregations to agree to a process for dealing with clearly prejudicial comments and/or discriminatory behaviours (see, for example, Matthew 18.15–17).

Nevertheless, regular reminders to ourselves that we were formed in a narrative filled with prejudices and discriminatory practices can help us to be gentle with ourselves, even as we seek a more life-affirming way for ourselves and others. Regular reminders that members of our communities also were formed in similar spaces enables us to connect with their fears, understand their concerns and prepare for their resistance. Regular reminders that we all have been called to partner with God on the journey to a more compassionate, fully human place empowers us to name discrimination, offer a healing counter-narrative, and engage our individual and communal decision-making from that counter-narrative.

Finally, ministers need to remember that, because the roots of discrimination are formed and consistently nurtured by the forces of socialization and enculturation, they are pervasive, resilient and often imperceptible to the casual observer – thereby enabling the 'normalization' and institutionalization of discriminatory practices. Taking seriously the counter-narrative of equality under God will involve bold, consistent, courageous moves not only into the land of prophetic preaching and teaching but also into creative partnerships with unlikely companions. It will involve listening to stories describing discriminatory practices, and viewing films or reading books that are disconcerting. It will involve engaging in worship with people of different religious, ethnic, sexual, economic and political persuasions. It will involve dining with, and listening deeply to, those deemed 'other'. And it will involve living with the uneasy awareness that we may not get to the promised land. Yet, it involves the joy of knowing that God is with us and that God's grace will be sufficient for the journey.

33

Gender and ministry

EMMA PERCY

In 1994 *The Vicar of Dibley* became a hit television show in the UK. For the first time we had a fictionalized vicar who was a woman. People learned to laugh at, and with, Revd Geraldine Granger as she muddled her way through caring for her dippy parishioners. At the same time parishes were beginning to adjust to the reality that the local vicar might be a woman as legislation in the Church of England allowed women to become priests. For the majority of the Church, and the wider public, the adjustment did not take too long. People wanted a vicar who provided spiritual leadership and good pastoral care; for many the gender of the priest ceased to matter. Yet, for others, the reality of women priests was an oxymoron. Women cannot be priests, should not preach and ought not to be spiritual leaders over men.

The theological reasons for such arguments are grounded in tradition, church order, interpretations of Scripture, and a deeply held stance on the innate difference between men and women. When in 2014 the Church of England finally passed legislation to allow women to be consecrated as bishops, the ambiguity about ordained women was enshrined in 'The Five Guiding Principles'; this document outlined a paradoxical position in which the Anglican Church recognized women's orders and at the same time recognized the right of people not to recognize them.

With its complex breadth the Church of England holds together those shaped by Catholic theologies of ministry and those firmly from the reformed tradition. Thus the ambiguity over the question of gender and ministry within the Church of England offers insights into the debate about the issue across other denominations. For vast numbers of Christians the question of ministry and gender is not really on the table. Orthodox Christianity and Roman Catholicism do not ordain women to any kind of church order. Within these churches there are those raising the question about women and priesthood and trying to encourage debate, but it is not high on the agenda of those in authority.

Currently the Roman Catholic Church does not officially sanction debate on the issue.

Among the reformed churches many have, since the mid-twentieth century, ordained women, offering them the same status as men. Yet, there are also reformed churches where people are deeply opposed to ideas of women in positions of spiritual leadership, preaching and teaching mixed congregations. These would point to passages in the New Testament that appear to prohibit women preaching. The questions raised about gender and ministry thus rest on a number of key issues. Does the Bible forbid it? Tradition has maintained a male-only order; who are we to change it? Are women and men so fundamentally different that orders cannot be assumed by women? If women are ordained, is a woman priest different from a male priest, and if so, what does that mean?

In this chapter I will look briefly at the history of women's orders within the Church of England in order to explore their ambiguous nature. This can then lead to a wider discussion of complementary views of gender and the problems these ideas continue to pose for the churches as we move into the far more complex understanding of gender in the twenty-first century.

From deaconess to priest

An important part of the history of women's ministry is held by the religious orders. Women found a freedom within the restrictions of a vowed life to engage in a wide range of Christian ministry. The spiritual wisdom and theological understanding of religious women was sought out by many and their practical ministry was and is wide-ranging. At the Reformation religious orders ceased for those churches which followed the Protestant theology. Women no longer had a formalized way of engaging in ministry, though of course women continued to minister as lay women, often carrying out practical acts of charity in the name of the Church. The societal changes of the nineteenth century, with the increase of urban populations, brought challenges to the kind of pastoral ministry that had been practical in smaller parishes. Both men and women realized that different forms of ministry might be needed to work in the city slums and reach out to the poor, who were losing touch with the established Church.

In the Church of England, one response to women's growing desire to serve in a more structured way was to bring back religious orders. In 1845 the first Anglican sisterhood in the Church of England was founded to work in the poor area of Somers Town in London. The Sisters of the Holy Cross were followed by other communities of nuns founded to offer social and spiritual care for the poor, dispossessed and sick. These orders were viewed with some uncertainty by those in the Church who thought them too catholic. This seemed to be a return to medieval church practice and sat uneasily with those of a more reformed theology.

The Lutheran Church in Germany came up with a similar but importantly different model of women's ministry. Like the religious orders it involved women living in community and ministering out of that community to those in need, but it did not involve the same kind of life vows and it traced its roots to the New Testament, rather than the pre-Reformation Church. This was the order of 'deaconess', a revival, it was claimed, of the ministry of Phoebe and others mentioned in the letters of St Paul. The deaconess community at Kaiserswerth was visited by a number of English women exploring a sense of vocation, including Florence Nightingale.

In 1858 the Convocation of Canterbury discussed the possible revival of the deaconess order in the Church of England, though no conclusions were reached. Encouraged by Bishop Tait of London, Elizabeth Ferard visited Kaiserswerth in 1861, and on returning Bishop Tait ordained her as a deaconess, establishing the North London Deaconess Institution (NLDI). Initially, like the new religious orders, this provided a communal life for women. Yet, from very early on, non-community deaconesses existed alongside those who lived a common life.

In the 1880s Isabella Gilmore was asked to set up deaconess training in Rochester Diocese. She developed a pattern more akin to the education of male clergy. She argued that this was more in keeping with the primitive pattern of deaconess ministry. Women were centrally trained and then, after ordination, they were sent out to perform parish work. This, rather than communal living, became the more common pattern of deaconess ministry. It seemed to offer a constructive way of formalizing women's ministry in the Church.

> Keen to exploit women's vocation and labour, but wary of the romanism implicit in religious communities as well as their independence asserted by many of them, clergy and laity saw the deaconess as a better alternative. Explicitly under episcopal control, potentially part of the official ministry of the church, it was hoped that the Deaconess Order would avoid the traps of church-party politics and attract large numbers of women who wished to pursue a vocation and contribute to the mission of the church.[1]

---

[1]   Henrietta Blackmore, ed., *The Beginning of Women's Ministry: The Revival of the Deaconess in the Nineteenth-Century Church of England* (Woodbridge: Bodley Press), 2007, p. xvi.

Blackmore suggests that the reason large numbers were not attracted to the order was the continuing ambiguity over what this ministry actually was. It sat in an ill-defined place between lay ministry and clerical order. Deaconesses were ordained by the laying on of the bishop's hands, and most bishops used an adapted form of the prayer book service for ordaining a deacon. So were these simply female deacons? Some certainly thought so. Berdmore Compton, Chaplain to the NLDI, maintained in a Mansion House speech of 1887: 'Indeed there is more said about Deaconesses in the New Testament than about the episcopate or the priesthood . . . A Deaconess is simply a woman deacon, in the true sense of the word.' The argument from Scripture was then, as it still is now, an important counter to the suggestion that women's ministry was a modern phenomenon and a novelty for the Church. 'The deaconess's heritage as part of an apostolic order of ministry was stressed, different from that of a lay visitor and as an adjunct of the parochial clergy.'[2]

Yet, the claim that deaconesses were simply women deacons was a far more contentious statement. The role of deaconess may have been accepted as a New Testament order, but to suggest it was the same as that of male deacons, or even apostolic, was too unsettling for many. The ambiguity over this quasi-clerical order prevented the Church of England and the wider Anglican Communion from fully recognizing it. This did not happen until the 1920 Lambeth Conference. Many women opted for the less contentious title of Parish Worker, clearly a lay ministry.

It would not be until 1970, in the General Convention of the Episcopal Church in the USA, that the ambiguous nature of the deaconess was settled and a canon passed to allow men and women to be recognized as deacons. It took until 1987 for a similar decision to be made in the Church of England. Women could therefore be clergy, but in both churches the suggestion that they could then become priests was not automatic.

In 2016 Pope Francis suggested that the Catholic Church should reflect on the ministry of women in the Bible to see whether some kind of deaconess order would be compatible with Catholic teaching. This, though, is not intended to further the calls for women priests in that Church.

What is clear from this brief look at the history of deaconesses is that there has been resistance to seeing women's ministry as equivalent to men's, even when women are doing the same kinds of things. This is not about competency or qualification in a purely functional understanding of what that means. This is about the nature of men and women and the

---

[2] Blackmore, ed., *Beginning of Women's Ministry*, p. xvii.

assumption that the difference between them is significant in terms of ordination and spiritual office.

The first woman to be ordained as priest in the Anglican Church was Florence Li Tim Oi, a deaconess ordained in Hong Kong and licensed to work in the Portuguese province of Macau. The Japanese occupation of China meant that no priests were able to travel to Macau, and Florence was the only authorized minister. Bishop R. O. Hall, of Hong Kong, made the pragmatic decision to ordain her as a priest on 25 January 1944 so that she could provide a full sacramental ministry to the people of Macau. This irregular ordination was considered invalid by the Lambeth Conference of 1948 and Li Tim Oi resigned her licence. She was no longer able to minister as a priest.

It was many years before the next irregular ordinations, which took place in Philadelphia, in the Episcopal Church. On 29 July 1974, 11 women deacons were ordained priest by three retired bishops. These ordinations were regularized in 1976 when the General Convention approved the ordination of women. It would be two decades after the 'Philadelphia 11' before the Church of England ordained its first women priests in the spring of 1994. As of January 2015, of the 38 provinces of the Anglican Communion, 5 do not ordain women at all, 3 ordain them only as deacons, 8 ordain deacons and priests, while the others, in principle, ordain women to all three orders.

Discrimination and theological convictions

As in any of the professions that were traditionally male, women entering the world of ministry have had to contend with unconscious bias and other structural forms of discrimination that make it hard for them to progress. They face similar challenges to women in other walks of life as they try to find ways to move through the glass ceiling and be assessed on merit and not on gender. Again, like many women, they often have to juggle the expectations of caring roles at home alongside any paid work. Within the professional ministry of the Church this is further compounded by the lack of clear work boundaries and the theological imperative to be caring.

Yet, alongside these similarities with other professional women, they face deliberate discrimination sanctioned on the grounds of theological conviction. Such discrimination is based purely on the fact that they are not men. For those in the reformed tradition who hold to a very particular reading of the Bible, the arguments about female deacons do not counter Paul's statements in certain letters about the requirement for women's silence in church and subordination to their husbands. The apostles were male, and little significance is made of the women noted in the Gospels who followed Jesus. It is maintained that the biblical witness is clear: Jesus and the leaders of the early Church gave authority to preach and minister to men and not to women. Sexual difference, we are told, matters for far more than procreation.

Though this restriction of ministry to men may have been defended in the past by arguments about the inferiority of women, now it is about their 'otherness'. Men and women, it is maintained, are created by God as complementary beings with different callings and complementary gifts. Women have special roles in the home and in ministering to other women and children. They should not seek to usurp men's special roles of leadership.

This position is also strongly argued by the Roman Catholic Church, notably in the writings of Pope John Paul II: 'Womanhood and manhood are complementary *not only from the physical and psychological points of view*, but also from the *ontological*. It is only through the duality of the "masculine" and "feminine" that the human finds full realisation.'[3] In a Church where the sacraments, rather than preaching, are central to ministry, the masculinity of Jesus is stressed, as is the need for priests to be able to properly represent him:

> The same natural resemblance is required for persons as for things: when Christ's role in the Eucharist is to be expressed sacramentally, there would not be this 'natural resemblance' which must exist between Christ and his minister if the role of Christ were not taken by a man: in such a case it would be difficult to see in the minister the image of Christ. For Christ himself was and remains a man.[4]

This strongly held view of the complementary difference between men and women means that women are deemed unable to be authoritative preachers, church leaders or priests because they *are* women. It is not a matter of education, competency, appropriate gifts and skills but it is a matter of being. It is this that has made the debates around women and ministry so difficult and so hard, at times, for those beyond the Church to comprehend.

---

[3] *Letter of Pope John Paul II: To Women*, from the Vatican, 29 June 1995: <http://w2.vatican. va/content/john-paul-ii/en/letters/1995/documents/hf_jp-ii_let_29061995_women.html> (accessed 5 September 2016).

[4] Sacred Congregation for the Doctrine of Faith, *Inter Insigniores*, 15 October 1976: <http:// www.papalencyclicals.net/paul06/p6interi.htm>, paragraph 5 (accessed 27 November 2012).

We are told that women are called by God to be complementary to men, but it is hard to find a role of equal status that is defined as for women only. Christine Gudorf's excellent article on the ethics of a male-only priesthood in the Catholic Church challenges this lack of balance. She does not object to an ethics of difference but points out: 'The exclusion of one sex from a social role should be balanced by roughly parallel exclusions of the other sex from a role of approximately equal power and importance.'[5]

We do not find this balance in churches that argue for complementary roles, and the areas of women's ministry in such churches are usually clearly delineated by men.

Created in the image of God, male and female

This anthropology of complementary is expressed theologically with reference to the creation accounts in the book of Genesis. Chapter 1 refers to the creation of humanity in the image of God, male and female. In Genesis 2 we find a single human, Adam, who cannot find a companion until the creation from his body of the woman Eve. Adam and Eve are charged, along with all creation, to multiply, and the man and woman together produce children. There are different physical features between men and women necessary for procreation. These complementary features are used to read the creation stories, concluding that these differences are central to human life. Thus an anthropology of male and female complementarity has given rise to the notion of the 'opposite' sex and the essentially different nature of women and men, which suggests that anatomical differences point to different natural characteristics.

This is, of course, not the only way to read these stories. Many challenging those who seek to limit women's participation in the Church's ministry have stressed that in the Genesis account both male and female are declared to be made in the image of God. If men have been able to see this fully in their humanity, then so should women. If a man embodies the image of God in his bodily life and experience, then so does a woman. To say otherwise is to somehow limit the way in which women are fully human and thus fully made in the divine image. This raises other theological questions. If women are made in the image of God then can we and should we sometimes speak of the divine in female terms? Such questions

---

[5] Christine E. Gudorf, 'Probing the Politics of Difference: What's Wrong with an All-Male Priesthood?', *Journal of Religious Ethics*, vol. 27, no. 3 (Fall 1999), pp. 377–405.

only highlight the concerns of those who want to limit women's role in ministry.

The account of Adam and Eve's creation can also be read as an affirmation of common humanity rather than of opposites. Adam greets Eve with the words, 'here at last is bone of my bone, flesh of my flesh'; a clear recognition of the sameness they share. Yet, such a reading is rarely heard. Historically this text has been used to justify women's subordination and now is used as a basis for complementary theories of sex and gender. This binary understanding of sex and gender as opposites or complements tends to limit the opportunities deemed appropriate to women. Because this reading of Scripture is shaped by the sexual differences necessary for procreation, it also leads to an anthropology that is rigidly heterosexual.

Yet, importantly, complementary understandings of sex and gender do not necessarily lead to the exclusion of women from ministry. Equality and inclusion can be argued on the basis that the differing natures of men and women both need to be present. It has in fact been necessary for those campaigning for women in ministry to adopt a form of 'strategic essentialism', championing women in order to make the case for their inclusion and monitor their acceptance. Yet, there is a tension in speaking about women in ministry; it can be all too easy to perpetuate the idea of a normally male role that women now inhabit either in the same way as men or in a uniquely female way. It can also imply a generic idea of women, increasing stereotypical expectations. Are female clergy all going to be more nurturing and less assertive than male clergy?

Clearly, women in general bring into their experience of ministry all that comes from growing up and living in a society that emphasizes gender differences. Yet, they also bring a range of educational and social backgrounds, as well as differing life stories and religious experience. These may have as much impact on how they inhabit the role of a priest as their gender; indeed they may be far more important factors. In ministry, clergy are involved in myriad relationships and these bring with them assumptions and expectations on the part of others, which will include gender assumptions. A strongly held complementary anthropology of gender tends to strengthen stereotypes and reward those who conform to expectations. Thus Christian women can find themselves caught in the double bind of selfless service; an expectation of both their gender and their Christian calling. Challenging the stereotypes can be extremely difficult as it may require behaviour that is perceived as more assertive, unfeminine and lacking in humility.

Where are we now?

For the majority of Christians the ordained ministry of the Church, and consequently the authority of the Church, is still male. For the Orthodox churches and the Roman Catholic Church, ordination requires a male body. There are groups who challenge this and campaign for change; however, at the moment serious debate around the issues is not a priority for those in authority. Women continue to have important ministries as religious and as lay people but rarely have a significant voice in the major decision-making bodies.

Within Protestant churches the position differs. Some churches have fully embraced women in ordained ministry and church governance. Some still maintain exclusively male leadership on the grounds of biblical fidelity. For the Anglican Church the position is typically ambiguous.

As noted above, the majority of Anglican provinces do ordain women as deacons and priests, and more than half consecrate women bishops. Yet, in many provinces where women are ordained there are still parishes whose clergy reject the principle. The Church of England chose to enshrine legal protection for this position; in other provinces it is managed pastorally, though in some cases it has led to break-away denominations. In many of the provinces which do ordain women and potentially would consecrate a woman bishop, there are very few, if any, women who have actually been consecrated.

For some the exclusion of women is argued in pragmatic terms. Where ecumenism is a central part of the ministry, maintaining a male priesthood is seen as enabling easier relationships with Roman Catholic or Orthodox colleagues. Where the Church is ministering in a largely Muslim area it is argued that having women in leadership roles would be a detriment to the witness of the Church. Here it is assumed that challenging injustice around gender is not as important as other aspects of the ministry of the Church, and when women question this they can be seen as self-serving rather than mission-minded.

As the churches which do include women in positions of leadership adjust to this reality, changes will happen. One of the more worrying concerns is that as more women inhabit the roles, the status of such positions may well be devalued. This is a particular issue for parish clergy whose spheres of work are in many of the areas assumed to be more feminine. They see people in their 'non-work' environments and are concerned with domestic issues, children, the elderly and the ill. The work is relatively low paid and hard to articulate. With a male-only priesthood this was less of an issue. Anecdotally, there is evidence of a desire to play down the pastoral care aspect of ministry and emphasize the leadership and managerial roles. There is also a growing number of requests for women to conduct funerals, baptisms and other similar services because they are seen as more caring. Women often find it harder than men to move into more senior positions or to take on the leadership of larger churches. Some of this is no doubt due to the difficult process of changing a system which has been male for so long.

A question of gender

As the churches either welcome women into formal ministry, or hone their theological arguments for excluding them, the wider world is beginning to raise new questions about gender. As I have argued above, much of the theology around gender is rooted in a clear essentialist binary understanding of male and female with implications for women and for those who are not heterosexual. Such binaries are now being challenged. A wider understanding of those who come under the loose heading of 'intersex' challenges the idea that the sex of an individual is always clear. For a minority the reality is far from clear and previous policies of 'normalizing' infants so that they can fit into binary categories is rightly being challenged. Do we define a woman or a man in terms of chromosomes, genitalia, hormone levels or reproductive abilities?

Alongside this, the increasing profile of some transgender individuals raises complex debates about the connection between bodily sex and lived gender. Some individuals who are clearly identifiable, through chromosomes, genitalia and so on, as having either male or female bodies strongly identify as a gender different from their body sex. This article is too short to explore this in detail, but theological thinking about sex, gender and inclusion needs to take seriously the questions being raised. How do we define someone as a man or a woman?

It may well be that we need to rethink our theology of gender, starting from Paul's declaration that 'in Christ there is neither male nor female'. We need to draw distinctions between what is necessary for procreation – a clear preoccupation of the biblical narrative as a family became a people and a nation – and the diversity which can be celebrated as part of the rich resources of God's creativity. In terms of gender and ministry we need to move away from debates about what women should be allowed to do, and explore more creatively the ways in which diverse human beings can bring their gifts and experiences to God for the service of the Church and the world and find those gifts blessed, welcomed and used.

34

Missionary wives and women's distinctive contributions to mission

CATHY ROSS

Introduction

'One liners'[1] is how the history of women in mission could be described until recently because the role of women in mission has often been neglected and overlooked. Jane Austen pertinently observed that history consisted of 'the quarrels of popes and kings, with wars or pestilences in every page; the men all so good for nothing and hardly any women at all'[2]. Jane Austen's remarks resonate with feminist historians within the Church as they have also repeatedly encountered the issue of women's invisibility in church history. Even the reputable *A History of Christian Missions* by Stephen Neill (1964) and David Bosch's *magnum opus, Transforming Mission* (1991), largely ignored the vital contribution of women in mission over the centuries.[3] Lavinia Byrne argued that women's missionary history is 'subject to the same forms of suppression as [that] of other women spiritual writers and theologians'.[4] It is as though women have trained a camera lens through the ages of the Church and have found the women missing. As Patricia Hill commented, 'The women have simply disappeared.'[5]

Moreover, the term 'missionary' was considered a 'male noun [which] denoted a male actor, male action, male spheres of service'.[6] And yet women have always been involved in mission, of course, but until relatively

---

[1] Elaine Bolitho, 'Women in New Zealand Churches: Part 1, 1814–1939', *Stimulus* 1, no. 3 (August 1993), 25.

[2] Jane Austen, *Northanger Abbey* (Harmondsworth: Penguin, 1973; first published 1818), 123.

[3] In the Index of Neill's book there are only 16 names of women and six of these are royal women. Stephen Neill, *A History of Christian Missions*, 2nd edn (London: Penguin, 1986), 217.

[4] Lavinia Byrne, ed., *The Hidden Journey: Missionary Heroines in Many Lands* (London: SPCK, 1993), 10.

[5] Janet Crawford, 'Church History', in *An A to Z of Feminist Theology*, ed. Lisa Isherwood and Dorothea McEwan (Sheffield: Sheffield University Press, 1996), 27–30.

[6] Fiona Bowie, 'Introduction: Reclaiming Women's Presence', in *Women and Missions: Past and*

recently this has been an untold story. Three examples from the nineteenth century demonstrate that women were fully involved in recruiting, sending and supporting women to engage in mission overseas.

Women-only mission boards developed during the nineteenth century in North America because American mission boards were reluctant to recruit and send single women. Men were encouraged to marry pious wives – indeed wives were seen as indispensable for the success of the work – not only to provide a 'tolerable home' for their husbands but also to model devout domesticity in heathen lands.[7] The wife got little, if any, official recognition. Despite male fear and prejudice that this movement was masking the women's rights and suffrage movement, by the end of the nineteenth century nearly half of the mission sending boards in the USA were women's boards.[8] Women were on the move in mission, organizing and managing their own structures, sending women to be involved with women's issues. Women were raising financial support, interviewing candidates, corresponding with women overseas and educating their support base to be more intelligently involved with mission. Sadly, the existence of these boards was relatively short-lived and by the early decades of the twentieth century they had merged and integrated with the 'general boards', almost certainly to the detriment of the involvement of American women in mission. The women succumbed to a variety of pressures: appeals to denominational loyalty, criticisms about duplication of resources and inefficiency, assurances that they would be represented in decision-making structures and that their concerns would be acknowledged and served in the new 'integrated' structures. Unfortunately, the reality was very different. At the beginning of this millennium, Dana Robert even wondered if the collapse of the women's missionary movement led to a decline in the mission interest of mainline churches because of the removal of their greatest advocates of mission.[9]

A similar initiative in Britain was the establishment of the Zenana Bible and Medical Mission, now known as Interserve. This mission was founded in 1852 and its field staff remained all female until 1952. Medical work was an area which made a huge impact on women as only women missionaries

---

Present Anthropological and Historical Perspectives, ed. Fiona Bowie, Deborah Kirkwood and Shirley Ardener (Oxford: Berg, 1993), 1.

[7] R. Pierce Beaver, *American Protestant Women in World Mission: A History of the First Feminist Movement in North America* (Grand Rapids, MI: Eerdmans, 1980), 52.

[8] By 1900 41 of the 94 mission boards were women's boards. Beaver, *American Protestant Women*, 87–8.

[9] See Dana Robert, 'Women and Missions: Historical Themes and Current Realities', in *Twentieth Century Missions and Gender Conference* (unpublished paper presented at a conference at Boston University, March 2000), 1–15.

could have any contact with women secluded in 'zenanas'.[10] It seems that this was a sphere where it was acceptable for single women to be involved in mission, although in 1908 Richter acknowledged that the work done by women in India 'has for the most part been carried on in secret, and little of it has found its way into missionary reports'.[11] The third example is the Society for Promoting Female Education in the East (SPFEE, 1831) which was another society run entirely by women for educating and evangelizing girls and women in distant lands. Societies such as these enabled women to find a new role and status in society. This was not only true for the women and girls in distant lands but also for the women who established the society, as the creation of this society gave them new opportunities to serve in the home church.[12]

It was not until the end of the nineteenth century that most mission societies could even begin to countenance the idea of sending single women overseas in greater numbers, and the enlistment of large numbers of single women did give a boost to missionary recruitment.[13] But even in the twentieth century the work of missionary wives and women remained unacknowledged. Wives of Church Missionary Society (CMS) missionaries were not registered until 1950; until that time they were listed as an asterisk next to their husband's name and later that was modified to a little 'm', denoting 'married'. Dana Roberts writes:

> Probably the most significant ambiguity in the work of twentieth-century missionary women has been their lack of recognition. Outnumbering men by two to one on the mission field during much of the century, women's own distinctive contributions to mission practice and theory have been ignored by scholars until relatively recently.[14]

---

[10] The *zenana* was the curtain behind which high-caste Indian women were secluded, and therefore by extension all women were enclosed against the outside world. Only women were permitted into the enclosure.

[11] J. Richter, *A History of Missions in India*, trans. S Moore (London: Oliphant, Anderson and Ferrier, 1908), 332.

[12] Margaret Donaldson, "'The Cultivation of the Heart and the Moulding of the Will . . .": The Missionary Contribution of the Society for Promoting Female Education in China, India and the East', in *Women in the Church*, ed. W. J. Sheils and Diana Wood (Oxford: Basil Blackwell, 1990), 429–42.

[13] For example, the Church Missionary Society (CMS) had sent 43 lone women missionaries by 1851, 50 from 1852 to 1882, and 224 from 1884 to 1894. Nearly all of these women were single or widows; usually on their marriage their 'connexion closed'. Church Missionary Society, *Register of Missionaries and Native Clergy from 1804 to 1904, Part 1* (London: Printed for Private Circulation, 1896), 260–96.

[14] D. Robert, ed., *Gospel Bearers, Gender Barriers* (Maryknoll, NY: Orbis Books, 2002), xi.

Missionary wives: 'I should like you to know that a wife and mother can also burn with missionary enthusiasm'[15]

Protestant missionary women went out as wives and as such served several purposes in the thinking of the male mission strategists. First, the existence of a wife generally signified that the missionary had a peaceful intent. Second, she reduced her husband's temptation to sexual philandering. Finally, she provided an excellent example and role model of feminine behaviour and she could teach useful domestic skills to native women.

Missionary wives have also been seen as helpmeets, heroines and partners.[16] First, most missionary wives were helpmeets to their husbands, enlisted to join in their husbands' work and to support their husbands in their high calling. The CMS Secretary of the Women's Department, Georgina Gollock, claimed that women's work was to be distinctive and complementary:

> The primary office of a missionary's wife is that of being a helpmeet to her husband. Her life is merged in his, and both together stand as one to set forward the work of the Lord. This has first to be done within the home, then in sharing and aiding in her husband's sphere of labour, and beyond that in taking up such further service for the Master as time and strength allow.[17]

They were primarily to be providers of conjugal comfort and homemakers so their husbands could be the missionaries. Grimshaw argued similarly, 'From the commencement of the mission it was assumed that, however educated and capable wives might be, the men would undertake mission leadership and the major work which was perceived by them to be most important.'[18] This dovetailed nicely with Evangelical teaching on submission and the wife's role.

Second, missionary wives were portrayed as heroines, 'fighting the hostile forces of paganism in dangerous and exotic locations, bringing their feminine virtue to transform the domestic and gender arrangements of

---

[15] This was a heartfelt plea from Mrs Margaret Beharell, who felt aggrieved at the marked lack of interest shown in women's work by a visiting deputation. Diane Langmore, 'The Gracious Influence of Wise and Thoughtful Womanhood', in *Missionary Lives Papua, 1874–1914*, ed. Robert C. Kiste, Pacific Island Monograph Series, no. 6 (Honolulu: University of Hawaii Press, 1989), 166.

[16] Hilary Carey, 'Women's Peculiar Mission to the Heathen: Protestant Missionary Wives to Australia 1788–1900', in *Long, Patient Conflict: Essays on Women and Gender in Australian Christianity*, ed. Mark Hutchinson and Edmund Campion (Sydney: Macquarie University, 1994), 26.

[17] Georgina Gollock, *Missionaries at Work* (London: CMS, 1898), 131, 133.

[18] Patricia Grimshaw, *Paths of Duty: American Missionary Wives in Nineteenth Century Hawaii* (Honolulu: University of Hawaii Press, 1989), 113.

natives everywhere'.[19] Although the domestic environment of missionary wives may not conjure up heroic images, they were often called on to
exhibit bravery and resilience in ways more private than their husbands
but no less demanding. Regular childbirths, often in remote locations
with no medical assistance, frequent absences of their husbands, assuming
prime responsibility for the education of their children, offering hospitality in sometimes trying conditions, tiredness, language difficulties and
illness were just some of the issues to be faced with fortitude.

Third, they were also seen as partners whose labour was essential to the
work of the mission. They performed and directed the practical tasks such
as teaching, nursing, cooking and other tasks normally assigned to the
women's sphere, as well as providing the role model for a Christian family life. Norman Goodall in his history on the London Missionary Society
(LMS), wrote:

> there has always been rendered by missionaries' wives an immense volume
> of work in schools, dispensaries and cottage industries, in translation and
> literary work, in the training of women workers, and in experiments that
> bear the stamp of creative originality.[20]

Partners they certainly were, but they were usually regarded as the
junior partners of this relationship. So while the rhetoric of the mission
society may have moved on from 'helpmeet' to 'partner', the work lacked
any official support from the society, and the wives certainly remained the
subordinate partner.

Many of the missionary wives' achievements were credited not only to
their husbands but also to other male colleagues, so that women missionaries were not seen as exercising their gifts and talents in their own right.
So how did missionary wives, who were 'burning with enthusiasm', get
around the limitations of the private sphere and make themselves useful?

Missionary wives: the object lesson of a civilized Christian home

The Christian home became a conscious and intentional missionary strategy, an object lesson, in fact.[21] Dana Robert has written extensively on the
place of the Christian home as a strategy for mission for missionary wives.

---

[19] Carey, 'Women's Peculiar Mission', 33.

[20] Norman Goodall, *A History of the London Missionary Society 1895–1945* (London: Oxford University Press, 1954), 14.

[21] Dana Robert, 'The "Christian Home" as a Cornerstone of Christian Thought and Practice', in

She argues, in the North American context, that by the 1830s domesticity had become the dominating discourse and that the Christian home had become an 'object lesson' as a matter of necessity:

> But the exact method of using the Christian home as an 'object lesson' or comprehensive example of evangelical domestic practice, child-training, and marital relations, did not emerge until it became clear that missionary wives found it exceedingly difficult to care for their own children and do mission work at the same [time].[22]

The home, therefore, provided a rationale for the involvement of women in all aspects of mission work as well as validating an Evangelical lifestyle. 'The Christian home was a pragmatic, plastic concept that could be shaped according to national, class, and gender interests, even as its continuity made it comfortable and non-controversial.'[23] The ideal of the Christian home was thus turned into a missionary strategy. Robert's thesis is that this only happened when it became clear that missionary wives could not care for their own families and do missionary work at the same time.

This missionary strategy for reform therefore focused on home and family. It also had the great advantage of complementing, and not competing with, men's missionary involvement:

> It is the husband's role to work outdoors – he farms and builds the home and prepares that which concerns the welfare of the body. The role of the wife is to maintain the house and all that is within . . .. It is wrong to neglect work and to leave the husband to keep the household.[24]

This left the women with the central goal of reforming the family by role-modelling pious domesticity and a Christian family life. Missionary wives were expected to 'support [their husbands] in their work, run the household, bear and raise the children, and together provide the "object lesson of a civilised Christian home"'.[25] Thus the Christian home and Christian family life became the *raison d'être* of missionary wives. 'By

---

Christian Missions and the Enlightenment of the West: The Challenges of Experience and History (Boston, MA: North Atlantic Missiology Project, June 1998), 1–37.

[22] Robert, 'The "Christian Home"', 10.

[23] Robert, 'The "Christian Home"', 3.

[24] Patricia Grimshaw, 'New England Missionary Wives, Hawaiian Women and "The Cult of Womanhood"', in *Family and Gender in the Pacific: Domestic Contradictions and the Colonial Impact*, ed. Margaret Jolly and Martha Macintyre (Cambridge: Cambridge University Press, 1989), quoting E. Clark (1844), *A Word Relating to Marriage*, trans. Carol Silva (Honolulu, HI: Mission Press), 35.

[25] Diane Langmore, '"The Object Lesson of a Civilized Christian Home"', in *Missionary Lives Papua*, ed. Kiste, 73.

interpreting family life as a mission agency, the mission wives sacralized the myriad activities that ate up their strength and their days.'[26]

The Christian home became the missionary goal, but its relationship to colonialism was often unquestioned and indeed even sanctioned. The focal point of a Protestant mission station was the mission home and this offered the object lesson of a civilized, Christian home. Victorian British and North American Evangelical domesticity was based on a particular view on the role of women, and it was this that became associated with the missionizing of women.

Missionary wives: subverting separate spheres

The ideal of the Christian home, however, was ambiguous as a mission strategy and relied on the Evangelical understanding of men and women inhabiting separate spheres. Robert concluded that, depending on the context, 'the Christian home can be seen in retrospect as either a "colonization of consciousness" or a source of dignity and even social change for women in a changing world.'[27] However, the Christian home did remain an enduring element in mission theory where the role of the wife on the mission station was primarily as helpmeet to her husband and, second, as a role model to those around her. Many women often experienced a tension between homemaking and child rearing and their own notions of social reform and moral uplift. The 'cult of true womanhood' was a complicated affair for women dealing with their personal capacities and vocations.

Jocelyn Murray has noted that 'immense amounts of work in schools and training was done by wives, un-listed daughters as well as companions and governesses'.[28] She emphasized this yet again in an article for the CMS Bicentennial Publication where she noted that much work was done by wives but this was not clear because of the way it was recorded. She gave several examples of the work done by wives, widows and other women in families – perhaps a sister or niece who had gone out to assist the family and who became involved in mission work. She lamented that it was not until the end of the nineteenth century that women's missionary service began to be more readily accepted: 'Women were accepted reluctantly,

---

[26] Robert, 'The "Christian Home"', 13.

[27] Robert, 'The "Christian Home"', 28.

[28] Jocelyn Murray, 'Anglican and Protestant Missionary Societies in Great Britain: Their Use of Women as Missionaries from the Late 18th Century to the Late 19th Century', *Exchange* 21, no. 1 (April 1992), 7.

and their work inadequately recognised, whether they had been wives or female missionaries.' By 1899 wives made up 53 per cent of the women serving overseas with the CMS.[29]

The home may have been the primary site for the mission endeavours of the wives, but often much more was required of them. In the absence of their husbands, they were called upon to run the mission station, keep accounts and write reports. They provided hospitality and nursing care and were often involved in the schooling of not only their own children but also those of the local people as well. For some, this loss of focus on family life and homemaking was welcomed; for others it was a sacrifice.[30]

I believe that this very ideology of 'separate spheres', also known as 'the angel in the house' phenomenon, led to some ambiguity in the working out of woman's role and identity within an Evangelical worldview.[31] It was clear that women were supposed to be subordinate and that home and children were their sphere, yet they still had influence. In fact many women argued that if they were the upholders of Christian values they should be able to use their influence outside the home in philanthropic activities and in social reform. It was a small step from the love of family to the love of the larger human family, and this step was made easier by Christian teaching. Female reformers hailed Christianity as an emancipating influence which could give enormous scope to woman as wife and mother and, by extension, to society. This philanthropic impulse was readily linked with an evangelistic motive.

So while this ideology of domesticity was at one level deeply conservative, at another it held within it the seeds of its own subversion. Within the home women could exercise a certain amount of power. As Davidoff and Hall commented: 'If the moral world was theirs, who needed the public

---

[29] Jocelyn Murray, 'The Role of Women in the CMS 1799–1917', in *The Church Missionary Society and World Christianity 1799–1999*, ed. Kevin Ward and Brian Stanley (Grand Rapids, MI: Eerdmans, 2000), 66–90, esp. 89.

[30] T. O. Beidelman, 'Altruism and Domesticity: Images of Missionizing Women among the Church Missionary Society in Nineteenth-Century East Africa', in *Gendered Missions: Women and Men in Missionary Discourse and Practice*, ed. Mary Taylor Huber and Nancy C Lutkehaus (Ann Arbor: University of Michigan Press, 1999), 135.

[31] This is the title of a Victorian poem by Coventry Patmore where the woman is extolled as having traditionally feminine virtues such as love, intuition, virtue and beauty. 'As Patmore's title suggests, the angel brings a more than mortal purity to the home that she at once creates and sanctifies, for which her mate consequently regards her with a sentimental, essentially religious reverence.' C. Christ, 'Victorian Masculinity and the Angel in the House', in *A Widening Sphere: Changing Roles of Victorian Women*, ed. M. Vicinus (Bloomington: Indiana University Press, 1977), 146.

world of business and politics?'[32] It was believed that women were the moral regenerators of the home and the nation and this could have wider ramifications as women became involved in philanthropic activities and engaged in mission service. Although Evangelical theology was conservative and limiting in terms of a woman's role, it also provided an effective justification for women's involvement in social reform and philanthropy in the public arena as an extension of their moral and spiritual activities in the home. This influence was even acknowledged at the time, so that by the middle of the nineteenth century one writer in *The Christian Observer* commented:

> By maintaining the most kindly intercourse with the poor, by alleviating sorrow beyond the little circle of home, by guiding the work of education, by using life for its highest and most beneficent purposes, by self-dedication to God, by labours in the mission field as well as in their own country, women are employing an influence scarcely acknowledged until we see it in detail, but the aggregate of which entitles it, when comprehensively surveyed to rank amongst the highest human agencies which a merciful God is blessing to the benefit of men's souls and bodies.[33]

The increasing emphasis on separate spheres had another interesting consequence. It led women to reach out to other women in sisterhood, in solidarity, on the common ground of domesticity. They would create friendships with other women, and within this lay the beginnings of many women's organizations which over time developed and flourished in a more formalized way.

Women's involvement in charitable endeavours grew remarkably during the course of the nineteenth century. This has been referred to as the 'angel out of the house' phenomenon which recognized women's role in a wider context.[34] Anglican social campaigner Josephine Butler, in 1869, also claimed that 'the extension beyond our homes of the home influence' would regenerate society and thereby serve to enhance family life.[35] Anne Summers described women's philanthropic work as a 'home from home'.[36]

---

[32] L. Davidoff and C. Hall, eds, *Family Fortunes: Men and Women of the English Middle Class* (London: Hutchinson, 1987), 183.

[33] Sean Gill, *Women and the Church of England from the Eighteenth Century to the Present* (London: SPCK, 1994), 79.

[34] Elizabeth K. Helsinger, Robin Lauterbach Sheets and William Veeder, 'Sarah Lewis and *Woman's Mission*', in *The Woman Question: Society and Literature in Britain and America 1837–1883, vol. 1: Defining Voices*, ed. Elizabeth K. Helsinger, Robin Lauterbach Sheets and William Veeder (Chicago, IL: University of Chicago Press, 1983), xi–xvii.

[35] Helsinger et al., 'Sarah Lewis and *Woman's Mission*', 131.

[36] A. Summers, 'A Home from Home – Women's Philanthropic Work in the Nineteenth Century', in *Fit Work for Women*, ed. S. Burman (London: Croom Helm, 1979), 33.

Women were involved in a wide variety of charitable activities. Some of the most notable were Sunday school teaching, the Girls' Friendly Society, missionary auxiliary societies seeking to raise funds for overseas mission work, the temperance movement, a network of penitentiaries and houses of refuge for prostitutes, and parish visiting where spiritual and physical needs were ascertained and met. And of course we could also wonder if a public face did not in fact mask a private reality. As Keith Wrightson has so appositely asked, '[Did] theoretical adherence to the doctrine of male authority and *public* female subordination [mask] the *private* existence of a strong complementary and companionate ethos?'[37] In other words, what it might look like from the outside might in fact be experienced very differently from within.

Women's distinctive contributions to missiology[38]

A missiology of emptiness and hiddenness

As we have seen, women's involvement in mission is often experienced from a point of weakness, sacrifice and invisibility. Women are familiar with approaches that are hidden, less recognized and rarely celebrated. We *all* need to recover these perspectives in our missiology, not just women. Taken to an extreme, these could reinforce unhelpful patterns of domination for men and submission for women. However, I believe that Jesus' approach was one where he emptied himself for the sake of others, where he sometimes even asked people to keep his healing miracles secret, where he declared that the first would be last, and told his disciples that we all need to take up our cross to follow him. Jesus' approaches of being hidden, less known and less recognized are Christian approaches in keeping with meekness and humility and which we all (men and women) would do well to emulate.

A missiology of comforting, consolation and healing

A missiology of comforting draws from the power of the Holy Spirit to comfort, transform and heal – both humanity and creation. The Holy Spirit, also known as the Comforter, is the one who comforts the broken,

---

[37] Amanda Vickery, 'Golden Ages to Separate Spheres? A Review of the Categories and Chronology of English Women's History', *Historical Journal* 36, no. 2 (1993), 385.

[38] For further elaboration of these concepts, see C. Ross, '"Without Faces": Women's Perspectives on Contextual Missiology', in *Putting Names with Faces: Women's Impact in Mission History*, ed. Christine Lienemann-Perrin, Atola Longkumer and Afrie Songco Joye (Nashville, TN: Abingdon Press, 2012).

the afflicted, the suffering. God is a God of consolation who is with the HIV & AIDS sufferers, the abused women, the victims of the so-called Islamic State (IS), of war. Women and children are the victims of war and violence. Women struggle on to feed and protect their families, to live in reconciliation and peace, to bind up the wounded, to heal the broken-hearted. Chung Hyun Kyung claims that Asian women believe in Christ 'in spite of' – in spite of lack of protection from their fathers and brothers who may beat them or sell them into child marriage or prostitution. She writes, 'Some Asian women have found Jesus as the one who really loves and respects them as human beings with dignity, while the other men in their lives have betrayed them.'[39] In other words, women find consolation in their relationship with Jesus. They know that Jesus sides with silenced Asian women and can bring liberation and wholeness. Jesus is the one who can bring healing, solace and renewal for women.

A missiology of hospitality and relationship

A missiology of the house or a missiology of the kitchen table could be a necessary corrective to much of our missiology. This conjures up images of intimacy, homeliness, warmth, comfort, rootedness, safety and rela-tionship. Hospitality is a powerful metaphor with which to think about mission. It begins with God and is an essentially outward-looking practice and virtue. Hospitality involves listening, learning, seeing the other, and negotiation of space by all parties. Generous hospitality can lead to rec-onciliation and genuine embrace of the other. Again, hospitality is not a simple metaphor, and plays out in different ways in different contexts. So while for some it may indeed mean invitation, warmth, sharing of food, relationship, for others it may mean ongoing stress and virtual impover-ishment as hospitality is demanded and expected sometimes beyond the resources available.

The whole guest–host conundrum is a fascinating study for Christian mission. Who is the guest and who is the host? This very question is demonstrated and incarnated in the life of Jesus.

Jesus is portrayed as a gracious host, welcoming children, tax collectors, prostitutes and sinners into his presence and therefore offending those who would have preferred such guests not to be at his gatherings. But Jesus is also portrayed as vulnerable guest and needy stranger who came to his own but found his own did not receive him (John 1.11). Pohl comments

---

[39] Chung Hyun Kyung, 'Who Is Jesus for Asian Women?', in *Liberation Theology: An Introductory Reader*, ed. C. Cadorette et al. (Maryknoll, NY: Orbis Books, 1992), 124.

that this 'intermingling of guest and host roles in the person of Jesus is part of what makes the story of hospitality so compelling for Christians'.[40] Think of Jesus on the Emmaus Road as travelling pilgrim and stranger, recognized as host and for who he was in the breaking of bread during a meal involving an act of hospitality. Or think of the Peter and Cornelius story (interestingly, another story involving varieties of food) – who is the host and who is the guest? Who is the insider and who is the outsider? Both offer and receive, both listen and learn, both are challenged and changed by the hospitality of the other. So we can see the importance of not only the ambiguity but also the fluidity and reciprocity/mutuality of the host/ guest conundrum. We offer and receive as both guest or stranger and host.

> Hospitality questions one's way of thinking about oneself and the other as belonging to different spheres; it breaks down categories that isolate. It challenges and confuses margins and centre. Hospitality involves a way of thinking without the presumption of knowing beforehand what is in the mind of the other; dialogue with the other is essential . . . To welcome the other means the willingness to enter the world of the other[41]

Of course this is the magic of mission and the challenge of the gospel. When we encounter the other as guest or host, insider or outsider (like Peter and Cornelius); when we engage in deep listening, we too are trans-formed and changed. We learn new things about ourselves and about the gospel. The whole guest–host idea begins to break down and becomes much more fluid and blurry as we learn from and relate to one another in mutual exchange and reciprocity.

A missiology of sight, embrace and flourishing

The gifts of sight and insight, awareness and attentiveness, are gifts of the Holy Spirit. Just as the female disciples were the first to see Jesus, our eyes have to be opened to recognize Jesus also. Once we can see Jesus, the Holy Spirit enables us to see the other person. Christian mission requires that we actively see and welcome the guest and stranger in our worlds. So a missiology of sight must encourage Christians to acknowl-edge the identity of the other – the other who is full of potential to be real-ized in relationship with Christ. The actual and the potential must be seen and acknowledged together. And in this encounter with the other, I too am confronted with the truth of myself and all that I am capable of becoming.

---

[40] C. Pohl, *Making Room: Recovering Hospitality as a Christian Tradition* (Grand Rapids, MI: Eerdmans, 1999), 17.
[41] Lucien Richard, *Living the Hospitality of God* (New York: Paulist Press, 2000), 12.

When I embrace the other, in a small way I begin to die to myself and begin to see myself in the other. John V. Taylor comments:

> But no less necessary to the Christian mission is the opening of our eyes towards other people. The scales fell from the eyes of the convert in Damascus precisely when he heard one of those whose very lives he had been threatening say, 'Saul, my brother, the Lord Jesus has sent *me to you.* I-Thou.[42]

Flourishing refers not just to human flourishing but to our web of interdependency with all of creation, and so mission calls for a reimagination of our relationships within all of creation so that flourishing is for all of humanity and all of creation.

Conclusion: the promotion of women's ministries – a perilous road?

Is this a perilous road – to highlight difference, and to promote women's perspectives and approaches? Is this the way to essentialism and further embedding of injustice and social enmeshment? Or are men still seen as normative and women as 'other'? Do we need a missiology which promotes women's ministries?

Ironically, the home which, historically, has been seen as the locus of pious domesticity is now recognized as one of the most dangerous places for women.

Christine Lienemann-Perrin alerts us to the ambiguities and complexities of this public–private separation for women. She writes, 'We know that in all of our world's societies violence increases behind the excuse that what takes place in the home is of no public concern.'[43] Mexican feminist theologian, Marilu Salazar, reminds us that domestic violence is more common than we would like to think: 'Home, for millions of women, has become a place more dangerous than the streets.'[44] And in some parts of the Church, women are actively discouraged from leaving abusive and violent partners, usually because of distorted understandings of headship and authority. We now need to acknowledge that the gendering of the public–private split and the phenomenon of separate spheres is not healthy for women.

---

[42] J. V. Taylor, *The Go-Between God: The Holy Spirit and the Christian Mission* (London: SCM Press, 1972), 21.

[43] C. Lienemann-Perrin, 'The Biblical Foundations for a Feminist and Participatory Theology of Mission', *International Review of Mission* 93, no. 368 (January 2004), 31.

[44] Marilu Salazar, 'Missionaries' Commitment to Mexico: Women's Education and Resistance to Violence', in *Putting Names with Faces*, ed. Lienemann-Perrin, 302.

Perhaps what we need is a missiology of risk that enables a prophetic voice to challenge the forces that render women invisible, marginalized and exposed to violence. We need a missiology of resistance which will oppose oppression and domination in all contexts and allow both women and men to flourish in mission and ministry. Missiologies of risk and resistance can offer prophetic approaches that unmask the issues, raise awareness, and suggest creative ways of dealing with invisibility and injustice.

Still today, in most parts of the world, women bear the main responsibility for meeting the basic needs of the family but are often denied access to the basic resources to make this possible, such as adequate nutrition, healthcare and education.

> Women continue to face discrimination in access to work, economic assets and participation in private and public decision-making. Women are also more likely to live in poverty than men . . . Women earn 24 per cent less than men globally. In 85 per cent of the 92 countries with data on unemployment rates by level of education for the years 2012–2013, women with advanced education have higher rates of unemployment than men with similar levels of education. Despite continuous progress, today the world still has far to go towards equal gender representation in private and public decision-making.[45]

The cycle of poverty, violence and disease affects women all over the world. It would seem, then, that the promotion of women's ministries is not a perilous road but rather a necessary road to follow in order for women to be agents rather than those acted upon. However, it will take women, as well as men, to make this a reality, and to allow women to flourish everywhere.

---

[45] At <http://www.un.org/millenniumgoals/2015_MDG_Report/pdf/MDG%202015%20rev%20 (July%201).pdf>, 8 (accessed 22 January 2016).

513

35

The dynamics of power in churches

MARTYN PERCY

The purpose of this chapter is to give some brief insight into human relations and psychodynamic insights in the practice of ministry – group work, role-relations, organization and institution, leadership and management. So we begin with a problem set out by one educationalist, puzzled about how a minister has chosen to lead a church:

> [T]he 'church' so talked about in seminary is neat, tidy, and generally civilised. A particular congregation is never neat, sometimes barely Christian and only rarely civilised. Part of the 'culture shock' is due to the changed status of the student. There is a world of difference between being a member of a congregation, and carrying the weight of its symbolic meaning in the institutionalised role of 'priest', whether that word is understood in a high or low sense. In addition, the student emerging from theological college is a different person from the one who entered.
>
> Again what appears to be the case upon the surface is not necessarily the case. In one parish a prolonged conflict occurred over the practice of the ladies' guild of placing a vase of flowers on the communion table. The new minister, on the basis of sound theological principles and an impeccable liturgical viewpoint well supported in theological college, made strenuous efforts to remove them.
>
> The conflict proved to be an illustration of two world views passing each other. The practice had arisen in the particular congregation positively as a confession of God's grace in renewing the world daily, and negatively because of the attempt of a former minister to close the women's group down. A vase of flowers was, to the women's group, symbol both of their identity as a group and a confession of their faith as Christians. The new minister saw only a custom he could not affirm with integrity. That was all he saw, and before his outlook had become informed much damage had been done to the life of the parish. Similar stories can be told about attempts to remove national flags from churches, or to change the arrangement of

church furniture bearing brass plates in honour of deceased parents and grandparents.[1]

Typically, attention to power in denominations and local congregations focuses on abuse and the problematic. High-profile cases are often reported in the media: clergy who sexually abuse adults or minors; arguments over money and trust; disputes about promises made, and then broken.

Yet it would be a pity to become fixated on the pitfalls of power and to overly problematize it, since a deeper appreciation of the dynamics of power can reveal the hidden governance, resources and untapped potential in a congregation. Too often, it is the fear of power and its potential for harm that prevents many congregations from coming to a more assured appreciation of how they (as a body) might symbolize that power to the wider community. Understanding power is essential for mission, organization and transformation; its dynamics need ownership, not shunning.

In paying attention to the reality of power in the local church, it is virtually inevitable that a whole set of social and material relations will become subject to scrutiny. In turn, some of the theological rationales that support those relations will also need to be assessed. For example, the defence of a particular tradition or custom is not 'simply' a case of a group of people protecting what they know to be the truth. It is also a statement about a way of being; a preference for one type of tradition over another; a formula that affirms one pattern of behaviour, but at the same time resists others. Power, therefore, is not one 'thing' to be discovered and studied. It is, rather, a more general term that covers a range of ideas and behaviour that constitute the fundamental life of the local church.[2]

To help us think a little more about the study of power in the local church, we can begin by focusing on different types of leadership, which in turn tend to embody different views of power. Consider, for example, three different caricatures of how Church of England bishops might operate within a diocese. One may see their role and task as primarily *executive*: being a hands-on manager, making key strategic decisions on a day-to-day basis. This view of pastoral power thrusts the bishop into the contentious realm of management, efficiency and rationalization, where he or she operates as a kind of chief executive officer in a large organization. This is a

---

[1] Denham Grierson (1985), *Transforming a People of God* (Melbourne: Joint Board of Christian Education of Australia and New Zealand), p. 18.
[2] See Martyn Percy (1996), *Power in the Church: Ecclesiology in an Age of Transition* (London: Cassell).

form of *rationalized* authority, and it will typically empathize with reviews, strategies and appraisals.

Another may take a different approach, and see the power of bishops in primarily *monarchical* terms. There are two faces to monarchical power. One is to rule by divine right: like a monarch, the bishop's word is law. But the second and more common manifestation of monarchical law is manifested in aloofness. Like most monarchs, bishops seldom intervene in any dispute decisively, and choose to remain 'neutral' and 'above' any divisive opinions or decisions. This is not an abrogation of power. Rather, the adoption of the second type of monarchical model proceeds from an understanding that others ('subjects') invest mystique and meaning in the power of the ruler, which in turn leads many monarchs and bishops to be 'officially silent' on most issues that have any immediacy, or are potentially divisive. Their symbolic power is maintained through mystique, and ultimately reticence. This is a form of *traditional* authority, where the power is primarily constituted in the office rather than in the individual charisms of the person holding it.

Another model is more *distributive*, and is concerned with facilitation and amplification. In this vision for embodying power in any office, the bishop becomes an enabler, helping to generate various kinds of powers (e.g. independent, related) within an organization. He or she will simply see to it that the growth of power is directed towards common goals, and is ultimately for the common good. But in this case, power is valued for its enabling capacities and its generative reticulation (e.g. the energy derived from and through networking, making connections); it is primarily verified through its connecting and non-directional capacities. To a point, such leadership requires a degree of *charismatic* authority, since the organization constantly requires a form of leadership that is connectional and innovative.

To be sure, most bishops will move between these models of power (and their associated types of authority) according to each case, and with each situation dictating which mode of power is deployed. But most bishops will naturally favour one kind of model over another. The advantage of looking at power through models of leadership, though, is that it illuminates other issues. For example, how is power 'conceptualized' in this situation or place? Who is said to have any ownership of power? How is power shared or dispersed in a congregation or denomination?

These issues are important when one considers the perpetual puzzling that often persists in relation to the status of charismatic leaders. For power is at its most obvious when it is at its most concentrated, and is intensely experienced. For this reason, an understanding of the complexities of power in relation to the local church is an essential element within the study of congregations. There are at last three ways of 'mapping' the power as it is encountered.

In one sense (as theorists of power in organizations argue),[3] power can be understood as *dispositional*. This refers to the habits and worldview of a congregation, and will closely correspond to their normative 'grammar of assent'. Appeals to an almighty God and Lord will have direct social consequences in terms of the expectations set upon obedience and compliance. On the other hand, *facilitative* power describes the agents or points of access through which such power is accessed. Here, the status of those agencies will normally match the power that they are connected to. Then again, *episodic* power, however, refers to those events or moments in the life of a congregation that produce surges of energy, challenge or opportunity.

Putting this together – with a Charismatic congregation serving as an example – one could say that the worship is dispositional, the leaders are facilitative, and the invocation of the Holy Spirit a cue for episodic manifestations of power that are unleashed. This sequence, of course, quickly becomes a dynamic cycle: the episodic confirms the validity of the facilitative and dispositional, and in so doing, creates further expectations of episodic manifestations of power, and the strengthening of other kinds. There is a real sense in which the local church is a 'circuit of power', replete with connections, adaptors, converters and charges of energy. The local church is a complex ecology of power, where energy of various types can flow in different ways, be subject to increase and decrease, and be converted and adapted for a variety of purposes.

Closely related to power is the question of authority. All Christian denominations evolve over time, and their patterning of power and arrangements for agreeing on normative sources of authority are also subject to change. Again, given proper scrutiny, excavating models of authority and power can reveal much about the structure of a church or congregation. Following Paula Nesbitt's sociological observations, we might note that in the first evolutionary phase of denominationalism, or in specific congregational evolution (which can currently be seen in the early history of new house-churches), institutional relations usually can be governed through obedience, and, if necessary, punishment. We might describe this

---

[3] See Percy, *Power in the Church*; and Martyn Percy (2006), *Engaging with Contemporary Culture: Christianity and the Concrete Church* (Aldershot: Ashgate).

as the exercise of *traditional* authority, where power over another can be nakedly asserted.

However, in the second phase, interpersonal contracts emerge between congregations, regions and individuals. Here 'ecclesial citizenship' is born, and law and order develop into agreed rather than imposed rule. We might call this *rational* authority: it has to be argued for and defended in the face of disputes and questioning. Again, a number of new churches are now at the point where their power and authority needs explaining in relation to their context and other relations. In the third phase (postmodern, etc.), more complex social contracts emerge between parties, which require a deeper articulation of a shared ethos and an agreement about the nature of a shared moral community. To retain unity and cohesive power, authority must be *negotiated*. It is here that the denomination effectively crosses the bridge from childhood to adulthood. Congregations learn to live with the differences between themselves.

Finally, there is *symbolic* authority. This states that authority and power are constituted in ways of being or dogma that are not easily apprehensible. Networks of congregations may choose a particular office ('chief pastor') or event ('synod') or artefact of tradition ('Bible'), and position this as having supreme governance. However, the weakness of symbolic authority is often comparable to the dilemma faced by those who prefer monarchical power. By positing power in an office that seldom intervenes in a decisive way, symbolic authority normally has to justify its substance. If it can't, it loses its power and authority. And no amount of assertion can make up for the imprecision which people vest in symbolic or monarchical power. Attempts to compensate for this dilemma often end with accusations of capriciousness.

Unconventional thoughts on power

Locating the unconscious in power relations is not a precise science; but it is possible to make some educated guesses as to what might be happening. Here is something that happened to me quite recently. I found myself chairing a highly contentious university committee, set up to review some work that had been hugely expensive and overrun on budget; yet it had still produced poor results, and was, moreover, deeply unpopular with local citizens, who had mounted vociferous campaigns of protest. The committee's work – no easy task – was to find remedial solutions that were not too costly, engage with the objections of local people and find a workable compromise.

We set about our task with the aid of excellent consultants, who were good listeners, highly professional and, crucially, humble and emotionally intelligent when it came to engaging with local objectors – a number of whom still boiled with rage. The university officers involved in the work were accomplished diplomats and ambassadors, and also could not be faulted for always going the extra mile. They also knew their work, and were highly competent. And then the time arrived: the period of public consultation for the new plans. The atmosphere was extraordinary. It should have been febrile and tense. It wasn't, however. It was peaceful, measured, constructive, restrained and temperate. Yes, there were still some criticisms to be addressed. But it was a quite different atmosphere from what had gone before.

How was this done? There was a blend of factors to take account of: partly the passing of time; partly the consultants and officers involved. And partly the *location* of the consultation – and this was the 'unconscious' aspect. The only space public enough and large enough to display the plans was an immaculately restored chapel, once dedicated to St Luke – the patron saint of healing. The space was calming and capacious, and beautifully lit. Its continued spiritual and contemplative ethos, which had survived its conversion into a large hall for displays, somehow reverberated. It was public, yet numinous. The space calmed, hushed and held its people. The unconscious was well at work.

The use of this space was not any kind of deliberate Machiavellian act. It was a happy accident. But it highlights how power is at work in human social relations.[4] Be sure, locating instances of power and abuse is a fairly obvious way of studying the shape and cadence of a congregation. However, some attention to apparently 'neutral' phenomena is also useful when trying to sketch or map the power dynamics of the local church. At least one of Paulo Freire's aspirations was to help people achieve 'deep literacy' – to be aware of the far from innocent forces which can shape lives and institutions. Freire argued that deep literacy came through dialogue.[5] It is in conversation and reflection that we become aware of how we are *determined* by our cultural inheritance and the powers within them. For example, the power of a building, and the mystique invested in its capacity to mould and inspire, is a form of power that may operate restrictively in a certain context.

---

[4]   On this, see Anton Obholzer and Vega Zagier Roberts (1994), *The Unconscious at Work: Individual and Organizational Stress in the Human Services* (London: Routledge).

[5]   Paulo Freire (1972), *Pedagogy of the Oppressed* (Harmondsworth: Penguin).

Equally, one must also pay attention to the numerous instances of power relations that continually construct and reconstruct power relations in a congregation. Silence on the part of individuals or groups within a congregation, and in the midst of a dispute or debate, can be interpreted in a variety of ways: as defeat – they have nothing more to say in this argument; as withdrawal – a refusal to participate; as 'wisdom' – they are waiting for you to see their point of view; as an act of defiance, or disapproval; as a spiritual rejoinder to too much discussion. Silence, then – even in its informal guise – is seldom innocent. It is a form of power that needs to be 'read', understood and interpreted.

Another example of what educationalists term the 'hidden curriculum' in relation to power can also be detected in apparently ordinary phenomena, such as dress codes and manners. I have often remarked that an important hermeneutical key for understanding Anglican congregations is to appreciate that, at a deeper level, Anglicanism could sometimes be said to be a sacralized system of manners. In other words, any disagreements must be moderated by a quality of civility. The means usually matter more than the ends: better to chair a good but ultimately inconclusive discussion than to arrive prematurely at a (correct) decision.

Similarly, codes of dress in church can also carry theological meaning that is related to dynamics of power. For some, dressing in a relaxed style connotes disrespect, a lack of formality, and, ultimately, is unacceptable. It is not that a congregation will necessarily have any hard or written rules about how to dress (e.g. gentlemen must wear ties and jackets). The codes and expectations evolve over a period of time, and in their own way, act as a sieve within the congregation. Conformity in uniformity indicates a degree of acquiescence in the pattern of belonging. To 'not dress right' is to not only rebel against the prevailing code; it is also to question the formal or informal ascriptions of God that are symbolized in those dress codes. Thus, in the relaxed gathering of a house church, where God is deemed to be immediate, friendly and even neighbourly, relaxed dress codes will tend to 'fit' and symbolize the theological outlook. Where God is deemed to be more formal and distant, with worship to complement this, it is likely that, like the worship itself, the dress code will be much more 'buttoned up'.

To be sure, one would have to exercise considerable caution in pushing these observations too far. But my point is that by paying simple and close attention to what the laity chooses to wear when they come to church, one can begin to gain some understanding of how power relations and expectations are constructed locally, and how they, in turn, reflect upon the congregation's (often unarticulated) theological priorities. Furthermore, this is an area that can be rich with conflict.

For example, in a North American church that I was briefly involved with some years ago, the pastor presented the following problem. One of the newest additions to the team of 12 elders, a person elected by the congregation, was refusing to wear a suit and tie for Sunday worship as the others did. (The elders were all male by custom rather than rule.) The new elder was also late for weekly meetings, and sometimes failed to turn up at all. The other 11 elders petitioned their pastor to have the errant elder removed or 'brought into line', claiming that the casual mode of dress signified disrespect (to God), and was mirrored in 'sloppy attendance habits'. The pastor made enquiries of the dissenter, and discovered that he had his reasons for 'dressing down'. He wanted the church to be more relaxed and less stuffy; he thought that formal attire inhibited worship, and also suggested a stern, somewhat formal God. The dissenting elder added that he thought that God was more mellow and relaxed, and he was merely expressing this. It was to this God that he was committed – or at least thinking about being committed to. So he did not miss meetings to be rude, or to make an obvious point; he simply didn't think that it mattered that much, *theologically*, and in the wider scheme of things. And that, of course, is itself theologically significant.

This story leads me to conclude this brief section by underlining the importance of reflecting on stories. James Hopewell, in his alert and prescient study of congregations, discusses the extent to which congregations are 'storied dwellings'.[6] By this, Hopewell means that congregations are frequently in the grip of myths and narratives that reflect worldviews, which in turn determine theological priorities. Congregations seldom understand that they are often owned or 'performed' by these 'dramatic scripts', but the stories do shape a congregation, nonetheless. His book is too rich and complex to be discussed further here, but the agenda he sets is a teasing one for the subject that we are concerned with. More often than not, what makes a congregation are the powerful narratives and stories it collects, which then go on to construct and constitute its inner life. These may be heroic stories, or they may be tales of triumph over adversity. Equally, however, the preferred stories can be centred on struggle, or on the value of coping.

But in focusing on stories, Hopewell has understood that power in the local church is more than a matter of studying the obvious or official

---

[6] James F. Hopewell (1987), *Congregation: Stories and Structures* (Philadelphia, PA: Fortress Press), pp. 40–54, and 140–52.

lines of authority, or the authorized power constructions and relations. True, there is value in paying proper attention to what we might term 'formal' religious structures and apparatus. Who is the pastor or vicar, and how does that person's style mediate his or her authority and power? In what ways do people regard the clergy? And how do the laity perceive themselves – as passive receptors of power, or as generators of empowerment? This is important, to be sure.

But there is also value in paying attention to the less formal and 'operant' faith of a congregation. What is the scale of the gap between the 'official' teaching of a church, and the actual 'concrete' discipleship of a congregation and its individuals? What does that gap tell us about power relations between the macro denomination and the micro congregation? Quite independent of what congregations are supposed to affirm, what kinds of stories of faith do they commonly tell? Where does the congregation think power lies? With the clergyperson? Or perhaps with a committee or governing body? Or perhaps with named individuals who wield different kinds of power (e.g. 'a pillar of the church') – perhaps through patronage, age, skill, charisma or experience? Or perhaps because an individual has an alternative theological and spiritual agenda that attracts a significant part of the congregation?

Ultimately, stories have power because they give us a kind of knowledge that abstract reasoning usually cannot deliver. One of the advantages of 'story knowledge', as a conveyor of power, lies in its sheer concreteness and specificity. Stories give us individualized people in specific times and places doing actual things: so they speak to congregations with a force and a power that dogma sometimes lacks. Rationality and theological formulae can tend to sidestep the messy particulars of life; stories, however, immerse us in life. So, if Hopewell is right, it is the narratives we tell each other that build and make the church what it is, and determine its sense of power. In imagining that the local church is a 'storied dwelling', to borrow Hopewell's memorable phrase again, we are invited to contemplate the many different ways in which we become what we speak, as churches. It is the stories that churches tell – much like personal testimonies – that turn out to be reliable reservoirs of power and authority. Such vignettes can be midrash: creeds-in-waiting.

Conclusion

In many congregations and denominations, the fear of conflict and aggression makes it very difficult to air strong feelings; the neuralgic anxiety is that the manifestation of feelings leads to the loss of poise in ecclesial polity. And yet we live in a world and within a Church that are shaped by human failings, and if we truly love these institutions then we will inevitably be angry about the ways they fall short. So what we do with our strong feelings, and how we handle the aggression that moves for change, will depend on whether we can see them as a sign of life and growth, or whether we suppress them for fear they will rock the boat too hard. As Harrison and Robb state:

> The moral question is not 'what do I feel?' but rather 'what do I do with what I feel?' Because this is not understood, contemporary Christianity is impaled between a subjectivist and sentimental piety that results from fear of strong feeling, especially strong negative feeling, and an objectivist, wooden piety that suppresses feelings under pretentious conceptual detachment. A feminist moral theology welcomes feeling for what it is – the basic ingredient in our relational transaction with the world.[7]

In the Church, the desire to avoid conflict both in parochial matters and in relationships in the diocese can often be a recipe for atrophy. When situations arise which cannot be ignored, the scale of feelings aroused can surprise and disappoint those who believe that if we all try to love each other, we will all agree. To truly love is to take seriously the desire to deepen relationships and work against all that limits and devalues human worth. Harrison and Robb put it like this:

> Radical love creates dangerous precedents and lofty expectations among human beings. Those in power believe such love to be 'unrealistic' because those touched by the power of such love tend to develop a reluctance to accept anything less than mutuality and self-respect, anything less than human dignity, anything less than authentic relatedness. It is for that reason that such persons become powerful threats to the *status quo*.[8]

So discovering how to acknowledge and give voice to strong feelings – in ways that can enable radical working together for the growth of all – is a challenge that the Church needs to heed. In his ministry, Jesus listened to the voices of the marginalized all the time. Indeed, not only did he listen but he also assimilated such voices into his ministry, and often made the marginalized central, and placed those who were central on the periphery,

---

[7] B. Harrison and C. Robb (1985), *Making the Connections: Essays in Feminist Social Ethics* (Boston, MA: Beacon Press), p. 14.

[8] Harrison and Robb, *Making the Connections*, p. 19.

thereby reordering society, forcing people to witness oppression and the response of the kingdom of God to despair, anger and marginalization.

So in the Church, we need to allow the experiences of the oppressed to challenge and shape the way we hold power and broker relationships. The churches need to continually learn from the veritable panoply of liberation theologies: that marginalized people should not simply be made welcome in the Church, but that their anger and aggressive desire for justice might be allowed to reform the manners of the Church. Learning to listen to narratives that convey strong, powerful feelings, rather than seeking to dismiss such stories as 'uncultured' or as 'bad manners', is a major and costly task for ecclesial polity and pastoral praxis. Ultimately, the aggression of those who seek justice may help the churches to move from a 'domesticated' valuing of crucifixion and suffering for its own sake, and work instead 'not to perpetuate crucifixions, but to bring an end to them in a world where they go on and on'.[9]

We are conscious that an argument for a Church in which feelings are allowed to be given their full vent carries risk. What if the venting of feelings damages or even destroys human relationships? We are all well aware that there is rightful place for reticence, and for the withholding of emotions. All of us understand that a temperate ecclesial polity can, to some extent, depend on finding a non-emotive language for expressing views and communicating across divisions. But I am also struck by how many churches, at local, regional and national level, deliberately disenfranchise and marginalize the proper expression of strong feelings. I find this not only to be poor ecclesial and pastoral practice, but also theologically weak and urbane, rendering the Church into some kind of semi-detached realm, in which all the correct probity of manners and politeness are observed, but 'real' feelings are never mentioned or aired.

This cannot be a proper reification of a strong incarnational theology, and neither can it make for the Church being an especially genuine community of the redeemed. If one of the tasks of the Church is to make it possible for people to truly face one another, then strong feelings must be properly addressed so that they can be appropriately located in the body of Christ, and not suppressed as part of some kind of artful process of subordination.

How, though, do we discern when anger is a legitimate call for justice, and when it is a petulant reaction to not getting one's way? Here we need to look at patterns of power and the motivation of anger. The good news

---

9   Harrison and Robb, *Making the Connections*, p. 19.

of the gospel is about the accessibility of God: the welcoming in of the religiously marginalized, and the breaking down of barriers. So in any kind of aggression and anger, we need to be clear whether or not it constitutes a move towards a vision of the kingdom, and how it is motivated by the radical mutuality of love. The command to love God and to love our neighbour as ourselves ultimately defines the place of our aggression and anger. It demands action, and that action demands drive, which at times requires generative anger and aggression. The Church needs to find a way of holding and utilizing the strong feelings that are part of human loving, remembering, as Harrison and Robb put it, that 'the important point is that where feeling is evaded, where anger is hidden or goes unattended, masking itself, there the power of love, the power to act, to deepen relation, atrophies and dies'.[10]

Part of the ministry of Jesus involved the expression of anger, and was occasionally constituted in acts of wilful aggression. It is hard to imagine some of Christ's words being spoken in anything other than simmering rage. There can of course be something like a *creative* rage – the kind of rage that the poets and the prophets speak of – which is markedly impolite, but utterly godly. The task for the Church, therefore, is to find ways that do not to suppress or block out strong feelings of anger, or hurt and the aggression it arouses, but to help discern how to channel the energy they bring into the work of the gospel.

While it is commonplace to pay attention to abuses or collapses of power in churches, the purpose of this section has been to show that there are deeper reasons why a focus on power is important for the study of the local church. First, the contested nature of power means that its study is essential if one is to clarify the culture, theology or anatomy of the local church. Second, there are conventional understandings of power that can illuminate ecclesiological analysis. Third, there are unconventional ways of understanding the identity and location of power that also merit attention. To simply study 'official' authority in the Church is to only undertake half the task, since there are hundreds of subtle and unofficial forms of power and authority that are no less significant. Ultimately, it is only by immersing oneself in a local church that one can begin to understand the complex range of implicit dynamics that make and shape a congregation. And in the act of immersion, the scholar needs to develop a deeper literacy that is attentive to the multifarious dynamics of power.

---

[10] Harrison and Robb, *Making the Connections*, p. 15.

Every collation of human relations within a social system carries some risk. The risks in the Church, however, are perhaps more unusual than other institutions or organizations. In fundamentalist or sectarian congregations, a primary hazard is that of conflation – the danger of eliding the identity of the leader with God, or with Scripture. In other words, it is sometimes impossible for the congregation or individuals to separate out the difference between what the Bible says, and what the (anointed) preacher or charismatic leader says it must and can only mean. Such conflation means that to disagree with the preacher or leader is tantamount to questioning God. In fundamentalist and sectarian Christian communities, it is not the Bible that rules, but rather the interpreter. Further issues may follow. The danger of populism is that it forms a personality cult, and eventually a culture of narcissism: 'demagogue-danger'. Cultures of narcissism and populism have a nasty habit of becoming bullying and sectarian. The study of ministry needs to focus more on human power relations, if abuses of power and authority are to be corrected. Only then can healthy patterns of ministry develop that truly enable people to flourish, and to become free, as the truth of the gospel promises.

36

Safeguarding in the Church of England

RUPERT BURSELL

The film *Spotlight* is a biographical drama film issued in 2015 and concerned with the *Boston Globe*'s investigation into widespread child sexual abuse in and around Boston by numerous Roman Catholic priests. In the course of the film, comments are made by various characters pointing out that the Catholic Church thinks in centuries; that a survivor, being alive, is one of the lucky ones; and that the clerical sexual abuse was not 'just' physical abuse but, as importantly, also spiritual abuse. The original investigation on which it is based won the Pulitzer Prize for Public Service in 2003, and the film itself won both Oscar and BAFTA awards. This investigation and exposé led to further horrific discoveries of clerical sexual abuse throughout the USA and beyond and continues to resonate loudly.

In 2012 the UK was rocked by devastating revelations of the sexual predation of children by the then deceased television and radio personality, Jimmy Savile, over a period of some 20 years. This in its turn led to prosecutions of other well-known television personalities for similar offences. These were unconnected with the Church, but the Church of England has also been riven with offences of sexual abuse of children as demonstrated by the Archbishop of Canterbury's Commissaries' Visitation of the Diocese of Chichester who reported in 2012–13; the *Inquiry into the Church of England's Response to Child Abuse Allegations Made against Robert Waddington* commissioned by the Archbishop of York (2014); the apologies for sexual abuse of children by prominent deceased clerics (Bishop George Bell and Chancellor Garth Moore) (2015); the conviction and imprisonment of Bishop Peter Ball for offences against 18 young men (2016); and a review into the abuse at a children's home run by the Church at Kendall House, Gravesend (2016). This terrible catalogue of abuse and failure by the Church has led the Archbishop of Canterbury, the Right Reverend Justin Welby, to request the Independent Inquiry into Child Sexual Abuse (IICSA), led by Justice Lowell Goddard, to prioritize the Church of England in its investigations into the institutional and organizational failings in England and Wales in relation to the protection of children.

In the *Church Times* dated 29 July 2016 three different articles appeared relating to abuse within the Anglican Church: one concerning IICSA in England and Wales; one concerning complaints under the Clergy Discipline Measure 2003 against an allegedly abusive priest and five bishops who allegedly responded inadequately to reports of that abuse; and one concerning an admitted cover-up of serial abusive behaviour by clergy in the diocese of Newcastle, New South Wales. In the first of these articles the leading counsel to IICSA was quoted as saying that the Inquiry would consider the extent to which the Diocese of Chichester and the criminal prosecution of the Right Reverend Peter Ball were 'representative of the Church of England [in England and Wales] as a whole'. In the third article the present Bishop of Newcastle, the Right Reverend Greg Thompson, is quoted as saying: 'This is what "mates looking after mates" looks like in the Church at times. And that is an appalling thing to say for a Christian person.' The bishop went on to say that he was being criticized 'because I am opening the cupboards and we're finding the skeletons'.

From all this it is apparent that comments made in the film *Spotlight* are as relevant to the Church of England today as to the Roman Catholic Church in America in 2003. Indeed, the July 2016 issue of the *Crucible* (being the *Journal of Christian Social Ethics*) was almost exclusively taken up with articles about safeguarding. One welcome result of all this is that the Church is at last paying attention to the voices of those who have themselves been abused and therefore to such organizations as Minister and Clergy Sexual Abuse Survivors (MACSAS) and Mosaic II.

Safeguarding is concerned not only with young children but with all children up to the age of 18 as well as with vulnerable adults. However, the Church of England (along with other sections of British society) has been slow to acknowledge this fact. Society has been all too willing to embrace the erroneous belief that children – especially girls – are responsible for their own abusive situations once they have reached the legal age of consent. The fallacy of this view is recognized in *Protecting All God's Children: The Policy for Protecting Children in the Church of England*[1] and is now enshrined in the Safeguarding and Clergy Discipline Measure 2016.

---

[1] Archbishops' Council (2010), *Protecting All God's Children: The Policy for Protecting Children in the Church of England*, 4th edn (London: Church House Publishing; first issued in 2004).

The Measure also for the first time in the English Church provides a definition of a vulnerable adult:

> A person aged 18 or over whose ability to protect himself or herself from violence, abuse, neglect or exploitation is significantly impaired through physical or mental disability or illness, old age, emotional fragility or distress, or otherwise; and for that purpose the reference to being impaired is being temporarily or indefinitely impaired.

Although not spelt out in relation to children, this definition makes clear that safeguarding is not confined to sexual abuse but that it embraces, in addition, any violence, neglect or exploitation. It also spells out that an adult may go in and out of vulnerability at any particular period of his or her life. It follows that consideration of individual circumstances is paramount: for example, an adult may be vulnerable when grieving or living in poverty, however temporary. Training of the clergy and laity in recognizing, and responding to, such vulnerability is therefore absolutely essential. Nevertheless, only time will tell whether this provision will be followed through with the intensity that it and those whom it is aimed at protecting deserve. It is also essential that the present horrific revelations about clerical sexual abuse do not distract from the wider obligations of safeguarding. These obligations may manifest themselves within a church context but may nevertheless be concerned with safeguarding issues in the wider community, family or school.

The Church has been slow to face up to imperfections in its safeguarding systems, in part due to the financial and logistical implications involved. Particularly among the longer-serving clergy there are examples of clerics being unwilling to recognize the dangers which safeguarding is designed to combat. This seems to be the result either of an unfounded confidence that it could not happen in their parishes; or a conscious or subconscious belief that the present concerns over safeguarding are overblown; or in the short term will go away; or that the whole system has become 'too bureaucratic'. This has led to such clergy, including in one instance (it is believed) a bishop, being reluctant or unwilling to undergo checks by the Disclosure and Barring Service (DBS, formerly CBS) and safeguarding training. The facts nonetheless remain that the strength of a chain is only that of its weakest link and that it is absolutely essential for all clergy, whether stipendiary or non-stipendiary and whether licensed or in receipt of a permission to officiate (PTO), to undergo the stipulated safeguarding checks and training before they take any part in church services or activities in their clerical capacities. It is this at which the new provisions of the Safeguarding and Clergy Discipline Measure 2016 are aimed: 'A relevant person[2] must have due regard[3] to guidance issued by the House of Bishops on matters relating to the safeguarding of children and vulnerable adults' (see section 5(1)).

This new provision is necessary not only to widen the scope of the relevant duty but also to counter any argument in the future that the House of Bishops' guidance could only impose a moral, not a legal, duty.[4] What is not so obvious, however, is that the provision underlines that diocesan safeguarding regulations do not have a similar legal force to that of (future) House of Bishops' guidance;[5] this is especially necessary as not all diocesan regulations or guidelines have in the past cohered with national guidelines. It remains to be seen to what extent diocesan safeguarding officers will try to circumvent this (to some of them) inconvenient situation, especially as it may mean their scrapping training material that they have painstakingly prepared in the past.

It is not always remembered – even by those who have themselves been abused – that the effects of abuse are particularly personal and unique to those affected by it. Although many of the abused prefer to be described as 'survivors' rather than 'victims', even that description skates over the problem that many of such abused persons have not managed to survive – due either to suicide or to drug overdoses driven by the damage (including their own perceived guilt in what took place) caused by the abuse. Central to this is that all such surviving victims live with the results of that abuse for the rest of their lives: it is not something that can be sloughed off or just put aside. It is also far too easy to ignore the fact that each individual has different needs or coping tactics: some wish to be left alone because they cannot bring themselves to share with others what has occurred; others are satisfied with an apology, both from the perpetrator

---

2 Section 5(2) states: 'Each of the following is a relevant person – (a) a clerk in Holy Orders who is authorised to officiate in accordance with the canons of the Church of England; (b) a diocesan, suffragan or assistant bishop; (c) an archdeacon; (d) a person who is licensed to exercise the office of reader or serve as a lay worker; (e) a churchwarden; (f) a parochial church council.' It should be noted that this provision does not apply to religious communities in so far as their members are not ordained or authorized to officiate within the canons. Although their numbers are few, this may prove to be an Achilles' heel in the future.

3 'A duty to "have regard to" guidance means that the person under the duty is not free to disregard it but is required to follow the guidance unless there are cogent reasons for not doing so. This sets a high standard. It means that a person can only depart from the guidance if the reasons for doing so are clear, logical and convincing.' See GS 1952-3x, paragraph 16.

4 See R. Bursell, 'Are the Clergy Discipline Measure 2003 and the Safeguarding and Clergy Discipline Measure 2016 Fit for Safeguarding Purposes?', *Crucible* (July 2016), pp. 52–3.

5 Bursell, 'Clergy Discipline Measure 2003', p. 53.

and the Church itself; others want to see the perpetrator brought to some sort of justice (whether in the criminal, civil or ecclesiastical courts); yet others seek compensation and financial or practical support in seeking treatment for themselves or their families which have also been affected by what has occurred. Each is different and unique, and the Church must be prepared to listen and respond to the cry of each individual. A failure timeously to respond only increases the pain and is itself a continuation of the original abuse. For this reason it is also imperative that the Church does not enter into insurance agreements which may limit the Church's response to the pains and needs of the abused person.

Yet, just as justice is imperative for those who have been abused (including those who are no longer alive), so is justice essential for those accused of abuse (whether living or dead)[6]. The procedures of the criminal and civil courts, where those alleging abuse are still subjected to long and (in some cases) unnecessarily intrusive cross-examination, remain far from ideal for the adjudication of allegations of abuse. Similarly, the procedures under the Clergy Discipline Measure 2003 are too cumbersome and take too long in reaching a conclusion. It remains to be seen to what extent these latter procedures can, or will, be improved in the future; certainly, the legislative procedures for the amendment of church legislation are themselves very long-winded and cumbersome and it cannot be easy for those who have been abused to appreciate or accept that this is so. In any event it is extremely doubtful whether the Church would wish, or be permitted by the Houses of Parliament (who oversee ecclesiastical legislation), to replace those procedures with, for example, a psychiatric assessment of an accused cleric.[7] At the end of the day, if a cleric or other lay worker is to be removed from office and possibly from gainful employment, that person (together with his or her dependants) must be entitled to a proper legal scrutiny of the accusations levelled against them.[8] Even though

---

[6]   If the reputation of a deceased person, such as Bishop George Bell, is to be impugned, the grounds of any decision must be open to scrutiny. It is highly unsatisfactory if the evidence (for or against) the imputation cannot be made public if, for example, any legal settlement of a civil case against the relevant diocese were to be reached on the basis of confidentiality. Any decision reached should also ensure that the strict application of the civil burden of proof is adhered to and that it is in no way affected by a desire to protect the diocese or the Church from further blame or acrimony.

[7]   For a somewhat different view see J. A. Stein, 'Surviving the Crucible of Ecclesiastical Abuse', *Crucible* (July 2016), p. 31.

[8]   Section 18(3)(c) of the 2003 Measure states that a Clergy Discipline Measure hearing 'shall be in private, except that the tribunal or court, if satisfied that it is in the interests of justice so to do or the respondent so requests, shall direct that the hearing shall be in public'. However, the

professionals, such as psychiatrists, weigh evidence carefully before reaching decisions in their professional lives, it is doubtful whether such experience matches the expertise of professional judges; indeed, experience in the civil courts argues strongly against such a viewpoint.

Further difficulties remain, however, with regard to safeguarding complaints. If a complaint is to be made in relation to clerical abuse, that complaint must almost of necessity be made, at least in the first instance, to a diocesan bishop. However, the fact of the initial abuse having been made by a cleric may make it emotionally very difficult for the abused person to approach another cleric about it, even if it is not face to face. As a matter of justice the Church should at least consider whether another mechanism for making complaints should not be provided. In this regard such a mechanism need not necessarily run counter to the concept that 'every bishop is the chief pastor of all that are within his diocese, as well laity as clergy, as their father in God'.[9] After all, a large measure of delegation already occurs under the Clergy Discipline Measure 2003 and in other areas of church life.

There is also confusion as to whether, and when, an actual 'complaint' is being made. Does a letter drawing past abuse to the attention of the bishop amount to a complaint and, if so, what does the person making the complaint expect to flow from it? Is it merely 'for information'? Does it seek any form of redress? Is a disciplinary procedure expected to follow or is some purely pastoral response expected? Such confusion already occurs and in some cases has led to grave misunderstanding between the person making the 'complaint' and the diocesan hierarchy. The bishop may respond pastorally but the person making the complaint may well, then or later in the procedure, expect some disciplinary response, such as suspension, without appreciating that in law no suspension (other than in relation to those holding PTOs)[10] may occur outside disciplinary proceedings. Unfortunately, the diocesan authorities far too frequently overlook the provisions of the Clergy Discipline Measure 2003 Code of Conduct which necessarily draw a distinction between a complaint and a 'formal complaint'. As only the latter triggers procedures under the 2003 Measure, diocesan authorities should ascertain carefully (and pastorally) whether the person making a complaint wishes to trigger those

---

open hearing of criminal prosecutions has led to a number of cases in which other victims of the accused came forward to the police.

9   Canon C 18, paragraph 1.
10   See the Clergy Discipline Measure 2003, section 8(2).

formal procedures. This is of particular importance as 'the bishop should not do anything that could prejudice, or appear to prejudice, the fair handling of a formal complaint under the Measure that could be made subsequently'.[11]

For example, a bishop's pastoral decision that the cleric's behaviour is not such as to prejudice his or her remaining in a particular parish may undermine any subsequent arguments in disciplinary proceedings that the matters complained of are 'potentially sufficiently serious for referral to a bishop's disciplinary tribunal'.[12] Indeed, the provision that procedures under the 2003 Measure should only be about such 'potentially sufficiently serious' conduct raises the question: what conduct, if any, within the safeguarding context is not 'potentially sufficiently serious'? A hand on the thigh? A hand resting on the knee? A kiss on the lips? A kiss on the top of the head? The final arbiter in such a decision is the President of Tribunals and there is no appeal from his or her decision.[13] Bearing in mind the uniqueness of the damage caused to an individual by any sexual abuse, it may be doubted whether this situation remains satisfactory.

Yet a further problem arises if the person who has been abused wishes to draw the fact of the abuse to the attention of the church authorities but without having to become involved in disciplinary procedures. In such a situation the Church is left in a very difficult situation. If the complaint is, or may be, true, other persons may be left in danger of similar acts of abuse by the cleric concerned. For this reason the Code of Practice[14] states that the bishop 'should consider asking an appropriate person, such as the archdeacon, to look into it'. Setting aside the obvious difficulty that few, if any, archdeacons have sufficient experience or are qualified to make such an investigation, any investigation is bound to be hampered by the reluctance of the abused person to be involved.

A similar situation of danger arises if the abused person does not want the police or social services informed. The archbishops of Canterbury and York have expressed their opinion that all clergy should report allegations of sexual misconduct to the police. In addition, *Protecting All God's Children* states: 'If someone believes that a child may be suffering, or is at

---

[11] Clergy Discipline Measure 2003 Code of Practice (issued January 2006, revised and reissued with effect from 1 February 2014), paragraph 10.

[12] Clergy Discipline Measure 2003 Code of Practice, at paragraph 8.

[13] Clergy Discipline Rules 2005, rule 29(3).

[14] Clergy Discipline Measure 2003 Code of Practice, paragraph 10.

risk of suffering, significant harm, that person should always refer the concerns to local authority children's social care services.'[15]

Clearly, similar referrals should be made in respect of vulnerable adults. Again, as *Protecting All God's Children* spells out:[16]

> Where a child or adult is judged to be at risk of significant harm and in need of protection, it will normally be necessary to share all relevant information with the statutory agencies . . . You should, where possible, respect the wishes of children, young persons or families who do not consent to share confidential information. You may still share information, if in your judgment on the facts of the case, there is sufficient need in the public interest to override that lack of consent.

This in turn leads on to the ministry of absolution.[17] *Protecting All God's Children* states:[18]

> Canon Law constrains a priest from disclosing details of any crime or offence which is revealed in the course of formal confession; however, there is some doubt as to whether this absolute privilege is consistent with the civil law. Where a penitent's behaviour is at issue, the priest should not only urge the person to report it to the police or local authority's social care, if that is appropriate, but may judge it necessary to withhold absolution.

This advice, however, is inadequate as it does not deal with the situation where the penitent refuses (for whatever reason) to report the matter. Should the priest then report the matter in spite of the seal of the confession? If that seal exists in law it raises the question: what is a confession (such as to attract the protection of that seal)? The Archbishops' Council have commissioned 'further theological and legal work to enable it to review, in consultation with the House of Bishops, the purpose and effect of the unrepealed proviso to the Canon [113] of 1603'.[19] However, it seems

---

[15] At paragraph 6.10. See, too, The Convocations of Canterbury and York (2015), *Guidelines for the Professional Conduct of the Clergy*, rev. edn (London: Church House Publishing), Appendix 3: 'The Church of England . . . is committed to acting promptly whenever a concern is raised about a child or young person or about the behaviour of an adult, and will work with the appropriate statutory bodies when an investigation into child abuse is necessary.'

[16] At paragraph 6.11.

[17] See the Revised Canons Ecclesiastical, Canon B 29. It may be doubted whether the jurisdictional limitations placed on this ministry by Canon B 29, paragraph 4, are either observed or enforceable.

[18] At paragraph 6.19. See, too, *Guidelines for the Professional Conduct of the Clergy* (2015) at paragraph 3.6.

[19] See GS Misc 1085 and *Guidelines for the Professional Conduct of the Clergy* (2015), Appendix 1. Although the question of the seal of the confession does not rely solely on this provision

unlikely that, whatever is decided, it will satisfy the whole spectrum of church opinion.

Some priests argue that there is such a confession once the penitent adopts a formal process of confessing his or her sins and whether or not absolution is finally given. It may, for example, be thought that a joke confession should not be regarded as a 'confession' at all. The same may be said of sham confessions, for example, made by a 'penitent' who only approaches confession in an attempt to gag the priest to whom 'confession' is being made. Yet such suggestions raise the question of intention and, if the person making the confession is not prepared to report his or her conduct and so qualify for absolution, it may be argued that he or she had insufficient intention to make what amounts to a formal confession in the first place. At the end of the day – and whether or not there is a legal obligation on priests to honour the seal of the confessional – the priest's own conscience must ultimately dictate his or her course of action where the question of continued abuse is an issue.

Finally, there is necessarily a tension in church life caused by the fact that its doors must be left open even to the most hardened abuser. It seems right that a convicted abuser should be barred from contact with children and therefore his or her attendance at church monitored accordingly. Nonetheless, the question arises: how is this to be enforced? At present convicted abusers are encouraged to enter into contracts with individual churches as to their attendance at divine worship, but not all abusers will announce themselves as such to the church authorities. Even if they do, to what extent should members of the congregation be informed of their past wrongdoings? Equally, how can the abuser's attendance at other churches (whether on holiday or in a town or metropolis) be monitored? At the end of the day it will only be by the strict enforcement of everyday safeguarding principles that the innocent will be protected.

All this leads back to the question of forgiveness. The Church has always taught that it is able to forgive sins (however heinous) but that forgiveness is neither dependent upon nor permitted to sideline the forgiveness, or otherwise, of the person abused. Even if a cleric is genuinely ashamed of his or her behaviour and intends thereafter to live a sin-free life, that does not mean that he or she should therefore be allowed to exercise a clerical office, either publicly or in private. Forgiveness does not wipe away the consequences of past practices, and part of contrition should be an

---

(which in turn must reflect the pre-Reformation canon law on the subject), it is the usual starting point for such discussions.

acknowledgement of the need to live with those consequences. The Church needs to enter into an open debate on this question rather than leave it to individual decisions. When doing so, it must remember the continuing hurt of those who have been abused and the additional trauma added to them if those responsible for their abuse are permitted to return to active clerical life in however an attenuated form.

37

Ministerial stresses and strains

AMANDA BLOOR

When research released by the UK Office of National Statistics in 2014 showed that clergy topped the list of people satisfied by their jobs (publicans proved to be the least happy of those engaged in 274 different occupations), there was a tone of surprise in media reports of the story.[1] Could ordained ministers, living on a low income, in tied accommodation, meeting the endless demands of parishioners in an age where faith itself is in question, really be so content with their lot? For the majority of clergy themselves, the findings of the well-being survey were less startling. Having committed themselves to a lifetime of service to God and their parishioners, and having undergone a lengthy period of 'discernment' and testing of their vocation before being allowed to enter the profession, it might be expected that they were content to be engaged in the work for which they believed themselves to be called. An ordinand of middle years, having given up a significant secular career in order to enter the priesthood said this when being interviewed about his experiences: 'I want to do this until the day I die . . . I haven't made this change in my life not to.'

The fact that significant numbers of elderly priests work beyond retirement age, either, for those having the freehold of their parish, in full-time ministry, or, for others, in voluntary part-time roles with 'Permission to Officiate'[2] from their bishop, suggests that they consider their ministry important enough to continue beyond the point at which secular contemporaries have completed their careers. Although the *character* of priesthood is lifelong,[3] it is possible for the professional exercise of that priestly ministry to be laid down at any point: the Church of England states that

---

[1] See for example *The Guardian*, 21 March 2014, at <http://www.theguardian.com/money/2014/mar/21/vicars-greatest-job-satisfaction-publicans-least-happy>.

[2] A legal document allowing the public exercise of ministry.

[3] The theology of Christ's priestly ministry, upon which is based the understanding of the Church, is stated in Hebrews 7.17: 'You are a priest for ever, according to the order of Melchizedek' (NRSV).

ordained ministers are called, without any limit of time, as long as they live, to proclaim the glory of God in every part of their lives, not just in the exercise of celebrating public services . . . [but] the precise expression of that vocation in authorized public ministry is likely to vary during a cleric's ministry.[4]

Those who have chosen to continue to offer a public ministry are therefore making a clear statement not only about the value they place on that ministry, but also about the satisfaction they derive from it.

For some clergy, however, the picture is different because the things that make their colleagues happy are missing in their own ministries. Instead of feeling that they are doing a good and valued job, that they have adequate spiritual and practical resources to cope with problems that arise, and that God is present in the task, they feel let down, overwhelmed and uncared for. Ministries entered into with faith and determination become a source of difficulty and distress; a situation that is compounded by feelings of guilt and inadequacy. What they believe about God, the Church and their vocation affects the way in which they interpret and manage the issues, stresses and strains that inevitably arise throughout ministry. Unrealistic or unhelpful models of priesthood threaten to fatally undermine vocations that have barely begun to be lived out. One person said this:

> There's great confusion about what I should be doing for the Church, which is not an easy state of affairs . . . clear expectations [from the diocese] would be helpful . . . if there are ordinands who are not very clear about what ordination is for, what the essentials of the gospel are, if they're not sure about what they're meant to be doing, they will be sailing adrift.

The very nature of ordained ministry is itself a contested concept. Although the commonly stated belief that Britain is a secular society does not stand up in the face of the increasing tendency of people to describe themselves as 'spiritual' rather than 'religious',[5] or census data showing that while Christianity has declined in the UK, other religions, especially Islam, have increased their numbers,[6] it is becoming a country in which Christianity is likely to no longer be the majority religion. Grace Davie refers to the

---

[4] Archbishops' Council, 'The Deployment of Clergy with Licences and Permission to Officiate' (June 2014) at <https://www.ons.gov.uk/peoplepopulationandcommunity/crimeandjustice/datasets/thenatureofviolentcrimeappendixtables>.

[5] See, for example, Linda Woodhead's analysis in Linda Woodhead and Rebecca Catto (eds), *Religion and Change in Modern Britain*, Abingdon, Routledge, 2012.

[6] 2011 Census data, Office for National Statistics, <http://www.ons.gov.uk/ons/rel/census/2011-census/key-statistics-for-local-authorities-in-england-and-wales/rpt-religion.html#tab-Changing-picture-of-religious-affiliation-over-last-decade>.

concept of 'vicarious religion' and notes that non-churchgoers tend to be most critical of the Church and its leaders when they fail to perform their representative roles or tasks in an acceptable fashion.[7] What priests are for, as well as what they do, appears unclear to the Church as well as to its people (it's significant that the criteria for selecting candidates for ordained ministry in the Church of England[8] require them to 'reflect on the way patterns of ministry are changing'[9] without any detail about what this might imply), and rapidly changing models of priesthood[10] can bewilder experienced clergy and newcomers alike. There is tension between the increasing professionalization of ordained ministry in the Church of England, where in recent years employment legislation, safeguarding issues, review systems and codes of conduct have been introduced both to protect and oversee the work of clergy authorized by the Church to exercise their vocation, and the understanding that God's calling is uniquely heard by each individual and lived out in culturally specific contexts.

Becoming an ordained minister, as with any other professional role, can be difficult and demanding. The reduction in numbers of stipendiary priests, together with increasingly amalgamated benefices, suggests that Church of England priests of the future may be asked to fulfil a pseudo-episcopal role, overseeing a geographical area rather than a parish and enabling lay volunteers to take on many of the roles which have, in the past, been traditional duties of the clergy. Newly ordained priests can recognize that much of the time they are, in one man's words, 'trying to project competency', while more experienced ministers might express the exhaustion that comes with doing a never-ending job with few boundaries, but, as long as they feel useful, know that they are respected by at least some of those they serve, know that God is alongside them, and trust that they are, at the present moment, where they are called to be, they are able to cope with most things. A group of experienced clergy, tasked with managerial roles as well as their parish duties, described being tired and overworked, but accepted this as part of the job. Some of them, approaching retirement, talked about the sense of relief that comes with the thought

---

[7] Grace Davie, *Religion in Britain: A Persistent Paradox*, Chichester, Wiley-Blackwell, 2015, p. 6.

[8] Although the observations in this chapter are based upon study of priests in the Church of England, the conclusions drawn are applicable to ministers of other Christian traditions too.

[9] Ministry Division, *Criteria for Selection for the Ordained Ministry in the Church of England*, London, Ministry Division of the Archbishop's Council, 2011, p. 2.

[10] Ian Bunting recognized seven different models extant at the end of the twentieth century: Ian Bunting, *Models of Ministry: Managing the Church Today*, Grove Pastoral Series 54, Cambridge, Grove Books, 1996.

of 'not being available every hour of every day and not having to worry all the time', but they knew that they had, on the whole, enjoyed their ministries and would miss parochial life. It seems that it is not what clergy are asked to do that causes anxiety and unhappiness, but the way in which they interpret who they are and the things that happen to them.

There are increasing numbers of clergy couples working in the Church of England, which can bring particular issues and frustrations. Some women have recognized a calling to ordination after years as a clergy spouse, and many of those (although not all) find themselves working effectively as their husband's curate, usually as self-supporting – that is, unpaid – ministers. Even if they have chosen this route, it still involves adjustments to the marriage relationship, which can cause tension. One woman, who had maintained a part-time curacy alongside her secular career ('I didn't feel called to give up my work and practically we couldn't, as I'm paying the mortgage') discovered that her wider skills were helpful to her diocese. However, after retirement, she found that more was asked, until at a time when she had expected to 'slow down a bit' she was effectively being asked to work full-time for the Church in a demanding specialist role but still without any pay or, more importantly, with little recognition from senior clergy that she was doing a useful job. Faith asks *all* Christians, not only priests, to be prepared to live in a sacrificial manner, but if the Church bases its planning on the assumption that the ministerial life must *always* be sacrificial, then the self-giving that is the choice of the individual to offer when appropriate has instead been demanded, and the sense of freely offered gift has been destroyed. It is easy, in such cases, for resentment to grow.

Younger clergy couples often meet during training, which then gives them and their employing dioceses problems when finding suitable posts, especially if both wish to work in parish ministry; joint stipendiary posts are rare, vacancies in neighbouring parishes are unlikely to occur at the same time, and there are financial losses if sharing one vicarage when stipends are calculated on the basis of including a housing element. Parishes and dioceses alike can assume that the male partner's career will come first, particularly if the couple decide to have children, and although the flexible nature of the clergy working day can be beneficial to family life, being called out to urgent pastoral cases or evening meetings can cause childcare difficulties. One female priest described how it was 'an enormous shock' to move from her curacy to a new parish where she was regarded only as the 'vicar's wife'. Giving precedence to her husband's career while she brought up their small children, she offered her services part-time without a stipend, but discovered that she was in a place which was not supportive of women's ministry:

> I'm not on any clergy mailing lists, I'm not allowed to be in Chapter meetings, I've celebrated Holy Communion only once since my curacy . . . I can't even talk about it because no one's talking to me! It's been quite desperate and very lonely.

It's not only women who find combining ministry and parenthood to be problematic. Young male clergy often describe how they want to be involved in their children's upbringing, and are critical of very long working days and frequently disturbed days off. Clergy of both sexes view marriage and parenthood to be vocations in their own right, but it can be difficult for female clergy, aware that parts of the Church still have reservations about women's ordained ministry, to express concerns about assumptions that parochial clergy are continually 'on call', that they are increasingly seen as 'service providers' rather than spiritual leaders, or that they are – in the words of one deeply unhappy incumbent – 'never going to meet all of the expectations of the parish'. It is their male counterparts, confident that they are fully accepted by the Church as priests, who are able to raise these issues and who have the opportunity to shape future practice. Helen Thorne pointed out at the beginning of the millennium that the 'problem' that women priests, particularly those married to other priests, posed to the Church in terms of childcare and working arrangements would not decrease unless changes were made at an organizational level.[11] It seems that as yet, such changes have not been implemented.

Other self-supporting clergy can find the frequent assumptions of the Church that they will spend their career as assistants to paid clergy both insulting and frustrating. A priest who had taken early retirement from a highly remunerated secular career offered his services without expecting a stipend ('I have a pension; I don't need to be paid by the Church') in order to 'give something back' but then found after completing his curacy that he was not considered eligible for incumbent posts. Others reported that the skills and techniques honed in secular working life did not appear to be valued despite their relevance to ministerial tasks: 'It's as if I'm an 18-year-old fresh from school . . . I've effectively been deskilled.' Being limited in scope and regarded as subsidiary to their stipendiary colleagues can cause enormous frustration. Clergy who have been ordained later in life can find

---

[11] Helen Thorne, *Journey to Priesthood: An In-depth Study of the First Women Priests in the Church of England*, CCSRG Monograph Series 5, Bristol, University of Bristol, 2000, p. 74.

that ministry – including oversight from senior clergy – does not always measure up to professional practice. A curate who had previously held a responsible role in a professional organization described the Church of England and its clergy as 'terribly amateurish'. Her largest concern was the 'lack of clarity about the role of the ordained person', which caused difficulties for clergy and parishioners alike. 'They haven't got a clue about the Church, not a clue,' she said. 'They have no idea what I do.' It can, of course, be argued that there is value in *not* following secular models of leadership and that Jesus himself did not operate according to professional guidelines, but the anxiety caused by such reservations can threaten the establishment of good working routines and relationships. Even those enjoying their ministry can find their role to be isolating and lonely: a priest who had previously worked in a team situation with close supervision and feedback now mused that 'when you're watched and not affirmed or encouraged, that can feel quite hard . . . it would be quite nice if there was more affirmation or constructive criticism as well'.

Clergy with significant experience in other fields, including voluntary work and motherhood as well as professional careers, believe that God's calling of them is, at least in part, a calling to use in the service of the Church the skills that they already possess. Sociology has confirmed the importance of being able to utilize insight, reflexivity and experience in order to flourish within communities; Patricia Collins, for example, has written about 'outsiders within'[12] and their need to 'learn to trust their own personal and cultural biographies as significant sources of knowledge'.[13] If this ability is inhibited either by diffidence or by a lack of trust within the parish or diocese, then relationships and confidence can suffer. Gender issues and styles of church practice are less important than beliefs that transformation is possible (Sarah Coakley has written about the importance of 'patient practices of vulnerability'),[14] that God is present, and that learning and development will take place. Clergy need to feel well-supported and well-prepared for what will be asked of them, and confident enough to utilize their particular skills and gifts without feeling

---

[12] Curates, who now belong to a community of ordained ministers but who do not fully 'belong' because of their status as recently commissioned trainees, form excellent examples of the 'outsider within'.

[13] Patricia Hill Collins, 'Learning from the Outsider Within: The Sociological Significance of Black Feminist Thought', in Mary Margaret Fonow and Judith A. Cook (eds), *Beyond Methodology: Feminist Scholarship as Lived Research*, Bloomington, Indiana University Press, 1991, p. 53.

[14] Sarah Coakley, 'Fresh Paths in Systematic Theology', in Rupert Shortt (ed.), *God's Advocates: Christian Thinkers in Conversation*, London, Darton, Longman & Todd, 2005, p. 77.

the need to conform to the pattern of another's ministry. The breakdown of relationships with other clergy, particularly those who are supposed to have a supervisory or mentoring role, or with members of the parish, can be extraordinarily painful. A male priest, shocked by the speed with which things had deteriorated between him and his training incumbent, said, 'I don't think I'd expected to be pushed into a place of such pain and darkness by a fellow priest.'

Frustrations can usually be dealt with, although they can inhibit the satisfaction that should come from being engaged in a long prepared-for ministry. In cases where the inevitable stresses and strains of ministerial life do begin to fatally undermine priestly vocations, the problem is largely due to two things: an insurmountable gulf between expectations and experience, so that clergy no longer know who they are or what they should do, or the belief that they have been abandoned or are being 'tested' by God because of failings in their own faith or religious practice. An Evangelical ordinand, for example, underwent a period of ill health that convinced him he was being 'disciplined' by God, and it was only after being introduced to spiritual writings that allowed him to acknowledge that God felt distant that he was able to recover a sense of equilibrium. A member of the clergy with a more sacramental theology felt that God's calling to ministry had to be answered, despite her 'unhappiness' at the thought. Expecting that ontological change would enable her to operate adequately as a priest, she found that instead she was 'doing all the things that I don't enjoy and none of the things that I do enjoy'. Another priest, trained as a 'pioneer minister' and appointed as incumbent to a struggling parish ostensibly because of his entrepreneurial skills, found that his parochial church council (PCC) blocked every attempt to introduce change. He began to mistrust his own abilities and questioned if he was 'good enough' to continue to serve God. Each of these ministers felt increasingly isolated and their sense of 'failure' made it difficult for them to seek help or advice from others. Priesthood itself became a concept that no longer made sense.

Although I resist essentialist assumptions about gender and practice, the tendency of some people to assume that, for example, women will instinctively be pastorally minded and men will be confident in leadership can create expectations that clergy find difficult to fulfil. One curate described her training incumbent as musing aloud that 'a female-dominated church is really bad for men' while she inwardly fumed that 'all the rubbish jobs are done by women and all the management is done by men'. A task-focused woman was completely bewildered by the way in which her parishioners made 'twittery, silly phone calls' about trivial matters such as the choice of biscuits at a meeting: 'I think it's a waste of time . . . they're looking for affirmation and it's a distraction from what we're meant to be doing.' There were parish expectations that because she could cook, she would help to cater for most functions, and she believed that offers to help look after her garden or do other practical tasks in the vicarage were usually pretexts for accessing the house and 'pushing boundaries'. Another priest, in contrast, recognized when frustrations were threatening to spill over and affect her work ('the stress of this place affected my performance as a human being, let alone as a vicar') and developed a pattern of work and leisure that sustained her energies and enthusiasm: 'I keep a chunk of the day from twelve o'clock to about three for me and the dogs . . . partly because the dogs need it and partly because it's sanity space.'

Issues of sex and gender are hugely problematic for the Church. Young women seeking ordination have grown up within a society which assumes that women and men will be treated equally, and are usually not exposed during training to any academic assessment of gender politics or feminist theology. They then have no formal resources to draw upon when they are faced with exclusion or belittling within church settings where it is still perfectly acceptable to refuse ministry offered by a woman. Young ordinands of both sexes can express surprise at the standard of sexual ethics expected of them by the Church; the insistence that sex belongs only within marriage, as well as the demands of parochial ministry, can lead women in particular to believe that if they are single when they enter training or ministry, then they are likely to remain so ('no one will want to marry me'). Interestingly, this seems to be less of an issue for male candidates, perhaps due to the dominant model of 'the vicar's wife' rather than that of a male clergy spouse. They talk about loneliness and the hope to find a suitable partner, but tend not to assume that their vocation or celibacy will be a barrier to future relationships.

The inability of the Church to agree on the question of same-sex attraction can be an embarrassment to younger candidates, whose secular contemporaries generally see this as 'a non-issue', while the volume of discussion can lead people coming forward to offer themselves for ministry to believe, probably erroneously, that change will come quickly. To live out a public ministry while suppressing or concealing one's own sexuality comes at enormous cost.[15] Similarly, some very public scandals have made clergy

---

[15] Joanna Collicutt refers to the 'personal incoherence' that results from trying to do things that do not fit with one's own internal standards and the resultant 'psychological distress'. Joanna Collicutt, *The Psychology of Christian Character Formation*, London, SCM Press, 2015, p. 21.

anxious of assumptions about links with abuse; an elderly widowed priest described how after a lifetime of wearing a cassock he was now afraid to go out of his house dressed in clerical clothing. Schools, which can be locations of joyful ministry, are sometimes suspicious of priests – one curate complained that 'we can't get into the senior school because we represent the institution' – leaving clergy frustrated by the denial of an opportunity to share understanding and build links within the community. It is easy for ministers to believe that they are being attacked as individuals rather than as symbolic representatives of what is happening within the Church.

Some clergy, although thankfully relatively few, suffer actual rather than perceived aggression, abuse or intimidation. An inner-city cleric described the damaged nature of some people who arrived on his doorstep and in church: 'I've called 999 more times in the last year than I have in the rest of my life altogether.' If ministers live in a house in their parish, particularly if this is a house that has long been associated with clergy, then it is impossible to close the door on the outside world or to remain anonymous when at home. Married priests can find the behaviour of their spouse and children held up to scrutiny, while single clergy can find living alone in a large house a source of anxiety. Ordained women express particular concerns about becoming a public figure in their parish; one described an incident where a visitor to her vicarage made 'a very inappropriate [sexual] suggestion' which made her aware that 'there could be a little more training [in college] about safety'.[16] She was well supported by a colleague and so found ways of formulating strategies to avoid such a situation in the future, but was left shaken and upset. Another woman talked about the inappropriate and intrusive interest of some male parishioners, including one clearly ill person – 'my stalker' – who made threats against her that were investigated by the police. 'The insecurities come out, the disappointments in life,' she said. Although government statistics show that young men are the most vulnerable group in society to suffer incidents of random or directed violence,[17] male ordinands and clergy are less likely to think about the possibility of physical attack. The fact remains, though,

---

[16] She emphasized that her training incumbent had been a great source of support after the incident, but that although physical safety had been briefly covered during training, the psychological consequences of coming to terms with a traumatic incident – 'How do you then go into your next visit?' – had not.

[17] 'Table 1: Prevalence of Violence, by Type of Violence and Personal Characteristics, Year Ending March 2017 CSEW', *The Nature of Violent Crime: Appendix Tables*, Office for National Statistics, at <https://www.ons.gov.uk/peoplepopulationandcommunity/crimeandjustice/datasets/thenatureofviolentcrimeappendixtables> (accessed 18 October 2018).

that for some ministers, becoming a public figure is not only psychologically challenging but also potentially dangerous.

Unrealistic expectations about what ministry will involve can lead to
unhappiness and bewilderment. Sometimes this arises from the determination to follow what is believed to be God's calling despite fundamental
differences between the skills and hopes of individuals and the tasks and
roles that the Church requires of them. One curate, for example, had been
ordained despite never accepting that she was called to parish ministry.
She had a vision of a largely contemplative vocation, working alongside
congregations and individuals to develop spirituality, reflection and 'the
interface between the Church and culture'. The fact that the Church would
only ordain her if she served a title post in a parish was a source of deep
frustration and bewilderment,[18] and because she was forced to serve in a
setting which did not match with her internal vision of how her gifts could
be used on God's behalf, what Mary McClintock Fulkerson has termed 'the
grace of the place'[19] could not be recognized. It was hardly surprising that
despite the efforts of her training incumbent to meet her needs for space
and solitude, she felt increasingly stressed and guilty about the mismatch
between her role and her identity. 'I don't feel that I can walk away at any
time,' she said, 'because it's a vocation; it's not a job.' She came close to
mental collapse and knew that without a continuing awareness of God's
presence, she would be contemplating suicide: 'If there wasn't some hope
at the end of it, there would be no reason to keep going.' It was a desperate
situation, and she was desperately miserable.

If clergy feel inadequate to undertake the range of tasks asked of them at
a time when they are expected to be teachers and interpreters of faith and
culture as well as having the appropriate pastoral and practical skills, it is all
too easy to try to hide weaknesses by relying upon others. This can lead to
inappropriate relationships or unpredictable approaches to management
and leadership. An extreme example of such behaviour caused a female
priest, who felt that she did not have the intellectual abilities that were
expected of her by the Church, to begin asking the advice of her churchwarden in all matters until he was effectively running the parish. After this
alienated her PCC and her ministry colleagues, she panicked and refused
to speak to the warden, insisting 'I need to run things my way.' Increasingly

---

[18] Although there would now be the opportunity for this young woman to be ordained as a
'pioneer minister' and to work in more creative situations, that option did not exist when she
began ordination training.

[19] Mary McClintock Fulkerson, *Places of Redemption: Theology for a Worldly Church*, Oxford,
Oxford University Press, 2007, p. 246.

erratic behaviour, a lack of trust from parishioners and, eventually, a very public nervous breakdown led to her complete withdrawal from ministry. She admitted that she had expected that the process of ordination would automatically give her a privileged and respected role within the community, and that her control over what happened in the parish would be absolute. Research in fact suggests that the opposite is true: that congregations are happiest and most content when they have a role in decision-making, and that in order for ministers to have a secure position, they paradoxically need to hand over some control to their parishioners.[20]

It takes time to 'learn' a parish or context for ministry. Martyn Percy's investigation of those 'implicit' factors that both affect and shape church life and practice suggests that what is not made explicit or visible can be deeply significant; expectations, context, history and performance are all factors that help to sustain faith and bring about meaning.[21] This is something well known to ethnographers, who understand that only embedded familiarity with place, situation and community will help to explain what might appear straightforward but can easily be misunderstood. But clergy, most of whom want to do the best job possible, do not always give themselves that time. They can feel isolated too; as one woman commented, chatting during a parish visit is not the same as meeting with a friend. Having adequate support systems in place, and having strategies to respond to questions of authority, power, leadership, relationships, purpose or identity, are crucial if clergy are to cope with the stresses and strains of ordained ministry. There are formal structures that are supposed to provide just this sort of forum, particularly local gatherings of clergy in deanery chapters, but these can be dismissed by ministers as irrelevant, unhelpful or divisive. One curate described her deanery chapter as 'the most depressing thing ever'. Ministers who are able to ask for and receive appropriate support and advice from people they trust (family and friends, local networks, 'cell groups' of like-minded clergy), and who discover ways of sustaining a sense of identity and purpose, are those who continue to find their vocations a source of joy and satisfaction. Those who are not able to devise such strategies, believing that they have 'got to endure', or who view God as a demanding (if essentially benevolent) taskmaster, can struggle to survive.

---

[20] Malcolm Torry (ed.), *The Parish: People, Place and Ministry: A Theological and Practical Exploration*, Norwich, Canterbury Press, 2004, p. 68.

[21] Martyn Percy, *Shaping the Church: The Promise of Implicit Theology*, Aldershot, Ashgate, 2010, p. 4.

What clergy expect to be doing with their time, and how they see themselves as ordained ministers in a particular community, are important markers of satisfaction or frustration. If there is a disconnect between their expectations and their experience, they are likely to become demoralized or stressed, believing in extreme cases either that their vocation was imagined or misheard, or that God is no longer with them. It can lead them to make inappropriate relationships within their sphere of ministry in order to bolster their flagging confidence or to make allies where all they see is opposition to their plans, to become dictatorial or passive in leadership, and to be angry with the colleagues or senior clergy who they feel have let them down. The sadness is that it takes so little to turn around such a situation; a priest who admitted to lack of trust in the institutional Church after not receiving support during a difficult period in ministry said that a simple word of encouragement would have made all the difference.

If clergy can find the right balance between idealism, authenticity and meaning, they can respond well to the inevitable demands and inconsistencies of ministry. A late entrant to ordained ministry, who had been critical of many aspects of the institutional Church, was able to say this:

> Priesthood? It's fantastic. Priesthood is standing on the cusp of liminal theology, standing at the brink of things, between heaven and earth, or anointing someone with oil because you think they're about to die, and that's a huge moment. Or it's standing with someone when they tell you something that's secret and has never been told before, because the office that you hold is one of inviolable trust . . . Priesthood is interpretation, translation, interpreting the gospel, translating the theology, making it physical, viral stuff, and it's also challenge; it's about challenging mediocrity, familiarity . . . and helping people see their own vision of Christ.

What a wonderful affirmation.

38

Conflict, reconciliation and healing

SARAH HILLS

At its most basic, reconciliation is about how we do relationships. It is either reconcile or fight. This morning, for example, did you argue about who was going take the bins out; or make the tea? Or where should we go on holiday? How much of our diocesan budget can we spend on training this year? What is happening in Syria or Burundi or Israel–Palestine or . . .

The twentieth century was spent wondering if we would live or not – the two world wars, the Cold War. In the twenty-first century we now are asking, 'How do we live together?' We face, in the world, and in the Church, many challenges: violent conflicts abound; globalization means we are more connected and yet struggle to understand each other; we have a multiplicity of ways of communicating through social media, twitter, blogging, and so on . . . but we need help to really hear each other's stories – not least in our own context in the Church, thinking of human sexuality, interfaith challenges and our engagement with climate change.

I became interested in forgiveness and reconciliation first through my upbringing in South Africa and then Northern Ireland. I was born in South Africa, and my parents were both involved in anti-apartheid activities. We left when I was a young child. In Northern Ireland, where we moved to, I grew up rather confused. About whether my hair was so curly because I was African; about why, when we went back to visit my grandparents, only white people could go to the beach, or sit on public benches; about why my old nanny lived in a house with no running water. And then, as a medical student, I spent time working in a rural hospital in South Africa. While there, I found myself joining in protest marches with thousands of other South Africans, demonstrating against apartheid – and taking bullets out of people who had been shot while demonstrating: singing freedom songs with the others – 'Viva Mandela!', 'Amandla!' Mandela, then coming towards the end of his 27 years in prison, was the inspiration, the name on everyone's lips. In the years following, Mandela's commitment to reconciliation lived in my mind, in stark contrast to rumours of the vengeful tarring and feathering of two teenage sweethearts who lived near my family home in Northern Ireland. She lived in our village, which was Protestant; he came from a farm in what was known as 'IRA' country. Questions couldn't help but form.

After qualifying in medicine, I worked as a psychiatrist. These questions about the nature of reconciliation, retribution, forgiveness and justice were fuelled by that work, and particularly in a setting where we were treating long-term and often seriously ill people through psychoanalytical psychotherapy. Several patients seemed to start to make significant progress towards healing when they had forgiven the perpetrator in a number of different situations such as maternal neglect or physical assault. Why did forgiveness matter for some, and not others?

During ordination training, I spent some time back in South Africa researching for my MA in Theology and Pastoral Studies, looking at a reconciliation and restitution process. This link continued post ordination and I spent further time there following up this restitution process, while on placement at St George's Cathedral, Cape Town. During these times, I met many people who had been involved in the anti-apartheid struggle, some of whom are still active in reconciliation in South Africa. From discussion with them and observation 'on the ground', it became clear that despite the end of apartheid and the birth of the new 'rainbow nation', huge socio-economic, educational and indeed racial divides still operated. While the Truth and Reconciliation Commission (TRC), chaired by Archbishop Desmond Tutu, has enabled great strides along the road to reconciliation, and has certainly averted what many feared would be a 'bloodbath', many of its recommendations have not been implemented.

Since 2014, I have been the Canon for Reconciliation at Coventry Cathedral. Coventry Cathedral has a particular calling to the ministry of reconciliation. The cathedral was destroyed during the Blitz on the night of 14 November 1940. Provost Howard, looking at the destruction around him after the bombing, took the bold decision to not only remember the past but to look forward when he held two charred pieces of wood from the ruins and said, 'Father, forgive.' Three of the medieval roof nails found in the ruins were bound together into the form of a cross – the cross of nails. The new cathedral was built and the people looked forward with hope to a time of peace and reconciliation.

So how do we look forward from here with that hope with which the new cathedral was built? Well, to look forward we need to truly see what is happening today, in order to make an attempt to understand where we are being called forward on this great journey with God. Part of Coventry

Cathedral's reconciliation ministry is centred on the Community of the Cross of Nails (CCN). The CCN has three major strands:

- healing the wounds of the past;
- living with difference and celebrating diversity;
- building a culture of peace.

Reconciliation is a journey – from the past, through the present, to the future. And this journey of reconciliation involves all of us. Reconciliation journeys start with the same thing – our stories. Your story, my story, all our stories. We are not all the same, and we do not all need to agree on everything all the time. But how can we live with difference well if we do not know something about each other, if we do not share our stories, if we do not try to understand the other? Because not trying to understand the other, to stand in someone else's shoes, has potentially dangerous consequences. Fear of the other, power imbalance, hate can flourish when we are unable to live with difference. And so how do we start to address this? Well, we start with sharing our stories, sharing our selves, our lives, our ministries, our hopes and dreams. And so I am going to share with you a story of reconciliation, a story about how we live together, how we can build relationships and start to build a culture of peace.

This story is about a train journey. Two years ago, I was working in South Africa, and I travelled with 47 survivors of a bomb attack in Worcester, Western Cape. The bombs went off on Christmas Eve in 1996; four people died and 70 were injured. We journeyed to meet one of the perpetrators in Pretoria Prison. Stefaans, 17 at the time he planted the bomb, was a member of a white supremacist group that targeted black people. For years he has been asking to meet the survivors so that he can make an apology.

Setting off from Worcester station felt like the first stage of a pilgrimage – a journey to a place of encounter, and then returning to the ordinariness of life, yet with hope of transformation. Everyone was given a food parcel for the 28-hour journey (made by the women of the local Dutch Reformed churches – a powerful symbol in itself), and the travellers were blessed with interfaith prayers. Pilgrimage involves time apart to prepare for encounter, and as we slid past the barren Karoo landscape baking in the sun, the turmoil of people's emotions was palpable. Anger, fear, grief were contained by the rocking of the train and the growing sense of community as we met in groups to prepare the survivors for the encounter with 'the bomber'. 'Seeing' the person who left your family without the breadwinner; who took away your child; who left you scarred . . . this seemed to be very important. Some wanted to tell him how angry they were; some wanted to be able to forgive; all wanted to share their story of that 'black Christmas'. It felt crucial as we journeyed to help people understand that forgiveness was not expected of them – rather that we were travelling in the hope of a real encounter with 'the other', and a space to be heard at last. Of course, forgiveness may follow such an encounter, but the discovery of a common vulnerability between victim and perpetrator is the first step on a long journey towards healing.

And the 'encounter'? A hall in the prison filled with survivors, prison staff, the press, a choir . . . and then Stefaans enters. Thin, upright, tearful as he listened to their stories, and answered questions. Gasps as he said, 'We wanted to kill as many people as we could . . . we were extremely disappointed that so few people were dead' – but quickly added that he was shaken to the core when he realized that children had died. 'I am really sorry for what I have done. I don't deserve anyone's forgiveness.' Some of the survivors gave him their forgiveness; others said they were still very angry and could not yet forgive him. A queue of survivors embraced him before he was taken out. An encounter which felt truthful, hugely painful, embodied, hopeful, sacred.

Waking up in my cabin on the train the next morning on the journey back, I watched a herd of springbok jumping in the veld. The sense of relief on the train matched their light-footedness . . . 'I slept so well because my heart is now clear' and 'I have got to this old age and for the first time because of this train I feel like somebody', two of the survivors told me.

The journey is not over. But we learned about living with difference, and how lives could be transformed by sharing our stories, our selves. Economic inequalities, poor education, are realities, and Stefaans knows he cannot fix these things. But, for some on that journey – bomb survivors, support staff and Stefaans – a new way of being with 'the other', of living with difference, is forming, and that is a beginning. It was a huge privilege to journey with them. The journey of reconciliation is always risky; it takes courage, it takes faith, but in a world which is so broken, this peace train provides a beacon of hope.

Reconciliation has to start with story, with our humanity, with praxis. John de Gruchy sums up the way this work needs to be done:

> Reconciliation is, indeed, an action, praxis and movement before it becomes a theory or dogma, something celebrated before it is explained . . . reconciliation is properly understood as a process in which we become engaged at the heart of the struggle for justice and peace in the world. That is why any discussion of reconciliation must be historically and contextually centered, a reflection on what is happening on the ground by those engaged in

the process. Only then we can critically engage the rhetoric and practice of reconciliation.[1]

But a ministry of reconciliation, or its praxis, for which we have all been given a mandate ('God . . . reconciled us to himself through Christ, and has given us the ministry of reconciliation', 2 Corinthians 5.18),[2] must be based on theology. So what is the theological undergirding of reconciliation? Drawing principles of reconciliation ministry out of story, we see that reconciliation involves pilgrimage. On a pilgrimage we journey towards a place of encounter, bringing our lives in all their conflict and brokenness. The space of encounter is sacred . . . we meet God. And then we journey out again, changed and transformed, ready to share our new understanding and ability to act in the world.

We do that together, embodied and in a real space. We come from our lives, and then, in the sharing of our selves, our stories, we can walk together. We meet others and share our journey, in all its pain, woundedness and hope.

And we do that in fellowship, learning how to listen, to see, to experience the other. And we recognize our need for each other on this pilgrimage – we are linked in the spirit of *ubuntu*: 'I exist because you exist.' Our stories are linked. We need each other.

In the space of pilgrimage, we learn about the process (often a long process) of reconciliation, the component parts of the journey. These include truth, acknowledgement, remembering, storytelling, lament, repentance, forgiveness, justice, restitution . . .

And this is all undergirded by a spirituality of reconciliation. We surround the reconciliation journey in prayer, in Scripture, in the journey through the cross, and especially in the Eucharist. We share the body of Christ together as the broken, shared, blessed body of Christ in the world, the community of Christian people.

And then we take our selves out again to act as agents of transformation, as reconcilers.

There is a missional challenge for reconciliation work. We may know that reconciliation is a good idea and a necessary skill, but parish clergy and lay ministers may need help realizing the value of it in their own ministry, or may well be afraid of it – a bit like helping people to step across a church threshold for the first time. Reconciliation is also public theology.

---

[1]   John de Gruchy, *Reconciliation: Restoring Justice* (London: SCM Press, 2002), pp. 21–2.
[2]   All biblical quotations in this chapter are taken from the New Revised Standard Version (NRSV).

It is important for the Church to have a voice in reconciliation for the world, one which is both practically and theologically based.

> Reconciliation is not intuitive and it is not easy. As both a process and goal, its power must be cultivated and nurtured ... reconciliation and justice thus struggle to chart the course forward, turning the wounds of the past into the basis for learning to live together within the rule of law and in pursuit of a culture of human rights.[3]

The literature on reconciliation and related concepts, such as forgiveness, truth, justice, repentance, confession and reparations, is large and varied, encompassing fields such as politics, transitional justice, conflict resolution, sociology, anthropology, psychology, medicine, philosophy and, of course, theology. Theologically, the doctrines of reconciliation, dating from St Paul, the early Church Fathers, through the medieval period to the Reformation and beyond, have much to inform the current debates. Old and New Testament biblical scholarship is of course informative when discussing concepts such as covenant, *shalom* and forgiveness. Reconciliation is not an abstract 'word'-based paradigm; it needs to be embodied, in the 'real world', for it to have the power to be transformative. So, to regard the theoretical ethical thinking that needs to be done about this issue of moral life as sufficient to inform human well-being, without involving the praxis of it and the people on the ground engaged in the day-to-day process, is a mistake. Engaging with this practical knowledge, this 'doing', enables a more complete understanding and therefore potential for change which may be lost without this embodiment or grounding of the theory.

> There is a movement, not easily discernible, at the heart of things to reverse the awful centrifugal force of alienation, brokenness, division, hostility and disharmony. God has set in motion a centripetal process, a moving toward the Centre, towards unity, harmony, goodness, peace and justice; one that removes barriers. Jesus says, 'And when I am lifted up from the earth I shall draw everyone to myself', as he hangs from His cross with outflung arms, thrown out to clasp all, everyone and everything, in cosmic embrace, so that all, everyone, everything, belongs. None is an outsider, all are insiders, all belong. There are no aliens; all belong in one family, God's family, and the human family.[4]

Desmond Tutu articulates the hope of reconciliation for all. This is clearly a Christian hope, and places reconciliation firmly in the theological arena.

---

3. Charles Villa-Vicencio and Eric Doxtader, eds, *Pieces of the Puzzle: Keywords on Reconciliation and Transitional Justice* (Cape Town: Institute for Justice and Reconciliation, 2004), p. viii.
4. Desmond Tutu, *No Future without Forgiveness* (New York: Doubleday, 1999), p. 213.

Forgiveness is at the heart of Tutu's theology of reconciliation, and indeed the Christian gospel. However, forgiveness is not a straightforward subject, and views on it and its place within the reconciliation journey differ widely, even from within the Christian perspective.

Where, then, if at all, does forgiveness fit in the reconciliation paradigm? Hannah Arendt writes of Jesus being the 'discoverer' of forgiveness,[5] and, whether or not that is the case,[6] there is no doubting the role forgiveness can play in reconciling relationships, in both the secular and the sacred. And while forgiveness is one of the key concepts to consider, justice, repentance, truth, peace, remembering, not to mention restitution, are just some of the others. What then does reconciliation mean, and what are its component parts?

While I concentrate on the theological concepts, this is a multi-disciplinary field, especially in practice. It is appropriate therefore to place theology alongside fields such as politics, sociology, psychology, transitional justice, conflict resolution, peacekeeping. For example, there is a huge literature surrounding forgiveness from a psychological viewpoint.[7]

Unsurprisingly, then, with regard to reconciliation itself, there is a multitude of definitions. Charles Villa-Vicencio argues that reconciliation cannot be defined in a neat set of rules. It is more than theory. It involves grace. It is an art rather than a science.[8] Piet Meiring contends, however, that reconciliation needs a clear definition, although he notes that this

---

[5] Hannah Arendt, *The Human Condition: A Study of the Central Conditions Facing Modern Man* (Garden City, NY: Doubleday, 1959), pp. 212–13.

[6] Anthony Bash, 'Did Jesus Discover Forgiveness?', *Journal of Religious Ethics* 41, 3 (2013), pp. 382–99 <DOI: 10.1111/jore.12020> (accessed 4 July 2014).

[7] Mary Ann Coate, *Sin, Guilt and Forgiveness: The Hidden Dimensions of a Pastoral Process* (London: SPCK, 1994); S. Lamb and J. G. Murphy, eds, *Before Forgiving: Cautionary Views of Forgiveness in Psychotherapy* (Oxford: Oxford University Press, 2002); Fraser Watts and Liz Gulliford, eds, *Forgiveness in Context: Theology and Psychology in Creative Dialogue* (London: T&T Clark, 2004); Everett Worthington Jr, ed., *Dimensions of Forgiveness: Psychological Research and Theological Perspectives* (Philadelphia, PA: Templeton Foundation Press, 1998); Marilyn McCord Adams, 'Forgiveness: A Christian Model', *Faith and Philosophy* 8, 3 (1991), pp. 277–304; M. Cavell, 'Freedom and Forgiveness', *International Journal of Psychoanalysis* 84 (2003), pp. 515–31; D. Kaminer and others, 'The Truth and Reconciliation Commission in South Africa: Relation to Psychiatric Status and Forgiveness among Survivors of Human Rights Abuses', *British Journal of Psychiatry* 178 (2001), pp. 373–7; Ann Macaskill, 'The Treatment of Forgiveness in Counselling and Therapy', *Counselling Psychology Review* 20 (2005), pp. 26–33; Ann Macaskill, 'Defining Forgiveness: Christian Clergy and General Population Perspectives', *Journal of Personality* 73, 5 (2005), pp. 1237–65.

[8] Charles Villa-Vicencio, 'The Art of Reconciliation', *Publications for Peace Education, Life and Peace Institute* (2002), p. 4.

does not mean that reconciliation can be 'organised'. He writes, 'Microwave oven reconciliation does not last!', meaning that reconciliation is not straightforward, nor should it be taken for granted. He does not, however, provide a definition as such, arguing rather for the necessity of inclusion of truth, justice, confession, forgiveness and firm commitment.[9] Wendy Lambourne, in her research on post-conflict peace-building, provides a list of at least 12 definitions of reconciliation, in order to 'illuminate the many and varied aspects of reconciliation'.[10]

Rather than attempting to provide a single definition of what seems to be a variable phenomenon, over time and place and dependent on the people involved, I argue that reconciliation itself as process must in fact constantly change and adapt to the myriad of influences working on it. This speaks to the 'counterfactual', the surprising, nature of an embodied process, which, at best, should be lived and experienced before theorizing takes place.

Reconciliation, then, as we have begun to see, has a multitude of meanings, component parts and order. It can be seen as primarily between God and humanity; or interpersonal, social, national, international, ecological. Or more than one of those at the same time. It can be seen as process, or goal, or both. For instance, John Paul Lederach uses Psalm 85 as a model for reconciliation, drawing out truth, justice, mercy and peace, as necessary and transformative processes leading towards reconciliation, which is at once journey, encounter and place.[11]

Reconciliation can be described as radical, political, theological and social. It may come at the beginning of a process which includes forgiveness, or at the end of a process which focuses on justice. Or it can be an overarching paradigm which includes repentance, confession, truth-telling and reparations. It can be called unjust, cheap, disempowering or just too hard. Social cohesion may be thought to be good enough. It sometimes includes apology. It may lead to healing or transformation. Reconciliation can be any of these, it seems.[12]

---

[9] Piet Meiring, 'Forward, with Joy and Confidence: Some Thoughts on the Prerequisites for Reconciliation in South Africa', *Journal of Theology for Southern Africa* 134 (July 2009), pp. 102–30.

[10] Wendy R. Lambourne, 'Justice and Reconciliation: Post-Conflict Peacebuilding in Cambodia and Rwanda' (unpublished PhD thesis, University of Sydney, 2002), pp. 201–3.

[11] John Paul Lederach, *The Journey toward Reconciliation* (Scottdale, PA: Herald Press, 1999), p. 13.

[12] Roundtable discussion at the University of the Western Cape, Cape Town, 2012, resulting in a book edited by Ernst M. Conradie, *Reconciliation: A Guiding Vision for South Africa?* (Stellenbosch: Sun Press, 2013).

However, at the heart of reconciliation are relationships – connections or reconnections: between humanity and God; between me and you; us and them. Robert Schreiter captures what I take as the core theological meaning of reconciliation:

> To enter into a process of reconciliation is better described as entering *mysterion*, a pathway in which God leads us out of suffering and alienation into the experience of the grace of reconciliation. This grace is transforming, and creates the conditions of possibility not only for forgiving our enemies, but also helping them to rediscover their humanity.[13]

Reconciliation, then, is about transforming relationships, about reconnecting. Reconciliation, however, clearly does not just 'happen', even though, soteriologically, grace is foremost in the enabling of these transformative relationships. So what are the other processes or components necessary for these reconnections? Several core components which make up the reconciliation journey include acknowledgement; remembering; truth; lament; understanding of the effect on the other (and self); repentance; transformation; restitution; justice; forgiveness.

Some of these concepts may not be in every reconciliation journey, and will certainly have a different emphasis. They may appear in a different order, and they may overlap. Some will take a considerable time; others may not. Moreover, it is important to realize that reconciliation is not a linear process, but rather one that can be conceptualized as a spiral. But this list does at least give us somewhere to start to consider what might be happening. Of course, these may be very different, for example, in the South African context, in our church disputes, in domestic abuse in the UK, or in the reconciliation of first nation peoples in Australia.

Smyth and Graham argue that the interplay between God's saving purpose and human sin, where forgiveness and reconciliation are placed, has a long biblical heritage, in both Old and New Testaments. They quote examples of fidelity and treachery (Cain and Abel); the co-existence of goodness and betrayal (Hagar, King David); and the world as both the arena of grace (John 3.16) and grace rejected (John 1.11).[14]

---

[13] Robert J. Schreiter, *Reconciliation: Mission and Ministry in a Changing Social Order* (Maryknoll, NY: Orbis Books, 1992), p. 58.

[14] Geraldine Smyth and Stephen Graham, *Forgiveness, Reconciliation and Justice* (Belfast: Centre for Contemporary Christianity in Ireland (CCCI), 2003).

If we truly recognize the world as God's creation, we cannot designate it as beyond the realm of grace. The world of politics and public life falls within God's reconciling purpose.[15]

So what does the process of reconciliation actually look like amidst all this? John de Gruchy warns of speaking too easily of reconciliation, but adds that bearing in mind the potential power imbalances between one and 'the other', and the dangers inherent in speaking on 'their' behalf, we dare not keep silent 'in a world torn apart by hatred, alienation and violence. We dare not remain silent whether as citizens or as Christians.'[16] Liechty and Clegg argue that a true understanding of reconciliation has to be 'built on the interlocking dynamics of forgiveness, repentance, truth and justice, understood in part as religiously-rooted virtues, but also as basic dynamics (even when unnamed or unrecognised) of human interaction, including public life and therefore politics'.

Reconciliation is thus 'both the theological remainder of politics, the leap that comes when realism confronts total conflict . . . and the political remainder of theology, a form of action that endows hope with content.'[17]

John de Gruchy writes that the process of reconciliation is 'a human and social process that requires theological explanation, and a theological concept seeking human and social embodiment'.[18]

Reconciliation then, I would argue, is a process which must be theological and human, social and political.[19] It is a process that entails both understanding and action, or theory and praxis. How do these inform each other? John de Gruchy sees four interrelated ways of looking at the process of reconciliation. The first is theological, and refers to reconciliation between God and humanity, which then allows for 'a shared life and language'.[20] The second is interpersonal reconciliation, or the relationships between individuals. The third is social, such as between communities or local groups. The fourth is political, for example the Southern African case

---

[15] Smyth and Graham, *Forgiveness, Reconciliation and Justice*, p. 3.

[16] De Gruchy, *Reconciliation*, p. 17.

[17] Joseph Liechty and Cecelia Clegg, *Moving Beyond Sectarianism: Religion, Conflict and Reconciliation in Northern Ireland* (Dublin: Columba Press, 2001), p. 17.

[18] De Gruchy, *Reconciliation*, p. 20.

[19] See Duncan Forrester, 'Politics and Reconciliation', in *Reconciliation in Religion and Society*, ed. Michael Hurley SJ (Antrim: Institute of Irish Studies, 1994), pp. 111–22, (p. 121). Jürgen Moltmann argues that those who live in hope 'can no longer put up with reality as it is, but begin to suffer under it, to contradict it'. This leads to creative action to change society for the better. Jürgen Moltmann, *Theology of Hope*, trans. James W. Leitch (London: SCM Press, 1967), p. 21.

[20] De Gruchy, *Reconciliation*, p. 26.

post-apartheid. He writes, 'Reconciliation is, if you like, a journey from the past into the future, a journey from estrangement to communion, or from what was patently unjust in search of a future that is just.'[21] A theology of reconciliation which is about bringing a just future into communion with others lends itself to my view of reconciliation as being necessarily relational, and a process, rather than a static event.

In order to explore this further, I turn to Miroslav Volf's work. Miroslav Volf, a Croatian theologian, addresses this question in his book *Exclusion and Embrace*.[22] Volf writes that in order to address the problems we face in our world of exclusion and difference, of hatred and misuse of power over those who are not like us, there is a need for a cross-centred act of relationship, or what he calls 'the embrace of reconciliation'. This 'drama of embrace' encapsulates four moments: opening the arms, waiting, closing the arms and opening them again.

In this cross-shaped embrace, first, opening the arms signifies a reaching out for relationship with the other, a desire for a sharing of myself with the other. Second, waiting signifies 'non-invasion'. My desire has been made clear; now it is up to you, 'the other', to respond. Third, in closing the arms the goal of the embrace is reached, and it must be reciprocal, but not overpowering or unequal. Fourth, the final act of opening the arms again needs to happen if one's boundary is not to become subsumed into the other. This final opening of the arms also allows for further embrace as we look forward to the future.

When I left South Africa in 2013, I organized a Reconciliation Eucharist, a communion service, to say thank-you to the people I had been working with. One of the women from the black township baked the bread, one of the white wine-farmers brought his wine, and we all came together to bring the divisions, conflicts, hurts to the altar. We reflected on the cross-shaped realities of the need for ongoing reconciliation and how hard it was. But we brought it all together to the altar, where these cross-shaped realities are embodied, seen, embraced.

Reconciliation is hard and it is not fast. It is cross-shaped. And it needs to be embodied through the realities of relationship with God and with each other that we come to share at the altar.

Reconciliation is costly and it is often convoluted. But it is possible.

---

21 De Gruchy, *Reconciliation*, p. 28.
22 Miroslav Volf, *Exclusion and Embrace: A Theological Exploration of Identity, Otherness, and Reconciliation* (Nashville, TN: Abingdon Press, 1996).

39

Spirituality, health and ministry

MARK COBB

Contemporary healthcare is largely a secular matter that retains little of its historic association with religion, and yet a type of spirituality has begun to flourish in this seemingly arid clinical space dissociated from theological tradition or practice. The relationship between spirituality and health has become a growth area in contemporary health studies and one that has all the makings of a field in its own right. Spirituality in this context represents a fourth dimension to the physical, psychological and social aspects of health and contributes to attempts at rebalancing the dominant bio-medical model into something more explicitly holistic and humanistic. Concepts of spirituality have thus developed within the academic paradigms of health, and medicine in particular, that typically take reductive, functional and inclusive forms of spirituality that can be subject to scientific methods and applied broadly to the clinical population. All this has happened so far with very little input from or formal dialogue with the faith communities, and yet it represents a distinctive construct of spirituality much of which has been developed from the ground up and has an impact on practices of care. In this chapter I therefore aim to explore three interrelated themes: first, what the emerging healthcare discourse of spirituality might reflect about the pastoral practice of the Church; second, the extent to which pastoral ministry might be empirically responsible and capable of entering into dialogue with more evidence-based approaches; and third, how ministry might respond to the contemporary challenges of nurturing healthy persons and communities.

Discovering the spiritual dimension of health

Archie Cochrane was by all accounts a bright student who qualified in medicine in 1938. He joined the Royal Army Medical Corps and was subsequently captured as a prisoner of war on Crete and then served as medical officer in POW camps in Greece and Germany. Here he faced the dilemma of how he might treat the ailments of prisoners and he realized that there was a lack of evidence about which interventions might improve the disease rather than causing harm to the patient.[1]

Following the war Cochrane went on to pursue a career in epidemiological research and continued his interest in the treatment of tuberculosis. He came to prominence with a modest publication in 1972 on the effectiveness and efficiency of health services in which he challenged the use of medical opinion that underpinned much accepted practice of the time. For example, the surgical removal of tonsils (tonsillectomy) was a very common procedure in the treatment of various respiratory diseases in school-age children. The Medical Research Council in the 1930s concluded that there was a tendency for tonsillectomies to be performed 'for no particular reason and with no particular result',[2] and the operative rates eventually began to reduce following more rigorous evaluations of the procedure and the introduction of antibiotics. The received wisdom did not withstand critical empirical assessment, and Cochrane was clear therefore that the value of medical opinion

> must be rated low, because there is no quantitative measurement, no attempt to discover what would have happened if the patients had had no treatment, and every possibility of bias affecting the assessment of the result. It could be described as the simplest (and worst) type of observational evidence.[3]

Cochrane's legacy was to promote the testing of health interventions and treatments to determine their benefit in ways that avoided bias and ruled out the possibility of chance. The experimental approach Cochrane advocated was the Randomized Control Trial, which at its simplest is a technique that compares the effect of the trial treatment with an alternative placebo or no treatment across two or more similar groups of patients. In this way decisions could be made about the best treatment while harmful or useless interventions could be avoided, an approach that has become widely known as **evidence-based medicine**.

In honour of Archie Cochrane's impact upon medical practice and healthcare, the Cochrane Collaborative was named after him and builds on his legacy by promoting evidence-informed healthcare through the

---

[1] G. B. Hill (2000), 'Archie Cochrane and His Legacy: An Internal Challenge to Physicians' Autonomy?', *Journal of Clinical Epidemiology* 53: 1189–92.

[2] J. A. Glover (2008), 'The Incidence of Tonsillectomy in School Children', *International Journal of Epidemiology* 37: 9–19.

[3] A. L. Cochrane (1972), *Effectiveness and Efficiency: Random Reflections on Health Services* (s.l.: The Nuffield Provincial Hospitals Trust, 1972), 20–1.

systematic collection and critical review of empirical research. Drawing upon the most reliable studies, and following strict methods, the Cochrane Collaborative produces reviews of evidence on a wide range of interventions with the aim of informing best practice, and one subject has been the effect of intercessory prayer.

> Prayer is amongst the oldest and most widespread interventions used with the intention of alleviating illness and promoting good health. Given the significance of this response to illness for a large proportion of the world's population, there has been considerable interest in recent years in measuring the efficacy of intercessory prayer for the alleviation of ill health in a scientifically rigorous fashion.[4]

The scientific interest in prayer is nothing new; Francis Galton published a review on the efficacy of prayer in 1872 in which he makes statistical comparisons of the outcome of prayer across a range of groups who pray and are prayed for. The more recent studies of intercessory prayer, particularly by medical researchers, points to a new wave of interest in the relationship between religion, spirituality and health,[5] and one that attempts to derive its understanding from the empirical evidence. This is a challenge to research methodologies, including randomized control trials, and raises some complex epistemological and theological issues.[6] Nonetheless major studies have been undertaken and published in high-ranking medical journals. For example, *The Lancet* published the MANTRA II study of 748 patients undergoing a coronary procedure in which they were randomly assigned either to one of a number of off-site prayer groups of different religions, or to no prayer group, and at the same time patients were randomly assigned to a form of complementary therapy or to routine care without therapy. No significant differences were found in the outcomes,[7] and the Cochrane review of prayer studies involving 7,646 patients in total reports that:

> The studies that have been done, reported and included in this review do not show a clear effect of intercessory prayer. However, because this review highlighted no clear effects does not mean that intercessory prayer does not

---

[4] L. Roberts, I. Ahmed, S. Hall and A. Davison (2009), 'Intercessory Prayer for the Alleviation of Ill Health', *Cochrane Database of Systematic Reviews*, 1.

[5] W. Cadge (2012), 'Possibilities and Limits of Medical Science: Debates over Double-Blind Clinical Trials of Intercessory Prayer', *Zygon* 47: 43–64.

[6] R. Gill (2006), *Health Care and Christian Ethics* (Cambridge: Cambridge University Press).

[7] M. W. Krucoff et al. (2005), 'Music, Imagery, Touch, and Prayer as Adjuncts to Interventional Cardiac Care: The Monitoring and Actualisation of Noetic Trainings (MANTRA) II Randomised Study', *The Lancet* 366: 211–17.

work. The limitations in trial design and reporting are enough to hide a real beneficial effect and we found no data to contraindicate the use of prayer for seriously ill people.[8]

Testing prayer like a form of medication (with a prescribed dose, route of administration and frequency) may appear incongruous with the pastoral ministry of the Church and the devotional habits of individuals, but there are relevant questions here about the extent to which ministerial practice can and should be empirically responsible, and whether scientific methods can yield relevant and applicable knowledge for ministry. Similarly, medical practice is not simply a matter of applied science: promoting human flourishing and alleviating suffering is of mutual interest to practitioners of pastoral care and medicine, and medicine is similarly practised within an interpersonal relationship that addresses particular embodied human needs and concerns, and is attentive to the personal narratives of illness and injury. Evidence from relevant research trials is therefore insufficient for medicine in the service of caring relationships and requires medicine to engage 'with an ethical and existential agenda (how should we live? when should we accept death?) and with that goal in mind, carefully distinguishes between whether to investigate, treat, or screen and how to do so'.[9]

The evidence-based practice movement in healthcare is rightly influential and it has brought religion and spirituality into its view as it seeks to understand more about interventions and treatments that benefit patients and to distinguish them from those that do harm or are simply ineffective. In doing so it has applied research questions to the lived experience of the sacred and spiritual in order to frame objects of study whose properties can be quantified and analysed. Cochrane himself was alert to what he called the 'snags' and limitations of the Randomized Control Trial, and he recognized that there are other techniques useful to research that need to be used to answer different questions from those of treatment efficacy, such as those about quality of life. However, the growth in studies about the relationship between religion, spirituality and health gives credence to a particular form of knowledge derived from systematic empirical methods without any recourse to the forms of knowledge embedded in religious traditions, ecclesial life, canonical and classical religious texts, or theological discourses. Consequently, an evidence-based construct of

---

[8] Roberts et al., 'Intercessory Prayer for the Alleviation of Ill Health', 25.

[9] T. Greenhalgh, J. Howick and N. Maskrey (2014), 'Evidence Based Medicine: A Movement in Crisis?', *BMJ: British Medical Journal* 348. doi:10.1136/bmj.g3725.

religion and spirituality now exists within the secular context of health-care and provides a new source of knowledge added to that which has traditionally informed pastoral ministry.

This is typically knowledge about religion and spirituality that places it in a functional role in relation to health and seeks to explain whether religion and spirituality are contributing factors to health outcomes. For example, it is estimated that 11 per cent of the adult population suffer severe pain that can seriously disrupt their lives and have significant con-sequences for their well-being (National Pain Audit, 2012).[10] Pain is a complex multidimensional experience and there is evidence to suggest that for some people the spiritual dimension could play a significant role:

> Religious and spiritual coping strategies are associated with feelings of spir-itual support and connection as well as reduced depression and anxiety and a greater sense of peace and calm. This may be due to a number of factors, including the ability to ascribe meaning to the suffering, increased self-efficacy, spiritual and social support, distraction, relaxation, and positive reappraisal.[11]

This scientific view of religion and spirituality is not incongruent with the understanding and knowledge gained by those exercising a pastoral minis-try to people experiencing pain, but in the case of the former, it has been inferred from the systematic collection of empirical data and subject to particular interpretation and analysis in ways that are considered by the research community to be valid and reliable. Consequently, this is a way of understanding religion and spirituality that has no allegiance to a par-ticular faith tradition but seeks a fidelity to the reported experience and physiology of patients in search of a therapeutic benefit. This intentionally reductive and functional understanding is set within a privileged narrative of research-based knowledge that aims to present a robust picture of real-ity in terms of scientific evidence. In contrast the performative knowledge of pastoral ministry, and its basis of ecclesial beliefs and practices, appears to present a view of reality whose fidelity is to a particular tradition and lacks empirical responsibility. Taken to more extreme levels the differ-ences between these paradigms are seen as contrary and even irreconcil-able,[12] which suggests ministry is on the back foot when operating in the

---

[10] British Pain Society / Dr Foster Intelligence, *National Pain Audit Final Report 2010–12.* Available from: <https://www.britishpainsociety.org/static/uploads/resources/files/members _articles_npa_2012_1.pdf> (accessed 20 November 2015).

[11] P. J. Siddall et al. (2015), 'Spirituality: What Is Its Role in Pain Medicine?', *Pain Medicine*: 54.

[12] M. Midgley (2014), *Are You an Illusion?* (Abingdon: Routledge).

matter-of-fact world of healthcare. More generally ministry and the faith it relates to can be easily derided as groundless and of no relevance to the scientifically informed view of the world, if it were not for the caveat that, 'Science has its high priests, sacred cows, revered scriptures, ideological exclusions, and ritual for suppressing dissent. To this extent, it is ridiculous to see it as the polar opposite of religion.'[13]

Evidence-informed pastoral care

Reality is far more complex and rich than the simple pictures and particular views that certain research knowledge provides us, and there is ample scope to approach questions of reality both theologically and scientifically. However, looking at ministry from the perspective of the evidence-based movement in healthcare prompts us to examine the knowledge we use to construct and interpret the pastoral paradigm, to question the embedded and tacit assumptions that guide understanding and practice, and to be critical of how the goals of pastoral care are realized. This is not alien territory for ministry when it remains contextually sensitive, theologically reflexive and ethically accountable. Pastoral ministry in learning and discerning mode is ministry that is concerned with both theological and empirical fidelity through its openness to dialogue, its attentiveness to both the realities of the world as much as to the realities of faith, and its search for the truth. Pastoral care is practised in the world, and a world whose realities are misunderstood or unexamined limits pastoral care to bland generalities and gestures that impede deep engagement with humanity and transformative encounters with the sacred. At its worst, pastoral care that is disinterested in the world and occupied only with self-validating theological fidelity causes harm: first, to the world in mistakenly identifying problems and their underlying causes; and second, to the ecclesial community in inadequately contextualizing the practice of theology and being inattentive to the wisdom of empirical enquiry and its role in informing theology.

Kent Schaible was two years old when he developed bacterial pneumonia following a cold. His parents, Catherine and Herbert, members of the First-Century Gospel Church in North Philadelphia, had never received medical care and followed the teaching of their church in the power of faith healing and prayer. They did not seek medical advice or care for Kent, and as a

---

[13] T. Eagleton (2009), *Reason, Faith, and Revolution: Reflections on the God Debate* (London: Yale University Press), 133.

consequence the treatable infection resulted in the child's death. Catherine and Herbert were convicted of involuntary manslaughter and sentenced to probation that was conditional upon their surviving seven children receiving annual check-ups and follow-up visits as required, and upon the parents' seeking medical care if a child became ill.[14] Four years later their seven-month-old son, Brandon, developed bacterial pneumonia and dehydration and died in similar circumstances. The parents' reliance on divine healing had again resulted in the death of a child, and this time the court imposed prison sentences and placed their surviving children into foster care.[15] Many states in the USA continue to allow a religious defence for parents who withhold medical care from their children[16] despite the long-standing opposition from the American Academy of Pediatrics.[17] In the UK there is no such defence and the state has powers to act in the best interest of the child in similar situations of faith-based medical neglect.

This is a shocking case of empirical recklessness where a normative practice of praying for healing excluded or problematized other sources of knowledge and practice that had the potential to save lives. Whatever theological insights and interpretation pastoral ministry proceeds from, this cannot displace the ethics of care that requires the intentional engagement of the specific reality encountered with its many facets, layers, structures and interrelationships. Elements of this encounter may include the theological, but matters of belief and faith in pastoral terms are always embodied in actual human beings and grounded in their physical and social lives. Caring well therefore requires an understanding of this context in order to make reasonable sense of it, formulate responsible actions, and recognize the limitations of theological knowledge and practice. Simply abstracting a

---

[14] M. Dale (2010), 'Pennsylvania Couple Convicted after Using Only Prayer, Not Medicine, for Dying Toddler', *Associated Press*. Available at: <http://www.cleveland.com/nation/index. ssf/2010/12/pennsylvania_couple_convicted.html> (accessed 1 November 2015); J. A. Slobodzian (2011), 'Parents Get 10 Years' Probation in Child's Faith-Healing Death', *Philly. com*. Available from: <http://www.philly.com/philly/news/local/20110203_Parents_get_10_ years__probation_in_child_s_faith-healing_death.html> (accessed 1 November 2015).

[15] D. Usborne (2014), 'US "Faith Healers" Sent to Prison for Death of Second Sick Child' *Independent*. Available at: <http://www.independent.co.uk/news/world/americas/us-faith-healers-sent-to-prison-for-death-of-second-sick-child-9142463.html> (accessed 1 November 2015); D. Warner (2014), 'Philadelphia Faith-Healer Couple Sentenced to Prison in Son's Death', *Reuters*. Available at: <http://www.reuters.com/article/us-usa-crime-faith-healing-idUSBREA1I1XJ20140219> (accessed 1 November 2015).

[16] S. F. Peters (2008), *When Prayer Fails: Faith Healing, Children, and the Law* (New York and Oxford: Oxford University Press).

[17] American Academy of Pediatrics Committee on Bioethics, 'Religious Objections to Medical Care', *Pediatrics* 99 (1997): 279–81.

pastoral encounter of depth and complexity into an exclusively theological perspective short-circuits discernment and understanding and can isolate the minister and those being ministered to from the gifts and resources of the wider community. In contrast attentiveness to context, critical engagement with alternative perspectives, and an openness to learning and dialogue enables a ministry of collaboration with those who can bring necessary but different gifts to a pastoral situation.

Diverse fields of empirically based enquiry across the humanities and sciences have the potential to inform and enhance pastoral ministry with their knowledge. One such field concerns interpersonal communication, which is fundamental to the practice of pastoral and other forms of care and has been described as 'a complex situated process in which people who have established a communicative relationship exchange messages in an effort to generate shared meanings and accomplish goals'.[18] In healthcare, communication is recognized as pivotal to patient care to support both the therapeutic relationship and the wider processes and systems of care. Medical students, for example, are educated and assessed in communication skills, informed by theoretical and research evidence, to ensure a necessary level of competence.[19] While the context-specific purposes of health-based communication, such as taking a patient history or gaining consent for an operation, may not have direct parallels in pastoral ministry, there are principles and skills that are transferable across these contexts such as relationship building, listening and the exchange of information. Another example is the field of mental health where the prevalence of mental health problems in the population means that ministers will encounter many people living with psychological problems and mental illness. Pastoral care is not psychiatry or psychology, but developing a theologically informed pastoral approach to supporting people with, say, hallucinatory experiences or depression is likely to be more responsive and less difficult when it is informed by the understandings and practices of those working in the mental health field.

Healthcare researchers have also stepped into the field of religious studies and observed what people do, say, practise and experience in relation to spirituality and religion in situations where people face the glory and tragedies of the human condition. This is the 'lived' religion and spirituality

---

18 B. R. Burleson (2009), 'The Nature of Interpersonal Communication: A Message-Centered Approach', in C. R. Berger, M. E. Roloff and D. R. Roskos-Ewoldsen (eds), *The Handbook of Communication Science*, 2nd edn (Thousand Oaks, CA; London: Sage).

19 M. von Fragstein et al. (2008), 'UK Consensus Statement on the Content of Communication Curricula in Undergraduate Medical Education', *Medical Education* 42: 1100–7.

as it happens in real-world contexts where people are challenged by what it means to be human and relate to the sacred in the midst of physical and existential uncertainty. A minister with any modicum of curiosity and compassion will have direct insight of this reality without necessarily approaching it through a scholarly lens. This granular knowledge when subject to reflection can have its own practical and ethical purpose:

> a knowledge of lived religion expands our empathetic entry into the world of the care receivers. If our care givers' eyes are opened not only to feelings, family dynamics, and ways of emotionally and cognitively constructing a world, but also to the roles, rules, and cultural artifacts that relay meaning, comfort, belonging, and a connection to the transcendent, then our empathetic capacities are enlarged. Knowledge and fluency in a care receiver's lived religion expand our empathy.[20]

Empathy is critical to engaging with those in need and to caring for them, but so is the way that human reality and experience is interpreted. In Christian pastoral ministry this is necessarily oriented by the gospel, but it is also informed and framed by tacit and learnt knowledge to which the scholarly practice of researchers brings rigorous description and analysis. Empirical theology, for example, is a modality of practical theology that contributes scholarly narrative about how the sacred is experienced in the everyday with the aim of enriching the practice of pastoral ministry. This disciplined attention to context and praxis as part of the pastoral cycle inevitably prompts us to reflect critically on theological method and methodology, in other words to question how we should do theology grounded in the pastoral context. In response we can draw upon three delineated modes of practical theology: pastoral theology, empirical theology and public theology, whose objects of study extend beyond ecclesial institutions and forms to the wider contexts of life and the ways in which people relate to the sacred.[21] This empirical turn in theology is also evident in the move to appropriate the methodology and methods of action research with its aim of understanding particular situations and experiences, enabling change and cultivating practical wisdom.[22]

---

[20] S. J. Dunlap (2011), 'Culture-Coded Care: Ecclesial Beliefs, Practices, and Artifacts in Response to Illness', in J. F. Maynard, L. Hummel and M. C. Moschella (eds), *Pastoral Bearings: Lived Religion and Pastoral Theology*, paperback edn (Lanham, MD: Lexington Books), 87.

[21] R. R. Ganzevoort and J. Roeland (2014), 'Lived Religion: The Praxis of Practical Theology', *International Journal of Practical Theology* 18: 91–101.

[22] E. Graham (2013), 'Is Practical Theology a Form of "Action Research"?' *International Journal of Practical Theology* 17: 148–78.

Theological action research and other modes of practical theology can thus provide the basis for entering authentically into dialogue with other forms of evidence-based healthcare. Significantly, the commitment in action research to self-understanding or first-person reflexivity is for the pastoral minister a theological task that requires a critical and disciplined practice of understanding the habitual ways that received wisdom, interpretations and practices are applied uncritically to the contexts and situations of ministry. Developing self-insight and discernment is a challenging and demanding exercise and one that can help to acknowledge and transcend limitations, pastoral blind spots, theological biases and confusing the interests of those we seek to serve with self-interests. Evidence of the theological self in this context is as important as evidence of the world, for:

> Without such theological self-knowledge, exploration, discipline, and accountability [caregivers] are likely to harm care seekers by imposing their own unexamined beliefs and values on them and/or judging them in ways that are self-affirming and self-protective. Given the power differential that usually inflates caregivers' agential power, it is imperative that caregivers are accountable for finding relational ways of tracking what's going on in their lived theology, assessing when theologies are life-giving and life-limiting, and integrating liberative compassion into their practice of care.[23]

The role of ministry in healthy persons and communities

It is easy to regard health primarily as a matter of medical science, healthcare professionals, hospitals and clinics, and, in the UK, the amount of the public purse available to fund the National Health Service (NHS). Powerful assumptions and beliefs about health and illness frame the ways in which society understands people who are sick or injured or dying, and they shape the institutions and organizations that society authorizes to act on its behalf. In 1975, Michael Wilson identified six major assumptions that underpinned the dominant forms of hospital medicine and nursing care and which he suggested mirrored societies' attitudes to health, illness and death at the time:

1 the cure of disease is more important than the care of patients;
2 staff assume power over patients;
3 individuals are separate from one another;

---

[23] C. Doehring (2015), *The Practice of Pastoral Care: A Postmodern Approach* (Louisville, KY: Westminster John Knox Press), 86.

4 the provision of health is a task for experts;
5 every problem has a solution;
6 death is the worst thing that can happen to a person.[24]

More than four decades later and these assumptions remain largely indelible despite evidence about the wider determinants of health and the movements that have sought to humanize health, deinstitutionalize healthcare and reintegrate mortality as part of the human condition. The churches have become increasingly mute at a national level in debates about the nature of health and what healthy communities and a healthy society might mean, and where theology has sometimes offered a language to explore this contentious subject, ecclesial theology appears to limit itself largely to more particular debates with a strong ethical character.

Health remains a subject of keen interest to most people, and the Church in serving local communities still plays a role, inadvertently or explicitly, in the nurturing or diminishing of healthy persons and communities. Pastoral ministry in this context has the potential to engage in health beyond the individual body and the institutional clinic and to offer valuable insights from pastoral practice. This pastoral approach is ministry in the public domain that recognizes health as a public good with its associated concerns about justice and human flourishing. The motivation for this concern is no less than the commission of the Church to participate in God's mission to the whole *oikoumene* to affirm life and to transform by God's grace all that denies salvation:

> Actions towards healing and wholeness of life of persons and communities are an important expression of mission. Healing was not only a central feature of Jesus' ministry but also a feature of his call to his followers to continue his work (Matt. 10:1). Healing is also one of the gifts of the Holy Spirit (1 Cor. 12:9; Acts 3). The Spirit empowers the church for a life-nurturing mission, which includes prayer, pastoral care, and professional health care on the one hand and prophetic denunciation of the root causes of suffering, transformation of structures that dispense injustice, and pursuit of scientific research on the other.[25]

The role of churches in local communities aligns well with the primary health model and its values of social justice, inclusion and participation.

---

[24] M. B. Wilson (1975), *Health Is for People* (London: Darton, Longman & Todd).
[25] World Council of Churches (WCC) (2012), *Together towards Life: Mission and Evangelism in Changing Landscapes* (Geneva: WCC), sect. 50. Available at: <https://www.oikoumene.org/en/resources/documents/commissions/mission-and-evangelism/together-towards-life-mission-and-evangelism-in-changing-landscapes> (accessed 23 November 2015).

The pastoral ministry of the local church can contribute to a holistic understanding of health and efforts to tackle the determinants that lead to health inequalities. It is well evidenced that the major determinants of people's health include the conditions in which people are born, grow, live, work and age,[26] all of which are understood to some extent and witnessed by those engaged in pastoral ministry. In helping to tackle the root causes of illness and suffering, local churches have many assets that can contribute to human flourishing and health, including pastoral care, meeting places, educational activities, community development, sources of meaning and hope, people with skills and abilities, and recognition of ministers as community leaders. These rich resources when coupled with the participation of local people make churches and their ministries partners with other local agencies in nurturing health.

Healthy ageing and the care of older people is an aspect of public health that will be familiar to churches and other community-based agencies and provides an example of how ministry can respond to an ageing society. Beginning with a deep engagement and commitment to local people who are older and frail, hearing their stories and bringing critical reflection to their contexts and the practice of the Church may suggest ways in which the Church can act to promote their flourishing and diminish their suffering. In the community of Alton in Hampshire this resulted in developing an ecumenical community model of chaplaincy for older people known as Anna Chaplaincy, after the prophet 'of great age' (Luke 2.36–38). This is a pastoral service that reaches beyond congregations to the community, is intentionally a catalyst for change in attitudes and practices towards older people, and is informed by research and expert knowledge on ageing.[27]

Anna Chaplaincy is both an expression of pastoral ministry and an exercise in practical theology rooted in a particular context. Older people can often be at a disadvantage in relation to normative patterns of being church, and the status quo is unlikely to change without a theological stance of openness and critique that enables both a deep engagement with context and a form of critical discipleship that is capable of questioning

---

[26] World Health Organization (WHO), Commission on Social Determinants of Health (2008), *Closing the Gap in a Generation: Health Equity through Action on the Social Determinants of Health* (Geneva: WHO).

[27] Bible Reading Fellowship (BRF) (2014), 'Anna Chaplaincy to Older People', *The Gift of Years*: <http://www.thegiftofyears.org.uk/anna-chaplaincy-older-people> (accessed 20 November 2015).

received wisdom and practices.[28] Theology can also be a unique resource in shaping a public dialogue for, in relation to ageing, it offers:

> practices of lament and thanksgiving, grief and compassion, by which we transcend our factuality. Theology brings in the language of love, emotions, social relationships, and self-esteem. It draws on biblical narratives where dramatic life stories fuel reflections much more than abstract ideas or concepts do.[29]

When local churches use their resources to engage with the human and social dimensions of health, they can contribute to the healing and wholeness of life of persons and communities. Practical theology is a unique and generative approach that ministers can bring to this public agenda and which can open a critical and constructive dialogue between the ecclesial and civic agencies within a particular place. Ministers also have to offer first-hand experience of serving among a local community, sharing in its stories, enabling its meaning-making, expressing its joys and sadness, and witnessing to hope, all of which express and shape the nature of health.

Conclusion

Archie Cochrane brought a much-needed critical view to the medical opinion of his day which has since developed into the evidence-based movement in healthcare in which good practice is developed from the rigorous creation and interpretation of knowledge. Inevitably spirituality and religion have come under the gaze of health researchers, who have gone on to build an evidence-based construct of these phenomena as they relate to people living with disease and injury. This raises challenging questions about the extent to which ministry should be empirically responsible and what this might mean. It also asks us to review critically the normative claims of received wisdom embedded in the pastoral practice of ministry. To some this might appear a secular threat or a project in material reductionism, but empirically informed pastoral care can also be seen as a way of engaging more deeply and critically with the situations of daily living and social life in which ministry is practised, and bringing new pastoral knowledge into critical dialogue with existing ministerial habits and skills. The challenge from healthcare is to develop ministry that is empirically

---

[28] E. A. Stoddart (2014), *Advancing Practical Theology: Critical Discipleship for Disturbing Times* (London: SCM Press).

[29] F. D. Lange (2015), *Loving Later Life: An Ethics of Aging* (Grand Rapids, MI: Eerdmans), 11.

responsible, contextually sensitive, theologically reflexive and ethically accountable. In responding to this challenge it is likely that ministry is more able to contribute to the life-nurturing mission of the Church and better informed to work alongside all those who seek to bring healing and wholeness to our damaged world.

40

Chaplaincy and healthcare

MARK NEWITT AND SALLY ROSS

This chapter explores the ministry of healthcare chaplaincy from the perspective of adult acute and adult mental health inpatient settings. Although there will be similarities in the way ministry is expressed, it does not directly address more specialist contexts such as paediatric or hospice chaplaincy. Similarly, the chapter does not attempt to cover community healthcare settings, such as general practitioner (GP) surgeries, which are a more recent development and where chaplaincy practices are generally less developed and more idiosyncratic.

Chaplains have been employed within the UK's National Health Service (NHS) since its inception in 1948 with Ministry of Health circulars at the time stipulating that hospital authorities should give special attention to providing for the spiritual needs of both patients and staff.[1] Over the last 30 years, as medical treatment has progressed, patient expectation has risen and successive governments have attempted to control mounting costs, the NHS has gone through many changes. Chaplains today may well look different and do different things from their counterparts from nearly 70 years ago, but their core job description remains the same: to provide for the religious and spiritual needs of patients, relatives/carers and staff.

While some literature highlights a lack of clarity among chaplains as to how they carry out that role,[2] the task of accompanying people at a time of acute change or crisis is widely acknowledged.[3] Chaplains minister within a context of profound human experience: serious illness with

---

[1] HMC(48)62, BG(48)65 and RHB(48)76. Cf. James W. Woodward, 'A Study of the Role of the Acute Health Care Chaplain in England' (PhD thesis, Open University, 1998), 90.

[2] Derek J. Fraser, 'Clarity and Cost Effectiveness in Chaplaincy', *Scottish Journal of Healthcare Chaplaincy* 7, no. 1 (2004); Helen Orchard, *Hospital Chaplaincy: Modern, Dependable?* (Sheffield: Sheffield Academic Press, 2000).

[3] Michael Wilson, *The Hospital – a Place of Truth: A Study of the Role of the Hospital Chaplain* (Birmingham: University of Birmingham, 1971); Iain Macritchie, 'The Chaplain as Translator', *Journal of Religion and Health* 40, no. 1 (2001); Mark Cobb, 'Change and Challenge: The Dynamic of Chaplaincy', *Scottish Journal of Healthcare Chaplaincy* 10, no. 1 (2007).

its frightening and distressing effects; pain which can be emotional and spiritual as well as physical; sudden or slow, long-awaited death; losses at multiple levels such as control, independence, hope, and the vulnerability that those losses bring. In responding to these things chaplains draw alongside people and seek to offer pastoral care.

David Lyall describes pastoral care as involving

> the establishment of a relationship or relationships whose purpose may encompass support in a time of trouble and personal and/or spiritual growth through deeper understanding of oneself, others, and/or God. Pastoral care will have at its heart the affirmation of meaning and worth of persons and will endeavour to strengthen their ability to respond creatively to whatever life brings.[4]

How is such pastoral care expressed within a healthcare context? Mowat and Swinton's investigation into healthcare chaplaincy in Scotland concluded that, rather than a list of particular tasks, there is a process of chaplaincy which involves *seeking out* people who need chaplaincy support, *identifying* the nature of that need and then *responding* to the need through theological and spiritual praxis.[5]

Mowat and Swinton state that a central part of a typical day relates to what they term 'need-seeking'. This can vary hugely from place to place depending on historical practice and the size of the hospital and chaplaincy team. It will most likely involve both formal and informal strategies. Typically, most 'need-seeking' can be divided into one of three categories. The first is to respond to a referral from an external source. Most usually this would be a member of a faith community informing the chaplaincy department that the patient has been admitted and requesting its help in providing support, particularly if the person has been admitted to a hospital at some distance from where he or she lives or normally attends a place of worship.

Second, a patient may be referred by a member of the clinical team. For example, a member of staff may pick up signs that a patient is upset over something and suggest that he or she might like to talk things through with a chaplain. Of course, all patients should be asked about whether or not they have a faith or belief practice when first admitted. However, this is not a good source of referrals. Audits regularly show that this is the question

---

4   David Lyall, *Integrity of Pastoral Care* (London: SPCK, 2001), 12.
5   Harriet Mowat and John Swinton, *What Do Chaplains Do? The Role of the Chaplain in Meeting the Spiritual Needs of Patients* (Aberdeen: Mowat Research, 2005), 29–30.

least likely to be answered on admission forms.[6] Even if the question has been asked, and the patient has indicated that he or she is practising, there is no guarantee that a referral will be made to the chaplaincy team. In addition to non-referral of people who would like support maintaining their faith practice, there are a number of other issues with relying on ascertaining religion at admission as a 'need-seeking' mechanism. Principally, it misses out those people who do not practise or identify with a particular faith, but still have spiritual need. In addition, spiritual need is a dynamic concept and a person who has no need on admission may well develop need later; for example, on receiving an unexpected diagnosis following tests. Largely stemming from a North American chaplaincy context, there are screening tools that have been developed to help identify spiritual need.[7] However, screening tools are not regularly or widely used within the UK context.

The third and last method of need-seeking involves chaplains or chaplaincy volunteers identifying patients in need of continuing support as a result of their own visiting. This may be as a consequence of going to see one particular patient and getting into conversation with another patient in the same bay, or encountering a nurse who is prompted into mentioning that such and such a person might value a conversation. Alternatively, it could be as a result of carrying out a general ward visit; this is when chaplains or volunteers visit a particular area with the aim of introducing themselves and saying hello to most of the patients on the ward. Particularly in the light of the poor referrals from a clinical route discussed above, this is done with the dual aim of meeting basic human need for social interaction, and also screening for deeper spiritual need or distress.

Mention was made above of spiritual need-screening tools. Increasingly, healthcare chaplaincy tools are classified as spiritual screening, spiritual history-taking or spiritual assessment tools.[8] The majority probably fall into the assessment category and, as such, most are more suited to Mowat and Swinton's next process, that of *identifying* the nature of the spiritual

---

[6] Mark Cobb, 'Assessing Spiritual Needs: An Examination of Practice', in Mark Cobb and Vanessa Robshaw (eds), *The Spiritual Challenge of Health Care* (Edinburgh: Churchill Livingstone, 1998); Chris Swift, Sara Calcutawalla and Rosie Elliot, 'Nursing Attitudes towards Recording of Religious and Spiritual Data', *British Journal of Nursing* 16, no. 20 (2007).

[7] Cf. George Fitchett and James Risk, 'Screening for Spiritual Struggle', *Journal of Pastoral Care and Counseling* 63, no. 4 (2009), 1–12.

[8] George Fitchett, 'Next Steps for Spiritual Assessment in Healthcare', in M Cobb, C. M. Puchlaki and B. Rumbold (eds), *Oxford Textbook of Spirituality in Healthcare* (New York; Oxford University Press, 2012), 299.

need. Most formal tools are based around asking certain questions and are often arranged as acronyms to aid remembrance of areas to ask about.[9] Whether a formal tool is used or not, chaplains need to make some assessment of need. At a simple level this may be about identifying where the focus of care should be; for example, whether the need is primarily:

- *social*, e.g. helping relieve isolation;
- related to *providing help and/or comfort*, e.g. listening to a patient's concerns;
- *spiritual*, e.g. the person feels abandoned by God;
- *ritual or faith-based*, e.g. provision of the sacraments.[10]

As they sit and talk with a patient to help identify need, chaplains will be listening out for potential trigger words or themes; for example, does a middle-aged woman talk about being isolated, does she say she is feeling guilty or that she feels she is being punished, does she talk about no longer feeling herself?

Having identified the nature of the need, chaplains then need to *respond* to that need, and here we return to Lyall's description of pastoral care. The description starts with the establishment of a relationship. Hospital patients come from all walks of life: a retired judge may be sitting next to a destitute asylum-seeker in the ward lounge; a drug addict with a history of gang membership may be in a bed next to a devout member of the local mosque. As with any pastoral ministry, the ability to build a relationship of trust and respect with each person, regardless of background, is critical to the work of a chaplain. First impressions can be crucial as, particularly within an acute hospital, there may only be one chance to see a patient before he or she is discharged. Moreover, in a crisis situation, such as with a grieving family after the death of a baby, or a patient who is feeling suicidal, there can be a need to develop an almost instant rapport.[11]

Chaplains need, therefore, to be adept at swiftly assessing the type and level of support that is required in order to establish a therapeutic bond. Social trends, such as the rejection of religious authority and the high

---

[9]   E.g. HOPE, SPIRIT, FICA; see Gowri Anandarajah and Ellen Hight, 'Spirituality and Medical Practice: Using the HOPE Questions as a Practical Tool for Spiritual Assessment', *American Family Physician* 63, no. 89 (2001); Todd A. Maugans, 'The Spiritual History', *Archives of Family Medicine* 5, no. 1 (1996); Christina Puchalski and Anna L. Romer, 'Taking a Spiritual History Allows Clinicians to Understand Patients More Fully', *Journal of Palliative Medicine* 3, no. 1 (2000).

[10]   Developed from unpublished work by Derek Fraser.

[11]   Mark Newitt, 'Chaplaincy Support to Bereaved Parents – Part 2: Balancing Options, Openness and Authoritative Action', *Health and Social Care Chaplaincy* 3, no. 1 (2015), 23–40.

levels of ignorance of or indifference to the Church,[12] mean that chaplains cannot simply assume that their presence will be welcomed. Even where support has been requested, research has shown that patients have been concerned about chaplains being 'inappropriately formal, detached and paternalistic'.[13] In overcoming such expectations the manner and bearing of the chaplain – for example, a friendly smile or soft eyes[14] – can be as important as anything the chaplain, at least initially, says or does.[15]

Lyall's definition of pastoral care continues by stating that one purpose of establishing a relationship is to provide support in time of trouble. Alongside helping patients maintain their faith practice – for example taking them Holy Communion – much of the support a chaplain provides will be through active listening. Chaplains have time to sit, listen and simply *be* with people at a time of acute need. Noticeably, a chaplain may be one of the few people to whom a patient is able to tell 'the story' of what is happening. As Mark has argued elsewhere,[16] this is not to say that other members of the hospital staff do not have listening skills, but it is to recognize that, by coming with a therapeutic agenda, they have an input into the narrative in a way that the chaplain, responding to need as presented, does not. This fact is implicit in Mowat and Swinton's suggestion that 'chaplaincy is arguably one of the few roles within the hospital that could truly be needs-led'.[17]

While providing a listening ear might be enough for some, Lyall's description of pastoral care goes deeper and wider, stating that it can also involve facilitating personal and spiritual growth. Back in the 1970s, Michael Wilson described the hospital as 'a place of conflict and truth'.[18] Pastoral care in a hospital often has an intense immediacy to it. Patients rapidly cut to the chase of what matters to them. The superficial can be quickly swept away as they are brought face to face with the ultimate questions about life and meaning. Frequently, what they have always felt or

---

[12] Survey designed by Linda Woodhead and carried out by YouGov for the Westminster Faith Debates (2013), pp. 51–4, available at: <http://d25d2506sfb94s.cloudfront.net/cumulus_uploads/document/4vs1srt1h1/YG-Archive-University-of-Lancaster-Faith-Matters-Debate-full-results-180613-website.pdf> (accessed 29 November 2013).

[13] Ewan Kelly, *Marking Short Lives: Constructing and Sharing Rituals Following Pregnancy Loss* (Oxford: Peter Lang, 2007), 137.

[14] M. Scott Peck, *The Different Drum: Community Making and Peace* (London: Arrow Books, 1987), 69.

[15] Mark Newitt, 'Chaplaincy Support to Bereaved Parents – Part 1: Liturgy, Ritual and Pastoral Presence', *Health and Social Care Chaplaincy* 2, no. 2 (2014), 179–94.

[16] Mark Newitt, 'The Role and Skills of a Hospital Chaplain: Reflections Based on a Case Study', *Practical Theology* 3, no. 2 (2010), 169.

[17] Mowat and Swinton, *What Do Chaplains Do?*, 34.

[18] Wilson, 'The Hospital – a Place of Truth', 57.

thought about the world no longer seems to make sense, their vision of the future is shattered and the narrative by which they understand their life breaks down. For those with a faith, their beliefs about God may be profoundly challenged. It is not surprising, therefore, that some patients begin to reappraise their understanding of themselves, the world, and perhaps, their understanding of God.

In relation to the notion of developing faith, Jeff Astley and his co-authors liken faith to 'a shawl (of meaning) that we knit and wrap around ourselves'. They continue:

> It is not the job of the pastor or educator to slash at this with a knife or rip it from a person's shoulders. But sometimes the shawl starts to unravel of its own accord. And then we should step in to help: not by darning up the loose ends, but by rolling up the wool, standing by the wearer in his nakedness, and then encouraging him to knit a new shawl for himself.[19]

Chaplains seek to affirm the meaning and worth of patients by attending to the stories they tell and the hopes, beliefs and doubts that are explicitly or implicitly contained within those narratives. Standing, or perhaps better sitting, by the 'shawl-wearers' in their nakedness provides a moving description of much chaplaincy ministry. Stripped by the effects of illness or disability and their removal to an alien hospital environment, patients are separated from the busyness, the distractions and the routines of ordinary life. Sometimes their old beliefs will no longer 'fit' the new situation in which they find themselves. Sometimes they will be tormented by religious guilt or fear. Sometimes they will feel abandoned by God.

The chaplain seeks to embody the love, compassion and mercy inherent within his or her own faith tradition. Listening to patients, helping individuals to articulate their beliefs, doubts, worries and hopes, the chaplain creates a safe space for people to tell their stories. In the telling, and perhaps through the tears, a patient may begin to connect at a deeper level with his or her own sources of hope, strength and meaning. The chaplain may ask questions to help deepen the person's reflection: 'What is worrying or frightening you at the moment?' 'What is helping you to keep going?' 'What gives you a sense of peace?'

It is worth noting here that proselytizing is prohibited by the Healthcare Chaplaincy Code of Conduct.[20] Chaplains may well, though, understand

---

[19] Jeff Astley et al., *How Faith Grows: Faith Development and Christian Education* (London: National Society / Church House Publishing, 1991), 41.

[20] UK Board of Healthcare Chaplaincy (UKBHC), *Code of Conduct for Healthcare Chaplains* (Cambridge: UKBHC, 2010).

their work in terms of mission in its broadest sense. Mark has suggested the metaphor of the chaplain as an embedded apologist,[21] and in depicting their ministry chaplains often speak of it as 'incarnational', emphasizing the theological as well as the practical importance of presence and relationships.[22] Such a description is, we suspect, not that dissimilar to how many church-based clergy understand their calling and their ministry.[23] In many ways, hospital chaplaincy is not essentially different from church-based ministry. Much of the above might resonate with local clergy, even if it is not their everyday reality. There are, however, some distinctive features which differentiate it from church-based ministry.

Perhaps the most notable feature is the transient nature of the populations that are served and many of the relationships that are formed. Hospitals are places of constant change. Policies and protocols are regularly updated as understandings of better and/or safer ways of practising medicine develop. Every three months some staff in training posts, such as junior doctors, will rotate jobs. Large hospital trusts employ many thousands of staff members so even a healthy turnover will involve significant numbers. All this is before the changeover of the patient population is factored in. Within England, the mean length of stay for admitted care in any NHS hospital (acute and psychiatric) is five days, with one day being the median length of stay.[24] Numbers for just psychiatric hospital are more complex to determine, but are around 30 or 45 days depending on how calculated.[25] Although some patients return for regular short admissions, such as a course of chemotherapy, getting to know a patient over an extended period of visiting or chapel attendance is increasingly unlikely. Certainly, in an acute hospital, it is not far from the truth to say that if a patient is well enough to attend the chapel service then he or she is probably well enough to be discharged! In fact, the increasing trend is

---

[21] 'New Directions in Hospital Chaplaincy: Chaplains – the Church's Embedded Apologists?', *Theology* 117, no. 6 (2014), 417–25.

[22] Andrew Todd, Victoria Slater and Sarah Dunlop, *The Church of England's Involvement in Chaplaincy* (Cuddesdon: The Cardiff Centre for Chaplaincy Studies / The Oxford Centre for Ecclesiology and Practical Theology, 2014), 30.

[23] Cf. Mowat and Swinton, who write about a 'myth of difference' between chaplains and parish clergy (*What Do Chaplains Do?*, 28).

[24] NHS Digital, 'Hospital Admitted Patient Care Activity, 2015–16' (November 2016): <http://www.content.digital.nhs.uk/catalogue/PUB22378/hosp-epis-stat-admi-prov-leve-2015-16-tab.xlsx> (accessed 30 November 2016).

[25] Stephen Watkins and Zoë Page, 'Mental Health: What the Data Tells Us' (2016): <https://www.birmingham.ac.uk/Documents/college-social-sciences/social-policy/HSMC/presentations/masterclasses/13-May-London/S.Watkins-and-Z.Page-Mental-Health-What-The-Data-Tells-Us.pdf> (accessed 30 November 2016).

for hospitals not to have a regular Sunday service but focus, instead, on the provision of ward-based ministry.

Where communal worship is held, the number of patients attending is likely to be small. However, these patients could be drawn from a wide range of spiritualties and worship styles. The chaplain may need to try to balance the needs of a high Anglo-Catholic with a more Charismatic or Pentecostal patient. Patients may have cognitive impairments or, as a result of illness or injury, find sitting for extended times painful or tiring. To compensate, the liturgy may need to be short, simple and as accessible as possible. Illnesses, such as stroke or dementia, may make people more disinhibited than normal; as a result, worship may be more interactive than planned and the chaplain may need to be spontaneous and creative in response. Worship in a hospital can also throw up unusual theological and/or ethical conundrums which might not be readily faced in a parish setting. What, for example, do you do when a Muslim patient, in full understanding that it is a Christian service, wishes to attend communion and puts his hands out to receive the bread and wine? How do you dispose of a partly eaten wafer that a patient has handed back to you, saying that she does not like it?

Like collective worship, the occasional offices are also shaped by the particularities of the context. Any type of occasional office is very rare within a mental health setting. In an acute setting, these services normally take place with the word 'emergency' either explicitly or implicitly prefaced to them. Emergency weddings and baptisms take on an extra poignancy. Promises made about 'till death us do part' are made in the very real knowledge that death will part the couple sooner rather than later. Similarly, the prayer over the water in a baptism service about being 'buried with Christ in his death' is heard in a different way when life support is shortly to be removed from a baby.

Time for preparation, as would generally happen in a church setting, is frequently lacking. Weddings can be arranged with little more than a few hours' notice. Even when there is more notice there can be unusual complications; for example, making sure that a patient's drug regime is carefully adjusted so that he is awake and lucid enough to have the capacity to make the appropriate responses. Further ethical questions arise when a patient has capacity to answer, but not the strength or control in her hand to sign her name. With an emergency baptism there can be time to shape a simple service. However, when a baby is deteriorating rapidly, there may only be time and space for the bare minimum. It is not unknown for a doctor to move her hands out of an incubator porthole so that the chaplain can put his hands in, pour water and pronounce, 'N, I baptize you in the name of the Father, and of the Son, and of the Holy Spirit', before withdrawing so the doctor may continue her attempts at cardiopulmonary resuscitation.

Under the letter of the law, when a person dies in hospital and there is no one able or willing to take responsibility for disposal of the body, it is the duty of the local authority to arrange for the body to be buried or cremated.[26] In practice, however, it is often the hospital that takes responsibility. Typically, this may involve a chaplain being asked to conduct the funeral service. These can be sad occasions with few, or even no, mourners attending. If a patient or mental health service user is unable to attend a funeral, a chaplain may conduct a parallel service at the same time as the funeral. Where large numbers of people are unable to attend a funeral or are affected by a death, for example the death of a member of staff or that of a long-standing mental health inpatient, a chaplain may be asked to provide a memorial service. Particularly in an acute setting, staff deaths may contain bitter ironies; histopathology staff, for example, diagnosing a colleague's disease; or nurses being looked after by colleagues when suffering from the same illness as those they had previously cared for.

In all of these situations there is a need for sensitivity, creativity and flexibility. The chaplain needs to be skilled at assessing the pastoral need of patients and relatives while balancing this with his or her own theological convictions and Christian tradition. At these times of acute distress the chaplain seeks to embody the all-encompassing tender mercy and love of God, but there still can be occasions when theological understandings or beliefs come into conflict with pastoral need. The fairly recent development of naming and blessing services has led to fewer requests to baptize a dead baby, but baptism can still raise tricky issues. What do you do when you are called to baptize a dying baby but the parents cannot be contacted and it is a grandparent making the request? What do you do when the relatives of an unconscious adult say that the patient has not been baptized and they want you to baptize him before treatment is withdrawn? Alternatively, how do you respond when a suicidal mental health patient believes that she will go to hell if she takes her own life and this belief is so strong that it is both frightening her but also, seemingly, protecting her from taking such an action? In complex situations, decisions should be made in consultation with other hospital staff and with other members of the chaplaincy team.

---

[26] Public Health (Control of Disease) Act 1984, ch. 22, sect. 46: <http://www.legislation.gov.uk/ukpga/1984/22/section/46> (accessed 1 December 2016).

Most healthcare chaplains work within some form of a team, often including volunteers. These vary in size and may be small or very part-time. As chaplaincy teams are meant to reflect the communities that the hospitals serve, these teams are increasingly likely to be multifaith as well as ecumenical. Reflecting the diverse society we live in, alongside chaplains of different faiths, some teams now include secular or humanist chaplains and/or volunteers.[27] The act of praying together as a team and making decisions together can be deeply enriching, bringing to the fore the shared understanding of faith and spirituality as well as, at times, exposing the sharp differences in belief. A strong, mutually supportive and respectful team helps to enable the chaplain to undertake the work which can, at times, be very emotionally demanding. Chaplains also attempt to work in collaboration with other staff in the hospital. This might include liaising with nurses and doctors to ensure that the spiritual needs of a patient are integrated with the care given by the rest of the ward team, or leading groups in conjunction with occupational therapists or psychologists. Such multidisciplinary working is often easier to achieve in particular areas or disciplines; for example, in mental health or palliative care. When successfully achieved it can be stimulating, each staff member enriched by the distinctive skills and expertise of the others, and lead to truly holistic care.

As in local ministry, the work of a chaplain within a hospital is much wider than just pastoral care and conducting religious services. Many chaplains are involved in teaching other hospital staff about spiritual care, helping them to understand that holistic care involves helping patients to find a sense of hope and meaning in life, while also attending to their physical and mental health needs. Many teams employ chaplaincy volunteers as well as paid members of staff, and the volunteers will receive training, supervision and support from the chaplains. The formal structures of the NHS require that its staff receive annual appraisals and undertake mandatory training. Alongside this, regular supervision and other developmental opportunities are encouraged. This helps to provide chaplains with a focus both on and beyond their pastoral work. It also ensures that chaplains are generally well supported in their ministry.

Reflective practice and academic research are other ways in which the chaplain has the opportunity to think more deeply about his or her role and enhance the quality of the care offered. Many hospital staff now engage in regular reflective practice sessions. In chaplaincy, this will

---

27 For more details see the Non-Religious Pastoral Support Network website: <http://nrpsn.org.uk> (accessed 28 November 2016).

involve reflecting on an aspect of chaplaincy practice or a particular visit. In a non-judgemental and supportive manner the members of the team will consider what went well and what might have been done differently. They will seek to understand more fully the underlying dynamics of the encounter, both theological and psychological. Chaplains are also encouraged to make time to develop and maintain a research awareness. While some might wish to carry out research as an active part of their job, for most this simply means keeping abreast of relevant research that might have an impact on the way in which they understand or carry out their work. For example, it may be useful to know that a patient is more likely to respond positively to the offer of chaplaincy support if it is made by a chaplain rather than a nurse.[28]

The emotional demands of hospital work are being increasingly recognized by the NHS. High-profile scandals, and the subsequent reports commissioned by the UK government, have highlighted the need to support staff to provide consistently kind and compassionate care in an environment which can sometimes be very stressful, distressing and challenging. Some hospital trusts have set up structured forums – the best known being Schwartz Rounds[29] – within which staff members from across disciplines can attend and reflect with others on the emotional and psychological impact of the work which they undertake. As chaplains are employed and paid by their hospital trust to support staff, as well as patients and their families, they may be involved in helping to organize such forums. After a traumatic incident, such as an unexpected death or suicide, a chaplain may facilitate a debrief for a whole ward or clinical team. While some staff members will arrange a time to meet formally with a chaplain for support, much staff support takes place informally in the corridor or by the nurse's desk. When entering a ward, a chaplain will often ask staff members how they are or how things are on the ward; simple questions designed to enable staff to talk about the pressures and stresses of the day.

Hospitals are under increasing politico-economic pressure for evidence-based practice, and chaplains are not exempt from this. Research is one way of responding, but evidence is wider than that; for example, it is good practice to keep a record of cards and letters of thanks. Similarly, while numbers never tell the whole story, as part of their work chaplains

---

[28] Marco Martinuz et al., 'Do You Want Some Spiritual Support? Different Rates of Positive Response to Chaplains' versus Nurses' Offer', *Journal of Pastoral Care and Counselling* 67, no. 4 (2013), 1–10.

[29] Cf. <https://www.pointofcarefoundation.org.uk/our-work/schwartz-rounds> (accessed 28 November 2016).

should keep accurate records of things like the total number of episodes of patient and staff support. As part of the process of seeking, identifying and meeting need, as described above, many chaplains will also keep notes documenting the care given and ongoing care plans. The language of assessment, care plans, and so on, borrowing heavily from the clinical world as it does, may sit uneasily with some. However, even without the economic and political pressure, chaplains should be ethically motivated to provide the best possible care to patients and staff and this can only be done if they have an awareness of what they are doing and what difference their care makes. As Stephen Pattison, in his seminal work on pastoral care, cautions: 'if pastors have no perspective on their work they risk complacency, stagnation and possible complicity with that which is less than good or desirable. Ultimately, they risk harming those in their care.'[30]

At various points through this chapter we have compared and contrasted the work of a chaplain with that of a church minister. From day to day, the work of a chaplain is perhaps more emotionally intense than church-based work. A chaplain may return from taking a baby's funeral and, within a short space of time, be bleeped to help support the family of a dying woman. In a psychiatric hospital, a chaplain may visit a ward and speak with patients who are suffering from depression and can find no meaning or hope in life, followed by a patient who is deeply distressed by visual and aural hallucinations and believes himself to be possessed by the devil. In comparison with parish work, however, the work is generally more bounded. Most chaplains work set hours and, unless on call, will not be expected to work outside these hours. In contrast, a church-based minister's day could stretch from early Morning Prayer to a meeting that doesn't finish until after 10 p.m. In addition, a chaplain lives away from the work setting and, apart from when on call, can only be contacted by patients and hospital staff when on the hospital site; the boundaries between work and home life are much clearer.

We began this chapter by noting there is a process to chaplaincy of seeking, identifying and responding to spiritual need. For many chaplains it is, perhaps, the responding to need that lies at the heart of their ministry. While chaplains will be involved in moments of celebration, conceivably the hardest, yet most rewarding part, is the responding to pain and suffering. Sometimes the chaplain will be able to alleviate suffering by helping the person explore, understand and give words to it and so reconnect with his or her own sources of hope, comfort and strength. At other times,

---

[30] Stephen Pattison, *A Critique of Pastoral Care*, 3rd edn (London: SCM Press, 2000), 1.

the chaplain may only be able to sit alongside and stay with the darkness or fear that the patient is experiencing. It is a form of ministry that demands openness to the pain of others, an honest acknowledgement of the chaplain's own experiences of struggle and difficulty, and an ability to bring those experiences to bear in the pastoral encounter without trying to 'fix everything'.[31] The psalmist writes, 'Even though I walk through the darkest valley, I fear no evil; for you are with me; your rod and your staff – they comfort me' (Psalm 23.4 NRSV). Chaplains may only accompany individual patients for a short time, but in doing so they seek to embody the love and faithfulness of God so that each person they encounter does not feel that he or she journeys alone.

---

[31] Healthtalkonline, 'Ending a Pregnancy for Fetal Abnormality: Treatment, Care and Communication' (May 2012): <http://www.healthtalkonline.org/Pregnancy_children/Ending_a_pregnancy_for_fetal_abnormality/Topic/2006> (accessed 28 November 2016).

41

Ministers and employment law

NORMAN DOE

In recent years, the English courts have considered the employment status in civil law of ministers of religion, including Anglican clergy. What follows narrates these developments.[1] In civil law, employees enjoy several rights; for example, not to be dismissed unfairly or unlawfully; to be given reasons for dismissal; to be given an opportunity to put a case against dismissal; and provision for financial redress. An employee is a person who works under a contract of employment or under any other contract to 'do or perform personally any work or services for another party'.[2] A distinction exists between employees with a contract of employment (also known as a contract of service) and those with a contract for services.[3] If there is a contract, the courts decide whether it is a contract of employment on the basis of various tests,[4] such as the control test (when the employer exercises control in the selection of and over the work done by the employee), the organization or integration test (if the employee is 'part and parcel' of the business) and the economic reality test (if the agreement provides for remuneration). While none of these tests 'has won universal approval',[5] the current preferred test is the 'Economic Reality/ Multiple Test';[6] 'all the relevant facts need to be looked at in the aggregate';[7] and also: 'the object of the exercise is to paint a picture from the accumulation of detail' and the 'details may also vary in importance from

---

1 It is taken in the main from M. Hill, R. Sandberg and N. Doe, *Religion and Law in the United Kingdom*, 2nd edn (Wolters Kluwer, The Hague, 2014), 115–27. I am also very grateful to colleagues at the Centre for Law and Religion at Cardiff Law School for assistance with this piece, especially Mark Hill QC, Russell Sandberg and Frank Cranmer, particularly with the case of *Sharpe*.
2 Employment Rights Act 1996, sect. 230.
3 The term 'worker' is defined under sect. 230(3).
4 See e.g. *Ready Mixed Concrete v. Ministry of Pensions* [1968] 2 QB 497.
5 *Quashie v. Stringfellow Restaurant Limited* [2012] EWCA Civ 1735 at para. 6.
6 *Ready Mixed Concrete v. Ministry of Pensions* [1968] 2 QB 497 at 515.
7 *Warner Holidays Ltd v. Secretary of State for Social Services* [1983] ICR 440 at 453, 455.

one situation to another'.[8] Historically, office holders have not been considered employees: an office is 'a subsisting, permanent, substantive position which has its existence independently from the person who filled it, which went on and was filled in succession by successive holders'.[9]

The classical doctrine

General rule

Historically, ministers of religion have not been regarded as employees because they do not exercise ministry under a contract of employment. The classical doctrine proposed a fundamental incompatibility between, on the one hand, vocation and the spiritual nature of ministerial functions and, on the other hand, the existence of a contract.[10] There is generally no ministerial right to remuneration;[11] instead

> as [the minister] gives himself, leaving no time or energy to provide for the material needs of himself and his family, the Church undertakes the burden of their support and provides for each . . . according to his requirements. There is a basic stipend . . . committed to his own stewardship.[12]

This is regarded as a gift from God through the Church: a stipend is paid by the Church as from God, to enable the minister to live and to give some measure of freedom for his service.[13]

As such, ministerial functions arise by way of a religious act (e.g. ordination), treated as a spiritual event, not a contractual transaction. For instance, in *Rogers v. Booth* (1937) the Court of Appeal held that an officer in the Salvation Army is not an employee. The relationship between the officer and the Salvation Army superior (the general) was spiritual, not contractual. The Court consulted the Salvation Army's Orders and Regulations which stated: 'Every officer becomes such upon the distinct understanding that no salary or allowance is guaranteed to him'; he 'is pledged to his duty, with or without pay; he works from love to God and souls, whether he receives little or much'; and:

---

8   *Hall (Inspector of Taxes) v. Lorimer* [1992] 1 WLR 939 at 944.

9   *Great Western Railway Company v. Bater* [1920] 3 KB 256.

10 See N. Doe, 'Ministers of Religion and Employment Law in the United Kingdom: Recent Judicial Developments', *Anuario de Derecho Eclesiástico del Estado* (1997), 349–55.

11 *Daly v. CIR* [1934] SC 444: 'The [Roman Catholic] Church is under no obligation to pay him anything'; 'He has, indeed, no personal or independent right to maintenance.'

12 *Methodist Conference v. Parfitt* [1984] QB 368.

13 *Chalcroft v. Bishop of Norwich* (1995) 32040/95.

The army does not recognize the payment of salary in the ordinary sense . . . the Army neither aims at paying nor professes to pay its officers an amount equal to the value of their work; but rather to supply them with sufficient for their actual needs, in view of the fact that, having devoted themselves to full-time Salvation service, they are thereby prevented from otherwise earning a livelihood.[14]

Ministers, especially clergy of the established Church of England,[15] have been treated legally as office holders: their functions are not allotted or governed by contract but by ecclesiastical law. In *Re Employment of Church of England Curates* (1912) the curate (an ordained cleric) was appointed by the bishop on the nomination of the incumbent of a parish to assist that incumbent. The curate was licensed by the bishop to what was described as an office (the office of curate). The High Court held the curate was not an employee; the curate's functions and control over him were regulated by ecclesiastical jurisdiction, not by a contract.[16] In short, when ministerial appointments are made the parties do not intend to enter a contract of the type recognized in civil law – there is no intention to create legal relations.[17]

The possibility of a contract

Cases late last century challenged the classical doctrine to suggest that a contract was possible and that it might amount to a contract of employment. In *Barthope v. Exeter Diocesan Board of Finance* (1979) it was held that a stipendiary Reader in the Church of England (who was not ordained but a lay person licensed to minister) was an office-holder. However, it was also held that it was possible that a Reader potentially could at the same time hold a contract of employment. An office and a contract could co-exist. Barthope had been given 'Terms of Reference for Employment' and was subject to regulations of the bishop. The case was remitted to the Industrial Tribunal but settled before determination.[18] Similarly, in *Methodist Conference v. Parfitt* (1983) the Court of Appeal held that a minister was not an employee: no wage was paid; a minister cannot unilaterally resign from ministry; the minister was in a spiritual relationship with the

---

[14] [1937] 2 All ER 751.
[15] *Coker v. Diocese of Southwark* [1998] ICR 140: the 'legal framework for the work of a Church of England priest . . . is unlike that of any secular employee'.
[16] [1912] 2 Ch. 563.
[17] *Balfour v. Balfour* [1919] 2 KB 571; *J Evans & Son (Portsmouth) Ltd v. Andrea Merzario* [1976] 2 All ER 930.
[18] (1979) ICR 900.

Church; there was no intention to create legal relations; and at ordination, a minister does not undertake by contract to serve as a minister. However, undertaking to perform spiritual work did not necessarily preclude the existence of a contract: a contract could be drafted setting out remuneration, holidays and functions, but this would be unusual.[19] This case proved influential. In *Davies v. Presbyterian Church of Wales* (1986) the House of Lords held there was no contract: the spiritual nature of ministerial functions was incompatible with the existence of a contract, but it was possible for a contract to be made – but there was no evidence of one here.[20]

The presumption against a contract

In *Santokh Singh v. Guru Nanak Gurdwara* (1990) there was no contract between a Sikh priest and his temple, even though the constitution of the temple called the priest an 'employee of the temple'.[21] In *Guru Nanak Temple v. Sharry* (1990) a document passed between the priest and temple was entitled a 'contract'. The Tribunal held there was sufficient evidence of intent to create legal relations, but this was overturned by the Employment Appeal Tribunal: the parties had carelessly used language and there was no contractual intent.[22] And in *Birmingham Mosque Trust v. Alavi* (1992) the Tribunal held there was a contract between a *khaleeb* and the trust running the mosque (since there was certainty of terms, salary, hours of work and duties), but the Employment Appeal Tribunal reversed this: it was 'desirable that the same broad brush approach should be taken by all those faced with this issue . . . where religious factors are introduced'.[23]

The Court of Appeal in *Coker v. Diocese of Southwark* (1998) reinforced the classical doctrine. The case concerned a curate of the Church of England. The Industrial Tribunal held that letters exchanged between the curate and bishop clearly indicated a contract.[24] This was overturned by the Employment Appeal Tribunal whose decision was upheld by the Court of Appeal. There was no contract between the Church and the

---

[19] [1983] 3 All ER 747.
[20] [1986] ICR 280.
[21] [1990] ICR 309.
[22] (1990) EAT (145/90).
[23] [1992] ICR 435.
[24] It was held that the curate was an employee because there was evidence of service, control and organization; the bishop was a likely contracting party (along with the Diocesan Board of Finance, which paid the curate); there was no incompatibility between office and contract; the Church had chosen to use secular models and a visible organization and therefore could not escape secular standards; and for the Industrial Tribunal there was a presumption in favour of a contract and this must be rebutted to oust the jurisdiction of the Court.

minister by dint of lack of intention to create legal relations; the legal effect of ordination is a call to an office regulated by law and it is not necessary to enter a contract for the creation, definition, execution or enforcement of clerical functions. The Court also held that the curate's spiritual functions were matters for ecclesiastical jurisdiction and that his relationship with the bishop was regulated by canonical obedience, under 'the law of an established church which is part of the public law of England and not by a negotiated, contractual arrangement'.[25]

Recent developments in case law

There have been three recent cases which have had an impact on the classical doctrine. *Percy v. Church of Scotland Board of National Mission* (2005) concerned a sex discrimination claim brought against the Church of Scotland by a former minister.[26] The two main issues were whether Percy's relationship with the Church constituted employment for the purposes of the Sex Discrimination Act 1975 and whether the claim was a 'spiritual matter' under the Church of Scotland Act 1921, meaning that it was within the exclusive cognizance of the Church of Scotland and its own courts. Percy did not pursue her claim for wrongful dismissal at this level, accepting that she had not entered into a contract of service. Also, she had demitted status as a minister rather than being tried before her presbytery, so the matter had never come before a church court. Her case was that she was employed under a contract personally to execute certain work, namely a contract for services, not a contract of service.

The House of Lords ultimately held that her relationship with the Church constituted employment for the purposes of the Sex Discrimination Act 1975 and was not a spiritual matter. For Lord Nicholls:

1 'holding an office and being an employee are not inconsistent'; the fact that Percy's status might be described as an ecclesiastical office led nowhere;
2 although there were 'many arrangements . . . in church matters where, viewed objectively on ordinary principles, the parties cannot be taken to have intended to enter into a legally-binding contract', this principle 'cannot be carried into arrangements which on their face are to be expected to give rise to legally-binding obligations. The offer and acceptance of a church post for a specific period, with specific provision

---

25 [1998] ICR 140.
26 [2005] UKHL 73.

for the appointee's duties and remuneration and travelling expenses and holidays and accommodation, seems to me to fall firmly within this latter category';

3 it was 'time to recognize that employment arrangements between a church and its ministers should not lightly be taken as intended to have no legal effect';

4 on the facts, the documents on their face showed that Percy entered into a contract with the Board to provide services to the Church on the agreed terms and conditions. The House had been shown and told nothing to displace this prima facie impression.

The decision clearly does not mean that ministers of religion now have employment rights. It does, however, seem to show that the presumption against a contract is rebuttable; the comments of their lordships as to intention to create legal relations suggest that the presumption has been removed. The Court of Appeal judgment in *New Testament Church of God v. Stewart* is important in indicating how *Percy* is to be interpreted.

New Testament Church of God v. Stewart (2007) concerned a minister whose pastorate had been terminated. The tribunal held that the claimant was an employee for the purposes of section 230 of the Employment Rights Act 1996. The Church appealed, citing its rights under Article 9 of the European Convention on Human Rights (ECHR), which protects inter alia the right to manifest religious belief in worship, teaching, practice and observance (9(1)), but which enables the State to limit the exercise of this right in prescribed circumstances (9(2)), as incorporated into English law under the Human Rights Act 1998. The claimant submitted that the decision of the House of Lords in *Percy* involved a fundamental change and resolved the issue in his favour. The Court of Appeal dismissed the appeal but considered both the importance of *Percy* and the Article 9 argument. Pill LJ held that *Percy* did not overrule the earlier cases. Instead, it established that 'the fact-finding tribunal is no longer required to approach its consideration of the nature of the relationship between a minister and his church with the presumption that there was no intention to create legal relations'. *Percy* leaves it open to tribunals to find, 'provided of course a careful and conscientious scrutiny of the evidence justifies such a finding', that there is an intention to create legal relations between a church and a minister.[27]

---

[27] [2007] EWCA Civ 1004. See also *MacDonald v. Free Presbyterian Church of Scotland* [2010] UKEAT S/0034/09/B1 (10 Feb. 2010) and *Maga v. Trustees of the Birmingham Archdiocese of the Roman Catholic Church* [2010] EWCA Civ 256.

Pill LJ held that the statement in *Parfitt* that the spiritual nature of the work is a relevant consideration remained a principle of the law and reflected Article 9 ECHR. This requires that respect be given to the faith and doctrine of the particular Church, which may run counter to there being a relationship enforceable at law between the minister and the Church. The law should not readily impose a legal relationship on members of a religious community which would be contrary to their religious beliefs. Employment tribunals should carefully analyse the particular facts, which will vary from church to church, and probably from religion to religion. For Arden LJ, Article 9 was engaged here since one aspect of it is freedom of a religious organization from arbitrary state intervention. A religious organization may, as one of its beliefs, consider that ministers should not have contracts of employment or that the State should not interfere in the way they conduct their affairs. Interference with that belief might be a violation of Article 9, though the interference will not constitute a violation of Article 9 if the conditions in Article 9(2) are satisfied. Arden LJ rejected the submission that for Article 9 to be engaged it had to be an express tenet of the religion that no contract is formed between the minister and the religious body or some part of it. It was sufficient that the beliefs are found to be inconsistent with the implication of any contract or alternatively any contract of employment. Also, the fact that in an employment dispute one party to the litigation is a religious body or that the other party is a minister of religion does not of itself engage Article 9. The implication of a contract of employment is not automatically an interference with religious beliefs. Rather, it is within the fact-finding function of the court or tribunal. On the facts of this case, the tribunal came to a different conclusion, looking at the evidence as a whole, and it was entitled to do so.

President of the Methodist Conference v. Preston (2013) concerned a minister in the Methodist Church who wished to challenge the Church for unfair dismissal.[28] The original Employment Tribunal in *Preston*[29] had held that a Methodist minister could not be an employee because it was bound by the Court of Appeal decision in *The President of the Methodist Conference v. Parfitt*.[30] This was reversed by the Employment Appeal Tribunal[31] whose decision was upheld by the Court of Appeal: Preston had served under a contract of employment.[32] The Supreme Court reversed

---

[28] [2013] UKSC 29.
[29] The claimant's surname was Moore when proceedings began. She subsequently married.
[30] [1983] 3 All ER 747.
[31] [2010] UKEAT 0219101503.
[32] [2011] EWCA Civ 1581.

the Court of Appeal decision: the claimant was not an employee. However, although the Supreme Court ultimately agreed with the Employment Tribunal that Preston was not an employee, it was also clarified that *Parfitt* was no longer good law. For Lord Sumption, much of the earlier case law was 'influenced by relatively inflexible tests born of social instincts which came more readily to judges of an earlier generation than they do in the more secular and regulated context of today'. He held that earlier cases had erred in treating ministers of religion as an 'abstract categorisation'; rather, the 'correct approach is to examine the rules and practices of the particular church and any special arrangements made with the particular minister'. The decision of the House of Lords in *Percy* meant 'the question whether a minister of religion serves under a contract of employment can no longer be answered simply by classifying the minister's occupation by type: office or employment, spiritual or secular'. There was now no presumption 'against the contractual character of the services of ministers'. Instead, the 'primary considerations are the manner in which the minister was engaged and the character of the rules or terms governing his or her service' – this is a task which, like 'all exercises in contractual construction', needs to construe the parties' intentions 'against their factual background'. *Percy* confirmed that 'this factual background included the spiritual character of a minister's calling', but that this 'could not be conclusive'. The Supreme Court reversed the Court of Appeal decision, which had held that Preston had served under a contract of employment, on the basis that the judgment paid insufficient attention to the facts, the Deed of Union and Standing Orders 'which were the foundation of Ms Preston's relationship with the Methodist Church'. Their broad approach 'would mean that almost any arrangements for the service of a minister of religion would be contractual'. This underscores how such cases will be fact specific.

Sharpe v. Worcester Diocesan Board of Finance Ltd (2013–15)

In *Sharpe v. Worcester Diocesan Board of Finance Ltd* (2013) the Employment Tribunal held that an ordained minister in the Church of England was neither an employee nor a worker. However, the Employment Appeal Tribunal reversed the decision: *Preston* had clarified the law; it was 'now unnecessary to refer to all of the earlier cases'; it was 'abundantly clear that cases concerning the employment status of a minister of religion cannot be determined simply by asking whether the minister is an office holder or in employment'; and 'there is no presumption against ordained ministers being engaged under contracts'. Instead, 'each case will always be fact specific, and probably Church specific'. This meant the Employment Tribunal had failed 'to carry out the full analysis that *Preston* now establishes'. The Employment Appeal Tribunal held: the focus should have been on whether there was a contract between the claimant and the bishop, having regard to the Church's rules and practices and particular arrangements made with the claimant; the judge should have conducted a careful analysis of these rules and practices, the manner in which the claimant was engaged, and the particular arrangements made with him, as revealed by all the relevant documentation, to decide whether they were characteristic of a contract and, if so, whether it was a contract of employment.[33]

The Employment Appeal Tribunal decision in *Sharpe* was appealed successfully to the Court of Appeal,[34] which reinstated the Employment Tribunal decision that Sharpe was not an employee. Arden LJ held that 'the conclusion of the employment judge that there was no contract, or no contract of employment, between the parties was the result of a detailed examination of the facts and the law'. In so doing, Arden LJ explored the recent appellate cases. Her account is entirely in line with that presented in the cases following *Percy*. She states that, historically, ministers were not seen as employees, and then explains that many of the reasons no longer apply:

> Not long ago, no one entertained the idea that, at least in a church where individual churches are subject to an overarching organisation, a minister of religion could be an employee of the religious organisation for which he worked. Several reasons were given for this: that the duties of office were spiritual or that the minister held an office (and that holding of an office was exclusive of employment) or that there was a presumption that the parties did not intend to create legal relations or that the duties were prescribed by the special institutional framework of religious law. Slowly but surely . . . some of these reasons have been displaced. The law has developed and changed because it was difficult to justify the exclusion of ministers of religion from the benefit of modern employment protection legislation.

Moreover, Arden LJ accepted that:

1 there are now no special rules on the employment status of ministers: 'there is now no rule which applies only to ministers which does not also apply to other persons who claim to be employees, although of course the facts to which the law has to be applied are very different. It is the same principles which have to be applied';

---

[33] [2013] UKEAT 0243 12 2811.
[34] [2015] EWCA Civ 399.

2 'the question of employment status cannot be answered simply by discerning whether a minister is an office holder or in employment';

3 there is no presumption against contractual intent; on this, *Coker* is no longer good law;

4 'the spiritual nature of a ministry does not in any way prevent a contract of employment arising';

5 minister cases will be fact specific: 'The facts must be looked at in the individual case and in the round';

6 it is not determinative that ministers have a spiritual function, are office-holders or are governed by ecclesiastical law; 'the fact that a person is an office holder does not mean that he cannot be an employee';

7 'it would be wrong . . . to suggest that canon law might preclude or prevent an employment contract' but that this could be considered as being 'contra-indicative of an employment contract';

8 the whole issue is important for the autonomy of the Church and its ministers.

Arden LJ cited the first clause of *Magna Carta* (that the English Church be free) and states: 'The value placed on freedom by the institution is obvious. That would, I think, include freedom of thought and conscience for individual incumbents, free from interference by parishioners or the Church's hierarchy.'

The Court of Appeal found no reason to set aside finding of the Employment Tribunal that 'as a matter of fact that there was no contract, express or implied, between Reverend Sharpe and the Bishop'. It affirmed earlier tests on the nature of a contract of employment.[35]

Vicarious liability and ministers of religion

The employment status of ministers has been further affected by recent cases concerning the vicarious liability of religious groups for torts committed by those who work for them. Some concede that ministers should be treated as if employees for the purpose of vicarious liability,[36] others that the religious organization could not be vicariously liable for the actions of ministers since they were not employees. In *JGE v. The Trustees of Portsmouth Roman Catholic Diocesan Trust* (2012) Ward LJ held

---

[35] Namely, those in the *Ready Mixed Concrete* case: see above, n. 4.

[36] *Maga v. Trustees of the Birmingham Archdiocese of the Roman Catholic Church* [2010] EWCA Civ 25. See H. Hall, '*Maga* and Direct Liability for Negligence', and F. Cranmer, '*Maga* and Vicarious Liability for Sexual Abuse', 167 *Law and Justice* (2011) 20.

that, although 'completely satisfied that there was no contract' between the priest and the bishop, the Church remained vicariously liable for the priest's actions. Also, there was 'a need to adapt to current demands' and consider whether a bishop could be vicariously liable on the basis that the relationship was akin to employment. He concluded that 'the time has come emphatically to announce that the law of vicarious liability has moved beyond the confines of a contract of service'.[37]

This judgment was later approved by the Supreme Court in *The Catholic Child Welfare Society v. Various Claimants* (2012). Lord Phillips affirmed the principle that the 'relationship that gives rise to vicarious liability is in the vast majority of cases that of employer and employee under a contract of employment'. However, vicarious liability could also arise where the relationship between the defendant and the tortfeasor is akin to that between an employer and an employee. The Supreme Court was clear that the technicalities of whether ministers of religion are employees would not inhibit the finding of vicarious liability. There would be vicarious liability if the organization had 'facilitated the commission of the abuse by placing the abusers in a position where they enjoyed both physical proximity to their victims and the influence of authority over them both as teachers and as men of god'.[38]

Political developments: Church of England

A Department of Trade and Industry (DTI) Consultation Paper 2002 dealt with atypical workers (e.g. agency workers, casual workers and clergy) with a view to giving churches the option for clergy to have rights under the Employment Relations Act 1999, section 23. In 2004 the DTI set up a Clergy Working Group, including representatives from trades unions and faith-groups, to look at the broad issues of clergy employment. The Group developed a statement of standards as to terms and conditions of work, resolving disputes, development and personnel support, and information and consultation. As a first step, the DTI asked faith-groups to assess the current position in relation to the standards in the statement and stated that it would revisit the issue two years later – but it did not rule out legislative action. Its successor, the Department for Business, Innovation and Skills, returned to the matter in 2009 and asked faith-groups for an update on their situations.

---

[37] [2012] EWCA Civ 938.
[38] [2012] UKSC 56.

In response, the Church of England set up a Working Group which suggested giving certain clergy employment rights as if they were employees.[39] As a result, the Ecclesiastical Offices (Terms of Service) Measure 2009 and Ecclesiastical Offices (Terms of Service) Regulations 2009 came into force in 2011.[40] This legislation gives clerics on common tenure the right not to be unfairly dismissed from office on the grounds of capability and for this to be enforceable in employment tribunals. However, the Measure and Regulations state in clear terms that such clergy are not employees: they confer rights under the 1996 Act *as if* such clergy were employed, not *because* they are employed. Section 9(6) of the Measure makes it explicit: 'Nothing in this Measure shall be taken as creating a relationship of employer and employee between an office holder and any other person or body.' Therefore, although clergy with common tenure have employment rights under the relevant legislation, they are not employees but office-holders.[41]

Conclusion

It is now clear that all the old reasons why a minister could not be an employee are now simply part of the facts that need to be examined in their entirety, case by case, to determine whether this specific post in this particular context was contractual and, if so, whether that contract took the form of a contract of employment. Recent cases show that ministers *can* be employees: it all depends on the facts. The traditional wisdom that ministers of religion are office-holders, not employees, is questionable. Today, ministers are now in the same position as anyone who wants to prove employment status: they need to point to a contract of employment and, since at least *Percy*, it is clear that the simple claims that they are 'employed by God' or hold an ecclesiastical office would not in themselves mean that they would not be found to be employees. In short, ministers of religion are not *always* employees but *may* be employees – and whether they are or not depends on whether there is a contract.[42]

---

[39] Church of England, *Review of Clergy Terms of Service* (2004).

[40] Thus, the employment position of Church of England ministers has been superseded by ecclesiastical law; as Arden LJ accepted, the facts of *Sharpe* occurred before the Measure came into force.

[41] HMRC's guidance, *PAYE70230 – PAYE Operation: Specific Employments: Clergy and Ministers of Religion*, states not entirely accurately that 'Ministers of the Church of England are office holders'.

[42] R. Sandberg, 'Not a Sharpe Turn: A Note on *Sharpe v Bishop of Worcester*', *Law & Religion UK*, 4 May 2015: <http://www.lawandreligionuk.com/2015/05/02/not-a-sharpe-turn-a-note-on-sharpe-v-bishop-of-worcester>.

42

Canon law in global Anglicanism

NORMAN DOE

The juridical instruments of the churches of the Anglican Communion contain elaborate rules applicable to ordained ministers. Ordained ministers are understood to exercise a special ministry and they are conceived theologically and legally as set apart from the laity. The juridical instruments of churches deal with the process of ordination, the appointment of ordained ministers to and their tenure in ecclesiastical offices and other positions, the functions, duties and rights of clergy, clerical discipline, the care of clergy in terms of accommodation, remuneration and pensions, and the termination of ministry.[1] This chapter sets out norms operative on these matters in relation to ordained ministers who function at the most localized ecclesiastical unit, that of the parish with, where appropriate, reference to the diocesan ministry of bishops and beyond that of archbishops. It does so with regard to a wide range of Anglican churches globally in the context of the principles of canon law common to the churches of the Anglican Communion (2008).[2]

Ordination and appointment to office

The holy orders are bishops, priests and deacons, and this 'threefold ordained ministry accords with the practice and tradition of the church'.[3] No person is to be a priest or deacon unless called, tried, examined and admitted according to the rite of ordination, and the diocesan bishop has a special responsibility, assisted by the faithful, to provide sufficient clergy and to foster vocations to ordained ministry; the normal age for

---

[1] See N. Doe, *Canon Law in the Anglican Communion* (Clarendon Press, Oxford, 1998), ch. 5.
[2] *The Principles of Canon Law Common to the Churches of the Anglican Communion*: Anglican Communion Legal Advisers Network (Anglican Communion Office, London, 2008) (hereafter PCLCCAC).
[3] PCLCCAC, Principle 31. See e.g. England: Canon C1(1); Wales: Book of Common Prayer 1984, v.

the diaconate is 23 and that for the priesthood 24.[4] There is no right to ordination. Baptism and confirmation are qualifications and the authority to determine suitability of a candidate rests with the bishop, who must be satisfied the candidate has the necessary spiritual, moral, physical and mental qualities – both men and women may be ordained to the extent permitted by law.[5]

Progression from the diaconate to the priesthood is not automatic. Normally, a deacon may not be ordained priest for at least one year, unless the bishop has good cause to ordain earlier; norms provide for training, and the production of prescribed documents prior to ordination.[6] The ordination must be in accordance with the ordinal or other authorized form of service, and a candidate must assent to church doctrine, to use only lawful forms of service, to obey the lawful and honest directions of the bishop, and to comply with the law.[7] Valid ordination consists in fulfilment of what the Church universal intends with the free consent of the candidate through the imposition of hands by a validly consecrated bishop with the invocation of the Holy Spirit to give grace for the work of a priest or deacon, whichever particular order is bestowed. Ordination cannot be repeated; orders are indelible.[8]

To exercise public ordained ministry within a diocese, prior authorization must be obtained from the diocesan bishop or other designated authority.[9] The bishop may confer authority to minister publicly by means of appointment to a particular office or public ministry (such as that of parish priest), by licence, by written permission, or by such other process as may be prescribed by law, which usually involves the laity or their representatives. No bishop, priest or deacon coming from another diocese may exercise public ministry in the host diocese without the prior permission of the host diocesan bishop. Before they may be permitted by the bishop to minister in the diocese, clergy from another diocese must produce to the

---

[4]   PCLCCAC, Principle 32.1–2. See e.g. Philippines: Canons III.11; Korea: Constitution, Art. 108.

[5]   PCLCCAC, Principle 32. See e.g. The Episcopal Church USA (hereafter TEC): Canons III.4.1: 'No one shall be denied access to the selection process for ordination in this Church because of race, color, ethnic origin, sex, national origin, marital status, sexual orientation, disabilities or age, except as otherwise specified . . . No right to ordination is hereby established'.

[6]   See e.g. New Zealand: Canons G.XIII.3.4; England: Canon C7; West Indies: Canons 16–17.

[7]   PCLCCAC, Principle 32.12–14. See e.g. Ireland: Constitution, IX.17.

[8]   PCLCCAC, Principle 32.

[9]   PCLCCAC, Principle 42.1; 34.1: charge of a parish; 34.2: assistant clergy.

host bishop such satisfactory evidence of ordination and good standing as may be lawfully required.[10]

The functions of ordained ministers

Ministry itself is 'a gift of God exercised by persons, called by God and recognized as such by lawful authority, to serve the church in its mission and witness to the gospel', and public ministry is assigned formally to an ecclesiastical office, or other official position, exercised normally under episcopal authority, to which, like all offices, prescribed functions attach.[11] First, all clergy (1) should fashion themselves after the example of Christ and should not engage in any occupations, habits or recreations inconsistent with their sacred calling but lead a disciplined way of life appropriate to their clerical state; (2) must be diligent in liturgical life, particularly the Eucharist, personal prayer, self-examination and study, especially of Holy Scripture; (3) must not engage in any secular employment or other occupation without permission from the diocesan bishop; (4) must reside within the territory of the ecclesiastical unit to which they are assigned unless the bishop permits otherwise; (5) are subject to the jurisdiction of their diocesan bishop and must comply with that bishop's lawful and honest directions; and (6) should dress in a manner suitable to the performance of their ministry as may be a sign and mark of their calling both to those within their charge and to society at large.[12]

Second, a deacon must care for people in need and assist the priest (subject to the priest's direction), but must not exercise functions reserved to the order of priests.[13] Third, working with the bishop, a priest is to (1) proclaim the gospel through preaching and teaching, administer the sacraments and provide pastoral care; (2) preside at the Eucharist and pronounce absolution; (3) visit those within their charge for spiritual

---

[10] PCLCCAC, Principle 42.1–6. See e.g. England: Canon C10 and Patronage (Benefices) Measure 1986: appointment is by: presentation/nomination by the patron (e.g. bishop) consulting parish representatives (with appeal against refusal to the archbishop); institution; and induction.

[11] PCLCCAC, Principle 28.

[12] PCLCCAC, Principle 41: clerical discipleship. See e.g. Ireland, Constitution, IX.33: lifestyle; Scotland, Canon 19: secular employment; England, Canon C14(3): 'I swear by Almighty God that I will pay true and canonical obedience to the Lord Bishop of C and his successors in all things lawful and honest.'

[13] PCLCCAC, Principle 33.1–3. See e.g. Brazil, Canons III.11.

consultation and advice, prepare candidates for baptism, confirmation and reception, and instruct children within their care in the Christian faith.[14]

Fourth, a parish priest has the primary authority and responsibility for the care of souls exercised under the general authority, oversight and pastoral direction of the diocesan bishop.[15] Fifth, clergy must uphold the professional ethic of public ministry (e.g. honesty, integrity and efficiency) in pastoral care, respect for colleagues, and confidentiality.[16] A cleric may be authorized to exercise non-parochial ministry. In some churches, a bishop may appoint: an archdeacon who assists the bishop in governance within the archdeaconries of a diocese; and an area dean who must report to the bishop any matter in a parish in the deanery which it may be necessary or useful for the bishop to know (e.g. cases of illness of a cleric).[17]

Doctrine, liturgy and rites of passage

What is striking about Anglican laws is their pervasiveness in the life of ordained ministry. Norms apply to church governance, the administration of church property and finance, and the discharge of ecumenical commitments. What follows describes basic norms operative in relation to doctrine, liturgy/worship and rites of passage.

Doctrine and sermons

As at ordination, on admission to an office clergy must subscribe, assent or otherwise affirm publicly their belief in or loyalty to the doctrine of their Church.[18] The bishop has a special responsibility to uphold sound and wholesome doctrine. Clergy must not teach, preach, publish or profess doctrine or belief incompatible with that of their own Church.[19] Doctrinal

---

[14] PCLCCAC, Principle 33.4–6.

[15] PCLCCAC, Principle 34. See e.g. West Indies, Canon 15.1: 'the spiritual jurisdiction of a Parish is vested in the Incumbent or Priest-in-Charge subject to Canons and Regulations of the Diocese and the authority of the Bishop'.

[16] PCLCCAC, Principle 43: trust; 44: compassion and accessibility; 45: respect for diversity and custom; 46: disclosure of confidential information may be subject to disciplinary process.

[17] PCLCCAC, Principle 33.6. See Melanesia: Canon C.8; Ireland, Constitution, II.38–42.

[18] PCLCCAC, Principle 53.1–3. AR, Art. 20: 'it is not lawful for the Church to ordain anything that is contrary to God's Word written'. See e.g. England: Canon C15.

[19] PCLCCAC, Principle 53.5–7. See e.g. Southern Africa: Canon 37: heresy ('false doctrine'), schism ('acceptance . . . in a religious body not in communion' with the Church) and apostasy (abandonment of 'the Christian faith'); the accused must have 'taught, published, or otherwise publicly promulgated, some doctrine or opinion repugnant to or at variance with the Faith and Doctrine of the Church'.

dissent may be subject to disciplinary process.[20] Priests and deacons have a responsibility to preach. In sermons they must 'endeavour with care and sincerity to expound the word of truth according to Holy Scripture, to the glory of God and to the edification of the people'.[21] Ministers should ensure that biblical texts are treated respectfully and coherently, building on tradition and scholarship, and bring new insights and knowledge to the interpretation and application of Scripture, so the gospel is proclaimed to this age as the good news it has been to ages past.[22] Clergy must also instruct those in their charge, especially children and young persons, in the doctrine, sacraments and discipline of Christ, as the Lord has commanded and as found in Holy Scripture, and the teaching and catechism of a Church.[23]

Worship

The worship of God is 'a fundamental action and responsibility of the church'.[24] A minister must use in public worship only those forms of service authorized or otherwise permitted by lawful authority. A church may require uniformity of a single liturgical use throughout that church or conformity with a number of alternative services. However, liturgical life should be characterized by flexibility (as authorized by law), and so ministers may use their own sensitivity and discretion to conduct worship so the faithful participate with sincerity and understanding. A minister may make variations in an authorized form of service which are lawful, reverent and seemly, and not contrary to the doctrine of the Church,[25] preparing services thoughtfully, carefully and collaboratively, considering the needs of locality and people, especially the disabled or disadvantaged.[26] The right to supervise public worship in a parish vests in the cleric responsible for that parish. No minister, lay or ordained, from another parish or diocese may conduct divine services publicly within a parish without the prior consent of its clergy. The oversight of public worship in the diocese

---

[20] PCLCCAC, Principle 53.8–10.
[21] PCLCCAC, Principle 48.
[22] PCLCCAC, Principle 51.
[23] PCLCCAC, Principle 48. See e.g. Ireland: Constitution, IX.27.
[24] PCLCCAC, Principle 54.1.
[25] PCLCCAC, Principle 56.1–9. See e.g. England: Canon B1, C15: '[e]very minister shall use only the forms of service authorised'; Australia: Canon P6 1992: [t]he minister may make and use variations which are not of substantial importance in any form of service'.
[26] PCLCCAC, Principle 57.1–4.

is subject to the general direction of the bishop,[27] who may prohibit any unlawful practice.[28] Any minister who fails to use lawful liturgical ritual or ceremonial, according to the order and use of a Church, may be the subject of disciplinary proceedings in the church courts or tribunals.[29]

Baptism and confirmation

As well as responsibilities with regard to the valid administration of baptism, godparents (or other sponsors) and the instruction of parents,[30] no minister may without lawful cause refuse or unduly delay baptism of a child if the parents of the child desire baptism. However, a minister may postpone it until the parents and sponsors are instructed and able to undertake their obligations. A minister should not baptize a child without parental consent. If a minister refuses or unduly delays to baptize any child, the parents may apply to the bishop for directions. A minister who refuses to baptize without lawful cause may be subject to disciplinary process.[31] Due to the indelibility of baptism, if there is uncertainty or other reasonable doubt as to whether a candidate has been baptized previously, such person may be baptized conditionally.[32] There are also norms on confirmation.[33]

Holy Communion

Presidency at the Holy Communion is reserved to a priest or bishop who, when present, is the principal celebrant; a deacon or authorized lay minister may assist in distributing the elements.[34] The sacrament may be

---

[27] PCLCCAC, Principle 59. See e.g. Southern Africa: Canon 24: 'Incumbents are recognized as leaders . . . in regard to . . . liturgical worship, under the authority of the bishop'.

[28] PCLCCAC, Principle 60.1–2. See e.g. Ireland: Constitution, IX.2: '[it] shall be competent for the ordinary to restrain and prohibit in the conduct of public worship any practice not enjoined in the Book of Common Prayer, or in any rubric or canon enacted by lawful authority of the Church of Ireland'.

[29] PCLCCAC, Principle 60.3–6. See e.g. New Zealand: Canons D.II.2: it is an offence to 'refuse or neglect to use . . . services authorised', 'except so far as shall be otherwise ordered by lawful authority'.

[30] PCLCCAC, Principles 61 and 62.

[31] PCLCCAC, Principle 63. See e.g. England: Canon B22.4: 'No minister shall refuse or . . . delay to baptize any infant within his cure that is brought to the church to be baptized'; Ireland: Constitution, IX.26.2: in the case of a refusal or an undue delay, 'the parents or guardians may apply to the bishop who shall, after consultation with the minister, give such directions as he shall think fit'.

[32] PCLCCAC, Principle 64.

[33] PCLCCAC, Principle 65.

[34] PCLCCAC, Principle 66.

reserved for the sick and housebound, those dying or in special need, and for devotional services, with the permission of the bishop.[35] In order to receive Holy Communion, a person must be baptized and, where required by law, confirmed or ready and desirous of being confirmed. Where confirmation remains a requirement, a bishop may authorize admission of baptized but unconfirmed persons to the extent lawfully permitted.[36] No minister shall without lawful cause deny the Holy Communion to any baptized Christian who devoutly and humbly desires it. However, a person, in the absence of repentance and amendment of life, may be denied Holy Communion, for living openly in grievous sin or contention, causing scandal to the congregation or bringing the Church into disrepute.[37] Norms provide for appeals to the bishop.[38]

Marriage

Marriage, an honourable estate instituted by God, is an exclusive life-long union, signifying the mystical union that is between Christ and his Church.[39] Ministers must comply with civil law as to the formation of marriage and with church law as to its solemnization.[40] An ecclesiastical marriage is presumed valid if the requirements of civil law and canon law are satisfied.[41] Generally, a minister may refuse to solemnize a marriage for such cause, which may include conscientious objection, as is provided by the law.[42] As to preliminaries, inter alia, a minister should instruct prospective spouses in the nature, significance, purpose and responsibilities of marriage in a manner consistent with church doctrine and any

---

[35] PCLCCAC, Principle 67. See e.g. West Indies: Canon 32.4; Ireland: Constitution, IX.14.

[36] PCLCCAC, Principle 68. See e.g. England: Canon B15A: 'There shall be admitted . . . members of the Church . . . who have been confirmed . . . or are ready and desirous to be confirmed'.

[37] PCLCCAC, Principle 69. See e.g. England: Canon B16: summary exclusion to avoid e.g. scandal; Scotland: Canon 26: 'it is the inherent right of a Bishop . . . to repel offenders from Communion'.

[38] PCLCCAC, Principle 69.6–9. See e.g. Southern Africa: Canon 35.8: investigation by the bishop and restoration; Scotland: Canon 26: appeal against the decision of the bishop to the College of Bishops.

[39] PCLCCAC, Principle 70.

[40] PCLCCAC, Principle 71.1.

[41] PCLCCAC, Principle 71.3. See e.g. West Africa: Canon 7.4; England: Canon B31–2.

[42] PCLCCAC, Principle 71. See e.g. Church of England Marriage Measure 2008: the common law right of parish residents extends to persons with a 'qualifying connection' to the parish; New Zealand: Canon G.III.2.8: 'No minister shall solemnize matrimony between two persons neither of whom has been baptized'; West Africa: Canon 7.3: if one/both are non-baptized, 'a dispensation [may] be granted by the Bishop' if e.g. they see it as 'a Christian marriage identical' to one between two baptized persons.

requirements prescribed by ecclesiastical authority.[43] A marriage is created by the free, competent and open consent of the parties in the presence of at least two witnesses, and is recorded in registers maintained in the church for this purpose.[44] Following the civil dissolution of a marriage, a Church may permit a person whose former spouse is still alive to be married in church, and may stipulate conditions required for solemnization of such a marriage which it judges necessary to safeguard the holiness of marriage and the respect due to it. An ordained minister may refuse for reasons of conscience or other lawful cause to solemnize the marriage of a divorced person whose former spouse is still alive to the extent allowed by law.[45]

Funerals

Most churches have the most rudimentary of rules on funerals. To prepare a person for death a Church may offer anointing or imposition of hands. Disposal of a body may be by burial or cremation. No minister may without lawful cause refuse or delay disposal, in accordance with the funeral rites of a Church, of the remains of any person brought to the designated place. The administration of funeral rites for the non-baptized, suicides and excommunicates may be subject to direction from the diocesan bishop. The choice of funeral rites, when alternatives are authorized, belongs to the officiating minister in consultation with the family or friends of the deceased. The remains of a Christian should be disposed of in a consecrated place or, if not consecrated, in a place which has been blessed.[46]

Clerical discipline

Discipline exists to enable the Church to fulfil its mission, to preserve unity and peace, and to cure the failings of the faithful, among whom the bishop is, generally, 'the guardian of discipline'.[47] Discipline may be enforced by:

---

[43] PCLCCAC, Principle 72. See e.g. Southern Africa: Canon 35.6: there is no marriage 'until [the parties] have received such instruction on Christian Marriage as ... approved by the Bishop'.

[44] PCLCCAC, Principle 73.

[45] PCLCCAC, Principle 75.5–9. See e.g. Australia: Canon 7, 1985, 4: 'A minister ... may refuse to solemnize the marriage of any divorced person during the life of the person's former spouse'.

[46] PCLCCAC, Principle 79. See e.g. England: Canon B38.2: it is 'the duty of every minister to bury, according to the rites of the Church of England, the corpse or ashes of any person deceased within his cure of souls or of any parishioners or persons whose names are entered on the electoral roll'.

[47] PCLCCAC: Principle 37.1: the bishop is 'guardian of discipline' and (38.6) is to 'maintain ecclesiastical discipline'; 48.8: clergy should follow the 'discipline of Christ'.

hierarchical recourse; visitation; or disciplinary process in the courts or tribunals of a Church.

Hierarchical recourse

Some churches provide for the referral of complaints and disagreements to the bishop or other diocesan authority for quasi-judicial determination over a variety of different matters; for example: a churchwarden's complaint of a cleric's conduct; or the refusal by a cleric to provide liturgical facilities.[48] Indeed, the Scottish Episcopal Church has a canon 'Of Differences and Disputes and Appeals'; this applies to all appeals allowed under the canons to the diocesan bishop or to the Episcopal Synod, as well as 'to any disputes between clergy or other members of this Church as to questions affecting Congregations, Dioceses or the Province'. The decision of the bishop or of the Episcopal Synod is final; moreover, 'the Bishop in dealing with disputes shall have full power and absolute discretion' to regulate the procedure, hear parties or dispense with a hearing, require oral or written contentions, take evidence formally or informally, and generally control the process. All parties may be represented.[49]

Visitation

There are three forms of visitation.[50] In several churches, the law imposes a duty on the primate, metropolitan or archbishop to visit the dioceses of the province regularly.[51] In some churches the diocesan bishop has a right and in others a duty of visitation over the parishes and congregations of the diocese at prescribed times (usually at intervals of every three years); the pastoral and liturgical side of visitation is stressed as well as an examination of the life and ministry of clergy and laity and the administration of the parish or other unit in question; some laws require an episcopal

---

[48] E.g. Southern Africa: Canon 28: churchwardens; England: Canon B3(4): liturgy; Canada: Canon XXI.26: if remarried persons seek Holy Communion, the bishop issues a 'judgment' for their 'spiritual welfare'.

[49] See e.g. Scotland: Canon 55: a bishop 'so personally concerned that it is expedient that another should act', or parties, may apply to the College of Bishop for one of its members to resolve the case.

[50] PCLCCAC, Principle 23: visitation enables the exercise of a supervisory jurisdiction or a pastoral ministry, including enquiry into and assessment of the condition of an ecclesiastical entity; only those entities may be visited which are prescribed by law; visitations may be held at such intervals, in such form and with such consequences as may be prescribed under the law.

[51] See e.g. England: Canon G5; Uganda: Constitution, Art. 9.

report following the visitation to the diocesan assembly.[52] Other churches
provide for a visitation by the archdeacon who is required to examine
prescribed matters (typically as to church property).[53] Anglican laws also
provide procedures to address the breakdown of pastoral relations in a
local church unit.[54]

Courts

Church courts and tribunals are independent from external interference
and must uphold the rule of law in the Church. Some churches have a
three-tier hierarchy of courts, with the diocesan court as the tribunal of
first instance, the provincial court as an appellate tribunal, and a further
final court of appeal; other churches have a two-tier system, a diocesan
court and an appellate provincial court. The diocesan tribunal is in some
churches styled the Court of the Bishop (and the bishop presides, assisted
typically by an appointee of the diocesan assembly), and in others the
Diocesan Court or Tribunal, sometimes presided over by the bishop or
by a judge elected by the diocesan assembly. Diocesan courts usually have
original jurisdiction over the discipline of priests and deacons and in several churches over the laity (and the commission of ecclesiastical offences
by them). With respect to appeals, the laws provide for: limitation periods;
grounds of appeal; leave to appeal; and powers of the appellate tribunal.
The superior tribunals have an original jurisdiction over, typically, the trial
of bishops, and constitutional, doctrinal and liturgical matters.[55]

Disciplinary process

Procedures in disciplinary and other trials make provision for: the right
to bring a complaint; notice; the charge; a preliminary enquiry (usually
by the bishop or an appointee of the bishop); interim suspension of the
accused; the trial; the right to be heard; legal representation; holding
the hearing in public or private; and the right to appeal. Ordinary jurisdiction in matters of discipline rests either with the bishop or with such
other ecclesiastical person, court or tribunal as may be prescribed by law.
Church disputes should be resolved equitably, and, in the first instance,
the parties should seek to resolve their differences amicably. Courts and

---

[52] See e.g. Southern Africa: Can 39 and England: Canon C18: discretion; Wales: Constitution, XI.27: duty; Scotland: Canon 6.1: congregations; Philippines: Canons III.15.5: report to the diocesan assembly.
[53] See e.g. England: Canon C22(5); Southern Africa: Canon 15.4; Wales: Constitution, XI.17.
[54] See e.g. England: Incumbents (Vacation of Benefices) Measure 1977 (as amended 1993).
[55] See Doe, *Canon Law in the Anglican Communion*, ch. 3.

tribunals are to be available as necessary to resolve disputes and accessible to such of the faithful, ordained or lay, as may be prescribed by law. Judicial officers are to exercise their office impartially, without fear or favour. In disciplinary and other cases, the procedure is at all times to be fair and just, and is to protect rights of the parties to notice of proceedings, to adequate time for preparation of a defence, to a presumption of innocence, to be heard within a reasonable time, to question evidence, to representation and to appeal in appropriate cases on a matter of fact or law. Church courts and tribunals must give their decisions, and the reasons for them, in writing, and both decisions and reasons must be based on fact and law.[56]

Offences and sanctions

'In disciplinary cases, ecclesiastical offences and defences to them are to be clearly defined and set out in writing.'[57] Thus, bishops, clergy and (in some churches) the laity may be tried for a number of ecclesiastical offences; typical are: the commission of a crime under state law; 'immorality' or immoral conduct; teaching doctrines contrary to those of the Church; violation of the law of the Church or of ordination vows; habitual or wilful neglect of duty; conduct unbecoming the office and work of an ordained minister; and disobedience to the lawful directions of a bishop.[58] Censures include deposition, deprivation, suspension, inhibition, admonition and rebuke.[59] Deposition from holy orders is the permanent taking away of the right to perform holy orders; deprivation, a permanent removal of the right to hold an office or appointment; suspension, a temporary taking away of the right to perform prescribed functions; inhibition, a prohibition against prescribed acts; admonition, a formal warning; and rebuke, a severe censure; excommunication may also be imposed in the case of both clergy and laity.[60]

---

[56] PCLCCAC, Principle 24: due judicial process.

[57] PCLCCAC, Principle 24.9.

[58] See e.g. West Africa: Constitution, Art. XXII.6: crime; Ireland: Constitution, VIII.53: immorality; West Indies: Canon 25: doctrine; Wales: Constitution, XI.18: disobeying law; Canada: Canon XVIII.8: neglect of duty; Scotland: Canon 54.2: conduct unbecoming; New Zealand: Canon D.II.4: disobeying episcopal directions.

[59] PCLCCAC, Principle 24.9, 11 and 15.

[60] E.g. New Zealand: Canon D.II.1: deposition; Nigeria: Canon XL(c): deprivation; TEC: Canons IV.12: suspension; West Indies: Canon 25: inhibition; Southern Africa: Canon 40: admonition and rebuke.

The termination of ministry

The withdrawal or termination of the exercise of public ministry must be carried out in accordance with the grounds and procedures prescribed by law.[61] Clergy may tender a resignation to the bishop but must resign or may be removed if their incapacity or unfitness to discharge ministry is lawfully established. Clergy must retire from office at such age as is fixed by law but may continue in public ministry with the approval of the bishop or other competent authority in the manner and to the extent prescribed by law. A person may voluntarily relinquish the exercise of holy orders. Relinquishment may be reversed in such circumstances as may be allowed under the law. A person may be deposed from holy orders by lawful pronouncement of a competent ecclesiastical authority. Deposition disables the exercise of holy orders, either irreversibly or reversibly, as the case may be, according to the law.[62]

Churches also provide for the material care of clergy by means of accommodation, remuneration and pensions. As well as the provision of accommodation for clergy in full-time ministry,[63] a Church should provide for the financial maintenance of ministry. Ministers in full-time ministry have a legitimate expectation to a stipend or other remuneration payable by virtue of the office or other position held by them. Stipend funds may be held and administered at a national, regional, provincial, diocesan or other level, and, in turn, stipend rates may be determined by a national, regional, provincial, diocesan or parish assembly. Provision for non-stipendiary ordained ministry may be made within a Church.[64] Ministers in receipt of a stipend are entitled to a pension upon their retirement on the basis of contributions made to and their membership of a clergy pension fund. A clergy pension fund should be set up at national, regional or provincial level in order to provide for pensions on retirement, maintenance for spouses and dependants, and awards during periods of illness. A proper actuarial relationship should be maintained between

---

[61] PCLCCAC: Principle 42.7.

[62] PCLCCAC, Principle 47. See e.g. Southern Africa, Canon 25: revocation by the bishop if 'the work of God in a Pastoral Charge demands . . . a change of Incumbent'; Canada, Canon XIX: abandonment of ministry is 'presumed' on e.g. 'public renunciation of its doctrine or discipline'.

[63] PCLCCAC, Principle 82; e.g. Ireland: Constitution, IV.51.5: a vicar is 'entitled to . . . a free residence'.

[64] PCLCCAC, Principle 91. See e.g. Ireland: Constitution, IV.51: 'stipends . . . paid to [the minister] by right of his office for the performance of his duties' are those 'he might reasonably be expected to have'.

contributions made, levied and collected for, and the several benefits paid from, a pension fund.[65]

Conclusion

The principles of canon law common to the churches of the Anglican Communion, and the regulatory instruments of churches from which those principles are derived, indicate that while ordained ministry is instituted by God, its public exercise is regulated by a complex and pervasive body of ecclesial norms: they touch upon a broad range of issues to facilitate and to order the exercise of ministry. Moreover, the principles of canon law are useful for theological reflection: each one represents a fundamental proposition of general applicability which has a strong dimension of weight, is induced from the similarities of laws of churches, derives from the canonical tradition of the Church, and expresses a basic theological truth or ethical value about ministry. They also share profound similarities with the norms of, and thus generate common ministerial action among, ecumenical partners of Anglicans.[66]

---

[65] PCLCCAC, Principle 92. See e.g. Korea: Canon 40: clergy pensions and severance pay are determined by the National Synod; TEC: Canons I.1.8: the Church Pensions Fund, a corporation under civil law.

[66] See N. Doe, *Christian Law: Contemporary Principles* (Cambridge University Press, Cambridge, 2013).

43

Money and ministry

BARNEY HAWKINS

Lay and ordained leaders of the Church are often terrified by the need to fund the Church's ministry. Vestries or governing bodies spend hours working on the annual budget and allocating resources. Money and ministry get so woven together that ministry becomes about limitations, not about opportunities. Funding the ministry of the Church is often 'eaten up' by matters of bricks and mortar. Yet, caring for the parish's buildings and grounds is a ministry in itself. It is about being a good steward of that which has been entrusted to the next generation. Ministry for many of us is more about what we do than where we worship, but most often the two go together in today's Church. It would be well to think about two ways of doing church and funding its ministry: in traditional settings and in new and innovative places, like coffee houses in shopping precincts.

If ministry is about what we do, then funding matters a great deal, especially when you consider most models of parish or diocesan life. Salaries and benefits more often than not consume 60 per cent of most annual budgets. We (and my perspective is of the Episcopal Church in the United States) are a Church driven by 'professionals'. Clergy for the most part have seminary training and most dioceses have minimum salaries. Benefits can be more than 40 per cent of the cash compensation for full-time clergy. Episcopal institutions are required to pay 18 per cent of compensation, including housing, to the Church Pension Fund. This is an onerous burden for many parishes. One of our largest dioceses, for example, has 50 per cent of its parishes with fewer than 100 members. Clergy consume much of the funding of many parishes.

Funding the ministry of the Church also involves leaders who most often are not ordained. Musicians, administrators, sextons and others are often volunteers. If salaries and benefits are paid, then funding the ministry of a congregation gets more complicated. Often, personnel eat up so much of the funds or budget that there is little left for programmes and outreach/service.

If money and ministry are necessary topics in parishes, the same is the case in other institutions and dioceses. The Episcopal Church has encountered many challenges in funding non-profits like seminaries; hospitals; schools; college and prison chaplaincies; camps and conference centres; and diocesan staff teams. Endowments are sometimes the lifeblood of an institution, and without such resources many church ministries are ill-equipped to serve. Often, funding ministry cannot depend on annual giving. Campaigns to raise money are not uncommon and many times the need is urgent. Special appeals are part of the landscape as leaders or 'professionals' scramble to find resources for ministry. Many times the very mission of an institution is obscured by the fixation on money because the need is so great. Ministry will fail without a clear mission articulated. Even money cannot fund or enable a ministry which has no clear purpose.

This brief introduction to the current 'lay of the land' in the Episcopal Church is not a new chapter in the Church's history. In fact, funding ministry is much older than the Church. This chapter will look at our roots in temple sacrifice which was at the very heart of Jewish identity and national life. We encounter the connection between money and ministry throughout the biblical narrative. In the New Testament money and ministry are connected in the very life, death and resurrection of Jesus Christ. Church history provides insights into the theology of money and the practice of ministry.

Finally, this chapter will offer some practical 'habits' as modern-day 'professionals' navigate the choppy waters of money and ministry in an effort to fund the ministry of the Church. No church leader can throw up his or her hands and say 'That's for others to do. I do not raise money.'

Sacrifices and offerings were the earliest forms of funding. Maimonides (*Guide for the Perplexed*) reminds us that in ancient times animal sacrifices were common as expressions of the human need for religious experience and an encounter with the Holy, the Other. The Torah did not invent temple sacrifices and the elaborate system which undergirded them. Human beings have always looked for a way to worship; to present an offering. In due course the Israelites connected 'sacrifice' to animal offerings only. Offerings and sacrifice occurred inside and outside the sanctuary of the Temple. In Exodus 20.24–26 we encounter altars in the land of Canaan, places for offerings. Even as early as Genesis 4.3–5 Cain delivered a fruit offering from the land to the Lord. Abel brought a lamb of his own flock.

In Genesis 8.20 'Noah built an altar to the LORD and, taking some of all the clean animals and clean birds, he sacrificed burnt offerings on it.'[1] Sacrifice and offering were part of the covenant-making by the ancient Israelites. The acceptance of the covenant on Mount Sinai finds Moses getting up early in Exodus 24.4–5 to build an earthen altar at the foot of the mountain. They sacrificed young bulls and offered burnt offerings to the Lord.

With the building of tabernacles, the Israelites began to develop a more elaborate system for funding temple work. Leviticus chapters 1—3 becomes the handbook for the earliest Jewish sacrificial system. There were five Levitical offerings: burnt, meal, peace, sin and trespass. The Jewish people have never been careless or carefree about their offerings. With the burnt offering they believed that the altar fire should never go out (Leviticus 6.13). Not just any animal was offered. 'Let him offer a male without blemish; he shall offer it of his own free will at the door of the tabernacle of meeting before the LORD' (Leviticus 1.3 NKJV). In Leviticus chapter 2 we find that meal offerings consisted of four types of cereal, made with oil and salt and no honey. Meal offerings also included incense (frankincense). With meal offerings a memorial portion was offered, with the temple priests eating the remainder.

Sin offerings in ancient Israel made right human weakness and failure before the Lord. With sin offerings we see the beginning of orders within worshipping communities. Each class of people in Israel had different practices. The high priest was required to offer a bull – with the bull's blood sprinkled seven times on the altar (Leviticus 4.17). For their sins the leaders offered a male goat. The blood was sprinkled on the altar only once, with the remainder around the offering. The common people in ancient Israel were justified before the Lord with offerings of female animals, goats, lambs, pigeons and turtledoves. The very poor brought to the altar a morsel of grain. Trespass offerings were very much like sin offerings. The sin offering, however, was more about cheating when it came to money and property. The sacrifice of a trespass offering was to be equal to the amount taken, with the priest getting a cut (Leviticus 6.5–7).

Sacrifice and offering in ancient Israel was a ritualistic system which was detailed and specific. For example, the Talmud describes with extreme care the slaughtering of animals for sacrifice. There was provision for the

---

[1] Unless otherwise noted, all quotations from the Bible in this chapter are taken from the New International Version (NIV) © 1984.

proper care of and respect for animals – indeed people should feed their cattle before eating themselves.

The precision of sacrifice and the centrality of sacrifice are at the centre of Old Testament theology. Sacrifice was about atonement, bringing offerings and sins to the altar to make right a relationship with God for the individual and the community. Continual sacrifice was required in order for a people or a man or a woman to be generous and giving, kind and faithful. In time there was a Day of Atonement (Yom Kippur) when the high priest would sprinkle blood on the altar, on the mercy seat, for his own sins and for the sins of the nation, the people of the Lord. The Jewish people made a sanctuary and brought offerings to draw close to the Lord. In Exodus 25.8 we find the purpose of the Mosaic law and the connection between 'money' and ministry: 'Then have them make a sanctuary for me, and I will dwell among them.' Sacrifices and offerings were faithful encounters with the God of Creation, the God of the Covenant, the God of Israel.

The incarnation of Jesus is part of an unbroken 'movement' which draws humankind into a lasting relationship with the God of all creation. Jesus himself honoured the Mosaic sacrificial system (Mark 1.44). He lived as a Jew, and in Matthew's Gospel (5.18) he respects the precision of the law, the 'smallest letter'. He encountered 'loopholes' in the law and set out to change, to transform, his followers. Jesus' life embodied the Levitical sacrifices of ancient Israel. He became the Passover sacrifice. His death on the cross was a 'guilt offering', a sin offering for others, the Passover lamb. At his last meal with his friends he offers a peace offering, a new meal (Luke 22.1–23). With his final Passover, Jesus becomes Israel's Passover with his bread being his body; the wine, his own blood. The wine or the cup for Jesus was the 'new covenant in my blood'. He must have been saying to himself the words of Jeremiah 31.31–37.

The theology of the New Testament interprets the incarnation of Jesus as the holy one who is the 'atoning sacrifice . . . for the sins of the whole world' (1 John 2.2). Paul (who offered temple sacrifices after he became a Christian) made it clear in Romans (3.24–25) that we are justified 'through the redemption that came by Christ Jesus. God presented him as a sacrifice of atonement, through faith in his blood'. The sin offering of the Old Testament is now, in the new Covenant, the forgiveness which God gives in the saving work of Jesus Christ. Hebrews 9—10 provides a summary of the Old Testament sacrificial system in the sanctuary of the Temple. Old Testament sacrifice and the death of Jesus are not disconnected. The veil was torn (Matthew 27.50–51) and the earth quaked when Jesus was on the cross. Yet, the story from Cain and Abel to Jesus is a seamless 'practice' of faithful people encountering the God of Abraham and Sarah and all their offspring, even the Church.

In the preaching of the early Church we soon discover that Paul and others use the sacrifices and offerings of the Old Testament as foundations for teaching about the new Covenant in the Temple not made with human hands. The sacrifices of ancient Israel are the words of the psalmist and the words of the New Testament: 'The sacrifices of God are a broken spirit; a broken and contrite heart, O God, you will not despise' (Psalm 51.17). In Romans (12.1) Paul tells us to 'present your bodies a living and holy sacrifice, acceptable to God, which is your spiritual service of worship' (NASB). The early apostle saw his ministry to the Gentiles as 'an offering acceptable to God, sanctified by the Holy Spirit' (Romans 15.16). The early teachings just after the death of Jesus were clear: 'to do good and to share with others, for with such sacrifices God is pleased' (Hebrews 13.15–16).

In the Episcopal Church's Book of Common Prayer, the Great Vigil of Easter celebrates the deep connection between us and the ancient Israelites. We call that 'most holy night' the 'Passover of the Lord, in which by hearing his Word and celebrating his Sacraments, we share in his victory over death'. In word and sacrament Christians have the Paschal feast, 'for he is the Paschal Lamb, who at the feast of the Passover paid for us the debt of Adam's sins, and by his blood delivered your faithful people'. In Jesus is the 'evening sacrifice, the offering' at the Great Vigil of Easter, the night 'when you brought our fathers, the children of Israel, out of bondage in Egypt, and led them through the Red Sea on dry land'. The 'Passover of your Son', we say in the prayers, brought us from sin into righteousness, 'out of death into life'.

This seamless history of sacrifice and offering, of 'funding' the Temple and the Church, is not a story with two chapters. It is a like a 'short story', a novella which has a straightforward, uncomplicated theme or plot. In the last prayer of the Great Vigil of Easter, there is a prayer which appears a number of times in the Book of Common Prayer. In this prayer we say:

> O God of unchangeable power and eternal light: Look favorably on your whole Church, that wonderful and sacred mystery; by the effectual working of your providence, carry out in tranquility the plan of salvation; let the whole world see and know that things which were cast down are being raised up. And things which had grown old are being made new, and that all things are being brought to their perfection by him through whom all things were made, your Son Jesus Christ our Lord. Amen

This poetic prayer makes clear that nothing is discarded in the 'plan of salvation'. Things cast down (sacrifices of old?) are being raised up, raised up on a cross for the world to see. Things which had grown old (the Levitical code of many laws?) are being made new, not discarded. The 'perfection' of the sacrificial system from before the Temple is being realized in the life, death and resurrection of Jesus Christ. The Incarnation in the joy of the resurrection sums up ancient Israel's long yearning for the Lord, the God whom the people encountered on Mount Sinai.

We know from the New Testament that the members of early Christian communities shared everything they had as they waited on the Lord, the promised Messiah. Through Paul and others, the gospel was delivered to more and more Gentiles (non-Jews). They met on the first day of the week and their gatherings were often in homes around a table, not in the Temple. Soon, as the Lord tarried, organization was required. There were elders (*presbyteros*) or overseers (*episcopas*). Elders were assisted by deacons, who handled the blessings of the community for all. In Acts and 1 Timothy we see the body of Christ becoming the institutional Church in, and increasingly of, the world. Deacons collected and distributed money and food for the poor.

John Chrysostom, in the fourth century, understood that a Christian ministry had become more complex. He wrote:

> So the shepherd needs great wisdom and a thousand eyes to examine the soul's condition from every angle . . . The priest, therefore, must not overlook any of these considerations, but examine them all with care and apply all his remedies appropriately for fear his care should be in vain . . .

Chrysostom writes as a priest, a leader, a 'professional' who is concerned about 'every angle' as he cares for his flock. Liturgical responsibilities have always included administrative duties. This care of the whole being, of the body of Christ, calls, according to this fourth-century saint, for 'a lot of concentration, perseverance, and patience'. He is talking about more than presiding, preaching or teaching. He offers, early on, a 'wide angle' view of the pastoral leader, the pastoral priest. It can be said that rather quickly, and certainly by the fourth century, the followers of Jesus were gleaning from Jesus' words the deep connection between things earthly and things heavenly, between money and ministry.

Actually, from the third century, there was some form of indulgences or penance associated with prayers, alms, fasts and payments of fixed sums depending on the sins or offences. Pilgrimages to holy sites often included pious donations. The practice of payment for sins deteriorated over time.

As the soul's journey in the afterlife, including purgatory, became more and more part of teaching and preaching, indulgences became a way to 'buy yourself' out of purgatory. Salvation itself was linked to money, as ministry had long been.

Canterbury Cathedral in England, the mother church of Anglicanism, dates from the Roman occupation of Britain. This sacred space was destroyed by fire and rebuilt by the Normans in 1070. It is a visual reminder that the Church required more and more funds for its buildings and organizational structure. Notre Dame in Paris from the thirteenth century is another example of the physical requirements of the body of Christ as Christians moved further and further from first-century Galilee and house worship.

The medieval Church faced more and more the need for money. The wealthy were courted to fill the offering plates. Perhaps the marriage of money and ministry is seen no more clearly than in the influence of the Medicis, an Italian banking family and political dynasty in the first half of the fifteenth century which shaped our understanding of art and architecture for all time. They were the patrons of Raphael and it was out of their coffers that the Pope found the money to commission Michelangelo to paint the altar wall of the Sistine Chapel in Rome in 1534.

The Sistine Chapel embodies the Renaissance which came upon Europe after the plagues in the fourteenth and fifteenth centuries. The Middle Ages of dark and gloom became years of gold and gilt in Church and society. The Church became a patron of art and architecture and this required more and more money for 'ministry'.

In 1445 the printing press was the 'Grand Invention'. The faithful were finding out the truths of life and death on their own. Martin Luther did his own printing in 1517 with his work *The Ninety-Five Theses*. Luther started his 'reformation' by criticizing the selling of indulgences. He was brave enough to say that the pope could not control purgatory with gifts. Luther's *Theses* opened the door to human reason and many say to humanism and scepticism about all authority.

Even a Reformation, however, could not sever the need that the Church has for money. In colonial America, the Church struggled to find resources for new buildings and for ministry. Letters to the colonial commissaries or representatives of the Bishop of London from the first American priests reveal a concern about funding Anglicanism in the new world. Strong vestries emerged because of the need for lay authority and fiduciary responsibility in the fledgling American Church. Indeed, a form of congregationalism was born under the banner of Anglicanism. In the seventeenth century, poor boxes were placed in the entrances or narthexes of most parish churches. Poor boxes were a way to fund outreach, to give to the poor.

It was not until the nineteenth century that American churches made the collection of money part of worship. There had always been the offering of bread and wine; but not a collection. The collection was not initially necessary. Like their cousins in Europe, churches in America were dependent on funds from the sending churches and from the state. Taxes and fees were collected from the people to support the work of the Church. The religious tax remained after the American Revolution. The churches remained established for all practical purposes after the Establishment Clause of the First Amendment of the US Constitution. The Commonwealth of Massachusetts did not repeal the religious tax until 1833. Every other state soon followed.

Pew rents became one source of funding the salary of the priest and the upkeep of the buildings. Some pews were bought by the wealthy. In due course pledges were encouraged in American churches as they became more and more disestablished and cut off from guaranteed income. Budgets followed pledges. In many parishes it was the largesse of the 'current' Medicis who funded the priest and the ministry of the Church. By the 1950s most American churches were having a pledge season in the autumn of each year. Money and ministry became 'stewardship'.

When I was growing up in the 1950s and 1960s in the southern part of the United States, I heard a lot about the 'tithe'. Sermons focused on the biblical tithe as the way to give as a faithful Christian. The biblical tithe was what God required of us, as found in Leviticus and Numbers. A theology of stewardship emerged in the Episcopal Church with the tithe as the biblical minimum. While the requirements of giving in Leviticus and Numbers are quite demanding, most Protestants and many Episcopalians heard that the tithe was 10 per cent of your income. As income taxes and property taxes took more and more income and benefited the 'common' good, many church leaders and peoples in the pew decided that the tithe to the Church should be more like 5 per cent.

The theology of stewardship has always been an awkward exercise. It is so often about self-preservation. It is about 'keeping the doors open' and not about service, outreach or mission. Many priests preach to raise their own salaries and not much more. Jesus' words about money and stewardship are often 'used' to raise money, not to inspire mission. For Jesus, money and ministry or stewardship are about what is God's – not ours, not Caesar's. What we give is not ours. It is God's.

No one in the United States in the twentieth century delivered a clearer message about money and ministry than William Stringfellow, born in 1928 on the eve of the Great Depression in the USA (he died in 1985). This lay theologian, lawyer and social activist had an inconvenient theology. He ran against the grain as he articulated a 'social gospel' which was informed by F. D. Maurice, the English Christian Socialist whose book, *The Kingdom of Christ*, was published in 1838 and shaped a generation seeking to do the work of the gospel. In his essay 'Money', Stringfellow warns against making money an idol.[2] He was concerned about a Church and a society 'where money is an idol [and] to be poor is a sin'. Stringfellow accepts the 'interdependence of rich and poor' but asks the provocative questions: 'Where . . . do the profits that enable great corporations to make large contributions to universities and churches and charity come from?' He concludes that 'such private beneficences' are 'in fact the real earnings of some of the poor of the world'.

Stringfellow preaches that the idolatry of money allows the rich to give money which will preserve their memory. He is bold to say that money left to institutions to avoid taxes is a 'grotesque form' of immortality. He laments: 'The poor just die and are at once forgotten.'

Jesus' encounter with the rich young ruler (Mark 10.17–27) is a parable which Stringfellow uses to address the temptation to make money an idol, even in funding the Church. He writes:

> Remember, it is not that money is inherently evil or that the possession of money as such is sin. The issue for the Christian (and ultimately everyone) is whether a person trusts money more than God and comes to rely on money rather than on grace for the assurance of moral significance, both as an individual and in relationship with the whole of humanity.

Stringfellow had harsh words for churches in the United States. He concluded that most of them were like the rich young ruler in loving money more than God: they were 'rarely in a position to preach to prosperous Americans, much less the needy'.

Indeed, the danger of stewardship is that it is more about money than ministry, more about survival than service. For the 'professional' priest or minister, or for every Christian, Stringfellow invites the Church to have

---

[2] Quoted in *A Keeper of the Word: Selected Writings of William Stringfellow*, ed. Bill Wylie Kellerman, Grand Rapids, MI, Eerdmans, 1994, pp. 247–8. All further references to this essay are to these pages.

the freedom 'to have money, to use money, to spend money without worshipping money, and . . . the freedom to do without money'. This New York lawyer saw that conversations about money were the duty of every church leader. In the final analysis, Stringfellow calls Christians who are leaders to use money sacramentally 'in both the liturgy and the world'. He calls on the faithful, 'the members of the Church', to confess that 'their money is not their own because their lives are not their own but, by the example of God's love, belong to the world'. So, money is part of God's 'own love' for the world, the world for which God gave his only Son. Stringfellow understands the Church as the body of Christ – and so members must lose 'their life in order that the world be given life'.

Rowan Williams, the 104th Archbishop of Canterbury, echoes the wisdom of William Stringfellow. In 'The Christian Priest Today', a lecture given in May 2014 on the occasion of the 150th anniversary of Ripon College Cuddesdon, Oxford, he offers the view that: 'The Church is . . . always a body which has built into its very structure a twofold measure of its honesty and fidelity, a twofold means of self-questioning and self-criticism, Bible and public ministry.'

Perhaps we could add a 'twofold measure' of money and ministry for funding the ministry of the Church. The Archbishop says that being in the Church is being in the middle of a 'sacrificial action, the act of Christ's giving'. The self-sacrifice of Jesus Christ is what connects money to ministry, and ministry to money. That same sacrifice, shaped in the literature of the Israelites, is the Incarnation, which unites the spiritual to the physical. A theology of stewardship is about what God is doing in God's creation. It is about what God is doing with what God has, which is what we have and so much more. This majestic God of all creation does not need our money, which is God's already. But in giving of our bounty we are, in a small way, with Jesus in his self-giving of himself.

Church leaders must find ways to connect money and ministry. Stewardship is not a seasonal obligation. It is a way of being as a leader. First and foremost, leaders are stewards of themselves; of creation; of vocation; and of the Church. A steward's way is not easy. The Church and its leaders cannot be of the world; yet, they cannot be separate from the world. So, stewardship is about Christian formation. What does it mean to give? What does it mean to save? Why should I have a will? How do I give back and give forward? Should I plan my gifts and think about God's mission in the world when I am no longer serving? These and many more questions are being asked by faithful people in the pew. Church leaders must preach a theology of stewardship which is honest and compelling.

Those same leaders must offer practical ways to help people with their money and in their ministry. Stewardship of money and ministry is finally not about funding the ministry of the Church. As in the beginning itself, stewardship is about creation and our use of God's gifts now and for the future. Stewardship is about our being in the image of God and not about what we give or do. It is about who we are, about our identity, about our very being as a child of God.

Conclusion

Interdisciplinary methods – the role of the minister and the study of ministry

FRANCESCA PO AND DAVID GORTNER

This volume started with an Introduction by Martyn Percy titled 'The history and development of ministry', which aimed to answer the question, 'What is "ministry"?' The bulk of the volume continued by exploring the concept of ministry from a variety of different disciplines by scholars and specialists from around the world. This conclusion, then, aims to answer two underlying questions: 'Why study ministry?' and 'Why undertake an interdisciplinary study of ministry?'

The problem, however, with 'why' questions is selecting the location from which to begin answering them. The image of the ever-familiar caricature of an inquisitive child asking its parent a successive list of 'why' questions, starting from something mundane, and ultimately leading to questions about the human condition and the creation of the universe, then emerges. So, why study ministry? Well, first of all, one must ask, 'What is a "minister"?'

The minister

In the Church of England, candidates for ordained ministry are assessed according to nine criteria, known as the Criteria for Selection:

1 **Criterion A: Vocation.** 'Candidates should be able to articulate a sense of vocation to the ordained ministry and reflect on the effect of this on their life. They should be able to speak of the development of their inner conviction and the extent to which others have confirmed it. They should be able to show an understanding of what it means to be a deacon or a priest. Their sense of vocation should be obedient, realistic and informed.'
2 **Criterion B: Ministry within the Church of England.** 'Candidates should show an understanding of their own tradition within the

Church of England, an awareness of the diversity of traditions and practice, and a commitment to learn from and work generously with difference. They should be able to speak of the distinctiveness of ordained ministry within the Church of England and of what it means to exercise public ministry. They should be able to reflect on changes in contemporary society and the implications of this for ministry and the Church.'

3 **Criterion C: Spirituality.** 'Candidates should show evidence of a commitment to a spiritual discipline, which involves individual and corporate prayer and worship. They should be committed to a developing pattern of disciplined prayer, Bible study and the regular receiving of Holy Communion. They should be able to show how they discern God's activity in their life, how their spiritual practice may have changed over time and how it is changing them. They should be able to reflect on how engagement with the world and others both affects, and is affected by, their practice of prayer. Their spiritual practice should be able to sustain and energise them in daily life and future ministry.'

4 **Criterion D: Personality and Character.** 'Candidates should be sufficiently self-aware, mature and stable to show that they are able to sustain the demanding role of an ordained minister. They should be able to demonstrate how they have faced change and pressure in a balanced and flexible way and how they manage stress. Candidates should be seen to be people of integrity who can generate trust and display honesty. They should be able to speak of how they have coped with difficult life experiences, how they have reflected upon them and incorporated them within their life and understanding.'

5 **Criterion E: Relationships.** 'Candidates should show the capacity to build healthy personal, professional, and pastoral relationships. They should demonstrate an awareness of the need for, and ability to establish and sustain, appropriate boundaries between personal and professional life and within pastoral relationships. They should be able to manage conflict and show an ability to negotiate difficult relationships. Candidates should demonstrate good interpersonal skills, the willingness to learn from experience, and a commitment to building inclusive relationships within diversity. They should show the potential to exercise effective pastoral care. Candidates must be willing to live within the discipline of *Issues in Human Sexuality.'*

6 **Criterion F: Leadership and Collaboration.** 'Candidates should demonstrate an ability to offer leadership in the Church community and in the wider community as appropriate. This ability includes the

capacity to offer an example of faith and discipleship, which is inspiring to others and witnesses to the servanthood of Christ. They should show a commitment to identifying and nurturing the gifts of others and be able to collaborate effectively. Candidates should be able to identify their own leadership style, and reflect on the strengths and weaknesses of this and of the different ways in which leadership may be exercised within the Church. They should be able to be flexible and adaptable in leadership and demonstrate ability to guide and shape the life of the Church community in its mission to the world.'

7 **Criterion G: Faith.** 'Candidates should show an understanding of the Christian faith and a desire to deepen their understanding. They should demonstrate a personal commitment to Christ and a mature, robust faith, which shapes their life and work. Candidates should show an ability to reflect critically on their faith and make connections between faith and contemporary life. They should demonstrate a capacity to communicate their faith engagingly and effectively.'

8 **Criterion H: Mission and Evangelism.** 'Candidates should demonstrate a personal commitment to mission that is reflected in thought, prayer and action. They should show a wide and inclusive understanding of mission and the strategic issues and opportunities within contemporary culture. Candidates should be able to articulate the good news of the Kingdom appropriately in differing contexts and speak of Jesus Christ in a way that is exciting, accessible, and attractive. They should enable others to develop their vocations as witnesses of the good news. They should show potential as leaders of mission.'

9 **Criterion I: Quality of Mind.** 'Candidates should have the necessary intellectual capacity and quality of mind to undertake satisfactorily a course of theological study and ministerial preparation and to cope with the intellectual demands of ministry. They should demonstrate a desire to learn through the integration of academic study and reflection on experience and a commitment to this as a lifelong process of learning and formation. Candidates should show flexibility of mind, openness to change and challenge, and the capacity to facilitate learning and theological reflection within the Church community.'[1]

Furthermore, these nine criteria are assessed by three different 'advisers': (1) the Vocational Adviser, who assesses the Vocation, Ministry within the Church of England, and Spirituality criteria; (2) the Pastoral Adviser, who

---

[1] See Archbishops' Council, *Going to a Bishops' Advisory Panel: Selection for Training for Ordained Ministry*, London, Ministry Division of the Archbishops' Council (2014), pp. 24–8.

assesses the Personality and Character, Relationships, and Leadership and Collaboration criteria; and (3) the Educational Adviser, who assesses the Faith, Mission and Evangelism, and Quality of Mind criteria. These three categories – vocational, pastoral and educational – represent three primary dimensions to ministerial life. The three dimensions, including the criteria that they represent, are a dynamic set of qualities and responsibilities that interact as a cohesive whole, ultimately characterizing the role of a minister.

While these lists comprehensively state the qualities and responsibilities of a minister – what a minister is – in the Church of England specifically, I would think it safe to assume that most Christian minsters would, to the most part, agree with it. Considering my work in religious studies, I, Francesca Po, found the Criteria for Selection to be particularly interesting when conceived as these three dimensions, and the minister as a human archetype.

First, the Vocation criterion, in particular, is the criterion that demonstrates the authenticity of an individual's calling towards ministry – a persistent and almost inescapable calling coming from one's inner life, spiritual life and social life. To many, if not all ministers, the calling towards ministry is something that is experienced paradoxically as a personal choice and a divine command. Going back to the Criteria for Selection, the criterion of Ministry within the Church of England discusses one's understanding of a particular faith tradition and one's place within it, while the criterion of Spirituality demonstrates a commitment to a spiritual life and how it is mutually sustaining to and sustained by the rest of the world as a whole.

Second, the pastoral dimension, which includes the Personality and Character, Relationships, and Leadership and Collaboration criteria, parallels the recurring theme that the pastoral dimension of ministry is the dimension that pays close attention to an individual's ability to be a pastor – from the Latin word for 'shepherd' – one who is responsible for watching over and taking care of others, especially those most vulnerable. A pastor watches over and takes care of all kinds of people in various contexts of their lives, such as the underprivileged, the physically sick and the mentally ill, in addition to the assumed responsibilities towards the spiritually weak. Another way to look at the role of a pastor is one who is a holistic healer – that is, a healer of all aspects of life: emotional, mental, psychological, physical and spiritual. That said, the Personality and Character criterion focuses on the emotional, mental and psychological well-being of a potential minister; the Relationships criterion focuses on one's capacity to build healthy relationships in all contexts of life; and the Leadership and Collaboration criterion focuses on one's ability to lead others in such a way that is inspiring and effective – all qualities that are imperative to being a good pastor.

Third, the educational dimension of ministry is the dimension that focuses on a minister's personal as well as professional capacity to be a specialist in Christianity. Christianity, among many things, is a way of being, which includes a deep inner life in Christ; an outer life that reflects it, that is, by building God's kingdom; as well as a continuous understanding of how to live it as wholly as possible. A minister, then, is expected to demonstrate strength in: the criterion of Faith, a personal commitment to an inner life; the criterion of Mission and Evangelism, reflecting the way in which faith feeds and sustains a proactive passion in making the world a better place; and the criterion of Quality of Mind, which places a rigorous intellectual expectation on a minister, not least because a primary role of a minister is to teach others about living a whole, intentional and committed Christian life. A minister, as a specialist in Christianity, is not only a figure who exemplifies what it is to be a good Christian, but does so in faith, word and deed.

In my attempt to answer the question, 'What is a "minister"?' I hoped to describe a role that, stripped of the context of religion, is still something that is crucial in human life. A minister, then, is a human archetype consisting of three dimensions: (1) one who is divinely called to the role and everything that comes with it, (2) has special gifts in holistic healing, and (3) is an expert in divine cosmology. However, the specificities and actualities of the role are different in every context. Thus, we turn to David Gortner with some insights from congregational studies.

Some elements in the study of congregations

In congregational studies, one must first investigate the primary field in which ministers find themselves: the congregation, parish or community (e.g. chaplaincy) that they serve. In other words, their context. Simultaneously, one then engages in the task of decoding what the minister might be in such a place – his or her role and identity.

In terms of contextual factors, it was stated earlier that congregational studies emerged as a field of enquiry and research to explore, test and establish sound and consistent methods to catalogue and understand the dynamic and complex world of a congregation, parish or community that a minister serves. For decades, and especially since the first Congregational

Studies Consultation in 1982,[2] scholars and practitioners have gathered insights from various fields of theory and research to construct a distinct field of study devoted to understanding congregations in community context. These tools offer better assessment of congregational vitality and suggest pathways for change and growth.

Contextual exegesis is fundamental for grasping and framing local theology (Schreiter),[3] and for engaging in sound theological reflection on local realities in relation to theological traditions and broader cultural sources of insight (Whitehead & Whitehead).[4] It undergirds practices of mission,[5] pastoral care[6] and practical theology[7]. Richard Osmer describes practical theology in ministry as a continuous cyclical process of descriptive enquiry, interpretative investigation, prescriptive evaluation and pragmatic solution.[8] Descriptive enquiry seeks to answer the question 'What (really) is going on?' through purposeful, sustained listening, and observing that is both expansive and incisive.[9] Osmer echoes Don Browning, a principal architect of contemporary practical theology, who summarized the process this way:

> For a practical theology to be genuinely practical, it must have some description of the present situation, some critical theory about the ideal situation, and some understanding of the processes, spiritual forces, and technologies required to get from where we are to the future ideal, no matter how fragmentarily and incompletely that ideal can be realized.[10]

---

[2] Jackson Carroll, Carl Dudley and William McKinney (eds), *Handbook for Congregational Studies*, Nashville, TN, Abingdon Press (1986). The Preface contains a brief history of congregational studies' emergence as a field of applied research, bringing together American scholars 'from the Alban Institute, Auburn Theological Seminary, Candler School of Theology, Hartford Seminary, McCormick Theological Seminary, and the research offices of the Presbyterian Church (USA) and the United Church Board for Homeland Ministries'. This handbook was an early result of their work.

[3] Robert J. Schreiter, *Constructing Local Theologies* Maryknoll, NY, Orbis Books (1985/1999).

[4] James D. Whitehead and Evelyn Eaton Whitehead, *Method in Ministry: Theological Reflection and Christian Ministry*, New York, Seabury Press (1981/1995).

[5] David J. Bosch, *Transforming Mission: Paradigm Shifts in Theology of Mission*, Maryknoll, NY, Orbis Books (1991/2011).

[6] Margaret Kornfeld, *Cultivating Wholeness: A Guide to Care and Counseling in Faith Communities*, New York, Continuum (2000/2012); Charles W. Taylor, *The Skilled Pastor: Counseling as the Practice of Theology*, Minneapolis, MN, Fortress Press (1991).

[7] Don S. Browning, *A Fundamental Practical Theology: Descriptive and Strategic Proposals* Minneapolis, MN, Augsburg (1996); Bonnie J. Miller-McLemore (ed.), *The Wiley-Blackwell Companion to Practical Theology*, Malden, MA, Wiley-Blackwell (2014).

[8] Richard R. Osmer, *Practical Theology: An Introduction*, Grand Rapids, MI and Cambridge, Eerdmans (2008), p. 4.

[9] Osmer, *Practical Theology*, pp. 31–76.

[10] Don S. Browning, 'Practical Theology and Political Theology', *Theology Today* 42(1), April 1985, p. 15, emphasis added.

Both Osmer's and Browning's starting place reveals a fundamental hermeneutical principle in contextual exegesis: that a context, like a text,
must be read and understood *from within*. For this reason, Moschella, in
Ethnography as a Pastoral Practice,[11] presents contextual exegesis ethnographic methods as essential for wise, faithful and insightful pastoral ministry and leadership – and argues for a process of balanced emic (insider)
and etic (outsider) discovery. This embraces the hermeneutic circle
involved in the deep sympathetic reading and interpretation of, and conversation with, a text.[12]

The importance of a multi-focal approach

In *Reframing Organizations*, Lee Bolman and Terrence Deal argue that
most leaders do not get themselves and their organizations into trouble
because of ineptness, but because of over-adeptness at one way of perceiving, analysing and intervening in the life of their organizations.[13] There
is an old saying, attributed to Abraham Maslow (1966)[14] and Abraham
Kaplan (1964),[15] that such over-adeptness in one way of seeing and doing
is all too easy a human tendency: 'if all you have is a hammer, then everything becomes a nail'. The British term, 'Birmingham screwdriver', refers
similarly (if pejoratively) to simplistic overuse of one tool. Bolman and
Deal argue convincingly that organizational leaders become adept simple-
tons by over-applying one theory, framework, perspective or set of tools as
the means to exegete, interpret and intervene in any context and situation.
In leadership, this degenerates into a canned response, and frequently does
at least as much damage as good, if not simply failing to address the real
issue.[16]

---

[11] Mary Clark Moschella, *Ethnography as a Pastoral Practice: An Introduction*, Cleveland, OH,
Pilgrim Press (2008).
[12] The process of 'getting inside' a text and its world of meaning ultimately leads to transformation of the reader. See Hans-Georg Gadamer, *Philosophical Hermeneutics*, ed. and trans. David
E. Linge, Berkeley, CA, University of California Press (1977).
[13] Lee G. Bolman and Terrence E. Deal, *Reframing Organizations*, San Francisco, CA, Jossey-Bass
(2013).
[14] Abraham H. Maslow, *The Psychology of Science: A Reconnaissance*, New York, Harper & Row
(1966), p. 16.
[15] Abraham Kaplan, *The Conduct of Inquiry: Methodology for Behavioral Science*, New York,
Harper & Row (1964), p. 28.
[16] Chris Argyris spent much of his career unpacking the problem he titled 'skilled incompe-
tency' among leaders across fields. His article, 'Teaching Smart People How to Learn' (*Harvard
Business Review*, 1991), is a classic. His deeper work, in *Overcoming Organizational Defenses:
Facilitating Organizational Learning*, Needham Heights, MA, Allyn & Bacon, 1990, has been
applied to ministry by Anita Farber-Robertson in her text, *Learning while Leading: Increasing*

Bolman and Deal present four distinct frames as assessment guides: structural, human relations, power and ritual.[17] Each has its purposes. Each in isolation can blind leaders to the complexity of organizational life and purpose. Like other leaders, clergy are vulnerable to monocular vision and mono-focal approaches based on their own preferences, education, and preceding habits that include earlier successes. But, woven together, these multiple frames help leaders to exegete their contexts, yielding richer insight and thus enabling them to work towards more nuanced efforts for development in congregational life.

For those using a *structural* frame, the dominant perspective is the organization as a machine, expressing a deep interest in how things work, what makes for smoother operation, and what the organizational structures and products reveal about the organization in terms of purpose and quality. The leader comes to view his or her primary role as a 'social architect' who helps build smooth and consistent structures and procedures within which projects – and people – can thrive. This is a typical default perspective for corporate managers and mid-level executives, and has useful application in many fields of work, including the Church, in mapping committee structures, staff responsibilities, chains of command and decision-making and implementation, and budgetary allocation. The structural frame applied to a congregational study guides leaders towards serious reading of data, including church attendance records, membership and demographics; comparison of congregational demographics with wider community (neighbourhood, 'parish') demographics; organizational charts of staff, lay leadership, committee structures and ministries; budget allocation and monetary flow; leadership and volunteer 'trees' that map pathways of leadership development; and the history of various structures and organizations in the congregation and broader community, and their impact. Church leaders ignore such realities at their own peril.

The *human relations* frame focuses on patterns of communication and participation. The organization is viewed more as a family or community. The goal is to see how individuals and groups thrive and find satisfaction in their life within the organization. The leader's main task is as an 'empowerer' who releases potential, unbinds interpersonal snags, opens communications, and strengthens satisfaction and thriving in organizational life. Social service and non-profit organization leaders

Your Effectiveness in Ministry, Herndon, VA, Alban Institute, 2000. One challenge facing leaders is the need to truly explore the question, 'What am I not seeing about my own assumptions and behaviours that is contributing to the systemic problems I am trying to address?'

[17] Bolman and Deal, *Reframing Organizations*.

often default to this frame, as will many church leaders oriented primarily towards therapeutic forms of pastoral care. But these are also increasingly primary concerns among leading executives in corporations, as they attend to organizational climate, emotional tone, motivational environment, and employee health and growth. In a congregational study, the human relations perspective helps leaders focus on signs of the emotional and motivational life of the congregation, through survey and interview methods, and as observed in informal settings like coffee hours, potluck dinners and patterns of interaction in meetings. Leaders using this frame seek out more intentional conversation with individuals about their own spiritual narratives, their personal experiences and their impressions of the congregation.

The *power* frame focuses analysis on the dynamics of power and influence in an organization, community or group. The leader operates as an 'advocate' and 'alliance-builder' who helps realize a vision and produce change by bringing together the right people at the right moment. Here, the organization is viewed as an arena, game-board or playing field. Attention focuses on people's mobilization around issues and concerns, emerging resistance, movement of power and influence through a community or organization, efforts that sustain or change that movement, and individuals' engagement level. Political leaders often default to this frame – as will some clergy and religious leaders charged with (or who take on a personal mission towards) congregational transformation and redevelopment, conflict resolution or social impact. Tools for reading power dynamics include records of elected and appointed positions, voting patterns, and initiatives that were supported or unsupported. Subtler but equally important patterns are found in communications (written and verbal), flow of influence in informal social networks, different demographic and contingency groups represented or not represented, values motivating different groups, and levels of transparency in decision-making.

Power is a dimension of human life that many Christians do not willingly acknowledge, except perhaps with that dismissive statement by Lord Acton: 'Power tends to corrupt, and absolute power corrupts absolutely.' But withdrawal from constructive consideration of the reality of power can lead to a lack of watchfulness and appropriate assertiveness, opening doorways for those who look to abuse it.[18] In *Transforming Power*, Robert

---

[18] David Gortner, 'Devolution: The Dynamics of Power and Permission', *Network of Episcopal Clergy Associations* (2014): <http://episcopalclergy.org/community/topic/devolution-the-dynamics-of-power-and-permission-by-the-rev-dr-david-gortner/>.

Linthicum helpfully summarizes a perspective for community organizers and organizational leaders alike:

> Power is always present in all human situations, because power is nothing more than the ability, capacity and willingness of a person, a group of people or an institution (whether it is a church or nation) to act. The ability, capacity and willingness to act is, in itself, neither good nor bad. What makes power constructive or destructive is how it is used and for what purpose it is used[19]

Finally, there is the *ritual* frame. Already, by its name, it appeals to the cleric – but Bolman and Deal view ritual more broadly. Ritual encompasses the meanings implicit and rendered explicit in an organization's routines, the roles and masks employed in those routines, and the ways such routines project, channel and direct energy, serving to promote and clarify identity for people inside and outside the organization. The leader's role is as a 'signifier' and 'inspirer' – a theatre director, orchestral conductor, master of ceremonies – who anchors diverse efforts around a common purpose, with a consistent message, for common impact and effect. Event planners and coordinators use this frame, as do performing arts directors, and organizers of political rallies and religious gatherings. Such leaders scan for patterns, symbols and routines in formal and informal gatherings that convey consistent or inconsistent messages about 'who we are', 'why we are here' and 'what we aspire to', as well as 'how we will move forward'; they also look for ways in which an organization or community characterizes the world around them.

An essential fifth frame needs consideration – the *newcomer* or *outsider* frame. A leader must invite congregation members to adopt this perspective with fresh eyes, in order to see what may otherwise lie hidden in plain sight because it is taken for granted. Someone with fresh eyes and ears will scan a congregation for energy level and emotional tone, how people think about the life of faith, who is present and who is missing (demographically), what the congregation cares about and does not care about, clarity of message, what people get from and give to congregational life, and the congregation's collective impact.

Congregational studies architects like Nancy Ammerman, Jackson Carroll, David Roozen and Loren Mead have similarly emphasized a multi-focal approach. The *Handbook for Congregational Studies* urges clergy and researchers towards an integrated, holistic study that includes

---

[19] Robert C. Linthicum, *Transforming Power: Biblical Strategies for Making a Difference in Your Community*, Downers Grove, IL, IVP, (2003), p. 12.

examination of a congregation's programme, process, surrounding context, and identity. These architects argue that clergy and congregations typically gravitate towards solitary, primary, or at least initial focus on programme (structure) and process, thus investing less effort learning about their surrounding community and their own identity and culture.[20] Such a focus yields only partial insight into congregational life and vitality, and skews leaders' perceptions and decisions towards the over-adept, single-focused model. The more ethnographic, qualitative approach (as articulated by Moschella, Lytch, and Savage and Presnell)[21] argues that without careful attention to nuances of behaviour, interpersonal interactions, decision processes, and themes of interest and disinterest, one will not grasp the depth and subtlety of life in a congregation.

A rich array of perspectives has emerged in congregational studies, exploring patterns and effects related to congregations' size, life cycle, spiritual and emotional climate, community engagement, demographic composition and geographic location, finances, and theological and social identity.[22] Nancy Ammerman's more recent handbook provides a solid introduction to studies that continue to expand in a variety of fields.[23] Paul Wilkes's case studies of 'excellent congregations' among Protestants and Catholics in the United States provide helpful insights into best practices that support congregational vitality.[24] These are joined by a range of helpful sociological and anthropological studies of religious communities by scholars such as Rodney Stark, Wade Clark Roof, Andrew Greeley, Tonya

---

[20] Carroll et al. (eds), *Handbook for Congregational Studies*, p. 12.

[21] Moschella, *Ethnography as a Pastoral Practice*; Carol E. Lytch, *Choosing Church: What Makes a Difference for Teens*, Louisville, KY, Westminster John Knox Press (2003); Carl Savage and William Presnell, *Narrative Research in Ministry: A Postmodern Research Approach for Faith Communities*, Louisville, KY, Wayne E. Oates Institute (2008).

[22] Regarding congregational dynamics related to size, see Arlin J. Rothauge, *Sizing Up a Congregation for New Member Ministry*, New York, Episcopal Church Center (1986); Alice Mann, *Raising the Roof: The Pastoral-to-Program Size Transition*, Herndon, VA, Alban Institute (2001); Anthony G. Pappas, *Entering the World of the Small Church*, Herndon, VA, Alban Institute (1989); and Scott Thumma and Dave Travis, *Beyond Megachurch Myths: What We Can Learn from America's Largest Churches*, San Francisco, CA, Jossey-Bass (2007). On spiritual engagement and discipleship, see Diana Butler Bass, *The Practicing Congregation: Imaging a New Old Church*, Herndon, VA, Alban Institute (2004). Regarding community engagement, see John M. Perkins, *Restoring At-Risk Communities: Doing It Together and Doing It Right*, Grand Rapids, MI, Baker (1996).

[23] Nancy Tatom Ammerman, Jackson W, Carroll, Carl S. Dudley and William McKinney (eds), *Studying Congregations: A New Handbook*, Nashville, TN, Abingdon Press (1998).

[24] Paul Wilkes, *Excellent Protestant Congregations: The Guide to Best Places and Practices*, Louisville, KY, Westminster John Knox Press (2004) and *Excellent Catholic Parishes: The Guide to Best Places and Practices*, Mahwah, NJ, Paulist Press (2001).

Luhrmann, Michael Hout and Keith Pargament. Readings from such studies provide new insights, external reference points, and benchmarks for the local congregation as it embarks on a study of itself.

At this point, the study of ministry reveals its complexity: it is the study of a broad role that requires narrow considerations. With that in mind, I, Francesca Po, turn to the interdisciplinary structure of this book.

Interdisciplinary studies and chapter summaries

The second underlying question to this volume on ministry is 'Why undertake an interdisciplinary study of ministry?' As mentioned earlier, my academic background is in religious studies – the discipline that is, for better or worse, anecdotally a non-discipline and, by its very nature, interdisciplinary. Religion is unique among other subjects because it is one that can be studied within nearly any other – from theology, philosophy and psychology, to anthropology, politics and economics, to more contemporary studies in cognitive science, environmental science and theoretical physics. Ministry, as this volume has demonstrated, like religion, is much the same. This volume is interdisciplinary not by intention, but by circumstance. Though ministry, like religion, may have a background in the discipline of theology, considering the very way that a minister permeates the entirety of life – the personal and social, the physical and metaphysical – as described in the previous section, there really could not be any other way to study ministry comprehensively than via an interdisciplinary route.

The first section of this volume is titled 'Understanding ministry', and sets the stage in the study of ministry though the lens of disciplines including and beyond theological norms. Chapter 1, 'The developing philosophy of ministry', the first of two chapters by John Fitzmaurice, narrates the development of the study of ministry throughout modernity and postmodernity and gives suggestions on how to move forward in the contemporary context. Chapter 2, 'Hermeneutics of ministry' by Ian Tomlinson, looks at ministry through the lens of interpretation, and suggests that it is simultaneously an ontological, functional, dependent and representative calling. Chapter 3, 'Anthropology of ministry' by Abby Day, gives practical examples of how anthropological methods are beneficial for studying ministry, particularly for the contemporary context. Chapter 4, 'Sociology of ministry' by Douglas Davies, highlights that ministry is legitimized by theological traditions, and influenced by wider socio-political, economic and gender factors. Chapter 5, 'Congregational studies and ministry' by David Gortner, makes a case for the importance of the study of congregations and organizations for ministry. Chapter 6, 'Psychology of ministry' by Fraser Watts, makes a case that the study of ministry and the discipline of psychology can be mutually beneficial to one another in the development of knowledge. Chapter 7, 'Ministry in fiction' by Catherine Wilcox, narrates how the image of the minister has changed from classical to contemporary literature, and what that may mean for ministers today. Chapter 8, 'Ministry in television and film' by Joshua Rey and Jolyon Mitchell, summarizes the various different archetypes that a minister may take in the medium of film, and compares it to what ministry is in real life.

The second section of this volume is called 'Models, methods and resources', and offers the basic tools necessary in the study of this subject. Chapter 9, 'Global and ecumenical models of ministry', the first of two chapters by Ian S. Markham, highlights the differences between the global, practice-focused, and ecumenical, theology-focused, perspectives of ministry. Chapter 10, 'Clerical and lay models of ministry' by Andrew Todd, shifts away from the academic perspective of ministry towards a more lived perspective. Chapter 11, 'Non-parochial forms of ministry' by Chris Swift, gives an overview of the different types of ministries, particularly, chaplaincies, and the value of studying each type. Chapter 12, 'A collaboratively shaped ministry for the coming Church' by Stephen Pickard, addresses the ever-diversifying global landscape, and suggests a collaboratively shaped ministry as an effective way forward for the future of the Church. Chapter 13, 'Psychotherapy and ministry' by Robert Roberts and Ryan West, discusses the specific type of psychotherapy that Christians use, namely, Pauline therapy. Chapter 14, 'Leadership studies and ministry' by Keith Lamdin, looks specifically at the complexity of the training and professional development of ministers in the contemporary context. Chapter 15, 'Digital media for ministry: key concepts and core convictions', the first of two chapters by Kyle Oliver and Lisa Kimball, highlights the inescapability of the use of new media in ministry, and how to go about using and understanding it. Chapter 16, titled 'Digital media for ministry: portraits, practices and potential', the second of two chapters by Kyle Oliver and Lisa Kimball, gives practical advice on how to use digital media in ministry, grounded in empirical case-studies.

The third section of this volume is called 'Ministry in Christian tradition', and focuses on major areas in which ministry is prevalent in its home tradition. Chapter 17, 'Scripture and ministry' by Hywel Clifford, analyses the study of ministry in sacred Christian Scripture through the five prisms of revelation, worship, ministry, mission and learning. Chapter 18, 'Liturgy and ministry' by James Farwell, compares the study of ministry to sacred praxis. Chapter 19, 'Missiology and ministry' by Robert Heaney, also looks at Christian practice, but addresses the more modern practice of global evangelization and development. Chapter 20, 'Ethics and ministry: witness or solidarity?' by Robin Gill, focuses on the current polarized perspectives in ministry and offers a Pauline perspective to the issues. Chapter 21, 'Politics and ministry' by Susanna Snyder, makes the case for the further integration of politics and political theory in the study of ministry. Chapter 22, 'An ecumenical theology of ministry' by Robin Greenwood, indicates leading implications for ministerial theology and practice while considering the tensions in contemporary theology.

The fourth section of this volume, titled 'Styles of Christian ministry', takes a turn from the theoretical and disciplinary studies of ministry to the actual issues in the real-life practice of ministry. Chapter 23, 'Roman Catholic pastoral theology' by Tom Hughson, gives an overview of the study of ministry from the scholarship of the largest denomination of Christianity: Roman Catholicism. Chapter 24, 'Pentecostal-style ministries' by Benjamin McNair Scott, is an overview of the Pentecostal–Charismatic movement (PCM) and the role of healing in these ministries. Chapter 25, 'Anglican theologies of ministry' by Tess Kuin Lawton, is also an overview of the study of ministry from another major denomination of Christianity: Anglicanism. Chapter 26, 'The parish church' by Alan Billings, adds the form of ministry that is familiar to most, and discusses its importance and relevance to the world today. Chapter 27, 'Contested Church: mission-shaped, emerging and disputed' by Justin Lewis-Anthony, covers the complexity of ministry, among other things, in one of the newest and most well-known manifestations of Christianity. Chapter 28, 'New ministries – new ministers' by Tom Keighley, focuses on ministries such as those of worker-priests, Readers, industrial mission ministers and female priests, and offers insights into how they compare to other forms of ministry. Chapter 29, 'Critical paradigms of ministry', the second of two chapters by John Fitzmaurice, seeks to develop pastoral theology by recognizing the importance of paradigm-challenging perspectives.

The fifth and final section of this volume, titled 'Issues in Christian ministry', stays within the context of the real-life and contemporary practices of ministry, but shifts back to broader issues that most, if not all, ministers encounter today. Chapter 30, 'The challenge of preaching' by Ruthanna Hooke, looks at contemporary culture and how forms of ministry are also very much a product of this culture. Chapter 31, 'Ministry among other faith traditions' by Bonnie Evans-Hills, addresses forms of ministry in other religions and compares them to Christian ministry.

Chapter 32, 'Discrimination and ministry', the second of two chapters by Ian S. Markham, now joined by Allison St Louis, addresses the politics of discrimination and how to manage it within oneself as well as within a congregation. Chapter 33, 'Gender and ministry' by Emma Percy, addresses the very important and controversial topic of gender in ministry. Chapter 34, 'Missionary wives and women's distinctive contributions to mission' by Cathy Ross, offers another perspective on women's contributions and sheds light on the important work of the ever-influential 'women behind the men'. Chapter 35, 'The dynamics of power in churches' by Martyn Percy, addresses the problem of the abuse of power, but ultimately highlights the importance of serving the most needy and vulnerable. Chapter 36, 'Safeguarding in the Church of England' by Rupert Bursell, directly addresses the grave and complex issue of sexual abuse in the Church. Chapter 37, 'Ministerial stresses and strains' by Amanda Bloor, addresses the inevitable demands and inconsistencies of ministry, suggesting the right balance between idealism, authenticity and meaning. Chapter 38, 'Conflict, reconciliation and healing' by Sarah Hills, focuses on the concept of reconciliation and its critical role in life in general, contextualized in personal experience. Chapter 39, 'Spirituality, health and ministry' by Mark Cobb, looks at the phenomenon of spirituality in contemporary healthcare, and how Christian ministry fits into this narrative. Chapter 40, 'Chaplaincy and healthcare' by Mark Newitt and Sally Ross, offers insights about healthcare chaplaincy, particularly in adult acute and adult mental health inpatient settings. Chapter 41, 'Ministers and employment law', the first of two chapters by Norman Doe, narrates the development of the employment status in civil law of ministers of religion in the UK. Chapter 42, 'Canon law in global Anglicanism', the second of two chapters by Norman Doe, is an overview of canon law in the Anglican Communion and how it functions. Chapter 43, 'Money and ministry' by Barney Hawkins, completes the volume by calling for the importance of recognizing the reality of funding in all aspects of church life.

As one can see from this summary, the study of ministry is vast – and not restricted to either Christianity or theology. Unlike previous incarnations of this survey, Percy says:

> it takes an intentional 'binocular' methodology to the field of the study of ministry. One lens is naturally concerned with the classical principles of theological reflections on the nature of ministry – past and present. This provides clergy and congregations with their classic resources for pastoral theology. The second lens is primarily concerned with more 'objective' and 'subjective'

perspectives, with a focus on how ministry might be studied – through the social sciences, for example, or in literature, histories and cultural studies.[25]

The territory of ministry is thus one that is relevant to a wider audience than previously studied.

Concluding remarks

Studied in breadth as well as in depth, it is evident that there is a place for a minister in all aspects of human life, throughout society, culture and history. That considered, many argue that one's religion *sensu stricto*, or the religious impulse *sensu lato*, is our species' definitive feature. In fact, the *Catechism of the Catholic Church* says:

> The desire for God is written in the human heart, because man is created by God and for God; and God never ceases to draw man to himself. Only in God will he find the truth and happiness he never stops searching for.[26]

Similarly, renowned scholar of new religious movements, Eileen Barker, argues that 'religion' can be defined simply as any individual seeking answers to 'questions of ultimate concern'.[27] Thus, one can interpret these two positions as follows: the human being having 'the desire for God' is the reason for 'seeking answers to "questions of ultimate concern"', or vice versa, the human being 'seeking answers to "questions of ultimate concern"' is because 'the desire for God is written in the human heart'. Whichever the position, the religious impulse is something that indeed has a long history with humanity.

For the final time, then, why study ministry? For as long as humans have religious needs, there probably will always be a need for ministers – and, one would hope, good ones. Furthermore, the study of ministry, and an inevitable interdisciplinary study of it, would be crucial in the continuous professional development of the role that caters to not only a very basic aspect of being human but also every aspect of being human.

---

[25] M. Percy, I. S. Markham and E. Percy, 'Book Proposal: SPCK's *The Study of Ministry*', 2015, p. 1.

[26] Libreria Editrice Vaticana, 'Catechism of the Catholic Church' (2003), p. 9, <http://www.vatican.va/archive/ENG0015/_INDEX.HTM>.

[27] E. Barker, 'Credo, Credis, Credit, Credimus, Creditis, Credunt', presented at the *What Does It Mean to Believe?* Symposium, University of Kent, Canterbury, 2012.

Afterword

The future shapes of ministry

MARTYN PERCY

The study and understanding of ministry can never be easily divorced from the eras and contexts in which such ministry is practised. In the twenty-first century, ministers – at least in the developed world – are facing a range of challenges. Each of these, on its own, will have some bearing on how the field of the study of ministry emerges; and, indeed, on how ministers are prepared and trained by their respective denominations. There are many contextual factors to note, and I briefly list ten of the most significant ones that look set to play some part in how ministry might evolve and be understood in the years to come.

First, there is growing demand for ministry to be more publicly accountable and transparent. Ecclesial traditions with significant investment in the 'mystique' of ministers and a culture of clerisy or 'priestly' privilege will find this increasingly hard to justify and defend. This may be caused by an increasing awareness of safeguarding issues around children. But there is also a growing sense that the Church cannot put the reputation and interests of the institution above the pastoral needs of the people it serves.

Second, the initial education of clergy, and their spiritual formation as ministers who serve in communities, requires a level of training that corresponds to some kind of public-professional standards. Ministerial formation is no longer – if it ever was – about producing the 'holy amateur' at the end of a training process. Increasingly, public ministry requires some acceptance that public standards are being adhered to. This is especially the case for chaplains who hold public office in education, healthcare, prisons or the military.

Third, ministers in congregations, parishes and chaplaincy contexts are dealing with increasing levels of religious illiteracy among the people they are ministering to. But, at the same time, this is coupled to growing demands in relation to spiritual consumerism. Clergy are under increasing pressures here to innovate, and to try to address the growing gap between the religious faith they represent and the spiritual appetites of those to whom their ministry is directed.

Fourth, ministry faces significant organizational and financial challenges. Despite the inexorable move towards greater professionalism, the infrastructure of the Church, and its financial resources, lack the capacity to enable ministry to become a serious vocational or employment option for some. Greater organizational and centralized control of clergy tends to produce cultures of compliance, and as ministry is usually a low-wage (or sometimes unpaid) vocation or profession, this threatens the traditional and cherished freedoms that earlier generations of clergy could afford to take for granted.

Fifth, while it is doubtful that the modern world is becoming more secular, we can say with some certainty that it is becoming more pluralistic and consumerist. Baptisms, weddings and funerals – those three key traditional 'rites of passage' – now all face stiff competition from purveyors of humanist or secular spirituality. The growth in spiritual consumerism has meant that churches now only account for one option among a range of possibilities.

Sixth, ministry currently finds that it faces growing demands to correspond to the 'elasticity' of contemporary ecclesiology, and the actuality of what Pete Ward terms 'liquid church'. Under such conditions, the Church and its ministers need to be increasingly nimble and innovative in their approach, recognizing that the unyielding sodalities of the churches of bygone eras will present little that is attractive to new generations of churchgoers.

Seventh, the churches continue to have their public witness and local presence rendered ineffective due to changes of stance in public life in general fields such as gender and sexuality. The emerging gap between the polity of the Church and its theological proclivities on the one hand, and standards in public life on the other, renders the Church more marginal. At the same time, this then squeezes the Church into becoming less of a public institution (or utility), causing it to behave more like an organization undertaking some self-marketing. This only causes the public to retreat even further, enlarging the gap between the smaller group of committed members and the larger mass of uncommitted supporters.

Eighth, increasing social diversity challenges the churches, ministers and ministries to cater for a greater range of people. Churches may wish to claim distinctive confessional grounds for excluding same-sex or transgender married couples from congregations, for example. But it is harder to extend this exclusion to the children or wider family of such couples.

Social diversity challenges the churches and ministers to think seriously about how congregations might host families of difference, the growing bulge in our older population, and younger generations who are spiritual but not religious, and by instinct, believers but not belongers.

Ninth, the older 'certainties' that once provided some kind of ecclesial map – 'liberal' and 'conservative', 'left' and 'right', and so forth – are no longer pertinent to the emerging spiritual-religious landscape. The emergent culture of spiritual consumerism and 'liquid church' has given the population wide access – through social media, partly – to a range of spiritual and religious resources. Religious leaders and ministers no longer control 'supply-and-demand'; now, 'the customer is king'. Thus, Evangelicals will happily take themselves off to a spiritual retreat at Taizé or Santiago de Compostela. Anglo-Catholics might, equally, book into one of the many Evangelical or Charismatic festivals available.

Tenth, there is little agreement on the priorities of the churches. Mission, evangelism, ministry, viability – or some other radical future rooted in alterity – all compete for the attention of ministers, and are subject to congregational negotiation. Increasingly, churches find – much like ministers – that their very identity is a subject of opinion in public life, and not an object that is above scrutiny and opinion. The increasing pressure for flexibility in the patterning of ministry suggests insecurity and uncertainty as much as it hints at innovation and confidence. In such circumstances, 'traditional' patterns of ministry become rarer, and also harder to define and defend in a pluralized and crowded 'market'.

This survey has sought to introduce the study of ministry, and provide a kind of 'field guide' for readers. Inevitably, there will be new issues to attend to in the future that are not covered here. However, the authors and editors have strived to provide sufficient coverage of the present to help navigate future challenges and issues. In so doing, we hope that readers will have been well-equipped by a survey that has sought to strike a blend between the generic and detailed, and enable as many as possible to benefit from the range of articles and reflections.

We conclude with three observations. First, it does seem that we can still express some generic, timeless truths about ministry. Namely that it continues to be perceived as public, valuable, vicarious and sacrificial. Ministers are dedicated and dutiful; they serve their community, and attempt, insofar as this is possible, to serve the God they worship. Ministers seek to embody the God they worship in order to serve the people and places they are called to. It is a selfless vocation that remains rooted in the development of a quality of spiritual life, rather than in any quantification criteria for success.

Second, ministry still appears to have public value, and is part of the social capital of society. The recent rise in the range and level of chaplaincy provision – much of which is publicly funded – suggests that religious, spiritual and pastoral support remains publicly valued and cherished beyond the frontiers of congregational life. Hospitals, prisons, schools, communities, healthcare and welfare contexts – with multi-denominational and interfaith provision – point to ministry being recognized as a valued service within society. Moreover, we anticipate new partnerships between faiths and public life developing such provision in the future, with new patterns in chaplaincy and ministry seen as positive initiatives for society as a whole.

Third, the future study of ministry will, undoubtedly, have to pay due attention and regard to the new landscapes and contexts in which ministers now function. At the same time, the study of ministry will also have to take account of the consistency of vocations that somehow seem to transcend cultures and contexts, and be firmly rooted in the God who continues to call – no matter what times and places we may dwell in.

Selected bibliography

Aagedal, Olaf (2013). *Deconstructing Death: Changing Cultures of Death, Dying, Bereavement and Care in the Nordic Countries* (Odense: University Press of Southern Denmark).

Adam, P. (2004). *Hearing God's Words: Exploring Biblical Spirituality* (Downers Grove, IL, and Leicester: IVP).

Advisory Council for the Church's Ministry (ACCM) (1987), 'Education for the Church's Ministry', Occasional Paper no. 22 (London: Church House Publishing).

Agamben, Giorgio (1998). *Homo Sacer: Sovereign Power and Bare Life*, trans. D. Heller-Roazen (Stanford, CA: Stanford University Press).

Alexander, Michelle (2012). *The New Jim Crow: Mass Incarceration in the Age of Colorblindness*. Rev. edn (New York: New Press).

Ali, Mansur, Stephen Pattison and Sophie Gilliat-Ray (eds) (2013). *Understanding Muslim Chaplaincy* (Farnham: Ashgate).

Allen, R. (1912). *Missionary Methods – St Paul's or Ours?* (London: Robert Scott).

American Academy of Pediatrics Committee on Bioethics (1997). 'Religious Objections to Medical Care'. *Pediatrics* 99, pp. 279–81.

Ammerman, N. T., J. W. Carroll, C. S. Dudley and W. McKinney (eds) (1998). *Studying Congregations: A New Handbook* (Nashville, TN: Abingdon Press).

Anderson, A. (2004). *An Introduction to Pentecostalism: Global Charismatic Christianity* (Cambridge: Cambridge University Press).

—— (2011). 'Deliverance and Exorcism in Majority World Pentecostalism'. In W. K. Kay and R. Parry (eds), *Exorcism and Deliverance: Multi-Disciplinary Studies* (Milton Keynes: Paternoster), ch. 5.

Anglican-Reformed International Commission (1984). *God's Reign and Our Unity: Report* (London: SPCK).

Appadurai, Arun (1996). *Modernity at Large: Cultural Dimensions of Globalization* (Minneapolis: University of Minnesota Press).

Appiah, Kwame Anthony (2005). *The Ethics of Identity* (Oxford: Princeton University Press).

—— (2007). *Cosmopolitanism: Ethics in a World of Strangers* (London: Penguin).

Aquinas, Thomas (2006). *Summa Theologiae*, ed. Thomas Gilby (Cambridge: Cambridge University Press).

Archbishops' Commission on Evangelism (1945). *Towards the Conversion of England: Report of the Archbishops' Commission on Evangelism* (London: Press and Publications Board of the Church Assembly).

Archbishops' Council (2014). *The Deployment of Clergy with Licences and Permission to Officiate*: <https://www.ons.gov.uk/peoplepopulationandcommunity/crimeandjustice/datasets/thenatureofviolentcrimeappendixtables> (accessed 12 October 2018).

Archbishops' Council (2014). *Going to a Bishops' Advisory Panel: Selection for Training for Ordained Ministry* (London: Ministry Division of the Archbishops' Council).

Archbishops' Council (2014). *Talent Management for Future Leaders and Leadership Development for Bishops and Deans: A New Approach*: <http://www.thinkinganglicans.org.uk/uploads/TalentManagement.pdf> (accessed 12 October 2018).

Archbishops' Council (2015). *Senior Church Leadership: A Resource for Reflection*: <https://www.churchofengland.org/sites/default/files/2017-10/senior_church_leadership_faoc.pdf> (accessed 12 October 2018).

Arendt, Hannah (1951). *The Origins of Totalitarianism* (San Diego, CA: Harcourt Brace Jovanovich).

Argyris, Chris (1990). *Overcoming Organizational Defenses: Facilitating Organizational Learning* (Needham Heights, MA: Allyn & Bacon).

—— (1991). 'Teaching Smart People How to Learn'. *Harvard Business Review* 69.3, pp. 99–109.

Arnold, T. (1833). *Principles of Church Reform* (London: SPCK).

Augustine (1972). *City of God*, trans. Henry Bettenson (London: Penguin).

Avis, Paul (2002). *Anglicanism and the Christian Church: Theological Resources in Historical Perspective*. 2nd edn (Edinburgh: T&T Clark).

—— (2007). *The Identity of Anglicanism: Essentials of Anglican Ecclesiology* (London: Continuum).

Bacote, V., L. C. Miguelez and D. L. Okholm (eds) (2004). *Evangelicals and Scripture: Tradition, Authority and Hermeneutics* (Downers Grove, IL: IVP).

Bakke, Raymond (1997). *A Theology as Big as the City* (Downers Grove, IL: IVP).

Ballard, P. (2009). 'Locating Chaplaincy: A Theological Note', *Crucible* (July–September), pp. 18–24.

Ballard, P., and J. Pritchard (1996). *Practical Theology in Action: Christian Thinking in the Service of Church and Society* (London: SPCK).

Ballard, P. H., S. R. Holmes and W. Elkins (eds) (2005). *The Bible in Pastoral Practice: Readings in the Place and Function of Scripture in the Church* (London: Darton, Longman & Todd).

Barker, Eileen (2012). 'Credo, Credis, Credit, Credimus, Creditis, Credunt'. Symposium, University of Kent, Canterbury, 2012.

Barrett, D. B. (2001). 'The Worldwide Holy Spirit Renewal'. In V. Synan (ed.), *The Century of the Holy Spirit: 100 Years of Pentecostal and Charismatic Renewal, 1901–2001* (Nashville, TN: Thomas Nelson), ch. 15.

Barry, F. R. (1998). 'Who Are Fit Persons?' In J. M. M. Francis and L. J. Francis (eds), *Tentmaking: Perspectives on Self-Supporting Ministry* (Leominster: Gracewing), pp. 77–80.

Barthes, Roland (1973). *Mythologies* (London: Paladin).

Barton, J. (1993). *People of the Book? The Authority of the Bible in Christianity*. Rev. edn (London: SPCK).

—— (ed.) (1998). *The Cambridge Companion to Biblical Interpretation* (Cambridge: Cambridge University Press).

Bass, Diana Butler (2004). *The Practicing Congregation: Imagining a New Old Church* (Herndon, VA: Alban Institute).

Bass, Dorothy C. (2010 (1997)). *Practicing Our Faith: A Way of Life for a Searching People* (San Francisco, CA: Jossey-Bass).

Beal, T. K. (ed.) (2015). *The Oxford Encyclopaedia of the Bible and the Arts* (New York: Oxford University Press).

Beavis, M. A., and M. J. Gilmour (eds) (2012). *Dictionary of the Bible and Western Culture* (Sheffield: Sheffield Phoenix Press).

Bechard, D. P. (ed., trans.) (2002). *The Scripture Documents: An Anthology of Official Catholic Teachings* (Collegeville, MN: Liturgical Press).

Bell, Duncan (2014). 'What Is Liberalism?', *Political Theory* 42.6, pp. 682–715.

Bellah, Robert (1985). *Habits of the Heart: Individualism and Commitment in American Life* (New York: Harper & Row).

Benhabib, Seyla (2004). *The Rights of Others: Aliens, Residents and Citizens* (Cambridge: Cambridge University Press).

Bialecki, J. (2011). 'Quiet Deliverances'. In M. Lindhardt (ed.), *Practicing the Faith: The Ritual Life of Pentecostal-Charismatic Christians* (New York and Oxford: Berghahn Books), ch. 9.

Bible Reading Fellowship (BRF) (2014). 'Anna Chaplaincy to Older People', *The Gift of Years*: <http://www.thegiftofyears.org.uk/anna-chaplaincy-older-people> (accessed 20 November 2015).

Billings, Alan (2009). *God and Community Cohesion: Help or Hindrance?* (London: SPCK).

Board for Mission and Unity (1986). *Priesthood of the Ordained Ministry* (London: Board for Mission and Unity).

Boff, Leonardo, and Clodovis Boff (1987). *Introducing Liberation Theology* (Maryknoll, NY: Orbis Books).

Boland, V., and T. McCarthy (eds) (2012). *The Word Is Flesh and Blood: The Eucharist and Sacred Scripture* (Dublin: Dominican Publications).

Bolman, Lee G., and Terrence E. Deal (2013). *Reframing Organizations* (San Francisco, CA: Jossey-Bass).

Bonzo, J. M., and M. R. Stevens. (2008). *Wendell Berry and the Cultivation of Life: A Reader's Guide* (Grand Rapids, MI: Brazos Press).

Bosch, D. (2011 (1991)). *Transforming Mission: Paradigm Shifts in Theology of Mission* (Maryknoll, NY: Orbis Books).

Bretherton, Luke (2010). *Christianity and Contemporary Politics* (Malden, MA, and Oxford: Wiley-Blackwell).

—— (2014). *Resurrecting Democracy: Faith, Citizenship, and the Politics of a Common Life* (Cambridge: Cambridge University Press).

Brettler, M. Z., P. Enns and D. J. Harrington (2013). *The Bible and the Believer: How to Read the Bible Critically and Religiously* (New York and Oxford: Oxford University Press).

Briggs, R. (2003). *Reading the Bible Wisely* (London: SPCK).

British Pain Society / Dr Foster Intelligence, *National Pain Audit Final Report 2010–12*. Available from: <https://www.britishpainsociety.org/static/uploads/resources/files/members_articles_npa_2012_1.pdf> (accessed 20 November 2015).

Bromiley, G. W. (1957). *Sacramental Teaching and Practice in the Reformation Churches* (Grand Rapids, MI: Eerdmans).

Brophy, Don (2010). *Catherine of Siena: A Passionate Life* (New York: BlueBridge).

Brown, Callum G. (2001). *The Death of Christian Britain* (London: Routledge).

—— (2015). 'An Oral History of Becoming Secular: How Anglicans Lose Religion'. In Abby Day (ed.), *Contemporary Issues in the Worldwide Anglican Communion: Powers and Pieties* (Farnham: Ashgate), pp. 245–66.

Brown, Callum G., and Michael Snape (eds) (2010). *Secularisation in the Christian World* (Farnham: Ashgate).

Brown, Candy Gunther (ed.) (2011). *Global Pentecostal and Charismatic Healing* (New York: Oxford University Press).

Brown, J. (2011). 'Pentecostalism and Deliverance or Exorcism? Narratives from the Beneficiaries and Benafactors (*sic*) in Lagos, Nigeria'. Paper presented at the Nigeria Pentecostal and Charismatic Research Conference, 12–13 December: <http://www.academia.edu/5210947/PENTECOSTALISM_AND_DELIVERANCE_OR_EXORCISM_NARRATIVES_FROM_THE_BENEFICIARIES_AND_BENAFACTORS_IN_LAGOS_NIGERIA> (accessed 14 April 2016).

Browning, D. S. (1996). *A Fundamental Practical Theology: Descriptive and Strategic Proposals* (Minneapolis, MN: Augsburg).

Browning, Don (1985). 'Practical Theology and Political Theology'. *Theology Today* 42(1), pp. 1–5.

Brueggemann, Walter (2004–7). 'Scripture: Old Testament'. In Peter Scott and William T. Cavanaugh (eds), *The Blackwell Companion to Political Theology* (Oxford: Blackwell), pp. 7–20.

Brugger, E. Christian (2014). *Capital Punishment and Roman Catholic Moral Tradition*. 2nd edn (Notre Dame, IN: University of Notre Dame Press).

Bunting, Ian (1996). *Models of Ministry: Managing the Church Today*. Grove Pastoral Series 54 (Cambridge: Grove Books).

Burleson, B. R. (2009). 'The Nature of Interpersonal Communication: A Message-Centered Approach'. In C. R. Berger, M. E. Roloff and D. R. Roskos-Ewoldsen (eds), *The Handbook of Communication Science*. 2nd edn (Thousand Oaks, CA, and London: Sage), pp. 145– 63.

Cadge, W. (2012). 'Possibilities and Limits of Medical Science: Debates over Double-Blind Clinical Trials of Intercessory Prayer'. *Zygon* 47, pp. 43–64.

Cahill, Lisa Sowle (2013). *Global Justice, Christology and Christian Ethics* (Cambridge and New York: Cambridge University Press).

Carens, Joseph (2013). *The Ethics of Immigration* (Oxford: Oxford University Press).

Carr, W. (2008 (1989)). *The Pastor as Theologian: The Formation of Today's Ministry in the Light of Contemporary Human Sciences* (London: SPCK).

—— (ed.) (1992). *Say One for Me: The Church of England in the Next Decade* (London: SPCK).

Carroll, Jackson W., Carl S. Dudley and William McKinney (eds) (1986). *Handbook for Congregational Studies* (Nashville, TN: Abingdon Press, 1986).

Cartledge, M. (2011). 'Demonology and Deliverance: A Practical-Theological Case Study'. In W. K. Kay and R. Parry (eds), *Exorcism and Deliverance: Multi-Disciplinary Studies* (Milton Keynes: Paternoster), ch. 12.

Castells, Manuel (2000). *The Rise of the Network Society: The Information Age: Economy, Society and Culture, vol. 1.* 2nd edn (Oxford: Blackwell).

Castles, Stephen, and Mark J. Miller (2009). *The Age of Migration: International Population Movements in the Modern World.* 4th edn (New York and London: Guilford Press).

Cavanaugh, William (1998). *Torture and Eucharist: Theology, Politics, and the Body of Christ* (Malden, MA and Oxford: Blackwell).

—— (2011). *Migrations of the Holy: God, State, and the Political Meaning of the Church* (Grand Rapids, MI: Eerdmans).

Chagnon, Napoleon A. (1981 (1968)). *Yanomamö: The Fierce People* (New York: Holt, Rinehart & Winston).

Chapman, M. D. (2015). 'Liberal Readings of the Bible and Their Conservative Responses'. In J. Riches (ed.), *The New Cambridge History of the Bible: From 1750 to the Present* (Cambridge: Cambridge University Press), pp. 208–19.

Cheng, Patrick (2011). *Radical Love: Introduction to Queer Theology* (New York: Seabury Press).

Clark-King, Ellen (2004). *Theology by Heart: Women, the Church and God* (Peterborough: Epworth Press).

Cobb, Mark, Chris Swift and Andrew Todd (2015). 'Introduction to Chaplaincy Studies'. In C. Swift, A. Todd and M. Cobb (eds), *A Handbook of Chaplaincy Studies: Understanding Spiritual Care in Public Places* (Farnham: Ashgate).

Cochrane, A. L. (1972). *Effectiveness and Efficiency: Random Reflections on Health Services* (s.l.: The Nuffield Provincial Hospitals Trust).

Cohen, M. Z., and A. Berlin (eds) (2016). *Interpreting Scriptures in Judaism, Christianity, and Islam: Overlapping Inquiries* (Cambridge: Cambridge University Press).

Coleman, Simon, and Peter Collins (2006). *Locating the Field? Changing Contexts of Fieldwork and Ethnography.* ASA Series (Oxford: Berg).

Coleman, Simon, and Pauline von Hellermann (2011). *Multi-sited Ethnography: Problems and Possibilities in the Translocation of Research Methods* (London: Routledge).

Coles, Romand (2005). *Beyond Gated Politics: Reflections for the Possibility of Democracy* (Minneapolis: University of Minnesota Press).

Collicutt, Joanna (2015). *The Psychology of Christian Character Formation* (London: SCM).

Collins, J. (2011). 'Deliverance and Exorcism in the Twentieth Century'. In W. K. Kay and R. Parry (eds), *Exorcism and Deliverance: Multi-Disciplinary Studies* (Milton Keynes: Paternoster), ch. 4.

Collins-Mayo, Sylvia, Andrew King and Lee Jones (2012). Faith in Action: Street Pastors Kingston Social and Spiritual Impact Project (London: Kingston University).

Cone, James H. (1977). *God of the Oppressed* (London: SPCK).

—— (1990). *A Black Theology of Liberation* (Maryknoll, NY: Orbis Books).

—— (1997). *Black Theology, Black Power* (Maryknoll, NY: Orbis Books).

—— (2011). *The Cross and The Lynching Tree* (Maryknoll, NY: Orbis Books).

Congar, Yves (1967). *True and False Reform in the Church* (Collegeville, MN: Liturgical Press).

Corsini, Raymond, and Danny Wedding (2010). *Current Psychotherapies* (Belmont, CA: Cengage Learning).

Cotterell, John (2007). *Social Networks in Youth and Adolescence* (Hove: Routledge).

Cox, Harvey (1965). *The Secular City: Secularization and Urbanization in Theological Perspective* (New York: Macmillan).

Craig, W. L., and J. P. Moreland (2003). *Philosophical Foundations for a Christian Worldview* (Downers Grove, IL: IVP).

Cranmer, F. (2015). 'Chaplaincy and the Law'. In C. Swift, A. Todd and M. Cobb (eds), *A Handbook of Chaplaincy Studies: Understanding Spiritual Care in Public Places* (Farnham: Ashgate).

Crenshaw, Kimberlé (1989). 'Demarginalizing the Intersection of Race and Sex: A Black Feminist Critique of Antidiscrimination Doctrine, Feminist Theory, and Antiracist Politics', *University of Chicago Legal Forum* 140, pp. 139–67.

Croft, S. J. L. (2008). *Ministry in Three Dimensions: Ordination and Leadership in the Local Church* (London: Darton, Longman & Todd).

Cushman, Philip (1995). *Constructing the Self, Constructing America: A Cultural History of Psychotherapy* (Boston: Addison-Wesley).

Dale, M. (2010). 'Pennsylvania Couple Convicted after Using Only Prayer, Not Medicine, for Dying Toddler'. *Associated Press*: <http://www.cleveland.com/nation/index.ssf/2010/12/pennsylvania_couple_convicted.html> (accessed 1 November 2015).

Daniélou, J. (1960 (1951)). *The Bible and the Liturgy* (London: Darton, Longman & Todd).

Davie, Grace (2015). *Religion in Britain: A Persistent Paradox* (Chichester: Wiley-Blackwell).

Davies, Douglas J. (2002). *Anthropology and Theology* (Oxford: Berg).

Day, Abby (2005). 'Doing Theodicy: An Empirical Study of a Women's Prayer Group', *Journal of Contemporary Religion* 20.3, pp. 343–56.

—— (2012). 'Extraordinary Relationality: Ancestor Veneration in Late Euro-American Society', *Nordic Journal of Religion and Society* 25.2, pp. 57–69.

—— (2015). 'The Spirit of "Generation A": Older Laywomen in the Church', *Modern Believing* 56.3, pp. 313–23.

—— (2017). *The Religious Lives of Older Laywomen: The Last Active Anglican Generation* (Oxford: Oxford University Press).

Day, Abby, and Simon Coleman (2016). 'Textbooks for Teaching the Anthropology of Religion: A Review', *Religion* 46.2, pp. 209–20.

DeArteaga, W. (1996). *Quenching the Spirit: Discover the REAL Spirit behind the Charismatic Controversy* (Orlando, FL: Creation House).

Doehring, C. (2015). *The Practice of Pastoral Care: A Postmodern Approach* (Louisville, KY: Westminster John Knox Press).

Donnelly, M. (2005). *Sixties Britain: Culture, Society and Politics* (Harlow: Pearson Education).

Dorrien, Gary (2008). *Social Ethics in the Making: Interpreting an American Tradition* (Oxford: Wiley-Blackwell).

Dudley, Carl S. (2003). *Effective Small Churches in the Twenty-first Century* (Nashville, TN: Abingdon Press).

Duffy, Eamon (1992). *The Stripping of the Altars: Traditional Religion in England 1400–1580* (New Haven, CT: Yale University Press).

Dunlap, S. J. (2011). 'Culture-Coded Care: Ecclesial Beliefs, Practices, and Artifacts in Response to Illness'. In J. F. Maynard, L. Hummel and M. C. Moschella (eds), *Pastoral Bearings: Lived Religion and Pastoral Theology*. Paperback edn (Lanham, MD: Lexington Books).

Eagleton, T. (2009). *Reason, Faith, and Revolution: Reflections on the God Debate* (London: Yale University Press).

Ecclestone, Giles (ed.) (1988). *The Parish Church? Explorations in the Relationship of the Church and the World* (London and Oxford: Mowbray).

Etchells, R. (1995). *Set My People Free: A Lay Challenge to the Churches* (London: Fount/HarperCollins).

Evans-Hills, Bonnie, and Michael Rusk (2015). *Engaging Islam from a Christian Perspective* (New York: Peter Lang).

Evans-Pritchard, E. E. (1976 (1937)). *Witchcraft, Oracles, and Magic among the Azande* (Oxford: Clarendon Press).

Fant, C. E., and M. G. Reddish (2008). *Lost Treasures of the Bible: Understanding the Bible through Archaeological Artifacts in World Museums* (Grand Rapids, MI, and Cambridge: Eerdmans).

Farber-Robertson, Anita (2000). *Learning while Leading: Increasing Your Effectiveness in Ministry* (Herndon, VA: Alban Institute).

Fitchett, G., and S. Nolan (2015). *Spiritual Care in Practice: Case Studies in Healthcare Chaplaincy* (London: Jessica Kingsley).

Fitzmaurice, J. (2016). *Virtue Ecclesiology: An Exploration in the Good Church* (Farnham: Ashgate).

Floyd-Thomas, Stacey (ed.) (2006). *Deeper Shades of Purple: Womanism in Religion and Society* (New York: New York University Press).

Fonow, Mary Margaret, and Judith A. Cook (1991). *Beyond Methodology: Feminist Scholarship as Lived Research* (Bloomington: Indiana University Press).

Ford, D. (2007). 'An Interfaith Wisdom: Scriptural Reasoning between Jews, Christians and Muslims'. In *Christian Wisdom: Desiring God and Learning in Love* (Cambridge: Cambridge University Press), pp. 273–303.

Foster, Charles R., Lisa E. Dahill, Lawrence A. Golemon and Barbara Wang Tolentino (2006). *Educating Clergy: Teaching Practice and Pastoral Imagination* (San Francisco, CA: Jossey-Bass).

Foster, Richard (1998 (1978)). *Celebration of Discipline: The Path to Spiritual Growth* (San Francisco: HarperSanFrancisco).

Fowler, Chris (2004). *The Archaeology of Personhood: An Anthropological Approach* (London: Routledge).

Fowler, J. (1981). *Stages of Faith: The Psychology of Human Development and the Quest for Meaning* (San Francisco, CA: Harper & Row).

Francis, Leslie J., Peter Hills and Christopher J. F. Rutledge (2008). 'Clergy Work-related Satisfactions in Parochial Ministry: The Influence of Personality and Churchmanship'. *Mental Health, Religion & Culture* 11.3 (April), pp. 327–39.

Francis, Leslie J., and S. H. Jones (1996). *Psychological Perspectives on Christian Ministry: A Reader* (Leominster: Gracewing / Fowler Wright).

Francis, Leslie J., and William K. Kay (1995). *Teenage Religion and Values* (Leominster: Gracewing / Fowler Wright).

Freire, Paulo (1972). *Pedagogy of the Oppressed* (Harmondsworth: Penguin, 1972).

—— (1973). *Education for Critical Consciousness* (New York: Seabury Press).

Fretheim, T. E. (1999). 'To Say Something – about God, Evil, and Suffering'. *Word and World* 19.4, pp. 339, 345–50.

Freud, Sigmund (1964 (1937)). 'Constructions in Analysis'. In *The Standard Edition of the Complete Psychological Works of Sigmund Freud: Volume XXIII (1937–1939)* (London: Hogarth Press).

Frey, John Carlos (director) and Daniel G. Groody (executive producer) (2008). *One Border, One Body: Immigration and the Eucharist* (Gatekeeper Films).

Frye, Northrop (1957). *Anatomy of Criticism: Four Essays* (Princeton, NJ: Princeton University Press).

Fulkerson, Mary McClintock (2007). *Places of Redemption: Theology for a Worldly Church* (Oxford: Oxford University Press).

Gadamer, Hans-Georg (1977). *Philosophical Hermeneutics* (Berkeley: University of California Press).

Ganzevoort, R. R., and J. Roeland (2014). 'Lived Religion: The Praxis of Practical Theology'. *International Journal of Practical Theology* 18, pp. 91–101.

Gardner, Howard, Mihaly Csikszentmihalyi and William Damon (2001). *Good Work: When Excellence and Ethics Meet* (New York: Basic Books).

Gecan, Michael (2008). *Effective Organizing for Congregational Renewal* (Skokie, IL: Acta Publications).

Gecan, Michael (2012). *Going Public* (Boston, MA: Beacon Press).

Gibson-Graham, J. K. (2006). *A Postcapitalist Politics* (Minneapolis: University of Minnesota Press).

Gill, Robin (2006). *Health Care and Christian Ethics* (Cambridge: Cambridge University Press).

—— (2012). *Theology in a Social Context: Sociological Theology, vol. 1* (Farnham: Ashgate).

—— (2013). *Society Shaped by Theology: Sociological Theology, vol. 3* (Farnham: Ashgate).

Gilroy, Paul (2002 (1987)). *There Ain't No Black in the Union Jack: The Cultural Politics of Race and Nation* (London: Routledge).

—— (2005). *Postcolonial Melancholia* (New York: Columbia University Press).

Glover, J. A. (2008). 'The Incidence of Tonsillectomy in School Children'. *International Journal of Epidemiology* 37, pp. 9–19.

Gooder, P., and M. Perham (2013). *Echoing the Word: The Bible in the Eucharist* (London: SPCK).

Gortner, David (2003). 'How Congregational Size Changes Congregational Climate', presented at the American Psychological Association Annual Meeting, Toronto, Ontario.

—— (2009). *Around One Table: Exploring Episcopal Identity* (Stanford, CA: College for Bishops / CREDO Institute Inc.): <https://www.episcopalchurch.org/files/aot_report.pdf> (accessed 21 December 2018).

—— (2013). *Varieties of Personal Theology* (Burlington, VT: Ashgate/Routledge).

—— (2014). 'Devolution: The Dynamics of Power and Permission'. *Network of Episcopal Clergy Associations*: <www.forma.church/blog/devolution-the-dynamics-of-power-and-permission-by-the-rev-dr-david-t-gortner/>.

Graham, E. (2013). 'Is Practical Theology a Form of "Action Research"?' *International Journal of Practical Theology* 17, pp. 148–78.

Graves, Mike (ed.) (2004). *What's the Matter with Preaching Today?* (Louisville, KY: Westminster John Knox Press).

Green, L. (1990). *Let's Do Theology: A Pastoral Cycle Resource Book* (London: Mowbray).

Green, M. (2004). *I Believe in the Holy Spirit* (Eastbourne: Kingsway Communications).

Greenhalgh, T., J. Howick and N. Maskrey (2014). 'Evidence Based Medicine: A Movement in Crisis?' *BMJ: British Medical Journal* 348. doi:10.1136/bmj.g3725.

Greenwood, R. (1994). *Transforming Priesthood: A New Theology of Mission and Ministry* (London: SPCK).

Gregory, Eric (2008). *Politics and the Order of Love: An Augustinian Ethic of Democratic Citizenship* (Chicago, IL and London: University of Chicago Press).

Grierson, Denham (1985). *Transforming a People of God* (Melbourne: Joint Board of Christian Education of Australia and New Zealand).

Groody, Daniel (2007). *Globalization, Spirituality, and Justice: Navigating the Path to Peace* (Maryknoll, NY: Orbis Books).

The Guardian (2014): <http://www.theguardian.com/money/2014/mar/21/vicars-greatest-job-satisfaction-publicans-least-happy> (accessed 21 October 2015).

Gutiérrez, Gustavo (1974). *A Theology of Liberation* (London: SCM Press).

—— (2003). 'The Situation and Tasks of Liberation Theology Today', trans. J. B. Nickoloff. In Joerg Rieger (ed.), *Opting for the Margins: Postmodernity and Liberation in Christian Theology* (Oxford: Oxford University Press).

Hadot, Pierre (1995). *Philosophy as a Way of Life* (Malden, MA: Blackwell).

Hahnenberg, Edward (2010). *Awakening Vocation: A Theology of Christian Calling* (Collegeville, MN: Liturgical Press).

Haker, Hille (2009). 'Narrative Ethics in Health Care Chaplaincy'. In Walter Moczynski, Hille Haker and Katrin Bentele (eds), *Medical Ethics in Health Care Chaplaincy* (Münster: Lit Verlag).

Hale, W. H. (1850). *The Duties of the Deacons and Priests in the Church of England Compared: With Suggestions for the Extension of the Order of Deacons and the Establishment of Sub-Deacons* (London: Francis and John Rivington).

Haraldsson, Erlendur (2006). 'Popular Psychology, Belief in Life after Death and Reincarnation in the Nordic Countries, Western and Eastern Europe'. *Nordic Psychology* 58.2, pp. 171–80.

Hardt, Michael, and Antonio Negri (2001). *Empire* (Cambridge, MA: Harvard University Press).

Hardy, A. C. (1979). *The Spiritual Nature of Man: A Study of Religious Experience* (Oxford: Oxford University Press).

Harris, H. A. (1998). *Fundamentalism and Evangelicals* (Oxford: Oxford University Press).

Harrison, B., and C. Robb (1985). *Making the Connections: Essays in Feminist Social Ethics* (Boston, MA: Beacon Press).

Hauerwas, Stanley (1981). *A Community of Character: Toward a Constructive Christian Ethics* (Notre Dame, IN: Notre Dame University Press).

—— (2001). *With the Grain of the Universe: The Church's Witness and Natural Theology* (Grand Rapids, MI: Brazos and London: SCM Press).

—— (2004). *Performing the Faith: Bonhoeffer and the Practice of Nonviolence* (London: SPCK).

Hauerwas, Stanley, and William Willimon (1989). *Resident Aliens: Life in the Christian Colony* (Nashville, TN: Abingdon Press).

Hay, David (1982). *Exploring Inner Space: Scientists and Experience* (Harmondsworth: Penguin).

Headlam, Stewart (1921). *Theological Education at the Universities* (Oxford: Blackwell).

Healy, Nicholas M. (2014). *Hauerwas: A (Very) Critical Introduction* (Grand Rapids, MI: Eerdmans).

Hebden, Keith (2017). *Re-enchanting the Activist: Spirituality and Social Change* (London: Jessica Kingsley).

Heifetz, Ronald A., Marty Linsky and Alexander Grashow (2009). *The Practice of Adaptive Leadership: Tools and Tactics for Changing Your Organization and the World* (Cambridge, MA: Harvard University Press).

Henderson, Stewart (1996). 'Priestly Duties', *Limited Edition* (London: Plover Books).

Hill, G. B. (2000). 'Archie Cochrane and His Legacy: An Internal Challenge to Physicians' Autonomy?' *Journal of Clinical Epidemiology* 53, pp. 1189–92.

Hill, M., R. Sandberg and N. Doe (2014). *Religion and Law in the United Kingdom*, 2nd edn (The Hague: Wolters Kluwer).

Hills, Sarah Ann (2015). 'A Theology of Restitution as Embodied Reconciliation: A Study of Restitution in a Reconciliation Process in Worcester, South Africa' (unpublished PhD thesis, Durham University).

Hoggarth, P. et al. (eds) (2013). *Bible in Mission* (Oxford: Regnum Books International).

Holifield, E. Brooks (2005). *A History of Pastoral Care in America* (Eugene, OR: Wipf & Stock).

Hook, W. F. (1851). *What Are the Best Means of Reclaiming Our Lost Population? A Report Presented to the Ruri-Decanal Chapter of Leeds from a Committee of That Body* (Leeds: Thomas Harrison).

Hooker, Richard (1902 (1597)). *Of the Laws of Ecclesiastical Polity: The Fifth Book* (London: Macmillan).

Hoover, Stewart M. (2001). 'Visual Religion in Media Culture'. In David Morgan and Sally M. Promey (eds), *The Visual Culture of American Religions* (Berkeley: University of California Press), pp. 146–59.

Hopewell, James (1987). *Congregation: Stories and Structures* (Philadelphia, PA: Fortress Press).

Horrell, David G. (2016 (2005)). *Solidarity and Difference: A Contemporary Reading of Paul's Ethics.* 2nd edn (London: Bloomsbury T&T Clark).

House of Bishops (1997). *Eucharistic Presidency* (London: Church House Publishing).

Inglehart, Ronald (1990). *Culture Shift in Advanced Industrial Society* (Princeton, NJ: Princeton University Press).

Isasi Díaz, Ada María (1998). 'Solidarity: Love of Neighbor in the 21st Century'. In Susan Brooke Thistlethwaite and Mary Potter Engels (eds), *Lift Every Voice: Constructing Christian Theologies from the Underside.* Rev. edn (Maryknoll, NY: Orbis), pp. 30–9.

Jacobsen, Dennis A. (2001). *Doing Justice: Congregations and Community Organizing* (Minneapolis, MN: Fortress).

Janis, I. (1982). *Groupthink: Psychological Studies of Policy Decisions and Fiascos.* 2nd edn (Orlando, FL: Houghton Mifflin).

Jenkins, Willis (2013). *The Future of Ethics: Sustainability, Social Justice, and Religious Creativity* (Washington, DC: Georgetown University Press).

Johnson, B. (2003). *When Heaven Invades Earth: A Practical Guide to a Life of Miracles* (Shippensburg, PA: Destiny Image).

Johnson, T. M. et al. (eds) (2002). *World Christian Encyclopedia: A Comparative Survey of Churches and Religions in the Modern World.* 2 vols (New York: Oxford University Press).

Jones, A. (2000). *A Thousand Years of the English Parish: Medieval Patterns and Modern Interpretations* (Moreton-in-Marsh: Windrush Press).

Kadushin, Charles (2012 (1966/1968)). *Understanding Social Networks: Theories, Concepts, and Findings* (Oxford and New York: Oxford University Press).

Kaplan, Abraham (1964). *The Conduct of Inquiry: Methodology for Behavioral Science* (New York: Harper & Row).

Karamanolis, G. E. (2013). *The Philosophy of Early Christianity* (Durham: Acumen).

Kay, W. K. (2007) *Apostolic Networks in Britain: New Ways of Being Church* (Milton Keynes: Paternoster).

—— (2009). *Pentecostalism* (London: SCM Press).

Kelly, H. H. (1916). 'The Pattern of the Early Church: The Formation of Ministry'. *The East and the West* 14, pp. 429–39.

Kevern, P., and W. McSherry (2015). 'The Study of Chaplaincy: Methods and Materials'. In C. Swift, A. Todd and M. Cobb (eds), *A Handbook of Chaplaincy Studies: Understanding Spiritual Care in Public Places* (Farnham: Ashgate).

King Jr, Martin Luther (1964). 'Letter from Birmingham Jail'. In *Why We Can't Wait* (New York: Harper & Row).

Kornfeld, Margaret (2012 (2000)). *Cultivating Wholeness: A Guide to Care and Counseling in Faith Communities* (New York: Continuum).

Kraft, C. H. (2002). 'Spiritual Warfare: A Neocharismatic Perspective'. In S. M. Burgess (ed.), *The New International Dictionary of Pentecostal and Charismatic Movements*. Rev. edn (Grand Rapids, MI: Zondervan), pp. 1091–6.

Krucoff, M. W., S. W. Crater, D. Gallup, J. C. Blankenship, M. Cuffe, M. Guarneri, R. A. Krieger, V. R. Kshettry, K. Morris, M. Oz, A. Pichard, M. H. Sketch Jr, H. G. Koenig, D. Mark and K. L. Lee (2005). 'Music, Imagery, Touch, and Prayer as Adjuncts to Interventional Cardiac Care: The Monitoring and Actualisation of Noetic Trainings (MANTRA) II Randomised Study'. *The Lancet* 366, pp. 211–17.

Kwok Pui-lan (2005). *Postcolonial Imagination and Feminist Theology* (Louisville, KY: Westminster John Knox Press).

—— (ed.) (2010). *Hope Abundant: Third World and Indigenous Women's Theology* (Maryknoll, NY: Orbis Books).

Kymlicka, Will (2001). *Politics in the Vernacular: Nationalism, Multiculturalism and Citizenship* (Oxford: Oxford University Press).

Lambek, Michael (ed.) (2002). *A Reader in the Anthropology of Religion* (Malden, MA: Blackwell).

Lambert, Michael (2013). 'The Efficacy and Effectiveness of Psychotherapy'. In *Bergin and Garfield's Handbook of Psychotherapy and Behavior Change*. 6th edn (Somerset, NJ: John Wiley & Sons), pp. 169–218.

Lambeth Conference (1958). *Resolution 89* (The Lambeth Conference: London).

Lange, F. D. (2015). *Loving Later Life: An Ethics of Aging* (Grand Rapids, MI: Eerdmans).

Lasch, Christopher (1979). *The Culture of Narcissism: American Life in an Age of Diminishing Expectations* (New York: W. W. Norton).

Law, D. R. (2012). *Historical Critical Method: A Guide for the Perplexed* (London: T&T Clark).

Lechner, Frank J., and John Boli (eds) (2008). *The Globalization Reader*. 3rd edn (Oxford: Blackwell).

Leech, K. (1997). *The Sky Is Red: Discerning the Signs of the Times* (London: Darton, Longman & Todd).

Levenson, J. D. (1993). *The Hebrew Bible, the Old Testament, and Historical Criticism: Jews and Christians in Biblical Studies* (Louisville, KY: Westminster John Knox Press).

Lévy-Bruhl, L. (1926). *How Natives Think* (London: George Allen & Unwin).

Lewin, Kurt (1951). *Field Theory in Social Science: Selected Theoretical Papers* (New York: Harper & Row).

Lewis-Anthony, J. (2009). *If You Meet George Herbert on the Road, Kill Him: Radically Re-thinking Priestly Ministry* (London: Mowbray).

—— (2013). *You Are the Messiah and I Should Know: Why Leadership Is a Myth (and Probably a Heresy)* (London: Bloomsbury).

Liardon, R. (1996). *God's Generals: Why They Succeeded and Why Some Failed* (Tulsa, OK: Albury).

Libreria Editrice Vaticana (2003). 'Catechism of the Catholic Church': <http://www.vatican.va/archive/ENG0015/_INDEX.HTM>.

Lin, Nan (2001). *Social Capital: A Theory of Social Structure and Action* (New York: Cambridge University Press).

Lindhardt, M. (ed.) (2011). *Practicing the Faith: The Ritual Life of Pentecostal-Charismatic Christians* (New York and Oxford: Berghahn Books).

Linthicum, Robert C. (2003). *Transforming Power: Biblical Strategies for Making a Difference in Your Community* (Downers Grove, IL: IVP).

Long, S. S., and J. F. A. Sawyer (2015). *The Bible in Music: A Dictionary of Songs, Works, and More* (Lanham, MD: Rowman & Littlefield).

Lorde, Audre (2007). *Sister Outsider* (Berkeley, CA: Crossing Press).

Lovin, Robin W. (1995). *Reinhold Niebuhr and Christian Realism* (New York and Cambridge: Cambridge University Press).

—— (2003). 'Reinhold Niebuhr in Contemporary Scholarship: A Review Essay'. *Journal of Religious Ethics* 31.3, pp. 489–505.

—— (2008). *Christian Realism and the New Realities* (New York and Cambridge: Cambridge University Press).

Luhrmann, Tanya M. (1989). *Persuasions of the Witch's Craft* (Cambridge, MA: Harvard University Press).

—— (2007). 'How Do You Learn to Know That It Is God Who Speaks?' In D. Berliner and R. Sarró (eds), *Learning Religion: Anthropological Approaches* (New York and Oxford: Berghahn Books), pp. 83–102.

Lyall, D. (2001). *The Integrity of Pastoral Care* (London: SPCK).

Lytch, Carol E. (2003). *Choosing Church: What Makes a Difference for Teens* (Louisville, KY: Westminster John Knox Press).

McAdams, Dan P. (2013). *The Redemptive Self: Stories Americans Live By*. Rev. edn (New York: Oxford University Press).

Macchia, F. D. (2002). 'Theology, Pentecostal'. In S. M. Burgess (ed.), *The New International Dictionary of Pentecostal and Charismatic Movements*. Rev. edn (Grand Rapids, MI: Zondervan), pp. 1120–41.

McGee, G. B. (2001). 'To the Regions Beyond: The Global Expansion of Pentecostalism'. In V. Synan (ed.), *The Century of the Holy Spirit: 100 Years of Pentecostal and Charismatic Renewal, 1901–2001* (Nashville, TN: Thomas Nelson), ch. 4.

MacIntyre, Alasdair (1981). *After Virtue: A Study in Moral Theory* (London: Duckworth).

McKenzie, S. L. (ed.) (2013). *The Oxford Encyclopedia of Biblical Interpretation*. 2 vols (New York: Oxford University Press).

McKim, D. K. (ed.) (1988). *Historical Handbook of Major Biblical Interpreters* (Downers Grove, IL, and Leicester: IVP).

McKnight, John, and Peter Block (2010). *The Abundant Community* (San Francisco, CA: Berrett-Koehler).

McNair Scott, B. G. (2014). *Apostles Today: Making Sense of Contemporary Charismatic Apostolates: A Historical and Theological Appraisal* (Eugene, OR: Pickwick).

MacNutt, F. (1989). *Healing* (London: Hodder & Stoughton).

—— (1996). *Deliverance from Evil Spirits* (London: Hodder & Stoughton).

Malinowski, Bronislaw (1961 (1922)). *Argonauts of the Western Pacific* (New York: E. P. Dutton).

—— (1967). *A Diary in the Strict Sense of the Term* (London: The Athlone Press).

Malphurs, Aubrey (2011). *The Nuts and Bolts of Church Planting: A Guide for Starting any Kind of Church* (Grand Rapids, MI: Baker).

Mann, Alice (2001). *Raising the Roof: The Pastoral-to-Program Size Transition* (Lanham, MD: Rowman & Littlefield).

Mansfield, S. (2005). *Derek Prince: A Biography* (Milton Keynes: Authentic Media).

Mantle, J. (2000). *Britain's First Worker-Priests: Radical Ministry in a Post-War Setting* (London: SCM Press).

Markham, Ian, and Oran Warder (2016). *An Introduction to Ministry: A Primer for Renewed Life and Leadership in Mainline Protestant Congregations* (Oxford: Wiley-Blackwell).

Marlow, K., B. Winder and H. J. Elliott (2015). 'Working with Transgendered Sex Offenders: Prison Staff Experiences'. *Journal of Forensic Practice* 17.3, pp. 241–54.

Marriott, McKim (1976). 'Hindu Transactions: Diversity without Dualism'. In B. Kapferer (ed.), *Transaction and Meaning: Directions in the Anthropology of Human Issues* (Philadelphia, PA: Institute for the Study of Human Issues), pp. 109–42.

Marwick, A. (1998). *The Sixties: Cultural Revolution in Britain, France, Italy and United States, c.1958–c.1974* (Oxford: Oxford University Press).

Maslow, Abraham H. (1966). *The Psychology of Science: A Reconnaissance* (New York: Harper & Row).

Mead, Loren (2004). 'Lay Ministry Is at a Dead End'. *LayNet* 15.

Mead, Margaret (1928). *Coming of Age in Samoa: A Psychological Study of Primitive Youth for Western Civilisation* (New York: W. Morrow & Co.).

Mercer, Joyce Ann (2008). *Girltalk, Godtalk: Why Faith Matters to Teenage Girls –
and Their Parents* (San Francisco, CA: Jossey-Bass).

Meyer, Birgit (2015). *Sensational Movies: Video, Vision, and Christianity in Ghana*
(Berkeley and Los Angeles: University of California Press).

Midgley, M. A. (2014). *Are You an Illusion?* (Abingdon: Routledge).

Miles, Sara (2008). *Take This Bread: A Radical Conversion* (New York: Ballantine).

Miller, D. E., and T. Yamamori (2007). *Global Pentecostalism: The New Face of
Christian Social Engagement* (London: University of California Press).

Miller-McLemore, Bonnie J. (ed.) (2014). *The Wiley-Blackwell Companion to
Practical Theology* (Malden, MA: Wiley-Blackwell).

Ministry Division (2011). *Criteria for Selection for the Ordained Ministry in
the Church of England* (London: Ministry Division of the Archbishop's
Council).

Mitchell, Jolyon (2004). 'From Morality Tales to Horror Movies'. In Peter Horsfield,
Mary E. Hess and Adán M. Medrano (eds), *Belief in Media: Cultural Perspectives
on Media and Christianity* (Aldershot: Ashgate), pp. 107–20.

—— (2007). *Media Violence and Christian Ethics* (Cambridge: Cambridge
University Press).

—— (2007). 'Questioning Media and Religion'. In Gordon Lynch (ed.), *Between
Sacred and Profane: Researching Religion and Popular Culture* (London and
New York: I. B. Tauris), pp. 34–46.

—— (2007). 'Towards an Understanding of the Popularity of West African Video
Film'. In Jolyon Mitchell and S. Brent Plate (eds), *The Religion and Film Reader*
(London and New York: Routledge), pp. 103–12 (abbreviated and updated ver-
sion of previous longer essay).

—— (2014). 'Filming the Ends of Martyrdom'. In Dominic Janes and Alex Houen
(eds), *Terrorism and Martyrdom from Pre-Modern to Contemporary Perspectives*
(Oxford: Oxford University Press), pp. 271–90.

Moberly, R. C. (1897). *Ministerial Priesthood* (London: John Murray).

Modood, Tariq (2005). *Multicultural Politics: Racism, Ethnicity and Muslims in
Britain* (Edinburgh: Edinburgh University Press).

Moriarty, G., and L. Hoffman (2007). *God Image Handbook for Spiritual Counseling
and Psychotherapy: Research, Theory and Practice* (Binghamton, NY: Routledge/
Haworth).

Morton, Nelle. 'The Journey Is Home': <http://actsofhope.blogspot.co.uk/2007/08/
hearing-to-speech.html>

Moschella, Mary Clark (2008). *Ethnography as a Pastoral Practice: An Introduction*
(Cleveland, OH: Pilgrim Press).

Myers, Ched (1988). *Binding the Strong Man: A Political Reading of Mark's Story of
Jesus* (Maryknoll, NY: Orbis Books).

Newitt, Mark (2014). 'New Directions in Hospital Chaplaincy: Chaplains – the
Church's Embedded Apologists?' *Theology* 117.6, pp. 417–25.

Niebuhr, Reinhold (1945). *The Children of Light and the Children of Darkness*
(London: Nisbet).

—— (1951). *Christ and Culture* (New York: Harper & Brothers).

—— (1953). *Christian Realism and Political Problems* (London: Faber & Faber).

Novak, Michael (1982). *The Spirit of Democratic Capitalism* (New York: American Enterprise Institute / Simon & Schuster).

Nussbaum, Martha (1994). *The Therapy of Desire: Theory and Practice in Hellenistic Ethics* (Princeton, NJ: Princeton University Press).

Nye, R. (2009). *Children's Spirituality: What It Is and Why It Matters* (London: Church House Publishing).

Nynäs, Mika Lassander, and Terhi Utriainen (eds) (2015). *Post-secular Society* (New Brunswick, NJ, and London: Transaction).

O'Donovan, Oliver (1996). *Desire of Nations: Rediscovering the Roots of Political Theology* (Cambridge: Cambridge University Press).

O'Neill, William (2016). 'The Place of Displacement: The Ethics of Migration in the United States'. In Agnes Brazal and María Teresa Davíla (eds), *Living With(out) Borders: Catholic Theological Ethics on the Migration of Peoples* (Maryknoll, NY: Orbis Books), pp. 67–77.

Obholzer, Anton, and Vega Zagier Roberts (1994). *The Unconscious at Work: Individual and Organizational Stress in the Human Services* (London: Routledge).

Oden, T. (1978). 'The Theology of Carl Rogers'. In *Kerygma and Counseling* (New York: Harper & Row), pp. 83–113.

Office for National Statistics (2011). Census: 'Changing Picture of Religious Affiliation over the Last Decade': <http://www.ons.gov.uk/ons/rel/census/2011-census/key-statistics-for-local-authorities-in-england-and-wales/rpt-reli gion.html#tab-Changing-picture-of-religious-affiliation-over-last-decade> (accessed 22 October 2015).

—— (2018). 'Table 1: Prevalence of Violence, by Type of Violence and Personal Characteristics, Year Ending March 2017 CSEW', *The Nature of Violent Crime: Appendix Tables*: <https://www.ons.gov.uk/peoplepopulationandcommunity/crimeandjustice/datasets/thenatureofviolentcrimeappendixtables> (accessed 18 October 2018).

Onyinah, O. (2010). 'Deliverance as a Way of Confronting Witchcraft in Modern Africa: Ghana as a Case History', *Cyberjournal for Pentecostal-Charismatic Research*, issue 10 (July): <http://www.pctii.org/cyberj/cyberj10/onyinah.html> (accessed 13 April 2016).

Osmer, Richard (2008). *Practical Theology: An Introduction* (Grand Rapids, MI and Cambridge: Eerdmans).

Owens, R. (2001). 'The Asuza Street Revival: The Pentecostal Movement Begins in America'. In V. Synan (ed.), *The Century of the Holy Spirit: 100 Years of Pentecostal and Charismatic Renewal, 1901–2001* (Nashville, TN: Thomas Nelson), ch. 3.

Paget, J. C., et al. (eds) (2012–16). *The New Cambridge History of the Bible*. 4 vols (Cambridge: Cambridge University Press).

Pappas, Anthony G. (1989). *Entering the World of the Small Church* (Herndon, VA: Alban Institute).

Pargament, K. I. (2011). *Spiritually-Integrated Psychotherapy: Understanding and Addressing the Sacred* (New York: Guilford Press).

Parker, R. (2001). *Healing Wounded History: Reconciling Peoples and Healing Places* (Cleveland, OH: Pilgrim Press).

Paterson, M. (2015). 'Supervision, Support and Self Practice'. In C. Swift, A. Todd and M. Cobb (eds), *A Handbook of Chaplaincy Studies: Understanding Spiritual Care in Public Places* (Farnham: Ashgate).

Pattison, S. (1997). *The Faith of the Managers: When Management Becomes Religion* (London: Cassell).

Pattison, S., M. Cooling and T. Cooling (2007). *Using the Bible in Christian Ministry: The Workbook* (London: Darton, Longman & Todd).

Paul, L. (1964). *The Deployment and the Payment of the Clergy* (London: Church Information Office).

Paulsell, Stephanie (2002). *Honoring the Body: Meditations on a Christian Practice* (San Francisco, CA: Jossey-Bass).

Percy, Emma (2014). *Mothering as a Metaphor for Ministry* (Farnham: Ashgate).

—— (2014). *What Clergy Do: Especially When It Looks Like Nothing* (London: SPCK).

Percy, Martyn (1996). *Power in the Church: Ecclesiology in an Age of Transition* (London: Cassell).

—— (2006). *Clergy: The Origin of Species* (London: Bloomsbury/Continuum).

—— (2006). *Engaging with Contemporary Culture: Christianity and the Concrete Church* (Aldershot: Ashgate).

—— (2010). *Shaping the Church: The Promise of Implicit Theology* (Aldershot: Ashgate).

—— (2011). 'Adventure and Atrophy in a Charismatic Movement: Returning to the "Toronto Blessing"'. In M. Lindhardt (ed.), *Practicing the Faith: The Ritual Life of Pentecostal-Charismatic Christians* (Oxford: Berghahn Books), ch. 5.

—— (2015). 'Theological Education and Formation for an Uncommon Occupation'. In Abby Day (ed.), *Contemporary Issues in the Worldwide Anglican Communion: Powers and Pieties* (Farnham: Ashgate), pp. 229–43.

—— (2016). 'On Not Re-arranging the Deckchairs on the *Titanic*: A Commentary on Reform and Renewal in the Church of England': <https://modernchurch.org.uk/worship/prayer-liturgy/cremation-rite-for-unborn-children/send/32-articles/768-on-not-rearranging-the-deckchairs-on-the-titanic> (accessed 2 March 2016).

Percy, Martyn, Ian Markham and Emma Percy (2015). 'Book Proposal: SPCK's *The Study of Ministry*'.

Perkins, John M. (ed.) (1995). *Restoring At-Risk Communities: Doing It Together and Doing It Right* (Grand Rapids, MI: Baker).

Peters, S. F. (2008). *When Prayer Fails: Faith Healing, Children, and the Law* (New York and Oxford: Oxford University Press).

Peterson, E. H. (1992). *Under the Unpredictable Plant: An Exploration in Vocational Holiness* (Grand Rapids, MI: Eerdmans).

Phillips, Elizabeth (2012). *Political Theology: A Guide for the Perplexed* (London and New York: T&T Clark).

Pickard, Stephen (2009). *Theological Foundations for Collaborative Ministry* (Farnham: Ashgate).

Pounds, N. J. G. (2000). *A History of the English Parish Church: The Culture of Religion from Augustine to Victoria* (Cambridge: Cambridge University Press).

Putnam, Robert D. (2001). *Bowling Alone: The Collapse and Revival of American Community* (New York: Simon & Schuster).

Raffay J., E. Wood and A. Todd (2016). 'Service User Views of Spiritual and Pastoral Care (Chaplaincy) in NHS Mental Health Services: A Co-produced Constructivist Grounded Theory Investigation', *BMC Psychiatry* 16.200: <https://bmcpsychiatry.biomedcentral.com/articles/10.1186/s12888-016-0903-9> (accessed 2 October 2018).

Rappaport, Roy (1999). *Ritual and Religion in the Making of Humanity* (Cambridge: Cambridge University Press).

Rasmussen, Arne (1995). *The Church as Polis: From Political Theology to Theological Politics as Exemplified by Jürgen Moltmann and Stanley Hauerwas* (Notre Dame, IN: University of Notre Dame Press).

Rawls, John (2001). *Justice as Fairness: A Restatement*. 2nd edn (Cambridge, MA: Harvard University Press).

—— (2005 (1971)). *A Theory of Justice* (Cambridge, MA: Harvard University Press).

—— (2005 (1993)). *Political Liberalism* (New York: Columbia University Press).

Reed, Bruce (1978). *The Dynamics of Religion: Process and Movement in Christian Churches* (London: Darton, Longman & Todd).

Rieff, Philip (1966). *The Triumph of the Therapeutic: Uses of Faith after Freud* (New York: Harper & Row).

Rieger, Joerg (2007). *Christ and Empire: From Paul to Postcolonial Times* (Minneapolis, MN: Fortress).

Rieger, Joerg, and Kwok Pui-lan (2012). *Occupy Religion: Theology of the Multitude* (Lanham, MD: Rowman & Littlefield).

Robbins, Joel (2004). *Becoming Sinners: Christianity and Moral Torment in a Papua New Guinea Society* (Berkeley: University of California Press).

—— (2013). 'Beyond the Suffering Subject: Toward an Anthropology of the Good'. *Journal of the Royal Anthropological Institute* 19, pp. 447–62.

Roberts, L., I. Ahmed, S. Hall and A. Davison (2009). 'Intercessory Prayer for the Alleviation of Ill Health'. *Cochrane Database of Systematic Reviews*.

Roberts, Robert (1995). *Taking the Word to Heart: Self and Other in an Age of Therapies* (Grand Rapids, MI: Eerdmans).

—— (2001). 'Outline of Pauline Psychotherapy'. In Mark McMinn and Timothy Phillips (eds), *The Care of the Soul: Exploring the Intersection of Theology and Psychology* (Downers Grove, IL: IVP), pp. 134–63.

—— (2001). 'Psychotherapy and Christian Ministry'. *Word and World* 21, pp. 42–50.

Rose, J. (2013). *Psychology for Pastoral Contexts: A Handbook* (Norwich: Canterbury Press).

Ross, Cathy, and Jonny Baker (2014). *The Pioneer Gift: Explorations in Mission* (Norwich: Canterbury Press).

Ross, M. (1988). *Pillars of Flame: Power, Priesthood and Spiritual Maturity* (New York: Harper & Row).

Rothauge, Arlin J. (1986). *Sizing Up a Congregation for New Member Ministry* (New York: Episcopal Church Center).

Russell, Anthony (1980). *The Clerical Profession* (London: SPCK).

Ryan, B. (2015). *A Very Modern Ministry: Chaplaincy in the UK* (London: Theos).

Sandbrook, D. (2006). *White Heat: A History of Britain in the Swinging Sixties* (London: Little, Brown).

Sanders, Theresa (2002). *Celluloid Saints: Images of Sanctity in Film* (Macon, GA: Mercer University Press).

Savage, Carl, and William Presnell (2008). *Narrative Research in Ministry: A Postmodern Research Approach for Faith Communities* (Louisville, KY: Wayne E. Oates Institute).

Savage, S. B. (2013). 'Head and Heart in Preventing Religious Radicalization'. In F. Watts and G. Dumbreck (eds), *Head and Heart: Perspectives from Religion and Psychology* (Philadelphia, PA: Templeton Press), pp. 157–94.

Savage, S. B., and E. Boyd-MacMillan (2007). *The Human Face of Church: A Social Psychology and Pastoral Theology Resource for Pioneer and Traditional Ministry* (London: SCM Press).

Schillebeeckx, Edward (1981). *Ministry: A Case for Change* (London: SCM Press).

—— (2014). *The Collected Works of Edward Schillebeeckx*, ed. T. Schoof and C. Sterkens. 11 vols (London: Bloomsbury T&T Clark).

Schreiter, Robert J. (1999 (1985)). *Constructing Local Theologies* (Maryknoll, NY: Orbis Books).

Scott, Peter, and William T. Cavanaugh (eds) (2004–7). *The Blackwell Companion to Political Theology* (Oxford: Blackwell).

Senior, D., and C. Stuhlmueller (1983). *The Biblical Foundations for Mission* (London: SCM Press).

Shiva, Vandana (2005). *Earth Democracy: Justice, Sustainability and Peace* (Boston, MA: South End Press).

Shopes, Linda (2002). 'Making Sense of Oral History'. In *History Matters: The U.S. Survey Course on the Web*: <http://historymatters.gmu.edu/mse/oral> (accessed 21 December 2018).

Siddall, P. J., M. Lovell and R. Macleod (2015). 'Spirituality: What Is Its Role in Pain Medicine?', *Pain Medicine* 16.1, pp. 51–60.

Slater, Victoria (2015). *Chaplaincy Ministry and the Mission of the Church* (London: SCM Press).

Slobodzian, J. A. (2011). 'Parents Get 10 Years' Probation in Child's Faith-healing Death'. *Philly.com*: <http://www.philly.com/philly/news/local/20110203_Parents_get_10_years__probation_in_child_s_faith-healing_death.html> (accessed 12 October 2018).

Smail, T., A. Walker and N. Wright (1994). *The Love of Power or the Power of Love* (Minneapolis, MN: Bethany House).

Smart, Ninian (1996). *Dimensions of the Sacred: Anatomy of the World's Beliefs* (Berkeley: University of California Press).

Smith, Christian, and Melina Lundquist Denton (2005). *Soul Searching: The Religious and Spiritual Lives of American Teenagers* (New York: Oxford University Press).

Smith, Huston (1991). *The World's Religions: Our Great Wisdom Traditions* (New York: Harper One).

Smith, J. K. A. (2014). *How (Not) to Be Secular: Reading Charles Taylor* (Grand Rapids, MI: Eerdmans).

Snowdon, Christopher (2014). *Closing Time: Who's Killing the British Pub?* (London: Institute of Economic Affairs).

Sounes, H. (2006). *Seventies: The Sights and Sounds of a Brilliant Decade* (London: Simon & Schuster).

Spittler, R. P. (2002). 'Spirituality, Pentecostal and Charismatic'. In S. M. Burgess (ed.), *The New International Dictionary of Pentecostal and Charismatic Movements*. Rev. edn (Grand Rapids, MI: Zondervan), pp. 1096–1102.

Spohn, William (1999). *Go and Do Likewise: Jesus and Ethics* (New York: Continuum).

Stark, Rodney (1999). 'Secularization, R.I.P.'. *Sociology of Religion* 60.3, pp. 249–73.

Stibbe, M. (2000). *Know Your Spiritual Gifts: How to Minister in the Power of the Spirit* (London: Marshall Pickering).

—— (2004). *Prophetic Evangelism: When God Speaks to Those Who Don't Know Him* (Milton Keynes: Authentic).

Stoddart, E. A. (2014). *Advancing Practical Theology: Critical Discipleship for Disturbing Times* (London: SCM Press).

Strathern, Marylin (1988). *The Gender of the Gift: Problems with Women and Problems with Society in Melanesia* (Berkeley: University of California Press).

Sullivan, Winnifred Fallers (2014). *A Ministry of Presence: Chaplaincy, Spiritual Care, and the Law* (Chicago, IL: University of Chicago Press).

Suna-Koro, Kristine (2014). 'The Sign of Unity and the Bond of Charity: On the Eucharist as a "Taskmaster" in the Context of Migration'. *Dialog* 53.2, June, pp. 138–48.

Sunstein, C. and R. Hastie (2015). *Wiser: Getting beyond Groupthink to Make Groups Smarter* (Boston, MA: Harvard Business Review Press).

Sutterfield, Ragan (2015). *This Is My Body: From Obesity to Ironman* (New York: Convergent Books).

Swift, C. (2014). *Hospital Chaplaincy in the Twenty-first Century: The Crisis of Spiritual Care on the NHS* (Farnham: Ashgate).

—— (2015). *NHS England Chaplaincy Guidelines 2015: Promoting Excellence in Pastoral, Spiritual and Religious Care* (Leeds: NHS England).

Swimme, Brian, and Thomas Berry (1992). *The Universe Story: From the Primordial Flaring Forth to the Ecozoic Era – a Celebration of the Unfolding of the Cosmos* (San Francisco, CA: HarperCollins).

Synan, V. (ed.) (2001). *The Century of the Holy Spirit: 100 Years of Pentecostal and Charismatic Renewal, 1901–2001* (Nashville, TN: Thomas Nelson).

Tan, Siang-Yang (2011). *Counseling and Psychotherapy: A Christian Perspective* (Grand Rapids, MI: Baker Academic).

Taylor, Bryony (2015). *More TV Vicar? Christians on the Telly: The Good, the Bad and the Quirky* (London: Darton, Longman & Todd).

Taylor, C. (2007). *A Secular Age* (Cambridge, MA: Harvard University Press).

Taylor, Charles W. (1991). *The Skilled Pastor: Counseling as the Practice of Theology* (Minneapolis, MN: Fortress).

Thorne, B. (2012). *Counselling and Spiritual Accompaniment: Bridging Faith and Person-centred Therapy* (Oxford: Wiley-Blackwell).

Thorne, Helen (2000). *Journey to Priesthood: An In-depth Study of the First Women Priests in the Church of England.* CCSRG Monograph Series 5 (Bristol: University of Bristol).

Thumma, Scott, and Dave Travis (2007). *Beyond Megachurch Myths: What We Can Learn from America's Largest Churches* (San Francisco, CA: Jossey-Bass).

Todd, A. (2002). 'Of Presbyters and Priests: An Anglican View'. In P. Luscombe and E. Shreeve (eds), *What Is a Minister?* (Peterborough: Epworth Press), pp. 104–16.

Todd, A., and C. Butler (2013). 'Moral Engagements: Morality, Mission and Military Chaplaincy'. In A. Todd (ed.), *Military Chaplaincy in Contention: Chaplains, Churches and the Morality of Conflict* (Farnham: Ashgate).

Todd, A., V. Slater and S. Dunlop (2014). *The Church of England's Involvement in Chaplaincy: Research Report for the Church of England's Mission and Public Affairs Council* (Cuddesdon: The Cardiff Centre for Chaplaincy Studies/The Oxford Centre for Ecclesiology and Practical Theology): <http://orca.cf.ac.uk/62257/1/Todd%2C%20Slater%20%26%20Dunlop%202014%20Report%20on%20Church%20of%20England%20Chaplaincy.pdf> (accessed 2 October 2018).

Todd, A., and L. Tipton (2011). *The Role and Contribution of a Multi-faith Prison Chaplaincy to the Contemporary Prison Service*: <http://orca.cf.ac.uk/29120/1/Chaplaincy%20Report%20Final%20Draft%20%283%29.pdf> (accessed 2 October 2018).

Torry, Malcolm (ed.) (2006). *The Parish: People, Place and Ministry: A Theological and Practical Exploration* (Norwich: Canterbury Press).

Towler, A., and A. P. M. Coxon (1979). *The Fate of the Anglican Clergy* (London: Routledge).

Trollope, A. (2013). *Barchester Chronicles*: e-artnow.

Tweed, Thomas (2006). *Crossing and Dwelling: A Theory of Religion* (Cambridge, MA: Harvard University Press).

Tylor, Edward Burnett (1958 (1871)). *Primitive Culture* (New York: Harper).

Urquhart, C. (2004). *The Truth That Sets You Free* (London: Hodder & Stoughton).

Usborne, D. (2014). 'US "Faith Healers" Sent to Prison for Death of Second Sick Child'. *Independent*: <http://www.independent.co.uk/news/world/americas/us-faith-healers-sent-to-prison-for-death-of-second-sick-child-9142463.html> (accessed 1 November 2015).

Valentine, Christine (2008). *Bereavement Narratives: Continuing Bonds in the Twentieth Century* (Abingdon: Routledge).

Vanhoozer, K. J. (2016). 'Holy Scripture'. In M. Allen and S. R. Swain (eds), *Christian Dogmatics: Reformed Theology for the Church Catholic* (Grand Rapids, MI: Baker Academic), pp. 30–56.

Vitz, Paul (1995). *Psychology as Religion: The Cult of Self-Worship* (Grand Rapids, MI: Eerdmans).

Volf, Miroslav (2013). *A Public Faith: How Followers of Christ Should Serve the Common Good* (Grand Rapids, MI: Baker).

Von Fragstein, M., J. Silverman, A. Cushing, S. Quilligan, H. Salisbury and C. Wiskin (2008). 'UK Consensus Statement on the Content of Communication Curricula in Undergraduate Medical Education'. *Medical Education* 42, pp. 1100–7.

Wall, B. A. (1946). *Visiting the Hospital: A Practical Handbook for Hospital Chaplains and Clergy Who Visit Hospitals* (London: A. R. Mowbray & Co.).

Walsh, J., Haydon, C., and Taylor, S. (eds) (1993). *The Church of England c.1689–1833: From Toleration to Tractarianism* (Cambridge: Cambridge University Press).

Walton, Heather (2014). *Writing Methods in Theological Reflection* (London: SCM Press).

Walzer, Michael (1984). *Spheres of Justice: A Defense of Pluralism and Equality* (New York: Basic Books).

Ward, Keith (2000). *Religion and Community* (Oxford: Clarendon Press).

Warner, D. (2014). 'Philadelphia Faith-healer Couple Sentenced to Prison in Son's Death'. *Reuters*: <http://www.reuters.com/article/us-usa-crime-faithhealing-idUSBREA1I1XJ20140219> (accessed 1 November 2015).

Watts, F. (2011). *Spiritual Healing: Scientific and Religious Perspectives* (Cambridge: Cambridge University Press).

—— (2016). *Psychology, Religion and Spirituality: Concepts and Applications* (Cambridge: Cambridge University Press).

Watts, F., R. Nye and S. B. Savage (2002). *Psychology for Christian Ministry* (London: Routledge).

Weber, Max (1922). *The Sociology of Religion* (Boston, MA: Beacon Press).

—— (1968). *Charisma and Institution Building* (Chicago, IL: Chicago University Press).

Webster, J. B. (1988). 'Ministry and Priesthood'. In S. Sykes and J. Booty (eds), *The Study of Anglicanism* (London: SPCK), pp. 285–96.

Wesley, John (ed. Albert C. Outler) (1964). *John Wesley* (New York: Oxford University Press).

West, Cornel (2001). *Race Matters*. New edn (New York: Vintage).

Westfield, N. Lynne (2001). *Dear Sisters: A Womanist Practice of Hospitality* (Cleveland, OH: Pilgrim Press).

Westin, Charles (1999). 'Regional Analysis of Refugee Movements: Origins and Response'. In Alastair Ager (ed.), *Refugees: Perspectives on the Experience of Forced Migration* (London and New York: Continuum, 1999), pp. 24–45.

Whitehead, James D., and Evelyn Eaton Whitehead (1995 (1981)). *Method in Ministry: Theological Reflection and Christian Ministry* (Lanham, MD: Rowman & Littlefield).

Wilkes, Paul (2001). *Excellent Catholic Parishes: The Guide to Best Places and Practices* (Mahwah, NJ: Paulist Press).

Wilkes, Paul (2004). *Excellent Protestant Congregations: The Guide to Best Places and Practices* (Louisville, KY: Westminster John Knox Press).

Williams, Mari Lloyd, Michael Wright, Mark Cobb and Chris Shiels (2004). 'A Prospective Study of the Roles, Responsibilities and Stresses of Chaplains Working within a Hospice'. *Palliative Medicine* 18.7, pp. 638–45.

Williams, Rowan (2000). *On Christian Theology* (Oxford: Blackwell).

—— (2004). 'The Christian Priest Today'. Lecture at Ripon College Cuddesdon, Oxford, 28 May.

Williamson, H. G. M. (1998). *Variations on a Theme: King, Messiah and Servant in the Book of Isaiah* (Carlisle: Paternoster).

Willimon, W. (2000), *Calling and Character: Virtues of the Ordained Life* (Nashville, TN: Abingdon Press).

Wilson, M. B. (1975). *Health Is for People* (London: Darton, Longman & Todd).

Wimber, J. (2001). *Power Evangelism* (London: Hodder & Stoughton).

Wind, James P. (1990). *Places of Worship: Exploring Their History* (Nashville, TN: American Association for State and Local History).

Wink, Walter (1992). *Engaging the Powers: Discernment and Resistance in a World of Domination* (Minneapolis, MN: Fortress).

—— (2000 (1998)). *The Powers that Be: Theology for a New Millennium* (New York: Galilee Doubleday).

Wogaman, J. Philip (2000). *Christian Perspectives on Politics*. Rev. edn (Louisville, KY: Westminster John Knox Press).

Wogaman, J. Philip, and Douglas Strong (eds) (1996). *Readings in Christian Ethics: A Historical Sourcebook* (Louisville, KY: Westminster John Knox Press).

Woodhead, Linda (2000). 'Can Women Love Stanley Hauerwas? Pursuing an Embodied Theology'. In M. T. Nation and S. Wells (eds), *Faithfulness and Fortitude: In Conversation with the Theological Ethics of Stanley Hauerwas* (Edinburgh: T&T Clark), pp. 161–88.

Woodhead, Linda, and Andrew Brown (2016). *That Was the Church That Was: How the Church of England Lost the English People* (London: Bloomsbury).

Woolmer, J. (1999). *Healing and Deliverance* (London: Monarch).

World Council of Churches (1982). *Baptism, Eucharist, and Ministry* (Geneva: World Council of Churches).

—— (2012). *Together towards Life: Mission and Evangelism in Changing Land-scapes*: <https://www.oikoumene.org/en/resources/documents/commissions/mission-and-evangelism/together-towards-life-mission-and-evangelism-in-changing-landscapes> (accessed 23 November 2015).

World Health Organization, Commission on Social Determinants of Health (2008). *Closing the Gap in a Generation: Health Equity through Action on the Social Determinants of Health* (Geneva: World Health Organization).

Worthington, E. L. (2006). *Forgiveness and Reconciliation: Theory and Application* (New York: Routledge).

Wright, C. J. H. (2006). *The Mission of God: Unlocking the Bible's Grand Narrative* (Nottingham: IVP).

Wuthnow, Robert (2007). *After the Baby Boomers: How Twenty- and Thirty-Somethings Are Shaping the Future of American Religion* (Princeton, NJ: Princeton University Press).

Yoder, John Howard (1994). *The Politics of Jesus.* 2nd edn (Grand Rapids, MI: Eerdmans).

Young, F. M. (2008). 'Interpretation of Scripture'. In S. A. Harvey and D. G. Hunter (eds), *The Oxford Handbook of Early Christian Studies* (Oxford: Oxford University Press), pp. 845–63.

Further reading

Bibliographical sources for the formation, presence and engagement of ministry

JAMES WOODWARD

Before an Anglican ordination service, in conversation with an experienced priest who was aware that I had recently taken up responsibility for a college that offers a diverse provision of theological learning, I was asked, 'What has equipped you to do this kind of work?' It was an insightful and challenging question. It offers a starting point for this essay. What are the resources that might equip the work of Christian ministry in the twenty-first century? Where are we to look for guidance, challenge, refreshment and renewal in the ever-demanding task of ministry today? We all know from our experience of hard-working professionals how easy it is to become tired, disconnected and disillusioned. We live in challenging and complex times.

This chapter will offer an overview of some of the range of publications that might equip ministry. There can be no claim to comprehensiveness, although, as the reader will note, the careful and insightful editors of this volume have drawn together a wide variety of perspectives and learning on the nature of ministry. In particular I have made no reference here to issues in ministry around gender and sexuality. Rooted in an informed historical perspective, this collection of essays reminds those in ministry that we should be aware of introversion and self-preoccupation. In other words there is a commitment to an outward-facing horizon that contextualizes the nature, purpose and practice of Christian ministry.

The various publications discussed below relate to what has emerged for this writer and practitioner over the last 30 years of ministry in a variety of contexts. It will be impossible to offer any comprehensiveness and we should be glad to hear from readers about obvious gaps in this outline for further reading. It is the aim of this chapter to encourage the reader to develop his or her own library and to especially examine how best to resource a lifelong commitment to learning for ministry. I have limited myself to books and include no other resources, particularly those available via the Internet. It is my intention to continue to expand this list by including such resources in due course. I can be contacted via my webpage: <www.jameswoodward.info>.

Readers will have their own way of organizing learning and resources. It follows here that an attention to theological knowledge and our own ongoing learning and development is a discipline and practice absolutely essential to keep the renewal and refreshment of ministry alive. The suggested hundred or so books that follow may not be on your shelves or ever find their way there, but the plea is to consider how best to keep connected with the shape, substance and wisdom of our theological tradition.

There are a number of ways in which you can do this. You can read or join others in a book group. You might want to attend study days or carve out a week for reading in the course of your year. There will be opportunities for you to connect with others in learning for ministry and you might want to explore the possibility of developing a particular area of interest or expertise. You might look for subscription to journals or indeed seek to connect with associations that feed or nourish you. For some the New Wine network is an essential part of their renewal in ministry, and for others it may be the Greenbelt Festival or a particular retreat or study centre. This chapter therefore is a stimulus to think through what your discipline might look like and whether it might need to be strengthened or changed.

I have had to review a substantial part of my library and learning as part of my preparation for this chapter. I have become acutely aware of my bias and limitations and particularly how much of my learning has been shaped by the voices and learning of men. In this book there is a commitment to opening ourselves up to the variety of voices, especially the voices of those who have been marginalized in the Church. We often learn more when there is difference, challenge and conflict.

The ministry of the Church continues to adapt and change. In many dioceses in England, at least, there are more licensed lay ministers at work than ordained ministers. While this chapter is written primarily for those who are ordained, it is not my intention to exclude the support and development of a range of other lay ministries. It is to be hoped that this book will be a resource to the whole people of God in their journey of deepening discipleship. There are resources here for those who wish to deepen their theological engagement with the world.

Theological dictionaries and encyclopaedias

Ministry needs to be put into context and especially within the long and rich tradition of Christian history and thinking. This first section asks the minister to consider the resource of our history. The following are to be considered. Dr Elizabeth Livingstone has revised the 1957 edition of F. L. Cross's *Oxford Dictionary of the Christian Church* (Oxford University Press, 1997). Two millennia are enshrined within this volume, which covers nearly 2,000 pages and offers a very wide range of articles on Christianity. It is a book to have close to hand and should be used as a starting point to open up history, doctrine and ethics. It is hardly to be rivalled in its scholarship and comprehensiveness.

John Bowden was for over 30 years the editor and managing director of SCM Press where he published the work of some of the most famous theologians from around the world. He puts his scholarship and learning to work in *Christianity: The Complete Guide* (Continuum, 2005). It is unique in so far as it approaches Christianity as a foreign land, which it is for a large number of people. Almost 200 contributors introduce the reader to a variety of forms of Christianity; to its geographical spread; to its history; to its great works of art, and to its values and ethical responses to significant issues of the day. It explores prayer and worship and the thinking that shapes how we use the Bible. It is particularly strong on how we should understand the nature of belief in God. Again this introduction combines scholarship with brevity and offers a way into a subject which may be unfamiliar or alien to its reader.

Finally the Oxford Companions have established themselves as key textbooks for students and teachers. *The Oxford Companion to Christian Thought*, edited by Adrian Hastings, Alastair Mason and Hugh Piper (Oxford University Press, 2000), sets out an ambitious organizing question: 'At the dawn of the third millennium what does it mean to be a Christian?' The reader will discover 600 articles that cover the roots of Christian belief in the Bible; major themes of belief and theology (creation, sin, resurrection, grace, justification, the Eucharist); key schools and concepts of philosophy; spiritualities, lifestyles and prayer; politics, social justice and ethics; major thinkers on the shape of Christianity; and topics such as globalization, medical ethics and sexuality. This volume will suit a general reader wanting to understand the profound pluralism of Christianity.

When it comes to applying theology to practice in ministry, what resource books might be a useful and stimulating starting point for the general reader?

Reference books – pastoral and practical theology

The Blackwell Reader in Pastoral and Practical Theology, edited by James Woodward and Stephen Pattison (Blackwell, 2010), though first published in 2000 still provides a useful overview of the field within a theoretical framework. The book includes six classic articles which might otherwise be difficult to locate, together with a number of articles which hold together both theory and practice. *The Wiley-Blackwell Companion to Practical Theology*, edited by Bonnie J. Miller-McLemore (Wiley-Blackwell, 2012), will remain for some years one of the most comprehensive introductions to practical theology. Carefully organized, it offers its reader an overview of key developments, themes, methods and future directions. The writing manages to maintain persistent creativity and always has a focus on the nature of applied theological knowledge. SPCK has a long tradition of resourcing ministry through its publications and *The New Dictionary of Pastoral Studies*, edited by Wesley Carr (2002), offers accessible and accurate information on a range of issues associated with ministry. The writing is succinct and focused and again always practical. Rodney Hunter is the general editor of the American *Dictionary of Pastoral Care and Counseling* (Abingdon Press, 1990), the publication of which should certainly be viewed as one of the most important events in the revolution of pastoral care and pastoral theology over the last three decades. There are 600 articles from around the world, representing a rich range of viewpoints. The writers balance theology with psychology and always contextualize the theory with a particular emphasis on under-represented aspects of pastoral care such as black pastoral care and feminist challenges to pastoral care. It is also strong on the way in which pastoral ministry has evolved. Inter-Varsity Press combine pastoral theology and Christian ethics in a similar dictionary edited by David Atkinson and David Field. *The New Dictionary of Christian Ethics in Pastoral Theology*, published in 1995, is again a carefully organized dictionary that falls into two parts. The first introduces users to the main themes of Christian ethics and pastoral theology, and the second part contains articles which stem from the main themes. The focus is always on how we might live out our faith meaningfully and ethically amidst the challenges of today's world.

The Bible

It may be that one of the most pressing challenges of ministry is to enable the whole people of God to handle Scripture in a way that is both liberating and life enhancing. In his book *Pedagogy of the Bible: An Analysis and Proposal* (Westminster John Knox Press, 2008) Dale Martin deconstructs historical criticism as inadequate for the interpretation of Scripture. He offers a new framework within which ministry might use the Bible for preaching and teaching. Ministers may wish to explore their own use of the Bible by reading Chapter 6 ('The Use of the Bible in Pastoral Care') in Stephen Pattison's *A Critique of Pastoral Care* (SCM Press, 1993). The work of James Barr continues to have significant relevance in helping us understand the Bible as literature and how the Bible is sometimes used to promote rigidity and fundamentalism in pastoral care. His books *The Bible in the Modern World* (SCM Press, 1973) and *Escaping from Fundamentalism* (SCM Press, 1984) continue to have a significant influence on biblical scholars. If we were to look for an example of how to read Scripture in a compelling, counter-cultural and challenging way, then the work of Ched Myers stands out as a model of uncompromising engagement; see *Binding the Strongman: A Political Reading of Mark's Story of Jesus* (Orbis, 1995). A final suggestion in this area would be from Michael Joseph Brown: *What They Don't Tell You: A Survivor's Guide to Biblical Studies* (Westminster John Knox Press, 2000). It is a clear and comprehensive overview about the shape of how to read Scripture.

Church history

The Penguin History of the Church (seven volumes), though dated, is a good starting point for an overview of the development of Christianity, especially in the early Church and Reformation period. Diarmaid MacCulloch has produced a one-volume study: *A History of Christianity* (Allen Lane, 2009). It is an horizon-setting book and puts much of the life of the Church into perspective. It is also a good starting point for providing references for further research and reflection.

There are two other books which offer historical insight into the shape of ministry from historians. In order to understand our modern age it is worth looking at Owen Chadwick's *Michael Ramsey: A Life* (Oxford University Press, 1990) as it describes the leadership of Ramsey through the 1960s and 1970s, providing a fascinating insight into change, conflict and the agendas that preoccupied Anglicanism during that period. Although technical and demanding, Diarmaid MacCulloch's *Thomas Cranmer* (Yale University Press, 1996) guides the reader through the crises that Cranmer negotiated during the reign of Henry VIII and the shaping of the Anglican Book of Common Prayer. It might be argued that it is not possible to understand Anglicanism without some appreciation of this period of church history.

Sean Gill adds to our appreciation of the substantial contribution women have been to the life of the Church in his *Women and the Church of England: From the Eighteenth Century to the Present* (SPCK, 1994).

Historical and systematic theology

Ministry will always engage with apologetics as in each generation we are called to proclaim the gospel afresh. Readers will have their own theological giants from across the centuries who have inspired, deepened and enlarged a sense of the shape and meaning of theological narrative. For an introduction to the shape of modern theology look at *The Blackwell Companion to Modern Theology*, edited by Gareth Jones (Blackwell, 2004). Combine this with David Ford's *The Modern Theologians: An Introduction to Christian Theology since 1918* (Blackwell, 2005). A trinity of books offering horizon setting and an overview would be completed with *Christian Theology: An Introduction* by Alister McGrath (4th edition, Blackwell, 2007). These books will be helpful starting points that might stimulate more detailed engagement with either historical periods of theological thinking or indeed particular theological thinkers.

The present writer offers the following authors as significant for reflecting on how best to communicate faith and belief. Jürgen Moltmann stands out as a person who has had a significant shaping influence on theology. His *The Crucified God* (SCM Press, 1974) offers a framework within which we might see the cross of Christ as the foundation and criticism of Christian theology. The Chicago theologian David Tracy takes seriously the context within which theology attempts to assert itself as a public narrative. His book *The Analogical Imagination* (SCM Press, 1981) excites the reader with both breadth and imagination in how we might talk about God. Other theologians should include Gordon Kaufman, *In Face of Mystery: A Constructive Theology* (Harvard University Press, 1993); Rowan Williams, *On Christian Theology* (Blackwell, 2000); John Milbank, *The Word Made Strange: Theology, Language and Culture* (Blackwell, 1997); and David Ford, *The Future of Christian Theology* (Wiley-Blackwell, 2011). Another long-standing textbook, by Daniel L. Migliore, is *Faith Seeking Understanding: An Introduction to Christian Theology* (2nd edition, Eerdmans, 2004), which succeeds in grounding doctrine in the life and practice of pastoral ministry. It is another useful starting point for readers, allowing them to take a step back and understand the history, themes and challenges of Christian belief.

Among writers who seem especially to have influenced ministerial identity and practice, John V. Taylor stands out for his book *The Go-between God: The Holy Spirit and the Christian Mission* (SCM Press, 1972). It is one of those rare books that is still being published and read across languages and cultures. Other resources that may be regarded as somewhat dated still manage to secure their authority as helpful guides to systematic theology. John Macquarrie offers a one-volume systematic theology which is well organized and accessible. In *Principles of Christian Theology* (revised edition, SCM, 2009) he explores the nature of theology and discusses issues of methodology, the relation of theology to other disciplines, and different theological perspectives. John Austin Baker in *The Foolishness of God* (Darton, Longman & Todd, 1990) narrates a systematic approach to what believing in God might mean with an unusual clarity and conviction which holds together learning and believing. Finally, a further writer who has had a significant influence on generations of Christian ministry is Nicholas Lash. In particular his *Theology on Dover Beach* (Darton, Longman & Todd, 1979) and *Easter in Ordinary: Reflections on Human Experience and the Knowledge of God* (SCM Press, 1988) remind us of the importance of intellectual enquiry for the way we practise ministry. Lash continues to critique the modern, and notably Evangelical, view of the Christian life that tends to accentuate the inner spiritual life to the depreciation of the God-ordained whole – the thrilling and extraordinary to the detriment of any recognition of God's intimate relation to the everyday. Lash reminds those of us who explore theology that we need to be careful in our use of language and be very aware of words and phrases that fail to carry much meaning. In this respect ministry needs to grasp the shape and practice of religious knowledge. In formation we need to beware of the dangers of emphasizing process and experience to the detriment of the history, shape and substance of theology. Although I have never been especially attracted to substantial schemas of Christian theology, I respect those who turn to the works of Karl Barth, whose *Church Dogmatics* is largely regarded as one of the most important theological works of the twentieth century. His theology continues to influence new generations of pastors and academics worldwide. For an introduction to Barth's work see Karl Barth's *Church Dogmatics: An Introduction and Reader* (paperback edition, T&T Clark, 2012).

Sarah Coakley stands out as one of the most significant and insightful Anglican systematic theologians and philosophers of religion with wide

interdisciplinary interests. She has embarked upon a four-volume systematic theology; the first volume is *God, Sexuality, and the Self: An Essay 'On
the Trinity'* (Cambridge University Press, 2013). Her recent *New Asceticism:
Sexuality, Gender and the Quest for God* (Bloomsbury, 2015) concentrates
on contentious issues in contemporary theology – the role of women in
the churches, homosexuality and the priesthood, celibacy, and the future
of Christian asceticism – in a thesis about the nature of desire which may
start to heal many contemporary divisions.

Ethics

Christian ethics is a branch of theology that considers human behaviour
from a Christian perspective. Systematic theological study of Christian
ethics is called moral theology. Christian ethicists, like other ethicists,
approach ethics using different frameworks and perspectives. The approach
of virtue ethics has become popular in recent decades, largely owing to the
work of thinkers such as Alasdair MacIntyre and Stanley Hauerwas.

The following books offer an overview and introduction to this particular dimension of Christian thinking. William Schweiker has edited *The
Blackwell Companion to Religious Ethics* (Blackwell, 2005), which maps out
moral teaching and holds together both theoretical and practical issues.
Bernard Hoose brings together all the main themes in fundamental and
applied moral theology in *Christian Ethics: An Introduction* (paperback
edition, Continuum, 1998). John Mizzoni in *Ethics: The Basics* (Blackwell,
2010) provides the reader with a solid grounding in basic ethical principles, theories and traditions, as well as a set of conceptual tools necessary
to think about ethics and make ethical decisions.

Ministry, vocation and mission

Many of us have found ourselves drawn into particular vocational choices.
Among the books that those guiding vocation have found helpful are: John
Adair, *How to Find Your Vocation* (Canterbury Press, 2002); Francis Dewar,
Called or Collared (SPCK, 2000); Henri Nouwen, *The Road to Daybreak*
(Darton, Longman & Todd, 1989); Stephen Platten, *Vocation: Singing the
Lord's Song* (SPCK, 2007); and David Runcorn, *Choice, Desire and the Will
of God* (SPCK, 2003).

We would do well to continue to explore the changing shape of vocation
and develop reflectiveness about the nature of our ministry. Emma Percy,
What Clergy Do: Especially When It Looks Like Nothing (SPCK, 2014), offers

an insightful and refreshing overview of ministry. Other volumes worth considering are: Alan Billings, *Making God Possible: The Task of Ordained Ministry Present and Future* (SPCK, 2010); Christopher Cocksworth and Rosalind Brown, *Being a Priest Today* (Canterbury Press, 2002); and Ali Green, *A Theology of Women's Priesthood* (SPCK, 2009). A classic on the nature of ministry remains Michael Ramsey, *The Christian Priest Today* (SPCK, 1972) and, in this tradition, Christopher Moody, *Eccentric Ministry* (Darton, Longman & Todd, 1992).

Inextricably linked with the nature of vocation and the practice of ministry is an increasing energy and creativity around the necessity for mission and evangelism. The following books offer a number of theories, frameworks and stimulus for practice: Paul Avis, *A Ministry Shaped by Mission* (T&T Clark, 2005); Stephen Cottrell, *From the Abundance of the Heart* (Darton, Longman & Todd, 2006); Steve Hollinghurst, *Mission-Shaped Evangelism* (Canterbury Press, 2010); J. Andrew Kirk, *What Is Mission?* (Darton, Longman & Todd, 2002); and Ann Morisy, *Journeying Out: A New Approach to Christian Mission* (Morehouse, 2004).

Pastoral care

The work of ministry will take us into many dimensions of the struggle to flourish, given some of the challenges of our human living and experience. The practitioner would do well to be aware of the specialist areas of pastoral care that may need further particular support and resourcing. It might be helpful to consider the human lifespan and look at the organizing of specific resources through the following subject areas: birth, early years, childhood and parenting; wholeness, disability and healing; the ministry of healing; singleness; issues of suffering and faith; depression and mental health; death, dying and grief; sex and sexuality; marriage, divorce and remarriage; ageing and retirement; together with general books about the nature of the pastoral relationship and the shape of listening.

The SPCK New Library of Pastoral Care series covers many of the above issues. Particular models of excellence in guiding practice in this area of ministry include Michael Jacobs, *Swift to Hear: Facilitating Skills in Listening and Responding* (SPCK, 1985); Morton Kelsey, *Caring: How Can We Love One Another?* (Paulist Press, 1981); and Pamela Cooper White, *Shared Wisdom: Use of the Self in Pastoral Care and Counselling* (Fortress Press, 2004). For all those who engage in regular pastoral care it will be important to develop skills in reflective practice and to seek supervision. Jane Leach and Michael Paterson take an overview of this critical area of reflection in their book *Pastoral Supervision: A Handbook* (SCM Press, 2010). Sally Nash and Paul Nash pick up similar practical themes in their book *Tools for Reflective Ministry* (Library of Ministry series, SPCK, 2009). Barbara McClure offers an insightful reflection on pastoral care in *Moving beyond Individualism in Pastoral Care and Counselling: Reflections on Theory, Theology and Practice* (Lutterworth, 2011). Readers would also be well served by the range of books published by Jessica Kingsley whose writers focus on the resourcing of reflective practice. There is much to learn from the way in which care is theorized and practised across professional boundaries.

The sociological, cultural and geographical context of ministry

Ministers need to understand the rapidly changing culture within which they practise their life and work. In particular some of this work has concentrated on the reality of the relative decline of religion in some parts of the West. One of the more insightful writers in this area is Grace Davie, a sociologist of religion, who has examined patterns of religion in Europe. The notion of 'multiple modernities' enables us to make sense of the significance of religion in the modern world as pattern of believing without necessarily belonging. Her most recent book is *Religion in Britain: A Persistent Paradox* (Wiley-Blackwell, 2015). Steve Bruce adds particularly to our understanding of the character and place of religion in contemporary British society in his books *Religion in Modern Britain* (Oxford University Press, 1995) and *Religion in the Modern World: From Cathedrals to Cults* (Oxford University Press, 1996). The American writer Robert Coles helps us to see some of the context of secularism in *The Secular Mind* (Princeton University Press, 1999). The importance of our engagement and dialogue with cultural analysis and criticism is captured in the collection of essays edited by Delwin Brown, Sheila Davaney and Kathryn Tanner: *Converging on Culture: Theologians in Dialogue with Cultural Analysis and Criticism* (Oxford University Press, 2001). Probably one of the best books in this area, which traces theology as embodied in the midst of congregational life with an insightful use of ethnography and place theory, is *Places of Redemption: Theology for a Worldly Church* by Mary McClintock Fulkerson; she offers us a picture of the activities that constitute church life as a starting point for understanding the way in which belief is practised in any particular context.

The geographical context of ministry will certainly shape thought and practice. *Theology in the City*, edited by Anthony Harvey (SPCK, 1989), remains an insightful collection of reflections on the Church's attempt to recover its social and prophetic ministry in urban areas following the *Faith in the City* report in the 1980s. Rod Garner offers an eloquent and compelling discussion of urban life in *Facing the City: Urban Ministry in the 21st Century* (Epworth Press, 2004). Laurie Green harvests many decades of working in inner-city areas and especially on housing estates in his book *Blessed Are the Poor? Urban Poverty and the Church* (SCM Press, 2015).

Resourcing our reflection on the work of ministry in a rural context will be helped by Tim Gibson, *Church and Countryside: Insights from Rural Theology* (SCM Press, 2010); Leslie Francis, *Rural Life and Rural Church: Theological and Empirical Reflections* (Equinox, 2012); and Jill Hopkinson, *Reshaping Rural Ministry: A Theological and Practical Handbook* (Canterbury Press, 2009).

Ministry and leadership

The literature relating to the nature and practice of leadership in ministry continues to abound. The way ministers are trained for leadership and chosen for senior responsibility is an area of discussion and disagreement. Two books that help us to understand some of the questions and challenges of leadership are worth noting here. The first, *The Faith of the Managers: When Management Becomes Religion* (Cassell, 1997) by Stephen Pattison, challenges much of the manipulative technique and incomprehensibility of management jargon and warns against the dangers of managerialism in ministry. *Managing the Church? Order and Organization in a Secular Age*, edited by G. R. Evans and Martyn Percy (Sheffield Academic Press, 2000), explores the complex questions about how churches and other religious organizations attempt to order themselves in the secular age.

Evangelical writers continue to make a very distinctive contribution to the literature on leadership. Steven Croft, *Ministry in Three Dimensions* (Darton, Longman & Todd, 2008), critiques traditional models of mission and offers a thoughtful contribution to a more outward-looking Church in intentional mission.

Graham Tomlin adds to the literature with a scripturally grounded book, *The Widening Circle: Priesthood as God's Way of Blessing the World* (SPCK, 2014), which seeks to understand priesthood within a framework of Church, humanity and creation: the widening circle of blessing which priesthood brings to the Church, which the Church brings to humanity and which humanity brings to the whole of creation.

The questions and challenges in all of these books about how management is imported into the churches will continue to be an area of contestation in future years. In this debate I commend the work of the Australian theologian Gerald Arbuckle. His books, *Refounding the Church: Dissent for Leadership* (Geoffrey Chapman, 1993) and *From Chaos to Mission: Refounding Religious Life Formation* (Geoffrey Chapman, 1996), deserve to be much more widely read as they tackle fundamental questions about the nature of mission, the purpose and style of leadership, and what kind of Christian communities we are shaping and forming today.

Theological reflection, self-care and supervision

The challenges of standing back and reflecting on our ministerial experience in the light of faith in God remain significant amidst the many demands of our work. Patricia Killen and John de Beer describe the nature and practice of reflection in *The Art of Theological Reflection* (Crossroad, 2009) as does Judith Thompson in *Theological Reflection* (SCM Press, 2008). Laurie Green offers an overview of contextual theology in *Let's Do Theology* (Mowbray, 2009). Other resources in this area include John Patton, *From Ministry to Theology* (Abingdon Press, 1990); Howard Stone and James Duke, *How to Think Theologically* (Fortress, 2006). However, the most comprehensive, convincing and intelligent overview of this practice in ministry is *Christian Theology in Practice: Discovering a Discipline* by Bonnie J. Miller-McLemore (Eerdmans, 2012).

Kate Litchfield handles the issue of resilience and self-care in ministry in *Tend My Flock: Sustaining Good Pastoral Care* (Canterbury Press, 2006). Michael Jinkins deals with some of these issues of self-care in *Letters to New Pastors* (Eerdmans, 2006). Ronald Richardson offers a framework for the development of ministerial effectiveness in *Becoming a Healthier Pastor* (Fortress, 2005). Although writing from the perspective of psychoanalysis, Patrick Casement offers unique insights into how professional experience can shape and misshape us in *Learning from Life* (Routledge, 2006).

All those working in ministry will have been encouraged to engage in regular supervision. For a clear outline of the nature and practice of supervision see *Passionate Supervision*, edited by Robin Shohet (Jessica Kingsley, 2007). Appreciative enquiry as an approach to individual and organizational change has garnered a great deal of interest and respect. See Sue Hammond and Cathy Royal, *Lessons from the Field: Applying Appreciative*

Inquiry (Practical Press, 1998) and *The Power of Appreciative Inquiry* by Diana Whitney and Amanda Trosten-Bloom (Berrett-Koehler, 2003).

Spirituality

Three larger books that cover a great deal of ground in the area of Christian spirituality are worth noting before particular writers in this area are mentioned. Philip Sheldrake skilfully edits a collection of articles in *The New SCM Dictionary of Christian Spirituality* (SCM Press, 2005). *Love's Redeeming Work: The Anglican Quest for Holiness*, edited by Geoffrey Rowell, Kenneth Stevenson and Rowan Williams (Oxford University Press, 2001), guides the reader through writings from the Anglican tradition. It traces the diversity and depth of how spiritual awareness and knowledge of the Christian tradition has been a particular quest of Anglicanism in its service of the whole community. Gordon Mursell sets out a historical survey of English spirituality from earliest times to the present day in two volumes: *English Spirituality: From Earliest Times to 1700* and *English Spirituality: From 1700 to the Present Day* (both volumes SPCK, 2001).

Despite the relative decline in church numbers in parts of the West over recent decades, there is a marked interest in the area of spirituality. Books about the spiritual life and prayer continue to increase in number and scope. Some readers may be enriched by reading classical writers on spirituality like Thomas Merton, Evelyn Underhill, St John of the Cross, Teresa of Avila, Julian of Norwich, or John and Charles Wesley. Authors in recent years should include Kenneth Leech who has written widely about spirituality but does so within a social and political context and wherever possible attempts to integrate doctrine and history. Among his many books the particular exploration of spiritual theology lies in *True God* (Sheldon, 1985). The Roman Catholic Jesuit writer Gerard Hughes has written one of the great books of spiritual guidance, *God of Surprises* (Darton, Longman & Todd, 1985). Harry Williams, though now dated, has certainly influenced spiritual formation in his writing and particularly the way he uses human vulnerability. *Tensions* (Mitchell Beazley, 1976) continues to be read and used as an insightful examination of the very necessity of conflict in our life and love. W. H. Vanstone produced a spiritual classic, emerging out of his many years of pastoral ministry, in the shape of *Love's Endeavour, Love's Expense: The Response of Being to the Love of God* (Darton, Longman & Todd, 1977). The distinctive characteristic of this book is its combination of personal experience, intellectual discipline and a Christian concern that always struggles to be theological.

One of the giants of spiritual engagement in writing is Joan Chittister, an American Benedictine. Her introductions to the Rule of Benedict and reflections on women's spirituality are particularly worth reading. Her best writing is to be found in *Scarred by Struggle, Transformed by Hope* (Eerdmans, 2003) and, on the celebration of growing old, *The Gift of Years* (Darton, Longman & Todd, 2008).

Christian liturgy and worship

Paul Bradshaw edits an overview of a comprehensive range of articles in *The New SCM Dictionary of Liturgy and Worship* (SCM Press, 2013). George Guiver offers a comprehensive history of liturgical prayer in *Company of Voices: Daily Prayer and the People of God* (SPCK, 1989). Richard Giles considers the built environment within which worship takes place in his book *Re-pitching the Tent: Re-ordering the Church Building for Worship and Mission* (Canterbury Press, 2004). Jeremy Begbie brings his creative intelligence to music and worship in *Resounding Truth: Christian Wisdom in the World of Music* (SPCK, 2008). Doug Gay is at the forefront of the development of reflection on emerging ecclesiologies, particularly in relation to pioneer ministry. His book with Duncan Forrester, *Worship and Liturgy in Context: Studies and Case Studies in Theology and Practice* (SCM Press, 2009), offers grounded reflection on the possible future shape of worship.

Copyright acknowledgements

Bible acknowledgements

Scripture quotations marked ESV are taken from the ESV Bible (The Holy Bible, English Standard Version), copyright © 2001 by Crossway, a publishing ministry of Good News Publishers. Used by permission. All rights reserved.

Quotations marked NASB are taken from the NEW AMERICAN STANDARD BIBLE®, Copyright © 1960, 1962, 1963, 1968, 1971, 1972, 1973, 1975, 1977, 1995 by The Lockman Foundation. Used by permission.

Quotations marked NIV 1984 are taken from the HOLY BIBLE, NEW INTERNATIONAL VERSION. Copyright © 1973, 1978, 1984 by International Bible Society. Used by permission of Hodder & Stoughton Publishers, a member of the Hachette UK Group. All rights reserved. 'NIV' is a registered trademark of International Bible Society. UK trademark number 1448790.

Quotations marked NIV 2011 are taken from the Holy Bible, NEW INTERNATIONAL VERSION®, NIV®. Copyright © 1973, 1978, 1984, 2011 by Biblica, Inc.® Used by permission. All rights reserved worldwide.

Quotations marked NKJV are taken from the New King James Version. Copyright © 1982 by Thomas Nelson, Inc. Used by permission. All rights reserved.

Quotations marked NRSV are taken from the New Revised Standard Version of the Bible, Anglicized Edition, copyright © 1989, 1995 by the Division of Christian Education of the National Council of the Churches of Christ in the USA. Used by permission. All rights reserved.

Quotations marked RSV are taken from the Revised Standard Version of the Bible, copyright © 1946, 1952 and 1971 by the Division of Christian Education of the National Council of the Churches of Christ in the USA. Used by permission. All rights reserved.

Other acknowledgements

The publisher and author acknowledge with thanks permission to reproduce extracts from the following:

Index of names

Index of subjects